THE FOOD AND FOLKLORE READER

D0545843

THE FOOD AND FOLKLORE READER

Edited by Lucy M. Long

Bloomsbury Academic
An imprint of Bloomsbury Publishing Plc

B L O O M S B U R Y
LONDON · OXFORD · NEW YORK · NEW DELHI · SYDNEY

Bloomsbury Academic

An imprint of Bloomsbury Publishing Plc

50 Bedford Square
London
WC1B 3DP
UK

1385 Broadway
New York
NY 10018
USA

www.bloomsbury.com

BLOOMSBURY and the Diana logo are trademarks of Bloomsbury Publishing Plc

First published 2015

© Selection and Editorial Material: Lucy M. Long, 2015

Lucy M. Long has asserted her right under the Copyright, Designs and Patents Act, 1988,
to be identified as Editor of this work.

All rights reserved. No part of this publication may be reproduced or transmitted in
any form or by any means, electronic or mechanical, including photocopying,
recording, or any information storage or retrieval system, without
prior permission in writing from the publishers.

No responsibility for loss caused to any individual or organization acting
on or refraining from action as a result of the material in this
publication can be accepted by Bloomsbury or the authors.

British Library Cataloguing-in-Publication Data
A catalogue record for this book is available from the British Library.

ISBN: HB: 978-0-8578-5723-1
PB: 978-0-8578-5699-9

Library of Congress Cataloging-in-Publication Data
A catalog record for this book is available from the Library of Congress.

Typeset by Deanta Global Publishing Services, Chennai, India
Printed and bound in India

CONTENTS

Contents

ACKNOWLEDGEMENTS

This *Reader* represents years of discussions with, and learning from, numerous individuals. Some of those were teachers and mentors, including folklorists Jack Santino, Steve Zeitlin, Bill Ferris, Judy Peiser, Alan Jabbour, Dan Ben-Amos, Henry Glassie, Don Yoder, Roger Abrahams, and Margaret Mills. I especially thank Don Yoder, Barbara Kirshenblatt-Gimblett, Yvonne Lockwood, Simon Bronner: Tim Lloyd, and Michael Owen Jones, who have all provided encouragement and guidance to my pursuit of food as a subject within folkloristics. Yvonne, in particular, has been a friend and mentor, bringing me into the Foodways Section of the American Folklore Society and its publication, *Digest*. It was actually Yvonne who helped conceive this volume, guiding me in the proposal, the selection of articles, and reading through drafts of the introductions. Jack Santino also provided his insights and keen eye to drafts of this *Reader*.

Folklore colleagues Betty Belanus, Riki Saltzman, and Eve Jochnowitz, along with being friends, co-researchers, and sounding posts, also contributed much to the development of not only the *Reader*, but also of my thinking about food and foodways. Other folklorists may not be aware of the encouragement that they have given—in particular, Diane Tye, LuAnne Roth, Amy Shuman, Sue Eleuterio, and Tim Lloyd. I also owe a great deal of gratitude to colleagues in the world of food studies who have provided insights, feedback, and support, including Warren Belasco, Amy Bentley, Krishnendu Ray: Carole Counihan, Fabio Parasecoli, Alice Julier, Ken Albala, Alex MacIntosh, Lisa Heldke, Jeffrey Sobal, Jon Deutsch, Annie Hauk-Lawson, and others. We never know when a positive word or even just a smile or nod during a conference presentation helps someone keep their nose to the grindstone or follow an unknown path in scholarship.

Various people at Bloomsbury Press have guided me through the process of putting together this volume. Louise Butler originally worked on the proposal, and her enthusiasm lent an affirmation that was much appreciated—and needed. Others, including Jennifer Schmidt, Claire Cooper, Grishma Frederic, have also been instrumental along the way, and I much appreciate their insightful reading and careful editing. That includes a special thanks to Molly Beck who saw the project through from its stumbling beginnings to publication.

I also need to thank some of the people who worked behind the scenes in getting this volume in print. I could not have done this without Melissa Hill who helped with technical aspects of gathering articles and putting them in order, initially as a graduate assistant, then as a colleague and friend. Holly Howard patiently typed in entry after entry for the bibliographies, and Hannah Santino read initial drafts to give a college student's perspective. Although they were not always aware they were doing so, Ian Santino and Will Santino offered feedback to ideas, usually over meals, which as they should be, are frequently one of the most thought-provoking activities we share.

GENERAL INTRODUCTION

Food connects us all. It connects individuals to their pasts, places, and other people as well as to the larger culture and society surrounding them. It connects us in satisfying a universal biological need, but its forms, meanings, and functions are specific to each culture and group. Through its production and procurement, food connects us to the earth, physical spaces, and the natural cycles; and access to and distribution of food is shaped by and connected to politics, economics, religion, and every other construction of humankind.

The field of folklore, also called "folkloristics," recognizes and studies this connectedness of food—the processes by which it connects us; the products resulting from those processes; and the experiences, memories, and events surrounding food and eating.[1] Food has been included within folklore studies since the late 1800s. The focus originally was on "folk foods," those that were traditional to groups historically tied to the land, and on "folklore about food," beliefs and customs surrounding food. But beginning in the 1960s and 1970s, folklorists explored "food as folklore," a domain of cultural and social activity in which groups and individuals interactively and creatively construct, maintain, and negotiate meaningful connections to their pasts, places, and other people.[2] Expanding food to foodways, folklorists take a holistic view of the activities, beliefs, practices, and events surrounding the preparation and consumption of food, which they use to explore concepts of identity, performance, communication, artistry, group construction and maintenance, and power.[3] They also explore ways in which these perspectives, and the knowledge gathered by scholars, can be used in educating audiences about the complexity and richness of diverse cultures, in creating sustainable agricultural and economic systems, and in shaping and interpreting artistic and recreational, as well as economic and occupational, practices. Their work touches on, and has implications for, scholarship on cuisine (the repertoire of ingredients, flavors, cooking techniques, and serving and eating styles felt to represent and articulate quality within a food culture), food systems (the networks and institutions taking food from production to consumption), and food cultures (the underlying ethos and aesthetics of a group's foodways along with the historical resources and factors shaping possibilities within that foodways).[4]

Folkloristics recognizes that food reaches into every aspect of our lives and is interwoven into our daily activities, scheduling, socializing, rituals, beliefs, health, and more. Food crosses boundaries and borders, not only of the divisions we make of the universe, but also of academia. Like the proverbial elephant described by blind wise men according to the particular part they touched, food cannot be understood in its totality by any one discipline. Each has a perspective to add, and all of those perspectives are needed. Universities are now establishing food studies programs,[5] and numerous textbooks and encyclopedias attempt to bring together the range of perspectives and methodologies useful in studying food.[6]

Folkloristics has contributed significantly to the literature on food studies. This *Reader* is the first collection to bring together examples illustrating the wide range of work done by folklorists on food. It also serves as an introduction to the field of folklore, reviewing and explaining selected concepts, theories, and methodologies. It does not cover the entirety of folkloristics, but focuses on those aspects that are, in the opinion of the editor, the most useful in the understanding of food as a cultural, social, and personal construction[7] in which individuals and groups create, negotiate, and affirm identity, meaning, and connectedness with the past, place, and other people. It emphasizes American materials, an unfortunate reflection of the field itself as well as of the availability of the publications in English.

Folkloristics overlaps at times with other disciplines in subject matter, methodologies, and theories; however, it is distinct in its emphasis on individuals and their creative expressions as traditions reflecting personal agency within the larger dominant structures of life. It is described by the American Folklore Society as "a listening discipline that uses locally based qualitative research to understand culture and community through expressive life."[8] It is characterized by ethnographic (although not always) methodologies, with the interpretation of data focusing on what traditions mean to the people participating in them. Although it historically emphasized the verbal, musical, and material traditions of groups outside the mainstream, the field now looks at all forms of expressions among all types of groups throughout the world. It frequently includes a strong sense of commitment to the people studied, calling for them to be treated as research participants and community scholars, as well as a commitment to preserving and sustaining traditions among groups that seem in danger of being overshadowed or misrepresented. The resulting scholarship contributed significantly to the awakening of awareness of food as a subject for social science and humanities research.[9] As food studies emerged as an academic discipline in the late 1990s and early 2000s, it drew heavily from folklore publications and perspectives. Folklore continues to contribute to food studies, and its perspectives continue to be useful.

A variety of scholarly definitions of both folklore and folklorists exist. The *Reader* gives an overview of definitions in Part I. The editor draws upon these definitions as well as her own folklore training that emphasized a sociolinguistics and performance studies foundation to formulate a working definition: "Folklore is the processes and products through which an individual meaningfully connects with his/her past, place, and other people" (Long 2004).

The *Reader* is organized around a definition of folklore representative of the historical shift in the 1960s to contemporary scholarship—"artistic communication in small groups."[10] Framed by an overview of the history and methodologies of folkloristics and a section on public and applied folklore, the articles are organized around the themes of "artistic," "communication," and "small groups," exploring and expanding them for the study of food. Although many of the articles are excerpted in order to make them more accessible for the readers, some are given in their entirety.

How to use this *Reader*

The *Reader* is broken into five sections, with introductions to the particular concepts covered in each section. Discussion questions are also included along with a references and further readings section. In this way, the sections are self-contained and can be utilized apart from the *Reader* as a whole, according to the users' needs and interests.

Part 1: Foundations and frameworks

The Introduction to this section gives a brief overview of the history of folklore theories and methodologies, discusses their relevance for studying food, and expands upon the concept of foodways as introduced into folklore studies by Don Yoder. The two articles represent earlier ethnographic approaches to folklore by influential scholars who contributed significantly to the recognition of food as a scholarly subject and raised questions that set in motion further scholarship.

Part 2: Food in groups, communities, and identities

This section explores the role of food in constructing and maintaining social groups and identity. A cohesive group in which people feel a sense of belonging makes up a community, and food oftentimes acts as a tool for creating that feeling as well as for drawing boundaries for those not sharing such a feeling. Folklorists study groups formed around a variety of commonalities: family, ethnicity, region, religion, and other interests or values. Traditions then emerge out of these commonalities, further defining and strengthening the group as well as the identity of the individual members.

Part 3: Food as art, symbol, and ritual

Folklorists emphasize the aesthetic dimensions of everyday life, recognizing that individuals express their sense of order and beauty whenever they participate in even the most mundane activities in foodways. They approach cooking as an artistic activity that is both functional and "ornamental," in that cooks often use their creative judgment in making choices about ingredients, cooking methods, and presentation styles, and food itself is frequently intentionally treated as an art.

The interpretation of food as a symbol, as something standing for something else, is a significant aspect of folklore studies. A prominent theme in scholarship has been the cultural and social significance of particular food items or foodways activities. Similarly, extensive attention has been given to the role of food in rituals, celebrations, and festivals.

Part 4: Food as communication, performance, and power

Contemporary scholars see folklore as resulting from communication between performers (producers) and audiences (consumers). As such, each performance of folklore is a dynamic and creative expression of the particular individuals involved. Also, each performance is an enactment of larger cultural patterns as filtered through the individuals involved in the performance and the context in which it occurs. Issues of power come into play here, in terms of what resources are available, who gets to use them and when, and who has the authority to interpret or state the meanings of the specific performances. Specific acts or events of foodways, similarly, are performances of the larger cultural traditions and are shaped by the communications occurring in these specific instances.

Part 5: Food in public and applied folklore

Folklorists have long drawn from their training to address issues in areas outside of academia as well as for their own creative productions. The field of public folklore encompasses these applications and encourages expanding our own understandings of the potential usefulness of folkloristics.

Food has frequently played a role in public and applied folklore, particularly in relation to health and medicine, K-12 education, museums, cultural interpretation and cross-cultural communications, tourism, and environmental and cultural sustainability. While folklorists have generally not addressed the contemporary industrial food system, their work critiques parts of that system and contextualizes it, giving insights into the historical and cultural backgrounds that allowed the system to evolve as it did. This section introduces some of these works and encourages the readers in developing further applications of folklore theories and methods to better understand the issues and to offer solutions. It also includes a set of poems about food written by a folklorist and which is based on her fieldwork.

Conclusion

It is hoped that this *Reader* will be useful to anyone interested not only in food, but also in how individuals can see their own role in the course of history. Personal choices matter. They make a difference in creating relationships, in building communities, and in affirming groups and people. But they can also tear them down. Individuals can also build upon the past, learning from it and using it as a rich resource to forge better presents and futures. Similarly, place can offer a site to come home to, or become a prison from which individuals want to escape. By better understanding how folklore represents such meaningful connections, we can better understand ourselves.[11] Food, too, offers potential possibilities far beyond its nutritional and biological functions. Studying it from a folklore perspective helps us recognize its richness. This volume is meant to encourage further application and exploration, not only of that perspective, but also of food's other potential possibilities.

Notes

1. For a summary of definitions of folklore, see the American Folklore Society's website: http://www.afsnet.org/?page=WhatIsFolklore&hhSearchTerms=%22definition%22.

2. For more discussions on the different approaches to the relationship between food and folklore, see Lucy M. Long, "Myths and Folklore of Food," *Encyclopedia of American Food and Drink* (Oxford University Press, 2004).

3. Questions of authenticity were significant in folklore scholarship in the 1980s and 1990s and generally centered on whether or not cultural artifacts and products were the accurate representations of that culture. Scholars point out that authenticity itself is a popular and academic construct that arose in reaction to modernity and industrialization and the resulting move away from pastoral lifestyles in which individuals were involved in all aspects of the production of the materials they used. The concept tends, though, to idealize the past and crystallize cultures as defined by specific moments in time and place as representing, but not recognizing, the constantly fluid processes occurring within the cultural groups, the individuals involved in them, the beliefs and perspectives attached to them, and the practices and forms expressing those perspectives. An excellent summary and critique of the concept of authenticity from a folkloristic perspective is Regina Bendix's *In Search of Authenticity: The Formation of Folklore Studies* (University of Wisconsin Press, 1997). In relation to food, see Shun Lu and Gary A. Fine, "The Presentation of Ethnic Authenticity: Chinese Food as a Social Accomplishment," *The Sociological Quarterly* 36, no. 3 (1995): 535–53; Jennie German Molz, "Tasting an Imagined Thailand: Authenticity and Tourism in Thai Restaurants," in *Culinary Tourism*, ed. Lucy M. Long (Lexington: University of Kentucky Press, 2004), 53–75; M. De Soucey, "Gastronationalism: Food Traditions and Authenticity Politics in the European Union," *American Sociological Review* 75, no. 3 (2010): 432–55.

4. Foundational collections of essays on food by folklorists include: *Ethnic and Regional Foodways in the United States: The Performance of Group Identity*, ed. Linda Keller Brown and Kay Mussell (Knoxville: University of Tennessee Press, 1984); *The Taste of American Place: A Reader on Regional and Ethnic Foods*, ed. Barbara G. Shortridge and James R. Shortridge (Lanham, MD: Rowman & Littlefield, 1998); *Rooted in America: Foodlore of Popular Fruits and Vegetables*, ed. David S. Wilson and Angus K. Gillespie (Knoxville: University of Tennessee Press, 1988); *Foodways and Eating Habits: Directions for Research*, ed. Michael Owen Jones, Bruce B. Giuliano, and Roberta Krell (Los Angeles, CA: California Folklore Society, 1983); *We Gather Together: Food and Festival in American Life,*

ed. Theodore C. Humphrey and Lin T. Humphrey (Ann Arbor: UMI Research, 1988); and *Culinary Tourism*, ed. Lucy M. Long (Lexington: University of Kentucky, 2004).

5. For a listing of food studies programs, see the website of the Association for the Study of Food and Society. Both food cultures and food systems are now being taught in many undergraduate programs across a variety of disciplines.

6. Some of the most widely used texts that are suitable for use in the classroom and are also relevant to folklore studies include: *Routledge International Handbook of Food Studies*, ed. Ken Albala (London: Routledge, 2013); *The Food History Reader: Primary Sources*, ed. Ken Albala (London: Bloomsbury Academic, 2014); *Food and Cultural Studies*, ed. Bob Ashley, Joanne Hollows, Steve Jones, and Ben Taylor (London: Routledge, 2004); *Food in Society: Economy, Culture, Geography*, ed. P. J. Atkins and Ian R. Bowler (London: Arnold, 2001); *Sociology on the Menu: An Invitation to the Study of Food and Society*, ed. Alan Beardsworth and Teresa Keil (London: Routledge, 1997); *Food: The Key Concepts*, ed. Warren James Belasco (Oxford: Berg, 2008); *Consuming Geographies: We Are Where We Eat*, ed. David Bell and Gill Valentine (London: Routledge, 1997); Carole Counihan and Penny Van Esterik (eds), *Food and Culture: A Reader* (New York: Routledge, 2013); Darra Goldstein (ed.), *The Gastronomica Reader* (Berkeley: University of California, 2010); Amy Elizabeth Guptill, Denise A. Copelton, and Betsy Lucal, *Food & Society: Principles and Paradoxes* (Malden, MA: Polity, 2013); Peter Jackson (ed.), *Food Words: Essays in Culinary Culture* (New York: Bloomsbury, 2013); Carolyn Korsmeyer (ed.), *The Taste Culture Reader: Experiencing Food and Drink* (Oxford: Berg, 2007); Jeff Miller and Jonathan Deutsch, *Food Studies: An Introduction to Research Methods* (Oxford: Berg, 2009); Anne Murcott, Warren Belasco, and Peter Jackson (eds), *The Handbook of Food Research* (London: Bloomsbury, 2013); and Fabio Parasecoli, *Bite Me: Food in Popular Culture* (Oxford: Berg, 2008).

7. If we think of food as "matter considered appropriate for ingestion," we can look at it as a cultural construction (each group or culture develops notions of what can and should be eaten—edibility—and these notions reflect their worldview, history, natural environment, and moral system), social construction (each group or culture develops notions of what tastes good; what foods are desirable; and how, when, with whom, where certain foods should be eaten, reflecting social institutions and hierarchies of power within that group), and personal construction (every individual negotiates the larger cultural and social constructions with their own experiences, circumstances, tastes, values, and personality to create their own universe of food.) The above definition of food draws from anthropological and ethnological scholarship but is my own wording. The concept of construction is now common in cultural fields and owes much to the seminal work by Peter L. Berger and Thomas Luckman in their 1966 publication, *The Social Construction of Reality: A Treatise in the Sociology of Knowledge* (Anchor Books).

8. See the website of the American Folklore Society for a more detailed discussion on the folklore approaches and methodologies. http://www.afsnet.org/?page=AboutFolklore (accessed March 22, 2015).

9. See Lucy M. Long, "Nourishing the Academic Imagination: The Use of Food in Teaching Concepts of Culture," *Food and Foodways* 9, no. 3–4 (2001): 235–62; and *Digest: Special Issue: Eating Across the Curriculum*, edited by Lucy M. Long (vol.19, 1999).

10. Dan Ben-Amos, "Toward a Definition of Folklore in Context," *Journal of American Folklore* 84 (1971): 3–15.

11. For an eloquent discussion on how folkloristics can contribute to a deeper understanding of the human condition, see William A. Wilson, "The Deeper Necessity: Folklore and the Humanities," *Journal of American Folklore* 101, no. 400 (1988): 156–67.

PART I
FOUNDATIONS: HISTORY, DEFINITIONS, AND METHODOLOGIES

INTRODUCTION TO PART ONE

History of the discipline of folklore[1]

Folklore began as a scholarly discipline in the European social and political movements of romantic nationalism of the late 1700s.[2] This was a time of great social and political upheaval in Europe. Industrialization and urbanization were beginning, both of which physically separated people from the land while also introducing technologies and new lifestyles that changed everyday life. Politically, much of Europe was in flux, with boundaries being redrawn, kingdoms uniting and breaking apart, and notions of individuals having the right to think for themselves challenging the authority of the church and monarchies.

Romanticism was the idea that peasants were remnants of earlier societies tied to the land and therefore were closer to the natural and spiritual identity of a place. By collecting stories, songs, and superstitions of peasants, scholars could get a glimpse into both the past ways of life and the essence of national identity. Nationalism was the idea that a group of people sharing a common place of origin could be a political entity with distinctive identity—and autonomy. This, in turn, meant that those who declared themselves a nation had a moral and spiritual right to ownership of that land. The traditions of the peasant groups living on that land could then be used as resources for constructing new art forms and customs that defined the character of the nation.

Germanic areas initially led the way in collecting peasant traditions, thanks largely to the Grimm brothers, who collected and published "*Marchen*" ("household tales") from the peasant women who served as nannies for many German children. Although a booklet of such stories had been previously published in France, it brought attention to "fairy tales" and "folk tales," popularizing them for general audiences as well as presenting them as fodder for scholars to study. One of the concerns for those studying these tales was their origin. Those looking for affirmation for nation constructing wanted to prove that the tales came from specific places, while others were interested in them as cultural artifacts. Scholars therefore began documenting and comparing tales and their variations, hoping to trace them to the original, or "ur," tale and its source. They developed ways of classifying and comparing tales, identifying themes and motifs (patterns) within the tales. The location of tale variants could then be mapped, so that its development could be traced over time and place. The historical-geographic method emerged from these concerns, providing a methodology that helped make folklorists into a "science," since it meant that data could be collected and theories tested objectively.[3] It was also used in the study of forms other than tales—riddles, proverbs, myths, ballads and folksongs, and even material culture, providing the foundation for the European field of ethnology (so called in the US folklife studies). Ethnologists throughout Europe, particularly in Scandinavia, developed cataloguing systems for the oral and customary forms and material artifacts they collected, establishing databases for the comparative and historical analysis of these materials.

Meanwhile, England during this time (1700, 1800s) was politically and economically powerful and felt no need to construct a new culture. Instead, they could look back fondly on the stories of the past, collecting and preserving them as a reassuring reminder of their current status. In 1846, an English scholar, William Thoms, suggested replacing the German word "volkskunde" with the English "folk-lore" (the hyphen was later dropped) to refer to these "popular antiquities." Another English scholar also contributed significantly to the study of folklore, when Edward B. Tylor applied the principles of biological evolution to cultures with societies evolving through three stages: savage, barbarism, and civilization (1871). Although his theory was later discredited, the effects of it have lingered, so that even today, nations are described as primitive or civilized, developed or underdeveloped (or developing). Also, Tylor's notion of "survivals"—people or customs left behind as cultures evolved—shaped folklore studies as well as popular stereotypes of the subject as being unscientific, useless, and trivial.

These European concepts of folklore were brought to the United States; but since "peasants" were lacking, scholars looked for groups that might display characteristics of peasants—groups that were outside the mainstream culture, but which had a strong sense of oral tradition and practices that seemed to reflect survivals from the past. These include people isolated by geography (mountaineers; islanders), ethnicity (Mexican-, Irish-, Italian-Americans), occupation (fishermen, loggers), religion (Amish), language (Cajuns, Hispanics, Native Americans), and race (African Americans, Native Americans). Also, rather than studying the "old ways," they shifted focus on the things that were "traditional"—that is, that had been handed down through oral tradition. In 1888, the American Folklore Society was established, and its journal published a new American definition: "Oral tradition and belief handed down from generation to generation without the use of writing" (Newell 1890: 134–6). This definition opened the way for scholars to see folklore as existing among all groups of people, an idea further developed in the 1930s, by anthropologist Robert Redfield, who suggested that every culture had a mainstream, powerful "Great Society" with numerous smaller cultures or "Little Societies." This meant that folk groups could exist within contemporary, modern societies, not just isolated ones. Folklore then was cultural forms and means of expression that existed outside the mainstream, official culture, even among the literate and the educated. "Folklore is a body of traditional belief, custom, and expression, handed down largely by word of mouth and circulating chiefly outside of commercial and academic means of communication and instruction (Botkin 1938)."

Folklore scholars in the 1960s continued refining definitions of folklore, drawing from a number of intellectual movements, including Russian formalism, structuralism, and studies such as linguistics, and sociolinguistics.[4]

Materials that circulate traditionally among members of any group in different versions, whether in oral form or by means of a customary example. (Brunvand 1968)

The hidden submerged culture lying behind the shadow of official civilization. (Dorson 1968)

Artistic communication in small groups. (Ben-Amos 1971: 13)

Communicative processes [and] forms . . . which evidence continuities and consistencies in human thought and behavior through time or space. (Georges 1983)

All of these definitions shift focus from the "stuff" (the text or product) of folklore to the processes through which folklore exists, so that the means and mediums of transmission are usually seen as a defining feature. Folklore is now understood as being about people communicating and interacting. This "paradigm shift," in folklore studies draws heavily from sociolinguistics and performance theories, in which folklore is "enacted" in specific instances within specific contexts and restraints. Contemporary folklore scholarship recognizes the dynamic, creative nature of human activities and the role of the individual acting within the larger cultural structures and power hierarchies.[5] It also recognizes that forms, contexts, and groups are all interconnected so that a single item or performance cannot be understood individually. Instead, each references another, and multiple identities shape the experience of the participating individuals.[6] Many folklorists now explore the folkloric elements within cultural productions, identifying those aspects—the product itself, the processes of transmission and distribution, the production methods, and the functions—in which personal creativity and meaning is possible. The discipline now includes the study of any social group, all forms of cultural expression—mass-mediated as well as personal creations—and issues of power shaping both the construction and the performance of folklore.

Food in the history of the discipline

Where was food in the history of folkloristics? Initially, it was not treated as a serious subject for scholarly study. European ethnology included cooking implements, farming and harvesting traditions, and common dishes and ingredients within its descriptive studies of peasant life, but it focused on the oral genres (narratives, proverbs, myths, riddles, and ballads) for developing classification systems and theorizing folklore.[7] Food was perhaps too mundane, private, and domestic (or female) to be considered a significant form of artistic expression or cultural practice. European, especially Scandinavian, German, and British, folklorists in the first half of the 1900s, however, began recognizing food's integral role in daily life as well as in rituals and celebrations. They conducted extensive documentation of the material culture, customs, and beliefs surrounding foodways as well as detailed descriptions of the foods themselves.[8]

In the United States, food was included within the American Folklore Society's 1888 inaugural mission statement to focus on "the fast vanishing remains of Folk-Lore in America" (JAF 1888, v1, p. 1). John G. Bourke's 1895 article in the Society's journal on the "folk-foods of the Rio Grande Valley and of Northern Mexico" illustrated the prevailing concern with traditions, such as foodways, that were being replaced by modern industrial ones. Interestingly, though, the journal did not publish another article on food for seventy years! This does not reflect a complete lack of interest in food. A number of influential scholars who overlapped with folklore and anthropology studied it: Margaret Mead, Robert Redfield, Audrey Richards, Raymond Firth, Claude Levi-Strauss, Roland Barthes, Mary Douglas, and others.[9]

Meanwhile, in the 1950s and 1960s, American folklorist, Don Yoder, promoted European ethnology approaches in the United States, suggesting the use of the term "folklife" to similarly include all the practices and forms of a group. Although he focused in his own research on a group that could easily be classified as folk—the Pennsylvania-Dutch, as a professor at one of the leading folklore programs in the United States from the mid 1900s until the early 2000s, he significantly influenced several generations of folklorists to look beyond the oral genres to the customary (religious, belief, medical, festivals, rituals) and material (clothing, art, food) ones. He also published widely on food traditions, borrowing the term "foodways" to replace "folk cookery" and encouraged numerous students to pursue the folkloristic study of food.[10]

Also during the 1970s, other influential graduates in folklore were encouraging the study of food—Michael Owen Jones and Robert Georges at the University of California, Los Angeles, Alan Dundes at the University of California, Berkeley, and European folklore scholars at Indiana University. A periodical for publishing this work on food, *Digest: An Interdisciplinary Review of Food and Foodways,* was established by students at the University of Pennsylvania in 1979, and in the 1980s a number of anthologies followed: *Foodways and Eating Habits: Directions for Research* (Jones, Giuliano, and Krell 1983), *Ethnic and Regional Foodways in the United States* (Mussell and Brown 1984), and *"We Gather Together": Food and Festival in American Life* (Humphrey and Humphrey 1988). These works grounded scholarship on food in ethnographic fieldwork and in the newer paradigms for folklore theory, exploring the role of food in constructing and negotiating group identity and boundaries, in expressing individual creativity and aesthetics, and in holding onto traditional patterns of life.

Contemporary folklorists throughout the world recognize food as a valid subject for scholarship. They not only study the food traditions themselves, but also use food to theorize about cultural processes, the nature of tradition and folkloric interactions, and the discipline itself. The American Folklore Society includes a Foodways Section, established in 1970s, which regularly sponsors panels at the annual meetings along with the journal, *Digest*. Academic folklore programs frequently include at least one course on foodways or the subject appears within other courses, and folklorists working in the public sector almost always mention food in some manner. Although much of the focus in the past has been on European and North American foodways, attention to other geographic regions is growing.

Folklore methodologies for the study of food

Methodology in folkloristics has historically focused on the procedures and issues surrounding the documentation and collection of folklore materials, and emphasis has been given to primary sources for that data—people and their artifacts. The historic-geographic method discussed earlier was long considered the primary method, and its emphasis on detailed descriptions, identification, cataloguing, and comparison of motifs and themes was carried over to the study of food traditions by European folklorists in the first half of the 1900s, resulting in documentation and archiving of recipes, ingredients, farming and cooking implements, and food customs, particularly around holiday and life cycle celebrations. Although the method is no longer emphasized in contemporary scholarship, it offers a useful model for studying the history and geographic distribution of foodways.

A significant aspect of folkloristics is its emphasis on ethnographic fieldwork and individual "tradition bearers" as carriers of tradition. Initially seen as straightforward representatives of their community or tradition, such individuals came to be recognized as active agents in interpreting and reproducing their cultures. Their life histories, then, could suggest the changing uses of tradition as well as the personal creativity and innovation displayed in adapting them (Titon 1980). The focus on individuals led to theorizing about the role of "tradition bearers" in their communities and how best to select them.[11] Now usually referred to as "community scholars," individuals are generally chosen as representative of a group (recognizing that folk groups are diverse and complex) but also as illustrative of the various processes involved in folklore.

Partly because of this attention to individuals, folklorists also recognized the potential for ethnography to change the very traditions being studied and to influence, even harm, the groups and the individuals participating in them. Folklorist Barre Toelken, in particular, wrote eloquently about the ethics of fieldwork and his own experiences (1976, 1979/1996, 1998). Folklore scholars drawing from feminist and other perspectives further explored these ethical dimensions but also pointed out that documentation and interpretation had historically been one-sided, representing only the scholars' perspectives. They suggested that scholarship would be more accurate as well as ethical and useful if ethnography were done in collaboration with the individuals being studied. Such collaborative and reciprocal ethnography (Brown 2000; Lawless 1991, 2000) is a significant aspect of effective studies of foodways.

Folklorists began theorizing about fieldwork itself in the 1960s, questioning the usefulness of collecting texts and artifacts without looking at their role and function within the cultural groups participating in them. Attention was then turned to context (both the immediate and the larger cultural-social surroundings of that text) and texture (the stylistic elements involved in the production of the text and its variations)[12] and reflected the confluence of interests between folklore and other disciplines addressing culture as a dynamic social production. Linguistics, sociolinguistics, and sociology were particularly influential, with much cross-fertilization with folklore and anthropology. Models that had direct influence on folklore theory included Goffman's presentation of self (1959) and frame analysis (1974), ethnopoetics (Tedlock 1992), and Dell Hymes's ethnography of speaking (1974). These methods reflected the paradigm shift in folklore, but also stimulated further theorizing on ethnography itself.[13]

One of the central questions addressed by this more recent folklore scholarship on food is that of meaning.[14] What do certain foods mean, not only on a large cultural and social scale but also to individuals. It is helpful here to distinguish between "meaning" and "meaningfulness." The former refers to an intellectual, cognitive understanding of what something represents that is created and shared publicly. "Meaningfulness" (sometimes called "felt meaning") refers to what it means personally to an individual; that is, what memories and emotions it evokes for them. For example, in the United States a cake with candles on it signifies a birthday celebration. Each individual, however, has one's own memories and experiences with cakes as well as personal beliefs about celebrations and birthdays. Some individuals may have negative associations with cakes and celebrations in their past, and therefore they do not want to relive those memories. Others may simply feel that birthdays are unimportant and that any celebration of them, including with cakes, are meaningless. At the same time, a cake made specifically for that individual by someone in a special relationship might take on entirely new and different associations and can become very meaningful. Meaningfulness represents what matters to individuals. It motivates them, can be a goal in participating in an activity, and provides purpose to traditions. Folklore scholarship, while attending to the more public meanings of food, generally emphasizes the meaningfulness of a product, practice, or tradition to specific individuals or groups. Two particularly useful methodological models for exploring food in this way are elaborations on Yoder's concept of foodways and an adaptation of Hymes "ethnography of speaking" to "ethnography of eating."

"Foodways" was mentioned above in the historical development of folkloristics, but here it is expanded on as both a theoretical construct and a methodological model. The term itself was used in the early 1940s, and even earlier, to refer to food habits and patterns of consumption.[15] Folklorist Don Yoder borrowed it from John Honigman (1948, 1961), who probably borrowed it from either anthropologist John William Bennett (1941) or from government documents of the National Nutritional Council for Defense (1941). Yoder used the term in place of the more common "folk cookery" in the early 1970s to refer to the whole range of activities and expressive forms surrounding food and eating within a cultural group: "For the total cookery complex, including attitudes, taboos, and meal systems—the whole range of cookery and food habits in a society—Honigman's term 'foodways' has become useful" (Yoder 1972: 325).

Foodways includes not only what people eat, but when, where, why, how and with whom. The term has since become common parlance outside of folklore, frequently overlapping with food habits, food culture, foodlore, and food traditions; however, its use within the discipline is distinctive, carrying particular theoretical and methodological implications. For one thing, Yoder coupled it with the concept of "folklife," emphasizing the totality of a group's practices and expressions, a departure from many American folklorists' emphasis at that time on only selected aspects of expressive culture, specifically the verbal arts. Furthermore, it was introduced during the overall paradigm shift in folklore from focus on text and product to context and process, and it carries those theoretical ramifications. It therefore offered a way to talk about food as a more complicated system of activities and as a domain for creativity, communication, and meaning-making.

Foodways has since been developed within the field of folklore as both a theory and a methodology. Folklorists working in the contexts of public folklore have particularly utilized it in educational presentations and exhibits.[16] Folklorist Charles Camp used it in his analyses of American food culture (1982), and I have drawn upon both Yoder and Camp in my own development of foodways as a conceptual and methodological framework for studying the meanings of food. (Long 2001, 2004, 2005) This *Reader* uses the following definition and model:

FOODWAYS—The total system of practices and concepts surrounding food and eating.
    PRODUCT—the food itself (ingredient, recipe, dish, meal, food culture, or cuisine)
    PRACTICES/PROCESSES (oral—narratives, instructions, vocabulary; customary (techniques, styles), material forms—implements)
        Production—growing, manufacturing of raw ingredients into "food"
        Procurement—obtaining those ingredients (garden, store, vendors, etc.)
        Preservation—the storage of food; methods and techniques of preserving food
        Preparation—preparing ingredients and cooking
        Presentation—serving, displaying, presenting food
        Consumption—eating, ingesting, tasting of food
        Clean-up/Disposal—cleaning up from preparation and consumption; disposing of unwanted food; use of left-over food
PERFORMANCE
    Performance—Intentional and unintentional functions and symbolism of food
    Conceptualizations—beliefs, evaluation systems, aesthetics and attitudes around food
    Contexts and Meal System—physical spaces, occasions, and types of events for specific aspects of foodways; expected routine of meals—times of day, menu, contexts

As a methodology, foodways provides a systematic way of observing and describing the full range of food-related activities. It can be applied to individual, single ingredient, meal, group, or culture. It then lends itself to conducting comparative studies of the foodways patterns of cultures, subgroups within a culture, historical eras, and individuals. Although some of them are self-evident and straightforward, these components need some explication. The basic questions of who, where, what, when, how and why can be asked of each component. Comparisons can also be made between paradigms, that is, the expected contents of a food, and the variations that occur in the actual performance of that paradigm.

As a theory, foodways posits an interpretive lens for the multifaceted and multi-vocal nature of food. First, in identifying the range of activities connected to food and eating, it demonstrates that food is integrated into our everyday and celebratory lives. Secondly, the foodways model recognizes the interconnectedness of these activities. Each part of the network shapes, informs, and influences the other. Thirdly, foodways recognizes food as a carrier and construction of meaning for individuals and groups. Cultural symbolism as well as personal meaning or "meaningfulness" can be attached to a food anywhere within this framework. Similarly, food products can carry meaning for an individual because of meaningful associations elsewhere in the foodways system. Foodways offers a way to identify where the meaning of a food lies for a given individual. An individual can and may insert his or her inventiveness, artistry, or creativity into any part of the system without noticeably changing the final product.

A second methodology for documenting, analyzing, and interpreting meaning in food is an adaptation of Dell Hymes's "ethnography of speaking" to an "ethnography of eating." Drawing upon linguistic theories, Hymes suggested that for every act of speech, an individual draws from one's pool of vocabulary and grammatical structures but then selects from that pool according to the specific context in which the speech is occurring and according to the specific meaning intended by that individual. Those options and the contexts within which choices are being made are shaped by numerous external factors (culture, race, ethnicity, gender, class, time and place), but every individual balances those factors with one's own immediate needs, intentions, and creativity in each specific circumstance.

Adapting the model to food calls for an initial ethnography of all the options available to an individual as well as in-depth observations of the actual choices made, the contexts in which they are made, the external factors shaping both the options and the choices, and the individual's own explanations of those choices. Such a model enables us to move away from food as static "text" with set meanings to better identify and understand the variety of meanings that can be attached to the activities, processes, and conceptualizations surrounding food by individuals in a variety of contexts or "food events" (Camp 1982). It approaches meaning as personally as well as socially constructed and acknowledges that external, political and historical issues of power, hierarchy, and status that shape the options available to individuals and the choices that they make.

Also significant in the folklore methodology, and applicable to food, is the attention given to personal creativity and innovation. Variations in recipes, cooking techniques, menus, ingredients, etc., may result from inexperience, incompetence, or ignorance, but it also can be the purposeful expression of an individual's identity and taste. Food is an aesthetic domain, as well as a biological, economic, or political one, and all aspects of foodways can be approached as an aesthetic experience to be evaluated in terms of beauty, engagement of the senses, or satisfying arrangement of components. Food itself has an obvious aesthetic dimension, but so do the ways in which individuals organize their pantry, plan their garden rows, arrange food on their plates, or even put away clean dishes. The potential for finding pleasure in such activities drives people choices, and folklorists recognize that—and attend to it in their fieldwork and observations.

Articles in *Reader*

Don Yoder is one of the foundational figures in the study of foodways in American folklore scholarship. In this essay, "Folk Cookery," published in 1972, he discusses the adaptation of European ethnological methods to American contexts, suggesting the word "foodways" to refer to the broader sweep of activities around food traditions. Using examples from his own fieldwork with Pennsylvania Germans, he then discusses American foodways as a layering of cultural traditions—Native American, ethnic, and regional— and suggests further areas of research.

Gunter Wiegelmann's 1974 article, "Innovations in Food and Meals," is credited by another significant scholar, Nils-Arvid Bringeus, as bringing European foodways studies into contemporary folklore scholarship (1971). Rather than a description of traditional customs and habits with the underlying assumption that folk cultures were static and in danger of dying out, Weigleman explored variations in in meal systems and menus as illustrating processes of innovation.

Discussion questions and activities

1. Follow a recipe or an ingredient over time and place. Can you see how it has been shaped by history and geography? Are there specific factors that have influenced its use and meaning? (Good examples are lobster, coffee, tomatoes, and chocolate.)

2. Can you create a map of your own city or neighborhood showing where certain foods are prevalent? Does the map reflect or display class, race, ethnicity, occupation, or religion in any way?

3. Identify a common food motif or theme (for example, dough wrapped around a filling) and compare that motif across cultures. What variations appear? Do those variations reflect different histories and geographies?

4. Explore the beliefs you hold about food, eating, and health. Where did they come from? How do they shape your food choices? Would they still affect your foodways if they were proven by medical science to be untrue? (Think of recent debates on carbohydrates, gluten, fats, vegan and vegetarian diets.)

5. Apply the foodways framework to yourself or another individual in order to develop a food-based life history. Can you identify occasions in the past in which certain foods or foodways activities became memorable or meaningful? What parts of foodways are the most significant to you now? Do any patterns appear? Can you compare them to patterns in the past as well as to larger national patterns?

Notes

1. Some excellent histories of the discipline have been published. The American Folklore Society sponsored a collection of essays (Clements 1988), Simon Bronner published an intellectual history of folklore in the United States (1986), and Rosemary Zumwalt analyzes the split between what she terms the "literary" and the "anthropological" folklorists (1988). A history of the discipline is frequently included in introductory texts to folklore: Blank (2013), Brunvand (1998), Dorson (1983), Georges and Jones (1995), Oring (1986, 1986a, 2012), Schoemaker (1990) Sims and Stephens (2005), Toelken (1979). Feintuch (2003) is oftentimes used for graduate courses as an introduction to key concepts in folklore.

2. Johann Gottfried von Herder is oftentimes identified as the "father" of the field in that his writings inspired individuals to look seriously at peasant traditions and to begin collecting them. See Wilson (1989) for an excellent overview of Herder and Romantic Nationalism. For a critique of how these ideas have shaped the development of the field see Bendix (1997).

3. The historic-geographic method is also referred to as the Finnish comparative method since it originated there with the study of folktales by Julius Krohn in the second half of the 1800s and by his son, Kaarle, in the early 1900s. The method was borrowed from philology (the study of words) and the study of the oral epics to develop a system for reconstructing an oral tradition and identifying the "ur" form (archetype) of a tale. The Finnish scholar Antti Aarne developed the initial classification system for folktales in the early 1900s (1910), which was then refined into a tale-type index with a numbering system (Aarne and Thompson 1961) by the American folklorist Stith Thompson. Thompson also developed an indexing system for tale motifs (1955).
   For an overview of the historic-geographic method as well as critiques of it, see Goldberg (1996), Meider (1987).

4. That scholars debated among themselves over the nature of the materials they studied is evident in a 1959 essay by Maria Leach, who gave twenty-one definitions in the Funk and Wagnalls's *Standard Dictionary of Folklore, Mythology, and Legend*, which she edited. Also see Bascom (1955, 1972) for an overview of these earlier debates. Also, a number of folklorists skirted the issue of definitions by emphasizing the characteristics of folklore (Dundes 1965; Sims and Stephens 2005: 1–12), an approach that was also critiqued (Oring 1986a: 1–22).

5. Among the folklore scholars considered foundational to this shift are Ben-Amos (1971), Hymes, Bauman, and Abrahams. Michael Owen Jones (1983), Robert Georges (1984), and Don Yoder (1972), and his students, Jay Anderson (1971) and Charles Camp (1978, 1979, 1980, 1982, 1989), Janet Theophano, Leslie Prosterman, Amy Schuman (1981), and Kathy Neustadt, among others) were instrumental in applying the shift to the subject of food. Sections III and IV of this *Reader* give more explanation of the ideas and theories in this shift.

6. This notion of the complexity of folkloric interactions is known as "intersectionality." It is a significant aspect of feminist, gender-, and post-colonial scholarship. For more explanation see Sims and Stephens (2005: 198–200).

7. For histories of food within folklore studies in Europe, see Breugel and Laurioux (2002), Bringeus and Wiegelmann (1971), Salomonsson (1990), Wiegelmann (1972). Although not specifically folkloristic, European food scholars

established a journal in 1985, *Food and Foodways: Explorations in the History and Culture of Human Nourishment*. Many US and Canadian-trained folklorists also worked with European materials and scholarship, continuing the emphasis on fieldwork and comparative studies that characterized ethnology. (I am indebted to American folklorist and food scholar, Yvonne Lockwood, for perspectives on European food and folklore studies.)

8. The role of belief in foodways activities was a significant area of study in European folklore scholarship. These beliefs were usually not founded on scientific knowledge, so were usually considered "superstitions." For an example of how such beliefs shaped food traditions, see Nils-Arvid Bringeus (1975).

9. A brief history of the role of food in cultural anthropology is given by Counihan and Van Esterik (2013) in the introduction to their edited volume, *Food and Culture: A Reader*, first published in 1997. A number of articles included here, particularly in the first section on "Food, Meaning, and Voice," are familiar to academically trained folklorists.

10. Among his students are numerous names that are mentioned in this volume, particularly Jay Anderson, Janet Theophano, and Charles Camp, who wrote some of the first folklore dissertations on food in the US. I also consider him a mentor. For his graduate class on Folklife, I conducted an ethnography of Korean restaurants to explore how they adapted their kimchi recipes for different audiences. Yoder's enthusiasm for the topic encouraged me to continue studying foodways.

11. See for example, Toelken (1979) and Goldstein (1975). The latter made the distinction between active and passive tradition bearers, pointing out that fieldwork needed to include a variety of individuals in a community, not just the "star performer" (best known or most acclaimed individual).

12. For the context, see Dundes (1964, 1965) and Ben-Amos (1993). A seminal publication on texture was again Dundes (1964).

13. For seminal examples, see Barbara Kirshenblatt-Gimblett (1975), Ben-Amos and Goldstein (1975), and Toelken (1976).

14. An excellent example of such work in food is Kathy Neustadt's *Clambake* (1992) in which she critiques and expands upon the structuralism of Claude Levi-Strauss to explore the meanings of this food tradition in New England. Also, the edited volume, *Rooted in America: Foodlore of Popular Fruits and Vegetables* (Wilson and Gillespie 1999), explores a variety of theoretical perspectives for interpreting the meanings of nine different fruits and vegetables usually perceived as iconic or somehow significant in American foodways: pumpkins, apples, oranges, tomatoes, watermelon, corn, bananas, potatoes, and tobacco.

15. See Camp (1997) and Adema (2007) for a fuller history of the term. Adema points to a 1904 use of it in reference to the alimentary canal in a medical journal. Camp states that it was adapted from the term "folkways," which was introduced in 1906 by William Graham Sumner. According to Camp, Sumner "intended to provide a way of describing the knitted wholeness of folk culture" (1997: 367). Its use and ownership are somewhat contested; however, it seems fairly clear that Yoder is responsible for introducing it into folklore and folklife studies (1972). Folklorists have used it since, with theoretical perspectives implied in it. Camp and Long have each discussed it as a theory of food and folklore.

16. I credit folklorists working with the Smithsonian Institution's Folklife Festival for developing the concept as a practice. They frequently included foodways demonstrations and displays in the festival.

References

Aarne, Antti Amatus and Stith Thompson. *The Types of the Folktale: A Classification and Bibliography*. Helsinki: Suomalainen Tiedeakatemia, 1973 (1961).

Abrahams, Roger D. *Everyday Life: A Poetics of Vernacular Practices*. Philadelphia: University of Pennsylvania, 2005.

Abrahams, Roger D. "Toward an Enactment Theory of Folklore." In *Frontiers of Folklore*, edited by William Russell Bascom, 79–102. Boulder, CO: Published by Westview for the American Association for the Advancement of Science, Washington, DC, 1977.

Adema, Pauline. "Foodways." In *The Oxford Companion to American Food and Drink*, edited by Andrew F. Smith, 232–33. Oxford: Oxford University Press, 2007.

Anderson, Jay. "The Study of Contemporary Foodways in American Folklife Research." *Keystone Folklore Quarterly* 16 (1971): 155–63.

Bascom, William R. "Folklore, Verbal Art, and Culture." *Journal of American Folklore* 86, no. 342 (October–December) (1973): 373–81.

Bauman, Richard. *Verbal Art as Performance*. Prospect Heights, IL: Waveland, 1977.

Ben-Amos, Dan. "Toward a Definition of Folklore in Context." *Toward New Perspectives in Folklore, Special Issue, Journal of American Folklore* 84 (1971): 3–15.

Ben-Amos, Dan. "The Seven Strands of Tradition: Varieties in Its Meaning in American Folklore Studies." *Journal of Folklore Research* 21 (1984): 97–131.

Ben-Amos, Dan and Kenneth S. Goldstein (eds). *Folklore: Performance and Communication*. The Hague: Mouton, 1975.

Bendix, Regina. *In Search of Authenticity: The Formation of Folklore Studies*. Madison, WI: University of Wisconsin, 1997.

Bendix, Regina. ed. "From Fakelore to the Politics of Culture: The Changing Contours of American Folkloristics." In *In Search of Authenticity*, 188–218. Madison, WI: University of Wisconsin, 1997.

Bennett, John W., Harvey L. Smith, and Herbert Passin. "Food and Culture in Southern Illinois—A Preliminary Report." *American Sociological Review* 7, no. 5 (1942): 645–60.

Beriss, David and David E. Sutton. *The Restaurants Book: Ethnographies of Where We Eat*. Oxford: Berg, 2007.

Blank, Trevor J. and Robert Glenn Howard. *Tradition in the Twenty-First Century: Locating the Role of the past in the Present*. Logan, UT: Utah State University Press, 2013.

Botkin, Benjamin A. *Supplementary Instructions to the American Guide Manual: Guide for Folklore Studies, Box* 69, Federal Writers Project. Records Group 69. National Archives, Washington, DC. August 15, 1938.

Bourke, John G. "Folk-Foods of the Rio Grande Valley and of Northern Mexico." *Journal of American Folk-Lore* 8, no. 28 (January–March 1895): 41–71.

Bringeus, Nils-Arvid. "Food and Folk-beliefs: On Prophylactic Measures Connected with the Boiling of Blood-sausage." *Ethnological Food Research—Reports*, 29–53. Finland: Helsinki, 1975.

Bringeus, Nils-Arvid and Gunter Wiegelmann. "Ethnological Food Research in Europe and the USA." *Ethnologia Europaea* 4 (1971): 6–13.

Bringeus, Nils-Arvid. Man, Food and Milieu: A Swedish Approach to Food Ethnology. Edinburgh: Tuckwell Press, 1971.

Bronner, Simon J. *American folklore Studies: An Intellectual History*. Lawrence: University Press of Kansas, 1986.

Bronner, Simon J. *Following Tradition: Folklore in the Discourse of American Culture*. Logan, UT: Utah State University Press, 1998.

Brown, Mary Ellen, ed. Issues in Collaboration and Representation. Special issue, *Journal of Folklore Research* 37, no. 2–3 (2000).

Brown, Linda Keller and Kay Mussell, eds. *Ethnic and Regional Foodways in the United States: The Performance of Group Identity*. Knoxville: The University of Tennessee Press, 1984.

Brunvand, Jan Harold. *The Study of American Folklore: An Introduction*. New York: W.W. Norton, 1968.

Camp, Charles. *American Food Ways: What, When, Why, and How We Eat in America*. Little Rock, Arkansas: August House, 1989.

Camp, Charles. "Food in American Culture: A Bibliographic Essay." *The Journal of American Culture* 2, no. 3 (1979): 559–70.

Clements, William M. *100 Years of American Folklore Studies: A Conceptual History*. Washington, DC: American Folklore Society, 1988.

Cocchiara, Giuseppe. *The History of Folklore in Europe*. Philadelphia: Institute for the Study of Human Issues, 1981.

Counihan, Carole M. and Van Esterik. eds. *Food and Culture: A Reader*. New York: Routledge, 1997.

Dégh, Linda. *American Folklore and the Mass Media*. Bloomington: Indiana University Press, 1994.

Dorson, Richard M. *Folklore and Fakelore: Essays toward a Discipline of Folk Studies*. Cambridge, MA: Harvard University Press, 1976.

Dorson, Richard M. *Folklore and Folklife, an Introduction*. Chicago: University of Chicago Press, 1972.

Dundes, Alan. "Texture, Text, and Context." *Southern Folklore Quarterly* 20 (1964): 251–65.

Dundes, Alan, ed. *The Study of Folklore*. Englewood Cliffs, NJ: Prentice-Hall, 1965.

Fenton, Alexander. "A Provisional Note on Ethnological Food Research in Britain." *Ethnologia Europaea* 5 (1971): 53–4.

Georges, Robert A. "Folklore." In *Sound Archives: A Guide to Their Establishment and Development*, edited by David Lance. Milton Keynes, England: International Association of Sound Archives, 1983.

Goffman, Erving. *Frame Analysis: An Essay on the Organization of Experience*. New York: Harper & Row, 1974.

Goffman, Erving. *The Presentation of Self in Everyday Life*. Garden City, NY: Doubleday, 1959.

Goldberg, Christine. "Comparative Approach." In *American Folklore: An Encyclopedia*, edited by Jan Harold Brunvand, 318–22. N.p.: Taylor and Francis, 1996.

Goldstein, Kenneth S. "On the Application of the Concepts of Active and Inactive Traditions to the Study of Repertory." In *Toward New Perspectives in Folklore*, edited by Américo Paredes and Richard Bauman, 62–7. Austin: Published for the American Folklore Society by the University of Texas, 1972.

Handler, Richard and Jocelyn Linnekin. "Tradition, Genuine or Spurious." In *Folk Groups and Folklore Genres: A Reader*, edited by Elliott Oring, 38–42. Logan, UT: Utah State University Press, 1989.

Humphrey, Theodore C. and Lin T. Humphrey. *We Gather Together: Food and Festival in American Life*. Ann Arbor: UMI Research, 1988.

Hymes, Dell. *Foundations in Sociolinguistics: An Ethnographic Perspective*. Philadelphia: University of Pennsylvania Press, 1974.

Jones, Michael Owen., Bruce B. Giuliano, and Roberta Krell. *Foodways and Eating Habits: Directions for Research*. Los Angeles, CA: California Folklore Society, 1983.

Kirshenblatt-Gimblett, Barbara. "A Parable in Context: A Social Interactional Analysis of Storytelling Performance." In *Folklore: Performance and Communication*, edited by Dan Ben-Amos and Kenneth S. Goldstein, 105–30. The Hague: Mouton, 1975.

Lawless, Elaine. "'Reciprocal Ethnography': No One Said It Was Easy." *Journal of Folklore Research* 37, no. 2–3 (2000): 197–205.

Lawless, Elaine. "Women's Life Stories and Reciprocal Ethnography as Feminist and Emergent." *Journal of Folklore Research* 28 (1991): 35–61.

Leach, Maria. "Folklore." In *Funk & Wagnalls Standard Dictionary of Folklore, Mythology and Legend*, edited by Maria Leach. Vol. 1, 398–403. New York: Funk & Wagnalls, 1959.

Long, Lucy M. "Foodways: Using Food to Teach Folklore Theories and Methods." *Digest* 19 (2005): 32–6.

Meiselman, Herbert L., ed. *Dimensions of the Meal: The Science, Culture, Business, and Art of Eating*. Gaithersburg, MD: Aspen, 2000.

Narváez, Peter and Martin Laba. *Media Sense: The Folklore-popular Culture Continuum*. Bowling Green, OH: Bowling Green State University Popular, 1986.

Neustadt, Kathy. *Clambake: A History and Celebration of an American Tradition*. Amherst: University of Massachusetts, 1992.

Newell, William Wells. "On the Field and Work of a Journal of American Folk-Lore." *Journal of American Folklore* 1, no. 1 (1888): 3–7.

Oring, Elliott. "On the Concepts of Folklore." In *Folk Groups and Folklore Genres: An Introduction*, edited by Elliott Oring. 1–23. Logan, UT: Utah State University Press, 1986.

Paredes, Américo and Richard Bauman, eds. *Towards New Perspectives in Folklore*. Austin: University of Texas, 1972.

Salomonsson, Anders. "Food for Thought. Themes in Recent Swedish Ethnological Food Research." *Ethnologia Scandinavica* 20 (1990): 111–133.

Schoemaker, George H. *The Emergence of Folklore in Everyday Life: A Fieldguide and Sourcebook*. Bloomington, IN: Trickster, 1990.

Shuman, Amy. *Other People's Stories: Entitlement Claims and the Critique of Empathy*. Urbana: University of Illinois Press, 1995.

Sims, Martha C. and Martine Stephens. *Living Folklore: An Introduction to the Study of People and Their Traditions*. Logan: Utah State University Press, 2005.

Stahl, Sandra Dolby. *Literary Folkloristics and the Personal Narrative*. Bloomington: Indiana University Press, 1989.

Tedlock, Dennis. "Ethnopoetics." In *Folklore, Cultural Performances, and Popular Entertainments: A Communications-centered Handbook*, edited by Richard Bauman, 81–5. New York: Oxford University Press, 1992.

Thompson, Stith. *Motif-index of Folk-literature; a Classification of Narrative Elements in Folktales, Ballads, Myths, Fables, Mediaeval Romances, Exempla, Fabliaux, Jest-books, and Local Legends*. Bloomington: Indiana University Press, 1955.

Thompson, Stith. *The Folktale*. New York: Dryden, 1946.

Titon, Jeff Todd. "The Life Story." *Journal of American Folklore* 93, no. 369 (1980): 276–92.

Toelken, Barre. *The Dynamics of Folklore*. Boston: Houghton Mifflin, 1979.

Toelken, Barre. "The 'Pretty Languages' of Yellowman: Genre, Mode and Texture in Navaho Coyote Narratives." *Folklore Genres*, edited by Dan Ben-Amos, 145–70. Austin: University of Texas, 1976.

Tylor, Edward Burnett. *Primitive Culture*. London: Murray, 1871.

Visser, Margaret. *Much Depends on Dinner: The Extraordinary History and Mythology, Allure and Obsessions, Perils and Taboos, of an Ordinary Meal.* New York: Grove, 1987.

Williams, Raymond. *Keywords: A Vocabulary of Culture and Society.* New York: Oxford University Press, 1976.

Wilson, William A. "Herder, Folklore, and Romantic Nationalism." In *Folk Groups and Folklore Genres: An Introduction,* edited by Elliott Oring, 21–37. Logan, UT: Utah State University Press, 1989.

Yoder, Don. "Folk Cookery." In *Folklore and Folklife, an Introduction,* edited by Richard M. Dorson, 325–50. Chicago: University of Chicago, 1972.

Yoder, Don. "Folklife Studies in American Scholarship." In *Discovering American Folklife: Studies in Ethnic, Religious, and Regional Culture,* 43–66. Ann Arbor, MI: UMI Research, 1990.

Zumwalt, Rosemary Levy. *American Folklore Scholarship: A Dialogue of Dissent.* Bloomington: Indiana University Press, 1988.

CHAPTER 1
FOLK COOKERY
Don Yoder

Introduction: Food in folk culture

Folk cookery can be readily defined as traditional domestic cookery marked by regional variation. As everyday, domestic, family cookery based on regional tradition, it is obviously the opposite of the commercial, institutional, and scientific-nutritional versions of cookery. Diffused regionally into folk-cultural "provinces," it varies from both national and international cuisines. The study of folk cookery includes the study of the foods themselves, their morphology, their preparation, their preservation, their social and psychological functions, and their ramifications into all other aspects of folk-culture. For the total cookery complex, including attitudes, taboos, and meal systems—the whole range of cookery and food habits in a society—Honigman's term "foodways" has become useful.[1]

Folk cookery as a research field within the discipline of folklife studies, an area of such obvious and basic relevance for everyday life, has been strangely neglected in the United States. Folklorists have scarcely touched it except for "collecting" a few miscellaneous recipes in connection with other fieldwork. Historians have scarcely looked at it either, except for the discussion of pioneer and frontier cookery in our older county histories and descriptions of middle-class table manners by social historians. Home economists have touched it only tangentially, counting calories and pursuing invisible vitamins, for their task has been that of the reformer and diet-prescriber and traditional foods and foodways have been for them only evidence of the unprogressive past. The most valuable work in folk cookery done thus far has been that of our cultural anthropologists, who, however, have normally concentrated on areas outside the United States.

European folk-cultural scholarship, on the other hand, has recognized the basic place of cookery in folklife. Starting from their regionally oriented bases. European scholars of the present century have produced impressive studies on folk foods, folk methods of food preparation, the use of foods in the home, the storage of food products, the names of dishes, the meal system—every phase of the relation of food to folk culture. Europe's folklife scholars have studied their national and regional cuisines through two methods, the ethnographic and the historical. As part of the national folk-cultural atlas programs that are sponsored by many European nations, the ethnographer, through questionnaire and interview programs carried on intensively over a period of decades, has determined the traditional aspects of cookery in the region under study. The historian, through investigation of the vast historical source materials that exist in Europe from the Middle Ages to the present, culls and collates references to food and foodways. From this joint ethnographic and historical research have come archives, atlases, and research monographs on many specific food subjects.

Of cross-cultural studies dealing with European and American cuisines, the first volume of *Ethnologia Scandinavica* (1971), which is devoted entirely to folk cookery, stands in the first rank and will be useful in courses dealing with the subject. The volume, in German and English, includes the papers read at the First

Don Yoder, 'Folk Cookery' in Richard M. Dorson (ed.), *Folklore and Folklife: An Introduction*, (Chicago: University of Chicago Press, 1972), pp. 325–350.

© 1972 by The University of Chicago. Reprinted with permission from the University of Chicago Press.

International Symposium on Ethnological Food Research, convened at the University of Lund in August 1970 with scholars representing the Scandinavian countries. Germany, Austria, Yugoslavia. Poland, Hungary, Czechoslovakia, Bulgaria, Scotland, Ireland, France, and the United States. The papers present a wide variety of subjects, from methodological problems of foodways research and types of source materials available for their study, to analyses of the relationships of biology and culture in the problem of hunger, studies of kitchen utensils, food habits, food complexes and individual food elements, and economic treatment of food distribution and changes in food consumption patterns. The symposium grew out of the researches of Professor Bringéus of the University of Lund, and represents an important advance in scholarship on food and foodways.[2]

A few samples of the best European historical scholarship on the subject of cookery follow: J. C. Drummond and Anne Wilbraham. *The Englishman's Food: A History of Five Centuries of English Diet* (London. 1939): L. Burema. *De Voeding in Nederland van de Middeleeuwen tot de Twintigste Eeuw* (Assen. 1953); Albert Hauser, *Vom Essen und Trinken im alten Zürich: Tafelsitten, Kochkunst und Lebenshaltung vom Mittelalter bis in die Neuzeit* (Zurich, 1961): Maria Dembinska. *Konsumpeja Zymnosciowa w Polsee Sredniowieeznej* [Food Consumption in Medieval Poland] (Wroclaw-Warsawa-Krakow. 1963); and Nils-Arvid Bringéus. *Mat och Miljö: En bok om svenska kostvanor* (Lund. 1970). Several of these works cover the national areas involved from the Middle Ages to the present day, include folk cookery as well as the cookery of all national classes and groups, and use the insights of the several disciplines dealing with food and foodways.

Of the recent European studies, the most important national survey, for its combination of historical, ethnographic, and cartographic approaches, is that by Günter Wiegelmann, *Alltags- und Festspeisen: Wandel und gegenwärtige Stellung* (Marburg, 1967). Professor Wiegelmann, who has recently accepted the chair of folk-cultural studies at the University of Münster, is Germany's leading authority on folk cookery and one of Europe's leading authorities on the subject. His book is based on the materials in the *Atlas der deutschen Volkskunde* (1930–1935) and deals with four historical periods in German foodways: (1) *1500–1680,* the post-medieval period, when medieval eating habits were still in evidence: (2) *1680–1770,* the era of the appearance of new foods among the upper classes, the potato, coffee, tea, rice, and sugar, for example: (3) *1770–1850,* the era that saw the general adoption of the new foods by the country population: and (4) *1850 to the present,* the age of world trade and technical food production. The book includes twenty-six detailed diffusion maps on folk cookery, dealing with such subjects as eating out of a common dish, potato dishes served on weekdays and festival days, wedding meals, the raising of millet and its use in cuisine, the influence of coffee on folk cuisine, the influence of foreign foods such as English pudding and goulash on German folk cuisine, the names of meals and the meal system, sour dishes, salads, and so on. A fully annotated text analyzes the diffusion problems presented by the maps, and a thoroughgoing bibliography (pp. 245–61) completes the book's major reference value.

The American scholarly world has not yet produced any books on American traditional cookery that can rank in thoroughness and authoritativeness with the European examples I have named, unless it is Richard Osborn Cummings, *The American and His Food: A History of Food Habits in the United States* (Chicago, 1940). The only national survey since Cummings, *The American Heritage Cookbook and Illustrated History of American Eating & Drinking* (New York, 1964), was planned as a commercial rather than an academic book, and unfortunately lacks the usual scholarly apparatus, notes and bibliography. Of the many Latin American studies, the most complete national survey deals with Brazil, Luis da Camara Cascudo's *Historia de Alimentação no Brasil* (São Paolo, 1967), vol. 1. This volume deals with the acculturation of the three major strands in the Brazilian diet, the native Indian, African, and Portuguese foods.

It is to the European studies, then, that we must look for guidance. They show us that among the historical determinants of cookery and foodways are environment and climate; settlement history and ethnic demography; changes due to urbanization and innovations in technology; economic history; sociological factors; and religion. Considering the reaction of man to his basic natural environment, the study of folk cookery covers such subjects as the influence of environment on cuisine, seasonal foods, and local crops and local foods of the various cultural landscapes studied by cultural geographers and ecologists. The economic historian adds aspects of food distribution, in such phases as marketing, droving, and shipping, which affect the local economy and the local foodways. The agrarian historian and the historian of technology study changes in rural technology and have contributed much pertinent data on the resulting changes in foodways.[3]

In our teaching we can therefore use folk cookery as a key element in folk culture, ramifying as it does into many aspects of the entire structure. The folklorist can join the historian of religion and the anthropologist in studying the relation of sacred and secular cookery, the folklore of food taboos, the psychology of foodways, and, in the wider folklife context, can profitably exchange research data with the other sociohistorical sciences mentioned above.

Research problems in American folk cookery

The student of American folk cookery has two major directions to pursue: (1) the regional variation of American domestic cookery, which deserves recording, historically and ethnographically, on the scale that European folklife research has set: and (2) the comparative study of the relation of American to European folk patterns of cookery.

While Americans today seem to be developing an eclectic "American" cookery that rises above the regions, in the past our cookery, like our speech patterns and our architecture, was divided into regional versions. Examples, which we will draw upon in our discussion, are the New England, the Southern, the Appalachian, the Pennsylvania German, and the Southwest Spanish cuisines.

All of these American regional cultures shared basic foods, but because of differing ethnic backgrounds and climatic conditions, they put them to different use. All areas used, for example, that greatest of American Indian gifts to the European settler, maize, grown in Indian fashion and formalized into foods that were borrowed from Indian culture (mush, hominy, johnny cake) but were also American adaptations, a shifting key, so to speak, of basic European foods.[4] Thus, colonial Americans from the British Isles translated their basic oats or wheaten porridge into the equivalent dish made of maize—and called it "hasty pudding" in New England (because it took so long to stir it correctly for supper), "suppawn" in New York state, and "mush" in Pennsylvania and elsewhere.[5] Mush became an almost daily staple in pioneer times. It remained a favorite food on many American rural tables into the present century, and, judging from supermarket shelves, has even recently made a comeback into respectability. In the South the second maize product, hominy—corn grains from which the hulls have been soaked in a solution of lye—has remained as popular, so popular in fact that, as "grits," it is still served in restaurants with most cooked breakfasts as a "side dish," *caveat viator,* whether one orders it or not. Early America's dependence on cornmeal was sung by one of the first of our native poets, Joel Barlow, in the amusing work, "The Hasty Pudding," in 1796.[6]

Another example of a dish with European roots as well as American regional variation is the pie. The round fruit pie, which has been the all-time favorite American dessert, has a long and complicated history. American housewives exercised their ingenuity on this essentially English dish and came up with an immense stock of variations. The foremost novelist of New England life. Harriet Beecher Stowe, in describing the orgy of pie-baking that preceded the principal New England holiday. Thanksgiving, leaves us in no doubt as to the importance of pie:

The pie is an English institution, which, planted on American soil, forthwith ran rampant and burst forth into an untold variety of genera and species. Not merely the old traditional mince pie, but a thousand strictly American seedlings from that main stock, evinced the power of American housewives to adapt old institutions to new uses. Pumpkin pies, cranberry pies, huckleberry pies, cherry pies, green-currant pies, peach, pear, and plum pies, custard pies, apple pies, Marlborough-pudding pies,—pies with top crusts, and pies without,—pies adorned with all sorts of fanciful flutings and architectural strips laid across and around, and otherwise varied, attested to the boundless fertility of the feminine mind, when once let loose in a given direction.

She describes the mixing, rolling, tasting, and professional consulting that went on between her mother and grandmother, and Aunt Lois and Aunt Keziah. Even the oven is described in detail:

In the corner of the great kitchen, during all those days, the jolly old oven roared and crackled in great volcanic billows of flame, snapping and gurgling as if the old fellow entered with joyful sympathy into the frolic of the hour: and then, his great heart being once warmed up, he brooded over successive generations of pies and cakes, which went in raw and came out cooked, till butteries and dressers and shelves and pantries were literally crowded with a jostling abundance.

Since not all of this pre-Thanksgiving pie crop would be consumed at the holiday tables, we are treated finally to this description of the original "deep-freeze" arrangement:

A great cold northern chamber, where the sun never shone, and where in winter the snow sifted in at the window-cracks, and ice and frost reigned in undisputed sway, was fitted up to be the storehouse of these surplus treasures. There, frozen solid, and thus well preserved in their icy fetters, they formed a great repository for all the winter months; and the pies baked at Thanksgiving often came out fresh and good with the violets of April.[7]

The pie as such, baked in a round pie shell with or without a top crust, is an English contribution to American culture. There are several analogues on the Continent, from the *pizza* to the *Kuchen*. The German *Kuchen* consisted of a thick dough base, usually rectangular rather than round, into which slices of fruit or vegetables were stuck before baking. The *Kuchen* tradition was brought to the American Colonies by the Pennsylvania Germans, among whom we hear of *Hutzelbrot* (plum bread) and *Zwiwwelkuche* (onion pie). But they also adopted the round English pie from their neighbors, calling it "*boi*" (as in the word *Schnitzboi,* dried apple pie), presumably because their neighbors pronounced it, dialect-fashion, "poy" rather than "pie."

The "pie" and the "Kuchen" existed in tension with each other for two centuries until the pie vanquished its more homely central European rival. The pastry department of Pennsylvania Dutch cookery, a veritable *Teigkultur,* is rich, literally and figuratively, with complexes of dishes centering around the noodle, the filled noodle, the dumpling, the half-moon pie (a giant cousin of ravioli, filled with fruit or corn), the vegetable pie, and the ubiquitous stew called "potpie." Apart from the borrowings from the British Isles, this heavy dough culture betrays the ethnic origins of the people in south Germany and Switzerland, where *Mehlspeisen* are the characteristic food.[8]

Pennsylvania is a representative area for comparative folk cookery research because of the mixed ethnic components of the population, the acculturation that took place between Continental and British Isles emigrants beginning in the eighteenth century, and the linkage of upstate (rural) Pennsylvania and Philadelphia (urban) foodways through the farmers' market system.[9] In a sense the Philadelphia versions of the staple foods—for example, "scrapple"[10] instead of up-country "panhaas"—became known commercially as a symbol of regional cookery, just as Philadelphia's "mummers parade" has become a folk-cultural symbol of Pennsylvania, supplanting the countless rural and village mummers' parades that used to be a part of the upstate culture until the period of World War I. The same problem exists for the cuisines of Boston, Baltimore, Charleston, and New Orleans. In each case, folk foods of the region have become standardized and commercialized in the principal cities, in a sense providing culinary symbols for present-day regionalism.

As is the case with Europe, the United States provides the student with important relict areas where earlier foodways have been preserved in the face of contemporary social change. The principal of these is Appalachia. Appalachian cookery contains elements from several cultural areas, settled as it was from both the Middle States and the Tidewater and Piedmont South. As a depressed area, it has also preserved into the twentieth century many aspects of American frontier cooking, both as to monotony of cuisine and the simplicity of food preparation. A well-known account from the 1920s describes mountain cookery as follows:

> The average cooking is bad and renders the food unwholesome. The frying pan is the most common weapon, though a stew-pot is a close second. In combination with the poor cooking, the restricted diet is responsible for a depleted physical condition. The range of foodstuffs is far too narrow for good health. "Bread" and "meat" are the staples of diet. This means corn and pork. The poorest renter or squatter plans to "raise me a crap" or to "raise me some bread" by which is always meant corn. And usually he slaughters a hog or two for his "meat." This, salted and sometimes smoked, provides the necessary supply of bacon, "ham-meat," and lard. A family with a supply of bread and meat faces the winter without anxiety. At least they will not starve. If further provender can be laid up, so much the better. They may "hole up" in the garden a pyramid of potatoes, another of cabbage, and another of turnips, and dig them out when the larder runs low.[11]

But even these frontier amenities had their analogues, and in most cases precedents, among the peasant cultures of Europe. The extreme monotony of peasant cuisine is discussed in a recent history of Scottish agriculture:

> The diet of the tenants was a monotonous one, inadequate in quality and quantity. Oatmeal of the poorest quality was the staple food. It was taken in the form of porridge eaten with thin milk or ale, as a kind of paste called *sowens*, and as bread in the form of thin, toasted cakes. The food was rendered insipid by the frequent absence of salt, the salt tax making that commodity a luxury. Oatmeal and pease-meal provided a dish called brose, made by pouring over it water in which greens had been boiled and stirring the mixture to consistency; and *kail*, or broth made from cabbage leaves, thickened with coarse barley or groats of oats, was in daily use. This diet was sometimes flavoured with a piece of salt meat but as a rule flesh meat, apart from special occasions such as a christening or a wedding, came the way of the ordinary peasant only when an animal died of starvation or disease, or a crock ewe was slaughtered; though the better-class farmer at the end of autumn killed and salted one or two animals for winter fare. A little dirty butter, an occasional egg—though both hens and eggs were kept primarily to pay the rent—a 'black pudding' made by bleeding the cows and boiling the blood mixed with oatmeal, and cheese of a poor quality from the mixture of the milk of ewes and cows eked out this scanty subsistence. Tenants living on the banks of a Highland stream had always the chance of supplementing their usual fare with a salmon, and seafish and shellfish were part of the diet of those who lived on the coast. In poorer parts of the country the food was even more scanty. In the Orkneys the daily fare consisted of a

"morning piece" of half a bannock of bread made from bere mixed with seeds of all kinds of weeds. The breakfast was porridge made from the meal of the native black oats and seeds of wild plants. Fish, with nettle broth occasionally, thickened with a little meal, formed the main repast. The water in which the fish or crustacea had been boiled also served to boil the cabbage for dinner. The scourings of the pots and platters were mixed with the following morning's porridge. Salt water supplied the only seasoning. *Reuthie* bread, made from the seeds of wild mustard, filled the gap between the exhaustion of the old crop and the appearance of the new grain.[12]

It is no wonder that under such circumstances undernourishment led to ill-health; also, one can explain and understand the reverence our ancestors had for food, the "holy daily bread," which has come down to the present generation, even in affluent America, in parental admonitions to "finish your plate." Wasting food in the rural context was sinful, and the prohibition of it carried with it conscious or unconscious memories of the ancient "hunger times" that had so often afflicted rural populations in Europe.

In these days of higher and higher American living standards, and year-round supplies of frozen summer foods, the study of the cookery habits of the past can help us to understand poverty and the prudential reasons for the waste-not, want-not philosophy of our forefathers. Even in peasant areas where food was relatively abundant, if monotonous, there were times in the year when certain types of foods were in low stock. E. Estyn Evans tells us that "in Ulster the name given to July was 'the blue month' because it was a time of scarcity between the old potatoes and the new crop, but generally speaking milk products were consumed during the summer months."[13] An historian of New York rural life gives us a similar term:

> My own mother, within my memory but before every country store had fresh vegetables all winter, used to speak of the "six-weeks' want," meaning the early spring period when the old vegetables and apples were gone and nothing new was available. No wonder the housewife scoured the spring fields for something green to cook. Pot herbs were a change and probably they corrected certain vitamin deficiencies, but after all they were mainly water and their caloric value low. Again, these familiar greens were commonly plants of old fields and gardens and probably would not be available to the pioneer homemaker.[14]

Viewed historically, each regional and national cuisine is a culinary hybrid, with an elaborate stratigraphy of diverse historical layers combined into a usable and evidently satisfying structure. American folk cookery, like European, has preserved some ancient methods of food preparation, such as pickling, souring, drying, and smoking, all of which have lengthy European histories and which in fact are identified with different historical strata of European civilization. Gösta Berg's study of Swedish folk cookery has shown that, historically speaking, Swedish peasant cookery recapitulates the stages of Swedish civilization.[15] The common methods of preserving food in northern Sweden (souring and drying) belong to an older cultural epoch than the "newer" methods of salting and smoking that are diffused over southern and middle Sweden. The northern Swedish methods link Swedish cuisine with Arctic Asia and primitive man, the middle and southern Swedish methods show relations to Denmark, Germany, and central Europe.

Among early American foodways the souring and fermenting methods of preserving foods are of particular interest. We can study these methods in a great many folk food products, from sauerkraut to vinegar itself. Most interesting, however, are the milk products, or byproducts, that were soured and used widely by many cultures. The names given them—"bonny clabber" and "thick milk" in early America, *dicke Milch* in German-speaking areas, *langmjölk* in Sweden—show their wide use in peasant cultures. In some cases the tastes for these foods, acquired by necessity from primitive food preservation facilities, have lingered on. In the twentieth century we have witnessed the return to our tables of certain sophisticated versions of these ancient and simple folk foods that our ancestors made in many divergent European cultures. Yogurt, sour cream, and buttermilk are all "in" as health and gourmet foods today. Yogurt in particular—an almost exact equivalent of the thickened sour milk dishes of peasant Europe—has made a spectacular return to respectability via Central Asia and Paris.

Another recent phenomenon related to folk cookery is the decline of regional cooking at home in favor of eclectic "American" cuisine and the rise of regional restaurants. From the Spanish-Mexican culture area,[16] the great American Southwest, where Mexican foods are still functional both in the home and the local restaurant. "Mexican" restaurants have recently invaded the North and East, for instance in Chicago. Washington, and New York. As such they are symbolic of our hybrid and interethnic twentieth-century American culture. If American regional restaurants are now offering a few good (and relatively authentic, if standardized) regional dishes or combinations of dishes, one can also sample regional dishes at the lunch counters of those common denominators of American popular culture, the 5-and-10 cent stores. In New Mexico one sees tamales and tortillas in Woolworth's, in Slavic neighborhoods one can sample pirogies and stuffed cabbage—in addition to the standard hamburgers, the bacon, lettuce, and tomato sandwiches, the canned soups, and the bakery pies. A recent development is the commercial chains of snack shops for specialty foods: "Taco House." "Pancake House," "Kentucky Fried Chicken" establishments, and now finally, returned from Germany where it was originally developed to bring American fried chicken to Europe, the Wienerwald restaurant.

American cookery today is eclectic or hybrid in a national sense. It shows deeply the effects of urbanization and food-processing technology, as well as an interest in selected foods from American ethnic cultures (pizza, bagels) and from world cuisine (smörgasbord, chow mein, sukiyaki, shishkebab). In this present state of eclectic variety, how do we study American folk cookery?

To use the two-pronged European folklife technique, we can approach American cookery (1) ethno-graphically, and (2) historically. Fortunately, enough of the regional specialties are still known and prepared by at least the older cooks who have not yet submitted to the TV dinner approach to family cooking that the questionnaire and direct interview methods can be used with profit in the subject of American cooking.[17] Even if the informant no longer prepares regional specialties, he can usually offer information on the change in foodways during his lifetime. One can often still record from older persons in the more tradition-oriented areas fond memories of food, food preparation, and the psychological and sociological aspects of foodways. For example, one area of research that can be assigned to students for questionnaires and interviews is the meal system in the folk culture under study. This involves (1) the number of meals per day, (2) the names given to the daily meals. (3) the foods served at these meals, and (4) food specialties served on specific days of the week.

The common three-meals-per-day system of most American homes contrasts with the earlier rural custom of five meals per day, at least in the summer, when men were working in the fields. Between early breakfast on the farm (6:00 or 7:00 A.M.) and "dinner" announced by bell, horn, or voice (at 12:00 M.), there was usually a mid-morning snack, around 9:00 or 10:00—carried to the men working in the harvest fields, as shown in the Brueghel paintings of harvesting in the Netherlands in the sixteenth century. European scholars have investigated thoroughly the *Zehnerbrot* or *Neunerbrot, Vorjausen* or *Halbmittag,* as German peasants called it, and analyzed the relation of the meal system of an area to the group's general sense of time.[18] An afternoon snack (compare the German *Vesperbrot*) balanced the morning snack, thus accounting for five meals a day. Americans traveling in Europe are often surprised by the formality of the survival of the five-meals-per-day arrangement, dramatized in the British Isles by the almost religious ritual of "elevenses" in the morning and the "teas" of late afternoon between the larger meals of breakfast, luncheon, and dinner. In a sense the urban American office "coffee-break" is restoring a five-meals-a-day rhythm to our eating habits.

What foods were served at the various meals? This depends on the area one is studying and the time-period involved. Breakfast is a fascinating research area in folk cookery because of the vast change that has taken place in the American breakfast in the past seventy-five years. Travel in Europe informs Americans that there is still a basic difference between the "Continental" (bread and coffee) breakfast and the "English" (or "meat") breakfast. The American breakfast, being essentially a meat breakfast, is derived from the English breakfast, and continued for generations because of the heavy work involved on American farms. After the Civil War, with the various food reforms, we have the "breakfast cereal" fad introduced, so that by 1900 some Americans *combined* the heavy cooked meat breakfast with the cereal reforms—a combination we still find reflected on restaurant menus, with the skimpy glass of juice added later, as a health-fad afterthought of the 1920s.

Recorded comments on such changes in meal patterns can and need to be sought out as basic historical documentation for American folk-cookery research. Farm periodicals are a particularly good source of such documentation, since the editors, because of their interest in "progressive" farming and living, are quite conscious of traditional ways. As an example of the value of this type of dated documentation, an editorial entitled "A Choice of Breakfasts" appeared in *The Country Gentleman*, 3 January 1907.

> The hearty meat breakfast, though still the usual thing, is not so much a matter of course in American families as it once was. Perhaps the various "breakfast foods" have done more than anything else to change our habits in this respect. These patented cereal preparations, many of them specially manufactured to be eaten without additional cooking, are generally believed to offer a wholesome economy in both labor and money. Their vogue and the resulting rich returns from their sale are attested by the constant production of new variations, each liberally and expensively advertised. As a partial substitute for a meat diet, there is much to be said in their favor. If, as some assert, much meat in the diet causes excessive stimulation of the nerves, the over-nervous American does well to be content with a cereal breakfast. Even a gritty cracker and a bunch of grapes or an apple will serve the turn of some of these enthusiasts for the new health, but most of us demand a hot breakfast, at least, especially in cold weather.

As a sample of the hot breakfast, the author recommended for Sunday breakfast: coffee, rolls, farina, stewed apricots, panned oysters, rice griddle cakes, and clover honey. This she calls "a light, delicate breakfast." For a winter Monday breakfast her recommendation is: coffee, oatmeal. Grape Nuts, apple sauce, pork chops, potato balls, fried parsnips, and buckwheat cakes with syrup. As to the latter, the early American favorite that travelers referred to as "the ubiquitous buckwheat cake," the editor has this to say:

> Rye drop cakes, whole wheat gems, muffins, or corn bread will be preferred in place of the buckwheat cakes in many families. But there are still plenty of farmers' homes in which buckwheat pancakes at this season of the year is considered quite indispensable as an adjunct of a good breakfast. In a perfectly light, sweet batter, raised with yeast, and with pure, delicious maple syrup to adorn it, it is to be admitted that few things suit a cold morning better.

The function of folk cookery

Folk cookery of course represents more than a mere primitive satisfying of elemental needs. Like all aspects of folk culture it was related, integrally and functionally, to all other phases of the culture, and in its elaboration became, like dress and architecture, a work of art. Let us look at two directions into which folk cookery ramifies, (1) religion, and (2) material culture.

The connection of folk cookery with religion includes positive elements (e.g., festival cookery), and negative elements (e.g., food taboos). The subject of festival cookery has occupied much European attention, with emphasis especially upon Christmas cookery, Easter breads, the Easter egg with its symbolic decoration and social function, wedding meals, and carnival cookery. In America the New England festival of Thanksgiving, Christmas traditions, Easter, and other festivals of the year have evoked monographs and articles from the various folk-cultural regions and ethnic enclaves. Even political festivals like Election Day produced in New England recipes for "Election Cake," along with election sermons: and the American camp-meetings—the true "festivals of democracy" as the French traveler Chevalier called them in the 1830s[19]—produced some cookery of their own, as evidenced by the recipes for "Camp-Meeting Cake" that appeared in nineteenth-century newspapers.

America's ethnic and sectarian communities have also produced some cookery associated with their temporal festivals. Accounts of early American Quakerism abound in descriptions of yearly meeting hospitality, when country Quakers partook of the bounty of the urban Friends during "yearly meeting week," and even Quaker "quarterly meeting meals" were memorable. While frontier Methodists lived on the meager side, as the journals of the circuit-riders testify, at a quarterly meeting in Wyoming Valley in 1809 the hostess served "half a barrel of potpie," with "other things on the same scale," as a prelude to the singing, the praying, and the shouting.[20] And the "love feasts" and "watch nights" of the pietist sects form a cookery spectrum from the full broth-and-bread meals of the Dunkards through the ecclesiastical coffee-breaks of the Moravians to the austere bread-and-water diet of Methodists, who were permitted only spiritual inebriation.[21]

Of the urban ethnic groups. American Judaism has reproduced in this country, sometimes in factory-made, "kosher" form, many of the traditional festival dishes of European Judaism. One of the earliest general American cookbooks to contain a section on Jewish cookery was *Jennie June's American Cookery Book . . . by Mrs. J. C. Croly (Jennie June). Author of "Talks on Women's Topics." etc.* (New York: American News Co., 1874. c. 1866), "Dedicated to the Young Housekeepers of America." Jennie June's section on "Jewish Receipts," described as "all original and reliable" and "the contribution of a superior Jewish housekeeper in New York," included the following: White Stewed Fish, Brown Fricassee Chicken, A Good Pudding, Purim Fritters, Codfish Fritters, Lemon Pudding, A Richer Lemon Pudding—1. Lemon Pudding—2. Apple Pudding, Albert Sandwiches. Meringues, Bread and Butter Pudding, Sally Lunn (2), Cup Cake, Hickory Nut Cake, Marmalade, Orgent, CocoaNut Pudding, Sweet Crackers. Almond Pudding, Lemon Dumplings. Light Pudding, Tomatoes for Winter Use, and Pickled Cucumbers.[22] In the past half-century, the Jewish Delicatessen-restaurant in metropolitan areas has been the channel through which eastern European specialties, such as lox, bagels, and borscht, have found their way into American menus.

Religion has also exercised a negative role in American foodways, particularly in what we may as well refer to as American "drinkways." American drinking habits within the family, in large areas of our population, are different from drinking habits in most European cultures. Taboos on liquor are usually, but wrongly, blamed on Puritanism. The split did not appear until the nineteenth century when the American temperance movement, one of the most curious examples of religious taboo in history, invaded most of the Protestant churches, which at that time set the dominant cultural tone in America. The temperance movement is, folk-culturally speaking, a kind of watershed in America in regard to domestic life. Actually it was a middle-class wedge separating the upper and lower classes, both of which continued the earlier general drinking habits of colonial America.[23] Hence one has to divide American folk-cultures, at least those under Protestant influence, into "pre-temperance" and "post-temperance" eras. In the colonial era, wine, beer, and hard liquor flowed freely as part of family entertaining as well as at larger social gatherings, e.g., baptisms, weddings, and funerals, where the folk community gathered.[24] After temperance reform, drinking, like some older folk-cultural amusements and recreations, was made a sin.

While certain classes in American society continued to "drink," and the colonial "tavern" in turn became the nineteenth-century "saloon" and the twentieth-century "bar," nondrinking Americans had to find their substitutes in the "temperance houses," "sarsaparilla stands," and "cake and mead houses" run by genteel ladies in nineteenth-century villages, and eventually in their twentieth-century counterparts, the "corner drug store" and the "Coke counter."

In addition to the basic temperance taboo, food faddism inspired by religion has had a long history in the United States. Yankees and Yorkers. Quakers and other nineteenth-century nonconformists and reformers often pressed their hardheaded logical versions of Protestantism into extremist measures. Vegetarianism, nature foods, graham bread, and the breakfast cereal movement all came out of the Protestant reformist mentality, first in New England, and in Philadelphia and the "burned over district" of New York State, and later centered in the national headquarters of the Seventh Day Adventists—Battle Creek. Michigan—where the Kelloggs, Posts, and others attempted to apply reform principles, based on their religious ideas, to American eating habits.[25] The best history of this welter of reformist activity is Gerald Carson's *Cornflake Crusade* (New York: Rinehart & Company, Inc., 1957).

Perhaps functionally these food fads operate, as Richard Weiss hints, as unofficial Protestant substitutes for the Catholic sacramentals, which were among the medieval buffers against insecurity. In the last century Protestant cultures have developed unchurchly, pseudoscientific, even magical means of controlling life, "from vitaminized bread and toothpaste to books on life-technique (think positively—live longer!)."[26] These rituals serve the faddist Protestant in much the same way that earlier folk-religious practices served the peasant.

Folk cookery and material culture

The study of folk cookery takes the student into many areas of folk-culture. The whole subject of food preparation, preservation, and storage, along with the actual cooking methods used and the consumption of food, is related to complexes of material objects, which should be viewed against the total culture.

Consider that most researched area of food, the history of the "daily bread" that our cultural forefathers in Europe counted their basic food.[27] In our bread cultures, the production, milling, and storage of grain and the baking and storage of breadstuffs involve specific architectural structures (mills, granaries, corncribs, storage houses, and bake ovens) and specific tools (querns or handmills, hominy blocks, husking pegs, flails, rolling pins, dough-trays, bread baskets, peels) —the list is almost endless.

Of these the *bake oven,* its types and uses, can here provide us with valuable examples of how to study the material aspects of folk cookery. Today, except for adventurous younger housewives and a few traditional bread-baking groups, "bought bread" or "baker's bread" is found on American tables and even the memory of homemade bread is lost. In early America, before the days of the kitchen range, bread was baked by three different techniques: before the open fire, in the form of johnny-cake, in the coals in a Dutch oven, or in a bake oven. The johnny-cake style of baking was not necessarily, as is often thought, an adaptation to the American frontier; it was a primitive baking method much and widely practiced in Europe. In his descriptions of the Irish peasant economy, E. Estyn Evans has discussed fireside breadbaking methods, which, like other aspects of Irish peasant life, belong to Europe's "Atlantic province" of folk-cultural phenomena. Ovens are essentially central European: hearth cookery is found around the Atlantic edge of Europe.

To understand the fireside appliances and methods of cooking certain facts should be borne in mind—the absence of the brick oven, the use of turf, a slow-burning fuel admirable for stewing and for things requiring a steady heat, and the universal preference for "thin-bread," or "bread in cakes," as English observers call it. Once more we have to remind ourselves that parallels to surviving habits can be found 40 centuries back, for pottery baking slabs are known from Neolithic western Europe and of course oatcakes are best baked in this way.[28]

Bake ovens were of two sorts. In New England and the South they were often built into the inside kitchen wall, in or beside the huge kitchen fireplace. In Pennsylvania, following European precedent, they were built as separate, freestanding buildings in the yard, with the oven openings protected from the weather by a shed roof. The obvious rationale of the outdoor bake oven was threefold: (1) to protect the house from fire. (2) to remove the elaborate baking process as well as the additional heat from the busy kitchen area, and (3) to increase the size of the baking area.

The outdoor bake oven seems to have been a central European institution. From what we now know of their geographical diffusion in the United States, the center of outdoor bake oven use was originally in the United States, principally in the Pennsylvania German culture area, although analogues are found in French Canada. Cajun Louisiana, and in the Indian pueblos of the Southwest.[29] At any rate, New Englanders and southerners did not originally have outdoor bake ovens. This is brought out amusingly in Henry Ward Beecher's novel. *Norwood* (1868), in which a New England soldier, wounded at Gettysburg, is billeted on a Pennsylvania Quaker farm. While the soldier lies recuperating in the farmhouse his New England girlfriend, who has come to nurse him, is shown the farm by the farmer's daughter Martha.

"What is that?" said Rose, pointing to a queer stack of bricks under a tile shed close by the house.
"That is our oven," said Martha.
"What—out of doors? We build ours into the kitchen chimney."
"It is the way of our fathers. The other perhaps is more convenient."[30]

Research into the bake oven should be of immediate concern. Pennsylvania's bake ovens began to fall into disuse in the first decades of the twentieth century, and already the great majority of them have fallen in or have been removed. One can scarcely drive anywhere in Pennsylvania Dutch country today without seeing a bake oven in process of removal. Since there were several types, including the "squirrel-tail" bake oven (so-called because of the S-shaped flue), they need to be photographed, measured, and carefully described. A prime need is a diffusion map of the outdoor bake oven, since it spread widely from eastern Pennsylvania.

We need studies not only of the permanent bake oven but also of the summer or temporary bake oven (the "mud oven") and the community or village bake oven. The latter is reported from a few mine patches in Pennsylvania's coal regions, presumably repristinated here as an institution remembered from the Slavic homelands of nineteenth-century emigrants in the mining counties. We need to collect memories of how the bake oven fire was made, what "oven wood" was used, how one knew when the oven was hot enough to bake and not too hot to burn. Fortunately, although the bake ovens are in disuse, thousands of persons can still provide the ethnographer with first-hand information on the basic uses of the bake oven.

Cookery's connections with American folk architecture are also easily seen in the whole area of food storage. The granaries in the barns, the corncribs once found on most American farms, the attic storage of grain and herbs, the vaulted cellars underneath house or barn, the smokehouses and ham closets, the springhouses or dairies for the storage of milk and dairy products—all deserve study as to type, construction, function, and diffusion. The excellent European historical and ethnographic researches on *Haus, Hof, Scheune,* and *Speicher* can be matched eventually, in the United States.[31]

When historical sources are abstracted for this purpose, nineteenth-century novels in particular contain interesting and usable material. Harriet Beecher Stowe, in describing the parson's farmhouse at Poganuc, speaks in detail of the house as an instrument for food storage:

> The parsonage had also the advantage of three garrets—splendid ground for little people. There was first the garret over the kitchen, the floors of which in the fall were covered with stores of yellow pumpkins, fragrant heaps of quinces, and less fragrant spread of onions. There were bins of shelled corn and of oats, and, as in every other garret in the house, there were also barrels of old sermons and old family papers. But most stimulating to the imagination of all the features of this place was the smoke-house, which was a wide, deep chasm made in the kitchen chimney, where the Parson's hams and dried beef were cured. Its door, which opened into this garret, glistened with condensed creosote, a rumbling sound was heard there, and loud crackling reverberated within.[32]

The juvenile heroine of the book, Dolly Cushing, would sometimes open this door and "peer in fearfully as long as her eyes could bear the smoke," and think with a shudder of the passage in *Pilgrim's Progress* that describes a "by-way to Hell," a door opening into a hillside from which came smoke and "a rumbling noise as of fire and a cry of some tormented, and . . . the scent of brimstone." Garret Number Two was the large central garret over the main part of the house, where in addition to old spinning wheels and other disused furniture, "and more barrels of sermons," there were "vast heaps of golden corn on the cob, spread upon sheets." This was the favorite rainy-day play garret of the parsonage children. Garret Number Three was Father's study with its Puritan theological library.

> But the mysterious areas of the parsonage were not exhausted with its three garrets. Under the whole house in all its divisions spread a great cavernous cellar, where were murky rooms and dark passages explored only by the light of candles. There were rows of bins, in which were stored the apples of every name and race harvested in autumn from the family orchard: Pearmains, Greenings, Seek-no-furthers. Bristers, Pippins, Golden Sweets, and other forgotten kinds, had each its separate bin, to which the children at all times had free access. There, too, was a long row of cider barrels, from whence, in the hour of their early sweetness, Dolly had delighted to suck the cider through straws for that purpose carefully selected and provided.

The American farmhouse kitchen is a subject long overdue for basic research. Here we need to study the layout of the kitchen, which in many farmhouses was also the dining room. The furniture and appliances that were in the kitchen deserve study, and here memory of living persons can help, as well as research into inventories and other historical documents. Functionally the farmhouse kitchen was "the" room of the house, where life and much domestic work centered around the hearth or, later, the kitchen stove. This centralizing of family life in the kitchen had significance for many other areas of life. Since in early American farmhouses the kitchen was sometimes the only heated room and occupied by the family every evening, courting couples were forced to court in the girl's bedroom, thus continuing the "bundling" system that had such long European roots. The American kitchen also restored the family, and the mourning community to normalcy after a funeral, when the "funeral dinner" or "funeral feast"[33]—subject of many ministerial jeremiads in the nineteenth century— united them all in the continued pursuit and celebration of life.

Another indication of the basic ramifications of kitchen life and foodways into religion and folk religion is the fact that in the kitchen the father, or some other older member of the family, served in a sense as family priest, in saying the table graces or blessings at the beginning and often at the end of a meal. In Protestant areas formal family worship. Bible reading and hymn singing, sometimes accompanied or preceded the meal. This sense of the holiness of everyday food and the holiness of eating together was earlier expressed in the orientation of the kitchen. In the Catholic farming areas of central Europe the *Kultecke* or devotional corner often has a well-defined relation to the table where the family eats.[34] All this can help the student to understand the meaning of life in the peasant or folk-cultural setting, a life that was linked in countless beliefs and practices to the spiritual world.

Traditional cookery in the twentieth century

The revolutionary technological changes of the twentieth century, following the Industrial Revolution, have radically changed cookery and food preparation as well as every phase of everyday living. All of the recent ethnographic studies of European and American communities make much of these changes, as in this observation from Cape Breton Island, Nova Scotia:

> Cookery—the woman's art—has undergone a great change since first the Highland women set up homes on these shores. The traditional diet of the Highlander in Scotland at the time of the emigrations is said to have consisted of fish and boiled potatoes. In the New World the immigrants amplified this diet considerably, although it is still limited by the refrigerating problem. In the heat of summer, fish, cured or freshly caught, is still the mainstay; but in the winter, when provisions can be preserved by freezing, meat makes its appearance. The repertoire of the menu has been enlarged, moreover, by the increased quantity of fruit and vegetables once unknown in the Highlands which are now available in the New World. Some traditional Highland dishes remain to lend individuality to the Gael's table, such as porridge and oat bread. Others have unaccountably become very rare, such as the meat sausage known as *iosban,* or the oatmeal sausage known as *marag gheal,* or the blood sausage known as *marag dhubh.* The art of preparing home-made cheese is almost forgotten; although, in a few exceptional districts such as Mabou, sufficient quantities of a firm, whitish cheese are produced by home manufacture to sell in the local stores.[35]

Nova Scotians jokingly sum up the radical alterations in the old way of life through which they have lived in an oft-quoted saying, "When I was a boy, I was brought up on porridge and the Bible. But now, all I see is corn-flakes and Eaton's catalogue."[36] That is, ready-made "cold" cereals have taken the place of the home-preparation of "hot" cereal, thus sparing the housewife the labor of preparing breakfast, and whatever else she needs for the household she orders from the mail-order catalogue.

Whether we are better off with our "enriched" bread and our often flavorless frozen foods is a question that the historian and the folklife scholar as well as the nutritionist and public health official can help to answer. An Illinois social historian, in recording the change of Midwestern farm diet from "home-baked bread, meat, potatoes and pie" to "baker's bread, fresh meat, salads, vegetables and fruit from Florida and California," concludes that the farmer "lives no better, as far as food is concerned than his forbears, perhaps not as well in some respects, but he too craves variety, or at least novelty, and must pay with the profits of his own labor for baking, mending, repairs and laundry once done by the farm women."[37] In some areas, such as Appalachia, and in Switzerland's more backward alpine villages, the old ways of the twentieth century are not quite as wholesome as the romanticists have maintained. Richard Weiss, in one of his last essays, published posthumously, points to loss as well as gain:

> Our city population is, in contradistinction, today healthy compared with those many residents of mountain valleys. Even the urban relationships with the surrounding world are in many respects hygienically better. In the city it is no longer the case that a great part of the families, as in Canton Wallis, sleep crowded together into one room, often in one chamber with trundle beds, which is at the same time general living room and bedroom and can scarcely be aired out. In addition there is the fact that where the ancient traditional economy of self-provision decays, a one-sided and unsound food system results, in which fruits and vegetables from the earlier system are lacking. Where the home-baked black bread is replaced by white baker's bread and the fresh milk by a coffee-like drink, deficiency illnesses take the upper hand. That tooth decay has gained ground in exact relationship to the decline of home bread production, is statistically documented for the Goms, the Upper Rhone Valley.[38]

Yet perhaps in the basic area of human nutrition it all balances out. The old foodways were not so bad after all, the newer ones are not perfect either. That would seem to be the conclusion of Richard Cummings in his basic history of American food viewed from the nutritionist's standpoint: "While Americans in the early nineteenth century knew no set principles of balanced diet, they appear, without conscious design, to have maintained food habits which cannot be definitively termed unhealthful."[39] Perhaps we could close with a paraphrase of a famous statement about religion—"Each nation, each culture, and each generation, creates for itself the cuisine it deserves."

Notes

1. John J. Honigman, *Foodways in a Muskeg Community* (Ottawa, 1961).

2. A good introduction to the world of Swedish folkways research is furnished by Nils-Arvid Bringéus. *Mat och Miljö: En bok om svenska kostvanor* (Lund: Gleerups. 1970), Vol. 1 of the Ethnological Handbook series edited by Bringéus and Rehnberg. The book includes historical and analytical essays on a wide variety of topics. The essays are by the major Swedish scholars who have worked on the subject of Swedish diet and are all thoroughly documented as well as illustrated. The book concludes with an extensive bibliography of Swedish folk cookery research.

3. Two studies in folk cookery, using European as well as American perspectives, are being done at present at the University of Pennsylvania under my direction. These are doctoral dissertations by Jay A. Anderson, on "Yeoman Foodways in Stuart England" (1971), and by Eleanor F. Reishtein, on "Historical Bibliography of American Regional Cookery." I am indebted to Dr. Anderson and Mrs. Reishtein for several helpful suggestions and bibliographical items in the preparation of this paper.

4. For Indian influences on frontier cookery see Roger Williams. *A Key into the Language of America. . .* (London, 1643), reprinted in *Collections of the Rhode-Island Historical Society* 1 (1827): John Josselyn. *New-England's Rarities. . .* (Boston, 1865); Fulmer Mood. "John Winthrop, Jr., on Indian Corn." *New England Quarterly* 10 (1937): 121–33; Clark Wissler. "Aboriginal Maize Culture as a Typical Culture-Complex." *American Journal of Sociology* 21 (1916): 656–60; A. Irving Hallowell, "The Impact of the American Indian on American Culture," *American Anthropologist* 59 (April, 1957): 201–17; and Louise O. Bercaw. *et al., Corn in the Development of the Americas: A Selected and Annotated Bibliography* (Washington, D.C., 1940), U. S. Department of Agriculture, Bureau of Agricultural Economics, Agricultural Economics Bibliographies No. 87.

5. For a relatively complete cultural history of this basic frontier food see Don Yoder, "Pennsylvanians Called It Mush," *Pennsylvania Folklife* 13 (Winter 1962–63): 27–[49], which uses ethnographic as well as historical materials on the backgrounds, preparation, use, vocabulary, and social customs associated with the dish.

6. Joel Barlow, The Hasty Pudding: A Poem in Three Cantos. Written at Chambery, in Savoy, 1793. Omne tulit punctum qui miscuit utile dulci. He makes a good breakfast who mixes pudding with molasses (New Haven: printed by Tiebout & O'Brien, 1796). The poem first appeared in the New York Magazine (January 1796): 41–49.

It was often reprinted in the nineteenth century; one of the most attractive editions appeared in Harper's New Monthly Magazine (July 1856) with some amusing engravings of Indian girls stirring huge mush pots, Barlow sniffing a mush bowl for inspiration for his poetry, and a husking bee that ended in a "mush party." Basic Americana.

7. Harriet Beecher Stowe. *Oldtown Folks* (Boston. 1869), pp. 340, 341–42.

8. For Pennsylvania Dutch cookery see Ann Hark and Preston A. Barba. *Pennsylvania Dutch Cookery: A Regional Cookbook* (Allentown, Pennsylvania, 1950), which is the best historically oriented regional cookbook issued in the United States. For historical and ethnographic details on two Pennsylvania German specialties, sauerkraut and schnitz (dried apples), see Don Yoder, "Sauerkraut in the Pennsylvania Folk-Culture." *Pennsylvania Folklife* 12 (Summer 1961): 56–69; and "Schnitz in the Pennsylvania Folk-Culture." *Pennsylvania Folklife* 12 (Fall 1961): 44–53.

9. John F. Watson, *Annals of Philadelphia* (Philadelphia, 1830) is delightful reading on the culinary relation of Philadelphia and upstate Pennsylvania. While Watson does not enlighten us on the scrapple-panhaas problem, he does inform us that the Quakers made "Poprobin Soup," which appears from its description to have been what the Pennsylvania Germans call "Rivvel Soup," a milk soup with addition of dough scraps rubbed with the hand into balls, "rivvels" in Pennsylvania Dutch dialect. For fuller discussion of urban-rural culinary relationships in Pennsylvania see Don Yoder. "'Historical Sources for American Foodways Research and Plans for an American Foodways Archive," *Ethnologia Scandinavica* 1 (1971): 41–55.

10. On scrapple, there is the famous Philadelphia joke, usually told on the Prince of Wales, later Edward VII, who reported after his visit to Philadelphia that he "had met members of a large family named Scrapple, and enjoyed for breakfast a new dish called Biddle."

11. James Watt Raine. The Land of Saddle-Bags: A Study of the Mountain People of Appalachia (New York, 1924), pp. 211–12.

12. James E. Handler, *Scottish Farming in the Eighteenth Century* (London, 1953), pp. 78–80, omitting footnoting.

13. E. Estyn Evans, Irish Heritage: The Landscape, the People and Their Work (Dundalk, 1949), p. 77.

14. Jared van Wagenen, Jr., *The Golden Age of Homespun* (New York, 1963), pp. 98–99.

15. Gösta Berg. *Rökt skinka, torkade gäddor och surströmming, Svenska Kulturbilder* 6: 11–12 (Stockholm. 1932), analyzed in Brita Egardt. "Kost," *Schwedische Volkskunde* (Stockholm, 1961), pp. 376–78. The original essay has been reprinted in Nils-Arvid Bringéus. *Mat och Miljö* (Lund, 1970), pp. 161–76.

16. See the early scholarly work on this culture's folk foods by John Gregory Bourke. "The Folk-Foods of the Rio Grande Valley and of Northern Mexico." *Journal of American Folklore* 8 (1895): 41–71.

17. Thus far there have been three formal American questionnaires on the subject of cookery: (1) Bruce Buckley's Questionnaire on Rural Foods, Cooperstown Graduate Program, Cooperstown, N.Y.: (2) Norbert Riedl's Questionnaire on Tennessee Folk-Culture, University of Tennessee, Knoxville: and (3) Don Yoder's series of Folk-Cultural Questionnaires published in *Pennsylvania Folklife*.

18. See Dietman Wünschmann. *Die Tageszeiten: Ihre Bezeichmung im Deutschen* (Marburg, 1966), chap. 5.

19. Michael Chevalier. Society, Manners and Polities in the United States: Being a Series of Letters from North America (Boston. 1839). p. 317.

20. George Peck. *Early Methodism Within the Bounds of the Old Genesee Conference* (New York, 1860). p. 167. Peck also refers to coon's flesh (pp. 308–9), not a favorite dish with the preachers; "slap-jack coffee," made of charred buckwheat bread (p. 149), and "sorrel pie" (p. 323). My favorite quotation from the book is Marmaduke Pearce's lament over the frontier food and living conditions that he had to put up with while preaching on the Holland Purchase Circuit in 1811. Looking back on it in 1850, he wrote: ". . .O the cold houses, the snow, the mud, the sage tea, the baked beans! These things, the recollection of them, is like 'the music of Carol, pleasant and mournful to the soul'" (p. 344).

21. Don Yoder. "Love Feasts," *The Dutchman* 7 (Spring 1956); 34–37. For the Dunkard Love Feast, often described by nineteenth-century travelers, see Moritz Busch. *Wanderungen zwischen Hudson und Mississippi, 1851 und 1852* (Stuttgart. 1854): and Phebe Earle Gibbons, "The Dunker Love-Feast," in *"Pennsylvania Dutch," and Other Essay,* (Philadelphia. 1872), pp. 109–38.

22. According to Arnold Whitaker Oxford, English Cookery Books to the Year 1850 (London, 1913), the first British Jewish cookbook appeared in 1846: The Jewish Manual: or, Practical Information in Jewish and Modern Cookery, With a Collection of Valuable Recipes & Hints Relating to the Toilette. Edited by a Lady (London, 1846).

23. For the temperance movement see Joseph R. Gusfield, *Symbolic Crusade: Status Politics and the American Temperance Movement* (Urbana, Illinois, 1963); and David Joshua Pittman and Charles R. Snyder, eds., *Society, Culture, and Drinking Patterns* (New York, 1962).

24. For drinking habits in the early republic see Alice Felt Tyler. *Freedom's Ferment* (Minneapolis, 1944), pp. 308–12; also Clifton J. Furness. *The Life and Times of the Late Demon Rum* (New York, 1965).

25. See *Seventh-Day Adventist Encyclopedia* 10 (Washington, D.C., 1966) for detailed biographies of the Kelloggs and discussion of Adventist "Health Evangelism."

26. Richard Weiss, "Grundzüge einer protestantischen Volkskultur." *Schweizerisches Archiv für Volkskunde* 61 (1965): 77–78.

27. Of the many fine treatments of bread-making and bake ovens in Europe, cf. Ake Camphell. Det svenska Brödet (Stockholm. 1936): Hans Miese, So backt der Bauer sein Brot: ein volkskundlicher Beitrag zum bäuerlichen Brotbacken und zur Entwicklung von Backöfen und Backhäusern (Bielefeld. 1959); Martha Bringemeier, Vom Brotbacken in früherer Zeit (Münster/Westfalen, 1961): Jozef Weyns, Bakhuis en broodbakken in Vlaanderen (Sint Martens-Latem, 1963); and Kustaa Vilkuna. "Brodet och bakningens historia in Finland," Folk-Liv 9 (1945): 17–56.

28. E. Estyn Evans, *Irish Heritage* (Dundalk, 1949) , p. 73. For the flat bread made by open-hearth cookery see also Caoimhin Ó Danachair, "Bread," *Ulster Folklife* 4 (1958): 29–32: O. Rhiner, *Dünne, Wähe, Kuchen, Fladen, Zelten. Die Wortgeographie des Flachkuchens mit Belag und ihre volkskundlichen Hintergründe in der deutschen Schweiz* (Frauenfeld, 1958); and A. Wurmbach, "Kuchen—Fladen—Torte," *Zeitschrift für Volkskunde* 56 (1960): 20–40.

29. The best treatment thus far of the outdoor oven in any geographical or ethnic context in the United States is Fred Kniffen. "The Outdoor Oven in Louisiana," *Louisiana History* 1 (1960): 25–35, which includes basic bibliography.

30. Henry Ward Beecher. *Norwood: or, Village Life in New England* (New York, 1868), p. 533.

31. The best introduction to American farm building types, based on wide comparative fieldwork in North and South, is Henry Glassie, *Pattern in the Material Folk Culture of the Eastern United States* (Philadelphia, 1969), No. 1. University of Pennsylvania Monographs in Folklore and Folklife. This basic work is profusely illustrated with photographs and architectural drawings and contains the best bibliography thus far on American folk architecture.

32. Harriet Beecher Stowe, *Poganuc People: Their Loves and Lives* (New York, 1878), pp. 167–68. Subsequent quotation p. 176.

33. For the funeral meal in Europe see A. Frevbe, *Das alte deutsche Leichenmahl in seiner Art und Entartung* (Gütersloh, 1909); also Arnold van Gennep. *Manuel de folklore français contemporam* 2 (Paris, 1946): 773–91.

34. For the European peasant sense of holy space within his own farmhouse see Gustav Ränk, *Die heilige Hinterecke im Hauskult der Völker Nordosteuropas und Nordasiens* (Helsinki. 1949), *Folklore Fellows Communications* 137.

35. Charles W. Dunn, Highland Settler: A Portrait of the Scottish Gael in Nova Scotia (Toronto, 1953), p. 156.

36. Ibid., pp. 115–16.

37. Earnest Elmo Calkins. *They Broke the Prairies* (New York. 1939), pp. 17–18.

38. Richard Weiss, "Alpiner Mensch und alpines Leben in der Krise der Gegenwart." *Schweizerisches Archiv für Volkskunde* 58 (1962): 241–42.

39. Richard Osborn Cummings, The American and His Food: A History of Food Habits in the United States (Chicago, 1940), p. 229.

References

The American Heritage Cookbook and Illustrated History of American Eating & Drinking. New York: American Heritage Publishing Company, Inc., 1964. A readable, popular collection of essays on various regional and ethnic cuisines of the United States, magnificently illustrated from historical sources.

Arnow, Harriette Simpson. *Seedtime on the Cumberland.* New York: Macmillan Company, 1960. This book, an historical study of the Cumberland Valley area of Kentucky and Tennessee, describes the entire food economy of pioneer Appalachia (chap. 14, "Around the Family Hearth," pp. 387–425).

Brothwell, Don and Patricia. *Food in Antiquity: A Survey of the Diet of Early Peoples.* New York: Frederick A. Praeger, 1969. Vol. 66 in the useful series "Ancient Peoples and Places," published in England by Thames and Hudson. Bibliography, pp. 193–200.

Burnett, John. *Plenty and Want: A Social History of Diet in England from 1815 to the Present Day.* London: Thomas Nelson, 1966; Pelican Books, 1968. Analysis of the changes in diet in rural and industrial England, fully documented with many hitherto unpublished source materials.

Coffin, Robert P. Tristram. *Mainstays of Maine.* New York: Macmillan Company, 1944. Evocative essays by the poet and littérateur on New England foods and their social setting.

Cummings, Richard Osborn. *The American and His Food: A History of Food Habits in the United States.* Chicago: University of Chicago Press, 1940. The only recommendable general scholarly historical and nutritional study of the American diet.

Drummond, J. C., and Anne Wilbraham. *The Englishman's Food: A History of Five Centuries of English Diet.* London: Jonathan Cape, 1939. The best single treatment of the changes in English diet, individual foods, meal systems, and food habits from the Middle Ages to the present.

Eckstein, Friedrich. "Speise." *Handwörterbuch des deutschen Aberglaubens* 8: cols. 156–234. Definitive article on the ramifications of diet into folk belief and folk custom.

Eidlitz, Kerstin. *Food and Emergency Food in the Circumpolar Area.* Studia Ethnographica Upsaliensia 32. Uppsala, 1969. Historical and dietetic study of the relationships of arctic and subarctic ecologies, economies, and food systems. Emphasis is upon alternatives to traditional western diet in a world threatened by hunger.

Gottschalk, A. *Histoire de l'alimentation et de la gastronomie depuis la préhistoire jusqu'à nos jours.* 2 vols. Paris, 1948. Standard European survey of diet and food preparation, on all levels of culture.

Honigman, John H. *Foodways in a Muskeg Community: An Anthropological Report on the Attawapiskat Indians.* Ottawa: Northern Co-ordination and Research Center, 1961. A model North American ethnography of food habits, based on fieldwork in a Canadian Indian community.

Lemon, James T. "Household Consumption in Eighteenth-Century America and Its Relationship to Production and Trade: The Situation among Farmers in Southeastern Pennsylvania." *Agricultural History* 41 (January 1967): 59–70. Important for its pioneer use of wills and inventories for food research in the United States.

Lévi-Strauss, Claude. "Le triangle culinaire." *L'Arc* 26 (1965): 19–29: "The Culinary Triangle." *Partisan Review* 33 (Fall 1966): 586–95. Analyzing cooking methods, the author constructs a triangle of which the points are "cru," "cuit," and "pourri," with an interior triangle formed by the methods of frying, smoking, and boiling, with discussion of the intermediate forms between the points.

Lincoln, Waldo. *American Cookery Books 1742–1860.* Revised and enlarged by Eleanor Lowenstein. Worcester, Mass.: American Antiquarian Society, 1954. A holding list of American imprints containing recipes, providing the scholar with an indication of the regional cookbooks that appeared in print before the Civil War, plus some indication of the impact of food reforms and taboos on cookbook editors (homeopathic, hydropathic, temperance, and total abstinence cookbooks).

Lucas, Anthony T. "Irish Food Before the Potato." *Gwerin* 3 (1960–62): 1–36. A thoroughly documented study of Irish diet before the eighteenth century, by the director of the National Museum of Ireland.

Nordland, Odd. *Brewing and Beer Traditions in Norway. The Social Anthropological Background of the Brewing Industry.* Oslo: Universitets-forlaget, 1969. Model introduction to domestic brewing, its history, technology, and vocabulary.

Richards, Audrey I. *Land, Labour and Diet in Northern Rhodesia: An Economic Study of the Bemba Tribe.* London: Oxford University Press, 1939. One of the model ethnographies of diet. See especially "Food and Drink," pp. 44–108, and "The Production of Food," pp. 228–351.

Root, Waverly, *The Food of France.* New York: Vintage Books, 1966. A readable, popular account, both historical and descriptive, of the culinary provinces of France, divided on the basis of the three materials used for cooking: butter, fat, and oil.

Simoons, Frederick J. *Eat Not This Flesh: Food Avoidances in the Old World.* Madison, Wisconsin: University of Wisconsin Press, 1963. A basic anthropological study of food taboos and their sociological and psychological meaning.

Sorre, Max. "La géographie de l'alimentation." *Annales de géographie* 61: 184–99. Reprinted in Philip L. Wagner and Marvin W. Mikesell, eds., *Readings in Cultural Geography.* Chicago: University of Chicago Press, 1962. "The Geography of Diet," pp. 445–56. Deals with the relation of diet to environment, climate, ecology, religion, and traditional production techniques. Important, among other reasons, for its use of the term "dietary regime," by which Sorre means the ensemble of foods and their preparation that sustains a human group throughout the year.

Vicaire, Georges. *Bibliographie Gastronomique: A Bibliography of Books Appertaining to Food and Drink and Related Subjects, From the Beginning of Printing to 1890*. Paris, 1890. Reprint. London: Derek Verschoyle Academic and Bibliographical Publications, Ltd., 1954. With Introduction by André L. Simon.

Wiegelmann, Günter. *Alltags- und Festspeisen: Wandel und gegenwärtige Stellung*. Marburg: N. G. Elwert Verlag, 1967. Atlas der deutschen Volkskunde, Neue Folge, Beiheft 1. Ranks at the very top of the best European historical and ethnological studies of regional diet. The bibliography (pp. 245–61) is the most useful compiled thus far on European dietary studies.

Wright, Lawrence. *Home Fires Burning: The History of Domestic Heating and Cooking*. London: Routledge and Kegan Paul, 1964. Particularly good on open-hearth cookery and the changes that were brought to the kitchen by the "iron monster," the kitchen range.

Yoder, Don. "Historical Sources for American Foodways Research and Plans for an American Foodways Archive." *Ethnologia Scandinavica* 2 (1971): 41–55. Discusses printed, manuscript, and iconographic source materials and illustrates their value by applying them to acculturation problems in Pennsylvania German cookery research. An expanded version, with illustrations, appeared in *Pennsylvania Folklife* 20 (Spring 1971): 16–29.

CHAPTER 2
INNOVATIONS IN FOOD AND MEALS
Günter Wiegelmann

I

The kind of research into innovations founded by American agricultural sociology, led to a considerable clarification of the processes and a theorization of the analyses. This was possible through the study of recent, precisely observable processes, disregarding the individual features, and seeking the most general rules and fundamental laws by concentrating the view on that aspect of innovation concerned with its adoption.

However, the well known and clearly demonstrated results of the adoption and diffusion researches by Everett M. Rogers and Torsten Hägerstrand[1] will be applied here only to some extent, for they are also concerned with matters other than cultural anthropological research. The main deficiency is that such general rules can give only very general ideas, and therefore can reflect the circumstances in culturally different systems only in a very abstract way.

Another point is that the rules have been based on the analysis of present-day processes, that is on the basis of the quickly passing processes of a highly civilized society. Innovation processes of the eighteenth or sixteenth century, however, were influenced by totally different sets of values and communication-structures, so that the analogy of rules originating from an industrial society is only partly applicable.

A third point is that research into adoption and diffusion only considers the period until adoption, but not the related incorporation and assimilation processes within the cultural systems. Yet this aspect is the focal point of cultural anthropological research. The following questions, therefore, will be investigated here:

1. Under which conditions are food innovations adopted? Since there have always been minor innovations, it would be better to ask, under which conditions *do innovations increase*? And; under which conditions are basic innovations adopted?

2. What are the *social starting-points* of innovations? Which social classes fostered innovation, who are the typical laggards? How does an innovation proceed in general through the social classes?

3. In which *meals* are new elements in general at first observable? What path do they then follow through the arrangement of the meals?

4. What *time-spans* are to be taken into account for such integration processes?

II

First I should like to look into the conditions for innovation frequency, and the social reasons. I shall start with two examples that have moved in opposite directions, the introduction of coffee and the potato. Both appeared almost simultaneously on the European scene, although they represent two quite different patterns.

Günter Wiegelmann, 'Innovations in Food and Meals', *Folk Life* 12 (1974), 20–30. Reproduced with permission of Maney Publishing in the format 'Book' via Copyright Clearance Center.

Coffee (or in England tea) is the standard example of an element of culture that comes down the social scale.[2] As an expensive import, at first it was only drunk by rich citizens and in court circles. In 1716 'this expensive tea and coffee' were considered unnecessary exotic plants for Middle Europe. Only 'in distinguished houses at this time had the custom been introduced of imbibing coffee or tea in the morning or afternoon.'[3] Shortly afterwards, coffee was accepted more generally by the ordinary citizens and at about 1750 it began to penetrate into the villages. After about two generations (or seventy years) the new drink passed on from the highest classes to farmers, labourers, and servants. Of course, at this period only the first steps had been taken by the lower classes. The great break-through for them came only during the last decades of the eighteenth century, very significantly only after a coffee-ersatz (chicory-coffee) began to be provided by factories in large quantities. This spread of coffee drinking in the form of a cheap substitute reflects exactly the social situation of this time. The farmers, due to the good agricultural situation, were then in a position to adopt numerous elements of the living and eating habits of the middle class. At the same time, the lower classes, in Germany for the most part living in the country, were very badly off. Because too many labourers were available due to the enormous population increase, they could not earn much money. They had, however, the example of the good living of the well-to-do farmers before them and this incited them to imitation. Yet their scanty financial means permitted no real keeping up with the Joneses, so they took to cheap substitutes like chicory-coffee and later on potato-gin.[4]

This gradual spread of coffee drinking from the tables of the courts and rich people to the poor tables of the day-labourers is characterized by some typical features. The expensive luxury drink was at first only adopted by the upper classes. But just because it was an excellent status symbol, the middle and lower classes tried to participate in it. They imitated the upper-class meals accompanied by coffee. These efforts at imitation are also shown by the fact that in many German territories as a reaction coffee drinking was forbidden. The importance of imitation is also observable in the fact that people took to substitutes even though they did not have the most essential ingredient, caffein, with its vitalizing effect. The gradual social descent of coffee-drinking in Northern Germany, lasted on the whole, for a little more than one century, from about 1680 to about 1800.

The potato took just the opposite path.[5] It was first introduced by the poorest rural population, in Central Europe by the small farmers and day-labourers in infertile mountain regions such as the Erzgebirge. In these regions there had always been a shortage of cereals, so people avidly took to the new plant. The first evidence in Middle Europe dates from about 1680.

For a long time the potato was despised by city dwellers and well-off farmers. People considered it below their dignity to touch this food for pigs and poor people. It took a severe famine to work a change. When in 1770–1 people were starving even in regions normally rich in cereals, they remembered the potato. As it then helped to keep them from starvation, middle-class circles began to be enthusiastic about it — Matthias Claudius wrote a poem *Kartoffellied*— and rich farmers began to acknowledge its existence. Since then, the potato has been an important part of the national food in Germany. Gradually it also reached upper-class tables.

The above examples characterize two typical innovation processes. On the one hand there is the path followed by an originally expensive luxury food. Besides coffee, other examples are tea, sugar, rice, chocolate, and fruits from the south. They generally sank down the social scale. The spread of such prestige goods was speeded up at times of growing prosperity.

On the other hand, former famine foods took the opposite path. Besides potatoes, they included buckwheat, margarine and also to some extent maize. They started at the lower end of the social scale and moved upwards. Times of destitution intensified their use, in the same way as prosperity affected luxuries.

These two social starting points and processes are often to be found with food innovations. But it must be remembered that they do not always pass through the whole scale, from the richest to the poorest or vice versa. For example, buckwheat was never served as a meal on the tables of wealthy people in spite of its use for five centuries. On the other hand, numerous delicacies — such as caviar and lobster — were restricted for an equally long time to well-to-do circles. Not every innovation comes into the mechanism of social competition and some of them only temporarily.

It must also be remembered that points of origin at the social extremes, with the richest and the poorest people, are not always applicable. Some innovations originated from the middle classes, for instance through contacts made by these classes in times of emigration or temporary migrations. Despite this fact, the upper and lower classes in general must be considered the most active innovators, while the farmers, artisans, and other middle-class citizens are usually more conservative.

III

The following figure is a graphic representation of the typical innovation trends (see Fig. 1).

The cultural anthropological rules of this scheme may be summarized as follows:

1. Expensive innovations are at first adopted by the upper classes. Through imitation they often move down the social scale or are imitated through replacement by substitutes (model of a *sinkendes Kulturgut*).[6]

2. Adoption by a lower class is often brought about in times of increasing prosperity. Later on, efforts are made to maintain this standard even in worse times (theory of cultural fixation).[7]

3. Emergency innovations are at first adopted by the lowest classes. Often they are only introduced to the higher classes in times of distress (model of an *aufsteigendes Kulturgut*).[8]

4. The social rise and fall of elements of food has an equivalent in the up and down movement within the arrangement of meals. The up and down fluctuations in the social field and in the meals depends on the price of food and of its evaluation.[9]

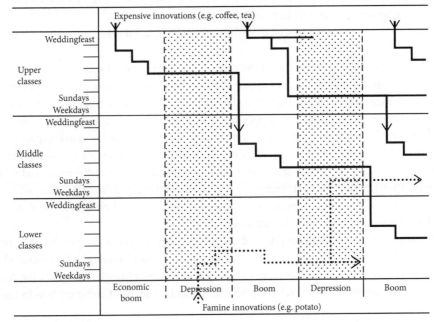

Figure 2.1 Innovations in classes and meals.

5. The meals of the actual upper classes and the festive meals of a social class aim at exclusiveness. As a result new food elements are often given up very quickly by the upper classes as soon as they fall into lower positions. The reverse is also true. Only those new victuals and preparations have a chance of being accepted in high social and festive positions, which have not yet been integrated in lower positions (differentiation efforts of social groups and meal arrangements).[10]

6. These differentiation efforts are the correlative to the mechanism of the *sinkendes Kulturgut*. Continuous imitation and sinking down the social scale would necessarily lead to a relatively uniform food culture if no further innovations were introduced. However, differentiation efforts repeatedly create new differences. Thus internal tensions in the system,[11] without direct influence from outside, cause innovations in food culture, mostly new preparations and eating customs.

The importance of the differentiation efforts depends on how strongly pronounced the social contrasts are and how richly differentiated the hierarchy of festive meals is. Therefore the extent of the differentiation efforts offers a reliable indicator for social barriers and for the spread of the arrangement of festive meals.

IV

In the foregoing, some conditions for the increase in food innovations — times of extreme destitution and times of increasing prosperity — have been indicated. Contacts through migration also give rise to innovation. For the settled population, close intercourse caused by trade, work and contacts at festivals has an effect similar to migrations. Both migrations and a high intensity of intercourse are, of course, general conditions for cultural contacts, not for food in particular.

A special condition, however, is a change in the availability of food. For the recent economic development of Europe it is characteristic that through expanding imports and increases in agricultural production, food is becoming available in ever-increasing quantities. At the same time there was an increase in and cheapening of consumption. This gave rise to special impulses for cultural processes.

An increasing consumption of one special food occasions two cultural reactions, which seem to be subject to a rule.

On the one hand there is an acceleration of the rate of downward spread within the social scales and the scales of meals, leading to a rapid adoption of upper-class elements by the lower social classes thus causing an innovation increase. Rice consumption is an example for this.[12] At the beginning of the nineteenth century rice porridge was still served as an expensive peculiarity at wedding meals of central European farmers. For city dwellers, however, it was already customary for Sunday meals. Due to the quick expansion of imports and the depreciation of rice, the principal conditions changed, however, at about the middle of the century. The suddenly lowered price of rice made it common for the every-day meals of the industrial worker. At this time, the reciprocal relationship between every-day food and food for high festivals also became very soon apparent. Since rice had become the common every-day food of the lowest classes, it could not maintain its exclusiveness for high festivals and the upper classes.

On the other hand, an increase in the range of dishes and their preparation goes hand in hand with an increase in consumption. This is a closely linked reaction, based on the physiologically motivated endeavours for change. The more a victual is consumed, that is, the more it is served in different meals, the more attempts are made to vary its preparation. This can be further demonstrated by meat consumption in the nineteenth century.

At about the middle of the nineteenth century, a quickly and continuously increasing meat consumption began in Germany.[13] Precisely at that time, people from all classes began to adopt new meat preparations, the French chop, the 'Wiener Schnitzel', and the Hungarian goulash, beefsteak and the custom of eating raw minced meat. In the context, I may also mention meat extract.

These conditions are probably the most important for innovation increases in food. It is not surprising that since a cultural element such as food is so closely related to economic conditions, the most important exogenous influences are of an economic nature.

V

An associated question is, in which cases are radical basic innovations, or smaller modifying innovations, to be expected, and to what extent are the structures of food and repast systems affected by them.

The question can hardly be answered in a general way, since in each case a concrete innovation process is involved which can only be roughly defined by rules. It can hardly be prophesied from the starting-point of a process, whether an innovation will eventually change the meals fundamentally. Thus about the year 1600, one could scarcely have foreseen the later diffusion of the potato and its revolutionary effect on Central European food since it was then still grown as a rarity in the botanic gardens of the princely courts. At that time no starting-points could be seen for the later central function of the potato as a famine emergency food for many classes.

Yet, some general tendencies may be indicated. Basic innovations are to be found mainly when famine innovations spread more generally. This happened to the potato, buckwheat and also to oats, which was also originally a famine cereal.[14] The later importance of former famine food has a certain consistency, for what stands the trial in extreme need when victuals are reduced to their most essential, may at other times also be considered as basic food.

On the other hand, it can be stated that the luxury innovations of the upper classes tend to be small. This accords with the nature of these innovations, such as marzipan, sugar and rice.

There is also a certain consistency in this group of food elements that diffuse downwards through the social scale, due to the fact that they involve modifying innovations, and are with respect to their function entirely exceptional things, prestige goods which otherwise would not inspire imitation.

Yet some of these innovations may also give rise to basic changes when conditions are such that the goods become available through reduction in price and mass production. This has been the case with sugar since the nineteenth century. At first its expense made it only a means of sweetening more refined than honey, but later the easy availability of cheaper cane-sugar and of beet-sugar soon made it a prevalent taste, largely determining the character of our food.[15]

VI

The question of which meals new elements are first introduced to, can be concisely treated. Unfortunately, the changes in the scales of meals are not so simple or regular that an innovation falling through the different social scales always begins at the top with very festive meals, which within one class then become common every-day meals, which in turn were seen by the next lower class as festive meals, and then the imitation and descent process continued as before. The co-ordination is more complicated, and not only because of the differentiation trends already discussed.

The following characteristics are observable. With the rural population, upper-class innovations often penetrated at first into Sunday meals, because every-day food was restricted in kind by the relatively constant nature of agriculture and a high degree of self-sufficiency, and because on the other hand festive meals sometimes tended to be of a fixed, traditional nature due to religious beliefs and customs. Of course, the ritual fixation of food — unless supported by church laws — seldom reached the constancy that can be observed with every-day food. Festive meals, characterized by numbers of participants and by prestige thinking which made the serving of especially good and outstanding dishes a kind of status symbol, were always prone to upper-class innovations.

It can also be said that in the social descent of new foods, not only the method of preparation, but in most cases also the timing and position of the upper-class meal was imitated by the lower classes. Coffee once more may be regarded as a model, for its middle-class position as a drink for visits, at breakfast and at tea-time was accurately imitated by the rural population.

But for the fuller clarification of this question we still lack an essential basis for almost all parts of Europe, that is a socially and regionally differentiated history of meals. Small clues may give us the diffusion of names of meals — such as 'lunch' and 'snack'. Hitherto, people have followed in their innovation studies mostly new food elements and eating customs through the different meal structures. For this purpose, meals were considered to be constant reference frames. This, however, is a premise, limiting the realistic analysis of the complicated innovation processes; for the meal systems also changed considerably in the course of the last centuries — from the daily two-meal system to the three-meal system and by the introduction of regular intermediate meals to a four-meal or five-meal system.

For this reason, the following up of innovation processes is complicated considerably. Let me explain the problem by an example. It was noted earlier that the middle-class meal positions of coffee were copied during the eighteenth century by the rural population. But can it be maintained that all these meals were already spread everywhere in the villages at that time? Were not some of them introduced only by the introduction of short meals with coffee or at least strengthened by it? In short, what influence had the coffee and tea innovations of the eighteenth century on the meal structure?

To be more precise: In Middle Europe, coffee drinking was at first adopted in a middle zone between the Rhineland, Saxony, and Mecklenburg. The quick spread of innovations in this zone was formerly explained by reference to the social structure, by the intermixture with a working population between the Rhineland and Saxony, and by the influence of the gentlemen farmers of Mecklenburg. But perhaps there was a more concrete condition for the speed of adoption, because breakfast and afternoon tea in these regions had already been formed before and had been institutionalized by the example of the middle class. And therefore the middle-class variants of these meals involving coffee were likely to be able to cross the social boundary easily.

VII

The last item — the time-span of the innovation processes — has already been outlined and we found that for the incorporation of coffee and the potato more than one century was needed for these to penetrate into the meals of all social classes.

Such time-spans of three to four generations for the integration process can be considered typical between the later seventeenth and the early twentieth century not only for coffee and the potato but also for eating customs, new meat dishes, for margarine, and the English floury pudding.

Of course, these time-spans are not valid for the twentieth century. There is at present a much more rapid sequence of innovations, for two reasons. On the one hand communication has been accelerated considerably. Advertising of new products reaches almost simultaneously millions of households, while the innovations in former times could be passed on only by numerous individual contacts from village to village, from region to region. Besides, the range of social differences and the meal hierarchy has been reduced recently. The food of the working people today is comparably closer to the rich people's food than at about 1800 and festive meals today no longer surpass every-day food as far as they did in former times. Therefore today's innovations no longer need as much time as formerly for the integration processes, even if the former communication processes still have to be applied. Of course, no comparable researches have yet been carried out for the last fifty years.

We have already mentioned the general exogenous conditions of economy, intercourse and so on for an acceleration of the processes. It must be added that internal cultural structures equally may have an accelerating or a retarding effect. I should like to indicate a few rules:

1. The more public the meal which brings an innovation, the greater the chance for a quick diffusion. Thus a wedding-meal or a meal in a restaurant has a better chance of becoming known, than food limited to family meals.[16]

2. Innovations proceeding from the upper classes have a better chance for a quick and general diffusion than lower-class famine innovations. This results from the more public character of the upper-class prestige goods and from imitation efforts[17] of the lower classes.

3. The better an innovation goes with the structures and changing trends of preparation, the better are the chances for a quick diffusion. This compatibility is valid particularly for every-day food. Thus the potato was taken on very quickly for the North German vegetable stew, and rice porridge replaced the former millet-gruel without a noticeable break. But it must be remembered that with festive meals often just the opposite proves to be true, and particular or extraordinary elements are preferred to those that go readily together. Therefore the frequently adduced argument of compatibility cannot be applied too much.

4. This does not prevent me from mentioning compatibility in relation to the meal organization. The less important the necessary changes in the meal organization are at the time of adoption, that is, the better a new food is adapted to the old meal structures and their changing trends, the greater is its chance for a quick diffusion. Thus the new modes of meat preparation of the nineteenth century (chop, cutlet, and so on) were easily introduced into the festive meals of Southern Germany, because they were characterized by a food succession consisting of several meat courses, while in Northern Germany they were not well received because the festive meals there consisted of only a few courses (sometimes only one course) and because sweet dishes were also important.

VIII

In this attempt to establish characteristics of innovation processes, generalizations have often been made, for this was unavoidable. What is characteristic is often general, and too much detail, for example of Middle European development, would obscure the present purpose. The international discussion on the approaches to and aims of ethnological food research must in my opinion be dealt with at a level of abstraction above the concrete.

Main circumstances governing food and meals

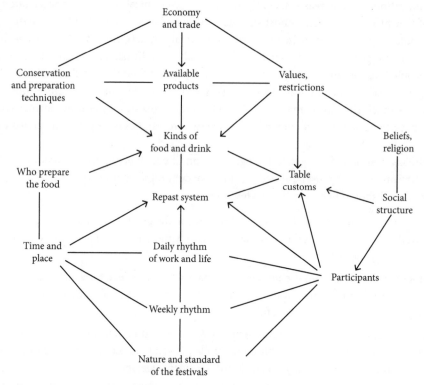

Figure 2.2 Main circumstances governing food and meals.

Only a part of the possible range of questions could be treated here,[18] and therefore a model has been devised, in which the conditioning structure for food and meals are indicated (see Fig. 2). By this means, further innovation impulses become obvious, for instance due to change in preparation and conservation techniques — almost the central subject of the twentieth century — and because of changes in the place of meals and of the persons preparing these meals. These and other questions cannot be dealt with at present.

Notes

1. Everett M. Rogers with F. Floyd Shoemaker, *Communication of Innovations. A cross-cultural approach,* second edition (New York, London, 1971); Torsten Hägerstrand, *Innovation-Diffusion as a spatial process,* translated by Alan Pred (Chicago, 1968).

2. Günter Wiegelmann, Alltags- und Festspeisen. Wandel und gegenwärtige Stellung (Beiheft 1 zum Atlas der deutschen Volkskunde, Neue Folge) (Marburg, 1967), pp. 157–90.

3. Paul Jacob Marperger, *Vollständiges Küch- und Keller-Dictionarium* (Hamburg, 1716), pp. 17, 186.

4. Hans J. Teuteberg and Günter Wiegelmann, *Der Wandel der Nahrungsgewohnheiten unter dem Einfluß der Industrialisierung* (Studien zum Wandel von Gesellschaft und Bildung im Neunzehnten Jahrhundert, iii) (Göttingen, 1972); Günter Wiegelmann, 'Tendenzen kulturellen Wandels in der Volksnahrung des 19. Jahrhunderts', *Ernährung und Ernährungslehre im 19. Jahrhundert* (Studien zur Medizingeschichte des neunzehnten Jahrhunderts, v), edited by Edith Heischkel (in print); John Burnett, Plenty and Want. *A social history of diet in England from 1815 to the present day* (Pelican Books, 1968).

5. Radcliffe N. Salaman, *The History and Social Influence of the Potato* (Cambridge, 1949); Gösta Berg, 'Die Kartoffel und die Rübe', *Ethnologia Scandinavica* (1971), pp. 158–66; Günter Wiegelmann, 'Alltagsspeisen' (see note 2), pp. 75–111.

6. Hans Naumann, *Grundzüge der deutschen Volkskunde* (Leipzig, 1922); Adolf Bach, *Deutsche Volkskunde*, third edition (Heidelberg, 1960), pp. 64–9, 435–6; Åke Hultkrantz, *General Ethnological Concepts* (Copenhagen, 1960), pp. 158–9.

7. Sigfrid Svensson, 'On the Concept of Cultural Fixation', *Ethnologia Europaea*, vi, 1972, (1973), 129–56 (with comments by G. Berg, B. Deneke, M. K. H. Eggert, S. B. Ek, A. Fenton, A. Gailey, T. Hofer).

8. Adolf Bach, *Volkskunde* (see note 6), pp. 437–40.

9. Brita Egardt, *Hästslakt och rackarskam* (Nordiska museets handlingar 57) (Stockholm, 1962); 'Hamburgare — hästkött; Svamp som föda', *Mat och miljö*, edited by Nils-Arvid Bringéus (Lund, 1970), pp. 205–24; Ulrich Tolksdorf, 'Pilze als Nahrung. Zu Vorurteil und Innovation eines Nahrungsmittels in Norddeutschland', *Kieler Blätter zur Volkskunde*, iii (1971), 5–26; 'Ein systemtheoretischer Ansatz in der ethnologischen Nahrungsforschung', *Kieler Blätter zur Volkskunde*, iv (1972), 55–72; 'Grill und Grillen. Oder: Die Kochkunst der mittleren Distanz', *Kieler Blätter zur Volkskunde*, v (1973), 113–34; Nils-Arvid Bringéus, 'Man, Food and Milieu', *Folk Life*, 8 (1970), 45–56.

10. Günter Wiegelmann, 'Möglichkeiten ethnohistorischer Nahrungsforschung', *Ethnologia Europaea*, 1 (1967), 185–94; 'Alltagsspeisen' (see note 2), pp. 75–165, 240–1.

11. Günter Wiegelmann, 'Theoretische Konzepte der Europäischen Ethnologic', *Zeitschrift für Volkskunde*, 68 (Jg. 1972), 196–212.

12. Günter Wiegelmann, 'Alltagsspeisen' (see note 2), pp. 131–48 (with fig. 7); Teuteberg/Wiegelmann, 'Wandel' (see note 4), pp. 227–9.

13. Teuteberg/Wiegelmann, 'Wandel' (see note 4), pp. 94–132.

14. *Reallexikon der germanischen Altertumskunde*, ii, edited by J. Hoops (Straßburg, 1913–15), pp. 357 ff.; Karl and Franz Bertsch, *Geschichte unserer Kulturpflanzen* (Stuttgart, 1947), pp. 78 ff.

15. E. O. von Lippman, *Geschichte des Zuckers seit den ältesten Zeiten bis zum Beginn der Rübenzucker-Fabrikation*, second edition (Berlin, 1929).

16. Günter Wiegelmann, '"Materielle" und "geistige" Volkskultur. Zu den Gliederungsprinzipien der Volkskunde', *Ethnologia Europaea*, iv, 1970 (1971), 187–93.

17. Günter Wiegelmann, 'Tendenzen' (see note 4).

18. *Mat och miljö*, edited by Nils-Arvid Bringéus (Lund, 1970). *Ethnologia Scandinavica 1971*; *Ethnological Food Research in Europe and USA*, edited by Nils-Arvid Bringéus and Günter Wiegelmann (Lund, 1972); *Ethnologia Europaea*, v (1971).

PART II
FOOD IN GROUPS, COMMUNITY, AND IDENTITY

INTRODUCTION TO PART TWO

Group

The concept of "folk group" is central to contemporary folkloristic approaches to the people who participate in folklore. While the folk were originally thought of as isolated, homogenous groups that lived their lives uncritically according to tradition,[1] scholars in the 1960s recognized that they could be any group that shared a commonality. Various scholars refined that definition, specifying that a folk group was one that developed expressive traditions from their shared commonality.[2] Richard Bauman examined the "social matrix" of folk groups, looking at how the "lore" of folklore functioned as "communicative interaction" that gave the group a sense of identity (1971). This shifted the focus from the product of that interaction to the processes surrounding it. It also meant that any group of people could develop that sense of communal identity and become a folk group. Dan Ben-Amos used the phrase "small group" for the type of group in which a "folkloric act" can occur: "Both the performers and the audience have to be in the same situation and be part of the same reference group (1971: 12)." By reference group, he means that the individuals "speak the same language, share similar values, beliefs, and background knowledge, have the same system of codes and signs for social interaction," so that there is an assumption of understanding within the group (1971). "Small" in the definition refers to a quality rather than a quantity in which the performers can adjust their performance according to the audience's reactions and there is communication between the two. Although initially that communication was assumed to be necessarily oral or imitative and face-to-face, later folklorists recognized that other mediums can be used and that folk groups can exist virtually as well as in physical space. In order to become a folk group, the group needs both the regular contact and the shared experience that allow the individuals to create shared traditions. It is the shared traditions that define them as a folk group, which is, in turn, used to express and negotiate the group's identity as well as to explore its characteristics (Noyes 2003).

The folk can therefore be any of us in any time or place. This is significant for food studies since it expands the perception of whose food can be studied as folklore. Food was of interest to early folklorists as another aspect of peasant life, with European ethnologists including its production, preservation, and preparation in their surveys of folk traditions. Beliefs around food were collected, as well as the material culture surrounding it. These were treated as artifacts showing national identity, regional variations, and superstitious worldviews. This approach was carried over in the United States, and the *Journal of American Folklore* published an article in 1895 on the "Folk-Foods of the Rio Grande and of Northern Mexico" (Bourke), establishing food as a viable subject for folklorists, but not challenging the notions of who were the folk or what could be learned through studying their food traditions. Even the attention brought to food in the 1960s by the American folklorist Don Yoder emphasized folk as marginal enclaves within the mainstream culture, since he focused on the Pennsylvania-Germans (1961a, 1961b, 1962, 1971). Yoder, however, did encourage applying the newer paradigm shift in folklore studies to the notions of who were the folk and the role of food in expressing that "folkness," and other folklorists, notably Michael Owen Jones (1983) and Robert Georges (1984), also began attending to food as a medium through which groups constructed and defined themselves.

It is obvious that people gather and interact around food constantly, and many develop social groups based on the shared interests and interactions. Not all food-based groups become folk groups, but all have the potential to do so, particularly since food, as a universal need, serves easily as a natural commonality. As mentioned above, several conditions need to exist in order for folk groups to develop.[3] Identifying these conditions enables us to understand how and why people sometimes feel connected to one another through food.

First, proximity, or regular contact, is a necessity for interaction (Noyes 2003; Sims 2005). Without it, a sense of shared commonality does not develop, nor does shared communication. It is out of this sharing that expressive traditions emerge that, in turn give the group its identity. Proximity usually happens by means of a shared geography—national, ethnic, regional, neighborhood—but it can also happen through virtual networks, through the Internet or telephone (Degh 1994). Furthermore, individuals can have proximity without becoming a folk group. People eat together all the time in restaurants or cafeterias without developing a sense of commonality and expressive forms with one another. Similarly, necessity, obligation, and circumstances, all offer the potential for a folk group to develop. Living in a family, attending school, or going to work forces us to be around other people and frequently to participate in activities with them. Sharing such contexts creates situations in which interactions, whether desired or not, occur. These interactions can, in turn, become representative expressions of the group and can give the members of the group a sense of common identity. Family, occupation, and peer groups, as well as some religious groups, can fit this type, and all frequently develop food traditions.

Secondly, regular interaction, not just regular contact, is needed for a group to become folk. As mentioned above, simply being together is not enough. Some type of interaction is necessary in order for individuals to feel that a group exists and that they are members of it. Interaction is also necessary in order for the third process to occur in which expressive forms are created that then give definition to the group. It is this last process that distinguishes a group of people from a folk group. These forms become the traditions that represent the group and in which members participate, making them aware of the shared references and the shared identity.

Foodways activities and events offer numerous opportunities for proximity, regular interaction, and the development of traditions. Similarly, folk groups based on other commonalities, such as ethnicity, region, religion, or occupation, usually include foodways activities, offering more opportunities for proximity, interaction, and the emergence of traditions. Food, then, according to the contemporary understanding of folk groups, is both a tool for their development and an expression of their commonality. As such, it can be a powerful medium for defining folk groups, showing who is a member and who is not, and illustrating the values and attitudes of the group. Folklorists in the 1970s and 1980s recognized this and explored food as central to a folk group being dynamic, fluid, constantly reconstructed as well as being used to both include and exclude individual members.[4]

Community

This brings us to the problematic concept of community. The term can refer to a concrete, physical entity—a bounded, defined geographic area, such as a neighborhood—but it also implies a welcoming atmosphere, a friendly neighborliness that goes beyond simple coexistence. It tends to serve as an ideal toward which groups should strive. As an academic construct, a fundamental feature of "community" is that it becomes a significant aspect of personal identity. Furthermore, other activities between members often develop that are secondary to the primary activity that initially brought people together (Jordan-Smith and Horton 2001). These secondary activities can develop into traditions that further strengthen relationships and connections between community members, creating "dense networks" of connections, in which individual members become connected in a variety of ways beyond the initial commonality. Foodways frequently offer some of those various ways. For example, pot-lucks at a dance become a tradition in themselves and may be the focus of another event that draws together that group, and they can even function as a common reference along with the primary activity. Meanwhile, participation in, and commitment to, the primary activity allows, in theory, for diversity and division, allowing like-minded individuals to come together in community and overlook other differences between those members (Jordan-Smith and Horton 2001).

It is easy to see how food can be the center of such voluntary communities, and foodways can be either a primary or a secondary activity, or both. Other folklorists, however, have questioned the use of "community" in place of "folk group," observing that the first carries a sense of responsibility toward the well-being of both the individuals and the community itself, a mutual obligation to look out for one another, that is oftentimes overlooked (Feintuch 2001). Identifying groups as "communities" may give a false sense of stability and security to the individuals participating in the activity and romanticizes relationships as well as human nature. It also celebrates the superficial feelings of connectedness without calling upon responsibility or the personal sacrifice that often goes along with caring for others. "Community gardens," "community supported agriculture," and other uses of community as an adjective imply a recognition and acceptance of the mutual obligations involved—but oftentimes fail because those responsibilities are not met.

Identity

Another key word and concept in folklore studies is identity. It can refer to the defining characteristics, the functions or roles, or the soul or essence of an individual or group. As commonly used today, it seems to refer to something stable that transcends time and place. However, as folklorist Roger Abrahams points out, personal identity is a Western concept growing out of romanticism and nationalism in which the self is a distinct and separate entity (2003). Its implications have been highly problematic, seeping into politics, psychology, and the legal system. "When used to refer to self or group of identification, the word seems to emancipate, yet when used to refer to others it too often imprisons (Abrahams 2003: 207)."

The concept of identity is equally problematic in speaking of food. Cuisines seem to have identifiable flavors and core ingredients, cooking styles, and values, but they also change over time and place. Recipes can be varied, but, at some point, no longer "belong" to the cooks originating with them; dishes can reflect a cook's identity, but can also be borrowed and adapted beyond recognition. These are not simply philosophical issues; they also have legal and commercial implications. Who "owns" Mexican cuisine and can open authentic restaurants? What ingredients and dishes define Italian cuisine and are therefore allowed within a site presenting Italian heritage? UNESCO designations of cultural heritage have raised such questions, as have copyright issues over recipes and cookbooks.[5]

Folklorists tend to see identity as an individual's or a group's sense of self, resulting from both the external forces shaping that self and the choices made for responding to those forces. Identity is made evident whenever an individual or a group acts, enacting, realizing, or performing that identity according to the specific time and place. It is also useful to think of identity as being socially, culturally, and personally constructed rather than as having a fixed and intrinsic quality.

This approach to identity also leads to the notion of multiple identities. We all have a variety of roles in life and ways of describing ourselves—race, ethnicity, class, gender, age, occupation, personality, personal interests, and so on. We can think about these various roles as our "multiple identities." Whenever we interact with other people, we are acting upon or highlighting only some of those identities, but not others. These are our "situational identities."[6] "Differential identity" is also shaped by the context, but it is based on the differences with other identities in that context (Bauman 1971). It emphasizes the differences, using them to define that identity and to select what aspects of it to perform. This means that differential identity is performed differently according to each context.

Foodways can easily be used to enact an aspect of our identity. Selecting one food over another in a grocery store may reflect a regional identity; cooking or eating with certain implements may represent an ethnicity; and abstinence from particular ingredients might express ethical values or religious affiliations. Since food is universal and ubiquitous, it offers numerous opportunities for the differences to be recognized and for choices to be made. As both domestic and commercial, everyday and celebratory, it also gives individuals and groups repeated chances to explore variations and adaptations—both in the food and in its public presentation—so that enactments of self can be tried and refined. Also, many of our food choices are made without intentionally performing aspects of our identity, but they are expressions of it just the same.

Conclusion

This *Reader* focuses on ethnic, regional, national, gendered, and religious/belief groups, but students are encouraged to look at other types of groups as well, particularly occupational, class-based, and age-related ones. Race can be its own commonality with shared histories and the potential for unique expressive forms, but it presents a quandary since it oftentimes overlaps with ethnicity and class. Also, groups and their foodways traditions do not always offer positive experiences. Both external factors (history, politics, and economics) and internal factors (human nature, emotional and psychological needs for status, security, and belonging) shape foodways practices, and these factors are neither fair nor gentle. Furthermore, every individual experiences their realities in unique ways and makes one's own choices about actions and meanings.

Articles in *Reader*

The articles in this section can be used as case studies for different types of groups as well as for the dynamic and complex character of groups, communities, and identity. In "'It's All from One Big Pot': Booya as an Expression of Community," Anne Kaplan discusses how a particular dish can represent a community. She points out that its processes of consumption and its preparation are communal, encouraging social interaction and the development of group identity and relationships.

Ethnic groups and their foodways have long been a subject for folklorists. In "Continuity and Adaptation in Arab American foodways," William G. Lockwood and Yvonne R. Lockwood examine the processes involved in "becoming ethnic." As a situational identity, ethnicity is constructed when individuals and groups move to an area in which they are different from the larger, more dominant culture. Exactly what characteristics constitute that identity and the forms expressing them are shaped by a number of factors, which are examined here through foodways. Based on an extensive fieldwork on the food culture of Arab Americans in the Detroit area, the article describes the changes that have been made to traditional foodways in various contexts, both public and private, and deals with some of the meanings of those changes. It also includes a description of holiday meals, including American Thanksgiving, as occasions for intentional performance of ethnic identity.

Regional identity can, at times, overlap with ethnic identity or even develop out of it. Tim Lloyd illustrates this process in his article, "Paterson's Hot Texas Weiner Tradition," about a New Jersey restaurant tradition of deep-fried hot dogs covered with a chili sauce that has Greek roots, similar to the distinctive regional commercial tradition of Cincinnati Chili (Lloyd 1981). The article also recognizes that symbolic foods can develop for pragmatic reasons, such as creating a successful business, but still become significant aspects of regional identity.

A European perspective is offered in Konrad Kostlin's article "A New Ascension on Regional Food." The popular interest in regional food in Europe reflects contemporary concerns about the safety and sustainability of the modern industrial food system. Kostlin identifies a theme of celebration of local foods, but he argues that this does not reflect an interest in performing or constructing regional or cultural identities. Instead, it demonstrates the use of foodways practices as expressions of ethical beliefs. At the same time, it redefines regional food as ethical food.

In contrast, in "Newfoundland and Labrador on a Plate: Bed, Breakfast, and Regional Identity," Holly Everett illustrates how the hospitality industry in these provinces of Canada, in serving food to tourists, negotiates which aspects of the local identity to highlight. Focusing on two bed-and-breakfast establishments, Everett discusses how the presentations of food were commentaries on the character of the local identity.

National identity is oftentimes represented by iconic foods. Robert Smith's article, "The Dog's Eye: The Pie in Australian Tradition," explores the long history of meat pies in Australia and the many variations of them as connected to specific places and makers. He argues that pies embody qualities that many Australians associate with their cultural identity—working-class origins, informal, unremarkable, ordinary, and presented with humor. It is these qualities that have allowed meat pies, although very commonplace and sold in commercial places rather than homemade, to stand as a national dish for Australians.

In "Balut: Fertilized Duck Eggs and Their Role in Filipino Culture," Margaret Magat demonstrates that national foods may develop from social and practical conditions rather than an intentional performance of identity. Ethnographic research led her to conclude that the consumption of this particular food is not motivated by nationalism or ethnic pride but by the more pragmatic interest in its qualities as an aphrodisiac. At the same time, though, it continues to embody beliefs, history, and practices of that culture. As discussed earlier, food can carry a variety of identities. In "Feeding the Jewish Soul in the Delta Diaspora," Marcie Cohen Ferris describes the foodways traditions of her Jewish family in Arkansas and how they used those traditions to negotiate their ethnic and religious as well as regional identity. The Jewish food culture that developed in the South was distinct from that in other American regions. It was simultaneously adapted to the region, but also maintained in selected contexts in order to create strong social ties and a sense of Jewishness. Ferris also emphasizes that individuals within the Jewish community varied in their adherence to the rules of Kashrut and the ways in which food was used to express identity.

Cooking is historically associated in American culture with females and domestic femininity. In "Boy Scouts and the Manly Art of Cooking," Jay Mechling analyzes how the Boy Scouts required boys to learn to cook and master other such "nurturing" tasks yet still presented these activities as masculine. Specific contexts for cooking, such as outdoors, in large groups, for celebrations, and specific types of foods, such as meats and hearty dishes, tend to be considered appropriate for men, but learning to cook also enables men to be less dependent on women, thus affirming their masculinity.

Discussion questions

Group

1. Identify the group(s) you belong to. They can be based on any commonality—national, ethnic, regional, religious, socioeconomic class, gender, occupational, recreational, age. What is the role of food in that group? How important is it? Does it define who belongs and who doesn't?

2. Is food the primary activity or focus for any social groups for you? Does that group meet the conditions for a folk group? Does the focus on food allow for diversity among the members of that group?

3. Can you think of ways in which you can apply the concepts of a folk group to construct or strengthen a social group you participate in?

Community

1. Do any of your groups fit the definition of "community" with the sense of mutual responsibility? What is the role of food in demonstrating that responsibility?

2. Can you think of any instances in which food has caused disagreements, hard feelings, or divisions within one of your communities or groups?

3. In your experience, does sharing food always automatically create a sense of belonging? Why not?

Identity

1. Do you intentionally use food to express your identity on any occasions?

    What identities are being performed through those foods?

    Which ones are highlighted (situational) for you as a student? Which are situational when you are with your family? Which are differential?

2.. Can you think of ways in which your food choices unintentionally express identity? How does a food that you commonly eat everyday express your identity? What variations do you apply to that food; what do those variations represent?

3. Select a common and popular food, such as, for Americans, chilis, pizzas, hot dogs, sandwiches. Explore the variations in recipes and ingredients you and your friends use for one of those foods. What do the variations say about your different backgrounds and identities?

4. Explore the diversity of identities brought to the table for your family or group celebration of a national meal, such as the American Thanksgiving dinner. What does your menu say about you and others in your group as well as your current circumstances?

Notes

1. The American Folklore Society described the folk as "the early settlers, in the colonies peopled from Great Britain," along with "Negroes in the Southern Sates of the Union . . . the Indian Tribes of North America . . . French Canada, Mexico, etc. . . ." *Journal of American Folklore* 1 (1888): 3.

2. For the overviews of the shift in definition see Toelken (1979), Oring (1986), Schoemaker, (1990). Alan Dundes defines the folk as any group sharing a commonality (1965).

3. In their textbook, *Living Folklore* (2005: 38–41), folklorists Martha Sims and Martine Stephens outline the different ways folk groups form.

4. The edited collection by Brown and Mussell emphasized regional and ethnic foodways and addressed theories defining those groups as well as the processes used in constructing them (1984). Their volume was extremely influential and is still used today as a basic textbook. Lynn Humphries and Ted Humphries also edited an influential volume of essays looking at the role of food in constructing and affirming social groups (1988). Food, while popularly seen as bringing people together harmoniously, can frequently create divisions, negative images, and conflict. In the US, for example, vegetable gardens are considered inappropriate in front of a house, as Italian immigrants to Utah discovered, much to their dismay (Raspa 1984). Similarly, Thanksgiving dinner, meant to celebrate family and national unity, oftentimes accentuates differences and causes emotional turmoil (Long 2000) and the social sharing of food between people can accentuate who is not included, making a public statement about exclusion. Integration at lunch counters in the American South in the 1960s were symbolic protests about larger racial divisions.

5. An excellent introduction and discussion of these issues is in the volume, *Edible Identities: Food as Cultural Heritage*, ed. Ronda L. Brulotte and Michael A. Di Giovine (Burlington, VT: Ashgate, 2014).

6. We feel ourselves free to be our true selves when we can enact or perform the identity we want to. This is often the one we feel most comfortable with, like the best, or do not have to perform consciously.

References

Abrahams, Roger D. "Identity." In *Eight Words for the Study of Expressive Culture*, edited by Burt Feintuch, 198–222. Urbana: University of Illinois, 2003.

Anderson, Benedict. *Imagined Communities: Reflections on the Origin and Spread of Nationalism*. London: Verso, 1983.

Avakian, Arlene Voski and Barbara Haber. *From Betty Crocker to Feminist Food Studies: Critical Perspectives on Women and Food*. Amherst: University of Massachusetts, 2005.

Bauman, Richard. "Differential Identity and the Social base of Folklore." In *Toward New Perspectives in Folklore*, edited by Richard Bauman. *Journal of American Folklore*. vol. 84/331 (1971): 31–41.

Ben-Amos, Dan. "Toward a Definition of Folklore in Context." *Toward New Perspectives in Folklore, Special Issue, Journal of American Folklore* 84 (1971): 3–15.

Bower, Anne. *Recipes for Reading: Community Cookbooks, Stories, Histories*. Amherst: University of Massachusetts, 1997.

Brown, Linda Keller and Kay Mussell. *Ethnic and Regional Foodways in the United States: The Performance of Group Identity*. Knoxville: University of Tennessee, 1984.

Brulotte, Ronda L. and Michael A. Di Giovine, eds. *Edible Identities: Food as Cultural Heritage*. Burlington, VT: Ashgate, 2014.

Chen, Yong. "Food, Race, and Ethnicity." In *The Oxford Handbook of Food History*, edited by Jeffrey M. Pilcher, 428–43. Oxford: Oxford University Press, 2012.

Counihan, Carole. *Food in the USA: A Reader*. New York: Routledge, 2002.

Counihan, Carole and Steven L. Kaplan. *Food and Gender: Identity and Power*. Amsterdam, the Netherlands: Harwood Academic, 1998.

Degh, Linda. *American Folklore and the Mass Media*. Bloomington: Indiana University Press, 1994.

Dubisch, Jill. "You Are Where You Eat: Religious Aspects of the Health Food Movement." In *Folk Groups and Folklore Genres: A Reader*, edited by Elliott Oring, 124–36. Logan, UT: Utah State University Press, 1989.

Dundes, Alan, ed. *The Study of Folklore*. Englewood Cliffs, NJ: Prentice-Hall, 1965.

Edison, Carol. "Roast Beef and Pit-Barbecued Lamb: The Role of Food at Two Utah Homecoming Celebrations." In *We Gather Together: Food and Festival in American Life*, edited by Theodore C. Humphrey and Lin T. Humphrey, 137–52. Ann Arbor: UMI Research, 1988.

Ellis, Bill, ed. "Journal of American Folklore." *Special Issue: Food and Identity in the Americas* 122, no. 483 (2009): 53–74.

Feintuch, Burt. "Longing for Community." *Western Folklore* 60, no. 2/3 (2001): 149–61.

Fine, Gary Alan. *Kitchens: The Culture of Restaurant Work*. Berkeley: University of California, 1996.

Gabaccia, Donna R. *We Are What We Eat: Ethnic Food and the Making of Americans*. Cambridge, MA: Harvard University Press, 1998.

Georges, Robert. "You Often Eat What Others Think You Are: Food as an Index of Others' Conceptions of Who One Is." *Western Folklore* 43, no. 4 (1984): 249–56.

Gillespie, Angus K. "A Wilderness in the Megalopolis: Foodways in the Pine Barrens of New Jersey." In *Ethnic and Regional Foodways in the United States: The Performance of Group Identity*, edited by Brown Linda Keller and Kay Mussell, 145–68. Knoxville: University of Tennessee, 1984.

Gutierrez, C. Paige. *Cajun Foodways*. Jackson: University of Mississippi, 1992.

Hall, Stuart and Paul Du Gay, eds. *Questions of Cultural Identity*. London: Sage, 1996.

Hauck-Lawson, Annie and Jonathan Deutsch. *Gastropolis: Food and New York City*. New York: Columbia University Press, 2009.

Humphrey, Lin T. "'Soup Night': Community Creating through Foodways." In *We Gather Together: Food and Festival in American Life*, edited by Theodore C. Humphrey and Lin T. Humphrey, 53–74. Ann Arbor: UMI Research, 1988.

Humphrey, Theodore C. and Lin T. Humphrey, eds. *We Gather Together: Food and Festival in American Life*. Ann Arbor: UMI Research, 1988.

Jones, Michael Owen. "'Tradition' in Identity Discourses and an Individual's Symbolic Construction of Self." *Western Folklore* 59 (2000): 115–41.

Jones, Michael Owen, Bruce Giuliano, and Roberta Krell, eds. *Foodways and Eating Habits: Direction for Research*. Los Angeles: California Folklore Society, 1983.

Jordan, R. A. and Susan J. Kalčik. *Women's Folklore, Women's Culture*. Philadelphia: University of Pennsylvania, 1985.

Jordan-Smith, Paul and Laurel Horton. "Communities of Practice: Traditional Music and Dance." *Western Folklore* 60, no. 2/3 (2001): 29–40.

Kalcik, Susan. "Ethnic Foodways in America: Symbol and the Performance of identity." In *Ethnic and Regional Foods in the United States: The Performance of Group Identity*, edited by Linda Keller Brown and Kay Mussell, 37–65. Knoxville: Univeristy of Tennessee Press, 1984.

Kaplan, Anne R., Marjorie A. Hoover, and Willard B. Moore. "Introduction: On Ethnic Foodways." In *The Taste of American Place: A Reader on Regional and Ethnic Foods*, edited by Barbara G. Shortridge and James R. Shortridge, 121–34. Lanham, MD: Rowman & Littlefield, 1998.

Kaplan, Anne R., Marjorie A. Hoover, and Willard B. Moore. *The Minnesota Ethnic Food Book*. Saint Paul: Minnesota Historical Society, 1986.

Kirlin, Katherine S. and Thomas M. Kirlin. *Smithsonian Folklife Cookbook*. Washington, DC: Smithsonian Institution, 1991.

Lloyd, Timothy C. "The Cincinnati Chili Culinary Complex." In *The Taste of American Place: A Reader on Regional and Ethnic Foods*, edited by Barbara G. Shortridge and James R. Shortridge. Lanham, MD: Rowman & Littlefield, 1998, 45–56.

Lockwood, William G. The Coney in Southeast Michigan: "Something More Substantial for the Working Man." In *Time for Food: Everyday Food and Changing Meal Habits in a Global Perspective*, edited by Patricia Lysagh, 143–56. Åbo Akademi University Press: Finland, 2012.

Lockwood, Yvonne R. and William G. Lockwood. "Pasties in Michigan's Upper Peninsula: Foodways, Interethnic Relations, and Regionalism." In *Creative Ethnicity: Symbols and Strategies of Contemporary Ethnic Life*, edited by Stephen Stern and John Allan Cicala, 3–20. Logan: Utah State University Press, 1991.

Long, Lucy M. "Holiday Meals: Rituals of Family Tradition." In *Dimensions of the Meal: The Science, Culture, Business, and Art of Eating*, edited by Herbert L. Meiselman, 143–59. Gaithersburg, MD: Aspen, 2000.

Long, Lucy M. "Learning to Listen to the Food Voice: Recipes as Expressions of Identity and Carriers of Memory." *Food, Culture and Society: An International Journal of Multidisciplinary Research* 7, no. 1 (2004): 118–22.

Long, Lucy M. *Regional American Food Culture*. Santa Barbara, CA: Greenwood, 2009.

Lysaght, Patricia, ed. *Time for Food: Everyday Food and Changing Meal Habits in a Global Perspective*. Åbo Akademi University Press: Finland, 2012.

McCarl, Robert. "Occupational Folklore." In *Folk Groups and Folklore Genres: An Introduction*, edited by Elliott Oring, 71–90. Logan, UT: Utah State University Press, 1986.

Noyes, Dorothy. "Group." In *Eight Words for the Study of Expressive Culture*, edited by Burt Feintuch, 7–41. Urbana: University of Illinois, 2003.

Oring, Eliot. "Ethnic Groups and Ethnic Folklore." In *Folk Groups and Folklore Genres: An Introduction*, edited by Elliott Oring, 23–44. Logan: Utah State University Press, 1986.

Oring, Eliot, ed. *Folk Groups and Folklore Genres: An Introduction*. Logan: Utah State University Press, 1986.

Oring, Eliot, ed. *Folk Groups and Folklore Genres: A Reader*. Logan: Utah State University Press, 1986.

Pilcher, Jeffrey M. *Que Vivan Los Tamales!: Food and the Making of Mexican Identity*. Albuquerque: University of New Mexico, 1998.

Raspa, Richard. "Exotic Foods Among Italian-Americans in Mormon Utah: Food as Nostalgic Enactment of Identity." In *Ethnic and Regional Foodways in the United States: The Performance of Group Identity*, edited by Linda Keller Brown and Kay Mussell, 185–94. Knoxville: University of Tennessee, 1984.

Ray, Krishnendu. *The Migrant's Table: Meals and Memories in Bengali-American Households*. Philadelphia: Temple University Press, 2004.

Shortridge, Barbara Gimla and James R. Shortridge, eds. *The Taste of American Place: A Reader on Regional and Ethnic Foods*. Lanham, MD: Rowman & Littlefield, 1998.

Sims, Martha C. and Martine Stephens. *Living Folklore: An Introduction to the Study of People and Their Traditions*. Logan: Utah State University Press, 2005.

Smith, Alison K. "National Cuisines." In *The Oxford Handbook of Food History*, edited by Jeffrey M. Pilcher, 444–60. Oxford: Oxford University Press, 2012.

Toelken, Barre. *The Dynamics of Folklore*. Boston: Houghton Mifflin, 1979.

Trubek, Amy B. *The Taste of Place: A Cultural Journey into Terroir*. Berkeley, CA: University of California, 2009.

Tuchman, Gaye and Harry Gene Levine. "New York Jews and Chinese Food: The Social Construction of an Ethnic Pattern." In *The Taste of American Place: A Reader on Regional and Ethnic Foods*, edited by Barbara G. Shortridge and James R. Shortridge. Lanham, MD: Rowman & Littlefield, 1998, 163–186.

Tuleja, Tad. "Making Ourselves Up: On the Manipulation of Tradition in Small Groups." In *Usable Pasts: Traditions and Group Expressions in North America*, edited by Tad Tuleja, 1–23. Logan, UT: Utah State University Press, 1997.

Tuleja, Tad. *Usable Pasts: Traditions and Group Expressions in North America*. Logan, UT: Utah State University Press, 1997.

Tye, Diane. *Baking as Biography: A Life Story in Recipes*. Montreal: McGill-Queen's University Press, 2010.

Vennum, Thomas. *Wild Rice and the Ojibway People*. St. Paul: Minnesota Historical Society, 1988.

Weaver, William Woys. *Sauerkraut Yankees: Pennsylvania Dutch Foods & Foodways*. Mechanicsburg, PA: Stackpole, 2002.

Williams-Forson, Psyche A. *Building Houses out of Chicken Legs: Black Women, Food, and Power*. Chapel Hill: University of North Carolina, 2006.

Yan, Nancy. "Un-defining Authenticity in Chinese Restaurants and Cuisine." In *Time for Food: Everyday Food and Changing Meal Habits in a Global Perspective*, edited by Patricia Lysaght, 88–94. Åbo Akademi University Press: Finland, 2012.

Yoder, Don. *Discovering American Folklife: Studies in Ethnic, Religious, and Regional Culture*. Ann Arbor, MI: UMI Research, 1990. (Includes articles: 1961a, 1961b, 1962, 1971).

Zeitlin, Steven J., Amy Kotkin, and Holly Cutting Baker. *A Celebration of American Family Folklore: Tales and Traditions from the Smithsonian Collection*. New York: Pantheon, 1982.

CHAPTER 3
"IT'S ALL FROM ONE BIG POT": BOOYA AS AN EXPRESSION OF COMMUNITY

Anne R. Kaplan

Libeled as "the goulash of the working class" and lauded as "the most nutritious life-sustaining stew around these parts,"[1] booya is both the name of a food and the boisterous community event at which it is consumed. Churches, clubs, volunteer fire companies, and neighborhood associations host annual booyas as fundraisers.[2] Making booya is always an undertaking of gargantuan proportions. A typical recipe for about 300 gallons, for example, calls for 300 pounds of beef bones, 150 pounds of chicken, 100 pounds of garlic, 3 pounds of pickling spice, 10 pounds of salt, 17 gallons canned tomatoes, 9 gallons each of canned peas, green beans, creamed corn, and whole-kernel corn, 100 pounds of oxtails, 300 pounds of potatoes, 100 pounds of celery, 75 pounds of carrots, 2 pounds of parsley, 3–4 pounds of allspice, 80 ounces of Worcestershire sauce, and 10 pounds of pepper. This does not include the secret seasonings, which are a major component of every booya recipe. "Exotic" tastes, however, are frowned upon, and no single flavor should dominate the finished product. Making booya that everyone will like is the goal.[3]

On the surface booya (the food and the event) bears some resemblance to a number of other traditional foodways. People familiar with Kentucky burgoo point out at least superficial similarities in the recipes and note that both booya and burgoo are made in large quantity, are usually consumed in public, and are the subject of familiar jokes about the disappearance of neighborhood pets, galoshes, bowling pins, and the like.[4] The setting, attendance patterns, and accompanying entertainments at most booyas are similar to those of midwestern fundraising food events such as corn feeds and church bazaars. Yet booya stands in a class by itself, distinguished not only by the food but also by certain traditions: the way the basic recipe is handed down, the secrecy of the vital seasonings, methods of preparation, and specialized gender and age roles. Not all booyas, of course, are the same; as with any living tradition, there is ample latitude for variation. Although the tradition is limited to particular neighborhoods of a few cities or small towns, mostly in Minnesota, specific booyas clearly bear the marks of their makers. In fact, making, selling, and eating booya can be a powerful expression of community on several levels. One could say that the pattern for a booya exists in the public domain as a generic tradition.[5] But as a group brews the food and hosts the event over years—often decades—the tradition is interpreted and elaborated; it is personalized. The group comes to view booya as its own tradition, a food and an event that helps focus and express those salient values and facets of identity, such as ethnicity, occupation, or neighborhood, that the group uses to define itself. In the end, booya (the food) becomes a badge of identity while the process of making it models or recreates community structure.

Two intrinsic aspects of the tradition help explain this symbolic process: the nature of fundraisers in general and the distribution of the booya tradition in particular. Both of these factors operate as givens; they are the backdrop before which every booya is enacted. Their interaction creates a complex sense of community that is both inclusive and exclusive.

Anne R. Kaplan, "'It's All from One Big Pot': Booya as an Expression of Community' in Theodore C. Humphrey and Lin T. Humphrey (eds), *Food and Fesitval in American Life*, (Logan: Utah State University Press, 1991), pp. 169–189. Reproduced with permission of Utah State University Press in the format 'Republish in a book' via Copyright Clearance Center.

Booya is unquestionably meant to be a social event, where the focus is on eating, drinking, playing games, and talking. Viewed from the top down, all who attend are participating in a community event and sharing the experience. But the underlying purpose is to raise money, and a fundraiser, by nature, creates insider-outsider distinctions among participants. Some people gather early and donate their time to prepare food for a specific cause; others come later to buy the food, thereby supporting the cause. Not only does booya comprise hosts and paying guests, then, but some customers will benefit from the sales, while others will get only a bowl of booya and perhaps a feeling of satisfaction in return. Yet the monetary success of the event depends on the smooth interaction of the sellers and buyers who are, on a social level, almost always friends and neighbors. Thus, the principle at work is one of inclusion-exclusion; "group-within-a-group" and insider-outsider distinctions are both created and integrated at a booya.

Likewise, the push-pull of inclusion-exclusion is at work in defining an ever more specific sense of community among people who participate in the entire booya tradition. All those who belong to the generic universe of booya feel a sense of camaraderie that comes from sharing specialized knowledge and experience. It is difficult for a total outsider to gain access to the tradition: one almost has to know about booya to learn more about it. Unlike more descriptive titles for fundraisers such as "corn feed," "bean feed," or "cake walk," the name itself tells one nothing.[6] Booyas are traditionally advertised by way of posters in neighborhood businesses and a banner at the park where the event is held. Poster text, however, is sparse, but this fact in itself is revealing. Often the cook's name appears along with the sponsoring organization's, the date, and park name—but no time or specific place. While this information might not get a stranger to the right place at the right time, it does imply a tight sense of community where one man's name—one cook's reputation—means enough to be advertised. Actually, the posters serve mostly as a memory jog. Most insiders learn of upcoming booyas because they belong to the sponsoring group, or by word of mouth from friends.

But within the unity of cognoscenti are many rival factions, for booya has been adapted and then further refined by regional, occupational, religious, ethnic, and neighborhood groups. Thus, while St. Paul booya makers as a community might compare themselves favorably to those from northern Minnesota, within St. Paul there is competition among firemen and church and neighborhood groups as to whose booya is best.

The nature of the food would seem to limit its consumption to members of an in-group who know and trust the cook. In her study of American food habits, Margaret Mead hypothesized that Americans' fear of strange foodways accounted for the tasteless foods found in most public eating places. She concluded that the safest preparation for a "mixed group" would be single foods cooked separately with a minimum of seasoning, served individually with condiments on the side.[7] Booya, on the other hand, is a hodgepodge of meats, vegetables, and seasonings cooked to an unrecognizable paste. In fact, its hallmark is this mysterious quality: "Good booya is just mush. You can—maybe [see] a few kernels of corn or a piece of bean. But no potatoes, no chunks of meat."[8] Traditional jokes about pets missing from the neighborhood on booya day and wild-animal tracks stopping right outside the cookshack door acknowledge and play on the anomalous quality of the food. These and more straightforward accounts of undesirable substances supposedly found in the booyas of rival groups—chicken bones, gizzards, or skin—point out that booya flirts with the line that divides order from chaos, purity from danger, edible from inedible. It is therefore not surprising that booya is a highly localized, community-based tradition controlled by well-known and respected members of a given group.

It is difficult to pinpoint the origins of booya. Ephemeral advertisements are rarely archived, and few organizations seem to maintain records of this sort of event. Evidence collected to date shows a cluster of booyas beginning in the 1930s. The North St. Paul Volunteer Firemen's booya, however, dates to 1922, and informants remember that in northern Minnesota the Vermillion Old Settlers Association hosted booyas at least as early as the Great Depression. In fact, booya figures prominently in the Depression-era memories of many informants, as well as in the writings from that era of populist-feminist author Meridel LeSueur and in the printings of her brother Mac. The Silver Fox Club, an all-male social group from West 7th Street, a blue-collar neighborhood in St. Paul, began its booya in 1936; the West 7th St. Pleasure Bowling League followed in 1938. That same year the Allied Czech Societies of St. Paul held a booya, but it is unclear whether this was a regular event.[9]

Most people trace booya to the French-Canadian fur traders who supposedly sustained themselves by stewing up vats of whatever wild game and vegetables were on hand. By dubious etymology they claim that the name "booya" is an Anglicized version of the French "bouillir" (to boil").[10] Such speculation aside, living memory dates booya to the late 19th century, when bars along West 7th St. began brewing booya to lure in customers. In fact, a minority of informants, pointing out the food's similarity to goulash, think "booya" is a corruption of an unknown Bohemian word.[11] After the turn of the century the food was appropriated by churches, clubs, and other organizations. Today booya is almost always used to raise funds, although occasionally a group of neighbors or a large family will host one, typically for a Fourth of July gathering or family reunion.[12]

The vast majority of booyas are held on summer Sunday afternoons in public parks; a few take place in VFW, church, or fire halls. In St. Paul, for example, the busiest facility is Highland Park, known as "the pavilion that booya built"; six gas-fired kettles are permanently installed in a cookshack and adjacent to a covered area complete with serving counters, concrete floor, and picnic tables. From May through August the pavilion is booked every Sunday for booyas. In North St. Paul the volunteer firemen built and donated to the city a booya building that holds 12 gas-fired vats.[13]

All booyas have the same basic structure, follow the same general rules for preparation, and depend on the same kinds of gender and age divisions of labor. Numerous levels of participation are available to potential booya makers. Men, and to some extent women and children, choose a role depending on their degree of commitment to the endeavor. People assigned to different tasks thus form the substrata of the group of insiders directly responsible for the food. As an event, booya has two distinct components: the preparation and the serving. For the insiders who make the booya, the preparation is the festive social occasion, much more so than the next day when the booya is sold and consumed.

The most apparent and widely shared facet of identity among booya makers is gender: booyas are held and managed by groups of men. The groups may exist for male-only recreation with some community service functions, for family-based recreation, to benefit various church functions, or purely for community service. When members of these male groups gather to make booya, various status rankings become apparent. "Old timers" are revered. They have their pick of the tasks or have the right to show up after the work is in progress simply to socialize. Middle-aged men are expected to carry the full weight of responsibility. The booya chef—the one man nominally in charge, who orders and inspects ingredients, who alone knows the secret recipe for spices, who supervises the process, and who tastes the concoction and pronounces it ready before it is served—this man usually comes from the ranks of the middle-aged. But he has apprenticed with the holder of the recipe, typically his father, father-in-law, or uncle, before the older man became too decrepit to pass it on. Thus he has close ties to the older generation and deep roots in the booya tradition. Young men are welcomed and they work hard at many of the same tasks as the older and middle-aged men, but they are clearly treated as beginners; their work is supervised. Teenaged boys are on the periphery. They may perform a few tasks such as sawing the bones for stock, but mostly they are onlookers. A boy who is 14 or 15 and has a father in the middle ranks may be allowed to spend the night at the pavilion with the booya crew. This rite of passage entitles him to join the ranks of the young men.

Single women do not help out with booya. When women are in attendance, they are the wives of the middle-aged male contingent and, occasionally, their pre-teen daughters. And their tasks as well as their socializing are clearly limited. To the women of St. Francis parish, for example, falls the task of peeling ten pounds of garlic. These women, gathered by the wife of the booya chef, meet at her house two nights before the booya is held. There they share food and wine or beer—and peel garlic. The next day they resume work at the booya pavilion where they peel potatoes while the men chop vegetables. Although they share in the beer and cigarettes, they do not mingle. The women work at a separate picnic table, several tables removed from the men's work.

This separation of the sexes is a prime example of the way in which making booya is a model of community structure. The preparation tasks are by no means assigned according to physical ability or dexterity; rather, the duties are culturally determined. Booya fits the American system wherein men are allowed to cook at outdoor, "roughing it" events—barbecues, picnics, pig roasts—whereas women cook in the home. More specifically, making booya is considered recreation and, among families interviewed for this study, men and women generally socialize in same-sex groups. It comes as no surprise, then, that for an event sponsored by all-male groups, the duties and responsibilities of women are both segregated and circumscribed.

Making booya is a time-consuming task. Starting at about 9:00 a.m. on Saturday, the day before the event, the vegetables must be cleaned and cut. All are chopped separately and stored, on ice, in metal trash cans lined with plastic garbage bags. Around six o'clock at night water is heated in the 30-gallon kettles. All of the meats are added and cooked at this point. At about midnight, with two men to a kettle, the meat is removed, boned, and returned to the pot. From here on, periodic checks are made for bones. The secret spices, in bags, are added in the night. Around dawn the vegetables and other flavorings go in. From this point on, the booya must be stirred constantly to prevent the potatoes from sticking to the bottom and burning. Around 10:00 a.m. on Sunday the chef begins tasting the booya and adjusting seasonings. Most booyas open to the public at noon, about 24 hours after the men's work began. And most like to claim that they are sold out by 2:00 p.m.

Different organizations handle the nighttime vigil differently. At some, work is done in four-hour shifts by different crews of men. At others, one crew cooks through the night and is relieved at dawn. At very few booyas are women present through the night;[14] night is the time for women to be home supervising the domestic scene. Among those at all familiar with booya, the social side of the nighttime work is well known. In this typically all-male event, beer and stories flow freely, often starting early in the afternoon and continuing at least until dawn. In the words of one fireman, "This is the one occasion that brings us all together. We used to bowl, drink a few beers, play cards. Now people don't have time, or the wives don't like it, or whatever. For this [booya] the retired come back. It's our biggest social function."[15]

The booya itself is an entirely different social occasion that emphasizes integration, not separation, of the sexes and ages. Unlike preparing booya, the public part of the event *is* family-oriented, and it is not unusual to see three generations lounging around a picnic table, or families pitching horseshoes, or teenagers gathered around a large radio.

Most people who attend a booya are part of the social network of the hosts. Thus, any given booya is overwhelmingly a neighborhood event, a parish event, or an organizational event. But as such social networks have long tentacles—friends who have moved away maintain neighborhood ties, families bring relatives and friends from the outside, and so forth—it is also a time for broadening and reintegrating community ties.

At the booya, attenders, of course, eat booya. They also have the opportunity to buy beer or soda, candy bars, hot dogs, potato chips; to play carnival-type games like show-down poker; to participate in a raffle; and, occasionally, to dance to a one- or two-piece band. While many people buy gallons of booya to take home and freeze for later consumption, insiders consider it boorish simply to purchase carry-out food. Booyas are meant for socializing, for mingling and lingering over beers, for spending money on hot dogs and games of chance after the booya is gone.

At the public event, thus, the inclusive side of booya is reasserted for reasons both economic and social. Booya sells for $1 per bowl, and most people estimate that it costs volunteers 80¢ a bowl to make it.

Organizations make most of their profit from beer, candy, and soda sales in addition to the income from games of chance. Therefore, it is better for the host group if people make a day of the event, talking, eating, drinking, and playing games for the entire afternoon.

In addition, booyas are a place and time for entire families to relax and visit with one another. People complain that their pace of life and leisure-time activities make it difficult to assemble the whole family around the dinner table, much less have time to see friends and neighbors with *their* extended families.[16] Booya is a time set aside for such socializing, for putting into practice the value of family and community that informants say they strongly believe but can rarely achieve. People demonstrate their commitment to community by choosing to devote a Sunday afternoon to booya rather than to fishing or watching television, gardening or painting the house. Merely purchasing a few quarts of food at the carry-out line would demonstrate a degree of financial support, but would also imply that other affairs are more important than community. In the words of one man who grew up in the West 7th neighborhood, "Booya is not just a bowlful of stew; it's a celebration that brings together the people. . . . You can't just eat booya. You go to a booya."[17]

While booya is all about community, however, it belongs to no one group in particular. Most observers of the tradition, including many who make booya, believe it expresses ethnicity. However, not only is it impossible to prove its French-Canadian origins, but also in St. Paul the "Bohunks on West 7th," "the Krauts on Rice St.,"[18] and the Czechs in South St. Paul all proudly claim booya as their own. And even this ethnic characterization is a gross overstatement, as the so-called West 7th Bohunks, for example, include Irish, Germans, and French Canadians within their ranks. The Finns and Slavs in northern Minnesota also participate in the rivalry over whose booya is best. And, furthermore, the suburban volunteer fire companies have members from a variety of backgrounds. Ethnicity is not even a salient factor in their group identity.

Nor can booya be tied to any single locale. Enthusiasts stoutly argue that theirs is a purely Minnesotan food. In fact, a South St. Paul florist, formerly a rodeo director, has undertaken a one-man crusade to add booya to the roster of state symbols. In 1985, for the third consecutive year, he organized an Annual World Booya Championship Contest, hoping, actually, to spread the gospel of booya statewide![19] In the process of promoting these events, it came to light that the Belgians and French Canadians of Green Bay, Wisconsin, also make something they call "booyah." There followed a nasty exchange of brags and name-calling in the hometown newspapers, in which loyalists sought to impugn the authenticity and quality of their rival's products, that ended abruptly when Wisconsin backed out of bringing its booya to the contest.[20] The fact that booyas also exist in Canada also confounds Minnesota's claim to the foodway, although the tradition is clearly confined to a fairly limited region of North America.

But even in Minnesota booya exists only in isolated pockets, in particular neighborhoods of particular cities in particular regions of the state. At first glance it appears to be an urban tradition, and even so, as far as research can show, booyas are only held in the metropolitan Minneapolis-St. Paul area and several hundred miles north, in the small towns in Minnesota's iron-mining district. In fact, class, more than anything else, seems to be the common denominator of booya, which flourishes in blue-collar neighborhoods and working-class Catholic parishes. Iron Range towns in northern Minnesota exhibit many urban characteristics precisely because they were established to house the workers of heavy industry; they are unlike Minnesota's rural small towns where booya is an unknown phenomenon.[21] Yet it is important to note that class is not stated as a salient factor for participants in the tradition. Rather, as mentioned above, communities that host booyas define themselves in terms of ethnicity, neighborhood, interest group, and so forth.

In any case, the shared traits of being workers in Minnesota do not work to forge much sense of community among members of these two regional groups. Instead, booya becomes a focus for rivalries between these two, re-expressing longstanding regional prides and hostilities wherein Twin Citians refer to the rest of the state as "out-state" with all the implications of being backward, unsophisticated, and quaint, while Iron Rangers hold

Twin Citians in contempt for their supposedly soft and favored existence, skimming the cream off of state programs. For example, when a native St. Paul newspaperman ventured to say in print that "Folks on the Iron Range occasionally sup of something called 'booyeh' that may be similar"[22] [to St. Paul's], an angry Iron Range resident replied:

The St. Paul variety is surely a far cry from the original. The voyageurs couldn't lay hands on those exotic ingredients such as pickling spices, parsley, garlic, etc. I don't know where they got that recipe, but unlike their recipe, which many dislike, I don't know anyone who has tasted the Iron Range Booyah who doesn't say it is utterly delicious. And the cost of our booyah is a great deal less than St. Paul's.[23]

Within the Twin Cities, St. Paul, which has the reputation of being the more ethnic, neighborhood-oriented of the two, hosts numerous booyas. Across the river in Minneapolis, the city that bills itself as "the Minneapple" and projects a cosmopolitan, cultured image, residents are largely ignorant of booya.[24] Yet even in St. Paul booyas exist only in isolated pockets, mostly in solid working-class neighborhoods of varying ethnicities. Catholicism is the predominant religion in these areas, but it is not correct to say that booya is a Catholic epiphenomenon, because booyas held outside of these neighborhoods show no such affiliation. Although the working-class link does not figure in community self-definition, it is important from an analytical standpoint, especially when considering that residents of the middle-class Macalester neighborhood, less than two miles from West 7th, hardly know of booya. And residents of the equally middle-class Highland area, which coincidentally houses the park pavilion where most of St. Paul's booyas occur, rarely if ever attend these events that are in, but definitely not of, their neighborhood and community.

The foregoing discussion briefly outlines the basic contours of the booya tradition. Examples of the annual booyas held by the parish of St. Francis de Sales and by the North St. Paul Volunteer Fire Department clearly demonstrate how specific communities use and adapt the generic tradition, making it a powerful medium for enacting and expressing a sense of community. The settings for these two booyas differ; the church is located in the heart of the booya belt in the West 7th St. neighborhood, while the fire company is in a late nineteenth-century town that has become a suburb of St. Paul. Likewise, the nature of the groups or premises for joining them are very different. The church has built a family-based community grounded in shared spiritual beliefs and strengthened through the continuity of generations of the same families from the same neighborhood regularly interacting at sacred and secular functions. The fire company, on the other hand, is composed only of men who volunteer a portion of their time for a specialized kind of community service. Membership is based on individual commitment to an ideal. The community they serve is a political entity, much broader than the social or cultural groups to which individual firemen belong. These men may not know the people they will help, nor, in that case, do they expect to establish relationships with their "clients."

St. Francis de Sales

The West 7th St. neighborhood in which the church is located is best characterized as a solid, stable, blue-collar enclave. "You have your upward mobility, but not here. Here people stay. Generations . . . families live in the same house or block. People might move away, but they come back."[25]

Cross-cut by railroad tracks and a freeway, bounded by downtown St. Paul to the east, the Mississippi River more or less to the south, the site of the Schmidt brewery, oil-storage tanks, a power plant, and numerous auto repair garages, second-hand stores, and small businesses, the neighborhood is one of St. Paul's oldest. Many men grew up there to work on street construction crews, for the railroad, meat-packing houses, or in trade unions as machinists, welders, assemblers, electricians, and the like. As in many traditional communities, women did not work outside of the home until fairly recently. In addition to churches of several Protestant denominations, the neighborhood houses three Catholic churches: St. Francis, originally the German parish; St. James, originally Irish; and St. Stanislaus, originally Bohemian (mostly Czech). Today church membership is mixed; people have been known to transfer allegiances among the three, but generally they stay with the family parish, a choice originally based on ethnicity and proximity to the church building. All three of the churches have held booyas; of them, St. Francis's is the most visible.[26]

The men and women of St. Francis make about 300 gallons of booya for their church picnic; theirs is the recipe quoted earlier in this article. Parish members can not date when the church began holding booyas; they speculate that the tradition goes back about 60 years. Since the late 1940s or early 1950s when Highland Park Pavilion was built, they have always used that facility.

The preparation process follows the age and gender rules listed above: the women gather in a home to peel garlic on Friday night and execute different tasks from the men's on Saturday at the Highland Pavilion. Youth has a special role at this booya; the son of one participant saws beef bones with a hacksaw under the supervision of an "old-timer." His is perhaps the most physically demanding job. Joe McDonough, the chef, oversees the work and takes "a lot of guff," both serious complaints from choppers about the quality of the vegetables, and light-hearted (the usual: "Hey Joe, someone's wondering where his cat is"). McDonough inherited the recipe from his father, who got it from Jim Kane, a janitor at St. James Church. While the amounts and kinds of vegetables and meats are a matter of public record, no one, not even his wife, knows the ingredients that flavor the mix. St. Francis booya makers credit him, aided of course by the recipe, for their superior booya. McDonough cooks the chicken in separate pots, "lets it settle, degreases the broth, and then just puts in stock. That way you're not picking out skin and bone."[27] This and the preparation of beef stock from bones is all accomplished before 6:00 p.m. mass. Thereafter, crews of men begin taking four-hour shifts, cooking the meats together, and adding the vegetables in proper sequence. Around 3:30 a.m. McDonough returns with the secret spices all mixed in a cloth bag.

The nighttime vigil is a social occasion that the men enjoy despite its grueling aspects. Crowding into a small outbuilding with six large, hot kettles of booya, constantly stirring massive amounts of thick, heavy food on a humid August night has strenuous moments. The old-timers tend to step back and let the middle-aged or younger men handle the toughest physical labor. But the work draws them together, and the vast amount of not-yet-finished booya, the reason for their gathering, is put to good use. The men float cobs of corn or polish sausage in the vats, and these snacks absorb some of the flavor and aroma of the brew. Thus, on this special occasion, the men share not only the beer, jokes, and stories that might be part of their everyday social interactions, but also ordinary food made special for, and because of, their participation in making booya.

The nature of the longstanding and intertwined family-neighborhood ties and traditional age and gender roles that characterize the church community make joining the inner circle of booya makers a slow and difficult, almost organic, process. The church, of course, welcomes new members. And the booya makers nominally encourage participation: many hands make light work. But newcomers get no closer than the Saturday-afternoon vegetable chopping for many years. In 1985, for example, one man, aged about 30, attended the afternoon session, but when the vegetables were all chopped and the workers pushed back from the tables, lit up cigarettes, and poured themselves more beer, he got up to leave. After his departure the old-timers and women spent considerable time trying to remember his name, place his face, and relate him to a known family.

At the booya on Sunday the principle of inclusion, or the larger community spirit, ascends. Booya makers mingle with the crowd. The men who stand behind the sale counters or circulate throughout the park retrieving trays and discarding empty bowls and plasticware wear no identifying clothing or buttons. The occasion is a parish picnic, attended also by close friends and neighbors of churchgoers. Outside of the church, word of the upcoming booya travels informally. Posters are not widely distributed or conspicuously displayed. As with most booyas, "People *know* when the booya is on. Word gets out—'The men are working at the booya. It's gonna be this weekend.'"[28]

In fact, the event highlights a larger-than-parish sense of community, owing to the fact that West 7th recognizes and presents itself as a solid booya enclave. Yet within it, the booya tradition is decentralized. Various groups hold booyas to raise funds for sundry, specialized purposes: church and ethnic fraternal organizations, recreational equipment, club operating funds, and so on. Many of the men of St. Francis belong to other social and recreational groups in the neighborhood. Thus, while rivalry exists about whose booya is best, membership in different organizations does not suggest a conflict. Members of the Silver Fox Club or West 7th St. Pleasure Bowling League, for example, come to the St. Francis booya because they like the food and because they or their friends also belong to the church.

These same people who may go to three different booyas in the span of eight weeks, however, do not attend those held outside of the neighborhood. People are well aware of other booya traditions; they volunteer information that Rice St. booya is greasy or the booya in North St. Paul is made in such quantity that it is thin (it is not), but this talk has the quality of legend. No one will admit to attending these other events; they simply have heard all the facts about the inferiority of the product outside the borders of their neighborhood community.

Thus, the annual St. Francis parish booya is a clear expression of both personal and group identity, of community on several levels that, like an inverted pyramid, grow ever broader or more inclusive. The unstated rules and roles for making booya model traditional family structure and values. The actual process of making booya enacts and reinforces these divisions, but it also draws participants together, forging a sense of group identity based on shared traditions and activity, family, neighborhood, and church membership. And attending the booya is, most of all, a powerful expression of community built on family, religion, friendship, and neighborhood allegiance: "You can't make a little of it. You can't make it yourself. It's all from one big pot. Everyone shares."[29]

North St. Paul

In North St. Paul the picture is somewhat different. Although the area today has become a suburb of St. Paul, it was founded in the late 1880s as a separate entity. "The town rose virtually overnight . . . to a bustling town containing more than a dozen factories."[30] Several decades later twenty-seven factories graced the area, ranging from several iron works and a brick company to furniture, piano, and casket manufacturers. A fire in 1933 destroyed much of the town.[31] The suburban appearance and aspects of North St. Paul are more prominent today than in 1922 when the volunteer fire company began holding booyas.

Change and mobility are themes that run through conversations with the volunteer firemen, whether they are discussing the community or their booya. Currently, people who live in the town may not work there. Likewise, people who now live there did not necessarily grow up in that area. Members of the fire department include men originally from Minneapolis, northern Minnesota, and even Chicago. These men—tradesmen and professionals—come from a variety of ethnic and religious cultures.

Volunteer firemen, of necessity, are derived from the immediate community, and their desire to join is motivated by several ideals: "It's the social function . . . and the chance to help with no commitment, no responsibility. If I get a fire call or an ambulance call, I go out, do my thing, and walk away from it. That's all. I don't need thanks. I've got the satisfaction, and that's it. It's over."[32] The larger community that the group serves is, in some ways, abstract. There need be no personal ties. Yet the group itself, formed for community service, does fulfill social needs for its members, some of whom join specifically as a means of establishing a sense of community in a new place.

This booya, like St. Francis's, follows the general pattern of age and gender role separation. The booya, however, is twice as big, filling thirteen kettles and totaling about 700 gallons. The nighttime stirring is handled by one crew—the same men who clean the permanently installed kettles. As in the West 7th neighborhood, nighttime is the prime social time: "A lot of the old-timers come back, sit around, drink a beer, and bull. It's real nice."[33] In North St. Paul, however, the old-timers and even middle-aged men ruminate frequently on changes in their tradition, rather than continuity. Before the department built and donated to the city its current pavilion in a park in 1981, the booya had been held in at least three different parks. The men cooked over wood fires in canvas tents, and, although all involved are pleased at the relative ease of using stationary kettles and gas flames, several people maintain that the booya flavor suffers without the wood smoke.

Over the years, booya ingredients have become more divorced from the community. Firewood used to be donated; vegetables at one time were all locally grown garden produce, except for the potatoes which were grown by the treasurer's relative about forty miles north of town. Currently the treasurer purchases all ingredients from a produce wholesaler and a meat market.

Perhaps the most discussed change, however, is the nature of female participation in the event. On Saturday afternoon, in the North St. Paul firehouse, a handful of women and young girls sit in a circle spatially segregated from the men's work just as at the St. Francis booya. Their sole task is to string and snap green beans. In 1985, there were too few women to complete the task in time; a young boy began cutting beans, but did so on the tables where the men were working. Asked about this discontinuity, one fireman replied: "Yeah. Used to be about a dozen women would be sitting around cutting beans, talking about whatever women talk about. And the men were real chauvinistic. Wouldn't cut 'em [the beans]. 'That's women's work!' Well, now the women would just say 'Sh—[doesn't complete the word].' You can read lips, can't you? . . ."[34]

Other commentary reveals the firemen's booya to be a microcosm of social change. "Used to be the backbone, the Ladies' Auxiliary. Now things are different."[35] According to department members, the wives of the younger firemen who have replaced the retired older generation of volunteers either work outside the home or have other commitments that preclude participation in the booya. In addition to preparing beans, women used to make pies and cakes; their auxiliary ran a bake sale at the booya. "Now we hardly have any, and it looks bad . . . I think it's better to have nothing than just a little."[36] The cookies and bars which women currently donate are easier to prepare than pies and cakes and possibly bespeak less time for commitment.

The social changes affecting the lives of the firemen as well as the nature and composition of the department makes the annual booya an especially significant event for members. As in other organizations that host booyas, the recipe is a secret part of the tradition that binds this group. In North St. Paul the lineage of recipe holders encompasses two families: William Weber, who started the booya, retired in the late 1950s or early 1960s and passed the secret spice combination on to his son-in-law. That man died young, and the recipe went to Weber's son, who is currently on the verge of retirement. "Who he's passing it on to, we don't know."[37] It is interesting to note that the department members cherish and respect the secrecy of the spice ingredients. The formula, for safekeeping, is locked in a bank safe-deposit box. "We could go look, but we choose not to. It's kind of a little tradition. Everyone needs traditions, you know."[38]

Advertising for the North St. Paul booya is a broader-spectrum affair than in the West 7th St. neighborhood. Rather than relying on posters in the windows of community businesses, in recent years the event has been announced over local radio, and, in 1985, on cable television. People are said to come from many of St. Paul's northern suburbs, but never from the city's well-known booya neighborhoods. The fact that all 700 gallons are usually sold within three hours attests to the success of the advertising.

At the booya, the firemen are clearly identified by their uniforms, including name tags. This garb is probably necessary to mark them as hosts, since people who attend the booya are not necessarily friends and neighbors who will recognize those in charge. In fact, in contrast to the St. Francis booya, this one, although it is a longstanding North St. Paul tradition, no longer serves as a community social event. "We try to make it a family day. People used to sit around and socialize more. People of today—I guess we're just in too fast a world—they just buy it and go. A few do stay, but not like they used to."[39]

Department members cite various reasons for this state of affairs. Some say that the booya sells out so fast that there is nothing to stay for. Others claim that since there are few or no games (these are a costly risk to rent if little participation is expected) and not much of a bake sale, there is nothing to tempt people to stay.[40] Still others claim that people prefer to buy vast quantities of booya and freeze it for use in cooler weather.[41] Whatever the reasons may be, the booya sells rapidly, but the attractive picnic grounds facing the lake are sparsely populated.

The nature and mission of the sponsoring group perhaps explains why this booya succeeds better as a fundraiser than as a social event. The community that the firemen serve is the entire city of North St. Paul, an abstract political entity rather than a personalized group of friends. The funds they raise go to the firemen's relief association general fund, to fire prevention posters, prizes for the city's Junior Fire Marshal program, to support civic doings like the Lions Club fishing contest and the local American Legion, to host regional firemen's meetings, to supply the fire station with beer and soda, to make donations to the city's athletic association, send flowers to funerals of past members, condolence and get-well cards, presents, and the like. The department spent $22,000 alone on the booya shelter which residents of the city may use throughout the year as a park building. "Everything has basically gone back into the city one way or another."[42]

The booya makers themselves, on the other hand, derive and reinforce a sense of community through their participation in the tradition. Membership in the department is a way for men to foster and share a sense of community in what they perceive as a highly mobile society where traditional values are in flux. Participating in the company booya intensifies their commitment to the group and their ties to its past. The North St. Paul Volunteer Firemen's booya is a totally different kind of social occasion set in a very different community context than the St. Francis parish event. Each group has shaped the generic booya tradition into a clear expression of its contemporary sense of self.

Notes

1. *Minneapolis Tribune,* September 6, 1981, p. 1B; *Minneapolis Star and Tribune,* December 8, 1984, p. 1B.

2. For a discussion of the social role of such organizations in promoting the consumption of foods not on grocery shelves, see Simon Bronner, *Grasping Things* (Lexington: University of Kentucky Press, 1986), Chapter 4 *passim.*

3. What constitutes "exotic," of course, is a matter of opinion. To members of other booya traditions, both the garlic and pickling spices mentioned above are offensive and too esoteric, respectively; Betty Wiljamaa to Editor, *Minneapolis Tribune,* September 27, 1984, p. 12A; interview of Howard Anderson, North St. Paul, August 8, 1985; interview of Ron Ritchie, North St. Paul, September 8, 1985.

4. Interviews of Arnie Leitner, Joe McDonough, and Joe Reichert (St. Francis de Sales Church), St. Paul, August 10, 1985; Frank Lewis, North St. Paul, September 8, 1985; *St. Paul Dispatch,* September 25, 1984, p. B1; Cathy Barton, "'It's Nothing But a Big Bowl of Soup!': Kentucky Burgoo and the Burgoo Supper," *Kentucky Folklore Record* 24 (July–December, 1978): 110.

5. In fact, new communities begin to hold booyas from time to time. The Apple Valley Volunteer fire company's event is only in its ninth year, and the tiny town of Finland, located about six miles west of Lake Superior in northern

Minnesota, attempted its first "Harvest Booya and Finn Fest" in 1985. Booya came to Finland through a former resident of St. Paul, who decided the food would be a welcome addition to the annual harvest party. The recipe was obtained from a man in South St. Paul who has been cooking booya for forty years.

6. Insiders tell jokes about how outsiders are puzzled by or sadly misconstrue the meaning of the name, thinking, for example, that the posters advertise a new dance craze, a terrorist group, or point to a taxidermist's: Body A (a misreading of a hand-lettered sign); *Minneapolis Star and Tribune*, December 8, 1984, p. 1B; *St. Paul Pioneer Press*, February 22, 1973, p. 19.

7. Margaret Mead, "The Problem of Changing Food Habits," in Committee on Food Habits, *The Problem of Changing Food Habits* (Washington, D.C.: National Research Council Bulletin No. 108, Oct., 1943).

8. Here to end of paragraph interview of Arnie Leitner, St. Paul, August 10, 1985; interview of Patrick Coleman, St. Paul, July 3, 1985; Mary Douglas, *Purity and Danger: An Analysis of the Concepts of Pollution and Taboo* (London: Routledge and Kegan Paul, 1966); Roger Abrahams, "Equal Opportunity Eating: A Structural Excursus on Things of the Mouth," in *Ethnic and Regional Foodways in the United States: The Performances of Group Identity*, Linda Keller Brown and Kay Mussell, eds. (Knoxville: University of Tennessee Press, 1984): 19–36.

9. Meridel Le Sueur, *The Girl*, reprint ed. (Minneapolis: West End Press and MEP Publications, 1982); Mac Le Sueur, "Untitled," painting ca. 1934–41; Allied Czech Societies of St. Paul, poster, Joseph Pavlicek Papers, Immigration History Research Center, St. Paul; West 7th St. Pleasure Bowling League, poster, collections of the Minnesota Historical Society, St. Paul; *The Community Reporter* (St. Paul), July, 1984, p. 3.

10. In fact, booyas are held in Canada's Ottawa Valley. The food and form of the event are different, but the communal base is consistent. Neighbors donate chickens to be raffled, and at the end of the raffle all fowl is stewed in a common pot and shared. I am indebted to I. Sheldon Posen for this information.

11. This theory appears to be the weaker of the two. Mrs. B. A. Ebert of LeCenter, Minnesota contributed a family recipe to a cookbook with the information that "a top favorite would be the Booya, or *'Vomachka'* as we Bohemians call it [my emphasis] made from the gizzards and hearts of ducks"; Virginia Huck and Ann H. Andersen, *100 Years of Good Cooking* (St. Paul: Minnesota Historical Society, 1958): 92.

12. Interview of Gene Gagner, St. Paul, July 28, 1985; Patrick Coleman, St. Paul, July 3, 1985.

13. Interview of Howard Anderson, North St. Paul, August 8, 1985; St. Paul Bark System Record Books for 1985; *Minneapolis Tribune*, September 6, 1981, p. 1B

14. Women do participate in the night vigil at the West 7th St. Pleasure Bowling League's and the Sokol Minnesota's (a Czech organization) booyas. Both of these groups stress that they are family oriented, clearly cognizant of their anomalous status within the tradition. Interviews of Gene Gagner and Brenda S., St. Paul, July 28, 1985; John Carl Hancock, Minneapolis, January 15, 1986.

15. Interview of Frank Lewis, North St. Paul, September 7, 1985.

16. See, for example, interviews of Gene Gagner, July 28, 1985; Nicholas J. Coleman, September 26, 1985; Dominic Cincotta, September 8, 1985.

17. Nicholas J. Coleman, in *Minneapolis Tribune*, September 6, 1981, p. 1B.

18. Interview of Robert Hess, St. Paul, August 2, 1985.

19. Minneapolis Star and Tribune, August 26, 1984, p. 4B.

20. *St. Paul Pioneer Press*, September 25, 1984, p. B1.

21. In this vein, however, it is curious that booya is also unknown in the city of Duluth, which perfectly fits the profile of a locale for the event. It will be interesting to discover whether the Finland booya takes root.

22. *Minneapolis Tribune*, September 6, 1981, p. 5B.

23. Betty Wiljamaa to Editor, *Minneapolis Tribune*, September 27, 1981, p. 12A.

24. Like most popular generalizations on booya, this one is not entirely correct. In the Minneapolis suburb of St. Anthony Village, the parish of St. Charles Boromel held booyas in the 1940s, and in nearby suburban New Brighton, St. John the Baptist Church has a vigorous booya tradition. Both parishes are composed of an ethnically mixed population which migrated out of the city's northeast, largely working-class, neighborhoods. I am indebted to Mark Haidet of the Minnesota Historical Society for this information.

25. Interview of Gene Gagner, St. Paul, July 28, 1985.

26. Connie X., for example, recently joined St. Stanislaus but continues to help cook for the St. Francis booya, as she has for twenty-five years; interview, August 10, 1985. St. Francis actually hosts two booyas per season, one as its parish picnic and the other, held by the Casinos, a men's club in the church, to benefit the church's athletic fund. This paper focuses on the parish event, which is more broadly representative of the community.

27. Connie X., August 10, 1985. She is contrasting St. Francis booya with others that do not use a stock but put all meats directly into the booya pot.

28. Interview of Nicholas J. Coleman, September 26, 1985.

29. Ibid.

30. North St. Paul Coordinating Committee, *Bicentennial Celebration, Souvenir Edition* (North St. Paul: The Committee, 1976): 2.

31. Linda Olson, An Abbreviated History of the Community of North St. Paul, n.p., n.d.

32. Interview of Frank Lewis, September 7, 1985.

33. Interview of Ron Ritchie, September 7, 1985.

34. Interview of Ray Z., September 7, 1985.

35. Interview of Frank Lewis, September 7, 1985.

36. Interview of Dominic Cincotta, September 7, 1985.

37. Interview of Frank Lewis, September 7, 1985

38. Here and the quote below, interview of Howard Anderson, fire chief, August 8, 1985.

39. Interview of Ron Ritchie, September 8, 1985. Ritchie has ties to West 7th through marriage and claims that although he has been to city booyas, none of the West 7th folk will ever come to his.

40. Interview of Howard Anderson, August 8, 1985.

41. Interview of Dominic Cincotta, September 8, 1985.

42. In fact, booya is so popular among deer hunters that the firemen hold a smaller booya in October strictly so hunters can stock up. At this latter event booya is sold only to carry out. Interview of Howard Anderson, August 8, 1985.

CHAPTER 4
CONTINUITY AND ADAPTATION IN ARAB AMERICAN FOODWAYS

William G. Lockwood and Yvonne R. Lockwood

THE PROCESS BY which immigrants become ethnic is long, gradual, and very complex. One can think of this process as ethnogenesis, or the creation of a new social group. Along with the development of a new ethnic group is a parallel development of a new subculture that both symbolizes the group's uniqueness to its members and marks off its social boundaries. The new subculture is created in the American context, altered to a greater or lesser degree from what was known in the homeland. Lebanese Americans are not the same as Lebanese in Lebanon, and Lebanese American culture is different from the culture(s) found in Lebanon. Neither do Lebanese Americans belong to a culture somewhere between American and Lebanese cultures, as might be surmised from the overly simple models of acculturation that have so far dominated thinking on the subject. Ethnicity exists only in specific contexts where one sort of people (Us) is brought into regular and intimate contact with people of other sorts (Them) (Barth 1969). In what follows, we are concerned with the cultural expressions that grow out of such contact, especially with regard to Arab American food and foodways and how these came to be the way they are.

The process by which immigrants become ethnic begins as soon as they board the boats and planes that carry them to the New World. Selective processes are already at work. No group of emigrants from any country represents a cross section of that country's population. They are always drawn from some regions more than others, some social strata more than others, and some communities more than others. Since each of these groups possesses a recognizable subculture (including distinctive foods and foodways), it is logical that immigrant communities cannot replicate exactly their old national culture in the New World.

Out of immigrant culture develops an ethnic culture that differs from it in significant ways. There are several primary sources on which this developing subculture draws. The first is the culture of the homeland. One aspect of the process is an amalgamation of the local, regional, and class-related subcultures that are represented in the immigrant community. A second source in the creation of an ethnic culture is the culture of mainstream America, such as it is experienced by immigrants and ethnics. The third source—too often overlooked—are the cultures of other immigrant and ethnic groups encountered in America. Most often, immigrants settle in neighborhoods and work in occupations associated with earlier immigrant groups. Yemeni immigrants in Detroit, for example, moved into houses vacated by Poles, Romanians, and Lebanese who were ready to move uptown or to the suburbs. An immigrant worker's foreman at the auto plant is likely to have been hired from a previous wave of immigrants. The creation of ethnic culture from these various sources takes place within the particular constraints of minority life: the homesickness, the prejudice, the sense of being different, the urge to assimilate or to resist assimilation, the need to recreate the Old World in the New or reject all possible reminders of the life that was. All shape the specific form taken by the new

William G. Lockwood and Yvonne R. Lockwood, 'Continuity and Adaptation in Arab American Foodways' in Nabeel Abraham and Andrew Shyrock (eds), *Arab Detroit: From Margin to Mainstream*, (Detroit: Wayne State University Press, 2000) pp. 515–549. Copyright © 2000 Wayne State University Press, with the permission of Wayne State University Press.

culture. Many anthropologists and folklorists refer to this cultural process as "creolization" (Abrahams 1980, 376–77) after the term for a similar linguistic process.

One can observe creolization in any aspect of ethnic culture, but it is particularly significant in food and foodways.[1] There are numerous reasons for this. First, cooking and eating are expressive behavior, relatively easy to observe, and heavily laden with symbolic meaning. Because cuisine is especially responsive to new environments, where some ingredients are unavailable, and because new social settings bring new ways of eating and cooking, foodways are especially quick to adapt and change. At the same time, however, perhaps no aspect of culture is so resistant to change, so tenaciously held. Generations after the loss of their mother tongue, ethnic Americans are still likely to be cooking and eating some version of the family's "mother cuisine."

In this essay we argue that in the creolization of Arab food and foodways (and quite possibly other aspects of culture) there are clear distinctions between the public, or commercial, and the private, or familial, spheres of behavior. For non-Arabs, it is invariably the public sphere that shapes the conceptualization of Arab American cuisine.

Food and foodways in the public sector

The first Arab restaurant in Michigan was located in downtown Detroit in what was then the Maronite community (Ahdab-Yehia 1983). Sometime after the First World War, Fadel Ganem, a Maronite immigrant from Lebanon (then part of Greater Syria), opened a small restaurant to serve his countrymen. At that time, the Maronite community still included a large number of single men, and Ganem's restaurant, like restaurants serving the earliest waves of other immigrant groups, provided familiar, inexpensive food. The restaurant had no name, only a small sign in the window that announced, in Arabic, "Arab Food." Nevertheless, non-Arabs would occasionally wander in for a meal. Ganem was forced to close during the Great Depression and remained closed through most of World War II. Then, in 1944, he reopened across the street from his original restaurant. This time he put up an English sign, "The Sheik: Syrian Food." At first he worked alone; customers would go to the kitchen to serve themselves. Later, as his restaurant became more popular, he hired a waiter and then a woman to help out in the kitchen. His children would come in after school to wash dishes. In 1956, Ganem received an "Outstanding Immigrant of the Year" award by Michigan's governor, G. Mennen Williams for, according to one version of family legend, "having introduced Arab food to the public in Detroit." When Ganem died, The Sheik was taken over by his oldest daughter's husband, who had started working at the restaurant as a waiter. When he died, his widow and one of her sisters ran the restaurant for many years. The restaurant closed in 1987. For many older Detroiters, The Sheik was the place where their conception of Arab food was created.

According to our best sources, the first Middle Eastern import grocery was established in 1954 by another Lebanese Maronite, Gabriel Wadia. The site, across the street from the Eastern Market, had been previously occupied by an American-style grocery owned by a Lebanese Muslim. Wadia established the first Middle Eastern import market in Michigan, renaming his store Gabriel's. Gabriel's has changed hands several times since, but it still carries on a Middle East import business in the same location under the same name. Today, it is owned by a Greek from Lebanon, and his customers are mostly Yugoslavs, Albanians, and other non-Arabs, but many older Arab Americans remember when Gabriel's was the only source for many of their culinary necessities.

In Detroit, the earliest shops served the Christian (especially Maronite) community from Greater Syria, who constituted the majority of early Middle Eastern immigrants. These businesses were located in downtown Detroit, where the first Syrian/Lebanese neighborhood emerged. By 1900 they had formed a small community around Congress Street just east of downtown Detroit. Many of these immigrants worked as peddlers. Others were day laborers in Eastern Market wholesale businesses. Once they secured their economic footing, many used their savings to open small retail businesses. It was decades, however, before stores serving the specific needs of the community were established. By the time The Sheik closed in 1987, there was little left of the original Maronite neighborhood. As early as 1920–25, Maronites and other Syrian/Lebanese Christians were moving to the eastern fringe of Detroit and to Grosse Pointe, St. Clair Shores, and Roseville. Today, they are a highly assimilated, middle-and upper-class community, dispersed among German Americans, Italian Americans, and others. Many attend the nearest Catholic Church rather than a Maronite Rite congregation.

There is no Arab American commercial district within this community, though there are a number of Lebanese markets and restaurants scattered throughout the area. Food tends to be excellent, but it reflects the acculturation of older Syrian/Lebanese families. Typical is Steve's Backroom, which was founded as a bakery and Middle Eastern import grocer and later opened a restaurant in the back room. The store now specializes in Middle Eastern products and gourmet foods (Celestial Seasonings teas, flavored coffee beans, fancy bottled salad dressings). The restaurant decor is chic and decidedly non-Arab: Monet prints on the wall, lemon slices in the water glasses, flowers on the table, and cookies with the bill. The menu includes all the Lebanese standards, but also "Greek" salad, Armenian *lahmajoun* ("Armenian-style open-face meat pie," topped with cheese at an extra price), pasta primavera, cheesecake, lots of vegetarian variants, and some Americanized versions of traditional foods such as *kibbeh* sandwiches and baked apricots with butter pistachio paste.

There were also a few Lebanese Muslims who immigrated at the end of the nineteenth century. They included both Sunni and Shia, though the difference was not as important in Detroit as it had been in Syria. The largest group settled in an ethnically mixed community of auto workers near the original Ford plant in Highland Park. In 1919 they established one of the first mosques in America. When Henry Ford moved his operations to Dearborn in the 1920s, the autoworker community moved also, and the neighborhood known as the Southend was established adjacent to Ford's River Rouge Plant. Until the 1970s this neighborhood housed a mixture of Lebanese Muslims and central and southern Europeans. During and after World War II, migrants from Appalachia were added. Over the years, Lebanese immigrants continued to arrive, as did a growing number of Palestinian refugees and Yemeni sojourners. This flow increased substantially after the reform of U.S. immigration laws in 1965 and with political troubles in the Middle East. Meanwhile, central and southern Europeans were moving elsewhere, and the Southend became increasingly Arab, reaching a majority by the late 1960s. Today, the Southend has the densest Arab population in America. The commercial district at its core is wholly Arab-owned and very Middle Eastern in character. The Southend is still probably the best known of Metropolitan Detroit's Arab neighborhoods, but relatively few non-Arabs patronize its stores.

Throughout the 1970s, problems developed between the Southend's more acculturated Lebanese and Palestinians and its more conservative, rapidly growing population of Yemenis. By the time a Yemeni cleric was hired in 1976 at the Southend mosque (built by Lebanese Muslims in 1934), many Lebanese and Palestinians had left the Southend for the more affluent neighborhoods of east Dearborn, nearer the Joy Road mosque, which was established during the 1960s.[2] This new community is served by a large, ever-expanding commercial district located east, west, and south of the intersection of Warren and Schaefer Avenues, which is quickly becoming the new epicenter.

A third Middle Eastern business district lies along Seven Mile Road, east of Woodward Avenue. It serves what was once the core of Detroit's large Chaldean community.[3] As the Chaldean community prospered financially in the 1970s and 1980s, the majority reestablished themselves in Detroit's affluent northern suburbs, especially Southfield, Birmingham, Oak Park, Bloomfield Hills, and Troy, where they live interspersed among the area's large Jewish population. Scattered restaurants and stores serve this suburban community, but many Chaldeans return to Seven Mile for their weekly shopping. Moreover, the Seven Mile neighborhood continues to serve as a "reception neighborhood" for newly arrived Chaldean immigrants (Agócs 1981, 135–36).

Thus there are three major commercial districts serving the Middle Eastern community of Greater Detroit: the Southend, now mostly Yemeni; Warren-Schaefer Avenues, entirely Levantine (mostly Muslim Lebanese with some Palestinians); and Seven Mile, entirely Chaldean. There is, in addition, one small cluster of businesses on south Joseph Campeau in the Yemeni enclave that developed along the Hamtramck-Detroit border near the old Dodge Main plant, and another small cluster in Livonia, in an area of Palestinian settlement. These districts, together with other businesses in Metropolitan Detroit and in the suburbs, constitute an infrastructure of the national communities they serve and of the Arab American community as a whole. Virtually anything one might want is available in the districts: appliance repair shops, Arabic-language bookstores, tuxedo rentals, doctors, lawyers, accountants, realtors. Here, community members can easily conduct all their business completely in Arabic. Of particular importance in this infrastructure are a variety of food-related businesses, including grocers, *halal* butchers, juice bars, fruit and vegetable stands, coffeehouses, bakeries, pastry shops, and, of course, restaurants.

Ethnic markets and national boundaries

Each of the three major Arab business districts has a distinctive feel. The Southend, with its prominent mosque, covered women, and arabesque architecture appears the most "Middle Eastern." Warren Avenue, a busy thoroughfare, has the most hustle and bustle. Seven Mile, set in an economically depressed area and subject to a constant siphoning off of more financially secure residents, is a bit rundown by comparison. But inside the stores and restaurants, at least to an uninformed outsider, the products offered appear much the same. On closer examination, of course, there are differences. This is most obvious in the Chaldean markets because Chaldean food, which reflects both the Iraqi regional cuisine of which it is part and specific Chaldean characteristics, is quite distinctive. Moreover, the Chaldean community tends to be composed (unlike the Yemeni—though this is gradually changing) of families with women there to cook, and the large Chaldean middle class can afford pricier imports when necessary.

A market serving a Chaldean clientele will almost always include *toorshi* (see glossary) along with the usual bulk olives and pickled vegetables, dried shallots used to season homemade toorshi, large jars of pickled mangos (from India but with labels printed partly in Arabic), frozen quail (a Chaldean delicacy), dates (four or five varieties, inevitably including the best available in Detroit, several brands of date syrup, date vinegar, and date confections), specific spice mixtures, and certain breads not seen elsewhere. By contrast, in Yemeni markets serving a clientele that is made up of a disproportionate number of males without families, is less financially secure, and is saving money to send home to Yemen instead of spending it on fancy foods, there is little difference from Levantine stores, except for less variety. This is so even though Yemeni food is as different from Levantine food as is Chaldean. In Yemen, for example, there is a large variety of regional breads (Alford and Duguid 1995, 24–25), yet none of these has ever been bought and sold in the Detroit market.

Similarly, there are certain items specific to Lebanese markets. Most Lebanese markets with Lebanese clientele will stock *yerba maté*, a tea imported from Argentina whose use was established in parts of Lebanon and Syria after immigrants returned from South America accustomed to its use.[4] Any larger Lebanese market will carry *faraykee* (smoke-dried green wheat), a local specialty of the Bekaa Valley. Neither *yerba maté* nor *faraykee* would be found in a Chaldean or Yemeni market. There is amalgamation at work here as Lebanese from other regions at least become aware of these local specialties after encountering them in Detroit markets.

We have no indication, however, that there has been any diffusion of *yerba maté* or *faraykee* to the local Palestinian, Yemeni, or Chaldean communities.

In nearly all respects, the stock of Palestinian markets cannot be distinguished from that of Lebanese markets even though they are sometimes marked by a distinctive name such as "Palestinian Food Market" or "Jerusalem Market." This is to be expected, since both groups are part of a larger Levantine culture area and share the same foodstuffs, if not always the same specific dishes. Much of what makes a cuisine distinctive has to do with recipes, techniques, and interpretations, even when this involves the same raw ingredients. This is especially true in the immigrant community, where a certain leveling takes place. Different national groups often make the same culinary accommodations. For some common ingredients, cooks from different backgrounds learn to make the same substitutions. The same item need not be imported from three different homelands. *Bulghur* is *bulghur,* after all. In fact, there may be an American producer of *bulghur;* no matter that he is an Armenian from California.

Not surprisingly, considerable amounts of shopping are done across national boundaries in Arab Detroit, the overriding objective being the acquisition of ingredients essential to home cuisine. Although patronizing a countryman may sometimes be a consideration, many others also determine where people shop, including proximity, convenience, service, and price. Arab markets serve a clientele far larger than the Arab American community. Many Greeks, Yugoslavs, Albanians, Romanians, Pakistanis, Indians, Jews, and especially Armenians find at least part of what they need to maintain their own culinary traditions in Arab markets. In fact, the failure to develop Armenian markets in greater Detroit, despite its large Armenian population, is probably a consequence of the excellent markets already available in the Arab community. A newly opened Armenian bakery, Arax Bakery in Warren, markets its products in Lebanese stores in the Southend and Chaldean stores in the suburbs, both of which are convenient to the principal Armenian residential areas.

Another reason for the similarity of stores in different neighborhoods is the strong emphasis on entrepreneurship in Levantine culture, coupled with the numerical and historical dominance of the Lebanese in Detroit. Nearly half the businesses in the Yemeni Southend, and these include all the larger markets, are owned by Lebanese. Markets in the small Yemeni neighborhood along the Hamtramck-Detroit border are also Lebanese.[5] This tendency in Yemeni neighborhoods has been reinforced by the perspective of many Yemenis who consider themselves sojourners who should make money quickly and send it back to Yemen, rather than invest it in stores in Detroit. But one also finds Lebanese markets in the Chaldean suburban neighborhoods (though not on Seven Mile, with one exception), where the stock includes all the Chaldean specifics found in Chaldean markets. This same entrepreneurial spirit can sometimes result in differentiation as well. Proprietors of stores will stock what they think their customers will purchase, whether these customers are of their own culture or not. One Lebanese baker in the Southend learned to make Yemeni specialties *samboosa* and *sabaya* for the Yemenis who form the majority of this community. When this same baker opened a second store uptown in Dearborn, where he hoped to attract non-Arab customers, he began to make broccoli pies, *halal* pepperoni rolls, and *zatar*-flavored croissants. Suburban Chaldean markets near Jewish residential areas make a point of stocking Israeli imports and certain foodstuffs of special interest to a Jewish clientele. Before Jewish holidays, they have special sales.

Before the proliferation of *halal* butchers in Detroit, some area Muslims used to purchase kosher meat. Now there are numerous *halal* butchers, with some in each of the three Arab commercial districts, including several wholesalers located near Eastern Market. All are more or less identical, with the same stock (including *basturma* and *soujouk*) and Middle Eastern-style butchering (cutting meat to order from carcasses rather than selling precut meat from cases). Chaldean butchers, being Christian, could sell pork. Yet patterns established in Iraq, where pork was not available, continue in Detroit, and pork is handled only by special order. Or, as one Chaldean butcher told us, "they buy their pork at Krogers." In fact, much of the meat sold by these

Christian Chaldean butchers is *halal,* since they purchase at least some of their stock from fellow Arabs, the *halal* wholesalers.

Pastry shops are a special case. With just one exception, every Middle Eastern pastry shop in the Detroit area is Lebanese. Pastry making represents a Lebanese hegemony within the Middle Eastern community, just as Chaldean supermarkets and Lebanese gas stations constitute ethnic hegemonies (Hannerz 1975, 48–54). Lebanese pastry is held in extremely high esteem throughout the Middle Eastern community, and non-Lebanese find it very difficult to compete. In the Southend, a small pastry shop opened recently; the owner was Yemeni, but his products were purchased from a Lebanese producer. Along Seven Mile, there is only one establishment not owned by a Chaldean; it is a Lebanese pastry maker. The repute of Lebanese pastries is such that he, despite being surrounded by Chaldeans, calls his shop Beirut Pastries.

The one pastry shop that is *not* Lebanese, Fabulous Masri Sweets, is an interesting exception and provides a useful example of cultural standardization in food commerce. The owner of Masri's is a Palestinian, Kader Masri, whose paternal grandfather founded a pastry shop in the West Bank town of Nablus, in 1902. Kader's father took over the business in 1936 and added a second shop just outside Jerusalem. Both shops are still open, owned and operated by one of Kader's five brothers. All of them grew up in the business, and their father insisted that they learn to make pastry before they went on to their chosen professions. Kader came to the United States in 1974 to study accounting at the University of Detroit. After graduating he worked as an accountant for eleven years, mostly in Arizona. He then returned to the Detroit area, in large part because he missed the large and lively Arab American community, and he opened a pastry shop in east Dearborn outside both the Arab commercial districts. Although his shop has no economic relationship with the family business, it bears the same name, uses the same recipes, and has a picture of "the founder," his grandfather, prominently displayed on the wall.

Kader's shop differs in significant ways, however, from the family shops in Palestine. Lebanese pastry shops, reflecting the long history of French political and cultural influence in Lebanon, always include one case of French pastries in addition to phyllo-based and other Middle Eastern-style sweets. The Masri shops in Palestine have a more limited stock; they specialize in *kanafa,* a specialty of Nablus, and also carry a line of phyllo-based Middle Eastern pastries, but no French-style pastries. Nevertheless, Kader felt obliged to offer them here because all his (Lebanese) competitors offer them. He took a couple of seminars in French pastry but learned mostly from a cousin trained in Germany and Greece, who now works as a pastry chef in Los Angeles. He worked with his cousin for several weeks and learned fast. "Once you have knowledge of baking, it's just tricks and recipes," he commented. When Kader first opened, he hired specialists to do his French pastry. Now he can tell *them* what to do. Similarly, there are several Middle Eastern-style sweets, such as fried sweets and farina cake, that in the Middle East are sold only at specialty shops. In Dearborn, however, Kader had to add them because his Lebanese competitors already offered them. In the same manner, all Lebanese pastry shops in Detroit now feel obliged to offer *kanafa,* Masri's specialty. As a consequence, every pastry shop in the area, including Fabulous Masri Sweets and all the Lebanese shops, tend to have the same stock differing only in some specific variations of the same dishes.

Restaurants

The context in which non-Arabs most often encounter Arab foodways is the restaurant. And restaurants in Detroit, even more than grocers and pastry shops, demonstrate the amalgamation of different Arab national culinary traditions. Menus of nearly all Arab American restaurants, no matter what national group they serve or are owned by, have a core of Lebanese dishes. These include all those dishes Americans have come to think of as Arab food, including *tabbouli, fattoush, kibbeh* (in several of its many forms), *hummus,* and *baba ghannouj.* There are several reasons for this, but most important is the fact that the Lebanese were the first to open Arab restaurants in the United States and for many years had a monopoly on them. Thus, it was Lebanese restaurateurs who developed and standardized the Arab American menu, establishing a set of fairly standard expectations.[6] Both an upscale Chaldean restaurant in the suburbs and a working-class Yemeni restaurant in the Southend arrange a few of their respective national dishes around a Lebanese core. The only exception to this pattern are the Chaldean restaurants along and near Seven Mile Road, which cater to new arrivals. Even these places invariably serve Lebanese-made pocket bread (pita) instead of the variety of fine Chaldean breads available just a few doors away.

The acceptance of Lebanese menus by Yemeni and Chaldean restaurants was made easier by the fact that Lebanese food is known and respected throughout the Middle East. The Lebanese are cited by Roden (1988, 3) as one of only two Middle Eastern societies—the other is Turkey—to have developed a restaurant culture. Detroit Chaldeans speak of having eaten in Lebanese restaurants in Iraq. In Detroit, many dishes considered by all to be Lebanese were already known elsewhere, at least by more sophisticated urbanites, as Lebanese. An Iraqi cookbook, for example, includes a recipe for *tabbouli,* noting that it is "originally Lebanese, but is popular in Baghdad" (Ing 1976, 28).

Pocket bread, which is widely known as pita or (in Detroit) as Arab bread and historically as Syrian bread, can now be bought in nearly every American supermarket. It is common in Levantine cities but is not known in Yemen and is only rarely eaten by Chaldeans in Iraq. Both the Yemenis and Chaldeans have a rich variety of other breads in their homelands. Yet every Yemeni and Chaldean restaurant serves pocket bread, with the exception of an upscale Chaldean restaurant in the suburbs, where they bake their own Chaldean rolls.

The diffusion of cuisine has not been one-way. All Lebanese restaurants in Detroit include one dish of Yemeni origin on their menu, *galaba.* The origins of this dish can be traced to the early period of Yemeni immigration to the Southend, before the development of Yemeni restaurants. Yemeni immigrants are said to have taught a Lebanese restaurant cook how to prepare their national dish. Once one Lebanese restaurant had it on the menu, it was only a matter of time before all Lebanese restaurants would have it, whether they had Yemeni customers or not. Similarly, a Lebanese restaurant, recently opened in the suburbs near a substantial Chaldean population, has several Chaldean specialties on the menu. Time will tell whether these dishes too will spread to other Lebanese restaurants.

The pattern, then, is one of considerable amalgamation of national cuisines in the public sector. While differences remain between restaurants, markets, and other food-related businesses associated with the different Arabic-speaking groups, and especially between Chaldean and all others, a general coalescence is obvious. The reasons behind the trend are numerous; they include Lebanese preeminence in Detroit, the vitality of Lebanese entrepreneurship, the sojourner status of Yemenis, specific cases of diffusion, and shared adaptations to American foods and foodways. The end result, albeit still incomplete, is the development of a new ethnic cuisine that is produced, consumed, and marketed in public contexts as Arab food. This New World cuisine is not the same as the national cuisines of Lebanon, Yemen, Iraq, Palestine, and other Arab homelands. As the next section will show, public versions of Arab American food are also unlike the foods Arab Americans eat at home in Detroit.

Food and foodways in the private sector

One should start at the beginning (of the meal, that is) with *mezzeh,* and so, too, *mezzeh* is an appropriate place to begin a discussion of Arab foodways in the home. *Mezzeh,* a varied selection of hot and cold appetizers, includes some of the best-known Arab foods. It is part of the culinary repertoire throughout the Levant, but it has been especially refined by the Lebanese. Some *mezzeh* dishes, but not *mezzeh* culture—that is, the body of ideas and practices surrounding *mezzeh*—have been adopted in the cuisine of most Arabic-speaking countries.

Mezzeh is consumed in both Arab American restaurants and homes. In the former context, it is more or less codified; in the latter, it is ever-changing and adaptive. As a system, *mezzeh* and the *mezzeh* culture are a legacy of the Ottoman Turks (*meze* is Turkish, meaning tidbit). As a culinary tradition, *mezzeh* extends beyond the Arab world as far west as the former Yugoslavia, where its function, structure, and practice are similar to the *mezzeh* of the Arab countries. Anyone buying a drink in Greece, for example, is automatically served a plate with something to nibble on as part of their order.[7]

Including in its very structure any number of small plates of varying foods, a *mezzeh* table often represents amalgamation and acculturation, as it contains foods from other regions or nations, a chef's invention, or adaptations of traditional foods. *Mezzeh* may be as simple as Arab bread and olives. For special occasions, it can feature dozens of dishes, including cheese, pickles, salads, savory pastries, stuffed vegetables, dips, and meats. Several *mezzeh* dishes, however, are regarded as Lebanese national foods, and their presence is almost mandatory except in the simplest *mezzeh*. *Tabbouli,* characterized by one Lebanese American as "the queen of the table," the ubiquitous *hummus, baba ghannouj,* and *kibbeh nayee* are all standardized *mezzeh* fare. They are available in Arab restaurants and are part of every Lebanese home cook's repertoire.

With its great variety of dishes, *mezzeh* invites new additions and easily lends itself to change. Women often add a platter of American-style raw vegetables and dip to the *mezzeh* table when they entertain. Consequently new combinations occur, such as when celery is dipped into *hummus* and *kibbeh* into mayonnaise-based dips. While cheeses and crackers are not strangers to an Arab American *mezzeh*, at one event, blue cheese mixed with *labneh* was such a success that it now appears on *mezzeh* tables throughout southeast Michigan. Cookbook writer Mary Laird Hamady (1987, 72) encourages readers to use their imaginations. "If we have Arabic bread," she writes of herself and her Lebanese American husband, "we could convert ordinary leftovers of any national origin into a respectable *mezzeh*." One Lebanese woman in Detroit occasionally includes Chinese egg rolls on her *mezzeh* table.

Today, the *mezzeh* served in Arab American restaurants and that served in homes can differ in its relationship to the rest of the meal. In restaurants one can eat *mezzeh* by itself, but when an entree is served, removing *mezzeh* from the table, leaving only the main dish, is a traditional pattern. In many homes, however, *mezzeh* consists of a limited number of dishes and is served along with other foods as side dishes. Other differences can be attributed to the distinctive Lebanese *mezzeh* culture. First, according to some Lebanese Detroiters, one cannot fully partake in *mezzeh* without *arak* or alcohol of some kind. Whether Muslim or Christian, Lebanese distinguish themselves from other Arabs by drinking alcohol with *mezzeh*.[8] Second, an elaborate *mezzeh*, consisting of a wide assortment of dishes, is more often served at holidays and to guests. It is used to create a social time during which diners eat, drink, and converse.[9] It is not everyday fare.

It is popularly thought by strangers to the Middle East that wine and alcohol are taboo and do not figure in the food cultures of the area. This is not entirely true. Prohibition came to be associated with Muslims, but drinking alcohol is common in much of Arab society, though it is done more discretely among Muslims. Alcohol has always been part of urban settings, and in sophisticated, literate, and prosperous circles, elaborate cultures and etiquettes grew up around drink (Zubaida and Tapper 1994, 15; Tapper 1994, 219). With or without alcohol, *mezzeh,* with its variations in content and performance, is a durable component of Arab American culture and cuisine.

Unlike *mezzeh,* in which amalgamation and acculturation occur and are even celebrated, overt signs of amalgamation in *kibbeh* are not. Although one may speak loosely of national cuisines, in reality, each locality and community within national boundaries has its own distinctive food styles, including dishes that are described in a common vocabulary but that differ from each other in definable ways. The same word for foods may cross numerous linguistic and political boundaries. The *kofte/kibbeh* category is one such example. *Kibbeh* exists in many *bulghur*-based versions throughout Lebanon, Syria, and Palestine, and in parts of Iraq, with *bulghur* and with rice (Zubaida 1994a, 35). Lebanese claim *kibbeh* as their dish, stating that each village makes a distinctive version and each cook has her special recipe, only a few of which seem to exist in Michigan. In most Arabic restaurants, the *kibbeh* menu is limited, offering at best baked, raw, and fried versions. In homes, there may be an amalgamation of types found in Lebanon, but there is still considerable variety.

Kibbeh takes many shapes. The stuffing can be placed between two layers of meat, filled into oblong shapes of meat, or mixed directly with the meat and *bulghur* and shaped into balls. It is served raw, baked, fried, simmered in yogurt, in broth, or in a tomato base. There also are variations with rice or potato. It can be simply spiced or it can use a special blend of many spices such as the mix from south Lebanon that includes (among other ingredients) rose petals. Another Lebanese variant includes pomegranate juice. This hardly exhausts all possibilities, but it does account for more versions than are found in restaurants. *Kibbeh* is one of those foods for which there are as many versions as there are cooks, and each prefers her own to that of others. For the time being, the amalgamation of even the Lebanese *kibbehs* (not to mention the Palestinian and Chaldean versions) seems unlikely in such an atmosphere of pride. Changes are taking place, nonetheless. The tradition of pounding lamb has given way to grinding it, a change that may have started in the old country, and lamb is being replaced by beef.

The widespread use of rice in the Middle East is relatively recent (Zubaida 1994b, 93). Except in a few rice-producing areas, rice was a luxury food for the tables of the wealthy and for special occasions. Today, the cultures of the region share similar methods of preparing rice. "Arab rice," a term denoting certain ingredients and preparations, is one example of a pan-Arab dish. In Greater Detroit, most Arab Americans refer to rice by equating it with their nationality—Lebanese Americans, for example, call it Lebanese rice. Yet Arab rice (whether it is called Lebanese or Palestinian) is essentially the same; it can be cooked simply with butter or elaborately with nuts, butter, spices, and lamb. Of course, many Lebanese Americans proclaim Lebanese rice to be the best. Every culture is ethnocentric about its food. Expressions of pride and boastfulness almost always focus on the basics, what Sidney Mintz (1989, 118) refers to as the core of a people's diet: the starchy center of a cuisine that must be eaten with every meal in order to feel as though one has eaten. Arab rice and bread are examples. An Arabic saying asks, "what do people in Paradise eat?" The answer is, "Rice and butter" (Zubaida 1994b, 93). Lebanese American ethnocentrism is not unusual, according to Mintz, but it does imply a lack of contact and experience with the rice of other Arab Americans in Detroit.

In the Middle East, rice was a staple only in limited rice-growing areas, the Nile delta, the Caspian provinces of Iran, and the southern marshlands of Iraq (Zubaida 1994b, 93). It was imported into other areas, where locally grown wheat was the primary staple. Rice is not served, for example, at every meal in the Middle East, but bread is, even when rice is also served. However, rice is a valued and important ingredient for celebrations in the Middle East. As in many other cultures, with affluence and availability, prestigious foods such as rice often become more everyday. *Bulghur,* though, when cooked as a pilav, is regarded by most Arabs as an inferior substitute for rice. This sentiment contrasts with that of the Chaldeans, who take great pride in the *bulghur* produced in northern Iraq and various dishes made with it.

While *bulghur* is not always regarded negatively in Greater Detroit, rice is held in high regard. In Dearborn, the first dish Lebanese grandmothers teach their granddaughters to cook is Lebanese rice.[10] For Thanksgiving, Lebanese rice with butter, nuts, spices, and meat is always present, sometimes as turkey stuffing, sometimes as a side dish. Lebanese rice is so central to the diet of one woman we interviewed that she eats it with almost everything, including Chinese food. An Arab American firefighter told us he is proud of having taught his fellow firefighters to cook Arab foods, especially Lebanese rice.

Sharing Arab foods and foodways

Every culture is proud of its food traditions and tends to be ambivalent about (or even contemptuous of) others. Others may eat foods similar to ours, but they do not cook them half as well, they use too much or too little spice, the fats are greasy, the oils smell, and so on. However, under conditions of social stability and harmony, people are curious about the foods of others and experiment with them. Within and between ethnic groups in Greater Detroit there exist formal and informal means of food exchange that contrast sharply with the formal distribution systems found in restaurants. The stability of Arab ethnic cuisines may be greatly affected by the nature of these nonmarket exchanges with non-Arabs and Arabs of other national backgrounds.

The foods traded over the backyard fence, at the workplace, and over coffee are regarded as "foreign" foods by the people who receive them, even when they can successfully reproduce them in their own kitchens. In Dearborn, neighbors frequently exchange gifts of cooked food and try each other's recipes. As a token of their friendship and hospitality, for example, Yemeni women give gifts of *sabaya* to their female neighbors. As in Yemen, offering this layered flaky pastry, lavished with clarified butter and honey, is a way of honoring a person (Maclagan 1994, 161). The women who receive this dish may not always understand the deeper meaning of the gesture. Nonetheless, a pattern of neighborly exchange and a sense of obligation are established through this gift of food.[11]

In one such demonstration of friendship, Fatme Boomrad, a Lebanese woman, reciprocated a Yemeni woman's gift of *sabaya* with a gift of spinach and meat pies. Failing miserably when she tried to make *sabaya* herself, Fatme and her neighbor agreed to continue exchanging Lebanese pies for Yemeni *sabaya*. In another exchange, Samiha Abusalah, a Palestinian woman, picked grape leaves from her Yemeni neighbor's fence and in return taught her to make stuffed grape leaves, a food unknown to the neighbor before she arrived in Dearborn. In exchange, the Yemeni woman occasionally sends *sabaya* to Samiha. An Italian/Polish American has built a close friendship with her Lebanese neighbor over coffee and Lebanese pastries during mid-morning visits. On occasion Samiha also makes Lebanese hot potatoes that a Lebanese coworker taught her. Similarly, Hana Khraizat, a Lebanese woman, learned to make apple pie from her Hungarian American neighbor.

When sharing special foods with other groups, one usually tries to maintain a balance—sometimes a delicate one—between what is distinctive and what is familiar enough to appeal. *Aseed,* an interesting Yemeni dish similar to several West African dishes, is a case in point. Flour is stirred in simmering water until it is very stiff. It is then turned out onto a platter and around it is poured *maraq,* a robust lamb broth. *Aseed* is eaten by tearing off a piece with the fingers and dipping it into the broth. Whereas it is normal for immigrant foods to change, the change in *aseed* in Michigan has been strictly ideological. In Yemen, *aseed* is considered poor food; in Detroit, it has acquired new meaning as an ethnic marker.[12] Yemenis do not make gifts of *aseed* as readily as they do *sabaya*, perhaps because they have realized the taste for *aseed* is acquired. In one case, a third-generation Lebanese American who received a gift of *aseed* and *maraq* liked the *maraq* very much but not the *aseed*. Now she makes *maraq* herself and prepares American-style dumplings with it instead of *aseed*.

Muslim women of the Southend also offer informal hospitality to their neighbors with mid-morning coffee and snacks. After chores are finished, women casually visit each other. The talk often comes back to the topic of food: "what are you cooking today?" Children present listen closely. If they don't like what is being cooked at home, they know they can eat with the neighbors instead. They just appear and are welcome. This open-door policy extends to one's married children as well, especially when the daughter works and has little time to cook properly for her husband and herself. They eat their main meal with her mother, or his.

Foods from the homeland

Although almost everything needed to cook and eat Arab food is readily available in Greater Detroit, some food items are just better in the homeland, and Arab Detroiters look to their kin back home for products they are accustomed to. Sumac, though available in the United States, is neither as strong nor as flavorful as that obtained from a trusted merchant back home. *Kishik* available in Detroit is generally not acceptable. Some families make their own, but the best is made from goat's-milk yogurt. *Kamuni* is a special combination of spices and rose petals added to the kinds of *kibbeh* made in south Lebanon, and the best *kamuni* originates in this region.[13] Two grades of *faraykee* are available in some Dearborn markets, but only one is regarded by south Lebanese women as the real thing. It should be greenish-brown and smoky, the result of being roasted over an open fire in the field. And only *faraykee* roasted by one's family will do. Women visiting relatives in the old country bring these essential foods back to the States in amounts sufficient to share with kin and neighbors. Relatives also mail seasonal packages when these valued foods are freshly prepared.

Until recently only dried and frozen *molokiyeh* (mucilaginous green leaf) were available in local markets. Not satisfied with its cleanliness, some women continued to bring from the old country *molokiyeh* dried by family members. At first grown only by a few, *molokiyeh* is now being grown in yards and gardens throughout Greater Detroit and shared with neighbors across the fence. It is beginning to appear in markets as well, although the seeds for this much-loved green are still not available commercially. This culinary link with people back home facilitates informal food exchanges that reinforce family ties and increase the stability of ethnic foods in Greater Detroit.

Innovation and change

Ethnic foodways are more than surviving relics or inferior versions of old country cuisine. Foods are constantly changing. By altering a dish, instead of refusing to make it for lack of proper ingredients, women demonstrate both their commitment to a food tradition and their creativity. Cuisines in the old country change too. Women often return from visits to the Middle East with new recipes they have learned from kin or with new ways to cook familiar foods. One of the first, almost imperceptible changes in ethnic food occurs as "substitution," a process about which there is very little ethnographic study (Mintz 1989, 119). Without access to traditional foodstuffs, cooks make substitutions. However, lack of ingredients is not the only reason for substitution. Today, despite the availability of raw materials, cooks are increasingly likely to substitute "foreign" ingredients for traditional ones. Ricotta or mozzarella are used in *kanafa*, lamb is replaced by beef, Mazola oil is substituted for clarified butter, pancake syrup for date syrup, Crisco or peanut butter for *tahini*, and pinto and navy beans for small fava beans. Some innovations are said to improve Old World recipes. Mayonnaise is added to *hummus* to make it creamier. Lamb is basted with soy sauce to enhance its color. Dried onion soup mix is combined with meat for Lebanese pies. In areas without Detroit's Middle Eastern culinary resources and overall ethnic infrastructure, much more substitution is necessary.

Children are the quickest to adapt to American culture and change the way their families eat. Through their school experiences, many kids come to like American food better than Arabic. Some women accommodate their children by cooking American food whenever they request it. Ehsan Mroui, for example, no longer prepares lamb brains, lamb stomach, stuffed casings, or green beans with lamb. Instead, she cooks mashed potatoes, gravy, hamburgers, hot dogs, and french fries for the children, and Arab food for the adults.

On the other hand, American experiences can strengthen Arab traditions. At home in Lebanon, Fatme Boomrad recalled how much she disliked *mujaddara*. The lentils were never cleaned well enough. In the United States, however, she found lentils to be grit free, and now she loves this dish. For some, traditional foods become a priority because of their nostalgic associations. Julia Najor speaks for many when she says, "We eat these old dishes more in America than we did at home—lentils, *bulghur*, wheat berries, barley. [They] bring memories. When you are poor, you want what you can't afford. When you can afford [what you had wanted], you want those dishes you ate when you were poor."[14]

Clearly, cultural heritage and identity are factors contributing to the perpetuation of some foods. Several Lebanese Detroiters (one of whom is a third-generation American) still make *dehen,* or *qawahrma,* a confit-like preserved meat. Before refrigeration, Lebanese village women preserved lamb by boiling pieces in the fat from the tail of sheep until the meat was dry. It was then placed in pottery jugs and covered with fat, which sealed out air and preserved the meat. Lamb prepared in this way has a distinctive flavor much loved by older people who grew up eating it. Today, Detroit women make *dehen* not to preserve the meat, but because it is a distinctive food with a special flavor and is part of their diet.[15] It is used in pies and with fried eggs. Many women make their own *maftool,* despite its availability in markets. Fatme Boomrad continues to make *khubuz markook* (mountain thin bread), baking it on a steel dome (*sajj*) brought from Lebanon, even though it also is available in nearby Arab bakeries.[16] In all these examples, the individuals are motivated by a desire to keep a tradition that consciously links them to their Lebanese American identity.

New traditions and old: Foodways at the holidays

Ethnic religious observances and holidays are also closely linked to heritage. The greatest stability in Arab American foods is seen in these contexts. Women who do not have time to cook Arab food every day gather with other family members and cook it for holidays. The dishes tend to be traditional, distinctive of one ethnicity, and have symbolic meaning. Christmas, for example, is the most significant Chaldean holy season and is widely celebrated with feasting and visiting. A special and very popular Chaldean Christmas dish is *pacha,* a great favorite among Chaldean Americans of all ages, who feel united spiritually by the knowledge that all Chaldeans are eating it at the same time.[17]

Among Muslims, Ramadan is the most holy observance. Although this is the month of fasting, it is also a time of communal feasting. The breaking of the fast, *fatur,* functions for Muslims as does *pacha* among Chaldeans. Symbolically, Muslims are united by the very act of breaking the fast according to the same proscriptions. Between sunrise and sunset there is total abstinence from food and drink. Breaking fast is done in a number of ways; the traditions vary from culture to culture, sometimes from family to family. At sunset, people might eat a date, drink water, coffee, or an apricot drink (made from apricot "leather"), or take a taste of salt, after which they pray and then eat a meal. Extended families gather to break the fast together. Except for specific sweets made for Ramadan, the meal does not necessarily consist of special foods (but the foods are usually traditional and ethnic); there is just more of everything and every attempt is made to prepare the food well. Women prepare many different dishes to ensure that everyone will find enough of what they like to eat.

Soup is often served at the *fatur*. At the Lebanese Muslim Mroui household, for example, the table was covered with dishes containing *fattoush, baba ghannouj,* south Lebanese *kibbeh nayee* and radishes, Lebanese rice, barbecued lamb, fried sardines with *tahini* sauce (*tarator*), pocket bread fried in the same oil as the sardines, roasted chicken, french fries, Pepsi, punch, and water.[18] Among the homemade sweets were *mamoul,* rice pudding, and *katayef.* Other sweets had been purchased at bakeries.

By contrast, at the first-generation Yemeni American Al-Mawri home, the menu had been prepared from familiar Middle Eastern ingredients, but the results were quite unlike Levantine fare. The *fatur* included the following: *shafoot* (a creamy souplike dish of yogurt, pieces of Arab bread, garlic, hot peppers, cilantro, cumin, salt, and liquid smoke), *samboosa* (fried triangles of Chinese egg roll dough filled with ground lamb, onion, parsley, garlic, cilantro, black pepper, green hot pepper, cumin, and salt), *aseed* and *maraq, fatoot* (Arabic bread, dribbled with hot clarified butter and a little liquid smoke and covered with meat broth), *ma'soub* (flour and water mixed to the consistency of thick cake batter, cooked on the stove until firm like bread, then broken up, mixed with hot clarified butter and honey, and eaten with fingers), *bagiah* (a falafel-like dish made from a "special bean," cilantro, onions, parsley, and deep fried as patties and eaten with bread and *sahawig,* a sauce with cumin and hot pepper), *zurbian* (rice with lamb, potatoes, yogurt, black pepper, cinnamon, cardamom, and garlic), *sabayah* (layers of paper-thin dough made from flour, water, eggs, milk, and black cumin seeds), *salata* (head lettuce, onions, tomatoes, cucumbers, radishes, carrots dressed with lemon juice, salt, and pepper), several types of Arab breads, fruits, and sweets (*mahalabiah,* a custard with fruit; *labanieh,* fruit custard served on cake; *kalaj,* cream-filled thin dough fried and covered with sugar syrup); sweet *samboosa* filled with dates, coconut, or raisins fried and dribbled with sugar syrup. Of this large menu, only *kalaj* was not Yemeni and, according to the family, is not known in Yemen. Rather, they learned it from Lebanese Americans after settling in Detroit. There is otherwise little indication of amalgamation in this Yemeni menu, a factor that may reflect limited contact with non-Yemenis.

Easter among Christian Arabs is also a time for feasting. Sylvia Freij and Yasmine Harb, first-generation Palestinian Americans from Ramallah, served their extended family a large Easter meal consisting of fourteen *mezzeh* dishes followed by meats, Arab rice, yogurt, and salad. The only break with Palestinian traditional cuisine was the inclusion of cheddar cheese as *mezzeh*.[19] In Ramallah, it is customary at Easter to have a whole roasted lamb stuffed with rice, and a salad. In Detroit, people are too busy to cook Arab food every day, and cooking an entire lamb is no longer convenient, even on special occasions. Therefore, instead of preparing a whole lamb for Easter, the extended family gets together to share an array of their favorite traditional Ramallah dishes. What used to be ordinary food in the home village has become, in Greater Detroit, the holiday food on which these Palestinians feast together.

One should consider, by way of contrast, the holiday dinner served by the Christian, extended family of Olivia and Lafi Khalil and Mary David. Family members include first- as well as fourth-generation Americans, great-grandparents as well as great-grandchildren, all of whom trace their ancestry to Syria, Palestine, or Lebanon. Their Christmas dinner reflects this mix of generations, decades of changes in the United States, and the periodic reinvigoration of old country food traditions by newly arrived family members. Appetizers were mainstream American (sliced cheese and crackers, nuts, sausages, and nachos). The main course, the same each year, was a conscious selection of traditional Levantine dishes, including traditional *mezzeh* served as side dishes. The menu consisted of baked *kibbeh, tabbouli* (served with head lettuce), grape leaves stuffed with rice and meat, yogurt, *hummus,* and *mansef.* Other dishes included sliced roasted turkey, mixed pickles, and Arab bread. *Mansef,* traditionally served at weddings and other celebratory events, was the centerpiece. Dessert included Arab pastries, American pies, cookies, and fruit. Covered with Levantine and ethnic American fare, this holiday table reflected the identities of all the celebrants gathered around it.

Thanksgiving

Thanksgiving, the all-American holiday, is eagerly adopted by immigrants as a way of participating in American culture and demonstrating their Americanness. Most ethnic groups participate in this day by intermingling holiday foods from their own cultures with symbolic American foods. In the process, however, the history, symbolism, and mythology of the day, as most Americans understand them, often do not transfer. What does carry over is the universally understood practice of feasting. The traditional Arab-style show of abundance at table coincidentally communicates a bountiful Thanksgiving meal.

The requisite turkey is always present. Its size a symbol of bounty, the Thanksgiving turkey would be appropriate for an Arab feast as well. Often, Arab American tables include one or two other large pieces of meat, such as a leg of lamb or beef roast, increasing the sense of boundless plenty. Arab rice is perhaps as essential as turkey; it may stuff the turkey (in the same way it stuffs a whole lamb), or it may be cooked separately. Among the symbolic Thanksgiving foods, Arabs in Detroit rarely eat cranberry sauce, most admit to disliking pumpkin pie, and many do not particularly like turkey. The Thanksgiving menu of Fatme Boomrad's multigenerational Lebanese Muslim family, for instance, includes the essential Arab dishes and illustrates their idea of what an American feast should be: "Lebanese" rice; turkey without stuffing; Lebanese rice with meat, spices, and nuts; yogurt; canned cranberries; corn; mashed potatoes; gravy; green and fruit salads (canned peaches on lettuce with cottage cheese). Desserts included homemade apple pie and Sara Lee pumpkin pies and cheesecake.

For a first-generation Yemeni family, the Thanksgiving meal also represents Arab and American cultures. Having once been married to an American, the head of the Hamdani household instructed his new Yemeni wife on how to prepare a Thanksgiving meal. She roasted a turkey with Stove-Top dressing and made potato salad, white rice, and salad with creamy French dressing. The husband purchased several JELL-O salads from a delicatessen. Served with this was a Yemeni lamb and vegetable stew with Arab bread. The turkey, stuffing, and JELL-O salads are appropriate foods for a Thanksgiving feast, which was consumed in the traditional Yemeni way. The male guests, who ate separately from the women and children, sat on the floor around a tablecloth laden with food. Each had a plate and tableware but soon dispensed with these and finished the American meal in traditional Yemeni village style, with bread and fingers.

The third-generation Palestinian/Lebanese Christian family of Frank and Sylvia Sophiea in the vicinity of Flint, celebrate their Thanksgiving in a consciously ethnic manner, evoking their heritage on this all-American occasion. The grandmother was introduced to Thanksgiving by an American friend soon after she arrived in the United States. The friend's turkey recipe is still the basis of this family's Thanksgiving meal, which, in 1995, consisted of turkey with American-style dressing, accompanied by Cornish hens stuffed with Arab rice and a salad of tomatoes, cucumbers, parsley, and lettuce. This was preceded by *mezzeh*—*hummus* and *baba ghannouj,* Arab bread, and sliced fresh vegetables. The meal concluded with fresh fruit followed by *harissa.* This celebration repeats a pattern seen among other ethnic groups. The turkey, as the center of the meal, is surrounded by ethnic dishes. On holidays, families several generations removed from the immigrants often go back to traditional ethnic foods; at Thanksgiving, these are the foods they want to eat.

Thanksgiving in Arab American homes does not differ radically from other American homes. The difference is in the meaning of the event more than its content. Arab Americans have taken up the turkey as a symbol of this American holiday and surrounded it with their traditional ethnic foods. However, Arab American Thanksgivings do not embody the Pilgrim mythology known to most other Americans. Consuming turkey, stuffing, cranberries, and JELL-O salads in itself symbolically demonstrates Americanness, but by including Arab foods at Thanksgiving, the families discussed here mesh two cultures, demonstrating their

Arab Americanness. Thanksgiving is an American family holiday rooted and observed according to family tradition. Consequently, it is unlikely that Arab American celebrations of Thanksgiving will amalgamate to become a kind of pan-Arab tradition. Rather, Arab Americans, like all Americans, will observe discrete family or ethnic Thanksgiving traditions that have been maintained across successive generations.

Conclusion

The foregoing has been a demonstration of ethnic cultural processes, specifically the evolution of Arab American food and foodways in both the public and private sectors. Within this context, it is possible to identify several specific types of culture change. Considerable debate has ensued in the past over the meaning of "acculturation." Here we will reserve the term for the simple meaning of one subordinate group adopting the culture traits of a dominant group. Ample example of this exists in both the private and public spheres of Detroit's Arab American community, from grocery stores selling Cheez Whiz and Cool Whip amidst the *tahini* and olive oil, to mothers preparing hot dogs for their kids. In some cases, the cultural exchange is accompanied by a change in meaning. The recently arrived Yemeni family gathered for the first time around a Thanksgiving turkey do not invest it with the symbolic load of the Pilgrims, Native Americans, and giving thanks but, rather, with the meaning "Now we are Americans."

Another common process is the diffusion of culinary traits from other ethnic groups. A Palestinian who makes tacos and burritos after eating them in a Mexican restaurant, a Lebanese woman who learns southern cooking from her Appalachian migrant husband and then passes recipes to her sister, a Lebanese cook who adds Chinese egg rolls to her *mezzeh* table: all are examples of diffusion at work. This process is not limited to the private sphere. One Arab-owned restaurant advertises "Arab, American and Italian Food." When asked "why Italian?" the owner's only answer was that there are many Italians in Dearborn. A newly remodeled Lebanese bakery-delicatessen on Warren Avenue has "welcome" written on the wall in Arabic, English, and Italian, presumably for the same reason. Yemenis who purchased a previously established pizza restaurant added *halal* pizza (though they have not listed it on the menu). Similar diffusion of foods occurs between different national groups, principally the Lebanese, Yemenis, and Palestinians, who most commonly are neighbors or work together.[20] They seem to regard foods from other Arabs much as they do foods received from non-Arabs: as exotic treats. In some cases, women incorporate such dishes into their own repertoire. But just as often, they do not try, or, if they do try, they are unsuccessful. In such cases, enduring trade partnerships are often established for continued exchange of "foreign" treats.

The process of amalgamation of culinary traditions has been of particular interest to us. In other words, to what degree have original differences between national cuisines decreased? Just how much diffusion has there been between them? To what extent is there a generalized Arab American cuisine? It is impossible to quantify such changes, but it seems that far greater amalgamation of food traditions has occurred in the public or commercial sector than in Arab American homes. Driven especially by commercialism and the need to keep up with competitors, an Arab American cuisine is emerging in most restaurants. Markets and butcher shops have more or less identical stock. There is a near monopoly of pastry shops by members of one national group, who supply the same pastry to all others.

Although some cultural exchange happens between national groups, each can be seen to constitute a separate but parallel process of creolization. Thus, to some extent, separate Lebanese American, Yemeni American, Palestinian American, and Chaldean American cuisines have developed. It is not surprising that Arab American amalgamation and national group distinctiveness can coexist at different levels of cultural integration. It is the cultural manifestation of the phenomenon called "nesting." Ethnic groups are almost never mutually exclusive. More often, one identity is nested within another more encompassing one, which sometimes lies within another more inclusive identity. Thus, to be Lebanese American or Yemeni American does not mean one is any less Arab American or vice versa. Individuals are free to choose their identifying label situationally, based on strategic considerations, from any number of such identities, including both nested ethnic identities and others based on occupation, class, region of origin, gender.[21] Each of these identities is associated with a particular subculture. It seems to us that a model of ethnic change based on parallel processes of creolization is much more in line with a view of America as a multicultural society, just as the acculturation model was more appropriate for the image of America as a melting pot or, predating that, as an Anglo-conforming society (Gordon 1964).

It must be emphasized that the cultural processes we have discussed above are ongoing, resulting in an ever-evolving situation. Even as we write, a new community of Iraqi Shia is taking shape in the Detroit area, new restaurants with new menus are opening, and a new group of immigrant homemakers are adapting their cooking to new and unfamiliar circumstances. Iraqi Shia will soon make their own contributions to ever-changing Arab American food and foodways in Greater Detroit.

ACKNOWLEDGMENTS: This work draws in part from informal contact with Metropolitan Detroit's Arab American community, particularly its public sector food and foodways, since our arrival in Michigan in 1969. More formal field research was conducted in 1988 and 1994–96 with the support of the National Endowment for the Humanities, National Endowment for the Arts, Michigan Council for Arts and Cultural Affairs, and Michigan Traditional Arts Program (Michigan State University Museum). We wish to acknowledge field-workers Barbara George Gallagher, Sally Howell, Haajar Mitchell, Rosina Hassoun, and Dawn Ramey, whose reports and discussions about food and celebration contributed to this paper. And last but not least, we thank the many community businesses and men and women who shared information and food with us.

Notes

1. See Sidney Mintz (1989) for a particularly eloquent statement of why anthropologists should study food and foodways.

2. This is an extremely abbreviated account of a complex series of events. For a more complete history, see Abraham, Abraham, and Aswad (1983, 171–75).

3. For further history and ethnography of Detroit's Chaldeans, see Sengstock (1982) and (1983).

4. For further data regarding the diffusion of *yerba maté* to Lebanon, see Luxner (1995).

5. In contrast, an entrepreneurial subculture is alive and well in some other migrant Yemeni communities, especially those in South Arabia, East Africa, and Southwest Asia (Nabeel Abraham, personal conversation, ca. 1998).

6. We have been amazed over the years at how fast and how thoroughly menus in ethnic restaurants become standardized in America. There is a strong tendency for all restaurants of any ethnic group to offer the same selection of dishes from what is inevitably a much larger repertoire. Afghani Americans provide a good example, one easier to document since the entire population came all at once relatively recently. Within just a couple of years, Afghani restaurants were opened up across America by people who had never previously owned a restaurant and with menus of the same ten to twelve dishes.

7. For the history and development of Arab foods, see Goody (1982, 127–33), Roden (1972, 1–29), and Zubaida and Tapper (1994, 1–17).

8. Our informant was a sophisticated, educated, urban, nonobservant Muslim. Her opinion, though shared by many, is denied by observant Muslims. Consumption of alcohol by Lebanese Americans dropped significantly after the Iranian revolution in 1979, which led to increased awareness and politicization of Islam in Detroit and Lebanon.

9. Some restaurants in Lebanon are known for *mezzeh* tables of over a hundred dishes. Only one upscale Lebanese restaurant in southeast Michigan offers a large and varied *mezzeh*.

10. With few exceptions, women we interviewed attributed their first cooking lessons to mothers-in-law, neighbors, and extended kin after they married. As unmarried teenagers their mothers regarded schooling and studies most important and discouraged their presence in the kitchen. Although education is still highly valued, we found a number of grandmothers in greater Detroit who insisted their granddaughters learn the basics of cooking while still living at home.

11. *Sabaya* is generically an old dish. The invention of layered pastries, such as baklava and *sabaya,* is attributed to the Turks. Nomadic Turks were making layered dough products as early as the eleventh century. Paper-thin layers of dough are thought to be the invention of the royal kitchens at the Topkapi Sarayi (Perry 1994, 87).

12. See Halpern (1958, 57) regarding a similar shift in Serbia with corn bread and wheat bread.

13. The "all spice" of the Lebanese and Palestinians and the "curry powder" of the Chaldeans are other mixtures of a variety of spices, up to seven spices for the all spice, and as many as thirteen for the curry powder. These are available in markets, premixed or mixed to order.

14. First-generation Chaldean woman, interview by authors, 1995.

15. The example of corned beef in the United States is analogous to this Lebanese preserved meat in that it is prepared for its taste long after the need for preservation is gone.

16. Talal's, an upscale Lebanese restaurant, employs a recently arrived immigrant woman, dressed in her village apparel, to make this bread in full view of customers.

17. Athir Shayota, a Chaldean artist, personal conversation, 1996.

18. One of the family said, "Our food goes best with Pepsi."

19. *Mezzeh* included: open-faced meat pies, ravioli-shaped meat pies, spinach pies, *kibbeh* meatballs, lamb stew, stuffed grape leaves, stuffed squash, *tabbouli, hummus,* raw vegetables, pickles, olives, Syrian white cheese, cheddar cheese, and leavened Arab bread. Entrees were lamb shoulder larded with garlic; chicken roasted with all spice and garlic; rice with pine nuts, lamb, and all spice; yogurt; and salad of lettuce, tomatoes, cucumbers, green onions, and mint, dressed with lemon and oil. Among the sweets were *mamoul* and date-filled cookies.

20. The first Chaldean immigrants settled among the Christian Lebanese, who were then still located in downtown Detroit. We assume that this same sort of culinary exchange prevailed between them at that time.

21. For further discussion of situational ethnicity, see Nagata (1974) and Okamura (1981).

Glossary

Culinary terms may vary according to regional dialect. The practice of transliterating Arabic in different ways also gives rise to variation in the spelling of food terms. The following terms appear here as they have been spelled in the text.

arak: anise-flavored distilled alcohol
aseed: stiff water and flour dough eaten with special, highly flavorful sauces and soups
baba ghannouj: a dip made from grilled eggplant mixed with *tahini* and lemon and eaten with Arabic pita bread
bagiah: Yemeni dish of falafel-like patties eaten with bread and special sauce
basturma: beef preserved with a coating of mixed spices, usually served in paper-thin slices as *mezzeh*
bulghur: cracked wheat available in fine, medium, and coarse grain
dehen (also *qawahrma*): pieces of lamb, sometimes beef, traditionally cooked and preserved in the fat from sheep tails in the manner of confit
faraykee: green wheat kernels roasted over an open fire making them greenish brown in color and smoky in flavor

fatoot: Arabic bread dribbled with clarified butter and liquid smoke and covered with meat broth

fattoush: originally a village salad mixed with baked or fried Arabic pita-bread pieces

galaba: pieces of meat, usually lamb, sauteed with vegetables, originally Yemeni but now widespread in the Detroit area

halal: term applied to meat slaughtered according to Islamic law

harissa: baked semolina, butter, and milk soaked with a syrup of sugar, honey, and water

hummus: a dip of mashed chick peas with *tahini* and lemon eaten with Arabic pita bread

kalaj: cream-filled thin dough fried and covered with sugar syrup

kamuni: a special combination of spices and rose petals

kanafa: a cheese and semolina confection served warm with rose-flavored syrup

katayef: crepe filled with cheese or nuts and fried

khubuz markook: mountain thin bread

kibbeh: pounded or finely ground meat, traditionally lamb, mixed with bulghur

kibbeh nayee: raw lamb

kishik: yogurt, wheat, and milk fermented and dried in cones

kofte: ground meat, traditionally lamb, mixed with onions, spices, and parsley for grilling

labanieh: custard with fruit

labneh: drained yogurt with consistency of sour cream

lahmajoun: Middle Eastern type of pizza, best known in America as its Armenian variant of the same name

maftool: a grainlike pasta resembling couscous

mahalabiah: custard with fruit

mamoul: molded semolina cookies filled with nuts or dates

mansef: a celebratory dish of rice topped with chunks of lamb cooked in *kishik,* nuts, and moistened with broth

maraq: robust lamb broth often eaten with *aseed*

ma'soub: baked flour and water dough eaten by dipping pieces into hot clarified butter and honey

molokiyeh: mucilaginous green leaf in the mallow family, usually associated with Egyptian cuisine

mujaddara: lentils with rice and onions

pacha: individual-sized "pockets" of tripe filled with rice and spices, Chaldean holiday food

pita: also called Syrian bread, Arab bread, or pocket bread

qawahrma (also *dehen*): lamb traditionally preserved in the fat from sheep tails in the manner of confit

sabaya: multilayered flaky pastry lavished with clarified butter and honey

sahawig: sauce with cumin and hot pepper

sajj: convex metal dome used for baking flat bread

samboosa: fried triangles of thin dough wrapped around mixture of ground lamb and spices or dates, coconut, and raisins

shafoot: souplike dish of yogurt with garlic, hot peppers, cilantro, cumin, liquid smoke, and pieces of Arabic bread

soujouk: Middle Eastern sausage

tabbouli: salad made of tomatoes, mint, parsley, cracked wheat (*bulghur*), and other vegetables

tahini: sesame-seed paste

tarator: sauce made with *tahini,* lemon, and garlic

toorshi: pickled vegetables with turmeric

yerba maté: a bitter, slightly smoky tealike drink made from the leaves of a small evergreen tree grown only in the semitropical lowlands of Brazil, Paraguay, and Argentina

zatar: thyme, or a spice mixture that includes thyme

zurbian: rice with lamb, potatoes, yogurt, garlic, and spices

References

Abraham, Sameer, Nabeel Abraham, and Barbara Aswad. 1983. The Southend: An Arab Muslim Working-Class Community. In *Arabs in the New World: Studies on Arab-American Communities,* edited by Sameer Abraham and Nabeel Abraham 164–81.

Abraham, Sameer, and Nabeel Abraham. 1983. *Arabs in the New World: Studies on Arab-American Communities.* Detroit: Center for Urban Studies, Wayne State University.

Abrahams, Roger D. 1980. Folklore. *Harvard Encyclopedia of American Ethnic Groups,* edited by Stephen Thernstrom. Cambridge: Harvard University Press.

Agócs, Carol. 1981. Ethnic Settlement in a Metropolitan Area: A Typology of Communities. *Ethnicity* 8:127–48.

Ahdab-Yehia, May. 1983. The Lebanese Maronites: Patterns of Continuity and Change. In *Arabs in the New World: Studies on Arab-American Communities,* edited by Sameer Abraham and Nabeel Abraham, 148–62.

Alford, Jeffrey, and Naomi Duguid. 1995. On the Flatbread Trail. *Aramco World* 46 (5):16–25.

Barth, Fredrik. 1969. *Ethnic Groups and Interethnic Relations.* Oslo: Universitetsforlaget.

Goody, Jack. 1982. *Cooking, Cuisine and Class. A Study in Comparative Sociology.* Cambridge: Cambridge University Press.

Gordon, Milton M. 1964. *Assimilation in American Life: The Role of Race, Religion and National Origins.* New York: Oxford University Press.

Halpern, Joel M. 1958. *A Serbian Village.* New York: Columbia University Press.

Hamady, Mary Laird. 1987. *Lebanese Mountain Cookery.* Boston: David R. Godine.

Hannerz, Ulf. 1975. Ethnicity and Opportunity in Urban America. In *Urban Ethnicity,* edited by Abner Cohen, 37–76. London: Routledge.

Ing, Daisy. 1976. *The Best of Baghdad Cooking, With Treats from Teheran.* New York: Saturday Review Press and E. P. Dutton.

Luxner, Larry. 1995. The South American Leaf. *Aramco World* 46 (6):28–29.

Maclagan, Ianthe. 1994. Food and Gender in a Yemeni Community. In *Culinary Cultures of the Middle East,* edited by Sami Zubaida and Richard Tapper, 159–72.

Mintz, Sidney W. 1989. Food and Culture: An Anthropological View. In *Completing the Food Chain,* edited by P. M. Hirschoff and N. G. Kotler, 114–20. Washington, D.C.: Smithsonian Institution Press.

Moerman, Michael. 1965. Ethnic Identification in a Complex Society: Who Are Lue? *American Anthropologist* 67:1215–30.

Nagata, Judith A. 1974. What Is a Malay? Situational Selection of Ethnic Identity in a Plural Society. *American Ethnologist* 1:331–50.

Okamura, Jonathan Y. 1981. Situational Ethnicity. *Ethnic and Racial Studies* 4:452–65.

Perry, Charles. 1994. The Taste for Layered Bread among the Nomadic Turks and the Central Asian Origins of Baklava. In *Culinary Cultures of the Middle East,* edited by Sami Zubaida and Richard Tapper, 87–91.

Roden, Claudia. 1972. *Book of Middle Eastern Food.* New York: Alfred A. Knopf.

—. 1988. Middle Eastern Cooking: The Legacy. *Aramco World* 39 (2):2–3.

Sengstock, Mary. 1982. *Chaldean-Americans: Changing Conceptions of Ethnic Identity.* New York: Center for Migration Studies.

—. 1983. Detroit's Iraqi-Chaldeans: A Conflicting Conception of Identity. In *Arabs in the New World: Studies on Arab-American Communities,* edited by Sameer Abraham and Nabeel Abraham, 136–46.

Staub, Shalom. 1989. *Yemenis in New York City: The Folklore of Ethnicity.* Philadelphia: Balch Institute Press.

Tapper, Richard. 1994. Blood, Wine and Water: Social and Symbolic Aspects of Drinks and Drinking in the Islamic Middle East. In *Culinary Cultures of the Middle East,* edited by Sami Zubaida and Richard Tapper, 215–31.

Zubaida, Sami. 1994a. National, Communal and Global Dimensions in Middle Eastern Food Cultures. In *Culinary Cultures of the Middle East,* edited by Sami Zubaida and Richard Tapper, 33–45.

—. 1994b. Rice in the Culinary Cultures of the Middle East. In *Culinary Cultures of the Middle East,* edited by Sami Zubaida and Richard Tapper, 93–104.

Zubaida, Sami, and Richard Tapper, eds. 1994. *Culinary Cultures of the Middle East.* London: I. B. Tauris.

CHAPTER 5
PATERSON'S HOT TEXAS WIENER TRADITION
Timothy Lloyd

Introduction

Twenty miles northwest of midtown Manhattan, Paterson, New Jersey, is the home of the Hot Texas Wiener. Each year, the members of the many cultural communities who populate this multicultural, multilingual city eat hundreds of thousands of deep-fried beef hot dogs, topped with spicy mustard, chopped onions, and a distinctive chili sauce.

Hot Texas Wieners are restaurant food, served at several dozen establishments throughout, but mostly limited to, Paterson and its neighboring cities. Greeks own a great many of these restaurants, but though the Hot Texas Wiener's chili sauce owes more to Greece than it does to Texas, the wiener is not locally thought of as a Greek food. Hot Texas Wieners are working people's food: they are inexpensive, and most of the older Hot Texas Wiener restaurants, including some no longer in business, were specifically located near industrial plants or along important truck routes through Paterson.

And, of course, Hot Texas Wiener restaurants are workplaces themselves. They are the home of several distinctive occupational traditions, and have been important immigrant-welcoming and economic-development sites for the Greeks and others who have worked there. Much less well-known than other American regional foodways, such as the New England clambake, the Southern fish fry, or the Southwestern barbecue, the Hot Texas Wiener is the most locally distinctive food tradition in the Paterson area, recognized, remembered, and argued about in loving and educated detail by present and former Patersonians.

In August 1994, I investigated the Paterson-area Hot Texas Wiener tradition by interviewing Nick Doris, a Greek-born part-owner of the Hot Grill on Lexington Avenue in Clifton, and Chris Betts, who with his brothers operated the Falls View Grill in Paterson.

The Hot Texas Wiener and its preparation

In its simplest, classic form, the Hot Texas Wiener is an all-beef hot dog "blanched" or par-cooked in 350-degree vegetable oil in a fry basket for a few minutes, cooked by another hot vegetable-oil bath in a tilted steel pan until done, and then placed in a bun, topped (in strict order) with a spicy, ballpark-style mustard, chopped onions, and a chili sauce containing ground beef, tomatoes, more onion, and a "secret" blend of spices, including (I believe) cayenne, cinnamon, allspice, and cumin. Hot Texas Wieners are available with any combination of these "classic" toppings (e.g., without onions, with only chili, and the like) as well as pickle relish and sauerkraut. The chili sauce is also sold in refrigerated pint- and quart-size containers, to take home.

The shorthand jargon used in wiener restaurants to describe orders for the many possible variations on the Hot Texas Wiener is a distinctive part of this local tradition. If you were to enter one of the area's many Hot

Timothy Lloyd, 'Paterson's Hot Texas Wiener Tradition', *Folklife Center News* 17 (1995), 8–11. Reprinted with permission of the author.

Texas Wiener restaurants and ask for "one," you would be served the food item I've described. If you were to ask for "a hot dog without onions," you would hear your counter-person yell back to the preparation line, "one no onions," and you would receive a wiener with mustard and chili sauce.

If you were to ask for "four hot dogs, two with everything, one with just mustard, and one with everything but no onions," you would hear your counter-person yell back, "one mustard, one no onions on four." "On (number)" at the end of a Hot Texas Wiener order indicates the total number of wieners ordered; in the example, subtracting the number of wieners ordered with special topping combinations (two, in this case) will tell those on the preparation line the number of wieners (two) to be served "with everything." On a simpler order, such as four wieners without mustard, the counterperson may shout back to the preparation line, "Four no mustard four," to emphasize the total number ordered.

Like many occupational traditions, the system of jargon used in Hot Texas Wiener restaurants has both a practical and an artistic importance. Practically, it standardizes orders so that they can be communicated clearly by voice (for the most part orders are not written down), especially in the midst of a lunchtime rush; but beyond this, knowing and using this folk speech has become the distinctive mark of the Hot Texas Wiener working world, and is stylistic evidence for those in the business of insider knowledge and occupational accomplishment.

The most common side dish for Hot Texas Wiener orders are French fries, which used to be ordered only plain or with ketchup, but in recent days are more often ordered with wiener-style toppings—mustard and chili sauce, and so on—and are also often served with gravy in a mid-Atlantic, urban style. Hot Texas Wiener restaurants customarily also serve a number of other foods, including hamburgers, cheeseburgers, bacon-lettuce-and-tomato sandwiches, and the like, along with soups and salads.

Some of these have been served at Hot Texas Wiener restaurants for many years. According to Chris Betts and Nick Doris, the five main foods of the old-time menu were wieners, hamburgers, cheeseburgers, French fries, and roast beef sandwiches. At Libby's, one of Paterson's oldest Hot Texas Wiener restaurants, a photograph visible today on the Pepsi machine, depicting that establishment in the 1940s, shows a long sign running along the restaurant's roof listing these five items in large letters. The other items on the typical Hot Texas Wiener restaurant menu are newer arrivals, added to satisfy a clientele more interested in "lighter" eating. Wieners, however, are by far the most important product, in terms both of sales volume and of local cultural significance.

Hot Texas Wieners are served in several dozen restaurants in the Paterson-Clifton area that specialize in them, most of which are owned and operated by Greek Americans, and many of which have been in business for some time. People in the Paterson-area Hot Texas Wiener business told me that this food is served only in the Paterson area and has never been successful elsewhere, but I have learned from natives of western Connecticut and Allentown, Pennsylvania, that Hot Texas Wieners are served there also: this probably represents the farthest geographic spread of this tradition to date.

The customary local term identifying a Hot Texas Wiener place is "grill," as in the Hot Grill, the Haledon Grill, the Colonial Grill, and so on. This usage is interesting, since the preparation method for Hot Texas Wieners does not include grilling: unlike many other wieners, Hot Texas Wieners are not grilled or boiled (in Hot Texas Wiener restaurant jargon, the "grill" is the part of the preparation line devoted to hamburgers and cheeseburgers) but, as described earlier, are deep-fried in two stages.

Most, if not all, Hot Texas Wiener businesses include the concocting of what is regarded within the business as its most important ingredient, the spice mixture for the chili sauce. At the Hot Grill, and at the wiener businesses with which Chris Betts was and is involved, and at many—if not all—other local wiener restaurants, only owners know how to perform this exacting task correctly and consistently. Both Chris Betts and Nick Doris, in talking about their work, repeatedly referred to this mixture as the "secret recipe."

As we discussed wiener preparation, both Betts and Doris listed a number of the ingredients that are included in the spice mixture: cayenne, chili powder, cumin, cinnamon, and the like. What it wouldn't have been appropriate for them to tell me was the proportions of each, and, perhaps, some especially important secret ingredient. In discussing the matter of secret recipes, they agreed that while the recipe for a given business was, or should be, consistent over time, the recipes differed from business to business.

As evidence for the importance of these recipes and their secrecy, Chris Betts told a story about his contribution to his son's Haledon Grill business, which opened in the late 1980s. The contract that established the business arrangement between Betts, his son, and his son's partner stipulated that Betts would not provide the spice recipe to the partners until the business had been in operation for five years, so he could be certain that the partnership would last. Until that time, Betts himself mixed the spices.

A brief history of the Hot Texas Wiener

According to Chris Betts, the Hot Texas Wiener was invented around 1924 by "an old Greek gentleman" who owned a hot dog "stand" (a restaurant-business term for a small restaurant) that sat ten or fifteen customers at a counter on Paterson Street in downtown Paterson. This gentleman was experimenting with various chili-type sauces to serve on his hot dogs, and apparently drew upon his own culinary heritage for the first Hot Texas Wiener chili-sauce recipe.

As Betts and Nick Doris mentioned when I questioned them about the sauce's origins, it resembles Greek spaghetti sauce, which contains tomatoes, meat, and a similar combination of spices. As Betts's account also suggests, the chili sauce is considered the crucial ingredient in this new food, its invention defining and separating the Hot Texas Wiener from the hot dogs the "old Greek gentleman" was serving before.

Two important aspects of this early history remain undocumented: the name of the "old Greek gentleman" and his business, and his reasons for naming his new food the "Hot Texas Wiener." Documentary research in newspapers, other local periodicals, and business directories of the period, as well as interviews with older workers, may well identify the Hot Texas Wiener's inventor and his place of business, although smaller businesses in working-class areas did not often receive much coverage in mainstream publications.

The specific reasons for his choice of "Texas," unfortunately, are more likely to remain unexplained. I suppose that, seeking to give a unique and, for Paterson, exotic name to his new and somewhat spicy food — itself characterized by a sauce whose name ("chili") carries Western, Latino, and cowboy associations — he might have chosen the "Texas" designation to give his creation what today we'd call an "image."

For several years the Paterson Street location was the major outlet for Hot Texas Wieners, but in 1936 a Paterson Street employee named William Pappas left and opened Libby's Hot Grill on McBride Avenue and Wayne Street, across the street from the Great Falls on the Passaic. Libby's — still in operation today in the same location — was extremely successful, in part because of the quality of its food and in part because of its location, near to its clientele of workers in Paterson's textile mills and other plants, and on one of the main highways to and from New York City.

In its heyday, Libby's employed over thirty people. Several of these employees took the knowledge and skills they gained at Libby's into their own Hot Texas Wiener businesses. For example, former Libby's employees opened Johnny and Hanges, on River Street, in the north end of Paterson, in 1940, and many long-time employees in other Hot Texas Wiener businesses received valuable experience at Libby's. (Johnny and Hanges is still in operation, though under different ownership.)

In May 1949, Paul Agrusti, another Libby's employee, left to open the Falls View Grill — two blocks east of Libby's, at the bottom of the hill where Market and Spruce Streets intersect, even more centrally located in the

Paterson Falls mill area — with three Greek brothers, Chris, George, and William Betts. After they returned from military service in World War II, the Bettses had gained experience in the Hot Texas Wiener business by leasing the Olympic Grill — which sat directly across McBride Avenue from Libby's — from John Patrelis, who had founded it in 1940. Also with an excellent location, convenient to working people from the mills and to major highways of the time, the Falls View was also quite successful for many years.

For two years, 1964 to 1965, the partners also operated a second location — the Falls View Grill East — in Elmwood Park, east of Paterson. Though the Bettses sold the business after a few years, it is still in operation as the Riverview Grill. Thus the three most-remembered Hot Texas Wiener restaurants of the post- World War II period — Libby's, the Olympic, and the Falls View — were located within a stone's throw of one another, of the mill buildings which were once the most important working-class workplaces in town, and one of the major east-west highways through Paterson.

Paul Agrusti left the Falls View in 1978 to open the Colonial Grill on Chamberlain Avenue; his son Leonard now runs it. The Betts brothers sold the Falls View business in 1984, but its buyers were not successful in operating the business and sold it in 1988. The building, in the midst of Paterson's historic manufacturing district, now houses a Burger King. Chris Betts's son now is part owner of the Haledon Grill on Haledon Avenue.

Nick Doris emigrated to the U.S. from Greece in 1954, and began working as a French-fry cook at the Falls View just after his arrival. Over the next several years he worked his way into knowledge of the whole occupation. In 1961, he and three partners — another Greek, Peter Leonidas, who has since passed away, and two Italians, Carlo Mendola and Dominic Sportelli — opened the Hot Grill on the site of Gabe's, a car lot and Hot Texas Wiener operation on Lexington Avenue, just over the city line into Clifton.

Since that opening day the Hot Grill has become quite successful, and is recognized throughout the area as perhaps the most authentic of Paterson's many Hot Texas Wiener restaurants. As Chris Betts said of the Hot Grill, "We were the old champs, and they're the new champs." The Hot Grill now employs thirty-five people, and the partners own two other restaurants, one serving Hot Texas Wieners, and the other more of a full-service restaurant.

Significance of the Hot Texas Wiener tradition

For many Patersonians, especially those who have lived in the area for some time, Hot Texas Wieners mean home. This "meaning" works in several different dimensions. Patersonians eat a great many wieners, of course, but they do much more: they may remember the time they met their spouses at a wiener counter, they may recall regular family trips to the neighborhood grill, they may recount regular lunchtime gatherings of working people at their favorite grill near work, they may chart the genealogy of wiener businesses emerging from one another over the past seventy years, they may know the neighborhoods of Paterson by the grills that carry their name and mark them, they may argue about which grill has the best wieners and whether wieners or the places that serve them were better in the "good old days," and, if they move away, they may make a beeline for the old familiar wiener place when they come home for vacations or holidays.

The Hot Texas Wiener tradition shows one of the ways in which people, faced with the demands of making a new way of life, creatively adapt and transform the cultural traditions with which they were raised. In Paterson, a Greek-derived food was made into the centerpiece and most important ingredient of a local culinary and occupational world, perhaps losing its specific ethnic associations — at least, in the setting of Hot Texas Wiener grills — but gaining over time a broader, more intense regional identification. Patersonians have made a new tradition using the raw materials of an old one.

CHAPTER 6
A NEW ASCENSION OF REGIONAL FOOD
Konrad Köstlin

Shopping and eating with a good conscience

There has been a heightened awareness of the impact of regional food, and also of traditional food, on identity in recent decades, and different aspects have been a matter of public discourse for some time.[1] Nowadays the debate about regional food tends to centre on modern ethics, with the aim of supporting small producers and entrepreneurs, and of strengthening regional economies, so that they are ecofriendly on the one hand, and support local identification demands on the other. The consumption of food has taken on the dimension of ethical advisor in everyday life, and also with regard to the care of one's own body. Eating and shopping have thus become a fact of modern ethics, and the performance of consumption with a good conscience has social and ecological implications, which are expressed in cultural forms and in culture's central codes. One of the newer code words is sustainability, something which is now related to our conscience.[2] As part of our mental waste management, the 'better life' seems to be linked to shopping and eating with a good conscience. Since shopping and consuming belong to modern identity practices, it is not only the choice of food that is important but much more so the stories and the arguments behind the choice that is made. These include matters such as the level of carbon-footprint and the waste of water involved, as well as logistical and transportation aspects, the methods of production used for fruit such as tomatoes, and the moral and socio-cultural aspects connected with the breeding of animals (animals as our brothers and sisters), and the production of crops. Products with ecological and social and cultural surplus-value are especially relevant in this context. Thus the Austrian government, among others, tries to convince people that by taking the right (Austrian) product from the food-rack, the consumer has the power to heal the world, while at the same time being a cultural-nationalistic shelf-patriot. So food has got new and manifold meanings.

It is noteworthy that the individual citizen is now being made responsible for the quality and state of the environment, for social working conditions in the surrounding region (and abroad), and for the appearance and physiognomy of the landscape, and the health of the region. The correct reach into the shelf to grasp the required products should lead to biological, regional and, as a matter of course, fair trade products — which are, as a matter of logic — more expensive than ordinary ones (whatever that may mean). Ordinary shopping, which means that a person buys the goods as cheaply as possible — which is the usual practice in most European countries — is thrashed in media discourses and food journals.

Responsibilities

Those who do not follow the new moral code in regard to the food which they consume are declassified — they are not regarded as being good citizens and they are disparaged. The making of the individual responsible

Konrad Köstlin, 'A New Ascension of Regional Food' in Patricia Lysaght (ed.), *Food and Meals at Cultural Crossroads: Proceedings of the 17th Conference of the International Commission for the Ethnological Food Research, Oslo, Nowray, September 15-19,* 2008 (Oslo: Novus Press, 2010), pp. 36–45.

Reprinted with permission from the author.

for the status of the environment worldwide seems to be a new trend in that it amounts to an outsourcing of responsibility for the management of the environment, a trend that can be observed in many fields. Textiles made from natural fibres such as local hemp and linen are being promoted since genetically-modified cotton imported from China, or the use of defoliants or herbicides such as Agent Orange, and the abuse of water in manufacturing, and in crop production and management, are under discussion and are being questioned. Bio-cosmetics which reproduced *'tierleidfrei'* (that is, without causing pain to animals), and bearing the national proof-seal *'Austria Bio Garantie'*, are increasingly found on the market, and finally, a ban on child labour has to be implemented.

All of this can be subsumed under the label 'regional quality'. Nearness has become the absolute preference. Since products (even biological ones) are often carried long distances around the world, the debate about CO_2 emissions intensifies the conflict between the local and the global. Since twenty percent of all of these emissions are connected to nutrition, the choice which people exercise in relation to food is said to be pivotal. And since men are supposed to be not only the grill-masters, but also to eat more meat than women, they are held to be responsible, to a greater degree than the female segment of world population, for the decline of the environment.

Region

It is not only in relation to food that the region has gained a new reality in western countries, as it is perceived as providing a symbolic vision of possible regional autonomy, resulting from moderation and conservatism as a form of deceleration. This includes ideas about autonomy and autarky in terms of electricity and energy, and, in some areas, concerning gas and oil production, for example, and runs contrary to the complexity of the world. It creates a microcosm, on the one hand, and it operates worldwide on the other. It offers energy-saving lamps instead of the former high-energy bulbs. It makes people feel responsible and oftentimes even guilty when using an old car or an old refrigerator and supports them when they buy new replacements.

Food which is called regional has reached a new dimension of explicitness. New tendencies – mostly called 'trends' – such as the interpretation of food as regional, national, ethnic, confession-, gender- or age-related, indicate the end of expressivity in food-consumption, and even attach to themselves new contours and characteristics, especially with regard to traditional local food and its explicit dimensions.

Identity, confessings, the body and the world

The selection and consumption of food has become one of the most important fields for the expression of self. And it is also one of the last remaining areas in which people can express their own identity by shaping their bodies in fitness studios, or by means of ascetic behaviour in accordance with certain ideals. This new form of individual competence has been invented in urban milieus. The urban connection is the most important reference point as preferences and trends have their roots in the metropolises and are mediated by them in their role as trend setters. This has to do with the new emphasis which has been placed on the body. Since people are told to be responsible for their bodies, the shaping of the body is a matter of discourse and thus not something which is self-evident to the individual any longer.

Following on that, the tendency toward the privatisation of the health-care-system can also be observed. The more the individual is made responsible for his health, the more food becomes a matter of debate. The discourses and the everyday practices put the body in focus: wellness and fitness, the shaping of the body, tattooing, piercing, colouring, and so on, as well as food, play an identity-producing role. Food turns out to be an expression of the individual's personality and his or her life-style, and is communicated as such. Thus one has to talk about it, explain it, and even defend one's own food habits. We live in a society of confessors who apparently have celebrated life-styles, and food is one of the few prominent means of expressing it. Food and food preferences can also serve as an expression of life-style which separates the sexes, especially if the individual's responsibility for his or her body is taken into account.

Since the expression of identity has reached the body as a whole, the body is one of the last remaining areas in which people feel a sense of self-determination and autonomy. In this respect western societies can be termed confession societies (with the confession sometimes printed on the front of a T-shirt).

Macs

Intellectuals are eager to blame MacDonalds for levelling the manifold nature and plurality of world kitchens. But it is also true that the 'Mac-attack' has helped to emphasise and to mark the (mostly lightly adapted) traditional kitchens which are articulated as being 'regional' and 'authentic'. The Mac-menu has spread all over the world with only slight modifications being evident with regard to its US descent. In this respect, a global interpretation is more than an excursus. From a biologist's point of view the Mac meal can be read and interpreted from a completely different perspective – one which converts the menu into a symbol of globalisation. Jana Vomosi, a biologist from Calgary, has counted a combination of twenty different food species in that menu. These include wheat, spices, milk, onions, pepper and coffee, potatoes, mustard, and so on. They all have been cultivated by people in different places on this earth. So the menu can be seen as exemplifying the broad repertoire which has been tapped into, by making non-edible stuff eatable by means of cooking and softening. 'So mankind became a general eater in the broadest sense'.[3] The artistry of interpretation!

Urban intellectuals

It is mostly in intellectual discourse that the preference for regional cuisine is explicitly stated. Ordinary people eat local or non-local food without offering explanations for the choices which they make. They just do it. They approach food in a general way without discussing the fact. In strict opposition to this applied general approach to food, people very often *think* about regional food, as a result of advertising campaigns run by regional or national marketing companies. Also, regional food can include different species of ingredients which can have different origins, but which have become adapted to the region in the course of time, and have become an obvious and accepted part of the region's food since then. The self-evident is something we do not normally argue about.

From that very point, that is, once food is *marked* as regional, a new spice – a cultural one – is added. The cultural taste of an ordinary dumpling changes when it represents a regional speciality on a menu-card and is thereby converted into a Tyrolean dumpling. Regional food has a label with a close connection to our lifestyles. These lifestyles are so demanding that they include the regional as a very special taste. The description 'regional' has left behind the idea of home and regionalism of the 1970s, even if a relic of this taste may still exist. It has lost its character of home-cooked and traditional food, which was planted, raised, and harvested nearby, and sold in a local market. Regional food has undergone a process of adaptation similar to that of exotic cuisines, and is to be cooked 'light' in restaurants, as a matter of 're-interpretation'. It is only on special occasions that it follows traditional recipes, such as at Christmas or at Thanksgiving, or with regard to the goose on St. Martin's Day, when, as part of a local ritual, people from neighbouring districts travel to Slovensky Grob, a village North of Bratislava and thus not far from Vienna, to eat a goose-meal in an explicitly traditional context.

This way of performing life-style by eating and food consumption is connected with a process of transformation that food has undergone in general terms. It is no more self-evident or, it is at least less self-evident, what people should eat. Eating has become one of the most discussed acts in one's life. Food and nutrition are matters of confession and expressive performance – as the set of designed modern water-bottles show (like the expensive water from Voss/Norway).[4]

Celebration

Celebration has thus become the keyword in relation to food consumption. Anybody who strolls through a market in a capital city will immediately be aware that there is not just one trend – such as the regional one. The main idea is to have authentic food – and this *may* be a regional one, from the region nearby, but it can also have another authentic origin with reference to its brand. These origins, which are marked as, and declared to be, authentic, are often a matter of worldwide consent. Only the slow food person, as part of the strict observation of his ideals, will insist on local authenticity which is conferred by the home region, and which includes being bred/grown locally, green grass, fresh water from a creek, humane slaughtering, and fair trade.

The story of authenticity

It is not only regional food that undergoes an apotheosis, a form of ascension. It is any kind of food which is linked to a plausible and convincing story, such as that connecting Mediterranean cuisine with olive oil, or cuisines with vegetarian or vegan orientations, or those whose authenticity is conveyed by stressing their biological origins, the kosher butchering mode used, and so on. This food authenticity – regardless of which kind of authenticity is involved – overlays the body of the individual. In the demand for authenticity, individuals are confronted with the need to select food. This involves a permanent type of discourse which the individual conducts with himself, a soliloquy or monologue. Discourse also means that the media involve the public in dealing with the body and its relation to food.

Gender and the body

A scene some days ago at a party: Two young men aged around twenty-five years sitting on a couch and talking about the best way to prepare pasta. Cooking has reached a position of special interest. And it is for the men to discuss the oil which has to be added to the pasta after it has been drained. This is the result not just of Jamie Oliver's 'Naked Chef' food programmes on TV, and his cookery books, but also because he is young, some would say charismatic, and courageous, and that he cooks simple meals of the highest quality. On looking through TV-Magazines, we find many slightly-different versions of Jamie Oliver. Cooking is described as being 'cool' and the cooking entertainers verify the attribute – they are cool. They put the meat in a plastic satchel and shake it until the marinade has reached the innermost part of the meat. Kitchen-barbarians? Fashion-victims?

TV cookery programmes reflect a male-oriented world in general; women are seldom to be seen in this context and seem to be a kind of decoration in these surroundings. Male writers are cooking on TV, as if writing and cooking were two sides of the same coin. So cooking men are artists; they do not just cook; they interpret, paraphrase and re-interpret the traditional cuisine anew.

Thus the pattern is as follows: Professional cooks, having experienced haute cuisine in a large establishment abroad, regularly return home to work: 'Here is a great master, who knows all the cuisines of the world, returned to his regional roots'. This 'back to the roots' elevates regional cuisine to the status of a new cuisine, a modern one, and locates it side by side with all the other cuisine movements of our day. With courage and witticism Buchinger offers forgotten, despised dishes, which he interprets with special lightness'.[5]

The regional is one of the many trends which are celebrated today – and if it is celebrated as such, it is mainly done by men. Men have often conquered the hearth-place since women seem to deny that they cook a 'real' meal. This is the point – a 'real' meal, regardless of the fact that women still do the main part of everyday-cooking – in Austria this is around eighty percent. The male celebration is important in that it again raises the gender question in relation to work in the home.[6]

The gender relationship has been converted into a development in which men prepare the special – even the regional – because it is not the food eaten everyday anymore. The extraordinary: A small, old country-*Gasthaus*, far away, no traffic, and only hand-cut French fries are offered, as well as entrails which, in a contemporary female context, are difficult to place. If the ascension of regional food exists, it is mainly a male domain. Men are the ones who feel creative and eager to experience adventure. Adult evening cookery courses are booked mostly by men.

Food poetry

Knowledge of regional gastronomy becomes important, not only in order to know its contours but also to be able to decipher a meal and its ingredients. *Eat Smart in Sicily* — a scientific book published by The University of Wisconsin Press — is subtitled 'How to Decipher a Menu. Know the Market Foods & Embark on a Tasting Adventure'. The book offers 'an historical overview of the people who have lived there and their contributions to Sicilian cuisine, with attention given to the fare distinct to the villages and urban centers of Sicily's four regions. A helpful guide to Sicilian menus, with English translations of Italian (or Sicilian) words, makes ordering food in Sicily an easy and immediately rewarding experience'.[7] This kind of food-poetry is frequently found – it is the story behind the food, it is the culture, that we eat. And it shows that disciplines like ours are the storytellers of our times. New cookery books tell stories about the country and its history, they illustrate the region by means of food, helping to make life and experiences more interesting, and they colour what is obvious and self-evident and convert it into a highlight, an event.

Identity debates

All of this is part of an identity-debate complex. Sustainability is related to social compatibility and is a matter of cultural acceptance with regard to who has produced the food, where, and under which conditions it has been produced. So food preferences may be seen as taking a position in relation to the problems of our world. Men — as the ones who prefer meat — can be accused of actively destroying the rainforests, while those who prefer green fodder are its saviours. Food preferences depict the individual's position towards the world. Explicit environmental awareness is a modern attitude that includes food as a manifestation of one's life-style, as well as one's body awareness. Eating behaviour is a part of our biographical exposure of the body, and illustrates our personal responsibility for its good shape and condition.

The ascension of regional food is one of the many determinants which combines the many food-trends that we know of. It is the search for authenticity which has become a basic factor in relation to food. Authentic, as a term, serves to describe the food as well as the person who eats it. Thus food has to be authentic, as the marker 'regional' promises.

Ethnologists

When we insist, as ethnologists, only on the regional, we have fallen into the trap of our 'deformation professionelle'. Our interest in regional food should not mean that we neglect existing food trends, such as convenience food, chilled food, take-away-food, ethnic and exotic food, functional food, anti-ageing and best-agers food, low-carb food, anti-fat food, organic and bio-food, and so on.

Many modes of consuming food are evident today. People — and it seems to be especially females — eat more often on the street, and in buses and trams, than was the case formerly. They eat snacks, fast food, or food-to-go at the baker's or butcher's shop which often serves meals, while men are standing – standing fast and elementary – as Ulrich Tolksdorf has pointed out.[8] Standing at snack boutiques, they eat more meat-oriented food, and prefer sausages. But the consumers can celebrate an explicit performance and an expressive consumption of food, which can include the so-called regional variety as one of the options available. And more and more people have adopted multiple competences in this regard, depending on the context.

'Regional' is a vague myth of the origin of good food, with the prediction that we can, thereby, root ourselves in a certain region[9] — contrary to the fact that our culture usually intensively masks the processing of food. People forget that meat does not grow at the butcher's shop. If an open air museum shows the slaughtering of an animal or the preparation of fish for eating, visitors regularly yell in shock at the sight.

Regional food has changed its character in recent decades; according to new contexts it has got new contours and raised new implications. As a result, it incorporates more than just simply nutrition from local sources and traditional localism.

Firstly, it has become part of a worldview and a philosophy of life. It is often a confession, influenced by the green movement with regard to the situation of our world in general. Visiting the shelf with regional food in a foodstore makes (some) people feel good, and amounts to the shelf informing you that you are in the right place.

Secondly, it is not only the green aspect of biological and healthy food that is included. Regional food belongs also to the celebration of the local, as is evident from the steep ascent of festivals, songs and folksy customs, and this may be interpreted as a counter-strategy to globalisation. In this respect, local food can mean that one grounds oneself symbolically in the local.

Thirdly, it can be argued that it is 'foreign' food which is a symbol of conquering globalisation. But that has helped to initiate the ascent of locality and its food in general, and has thus created a new market for regional food. MacDonalds as a 'Fast Food' phenomenon catapulted its European answer, 'Slow Food', into the market, as an expression of European anti-Americanism, and as a symbol of a strict distinction in cultural styles. All three aspects are intertwined in manifold ways.

Fourthly, the connection between sustainability and good conscience is influenced by the new ethics movement and so produces a new dimension of food relish. Food enjoyment is closely connected to responsibility towards the surrounding environment. This is also a part of the new dimension of discourses on *Heimat*, in which our former friendly perspective on cows has been converted into one of viewing them as the producers of CO_2, which is harmful to the environment.

Fifthly, the keyword which connects all four dimensions of regional food is *celebration*. The cultural setting in which regional food is to be consumed is a certain high-value time, which we call leisure-time. This time has become more and more pivotal for the expression of the self. Today, leisure-time is the cultural time in which we represent ourselves by means of eating, clothes, sport, and consumption in general. The criteria for being designated regional food are different according to scientific literature, market analyses, and popular meaning. Three dimensions of quality are involved: provenance of ingredients, product quality, and process quality – which refer – as already said – to the social aspects of the production process. Local actors share the definition of regional food that goes beyond the origin of ingredients or the location of processing – they are the interpretative authorities, and sometimes ethnologists are their storytellers – if the story fits in with their project.

The world can be seen in different ways. It is not only former ethnographers who have blamed women, especially mothers, for destroying the ethnic culture of the group. Among the German-speaking majority in the district of South Tyrol, Italy, women were held to have given up their German ethnic food traditions by opening the kitchen door to Italian spaghetti, which has penetrated the former dumpling-type cuisine of the area. A conservative male group in the region, the gun-club members, still avoid eating Italian pizza when wearing their uniforms. Among a Slavonic minority in Saxony, Germany, some of the Sorbs also accuse women of using the German language, the language of the majority, instead of speaking the former mother-tongue 'sorbisch', (Sorbian) which was supposed to be the language of home. So it would seem as if it is often women who are to be blamed for betraying the cause of identity. Consequently. it is then the duty of men to heal the world by promoting regional food in their celebrations.

The re-interpretation of regional food has turned out to be a new invention of food which is baptised as regional, and which includes sustainability as a new form of responsibility for the world in its entirety, and seeks to create this as a new and additional cultural taste of relish.

Notes

1. Köstlin, Konrad, 'Die Revitalisierung regionaler Kost', in *Ethnologische Nahrungsforschung. Vorträge des zweiten Internationalen Symposiums für ethnologische Nahrungsforschung* (= Kansatieteellinen Arkisto 26, Helsinki 1975, 159–66.

2. Zucca, Michela, Dubost, Michel, (eds.), *Learning Sustainability*, Lavis 2002 (= Centro di Ecologia Alpina, Recite II).

3. Vamosi, Jana C., 'Big Mac: The Whole World on Your Plate', http://www.eurekalert.org/pub_releases/2008-02/uoc-bmt020408.php. See also Proches, Serban, Wilson, John R. U., Vamosi, Jana C., Richardson, David M., 'Plant Diversity in the Human Diet: Weak Phylogenetic Signal Indicates Breadth', in *BioScience*, February 2008. http://www.aibs.org/bioscience/index.html.

4. See Köstlin, Konrad, 'Water, Spa and the Western Body: Paradigms, Lifestyles and Cultural Practices', in Lysaght, Patricia, (ed.), *Sanitas per Aquas. Spas, Lifestyles and Foodways*, Innsbruck 2008, 37–55, esp. 48–9.

5. Trebes, Klaus, 'Wo Wiener sich an Wachteln weiden', in *Die Woche* (Wien) vom 9. November 2001.

6. Köstlin, Konrad, 'Neue Männer an den neuen Herden', in *Schweizer Archiv für Volkskunde* 101 (2005), 91–102.

7. Peterson, Joan, Croce, Marcella, *Eat Smart in Sicily*, Madison WI, 2008.

8. Tolksdorf, Ulrich, 'Nahrung – Not und Überfluss', in Konrad Köstlin und Hermann Bausinger, (eds.), *Umgang mit Sachen. Zur Kulturgeschichte des Dinggebrauchs*, Regensburg 1983, 79–91.

9. Tschofen, Bernhard, 'Celebrated Origins: Local Food and Global Knowledge. Comments on the Possibilities of Food Studies in the Age of the World-Wide Web', in Lysaght, Patricia, (ed.), *Food and Celebration: From Fasting to Feasting.* Proceedings of the 13th Conference of the International Commission for Ethnological Food Research, Slovenia 2000, Ljubljana 2002, 101–12.

CHAPTER 7

NEWFOUNDLAND AND LABRADOR ON A PLATE: BED, BREAKFAST, AND REGIONAL IDENTITY

Holly Everett

Introduction

In late July 2002, my husband and I arrived in the Labrador Straits via the Blanc Sablon ferry after staying in bed and breakfast inns (B&Bs) across the island of Newfoundland. Our first stop, setting out from our home in St. John's, was Grand Falls-Windsor in central Newfoundland. Our last stop, before heading back home, would be Battle Harbour, a tiny island not far off the coast of Labrador. Altogether, we would travel over 2,100 kilometres.

Having developed an interest in foodways, and specifically culinary tourism, while studying for my Ph.D. comprehensive exams, I began research on the interplay between government and industry-based culinary tourism initiatives and Newfoundland and Labrador foodways in the summer of 2002. Particularly concerned with how traditional foods were being marketed to and received by tourists from outside the province, the project combined fieldwork with the analysis of electronic and print advertising, government and industry reports, vernacular travelogues on the Internet, survey and qualitative interview data, and tourist ephemera such as promotional brochures and flyers. The fieldwork included participant observation, primarily as a guest at B&Bs across the province, as well as qualitative interviews with tourists, business owners, and employees. All of the B&B hosts knew of my research prior to my arrival and I informed fellow guests upon meeting them.[1] In this discussion, I will focus on two of the B&Bs that so generously hosted me.

As I have studied the development of culinary tourism in the province, I have been increasingly interested in its dialogic aspects. While conducting fieldwork, I witnessed relatively informal social situations that facilitated significant intra- and intercultural exchanges. Such exchanges may also enable communication that supports, personalizes, disrupts, or deconstructs both esoteric and exoteric grand narratives,[2] narratives that utilize a range of vernacular strategies and are bounded by a particular metaculinary universe.[3] In this paper I will discuss the links between food production, place, and identity as manifest in B&Bs on Newfoundland's west coast and the Labrador Straits, focusing on conversations around the breakfast or supper table that provided owners and employees with an opportunity to perform local identities for their guests.[4]

Tourism in Newfoundland and Labrador

Newfoundland and Labrador, Canada's most easterly province, covers 405,720 square kilometres, more than three times the total area of the other Atlantic provinces (New Brunswick, Nova Scotia, and Prince Edward Island) combined. Its population, however, numbered just over 509,148 as of January 1, 2011, compared to

Holly Everett, 'Newfoundland and Labrador on a Plate: Bed, Breakfast, and Regional Identity', *Cuizine: The Journal of Canadian Food Cultures* 3 (2011), 12–22. Reprinted with permission of *Cuizine: The Journal of Canadian Food Cultures/Cuizine: revue des cultures culinaires au Canada* (www.cuizine.mcgill.ca).

Nova Scotia at 942,506, for example.[5] The majority of the province's population lives on the Avalon Peninsula, in or near the provincial capital of St. John's. Other commercial hubs include Grand Falls-Windsor in central Newfoundland, Corner Brook on the island's west coast, and Happy Valley-Goose Bay in central Labrador. A large segment of the population of Newfoundland and Labrador has until recently been employed in various fisheries, working either off or on-shore to procure and process cod, crab, lobster, and shrimp. The cod fishery—the industry that led to the settlement and development of the province—was severely curtailed by a moratorium on fishing northern cod in 1992. The fishing ban, "an economic tragedy of unprecedented proportions," continues to this day, and now includes capelin, salmon, and turbot.[6] Since the devastating moratorium, the province has looked toward high tech development, greater natural resource extraction, and tourism as important growth areas to offset the blow of the dwindling fishery. However, even with a promising economic turn and future prospects fueled by a rapidly developing oil industry, Newfoundland and Labrador suffers from emigration, as financially-strapped residents often leave the east coast for the oil fields of Alberta, one of Canada's wealthiest provinces.

Non-resident travel and tourism spending generated more than $400 million for the province by the end of 2010, representing a steady increase of about $100 million altogether since the late 1990s.[7] Over the last decade, I have witnessed the rapid development of tourism infrastructure as well as award-winning media campaigns that have brought the province to the attention of the wider world. In that time, the province has also worked to establish a brand with wide appeal that distinguishes Newfoundland and Labrador from the myriad other destinations clamouring for consumer attention. In fact, the provincial budget allocation for tourism has more than doubled in the last six years, bringing the figure to $13 million for 2010–2011.[8] Annual tourism campaigns have gone from an almost exclusive focus on "outdoor nature product"[9] to the promotion of nature *and* culture. For a century, the province has been carving a market niche as one of North America's last "unspoiled" destinations, offering a striking, rugged landscape with a unique people and culture to match.[10] As the 2009 provincial travel guide message from former premier Danny Williams states:

> Surprises wait around every corner and the list of things to do is endless. Hike the stunning coastline, visit UNESCO World Heritage sites, or attend a variety of festivals celebrating everything from traditional music, to live theatre, to blueberries and bake apples, to squid. You will be in awe of the graceful whales and majestic icebergs, all while meeting strangers who quickly become friends.[11]

Part of the branding of the province, as the above guide indicates, includes a renewed interest in traditional and emerging foodways that reflects both regional historical development and contemporary sensibilities.

My husband and I first drove across the province and into Labrador in July of 2002. The timing of this travel, during the high season, facilitated direct contact with numerous travelers, as well as observation of the local response to the high demand for tourist services. Travel across the province at this time also allowed me to participate in the first wave of tourism following the unexpected influx of airline passengers to Newfoundland on September 11, 2001, and the film and television premieres of *The Shipping News*, *Random Passage*, and *Rare Birds*, international dramatic productions centering on Newfoundland, all of which were expected to have a significant impact on provincial tourism.[12]

For the purposes of this discussion, I will focus on the region of western Newfoundland and the Labrador Straits as it encompasses a number of the province's major attractions. The island's Viking Trail, as it is called, begins in Deer Lake and boasts Gros Morne National Park at one end and the L'Anse aux Meadows National Historic Site at the tip of Great Northern Peninsula. Both are UNESCO World Heritage Sites. The year 2010 marked the 50th anniversary of the discovery of the L'Anse aux Meadows site, the earliest known European settlement in North America.[13] The main roadway for the area is provincial route 430. Other popular sites on the peninsula include the Port au Choix National Historic site, the Grenfell Historic Properties, and the Burnt Cape Ecological Reserve.

Common routes to the area from beyond the province include travel by ferry from Sydney, Nova Scotia, to Port aux Basques, and flights into Deer Lake. Less frequently, visitors fly into St. John's and drive across the island via rental car. The aforementioned ferry service to the Labrador Straits is also utilized for trips to see the Red Bay National Historic Site and the restored fishing premises of Battle Harbour. Smaller communities along these routes provide accommodation for the overflow from the busier tourist areas, as well as for travelers stopping en route. Moreover, the Main River region, to the east of the Viking Trail, is popular with hunters and fishers, and thus home to a number of lodges. Recreational vehicle (RV) owners sometimes leave their large vehicles and travel ahead by car, spending the night in a hotel or B&B. Together these factors form a dynamic complex of food needs and desires in the area, ranging from people who need food prepared for every meal to people camping in RVs or tents who are making many or all of their own meals.

As a result of both the popularity of the route and the geographical constraints of travel—one must use route 430 to reach L'Anse aux Meadows—tourists see each other again and again, and sometimes develop friendly relations on the basis of shared experiences. Meeting repeatedly by chance over a period of days or weeks, travelers pass on accommodation, sightseeing, and restaurant recommendations and warnings. In situations of unfamiliarity, travelers also exchange information about traditional Newfoundland and Labrador foods. Recognizing other tourists in the same eating establishment as people who have been encountered earlier in the journey, even without having spoken to one another, can also serve as a confirmation of the validity of dining choices. Such meta communication occurs not only within the physical confines of the restaurant, but also in the parking lot, as license plates and vehicles become points of recognition and affinity.

Due to the sheer number of tourists and the relatively small number of restaurants on the Viking Trail, a large proportion of B&Bs offer evening meals upon request. This is also true in the Labrador Straits. Many offer local specialties, and almost all emphasize "home cooking" in their advertising. While these meals may be served restaurant or "family" style, depending on the size of the establishment and the aesthetic of the proprietors, the most popular method is to serve individual portions of the same dishes at one large table. Thus, while everyone is eating the same things (although there may be exceptions made for vegetarians, children, or other individuals with specific dietary requirements), guests are not serving themselves from communal bowls or platters.

Again, depending on space and aesthetic, the proprietors may sit down with the guests, but even then may or may not eat with them. In some cases, one member of the host family may remain in the kitchen, while the other may sit at the table and participate in conversation, whether or not they eat (in the two examples presented here, men sit at the table as women continue to work in the kitchen). However, even in situations where the guests are served "restaurant-style" throughout the meal, the proprietors may attempt to control the social aspects of the meal by assigning seating.

Lucy Long has identified five main strategies for negotiating the production of cultural perspectives in culinary tourism: framing, naming or translation, explication, menu selection, and recipe adaptation.[14] In the examples below, I focus on the strategies of explication, menu selection, and recipe adaptation. "Explication" entails descriptions or explanations of particular foods, often with the goal of providing a native viewpoint of food items. Explication may be employed on menus, in cookbooks, or in person. For example, a number of my interviewees recounted that cod tongues had been described to them by servers at various restaurants or B&Bs, or by other tourists.[15] Menu selection is a process that involves highlighting dishes believed to be most acceptable to, and expected by, the target audience, or presenting unfamiliar foods alongside dishes identified with other regional specialties known to be familiar and popular to a general exoteric clientele. During my fieldwork I was served chicken with partridgeberry sauce, for example, which paired a widely familiar foodstuff, chicken, with the more exotic, locally prized partridgeberry.[16] Finally, recipe adaptation entails "the manipulation of the ingredients and preparation methods of particular dishes in order to adapt to the foodways system of the anticipated consumers."[17] In Newfoundland and Labrador, recipe adaptation is most employed in poaching or baking fish, namely cod, rather than frying it. Another example comes from the dinner menu of one B&B, which featured stir-fried root vegetables, rather than boiled ones, as is traditional.

Newfoundland and Labrador foodways

Culinary tourism in the province includes and builds on traditional foodways developed from regional adaptations of English, Irish, and Scottish culinary practices, with the important addition of indigenous flora, fauna, and *fruits de mer*.[18] There is an Acadian influence, too, as French fishers historically worked the waters of Newfoundland's south and west coasts, but this has not been as well-documented. In addition, the province is home to native peoples, including the Mi' Kmaq of Newfoundland, and the Inuit, Innu, and Métis of Labrador.

Area inhabitants have long relied on indigenous plants, utilizing blossoms, fruit, and greenery for both culinary and medicinal purposes. Caribou, moose, arctic hare, and snowshoe hare (locally referred to as "rabbit") have been the major game animals, with the moose remaining the most important today.[19] Game birds in the regional diet include duck, turr (murre), and partridge (ptarmigan). While imported foodstuffs are available in the province now as never before, hunted or fished game remains an important element of both diet and traditional social activity, as I will discuss in more detail later.

Fish and other sea creatures are perhaps the best-known element of the province's typical diet—and the most in demand among tourists—followed closely by moose and berries. Historically, cod has been king, and this is reflected in traditional meal patterns and cookbooks. Other fish locally caught and consumed include brook trout, caplin, halibut, herring, and salmon. The seal's place in traditional Newfoundland and Labrador foodways was established early, in the first half of the 19th century. Flippers, for seal flipper pie, are procured during the seal hunt, which has traditionally taken place each spring. The rich, dark meat is also used to make casseroles and sausage, and is sometimes bottled to ensure a supply outside of the hunting season.[20] Many speculate that the hunt is in its last days due to, among other things, the serious blow of the European Union's 2009 ban of seal products. Nonetheless, eating seal flipper pie is still an important seasonal activity for many in the province as a traditional rite of spring.

The early focus on harvesting the sea's bounty took precedence over agriculture. To prevent fishers being distracted from their primary occupation, farming was officially discouraged during early settlement of the area.[21] Large-scale agriculture was also restricted due to a short growing season and unfavourable soil conditions. This is not to say, however, that the cultivation of certain foods has not contributed to culinary practice. Cabbage, root vegetables including beets, carrots, onions, turnips, and potatoes, and small fruits such as currants, plums, and rhubarb have been and continue to be important domestic crops. Visitors to the province witness this continuing horticultural activity in the form of roadside and gravel pit gardens. As John T. Omohundro writes, "[s]elf-sufficiency, a basic axiom of Newfoundland culture for hundreds of years, is still valued by home producers."[22] Thus, canning and other means of preserving fruits, meats, and vegetables were valuable skills in the early days of settlement and continue to typify domestic practice.[23]

Perhaps the most beloved of the province's indigenous plants are the wide variety of berries, including strawberries, blackberries, currants, bakeapples (also known as cloud berries), raspberries, squashberries, blueberries, partridgeberries, marshberries, teaberries, gooseberries, and dogberries. As I have discussed in detail elsewhere, berry picking is an annual activity that local residents eagerly anticipate and enjoy.[24] The resulting berry stores are chiefly used in the home, but may also be sold by the roadside or to local grocery stores. Tourists are exposed to Newfoundlanders' and Labradorians' use of berries in the jams and jellies that often adorn B&B breakfast tables. These same jams and jellies often add flavour to other traditional dishes and are frequently used as pie filling and dessert sauces. Moreover, they are a frequent topic of conversation, as guests have the opportunity to sample berries they've never tasted, and sometimes never heard of, before. It is such conversation, centred on the province's foodways, to which I now turn my attention.

Foggy Cove Inn

My husband and I arrive at Foggy Cove Inn just before 6:00 pm.[25] The owners, Carl and Anne Young, are working on the evening meal along with hostess Ruth Anderson. A retired couple from Quebec arrives soon afterwards. A family with three young children from out west turns up much later, delaying everyone's supper, so the rest of us are offered a free glass of white wine. As supper is served, particular seating is suggested to accommodate the children. Our host, Carl, sits down and begins to eat with us while Anne and Ruth continue to work in the kitchen adjacent to the dining room. The meal (which includes local shrimp, salmon, partridgeberries, and root vegetables) is accompanied by water with iceberg chunks that Carl and Anne harvested themselves.[26] In selecting locally sourced products, the hosts showcase the island's bounty while adapting traditional ingredients to contemporary tastes. Shrimp and smoked salmon with tomato, mayonnaise, and capers serves as an appetizer. The main course, chicken in a pastry shell drizzled with partridgeberry sauce, is accompanied by stir-fried root vegetables and roasted potatoes. The accompanying conversation allows Carl numerous opportunities for explication of these and other traditional foodstuffs.

Thus, while we eat we talk primarily about food—what we're eating, what we've eaten, what we plan to eat, what we could never eat. The always controversial subject of seal flipper pie is raised, and while Carl notes that he grew up eating it, he reveals he never actually liked it and still doesn't. He adds, however, that you can buy seal flipper pie at Bidgood's, a grocery store in the Goulds that features traditional foods and crafts. A short drive from St. John's, the independent store is a tourist attraction in itself.[27]

After we finish our figgy duff—a traditional bread pudding and a local favourite—Carl directs us into the parlour down the hall from the dining room. He wants to show us part of a *Buddy Wasisname and the Other Fellers* DVD as a result of a guest's question about people camping by the side of the road in areas locally referred to as gravel pits. A musical comedy act featuring three talented Newfoundland musicians, *Buddy Wasisname and the Other Fellers* is beloved for their unflinching takeoffs on local vernacular culture and both emic and etic constructions of the "Newfie."[28] An excerpt from their song "Gravel Pits," penned by Wayne Chaulk, provides an example:

> We loves to go out in the good old gravel pits
> We loves to go out there when life gets smelly
> We can spray paint our names on the face of the cliff
> Go up to the Irving for a coke and chips
> Hitches up the camper and out of town we go
> Out on the highway with everything in tow
> The dog is in the back seat and Grandfather's drunk
> Youngsters in the trailer and the wife is in the trunk [29]

Watching the group perform in mixed company—by which I mean an audience of Newfoundlanders and non-Newfoundlanders—can be uncomfortable as the lines between praise, parody, and censure are often blurred. Audience members respond to the group's humour from different perspectives. This evening, there is an added layer of complexity, as everyone knows that I am a graduate student at Memorial University in St. John's, staying at the Inn while conducting research on tourism. The other guests are unsure whether or not it's proper to laugh at the group's comic depiction of Newfoundlanders and take their cues from Carl. I, too, wonder what the appropriate response is to lines such as, "The dog is in the back seat and Grandfather's drunk/Youngsters in the trailer and the wife is in the trunk." With weariness and a full belly pulling me into a rather groggy state, I cannot decide. Instead I ponder the contrast between the fine supper we've just consumed and the traditional gravel pit repast, "a bottle and a pot of moose stew," which I also know to be delicious.

Following the *Buddy Wasisname and the Other Fellers* clip, our host changes the tone by relating the story of a relative, a nineteenth-century Newfoundland sealing captain, and reads a recitation about his heroism in rescuing victims of a shipwreck.[30] He then passes out photocopies of the lyrics to a few Newfoundland songs, including "I'se the B'y" and the provincial anthem, "Ode to Newfoundland," and invites us to sing with him. With that, we all retire for the evening. It is 11:30 pm.

Shipwreck Bay B&B

Our education was much more informal, although no less instructive, at the Shipwreck Bay B&B in Labrador, which we reach by car following a ferry ride from St. Barbe, Newfoundland to Blanc Sablon, Quebec. At this point, I am sporting a bruised, scabby, and swollen right eyelid from a vicious black fly attack on the hiking trails near Foggy Cove Inn. Sharon and Doug Evans welcome us in anyway. Sharon appears quite outgoing, while Doug's initial reserve masks a gruff, but winning manner. Supper, booked weeks in advance and featuring caribou, will be ready at 6:30.[31]

Retired Floridians, originally from New York, and a trio of friends from British Columbia join us for caribou, cabbage, peas, potato, and turnip, smothered in caribou gravy. We are seated of our own accord at a large table in the kitchen. The arrangement allows Sharon to fully participate in conversation even as she works throughout the meal. The retirees have never had caribou before, nor bakeapples. Sharon explains that there are crucial differences between the caribou and bakeapples in Labrador, and those in Newfoundland. Having lived in both parts of the province, she can distinguish between caribou from Labrador and that from Newfoundland by the way the meat smells while it's cooking, a result of the differences in the animals' diet in each area. It is obvious that she prefers Labrador caribou. The steaks that we enjoy that evening are courtesy of Doug, who at 73 was still procuring various foodstuffs for the entire Evans family living in the immediate area, at least four households, as well as the B&B — berries, scallops, caribou, fish, and partridge. After supper, in the sitting room, Doug brings out photos of the caribou that we have just eaten, and shows us the bullets he prefers for hunting big game.

As the hour grows late and conversation turns to Canada's socialized health care system, in contrast to that of the United States, Doug slips away. But the lively discussion carries on as Sharon continues work in the kitchen, where she has been briskly multi-tasking since mid-afternoon. Her reminder that breakfast is at 8:00 am elicits rumblings of fatigue from the guests. We all head to our rooms around 10:30 pm.

The last to sit down at the table for breakfast the next morning (having also been last in line for the washroom), I notice that everyone is sitting in the same chairs as the night before, again with no direction from our hosts. The centrepiece that now occupies everyone's attention is an impressive display of jams and jellies, all picked and processed by Doug and Sharon. My fellow guests are particularly eager to sample the bakeapple jam.

Labrador bakeapples are believed by many to be superior to those on the island. Newfoundlanders living on the west coast of the island often traveled to the Labrador coast by skiff to pick bakeapples prior to Confederation. Women from Main Brook in western Newfoundland, for instance, accompanied their husbands to Labrador, to pick berries while the men fished.[32] Sharon often takes the opportunity to point out the difference in the bakeapple crops to guests through the foods she serves. If guests tell her that they don't like bakeapples, which can be quite tart, she immediately asks where they tried them, specifically wondering if it was on the island or in Labrador. Sharon attributes the differences in the taste of Newfoundland and Labrador bakeapples to variations in climate. She explained that the higher summer temperatures in Newfoundland (normally ranging from 15 to 25 degrees) essentially drain the berries of their flavour in a short period of time. Area residents know by the colour of the fruit when it is at its flavourful peak. She explains further, "when I serve bakeapples mine is a *deep* orange. [. . .], as opposed to yellowish or pale orange. When the berries are nice and orange, that's when the flavour's good."[33] Thus, Sharon encourages guests to give bakeapples another chance, assuring them of a different and more enjoyable culinary encounter. In the scenario Sharon describes, both explication and menu selection are brought to bear, highlighting differences between the two parts of the province that are often elided in tourism marketing materials.

Following the inevitable discussions about berries, icebergs, and Québec separatism, which occur at every B&B we visit, Sharon and Doug's daughter, Melissa, joins those of us still lingering over coffee. Doug and Melissa provide distinctly Labradorian views on natural resource extraction, highway construction and maintenance, the ferry system, the longstanding neglect of Labrador by Newfoundland politicians, and the handling of fish stocks.[34] Melissa begins shaking her head the moment her father starts to answer a guest's question about the causes of the fish stocks' collapse. Father and daughter agree to disagree on where the majority of the blame lies.

Conclusion

While both B&B experiences included the expected meal-time conversation, the stay at Foggy Cove was more structured and controlled. Supporting the widely promoted image of Newfoundlanders as stalwart, resourceful, musically-inclined, and "some of the funniest people on the planet,"[35] the formal, primarily unidirectional presentation of Newfoundland culture and identity was both reinforced and disrupted by the inclusion of the *Buddy Wasisname* DVD, inviting (or perhaps daring) guests to laugh at the "Newfie" stereotype parodied therein.

A contrasting view of the province was communicated at the Shipwreck Bay B&B. While also supporting the characterization of locals as strong and enduring, the conversation centred on practicalities such as quotidian food procurement, road maintenance, and health care. Moreover, Labradorian identity is at the forefront here. While sharing characteristics with emic constructions of Newfoundland identity, such as resourcefulness and perseverance, Labradorians not only inhabit a unique land, but a singular cultural and political space. While it is beyond the scope of this paper to address this in detail, it is important to recognize that these circumstances affect tourism in both obvious and subtle ways. As previously mentioned, guests at the Shipwreck Bay B&B are presented with a kind of running commentary on differences between the regions, something they may not encounter if their itinerary does not include Labrador.

Certainly, culinary tourism is a process of negotiation. Well aware of etic constructions of Newfoundland and Labrador culture, the individuated nature of tourism in the province currently provides a range of opportunities for its inhabitants to perform their culture *as they wish it to be perceived,* for as Phillip Crang notes, "Identity politics are at the heart of tourism labour processes."[36] Thus, the discourse presented at Foggy Cove Inn acknowledges cultural stereotypes, but ultimately emphasizes the most positive aspects of esoterically constructed identity, that of the "true Newfoundlander".[37] At Shipwreck Bay B&B, Labradorian identity is often presented in opposition to the more dominant, widespread image of the Newfoundlander, while still emphasizing vigour, ingenuity, and conviviality as integral aspects of local identity. Newfoundland and Labrador B&B owners construct and perform public identities as members of unique regional cultures. These oft-competing identities are shaped and maintained through formal and informal metaculinary discourse, verbal and non-verbal communication stimulated by encounters with unfamiliar food systems and the vernacular practices they encompass.

Through the maintenance and enlivening of centuries-old food practices as well as the incorporation of commercial goods into localized identities, Newfoundland and Labrador offers travelers a unique experience.[38] Thirty-something urbanites and retired RV enthusiasts alike find themselves at the same supper table in Labrador and are presented with the same plate of caribou, cabbage, peas, potato, and turnip. They do not completely forget their differences; indeed, their dissimilarities fuel conversation. But for the evening, their talk is enabled by the social conductivity of a shared meal. These brief but intimate gatherings are ideal settings in which B&B hosts may employ various strategies of culinary tourism to act out, and actively engage guests in, local identities. Much more than simply accommodations, B&Bs in Newfoundland and Labrador are sites of dynamic cultural production.

Notes

1. Holly Everett, *Class Acts: Culinary Tourism in Newfoundland and Labrador.* Ph.D. diss., Memorial University (2005).

2. See, for example, Jerry Bannister, "The Politics of Cultural Memory: Themes in the History of Newfoundland and Labrador in Canada, 1972-2003," in *Collected Papers of the Royal Commission on Renewing and Strengthening our Place in Canada* (St. John's: Government of Newfoundland and Labrador, 2003) 119–66; James Overton, "A Newfoundland Culture?" *Journal of Canadian Studies* 23 (1988), 5–22; Timothy J. Stanley, "Whose Public, Whose Memory? Racisms, Grand Narratives and Canadian History," in *To the Past: History, Education, Public Memory and Citizenship in Canada,* ed. Ruth W. Sandwell (Toronto: University of Toronto Press, 2006) 32–49.

3. Drawing on folklorist Don Yoder's pioneering work on foodways, Lucy Long explains that this universe encompasses "collecting cookbooks and recipes; producing and viewing televised cooking shows; participating in cooking classes *or in instances of teaching and learning techniques of food preparation, presentation and consumption*" (emphasis added). See Long, "Culinary Tourism: A Folkloristic Perspective on Eating and Otherness" in *Culinary Tourism,* ed. Lucy Long (Lexington: University Press of Kentucky, 2003), 23.

4. Pseudonyms are used for all hosts and their establishments.

5. Population figures are from the Newfoundland and Labrador and Nova Scotia provincial government websites at www.stats.gov.nl.ca/ and http://www.gov.ns.ca/finance/communitycounts/(accessed 8 May 2011).

6. Peter Narváez, "'She's Gone, Boys': Vernacular Song Responses to the Atlantic Fisheries Crisis," *Canadian Journal for Traditional Music* 24 (1997): 1.

7. Economic Research and Analysis Division, Department of Finance, *The Economy 2011* (St. John's: Government of Newfoundland and Labrador, 2011), 66–67.

8. Department of Tourism, Culture, and Recreation, *Annual Performance Report for Fiscal Year 2009-10* (St. John's: Government of Newfoundland and Labrador, 2010), 4.

9. Danette Dooley, "Known for His Hospitality: Roger Jamieson Satisfied with Term as HNL [Hospitality Newfoundland and Labrador] president," *The Express* [St. John's], February 12, 2002.

10. See, for example, Gerald Pocius, "Tourists, Health Seekers and Sportsmen: Luring Americans to Newfoundland in the Early Twentieth Century" in *Twentieth-Century Newfoundland Explorations,* ed. James Hillier and Peter Neary (St. John's: Breakwater, 1994) 47–77; James Overton, *Making a World of Difference: Essays on Tourism, Culture and Development in Newfoundland* (St. John's: Institute of Social and Economic Research, 1996).

11. Newfoundland and Labrador Tourism, *2009 Traveller's Guide* (St. John's: Government of Newfoundland and Labrador, 2009) 2.

12. Deana Stokes Sullivan, "Shipping News Tour Luring Tourists," *The Telegram* [St. John's], January 13, 2002. All three of these productions were based on novels: Annie Proulx's Pulitzer Prize and National Book Award-winning novel, *The Shipping News,* Bernice Morgan's *Random Passage,* and Edward Riche's *Rare Birds.* Both Morgan and Riche are Newfoundland authors. The set of *Random Passage*, in New Bonaventure, Trinity Bay, is now a tourist attraction. The 2002 provincial travel guide promoted all three productions and their sets or filming locations as popular culture attractions rooted in Newfoundland culture. As a major Hollywood production, *The Shipping News* received the most attention from both government and local media as significant to tourism in the province. I have addressed this in detail elsewhere (Everett, 2005), particularly with regard to the seal hunt.

13. Wayne Fife, "Semantic Slippage as a New Aspect of Authenticity: Viking Tourism on the Northern Peninsula of Newfoundland," *Journal of Folklore Research* 41, no. 1 (2004), 61–84.

14. Long, 37–44.

15. Cod tongues are usually quite unfamiliar to visitors from outside the province. Some wonder if the name really indicates what the dish is. It does. The tongues are usually fried on low heat, pressed and turned with a spatula, until crisp.

16. Holly Everett, "A Welcoming Wilderness: The Role of Wild Berries in the Construction of Newfoundland and Labrador as a Tourist Destination," *Ethnologies* 29, no. 1 (2007): 49–80.

17. Long, 42.

18. The most detailed, ethnographic work to date on traditional Newfoundland foodways is Pamela Gray's master's thesis, *Traditional Newfoundland Foodways: Origin, Adaptation and Change*, completed in 1977 at Memorial University.

19. Ibid.

20. John T. Omohundro, *Rough Food: The Seasons of Subsistence in Northern Newfoundland* (St. John's: Institute of Social and Economic Research, 1994), 256.

21. See Hilda Chaulk Murray, *Cows Don't Know It's Sunday: Agricultural Life in St. John's* (St. John's: Institute of Social and Economic Research, 2002) and G. M. Story, "Newfoundland: Fishermen, Hunters, Planters, and Merchants," in *Christmas Mumming in Newfoundland*, ed. Herbert Halpert and G. M. Story (Toronto: University of Toronto Press, 1990), 7–33.

22. Omohundro, 135.

23. Maura Hanrahan hypothesizes that aboriginal people aided European im/migrants in adapting to the unfamiliar environment and realizing the potential of incorporating hunting and gathering into their new lifestyle. See Maura Hanrahan and Marg Ewtushik, *A Veritable Scoff: Sources on Foodways and Nutrition in Newfoundland and Labrador* (St. John's: Flanker Press, Ltd., 2001).

24. Everett, 2007.

25. For the purposes of this discussion, I present excerpts from my fieldnotes.

26. Icebergs are an important element of the provincial tourism industry that has also been incorporated into culinary tourism. In addition to providing iceberg-viewing opportunities, locals go out in boats to procure iceberg chunks for guests at restaurants and B&Bs.

27. See Victoria Dickenson's review essay on Hanrahan and Ewtushik's *A Veritable Scoff* for more on Bidgoods and Newfoundland cuisine in general. Dickenson, "*A Veritable Scoff: Sources on Foodways and Nutrition in Newfoundland and Labrador* (review)," *CuiZine: The Journal of Canadian Food Cultures* 2.1 (2009), <http://www.erudit.org/revue/cuizine/2009/v2/n1/039522ar.html>.

28. As I have discussed elsewhere, the term "Newfie" and its various interpretations and usages continue to be debated. Depending on the context in which it is used, it may be perceived as a term of affection or a grave insult. See Holly Everett, "Vernacular Health Moralities and Culinary Tourism in Newfoundland and Labrador" *Journal of American Folklore* 122 (2009): 28–52; Pat Byrne, "Booze, Ritual, and the Invention of Tradition: The Phenomenon of the Newfoundland Screech-In," in *Usable Pasts,* ed. Tad Tuleja (Logan: Utah State University Press, 1997), 232–48; and Christie Davies, *Ethnic Humor Around the World: A Comparative Analysis* (Bloomington: Indiana University Press, 1990).

29. See the group's website, which includes a full discography and lyrics to all their songs, at www.buddywasisname.com (accessed 24 February 2010).

30. A significant type of regional folklore, a recitation is a monologue in poetic or prose narrative form, often recited from memory.

31. Due to the relatively small number of rooms available in the province, it is necessary to make reservations quite far in advance to be assured of having a room in any specific community or town. Both B&Bs discussed herein are fully booked months in advance.

32. Omohundro, 164–65.

33. Everett, 2007, 71–72.

34. The geographic separation of Newfoundland and Labrador is often echoed in the politics of the province.

35. Newfoundland and Labrador. Tourism Newfoundland and Labrador. *2009 Traveller's Guide*, 21.

36. Philip Crang, "Performing the Tourist Product," in *Touring Cultures: Transformations of Travel and Theory*, ed. by Chris Rojek and John Urry (London: Routledge, 1997), 152.

37. See, for example, Paul Chafe, "Rockin' the Rock: The Newfoundland Folk/Pop 'Revolution,'" *Newfoundland and Labrador Studies*, 22, no. 1 (2007), 345–60.

38. While I have presented a necessarily limited discussion here, B&Bs are rich sites for traditional foodways and culinary tourism research. As I have demonstrated, the physical sites provide excellent opportunities for participant-observation, whereas online research examining B&B websites and travelers' comments are important directions for further study.

CHAPTER 8

THE DOG'S EYE: THE PIE IN AUSTRALIAN TRADITION
Robert Smith

The subject of the Australian meat pie would be considered by some as being too familiar and too uniform a product to be more than of cursory interest. Even the foundational *Oxford Companion to Australian Folklore* notes only two aspects to Australian foodways: those within various national groups; and the 'pie-floater' in South Australia – a bowl of thick green pea soup in which floats a meat pie. The standard meat pie is so pervasive and unremarkable that in Australia even a sign with the single-word *Bakery* can be read as meaning that one could buy a pie there. Against this lack of discussion of the ordinary pie, some direction and support can come from Steve Zeitlan's description of contemporary folklore study, which can be paraphrased as "finding the meaning and the beauty in the ordinary".[1] In the choice of this topic and in the wide-ranging participant-observer survey to be followed, one might also take guidance from Joan Radner's description of folklore studies as being "eccentric by nature, marginal by choice, postmodern without ever having been modern".[2]

Also, so ordinary and widespread is the linking of the meat pie to our national imagery that it is almost a cliché. *Flikr.com*, the on-line site for images, has many instances of Australian pies, often posted by tourists, then supported by approving comments by overseas Australians, declaring how homesick they are and declaring their desire for this distinctive item of Australian culture. From these perhaps-temporary 'expats' the expressions have an intriguing mix of playful humour as well as deep sincerity. Michael Symons in his *One Continuous Picnic* looks to describe the same feelings for all Australians:

> With typical sardonic humour… Australians hold up the meat pie and tomato sauce as their national dish. It has everything: it's borrowed; it's crude; its contents are dubious; it's portable; it's factory-made; and even the manufacturers are now mostly foreign.[3]

While the scorn is more Symons' addition, here he touches several points of self-conscious humour and loyalty linked to the pie. One key reason that 'expats' feel such a link to the pie is that when overseas they find that a pie's size, contents and the language used to refer to it are all different. The familiar and ordinary is no longer present.

Specifically, the Australasian experience of *the pie* is very different from that of the rest of the world. In North America a pie is large (what Australians would call a *family pie*) and predominantly sweet. There the word *pie* is defined as "a baked dish of fruit, or meat and vegetables, typically with a top and base of pastry".[4] Looking back to Middle English, the word *pie* comes from the various combinations of ingredients typical of their product – and being compared to the objects randomly collected by a 'magpie'. In Britain today, a *pie* is "a baked dish of fruit, meat, fish, or vegetables, covered with pastry (or a similar substance) and frequently also having a base and sides of pastry".[5] By comparison, the Australian use is not so broad. Our dictionary

Robert Smith in 'The Dog's Eye: The Pie in Australian Tradition' in Graham Seal and Jennifer Gall (eds), *Antipodean Traditions: Australian Folklore in the 21st Century*, (Perth, WA: Black Swan Press, 2011), pp. 157–69.

Courtesy of Black Swan Press, Curtin University, Western Australia.

definitions continue some of the breadth of the British and much earlier meaning, but our vernacular usage shows a considerable narrowing of meaning. Here the single word, *pie*, does not have the sense of 'sweet', or of 'vegetable'. In Australia all such meanings require the addition of qualifying adjectives to vary the base meaning. In Australia the base word *pie*, when alone, most usually has the folk meaning which could be phrased as "meat pie – a pastry case enclosing meat and gravy, and as a single serve". This is what one would expect from all bakeries, the newer 'hot bread' shops, corner or convenience stores, take-away food stores, often at petrol stations (perhaps the only food available there that could be a meal) and so on – whenever one asked for *a pie*.

To have emerged as nationally ubiquitous and distinctive the Australian pie has met a need in the community. Pies were readily taken up by the working class – being self-enclosed (requiring no utensils), mobile (even able to be carried in the pocket of a workman's coat) and cheap (with low-cost ingredients, when produced in bulk) – the pie was broadly accessible and useful.[6] Its availability was aided by the large number of small bakeries and also by the increasing number of street vendors The latter emerged in early 19th century Australia, and in Sydney the most notable of these was the Flying Pieman.[7] Janet Clarkson notes that:

> The country's early love affair with the meat pie was shared across all ranks. . . [an 1850 Melbourne article] noted that the town councillors preferred meat pies from the local pub to the food provided in the council chambers.[8]

Those with wealth could always afford more exclusive food, but this example suggests the ready class mobility, where an increase in power does not overly change one's tastes or practices.

From such beginnings, today there are numerous codified practices on the eating of pies, starting with preference for the tomato sauce, present or not, and either being dispensed into the pie or into a small pool on the top. Some shared patterns are – the manipulation of the paper-bag, the application of sauce, the folding back of any foil base, the first bite of the crust only, and the cautious follow-up bite – all completed with a daintiness that can rival the use of silver service. Whether one is alone or in a small group is irrelevant, for eaters often exhibit a mix of embarrassment and pride/loyalty, or – if they burnt their mouth on the first main bite – of an anguish confidently shared with whosoever is nearest. Indeed, such is the abhorrence of a *cold pie* that eaters regularly prefer to risk the burning of their mouths. Even the author Patrick White was susceptible to this, and was also willing to use the painful experience for metaphorical effect:

> [after a particularly emotional encounter] I ran down the hill and bought a meat pie, and jumped on the Sydney train, scalding my mouth on hot gravy and remorse.[9]

In all, to eat the pie, or to be seen eating one, can be seen as an act of empowerment – it is a statement of commonality, of memory, of shared experience and values, and perhaps that thereby one might feel more authority to speak on behalf of a broader group.

Linked to the pie's working class accessibility, for many years the pie has been the usual food consumed by crowds at sporting events. As hot food purchased from an itinerant vendor, a pie was able to be eaten while standing in a crowd, sometimes with a pie in one hand and a beer in the other. A leading Rugby League footballer of the 1960–70s in Sydney, Artie Beetson, was specifically characterised in the media as well as more popularly for pie-eating. For a character who appeared undemonstrative, quiet and large, it was a mild and affectionate label. However, as his already large front-row-forward size increased even more over the years, so he began to express irritation with the repeated linking of his name with *pies*.[10] Still, over even more time, as he moved on from his playing/coaching career (and less reliant on physical condition and performance) and the media and public attention declined, so he came variously to embrace a link with *pies*.[11]

Affluence, social mobility, and healthy lifestyles, have in part changed the practice of pie-eating. A television advertisement of the middle years of this decade shows two workmen in the cab of a truck each engaged in eating a pie with delight. One of the workmen notices two suited businessmen in a restaurant, wining and dining in what is a parallel lunch for another class. After a seemingly long thoughtful pause, the workman turns to his partner, and says that the businessmen do not know what they are missing. He then resumes eating his pie with even greater relish. The pausing is a tense moment, containing the potential for class antagonism (the juxtaposition of the 'haves and the have nots', of the 'two cultures' and the taking advantage of the 'working poor' – the expression which so antagonised former Prime Minister Howard). The advertisement plays with the idea of the *pie* as a highly charged site of social difference – then coming down on the side of delight in the ordinary and familiar rather than of the elaborate or the pretentious. The advertisement has some ironic distancing, with the implication that it is actually the pie-eating workman who does not know what he is missing. Yet there is another level of irony, also beyond the workman, but which is implicit for Australian viewers, i.e. that the fine-dining Australian businessmen could themselves be hankering after a meat pie. All Australian businessmen of all eras would certainly be aware of pies, and when it suits them it is always a viable option as either a snack or a convenient small meal. While there is class tension in the advertisement's pause, the pie plays a countervailing role towards the egalitarianism that is largely seen to bind the nation. Adapting Barbara Kirshenblatt-Gimblett's observation – it is not just the "challenging foods" that are "highly charged"[12] for the ordinary can also at various times be "beloved, detested, stigmatised, or reclaimed".

A mix of affection and caution can be seen in the distinctive language used to describe pies in Australia.[13] The *dog's eye* of the title of this work is rhyming slang for the *pie*. It might appear in a combination as in wanting *a dog's eye and dead horse* – a pie and sauce. Underlining its importance, *dog's eye* is one of the most widely used items of rhyming slang in contemporary Australian usage.[14] Graham Seal notes *dog's eye* and *dead horse* for their humour, "colourful and generally visual nature", which indeed is true. Perhaps in looking for variety he then omits *dog's eye* and *dead horse* from his examples of "some startlingly colourful, whimsical and apt items", when the rhyming slang would seem to capture the on-going concern over the actual ingredients as well as the fears of contamination.[15] Rhyming slang also provides a link with football, so that if it were said that a player needed to *score a few more meat pies*, it would mean that he needed to score more *tries*.[16]

Similarly derogatory usages for the pie are the *rat's coffin, mystery bag, maggot case/bag* and so on.[17] While an impecunious baker could always vary the nature and amount of the ingredients (occasionally resulting in a rather flat, runny disappointing pie), actual examples of contamination always seem to be given a prominence well beyond their frequency. As with the rhyming slang, such pejorative expressions are not used to deter eaters. Rather, the terms are used by the eaters themselves in what is a form of self-deprecating humour and group-reinforcement.[18]

The origin of much Australian rhyming slang is located in the two World War periods with their large gatherings cutting across normal groupings, and in peril in exceptional circumstances. While it might give the impression of being old, *dog's eye* is however a relatively new usage and seemingly from the 1980s.[19] A closely related phrase has a much longer record – that of *tinned dog*, for 'canned meat'. As Ramson's *Australian National Dictionary* (1988)[20] records:

1896: Comestibles. . . took the form of tinned meats, 'tinned dog', as all the various preparations of beef and mutton in the bush are humorously. . . designated.

Ramson also records the steps of contraction, from *(tin) dog,* to the note that 'damper, *dog* and tea is served up, meal after meal'. The origin is one of rural workers in the period when canned meat became more available and convenient than slaughtering a beast – but where soon the tinned version, with its uncertain contents, became equally as monotonous, and deserving of humorous treatment.

Symons notes that it is not until World War 2 that "pie and tomato sauce" is referred to as a "national dish".[21] It is reasonable to see the transition from rural to urban worker, stimulated by the catalyst of a WW2 positioning with/against the British and Americans with a mix of cringe/assertion – all producing a broad need for national images, and having a specific expression in this case in a common food.[22]

The change from tinned food to shop-bought food, from eating *dog* to eating *pie,* charged by folk nationalist descriptions, found appropriately humorous new expression in *dog's eye.* When many think of rhyming slang as having an older cockney source, it is pleasing to see that this prominent term *dog's eye* has had a distinctive Australian and recent impetus/pedigree.

The commercial beginnings of the meat pie were in urban centres – whatever sized community could support a bakery. With increasing population numbers, a choice of bakers emerged, and the pies (just like the breads) were named after the particular bakers. I grew up in a 'two baker' town, and it seemed almost a point of honour to walk past the nearer bakery so that minor distinctions of preference could be exercised – over what was largely an identical product. For travellers there was the often-deprecated *railway pie* where its origins, reliability and accountability were always more suspect than that of local bakers.

Later there emerged broader distribution from regional, capital city and eventually national brands, where choice could be by reference to a distant/vague name, supported by local advertising hoardings. With such increasing variety, preference became more impersonal – with little scope for acknowledging the reliability or skill (or doubts about those) of a local baker. As one example for the features of this centralisation of production and distribution, one of the current major producers, *Four'N Twenty pies,* takes its name from the older English nursery rhyme, but its advertising images are all national – the red sauce on the pie presented in the shape of the Australian continent, the word *Australian* appearing prominently and more than twice on much of its packaging. It is as though the older rhyme used for the name simply adds an air of longtime authenticity to the related meaning of 'packs' or 'bulk', with echoes of the land of plenty.

Quicker to prepare and serve than sandwiches (the other standard school-lunch food), pies quickly became the staple for school-supplied/purchased food, once a pie-warmer was installed. In a 2011 ABC Radio National program on volunteers, the presenter, Richard Aedy, offered the statement that "There's more to working in a school canteen than turning on the pie-warmer".[23] For the students, the on-site availability of hot food marked a change from the often once-a-week practice of pies needing to be pre-paid by arrangement with a local bakery and then later delivered to the school for distribution. In the early years of high school, the consumption of two pies (instead of one) for a boy's lunch was a clear sign that he had reached maturity – a moment of transition, a schoolyard rite-of-passage, socially not so clearly noted elsewhere in this period of a boy's rapid growth. With this increased teenage hunger and notable performance, food-eating competitions in Australia have often focussed on pies. The pie's ubiquity, both prized and accessible, made it a suitable object for such endurance performances.

At the other extreme from quantity are the competitions for quality. So many advertise their achievement as winners of an award, in one of various categories, at regional, state or national levels, that it would appear all makers could be rewarded at one point over a span of years. This profusion of awards suggests that 'quality' must be regularly reaffirmed in the public's eye. Traditionally, at the local level, questions of 'quality' were shared across the community. For example, it is still not unusual for a non-pie-eater to proffer an opinion in answer to the question of "Who has the best pies in town?". This seeming anomaly continues and is one indication of the pie's community importance. Recently, social media have provided a means for consumer interest in such a search for quality to address a scale which is larger than the local – such as on-line discussion to declare 'Brisbane's best pie?'.[24]

Regardless of the contemporary generally uniform product, it must be said that *pies* still, as traditionally, have fallen victim to stories of occasional lapses in quality. Alarmist newspaper articles often take the lead in stirring concern on the nature and ratio of pies' ingredients, the potential for contamination, the preparation, freshness and service. With a fat content of up to 30 per cent, a healthy version would be a minor curiosity. Health/weight concerns provide any individual with an acceptable reason to decline/opt out, yet one could re-participate at any point – perhaps to gain the social benefits of egalitarianism. In health and social terms, the pie is not stigmatised in the way that, for example, are the multi-national fast-food chains.

Overseas visitors in Australia are often treated to a *pie* as an 'authentic' but baffling Australian experience. Two recent comedians from the United States have separately included items on *meat pies* in their television-broadcast routines. In these presentations neither could understand the Australian enjoyment of pies, and both were derogatory (e.g. one repeatedly describing the almost instant passage of a pie through the digestive tract). Perhaps because of this overseas' impression, there has been no take-up of meat pies by the multi-national fast-food chains in their offerings in Australia.

Still, some change has come. An increasing range of pies is becoming available, with choices including *steak and kidney pies, minted-lamb pies, Steak Diane pies, chicken mornay pies, Thai curry pies,* all in the same display/pie-warmer as that 'un-manly' newcomer the *quiche (pie).* Yet, while customers are offered this wide choice, several bakers have confided that their main sales are still those slight variations on the traditional pie (with names such as *plain pie, mince pie, beef pie, steak pie* and *chunky beef pie*). The recent availability of varieties of pies aids a sense of social mobility, where the offering of choice may disguise one otherwise being stigmatised by *ordering a pie.* It may be that the long lists of pie varieties now advertised in shops may not need to be fulfilled – they may be merely a type of 'social camouflage' for those still wishing to consume the basic pie.

Distinctive regional variation can only be observed when those regions are widely-dispersed. The *pie floater* of South Australia (and of Broken Hill, NSW) has its origins in Britain with its pie accompaniment there of 'mushy peas'.

There is a Tasmanian variation of *scallop pies,* reflecting that state's plentiful seafood. In New Zealand, until recent years the standard meat pie was made of minced mutton, with a strong odour characteristically different from that of beef-based pies. Otherwise, the New Zealand practice of pie-eating is largely indistinguishable from that of Australia. Indeed, on the evidence of their large number of their *pie carts,*[25] New Zealanders may be even more attached to the practice than are Australians. The smallness of this regional variation tends to throw into highlight the broad distribution, persistence and desirability of what is the standard *pie.*

So standard is the practice of Australian pie-eating, that increasing cultural diversity is also able to be accommodated within it. In the capital cities with large Islamic communities, halal meat pies have appeared and are increasingly available. The social impetus for this move can be observed in the collection of young people in schools. In a report on a particular school canteen introducing halal meat pies, the chairman of the Halal Certification Authority Australia, Mr El-Mouelhy, said:

Kids want to identify with their mates. It is Australian to eat a meat pie. The child is an Aussie. He was born here and when he is with his mates he wants to eat an Aussie meat pie.[26]

This is a cheering statement of unity, based upon traditional Australian food culture.

* * *

Culturally and socially, regional Australia is comparatively stable, and consideration of pie-eating and its presentation in the regions can help in discerning basic features of the modern practice. Across the long thin

North Coast region of New South Wales there is a sequence of local meat pie bakers and suppliers that have survived the expansion of metropolitan or national offerings. They have gained iconic status within their respective localities and often broadly across the region. While the prominent bakeries are spaced across the region in a pattern that is likely to attract at least one hungry tourist, these pie-eating sites have not been developed in the manner of 'tourist traps' – those other places more characterised by the proliferation of themed branding and tourist memorabilia. Rather, for the outward-bound city driver, these rural pie-outlets supply a 'taste of the local', an element of heritage, and so to some extent they satisfy a desire of the metropolitan Australian to support the concept of Australian rural/country tradition.

From the larger city of Newcastle, heading north, the more prominent sites with their distinctive naming and signage are:

- Heatherbrae's Pies: the name of the locality.
- Fredo's Famous Pies: in the village of Frederickton, long referred to by locals as 'Fredo'.
- Uncle Tom's Pies: attached to a petrol station at a T-intersection (now bypassed by the freeway), named after the original baker.
- Lismore Pie Cart: inland, named after the city and its pie facility.
- Mallanganee Pies: inland, named after the small hamlet.
- Humble Pies: on the freeway, at Billinudgel, using a halo as emblem.
- Yatala Pie Shop: named after the place. Also the site of a 'big pie', but no longer visible from the freeway.

One could trace a pattern of prominence and naming onward to Mocca's Pies in northern Queensland.

Throughout, the self-representations include the shopfront, signs on the approaching side, signage on vehicles, brochures and napkins. The language of these representations typically addresses three set elements:

- place names
- high quality
- fame

Occasionally, the year of establishment is presented. Significant omissions are claims of authenticity – all have largely identical products and so authenticity is taken for granted. Also mostly omitted are the names of the current proprietors/bakers – in earlier times as important a marker as place. Only long continuity transfers a baker's name to become a place name (e.g. 'Uncle Tom's'). In many cases the current bakers could all be new to the area – perhaps Vietnamese bakers bringing their fine-pastry French-style skills, aiding the consistency and quality of the product but where a Vietnamese name would break the illusion of long-time traditional continuity.[27]

The three most usual language elements have a particular effect. *Place names* draw upon local identity, loyalty and memory – perhaps long used as landmarks or reference points on journeys (e.g. "We always take a break at Uncle Tom's"). While representations of place-names can be humorous – as in the sign 'Eat Moore Pies'[28] – this 'place-name' function can be completely divorced from the concept of 'food'. For many years the slightly misleading signage at Uncle Tom's (also a garage) seemingly offered pies in 'leaded' and 'unleaded' varieties.

Official signage at Yatala for several years linked Yatala Pies with both the Crematorium and the Drive-in Theatre. This prominence of the place-name function is related to being long-established – where the tradition of many years at the site counts for more than does the actual food. *Quality* is repeatedly asserted – again, even though to a non-Australian the standard product is largely uniform across all producers.

Key words attesting to this quality are *hot* and *chunky*, but *prize, award* and *best* are common. Mallanganee Pies even advertise their wares as 'Best of the Best'.[29] Finally, one observes frequent use of the word *famous*. This element is almost as commonly found in the language for pie sites' representations as are the locality names. The assertion of fame is seeming justification for both the claims on quality as well as for the name's prominence, and encourages the process by which all will be reinforced. If one considers the discussion of the actual eaters, this usually centres on questions of the *quality,* which is nearly always affirmed, varying only in the amount of enthusiasm. They are already at the location, and are rehearsing stories which will be repeated with the name of the place. They have been partly drawn by the *fame,* and by reaffirming the *quality,* they again contribute to the *fame* – and the cycle continues.

* * *

Notwithstanding the humour and enjoyment which surrounds it, the Australian meat pie can be seen as a discrete folk marker of place, people, loyalty – and as a link with earlier times. Whether emblematic of national identity or of regional loyalty, the British theorist Raymond Williams' concept of culture as a "structure of feeling"[30] would seem to apply to the Australian meat pie. For Williams, much of what is termed 'culture' is felt, and these feelings are tested and transmitted to new generations. In our case the idea/feeling of the meat pie can be considered as so important to us as to largely dwarf the actual food – an experience which is more head/heart rather than digestive. Perhaps in all this the 'beauty in the ordinary' is in the shared humour and loyalty with which we hold our pies.

Notes

1. Steven J. Zeitlin, "I'm a Folklorist and You're Not: Expansive versus Delimited Strategies in the Practice of Folklore," *Journal of American Folklore* 112, no. 446 (1999): 4.

2. Joan Radner, "AFS Now and Tomorrow: The View from the Stepladder," (AFS Presidential Address, 28 October 2000), *Journal of American Folklore* 114, no. 453 (2001): 263.

3. Michael Symons, *One Continuous Picnic: A Gastronomic History of Australia,* 2nd ed. (Carlton, Victoria: Melbourne University Press, 2007), 300.

4. *Webster's New Twentieth Century Dictionary,* 2nd ed. (Cleveland; New York: World Publishing Company, 1964).

5. Pie, n.2, *Oxford English Dictionary,* 3rd ed., March 2006, online version June 2011, accessed 8 June 2011, http://www.oed.com/view/Entry/143537

6. Here there are parallels with the differently shaped *pasties* still more popular in Britain. See Janet Clarkson, *Pie: A Global History* (London: Reaktion Books, 2009), 98–99.

7. Warren Fahey, *When Mabel Laid the Table: The Folklore of Eating and Drinking in Australia* (Sydney: State Library of New South Wales Press, 1992), 4–5. For pies more generally, see elsewhere in this same work and also his *Tucker Track: The Curious History of Food in Australia* (Sydney: ABC Books, 2005).

8. Clarkson, *Pie: A Global History,* 93.

9. Patrick White, *Flaws in the Glass: A Self-Portrait* (London: Jonathan Cape, 1981), 16.

10. Perhaps there was also a lingering sense of the pejorative expression *pie-eater* meaning "someone who is 'small-time', of little account" – particularly used in horse-racing circles. See G. A. Wilkes, *Stunned Mullets and Two-pot Screamers: A Dictionary of Australian Colloquialisms,* 5th ed. (South Melbourne: Oxford University Press, 2008), 16. A British parallel for this derogatory / humorous usage is the soccer-style chant "Fat boy, fat boy. You ate all our pies". Pie, n.2, *Oxford English Dictionary.*

11. See pictorial overview in "The Changing Face of Sport," *Alpha,* January 2007, 24.

12. Lucy Long, *Culinary Tourism* (Lexington, K.Y: University of Kentucky Press, 2004), xiii.

13. For their distinctive Australianness, the examples which follow might be contrasted with the breadth of examples from elsewhere, which include a *funding pie, humble pie, easy as pie, fingers in the pie, American pie, apple pie,* etc.

14. Perhaps only exceeded in use by the *frog and toad* (road) of early Cockney origin.

15. Graham Seal, *Dog's Eye and Dead Horse* (Sydney: ABC Books/HarperCollins, 2009), 18, 19. Of course the two examples have already been given exceptional prominence in their being chosen as the title for the publication.

16. For example, see the article by Wayne Heming, 'Thorn Averts Nudie Run in Fond Farewell', *ninemsn,* August 26, 2007, accessed May 30, 2011, http://wwos.ninemsn.com.au/article.aspx?id=289813. This article presented the sentence 'Brisbane forward Brad Thorn hadn't scored a 'meat pie' all year.' The sentence was then repeated by numerous sporting websites. In the AFL football code, the Collingwood team ('the Magpies') is affectionately referred to as 'the Pies'.

17. Such derogatory terms extend to children's usage, with *dog's eye* appearing in June Factor's *Kidspeak: A Dictionary of Australian Children's Words, Expressions and Games* (Carlton South, Victoria: Melbourne University Press, 2000). They also extend across the Tasman with *maggot pack* appearing in Sonya Plowman's *Great Kiwi Slang* (Auckland: Summit Press, 2002).

18. It is similar to swearing at a mate, expecting the same in return.

19. It does not appear in Eric Partridge, *A Dictionary of Slang and Unconventional English,* ed. Paul Beale, 8th ed. (London; Melbourne; Henley: Routledge and Kegan Paul, 1984); nor in George W. Turner, ed., *The Australian Concise Oxford Dictionary,* 7th ed. (Melbourne: Oxford University Press, 1987); but is in Arthur Delbridge, ed., *The Macquarie Dictionary: Federation Edition* (Macquarie University, New South Wales: Macquarie Library, 2001); and in Tom Dalzell and Terry Victor, eds., *The New Partridge Dictionary of Slang and Unconventional English.* 2 vols. (London and New York: Routledge, 2006), citing published examples from 1988. The 1980s decade marks an increase in the numbers of young Australians travelling overseas – a wave subsequent to that of the Bazza MacKenzie generation, noted in Seal, *Dog's Eye and Dead Horse,* 14.

20. W. S. Ramson, ed., *The Australian National Dictionary* (Melbourne: Oxford University Press, 1988).

21. Symons, *One Continuous Picnic,* 158.

22. The 1944 guide to Australia for USA Servicemen described the meat pie as the Australian version of the US hotdog. See Symons, *One Continuous Picnic,* 195.

23. Richard Aedy, "School Food: The End of the Sausage Sizzle?" *Life Matters,* ABC Radio National, February 20, 2007, accessed May 30, 2011, http://wwwabc.net.au/rn/lifematters/stories/2007/1849833.htm

24. The online site of that title has now lapsed (last accessed January 13, 2010), but a Google search on the words *Brisbane best pies* currently yields over eight and a half million hits. Also see the attempted national coverage in "POI in Meat Pies," accessed July 9, 2010, http://www.poidb.com/groups/view-poi.asp?GroupID=465&region=2_0

25. Lindsay Neill, Claudia Bell and Ted Bryant, *The Great New Zealand Pie Cart* (Auckland: Hodder Moa, 2008).

26. Vikki Campion, "Now Students Tuck into Halal Meat Pies," *Daily Telegraph,* May 26, 2008, accessed September 15, 2009, http://www.news.com.au/dailytelegraph/story/0,22049,23755707-5001021,00.html. The article refers to Lurnea Public School in Sydney.

27. For contrast here, consider the situation with wineries where often the name of the proprietor is prominent, whether the time is long or short, e.g. Tyrrells (Hunter) or Cassegrain (Port Macquarie). Pies in the region are produced for a market that might be described as 'intensely local'.

28. Moore is a small town in the Esk shire to the northwest of Brisbane.

29. The expression *fresh pies* has been observed only on service station signage, here perhaps to dispel questions of the quality of the often maligned servo pie.

30. Raymond Williams, *The Long Revolution* (London: Chatto and Windus, 1961), 48–49.

References

Aedy, Richard. "School Food: The End of the Sausage Sizzle?" *Life Matters,* ABC Radio National, February 20, 2007. Accessed May 30, 2011. http://wwwabc.net.au/rn/lifematters/stories/2007/1849833.htm

Campion, Vikki. "Now Students Tuck into Halal Meat Pies." *Daily Telegraph,* May 26, 2008. Accessed September 15, 2009. http://www.news.com.au/dailytelegraph/story/0,22049,23755707-5001021,00.html

Clarkson, Janet. *Pie: A Global History.* London: Reaktion Books, 2009.

Dalzell, Tom and Terry Victor, eds. *The New Partridge Dictionary of Slang and Unconventional English.* 2 vols. London and New York: Routledge, 2006.

Davey, Gwenda Beed and Graham Seal. *A Guide to Australian Folklore.* East Roseville, New South Wales: Kangaroo Press, 2003.

Davey, Gwenda Beed, and Graham Seal, eds. *The Oxford Companion to Australian Folklore.* Melbourne: Oxford University Press, 1993.

Delbridge, Arthur, ed. *The Macquarie Dictionary: Federation Edition.* Macquarie University, New South Wales: Macquarie Library, 2001.

Factor, June. Kidspeak: *A Dictionary of Australian Children's Words, Expressions and Games.* Carlton South, Victoria: Melbourne University Press, 2000.

Fahey, Warren. *Tucker Track: The Curious History of Food in Australia.* Sydney: ABC Books, 2005.

Fahey, Warren. *When Mabel Laid the Table: The Folklore of Eating and Drinking in Australia.* Sydney: State Library of New South Wales Press, 1992.

Long, Lucy. *Culinary Tourism.* Lexington, K.Y: University of Kentucky Press, 2004.

Neill, Lindsay, Claudia Bell and Ted Bryant. *The Great New Zealand Pie Cart.* Auckland: Hodder Moa, 2008.

Oxford English Dictionary. 3rd ed. March 2006, online version June 2011. Accessed June 8, 2011. http://www.oed.com/view/Entry/143537

Partridge, Eric. *A Dictionary of Slang and Unconventional English.* Edited by Paul Beale, 8th ed. London; Melbourne; Henley: Routledge and Kegan Paul, 1984.

Plowman, Sonya. *Great Kiwi Slang.* Auckland: Summit Press, 2002.

Radner, Joan. "AFS Now and Tomorrow: The View from the Stepladder." (AFS Presidential Address, 28 October 2000), *Journal of American Folklore* 114, no. 453 (2001): 263–76.

Ramson, W. S., ed. *The Australian National Dictionary.* Melbourne: Oxford University Press, 1988.

Rolls, Eric. *A Celebration of Food and Wine: Of Flesh, of Fish, of Fowl.* St. Lucia, Queensland: University of Queensland Press, 1997.

Seal, Graham. *Dog's Eye and Dead Horse.* Sydney: ABC Books/HarperCollins, 2009.

Seal, Graham. *The Lingo: Listening to Australian English.* 2nd ed. Kensington, New South Wales: UNSW Press, 1999.

Symons, Michael. *One Continuous Picnic: A Gastronomic History of Australia.* 2nd ed. Carlton, Victoria: Melbourne University Press, 2007.

"The Changing Face of Sport." *Alpha,* January 2007, 24.

Webster's New Twentieth Century Dictionary. 2nd ed. Cleveland; New York: World Publishing Company, 1964.

White, Patrick. *Flaws in the Glass: A Self-Portrait.* London: Jonathan Cape, 1981.

Wilkes, Gerald Alfred. *Stunned Mullets and Two-pot Screamers: A Dictionary of Australian Colloquialisms.* 5th ed. South Melbourne: Oxford University Press, 2008.

Williams, Raymond. *The Long Revolution.* London: Chatto and Windus, 1961.

Zeitlin, Steven J. "I'm a Folklorist and You're Not: Expansive versus Delimited Strategies in the Practice of Folklore." *Journal of American Folklore* 112, no. 446 (1999): 3–19.

CHAPTER 9
BALUT: FERTILIZED DUCK EGGS AND THEIR ROLE IN FILIPINO CULTURE
Margaret Magat

Whoever discovered balut stumbled onto the fact that food has changing excellences (taste, texture) as it evolves and develops. Thus between the egg and the full-grown duck, there are stages that bear exploring—and eating. And the Filipino has explored them and evolved the culture of balut.

Doreen Fernandez in "The World of Balut"

This essay illustrates how consumption of one particular food, fertilized duck eggs, can reveal the interplay between food, beliefs, culture and history. Called *balut* in the Philippines or *hot vit lon* in Vietnam, fertilized duck eggs are also familiar in the food customs of Chinese, Laotians, Cambodians and Thais. Socio-cultural factors, not just nutritional reasons dominate its consumption. Using historical and literary sources, as well as fieldwork data culled from 25 balut eaters, two balut distributors and a duck farmer as well, I will explore what it is about balut that makes eating it desirable. Why ingest something that may already have bones, feathers and a beak? For Filipino and other Asian Americans, there are alternative sources of protein, (which is not the case for many in the Philippines who do not have the luxury of choice).

"Eating is usually a more complicated function than just taking nourishment" wrote food scholar Kurt Lewin. The complexities involved in the eating of balut, or any other food for that matter, has since been explored by a number of folklorists and anthropologists. Food scholarship has ranged from food as a semiotic system (Theophano 1991; Douglas 1966 & 1972; Weismantel 1988), to how consumption is tied to psychological and economic factors (Lewin 1942; Richards 1932), to the way food defines ethnicity (Brown and Mussell 1984; Georges 1984; Kalčik 1984). However, much of the debate between food scholars is between the materialists, led by Marvin Harris and Marshall Sahlins, and symbolic theorists such as Mary Douglas and Claude Levi-Strauss. Harris agrees that food may have symbolic meaning, but before anything else, "food must nourish the collective stomach before it can feed the collective mind" and whatever foods are eaten, "are foods that have a more favorable balance of practical benefits over costs than foods that are avoided (bad to eat)" (Harris 1985:15). For Douglas, however, food embodies a code, and the messages in it can be seen in "the pattern of social relations" (1972:61). Who is being excluded or included can be gleaned from the food categories and meal patterns; for example, drinks are reserved for strangers and acquaintances while meals are for intimate friends and family (Douglas 66).

In the case of balut, both symbolic and material explanations can illuminate the reasons why people would eat embryonic duck eggs. Although it is always eaten boiled, and never raw, eating balut requires the consumption of something in the fetal stage, and psychological, cultural, and socio-economic factors must all be considered. Generally sold late at night or early morning, balut is consumed by Filipino males for its alleged

Margaret Magat, 'Balut: Fertilized Duck Eggs and Their Role in Filipino Culture', *Western Folklore* 61 (1) (2002), 63–96. (Excerpt printed here: 63–74, 76–80, 85, 89–92. Omitted text is indicated by ellipses.)

© Western States Folklore Society.

aphrodisiac properties, while women eat it for reasons such as energy and nutrition, but never as a sexual stimulant. As one informant put it bluntly, balut as an aphrodisiac is *"para lang sa lalaki ito"* (it is just for men).

Eaten usually as a snack, and not a formal food, fertilized duck eggs have been described to be as "popular in Manila as hotdogs in the United States" (Maness 1950:10). Although at one point, balut may have been prevalent only in the Luzon region, and not in other areas of the Philippines, it has been hailed the country's "national street food" (Fernandez 1994:11). Balut is so deeply embedded in Philippine culture that it has inspired everything from a hit record song about the distinctive howling calls of balut vendors in the late night and early morning to dishes in Filipino haute cuisine. Indeed, the love affair of Filipinos with fertilized duck eggs has been carried by immigrants to the United States.

Estimating the number of balut businesses in the U.S. today is difficult. But wherever there are Filipinos, one can usually find balut. In California and Hawaii, businesses cater specifically to balut eaters. It is also easy to make balut in homes, where it is then sold to friends and co-workers. From Alaska to Rome, wherever Filipinos migrate for work, balut may be found.

Numerous articles on exotica have remarked upon balut, but now there seems to be a genuine interest in the eating of balut in its cultural context. The last decade has seen a flurry of articles on balut, including balut in Denver, Colorado (Kessler 1995); balut in Temecula, California (Hennessey 1995); interest in making balut by a Wellington, New Zealand duck farm (Lane 1995); balut served in Manila's cemeteries during the Day of the Dead (McIntosh 1994); and how Filipinos in Hong Kong eat it (Sheridan 1995). *The New York Times* ran a short story on the Filipinos' ongoing relationship with balut, describing it as a "national passion" (Mydans 1997).

According to the 2000 census, Filipino Americans number close to 1 million in California, the second biggest Asian group in the U.S., second to the Chinese Americans. Not surprisingly, the state is a leader in balut production. During the course of my fieldwork for my master's thesis, from which this article is derived, I visited Metzer Farms, which supplies an estimated fifty percent of the balut sold in the Bay Area. The farm also sells balut to other immigrant groups such as the Vietnamese, Cambodians, Laotians, and Chinese. In addition, Thais, Malays and Indonesians are known to eat it. Based on the closest Thai transliteration, balut is called *khaj luuk* or *khay luuk* (same in Laotian). For Cambodians, the closest transliteration in the Khmer language that refers to embryonic eggs is *pomtiakhong* or *pomtiakong*. Another spelling based on the sound of the word is *poomgpiakoong*.

What is balut?

Fertilized duck eggs sold as balut in the U.S. range from 16 to 20 days in age. The older the egg, the larger the chick and the more pronounced its feathers, bones, and beak. An embryo at 17 days has beak and feathers which are more developed at 20 days. Normally, after being fertilized, a chick hatches after 26 to 28 days of incubation.

The taste of the egg also depends on the breed of the laying duck. Different breeds of ducks supposedly produce balut varying in taste, with Muscovy ducks being hailed by some as the "cream of the crop" (Freeman 1996:53). The kind of balut sold in the U.S. is made from duck eggs. Chicken eggs may be made into balut as well, but duck eggs are preferred by the majority of Filipino Americans since they are larger and thought to be better in taste.

But whether the fertilized egg is chicken or duck, there are two types of balut. One is called *mamatong* by Filipinos. *Mamatong* balut has the embryo floating on top of the white and yolk and the consumer can easily detect it. Roughly translated to mean "the float," *mamatong* occurs between 14 to 16 days. The second is *balut sa puti* where the embryo is wrapped by a thin, whitish membrane and one cannot tell whether there is an embryo or not. In *balut sa puti,* the embryo is hidden by the albumen's white film. *Balut sa puti* is 17 to 18 days old and it is the preferred favorite of Filipinos in the U.S. and in the Philippines. A folk belief in the Philippines lets people know if an egg has developed into *mamatong* or *balut sa puti.* One takes a balut egg and drops it in water. If it floats, it is *mamatong,* but if it sinks, it is *balut sa puti.*

Just how good and fresh a balut is after it has been boiled can be determined by its broth, called "soup" by balut eaters. After cracking a hole in the wide part of the shell, the consumer usually sips the broth before he or she eats any part of the tiny chick and remaining yolk. If the balut is good, its soup has a sweet, clean taste. Fresh balut can be good for ten days to two weeks. Cooked balut if stored in the refrigerator will last for as long as a month. But the longer the balut is in the refrigerator, the more likely that its liquid will be dried out.

Nguyen is a balut distributor in Orange County. He has been familiar with fertilized duck eggs (which he calls balut instead of hot vit Ion), since he was a young child in Vietnam watching his father down three eggs with cognac during dinner. Nguyen says there are not too many big duck farms in Vietnam. If there are some, the eggs are usually hatched for the young. The *hot vit lon* that are available are boiled and sold by vendors who resemble the Filipino sellers, crying "hot vit lon" much like the way Filipino balut sellers sound. The eggs are sold in the afternoon, after work. However, Nguyen claims that *hot vit lon* is not believed in Vietnam to be an aphrodisiac. But now in the U.S., he and other Vietnamese believe it after hearing about it from Filipino friends.

Eating balut

In the U.S., balut is usually sold uncooked in Asian markets and sometimes cooked in Filipino restaurants. Once bought, raw balut is prepared by cooking it in boiling water for 20 to 30 minutes. It is eaten warm and never cold, and can be eaten by itself or accompanied with condiments. Filipinos eat it with salt, vinegar or soy sauce, while many Vietnamese Americans like Nguyen eat it with a green, mint-like herb called *rau ram* as well as salt and pepper. Nguyen also uses a spoon to eat the egg like many Vietnamese do, in contrast to Filipinos who do not.

Nguyen emphasizes that when he eats balut, it has to be accompanied by a drink, either cognac or beer. This is also true for Filipino male consumers. "I don't drink too much, but when I eat balut, I have to drink something," Nguyen said.

A good duck balut has four parts. There is the yolk, the white part called *bato* (rock) which is the tough-to-eat albumen, the embryo, and some liquid which aficionados sip with gusto before opening the egg. If the balut has a crack or if it is a chicken balut, it tends to not have the soup or liquid which is naturally present in duck eggs even after they are cooked.

There are numerous ways to eat the egg, but a usual method involves tapping the broad base of the egg on the table or with a spoon. Then the consumer removes the small cracked shell and breaks the delicate membrane to sip the liquid of the balut. As one sips the soup, one continues breaking the shell to expose the yolk, embryo and albumen. At this point, one can separate the pieces on a plate and salt them before eating. Others prefer to eat the egg straight from the shell, in two to three bites in order to not see the duck or chicken embryo. Those who like the taste of balut but cannot chew the embryo swallow it whole.

In his 15 years of distributing balut to stores as well as Filipino Americans and other Asian Americans in the Bay area, Butch Coyoca estimates that he has sold hundreds of thousands of eggs. In 1997, Coyoca states that he handled 5,000 to 10,000 fertilized eggs twice a week. Not surprisingly, he has come up with his own observations on why people eat balut.

According to Coyoca, about 60 percent of the people who buy balut from him believe that there is some medicinal value in eating it or that it creates a sex drive in males. When delivering balut directly to consumers during parties, he observes most balut eaters are males. This is similar to the Philippines. Of his customers, roughly 75 percent of Filipino American males and 25 percent of Filipino American women eat balut. Most of the Filipino American males who eat it are over 15 years old to seniors aged 55 and above.

But when it comes to Coyoca's Vietnamese American and Cambodian American consumers, eating balut is more evenly distributed, with 55 percent men and 45 percent women consuming balut. Thai Americans, however, do not eat as much as other groups. If they do eat balut, they prefer it to be made from chicken eggs.

Preferences for the age of the balut differ from group to group, although individual choices play a role as well. Vietnamese Americans generally prefer their eggs to be at least 17 days old and they along with Cambodians find 19-to-20-day-old balut to be more desirable, unlike Filipinos. In general, women prefer younger eggs with smaller embryos like 14 or 16 days old or *penoy* eggs. Penoy eggs range from 8 to 10 days of the incubation period, and they generally have no embryo.

Traditionally, men are what Coyoca terms the "hard-core balut eaters." This is the case for men no matter what race. Male customers usually want a bigger embryo aged 17 to 20 days. They tend not to be bothered with the appearance of the developed embryo.

A cheap, "super" food

The *Food Composition Table for Use in East Asia* (W. Leung et al. 1972:111) provides the following breakdown for nutrients in balut: embryonated duck egg—188 calories, 13.7 grams of protein, 14.2 grams of fat, 116 milligrams of calcium, 176 milligrams of phosphorous, 2.1 milligrams of iron, 875 micrograms of retinol, 435 micrograms of B-carotene equivalent, .12 milligrams of thiamine, .25 milligrams of riboflavin, 0.8 milligrams of niacin, 3 milligrams of ascorbic acid.

Balut is categorized in Filipino culture as a "hot" food, and therefore those with a fever are told not to eat it. A few informants mentioned limiting their balut consumption for fear of cholesterol. But for many, balut's reputed benefits more than outweigh its proscriptions.

Calling balut the cheapest nutritional substitute available to Filipinos, Butch Coyoca says that one can buy balut instead of buying vitamins. "It's like a powerbar, a superfood," he said. "If you stay up late at night and it's already morning, like 2 a.m., a lot of people would eat one or two before they go to bed because they would believe that (balut) would compensate for whatever losses they incurred for not sleeping enough." Coyoca also points to the ease in transporting balut, which makes it a convenient food to eat during long journeys when one cannot have a regular meal with rice, fish and vegetables.

The stark poverty in the Philippines is a definite factor in the consumption of balut. "Because most Filipinos have low incomes, they have learned to use all edible parts of a plant or animal product. . . the internal organs of chicken, hogs, cattle, which may look unappetizing, can be made into savory dishes" (Claudio 1994:6). A list of the items available as street foods shows this to be the case, especially illustrated by the barbecued items sold on skewers and flavored with condiments to the customer's preference. Many of the barbecued parts have given rise to their own folk names. Beside barbecued bananas and rice porridge, one can find chicken feet, nicknamed "Adidas," chicken wings called "PAL" (Philippine Airlines), chicken intestine called "IUD" for its appearance, pig's ears which are known as "walkman," and the combs on roosters, which are referred to as "helmet" (Fernandez 1994:10).

According to Fernandez, about forty years ago chicken breasts and thighs and pork meat were being sold. But as the economic crisis worsened, so did the food. By the 1970s, "almost every part of the pig and chicken came to be used: pigs' ears and intestines; chicken wings, necks, feet, heads, tails, combs, even intestines, meticulously cleaned and looped on thin skewers" (Fernandez 1994:9).

The consumption of balut, therefore, may in recent times be more tied to the economic situation in the Philippines since it is a relatively inexpensive source of protein and calcium. However, this cannot be the reason as to why Filipino Americans continue to eat balut. Other factors must be present. The fact is Filipino Americans choose willingly to eat a food that others consider exotic in a country full of steak and chicken. It may be that for them, balut is a luxury item, along the lines of oysters and caviar. But before expanding on the possible cultural factors involved, I will first turn to balut history.

The history of balut

It is impossible to date accurately when the custom of eating balut first began since pre-Spanish records written in syllabic writing by early Filipinos have not survived the burning zeal of the Spanish missionaries. This has forced scholars to consult ancient records of neighboring countries to find references regarding the Philippines. What is known is that long before the Spaniards set foot on the Philippine islands in 1521, Filipinos were already conducting maritime trade with Persia, Arabia, India (directly and indirectly through Indonesia from the 2nd century A.D.) and especially China beginning in 300 A.D. (Garcia 1979:8–34; Jocano 1975b:135–158).

Theorizing that many of the modern world's eating habits are a result of Columbus's journey to the New World in 1492, and the subsequent growth of the Spanish empire which involved the exchange of goods as corn, tomatoes, chilies and livestock, Raymond Sokolov points to the Philippines as being one of the main "centers for gastronomic change" (1991:14–22). Spain controlled the Philippines through Mexico, enabling the Spaniards also to partake in commerce with China. The effects of Spanish colonization as well as the history of exchanges with neighboring countries can be seen in Philippine cuisine with its Spanish, Chinese and Malay-influenced dishes that have been indigenized by the use of local ingredients and Filipino seasoning tastes.

Popular dishes like *adobo* betray their Spanish-Mexican origin with their names. *"dobo* is chicken or pork simmered with vinegar, soy sauce and bay leaves. There are rich desserts such as *leche flan* and a bread called *pan de sal*. The Philippines owes its noodle dishes, as well as its *lumpia* (egg roll) and *siopao* (*char su bao*, a white bun filled with meat), to the Chinese (Fernandez & Alegre 1988:17). For references to the Philippines in ancient Chinese records, see Wang 1952.

The influence of the Chinese may perhaps explain the presence of balut in the country. Many books on Chinese food tend to mention salted duck eggs, tea eggs and century-old duck eggs (see Chang 1977; Barer-Stein 1979; E. N. Anderson 1988), but a sprinkling of works do mention fertilized eggs. In his work *Food in China: A Cultural and Historical Inquiry* (1991), geographer Frederick Simoons provides a clue regarding fertilized duck eggs. "Perhaps also of nutritional relevance is the Chinese liking for fertilized eggs in which the embryo is well-developed, a preference they share with certain peoples in Southeast Asia and the Pacific region. Embryonated duck eggs . . . are substantially higher in calcium than ordinary ones" (Simoons 365). In addition to confirming that fertilized eggs were consumed by the Chinese, Simoons also verifies the widely held belief in the Philippines that balut is an important source of calcium, which explains why pregnant women and sick people are urged to eat it as well.

The earliest citation I was able to find regarding balut is an 1830 report on Siam and Cochin, China (Crawfurd 1830). It seems that "hatched eggs" were being eaten during great parties. The eggs "formed a delicacy beyond the reach of the poor, and only adapted for persons of distinction"; after 10 to 12 days when an egg is being hatched, they are "exactly in the state most agreeable to the palate of a Cochin Chinese epicure" (Crawfurd 1830:408).

M. Duval also mentioned incubated duck eggs in 1885, and so did geographer Friedrich Ratzel in *The History of Mankind* (1896–1898). "The Tagals are said to have learnt from the Chinese to eat eggs that have been sat upon, with the chick in them, as tit-bits" (Ratzel 1896–1898:432). In 1905, Jenks took note of the Igorots' liking for developing eggs and how they preferred to wait "until there is something in the egg to eat" (Jenks 1905:143). There are other works mentioning balut consumption; see Verrill 1946:211; and Schwabe 1979:399.

Before his 1979 work on Chinese food, Simoons included a paragraph on the eating of fertilized eggs in *Eat Not This Flesh* (1961). He speculates that this custom may have arisen long ago "when people gathered the eggs of wild fowl, any of which contained half-hatched birds, or it may be related to some primitive fear of undeveloped eggs. As eggs are widely considered to be a fertility symbol, primitive man may have been afraid to eat them before they had developed into some recognizable form of life, when their dangerous quality was presumably eliminated" (Simoons 1961:68).

I do not agree with this theory, for in my search through historical records of the Spanish chroniclers dating from 500 years ago, there is no mention of a fear of "undeveloped" eggs by early Filipinos; instead there was plenty of evidence that they enjoyed eating all kinds of eggs. For example, both Pigafetta and Loarca remarked on the tabon bird whose eggs in the sand were prized by Filipinos (Blair & Robertson 33:133; Blair & Robertson 5:167).

Describing his fascinating encounter with a native chief, Pigafetta writes in 1521 that the chief "was eating turtle eggs which were in two porcelain dishes, and he had four jars full of palm wine in front of him covered with sweet-smelling herbs and arranged with four small reeds in each jar by means of which he drank. . . then the king had us eat some of those eggs and drink through those slender reeds" (Blair & Robertson 33:149). Diego de Bobadilla also remarked on how he enjoyed eating those eggs as well (Blair & Robertson 29:303). Eggs were not only eaten but used in devotions to deities (Blair & Robertson 27:261), to honor the dead (Blair & Robertson 21:209), and hurled in rituals where the broken eggs cemented promises (Blair & Robertson 14:283–284).

As these records show, the early Filipinos were not afraid of eating eggs. Eggs for Filipinos were not things to fear but things to savor. Although there is no mention that the eggs were fertilized, it may well be that Filipinos may have been eating them long before the Spanish arrived. Filipinos have the most adventurous palates and consume many items which others, especially Westerners, may fear. In light of the brief historical mentions above, it may be assumed that by the 19th century, the Chinese truly did influence the Filipinos regarding the eating of balut.

If the practice of eating balut was already common in the 16th century, I am sure it would have been noted by the friars and explorers who were only too eager to mention all the seemingly gross eating habits they could find, such as the Filipino liking for what Spanish chronicler Antonio De Morga called "rotting" fish and shrimps (this may be *bagoong*, fermented shrimp not unlike fish sauce) (see Blair & Robertson 16:80).

It is my contention that balut-eating developed because it is an easy and relatively cheap protein source for people to eat. I also believe that the aphrodisiac belief attached to it was not originally a reason for people to eat balut, but I would suggest that this belief in balut as an aphrodisiac for men only came about when the Spaniards introduced the concept of "machismo," a notion I will expand on below.

[…]

The balut industry in the Philippines

To shelter themselves from typhoons, the early Chinese settlers in the Philippines constructed their settlements in the Luzon region by the shores of Laguna de Bay, which is a freshwater lake with an area of 350 square miles that is 25 miles in length and 21 miles in width. By the time the Spaniards arrived, one village in particular had an enormous number of ducks, and so it was christened "Pateros," meaning "duck-raisers." As late as the 1950s, Pateros had an estimated 400,000 ducks producing eggs, with production supplemented by millions of imported eggs (Maness 1950:10–13). For Pateros, which is 40 kilometres from Manila, producing balut became the number one industry and balut from this area was synonymous with the highest quality (Cunanan 1968; Zabilka 1963).

But by 1977, gone was the crystal-clear water where fishing was easy and ducks were free to roam and eat their favorite diet of snails. Pollution from factories and the dumping of garbage had taken their toll and blackened the waters of Laguna de Bay, infecting snails with algae which in turn has led to ducks having infertile eggs. The Pateros balut industry suffered as a consequence and many balut producers pursued other business ventures (Herrera 1977:24–25). One informant told of being forced to move from Pateros when the Laguna de Bay got polluted to other towns in Rizal in order to gather the fresh eggs needed for balut. Balut is now made in other places.

The word "balut" may have been derived from the traditional way that it was made. "Balut" is very similar to the Tagalog word *"balot,"* which means "wrapper" when used as a noun, or "to cover" when it is used as a verb (*"balutin mo"* translates to "cover it"). Balut made in the traditional way involves the eggs being covered by bags containing rice husks. The husks are heated in copper kettles until they become dry as well as extremely hot.

No matter what method is being used to make balut, the first step is to choose fertilized duck eggs that have thick, unbroken shells. In the Philippines, special men would be hired whose job consisted of selecting eggs with the thickest shell. This is no small feat as there are thousands of eggs that have to be looked at. These selected eggs must then be exposed to the sun for 3 to 5 hours to get them to "perspire" out the extra moisture before they are ready for incubation.

One common method utilized by balut-makers, called *mangbabalut,* involved the eggs being kept in woven bamboo incubators in the shape of barrels 3 feet high and 2 feet in width. The bamboo barrels were frequently used before the advent of artificial incubators and were designed to hold 10 bamboo trays, each of which could hold 100 to 120 eggs. One barrel could then contain 1,000 to 1,200 eggs (Maness 10). A variation on the bamboo trays was that the eggs would be placed in bags made of abaca hemp.

The eggs stay in the barrels to incubate for 18 days, and are "candled" using a candle or a lightbulb on the seventh, fourteenth and eighteenth days. A typical instrument for candling is the *silawan,* which is a box-like device in the shape of a triangle or a square. The Filipino balut-maker inserts the egg into a specially designed hole to hold it and by means of a light bulb inside the box, the contents of the egg can be seen. Something to watch out for while candling is a dark shape in the egg, which means an embryo has formed. If there are web-like veins, then the embryo is growing. If the light does not show anything but a whole yolk, then the egg is infertile. Sometimes, there is a crack on the egg or the embryo has died early. These are sold as penoy or made into salted eggs. In the U.S., the sale of eggs with dead embryos is prohibited.

[…]

Supernatural beliefs and balut

Many of my informants expressed strong feelings of disgust at seeing the embryo or catching a glimpse of the developed little chick. After studying the survey responses, I believe that the feelings of revulsion experienced by many at the sight of the fetus may be due to the idea of ingesting something that is clearly on the verge of being born. The notion of eggs as symbols of life can be demonstrated by the fact that many places, including parts of Africa, Europe and Australia, impose prohibitions on the eating of eggs (Newall 1971:113–115). Eggs were not to be consumed or destroyed because they had "universal significance . . . as an image of life force" (Newall 1971:113). This idea of eating something and ending its life as a chick seems to be a deep, disturbing issue for even those who choose to eat balut as well as for those who do not.

Several of the informants I interviewed mentioned that eating balut makes a person like an *aswang*. Also known as a *manananggal,* an *aswang* is a supernatural creature who craves human flesh and is afraid of salt and spice. Folklorist Maximo D. Ramos was convinced that "the Filipinos' decided preference for salt, sour, and spicy foods is likely due to their fear of the *manananggal* and similar preternatural beings" (1990b:148). I am not, however, insinuating that balut eaters are aswang. Rather, there seems to be a symbolic relationship between the belief in a balut's invigorating powers and the belief in the aswang. Perhaps the beliefs regarding balut may have been an effect or a result of the belief in the aswang.

[…]

Aswang: Creatures of the night

As early as 1582, Miguel de Loarca described the aswang belief among the Pintados of Panay, and in 1588 to 1591, Juan de Plasencia followed with an account of the Tagalogs and their belief in the aswang. However, it is Maximo Ramos who is credited for comprehensively defining not only several types of aswang but the numerous creatures of Philippine lower mythology.

According to Ramos, the aswang can be understood best if identified with similar European creatures. There are five types: the aswang who is usually female and likened to the blood-sucking vampire; the viscera-sucker who can remove its upper half from the lower half of its body; the weredog aswang who can change its shape; the aswang who is a witch capable of the evil eye and spells; the ghoul aswang who eats corpses. These five types share similar traits with each other and with other supernatural beings, leading to some confusion.

Various Filipino ethnic groups have different names for the aswang depending on its form and behavior, and the names proliferate even more with each type of aswang, such as the viscera sucker (see Lieban 1967:68; Ramos 1990c:xvi–xvii). Among the most well-known terms for viscera-suckers are: *aswang* (Bikol, Tagalog, Visayan); *abat* (Waray); *boroka* (Iloko, from Spanish word 'bruja'); *manananggal* (Tagalog); *mangalok* (Cuyonon); *aswang na lupad* (Bikol); *naguneg* (Iloko); *laman luob* (Tagalog) and *kasudlan* (West Visayan) (Ramos 1990b:142 and 1990c:xviii).

Viscera suckers are not limited to the Philippines but they can be found in Indonesia, Malaysia, Cambodia and Melanesia, including the Trobriand Islands. They are known as *tanggal* in Indonesia (*tanggal* means to "remove" or "take off something" in Tagalog and Indonesian. It also means "come apart," in that the top of the *tanggal's* body comes off). In Cambodia, it is known as *srei ap* and it feeds on human feces. It can fly using its hair or ears or pandanus leaves in Melanesia (Ramos 1990b:144). For clarity's sake, I will limit myself to the use of the word *aswang* as a general term for all five supernatural creatures.

It is significant that in Filipino folk belief, salt and seasonings play an important part in warding off creatures like the aswang or placating others like the dwende (dwarves), who prefer food without salt (see Ramos 1990a:40–41, 58). For example, ghoul aswangs, who are believed to feed on dead bodies which they often steal during wakes, are terrified of salt, spices, and vinegar. Vampire aswangs and viscera suckers are also driven away by the use of salt and spices like garlic. For more on the aswang's fear of salt and spices, see (Arens 1982:84; Ramos 1990c).

Salt also plays an essential role in eating balut. The overwhelming majority of balut eaters prefer salt sprinkled on their eggs. Other spices include pepper and vinegar with chilies. Perhaps salt is used by people as a sort of neutralizing agent when eating balut, unconsciously warding off the aswang effects. Since salt and spices are reputed to scare off various types of the aswang, presumably the person eating balut would not turn into an aswang.

In addition to being a neutralizer, salt may also be used unconsciously as a sort of purifying agent, to cleanse the balut eater from the impure action of eating and therefore ending the life of the baby chick. I speculate that if this is the case, the sprinkling of salt may be for the balut eater a way of atoning for the "sin" of ending another's life for the sake of continuing his/her own. The notion that a life must be ended to ensure that others may live could be applied here, with salt acting as an offering to the sacrificed life. However, salt should not be taken too seriously as an extension of the fear of the aswang or as a purifying agent; after all, supernatural beings aside, salt does tend to make everything taste better.

[…]

Sexual beliefs and balut

Whether balut is eaten for nutrition or avoided due to fear of becoming a terrifying aswang, the most common reason why balut is eaten as cited by my informants is the fertilized egg's alleged sexual energizing powers. Venetia Newall demonstrates that in many cultures, eggs are believed to restore virility to men but they can also bestow fertility to women (1971:113–141). It seems, then, that the sexual benefits of balut should apply to both men and women. But not so in the Philippines. I suggest that although the eating of fertilized eggs may have begun centuries ago at the same time as *pulutan,* the belief that it is an aphrodisiac strictly for men can be traced to the arrival of the Spanish in 1521. Christening the archipelago "Las Islas Filipinas" in honor of King Philip II of Spain, the Spanish conquistadors set about converting the natives. In addition to the morals and values of the Catholic religion, the Spaniards also brought with them their own set of values which they enforced on the natives. One of the lingering effects of more than 300 years of Spanish colonial rule is the machismo concept.

Tomas Andres's *Dictionary of Filipino Culture and Values* defines machismo as the "belief in male supremacy and the relegation of the women to a domestic role and as second-class citizens" (Andres 1994:97). It must be stressed at this point that not all women in the Philippines are treated in such a manner, and not all men believe in this concept.

[…]

What does all this data about sexuality have in common with balut? In my study of balut, I have attempted to show how sexual and cultural values of the Filipinos and Filipino Americans can be seen in the beliefs regarding the consumption of fertilized eggs. I argue that for Filipino men in the U.S., balut is eaten primarily for its powers to increase sexual potency and virility. It must be repeated that Filipino Americans who eat balut purchase their eggs raw, and not cooked since vendors selling balut are not present in the U.S. as in the Philippines. This means that eating this food is not a matter of convenience—the raw balut has to be boiled anywhere from 20 to 45 minutes. And one must first obtain some eggs from a farm or a market, that is, if there are even some fertilized eggs available to be sold. All of these factors are obstacles which may altogether discourage Filipino immigrants from seeking to eat balut in this country. But this is not the case as of now.

Although Filipinos of all ages and sexes in the Philippines eat balut, my informants stated that in the U.S., male balut eaters outnumber female eaters. The fact that female eaters, although a minority, continue to consume the fertilized duck eggs suggests that consuming balut is part of their ethnic identity. Food as a marker of ethnicity has been illustrated by numerous food scholars (see for ex., Theophano 1991; Brown and Mussell 1984; Staub 1989). But in addition to eating balut as enacting one's ethnic identity, I would like to suggest another reason why Filipinos, specifically Filipino American males, would want to eat it. Since nutritional needs for protein are not under consideration (indeed, many Filipino Americans have to limit their intake of foods like this which are high in cholesterol), it seems that balut as an aphrodisiac for men is the prime reason why Filipino Americans continue their consumption of balut. In a land where economic hardships do not necessarily distract Filipino American males in their pursuit of more sensual considerations, balut is sought for the belief that it can "rev up" one's sex life.

Appendix

Survey questionnaire

[Questions marked with an asterisk were considered especially important.]

Balut Survey: Please answer the following:

1. Name, age, occupation, ethnicity, (please also mention if first or second generation Filipino or other nationality)
2. Are you familiar with eating a fertilized egg called balut?
3. Do you know another name for it?
4. When and where did you first eat balut and how old were you?
5. When and where was the last time you ate balut? When did you eat it, morning, noon, or night?
*6. Why do you eat balut?
7. Where do you tend to eat it? ex. home, work, parties, dinner, snack during the day.
*8. How do you eat it? Please describe in detail from the moment you get it. Do you also put any seasoning or condiment on it?
9. Whom do you eat balut with, yourself or with others?
*10. Is balut good for anything? (ex. health, energy, sex). Please explain in detail what balut is good for according to your opinion and personal experience. If you are stating hearsay, please state this clearly as hearsay.
*11. If balut is good for something, do you think balut works?
12. How often do you eat balut?
13. Do you think everybody, male and female, young and old, eats balut or is there a specific age group that eats balut in the Philippines? What about in the U.S.?
14. What immigrant groups are you aware of eating balut?
15. Is there any reason or occasion NOT to eat balut?
*16. How did you feel after you ate balut? In other words, did you feel any effects and how soon did you feel those effects?

17. Does eating balut have any connection that you know of to Filipino supernatural beliefs ex. multo (ghosts), dwende (dwarves), aswang (witches) and other creatures of the night?

18. What was the effect of balut on your friends who ate it when it was prescribed to them by others (usually, friends urge others to eat balut for a reason, ex. telling newlyweds to eat it).

19. When is balut sold in the Philippines: morning, noon, or night? In U.S.? If sold at night in the Phil., why do you think this was so?

*20. Who was selling the balut, male or female? Why do you think it is sold the way it is in the Philippines, wrapped up like a baby?

*21. Can you think of any stories connected to balut from your experience or hearing from others about balut's supposed powers for the male? Please be detailed. (If this is something new to you, just say you have not heard it before).

22. What country and place do you think balut originated from?

23. If balut was easily available, how often would you eat it?

24. Optional: If you have further information about balut, please add it here. It could be anything from what you feel about balut or books and articles you came across that had information on balut.

[…]

References

Anderson, E. N. 1988. *The Food of China*. New Haven: Yale University Press.

Andres, Tomas Quintin D. 1994. *Dictionary of Filipino Culture and Values*. Quezon City: Giraffe Books.

Arens, Richard. 1982. *Folk Practices and Beliefs of Leyte and Samar: The Collected Articles of Fr. Richard Arens*. Gregorio C. Luangco ed. Tacloban City: Divine Word University Publications.

Barer-Stein, Thelma. 1979. *You Eat What You Are: A Study of Canadian Ethnic Food Traditions*. Toronto: McClelland & Stewart.

Blair, Emma Helen & James A. Robertson eds. 1903–1909. *The Philippine Islands 1493–1898*. Cleveland: The Arthur H. Clark Co. 55 vols.

Brown, Linda Keller & Kay Mussell. eds. 1984. *Ethnic and Regional Foodways in the United States: The Performance of Group Identity*. Knoxville: The University of Tennessee Press.

Chang, K. C. ed. 1977. *Food in Chinese Culture: Anthropological and Historical Perspectives*. New Haven: Yale University Press.

Claudio, Virginia S. 1994. *Filipino American Food Practices, Customs, & Holidays*. Chicago: American Dietetic Association.

Crawfurd, John. 1830. *Journal of an Embassy from the Governor-General of India to the Courts of Siam and Cochin China; Exhibiting a View of the Actual State of Those Kingdoms*. 2nd edition. vol. 1 of 2. London: Henry Colburn & Richard Bentley.

Cunanan, Agustina S. 1968. "Ang Industriya ng Balut" in *Intermediate Readings in Tagalog*. Berkeley and Los Angeles: University of California Press. p. 121.

Douglas, Mary. 1966. *Purity and Danger*. New York: Pantheon.

—. "Deciphering a Meal." 1972. *Daedalus* 101:61–82.

Duval, Mathias. 1885. "Sur les oeufs pourris comme aliment en Chine." *Bulletins de la Societe D'Anthropologie de Paris* troisieme serie vol. 8:209–300.

Fernandez, Doreen G. 1994. *Tikim: Essays on Philippine Food and Culture*. Pasig: Anvil Publishing.

—. "The World of Balut." Sept. 1996. *Food* 1.12:10–12.

Fernandez, Doreen & Edilberto Alegre. 1988. *Sarap: Essays on Philippine Food*. Aduana, Intramuros, Manila: Mr. & Mrs. Publishing Co.

Freeman, Nancy. July 1996. "Balut Brokering: Embryonic Enterprises." *Filipinas Magazine,* 53–56.

Garcia, Mauro ed. 1979. *Readings in Philippine Prehistory.* Manila: The Filipiniana Book Guild.

Georges, Robert A. 1984. "You Often Eat What Others Think You Are: Food as an Index of Others' Conceptions of Who One Is." *Western Folklore* 43: 249–255.

Harris, Marvin. *Good to Eat: Riddles of Food and Culture.* New York: Simon and Schuster, 1985.

Hennessey, Ann. January 5, 1995. "Growing Filipino Colony makes Riverside County Home." *Press Enterprise* Section B:8.

Herrera, Tetchie. June 1977. "Your Chance to go into Balut-Making." *Philippine Farmer's Journal* pp. 24–25.

Jenks, Albert E. 1905. *The Bontoc Igorot.* Manila: Bureau of Public Printing.

Jocano, F. Landa. 1975a. *The Philippines at the Spanish Contact.* Manila: MCS Enterprises.

—. 1975b. *Philippine Prehistory. An Anthropological Overview of the Beginnings of Filipino Society and Culture.* Diliman: Philippine Center for Advanced Studies.

Kalčik, Susan. 1984. "Ethnic Foodways in America: Symbol and the Performance of Identity." In *Ethnic and Regional Foodways in the United States: The Performance of Group Identity.* Brown and Mussell, eds. pp. 37–65. Knoxville: The University of Tennessee Press.

Kessler, John. Oct. 13, 1995. "Filipino Fare for the Open Mind and Bold Palate." *The Denver Post* p. 30.

Lane, Megan & Peter Logue & Colleen Logue. Dec. 1, 1995. "Frozen Ducks Fetch Cold Cash." *The Evening Post (Wellington)* Business Section p. 13.

Leung, Woot-Tsuen Wu & R. R. Butrum and F. H. Chang. 1972. *Food Composition Table for Use in East Asia.* Part 1. DHEW Publication No. (NIH) 73–465. Bethesda: U.S. Dept. of Health, Education and Welfare and the Food and Agricultural Organization of the United Nations.

Lewin, Kurt. 1942. "Forces behind Food Habits and Methods of Change" *Bulletin of the National Research Council,* pp. 35–65.

Lieban, Richard. 1967. *Cebuano Sorcery: Malign Magic in the Philippines.* Berkeley: University of California Press.

Maness, Hubert. June 1950. "BalutCa Duck Egg Delicacy." *World's Poultry Science Journal* pp. 10–13.

McIntosh, Alistair. Nov. 1, 1994. "Filipinos Party Among the Dead." *Reuter's World Service.*

Morga, Antonio de. 1559–1636. *Historical events of the Philippine Islands: published in Mexico in 1609 by Antonio de Morga, recently brought to light and annotated by Jose Rizal; preceded by a prologue by Ferdinand Blumentritt.* Centennial ed. Manila: Jose Rizal National Centennial Commission, 1962. Series title: Rizal, Jose, 1861–1896. Writings of Jose Rizal; v.6.

Mydans, Seth. Jan. 26, 1997. "The World: the Philippines—What the World Eats While It Watches; the Snacks Are Here: Duck!" *New York Times,* late edition, section 4, column 4: 3.

Newall, Venetia. 1967. "Easter Eggs." *Journal of American Folklore* 80:3–32.

—. 1971. *An Egg at Easter: a Folklore Study.* London: Routledge and K. Paul.

—. 1984. "Easter Eggs: Symbols of Life and Renewal." *Folklore* 95:21–29.

—. 1990a. *Legends of Lower Gods.* Quezon City: Phoenix Publishing House.

—. 1990b. *Philippine Demonological Legends and their Cultural Bearings.* Quezon City: Phoenix Publishing House.

—. 1990c. *The Aswang Complex in Philippine Folklore.* Quezon City: Phoenix Publishing House.

Ratzel, Friedrich. 1896–1898. *The History of Mankind.* vol. 1 of 3. London: Macmillan.

Richards, Audrey. 1932. *Hunger and Work in a Savage Tribe. A Functional Study of Nutrition Among the Southern Bantu.* Westport: Greenwood Press, 1985 edition.

Schwabe, Calvin W. 1979. *Unmentionable Cuisine.* Charlottesville: University Press of Virginia.

Sheridan, Margaret. Oct. 19, 1995. "Expatriates Have a Hunger for Home." *International Herald Tribune.* Section: Special Report. Dateline: Hong Kong. From Lexis Nexis database.

Simoons, Fredrick J. 1961. *Eat Not This Flesh: Food Avoidances in the Old World.* Madison: University of Wisconsin Press.

—. 1991. *Food in China: A Cultural & Historical Inquiry.* Boca Raton: CRC Press.

Sokolov, Raymond. 1991. *Why We Eat What We Eat: How the Encounter between the New World and the Old Changed the Way Everyone on the Planet Eats.* New York: Summit Books.

Staub, Shalom. *Yemenis in New York City. The Folklore of Ethnicity.* Philadelphia: The Balch Institute Press, 1989.

Theophano, Janet S. 1991. "I Gave Him a Cake: an Interpretation of Two Italian-American Weddings." In *Creative Ethnicity.* S. Stern and J. Cicala, eds. pp. 44–54. Logan: Utah State University.

Verrill, A. Hyatt. 1946. *Strange Customs, Manners and Beliefs.* Boston: L.C. Page & Co.

Wang, Teh-Ming. 1952. "An Early Mention of the Philippines in Chinese Records?" *Journal of East Asiatic Studies* 1:42–48.

Weismantel, Mary J. 1988. *Food, Gender and Poverty in the Ecuadorian Andes.* Philadelphia: University of Pennsylvania Press.

Zabilka, Gladys. ed. 1963. *Customs and Culture of the Philippines.* Rutland, VT: Charles E. Tuttle Publishing Co.

CHAPTER 10

FEEDING THE JEWISH SOUL IN THE DELTA DIASPORA

Marcie Cohen Ferris

Mention "The Delta" and vivid images come to mind of a dramatic, flat landscape etched by rows of cotton and bounded by the Mississippi River. One imagines catfish, juke joints, barbecue, and pick-up trucks in a world inhabited by white planters, poor white sharecroppers, and black blues musicians. Although the Mississippi and Arkansas Delta is largely populated by black and white working-class laborers and upper-class white landowners, the region is also shaped by a small group of Jewish southerners, now numbering no more than three hundred, whose families first arrived in the Delta in the late nineteenth century as peddlers and fledgling merchants.[1] Between the Mississippi River levee and Highway 61, amidst the shotgun houses, cotton fields, and Baptist churches of the Delta, are a handful of synagogues, Jewish cemeteries, Jewish-owned clothing stores, and businesses that were central to the economies of small Delta towns prior to the coming of discount stores like Wal-Mart. Less visible but nonetheless present are the adapted folklore and foodways of a transplanted culture, for feeding the Jewish soul, both spiritually and physically, has challenged Delta Jews from their first arrival in the region through today.

In the town of Blytheville in the Arkansas Delta, my family's Jewish identity separated us from our white and black Gentile neighbors. Contrary to popular belief, this division was more respectful than mean-spirited. Biblical identification of Jews as the "chosen people" carries weight in the South; because of our distant lineage to Moses, Jewish families had a special status in the Delta. Although there were violent incidents of antisemitism such as the 1960s temple bombings in Jackson and Meridian, Mississippi, most antisemitic expressions were far more benign actions such as exclusion from debutante parties, garden clubs, country clubs, and occasional comments about Jewish tightfistedness. My family attended synagogue—known to non-Jewish locals as "the Jewish church"—and offered up prayers to a deity, which helped to secure our acceptance in town. More than Judaism, it was the fact that we had not *always* lived in the community that separated us from the Gentiles. Because generations of history did not intimately link "our people" with "their people," our place in the local hierarchy of white society was never clear.[2]

My Jewish ancestors arrived in the Delta in the early 1920s. We lived within the Delta world of cotton planting, fall ginning, church socials, and football and the Jewish world of weekly Sabbath services, visiting rabbis, and preparation for the Passover seder in the spring and the High Holy Days of Rosh Hashanah and Yom Kippur in the fall. We ate *between* these two worlds in a complicated culinary negotiation of regional, ethnic, and religious identity. Within Jewish homes in the Delta, African American cooks and domestic workers set bountiful tables and prepared the cuisine for which the region is famous. Their meals featured elegant dinners of standing rib roast, as well as down-home southern Gentile meals of barbecue and fried catfish. Less familiar dishes served at Jewish tables in the Delta included matzah balls, kugels (dairy casserole),

Marcie Cohen Ferris, 'Feeding the Jewish Soul in the Delta Diaspora', *Southern Cultures* 10 (3) (2004), 52–85. (Excerpt printed here: 52–56, 58–60, 62–64, 68, 71–72, 76–85. Omitted text is indicated by ellipses.)

Copyright © 2004 by the Center for Study of the American South. Used by permission of the University of North Carolina Press. www.uncpress.unc.edu.

tortes, and tzimmes (baked sweetened vegetables and fruits), foods that tied Jewish worlds to central and eastern Europe.

Food writer Craig Claiborne was "initiated into the joys" of Jewish foods in the home of Sadie Wolf, who lived across the street from the Claiborne family in Indianola, Mississippi. Claiborne recalls visiting the Wolfs' home one Passover when daughter Anita had eaten her fill of traditional holiday foods. "If somebody feeds me one more matzah ball I'm going to kill them," protested Wolf. As Claiborne recalls in his memoir, it was the "talent and palate" of African American cooks who blended "soul food"—a mix of African and American Indian flavors—with creole cuisine that made the southern kitchen unique. Although separated by a gulf of race and class, African Americans and Jews in the Mississippi and Arkansas Delta were brought together by a culinary exchange that has existed since the late nineteenth century.[3]

Throughout the nation food strongly defines ethnic and regional identity. But in the South, and especially in the Delta, a region scarred by war, slavery, and the aftermath of Reconstruction and segregation, food is especially important. Historian David Blight suggests that the South was conquered during the Civil War, and afterwards the slow process of rebuilding and "re-imagining" the South began. Blight contends that while the South is no richer in history and memory than any other region, more of its collective energy is devoted to defining the past through literature, storytelling, and monument-making.[4] We should add food traditions to this list, because southerners also use food to define the history of their region. For generations, southerners, including southern Jews, have struggled to understand their experience through memory-making, and much of that struggle takes place at the dinner table. In this tradition Delta Jews connect to family and regional history at every meal, Oneg Shabbat, and Sisterhood luncheon.

Food historian Joan Nathan argues that because of their "wandering history" Jews always adapted their lifestyles and foodways to local cultures. Apart from matzah (the Passover unleavened bread), haroset (the Passover apple and nut spread), and cholent (a traditional slow-cooked Sabbath stew), she argues that there are no specifically Jewish foods; rather, foods are associated with Jewish countries of origin. Since more than two-thirds of American Jews trace their roots to eastern Europe, Polish and Russian foods such as rye bread, borscht, and herring in sour cream became known as Jewish foods in America.[5] Eastern European Jews were not the only Jews to learn to "make do or do without" while adjusting their tastes to regional food traditions and local ingredients. Earlier waves of Sephardic and Ashkenazic Jews left many culinary traditions in the Old World, but not all. After arriving in the South, Jewish immigrants revived their memories of stewed fish dishes flavored with lemon, olive oil, and almonds, bean soups, roasted goose, duck, chicken, kugels, challahs, kuchens (coffee cake), and tortes. Jewish women gave these recipes to African American cooks, who integrated these dishes into the culinary tradition of the South.

From the handful of Conservative and Orthodox Jews in the Delta, who closely adhere to the Jewish dietary rules, or *kashrut,* to the most liberal Reform Jews, who do not recognize these culinary restrictions, eating is inseparable from religion. Anthropologists, folklorists, and food historians agree that food is invested with symbolic meaning and that any food-related activity—from a simple meal at home to the most elaborate public celebration—is an act of communication.[6] In Judaism, food is both communication and communion. This concept is central to understanding the power of food in ethnic and regional communities like the Delta.

For observant Jews, eating is an act of divine law dictated from the Bible and expanded in the Talmud, the ancient rabbinic commentaries related to the Torah, the first five books of the Bible. As Blu Greenberg, an orthodox *rebbetzin* (wife of a rabbi) and an authority on the precepts of traditional Jewish life, explains, "Kashrut is not simply a set of rules about permitted and forbidden foods; kashrut is a way of life."[7] This way of life determines which foods are prohibited, how certain foods should be prepared, and how animals should be slaughtered. For example, Jews are allowed to eat meat only from animals that chew their cud and have cloven hooves, fish that have both fins and scales, and no combinations of dairy and meat dishes. Even this rudimentary explanation of kashrut hints at the predicament of Jews in the Delta, who are surrounded by a cuisine that celebrates *treyfe* (nonkosher) foods like pork, catfish, shrimp, crawfish, and wild game such as rabbit, squirrel, and deer. (Catfish is not kosher because it has no scales and is a nocturnal scavenger.)

Less observant Jews in the Delta ignore kashrut and eat Jewish foods like bagel and lox on Sunday morning as their only expression of Jewishness, a practice referred to as "kitchen Judaism."[8] For Delta Jews who position themselves between these two poles of observance, daily choices about food either connect them to or distance them from their Jewish identity. Thus, one encounters Jews who enjoy a pork barbecue sandwich at restaurants but avoid serving or eating pork at home. Some Jewish families keep separate dishes at home for serving nonkosher foods like shrimp and pork barbecue so that the "regular" dishes are not tainted by these forbidden foods—a "southernism" of kashrut that requires separate sets of dishes for meat and dairy items.

Sylvia Klumok Goodman and her sister Ann Klumok Bennett grew up in the Delta town of Moorhead, Mississippi, where their African American cook, Evalina Smith, prepared Jewish foods under the tutelage of their mother, Fannie Klumok. Smith created her own names for these foreign-sounding dishes. Gefilte fish was "filthy fish," chremslach (fried Passover fritter) became "himself," and haroset was "roses." "She might not have pronounced all these dishes correctly," said Sylvia, "but she could cook them as well as any Jewish *yenta* from the old country, actually better."[9]

The world of Delta families like the Klumoks, who lived "Jewishly" in a world dominated by the Mississippi River, cotton, churches, and the blues, reveals a unique expression of American Judaism. Although they were far removed from Jewish butcher shops, bakeries, grocery stores, and even synagogues, Delta Jews frequently drove to Greenville, Greenwood, Clarksdale, Vicksburg, and Blytheville to socialize and worship. Regular trips were made to Memphis to buy kosher meat and "kosher-style" and Jewish foods like bagels, rye bread, pastrami, and corn beef.[10]

Jewish foodways in small towns throughout the Delta illustrate how "country Jewish" life was distinctive from that of "city Jews" in Memphis, where it was possible to socialize almost exclusively with other Jews. Strong Jewish social ties in the Delta created a sense of Jewish community through monthly dinner clubs, Sisterhood and B'nai B'rith activities, deli lunches, seders, Jewish golf tournaments, dances, and youth activities that reinforced Jewish identity. Foodways of Delta Jews reveal a regional Jewish culture shaped by a deep sense of place, isolation, kinship ties, agricultural occupations, the influence of white and black Protestant cultures, and a long history of racial and class divisions.

"Cotton has been good to the Jewish people"

Morris Grundfest was born in Russia in 1869. He came to New York in the late 1890s, married Mollie Bernstein, and after the birth of their two children, the couple came to the Mississippi Delta. They were drawn by family already settled in the South and their belief that the South was an "open place" that presented opportunity with its many farms and plantations. Like so many southern Jewish immigrants, Morris Grundfest began as a pack peddler, walking between farms and plantations to sell goods to white and black families. Eventually, the Grundfests opened M. Grundfest's, a dry goods store in the nearby town of Cary. Later, stepping outside the retail sphere, Morris Grundfest purchased two hundred and twenty acres of Delta farmland and established himself as both a shopkeeper and a cotton planter.[11]

Betty Grundfest Lamensdorf, the great granddaughter of Mollie and Morris, and her husband, Ben, farm the original acreage known as "the Grundfest place." "People are surprised you're Jewish and a farmer," said

Ben Lamensdorf, who has raised cotton in the Delta for over forty years, "but we were farming a long time ago in Israel. We just went from sheep herders to raising cotton. Cotton has been good to the Jewish people who came to the Mississippi Delta."[12]

Morris's son Ike raised cotton in the Delta, ran his father's store after his death in 1925, and married June Flanagan, an Episcopalian. Their store was open six days each week, except for Rosh Hashanah and Yom Kippur, when Ike Grundfest closed it for half a day. Betty and her sister, Ann Grundfest Gerache, worked in the store after school and on Saturdays, the busiest shopping day of the week. "The labor would come in on Saturday to receive their pay, and then they'd buy their week's groceries. They usually ran about fifteen dollars," said Betty. "That would hold you for a whole week. And then, when everyone had gotten their groceries and visited and everything, we'd take the people and their groceries back to their houses."[13]

Despite the racial and class divisions that separated them, African Americans in the Delta found that Jews like the Grundfests were fair employers and shopkeepers. African Americans could try on clothes and shoes in Jewish-owned stores, and they were often employed as sales clerks. The Grundfests also provided transportation and housing for the black laborers who worked for them, an arrangement shaped by long-held Delta rules of race and class. "We knew that there was something different about them [Jewish southerners]," said writer Cliff Taulbert, an African American who grew up in nearby Glen Allan. "You didn't really expect them to do the same types of things that you'd expect a white person to do. And I guess, in our minds, we divided the two—there were white people in Glen Allan and there were Jewish people in Glen Allan. They may have felt they were white, but we never did."[14]

Some white gentile southerners may have questioned the racial status of their Jewish neighbors as well. Historian Leonard Rogoff argues that although southern Jews were accepted as white, their "precise racial place was not fixed," especially after Reconstruction with the arrival of thousands of eastern European Jews whose "swarthy" complexions concerned white southerners. The newly arrived Jews quickly realized that skin color in the South determined where they fell in the socioeconomic order. Jews in the Delta were accepted as white, and many joined local White Citizens' Councils during the 1950s and 1960s. Journalist Jack Nelson argues that the few resident Jews who became members of the councils did so either out of fear of antisemitism or because they too were "hard-rock segregationists."[15]

With their own racial identity questioned in a region plagued by nativism and growing antisemitism, Jews bridged the chasm between white and black cultures in their roles as merchants, cotton brokers, and music agents. A less visible but equally compelling source of identity was associated with food—at the Jewish dinner table, in the synagogue kitchen, and in Jewish-owned grocery stores and dry goods stores throughout the Delta. Here Jews encountered white and black Gentile neighbors, customers, domestic workers, cooks, and caterers, and southern and Jewish foods mixed. At times, the food choices emphasized Jews' "southerness," and at other times, the selections emphasized their "otherness."

With income from farming and their store, the Grundfests could afford to hire African Americans as cooks and domestic workers. Having full-time household help in the Delta—even with the meager salaries African American women were paid weekly—was often only possible for families where the wife worked in the family store and could not do the housework herself. In their Delta home, June Flanagan Grundfest supervised the work of African American employees, including Alice Watson, the family's cook, and Edna Davis, the housekeeper and the children's nurse.

Ann Grundfest Gerache described the family's daily meals as "southern country food." The Grundfest home was next door to the family store, and any ingredients Alice Watson needed were either found in the store or grown in the family's garden. "Mother didn't like to cook," said Ann. "She loved to garden. She did not like being inside cooking, because you worked half a day for every meal, and then it was gone in thirty minutes." Not allowed the luxury of "likes and dislikes," and limited to few options for work, African American cooks like Watson prepared three meals a day for white families like the Grundfests every day except Sunday. Watson worked a "double day," caring for the Grundfests during the day and beginning another round of labor with her own family when she returned home at night.[16]

In addition to her vegetable and flower gardens, June Grundfest raised squabs and chickens and tended a strawberry patch, plum and pear trees, and a fig tree from which she made delicious jams and jellies. The foods that Ann and Betty associate with their mother are a southern and Jewish mix of homemade jams and pickles, salted pecans, and blintzes, topped with June's homemade strawberry jelly, which their father, Ike, ate each Sunday evening. "If she put salted pecans on the table," said Ann, "it meant a celebration."[17] The pecans were grown locally on the place and were buttered, salted, toasted in the oven, and then put away for "company" and special occasions.

As Hortense Powdermaker observed in her sociological studies of Indianola in the 1930s, black domestic workers like Alice Watson were "the chief liaison agent between the races." The Grundfest girls were not allowed to help with the cooking, work considered inappropriate for well-to-do southern white women and girls, but after school they would slip into Watson's kitchen at the Grundfest home, where they sat on the kitchen counter and visited with Watson while she cooked. On occasion, Watson slipped the girls a forbidden cigarette. Ann and Betty recalled the cooking of "Ma Mary," who lived nearby and weighed cotton that the laborers picked in their cotton sacks during the fall harvest. "Ann and I used to walk down there and eat," said Betty. "She'd go out into her garden and pick the butter beans, peas, and okra. We'd sit at this little table and she'd bring the bread in a skillet from the wood-heated oven. That was the best food. It just stuck in my memory how good it tasted." Powdermaker collected a similar story from one of her female informants in the 1930s who said that the "happiest memory of her childhood" was when the family's black cook took her home, "across the tracks," to play with her children and eat turnip greens.[18] The narrative confirmed Powdermaker's belief that whites long cared for by black workers sentimentalized those relationships in their memories of nurturance and caring, often centered at the table.

The ample meals at the Grundfest table included several meats, bowls of fresh vegetables, rice and gravy, hot biscuits and cornbread, preserves, and two or three desserts. Ann found oppressive the amount of food and the ritual associated with their meals. "I'm not going to put all this food on my table," she brashly told her mother when she married. "We're going to have one meat, two vegetables, and I don't know if I'm going to have dessert."[19] In the Delta in the 1950s, Ann's declaration was considered a radical act.

Holidays were divided between June's Episcopal family in Blanton, Mississippi, where they celebrated Thanksgiving and Christmas, and Ike's Jewish family in Greenville and Clarksdale, where they visited on Sunday afternoons and at Passover and High Holy Days to attend religious services. The Grundfests belonged to temples in both Greenville and Vicksburg, which were fifty miles and thirty-seven miles respectively from Cary. At Christmas, June's aunt, Elizabeth Darden, oversaw an elegant dinner prepared by three African American cooks who were expected to work on the holiday. The feast included a turkey and all the trimmings, a coconut cake and ambrosia for dessert. Ike's sisters, Kate Grundfest Sebulsky and Hattie Grundfest Brownstein, worked in "ladies' ready-to-wear." During market trips to Memphis and St. Louis they bought kosher salamis, pastramis, and rye bread, treats that were served with home-made chopped liver when the family visited on Sundays.[20]

Beyond June's Sunday evening blintzes and the aunts' deli foods, Jewish foods were rarely eaten by the Grundfest family until they began to participate in the local community Passover seder, which was organized by Jewish families in the Rolling Fork area in the 1950s. Gefilte fish was bought in Jackson, and other dishes for the seder were prepared by Jewish women in Rolling Fork, Cary, and Anguilla. June always contributed a 1950s-style congealed salad. The dessert was individual "sham tarts," a Delta version of the German-Jewish shaum torte, a meringue served with fresh strawberries and whipped cream. Ann Gerache continues to serve the same dessert at family seders, where it has become known as "Mamaw's Slip and Slide Cake" because of its tendency to melt and slip on warm spring seder evenings.[21]

Living Jewishly in a gentile world of catfish and pork barbecue

Food traditions in the Grundfest family tell us much about the defining issue faced by Jews in the Delta since the late nineteenth century: the tension between the pull of assimilation as Jews began to make the Delta their home and the religious imperative to follow Jewish laws and foodways that by definition serve to set Jews apart from their Gentile neighbors. This tension touched all Jews in the Delta, regardless of their expression of Judaism and level of observance.

In the 1950s writer David Cohn, a native of Greenville, where his eastern European immigrant parents had opened a dry goods store, wrote that the Jews of the Delta had conformed so completely to the way of life of their Gentile neighbors that "they had not even clung to the many items of cookery gathered by their forebears during their peregrinations through Russia, Rumania, Hungary, Poland, Germany, and the Baltic States." Cohn underestimated the tenacity of food and the strength of food memories even in situations of great duress. In the Mississippi Delta Jews preserved food memories passed down by Jewish grandmothers and African American cooks alike. Despite intermarriage, a deep attachment to the South, and the strong influence of the white and black Protestant world in which they lived, Delta Jews preserved Jewish foodways in "the most southern place on earth."[22]

[...]

When Ann Grundfest married her first husband, Robert Emmich, a Vicksburg Jew, in the early 1950s, they agreed that a decision had to be made about their children's religion. "You can't have Christmas *and* Hanukkah," Robert told Ann. "You have to decide how you want to raise your children, and you must do one or the other."[23] They chose Judaism for their children, and with this choice came Jewish food. Ann learned to prepare Jewish foods rarely seen in her childhood home as she turned to Jewish cookbooks, in-laws, Sisterhood friends, and the rabbi for advice and their recipes.

[...]

Practicing Judaism in an overwhelmingly gentile world like the Delta was challenging, and for most Jews in the region, it meant adjusting religious practices to live in a farming society that conformed to both a southern and Protestant time table. For Jewish merchants like those in Vicksburg in the 1870s, this meant keeping their stores open on Saturdays—the Sabbath and holiest day of the Jewish calendar. In the 1940s and 1950s, Jewish retailers were overwhelmed with business from both white and black families that began early on Saturday morning and continued late into the evening. "This street on Saturday night when I was growing up," said Joe Erber of Greenwood's downtown, "'till one thirty, two o'clock in the morning would be packed with people. The Mississippi Delta was an agricultural-based economy, . . . and the farmers all paid off on Saturdays."[24] Jewish merchants did what they had to do to make a living, and those who kept their stores open on the Sabbath hoped that God might understand the business cycles of the Delta.

[...]

Obtaining Jewish food supplies in the Delta was one of the biggest challenges of being far from a center of Jewish population. Jewish women in the Delta never traveled without an ice cooler in the trunk of their cars to keep their foods fresh. No traveler went to Jackson, Memphis, St. Louis, Birmingham, New Orleans, and especially to New York, without promising to return with bagels, lox, corned beef, and dark loaves of pumpernickel. Women charged relatives and friends traveling outside the region with this task, and returning empty-handed required a good explanation. Cecile Gudelsky remembered her grandfather bringing Jewish foods with him on the train when he returned from St. Louis to Paragould, Arkansas. He sat with friends on the way to St. Louis, but on the return trip he sat alone because the smell of salami and pastrami was too much for his companions.[25]

Delicatessens and kosher butcher shops like the Old Tyme Delicatessen in Jackson and Rosen's, Segal's, and Halpern's in Memphis were known in the Delta by word of mouth as well as through advertisements in Jewish newspapers like the *Hebrew Watchman* and the *Jewish Spectator.* Advertisements guaranteeing "prompt attention given out-of-town orders" encouraged Delta Jews to mail-order foods that would be delivered by bus and train. Gilbert Halpern, the son of Thelma and Louis Halpern, who opened their Memphis delicatessen in 1946, remembered their busy mail-order business at Passover time.[26] After the restaurant closed at the end of the day, the building turned into a packing business at night. Gilbert personally delivered food supplies to families in the Delta and Arkansas, and he remembered the warm reunions when those same families visited his deli in Memphis.

Preparing for Passover posed challenging logistics for Jewish homemakers in the Delta. In Shaw, Bess Seligman did the trips to Memphis. "I was the 'delivery boy'," said Seligman. "I went to Memphis and took everybody's order and brought back the meat and the perishable foods. The matzah, the flour, the potato starch, and all that, we would ship by bus or by train, because we couldn't put it all in a car." In Moorhead, Fannie Klumok ordered her kosher meats and other Passover foods from Rosen's Delicatessen in Memphis. The primary Passover order arrived several days before Passover. "Each day as she assessed our needs," said Sylvia Klumok Goodman, mother "called Rosen's and they would send us the current day's request by Greyhound bus." Fannie Klumok hired two African American men and three additional African American women to help with the Passover cleaning and preparations. "Nonkosher and non-Passover foods were either given to the black workers or stored at a gentile's house until after Passover," said Sylvia.[27] Passover was the one week a year when the Klumok family observed the dietary laws of kashrut.

Because she worked at the family's store in Indianola and could not be home to oversee the kosher-keeping skills of her domestic workers, Fannie Klumok outlawed any dairy products in the home for that week. Relying on African American cooks to prepare daily southern fare was acceptable to her, but their involvement in Jewish tradition and dietary laws was another matter. Race and class shaped the Klumoks' daily decisions, including preparations for a southern Jewish Passover. "We had kosher meats and no dairy on Passover as my mother was afraid that our cook and maid wouldn't be able to keep the dishes separate. I never knew that you could eat matzah with butter until I went to college and learned that dairy wasn't prohibited during Passover."[28] Fifty Jews and Gentile friends attended the Klumok seder, for which Fannie annually prepared three hundred pieces of gefilte fish made from a mixture of locally available carp and buffalo fish.

[…]

The foods Jews chose to eat positioned them in Delta society, and these choices were not limited to the broader categories of "southern" and "Jewish." There were subcategories. Delta Jews could eat southern food, but it was important to eat only those foods associated with their own race and class, including foods prepared by African American cooks, who understood what was appropriate fare in a white home. Fried chicken was appropriate, chitterlings ("chitlins") were not.

A similar hierarchy existed for the Jewish foods a Delta Jewish woman would serve to her family and her gentile guests. Foods associated with higher class, German-Jewish tastes—roast chicken, tortes, sponge cakes, and kuchens—were acceptable to serve for family and Gentile company. Heavier foods of eastern European cuisine—kugels, kiskha, tzimmes, and cholents—were more questionable. Some Delta Jews avoided foods associated with Jews from the *shtetl,* the small villages of eastern Europe. Although outwardly accepted by the white society around them, Delta Jews were mindful of their "otherness" and vigilantly strove to maintain status in the community, even at the dinner table.

Because of their small numbers and the lengthy drives between home and synagogue, Jews in the Delta often gathered together at holiday time for community seders, Rosh Hashanah dinners, Yom Kippur break-the-fasts, and Hanukkah latke parties. Depending on the number of participants, these events might be held in private homes, at the synagogue, in a Jewish social club like Vicksburg's B.B. (B'nai B'rith) Literary Association, the Olympia Club in Greenville, or at a local restaurant. Jennifer Stollman observes that the annual Sisterhood-sponsored "deli lunch," still held in Greenville, not only raises money for the synagogue and brings members together but helps to "demystify" the Jewish community to the hundreds of Gentiles who come to purchase cornbeef sandwiches.[29]

[…]

Living in small communities where there were few other Jews—in some cases only a single family—Delta Jews developed networks to sustain their social and spiritual worlds. From formal dances at the B.B. Club in Vicksburg in the 1950s where Jewish youth were entertained by the music of the Red Tops, a popular African American band, to monthly dinner clubs and Sunday afternoon family visits, the dispersed Delta Jewish community gathered for friendship and courtship. The active calendar of Jewish social life reflected the lifestyle of the Gentile community in the Delta where both blacks and whites are known for their hospitality, high standards of entertaining, and love of a good time. Delta people have a sense of space and distance that distinguishes them from people in the city, and they willingly travel an hour or more on lonely Delta roads to attend a good party. Harry Ball describes the social life of Washington County in the Delta from the 1880s to the early decades of the twentieth century in his diary. Ball recalls a "full-dress ball" at the Jewish social club in Greenville, which was attended by two hundred people, "the largest public ball we have ever had."[30] Decades later during the Civil Rights movement of the 1960s, such hospitality was not extended to Jewish "freedom riders" from the Midwest and Northeast who threatened the Jewish community's tenuous position in the racially charged, violent state of Mississippi.

[…]

As Jewish population has diminished in the Delta, social functions have become even more important in sustaining Jewish life in the region. Delta Jews were hit particularly hard by the decline in the overall population of the Delta. This decline is associated with the arrival of the boll weevil in the early 1900s, the mechanization of cotton picking in the 1940s, the "great migration" of black laborers out of the Delta to industrial cities like Chicago, and the movement after World War II of veterans and young adults from their rural communities to cities like Memphis and Chicago. These changes, accompanied by the decline of downtown business districts and the growth of regional discount stores like Wal-Mart, pushed third and fourth generation Jews out of their small mercantile businesses in the Delta and into professions located in cities.

In the 1930s there were over two dozen Jewish-owned businesses in Blytheville.[31] Today there are no Jewish-owned businesses downtown. Temple Israel held its last service in the fall of 2004. Congregants donated the sanctuary's stained glass windows and a Torah to Congregation Beth Sholom in Memphis, a vital synagogue of 325 families, where several Blytheville residents now worship.

Jews who remain in Delta communities—older adults and sons and daughters who work with family businesses and farms—are bound together by kinship and the challenge of maintaining Judaism in their region. While their Judaism is different from that of Jews outside the South, for Delta Jews it is the "real thing" despite their different ritual practices, accents, and food traditions. Judaism in the South is not defined by "faith, theological principles, or affiliation only," says Carolyn Lipson-Walker, who argues that in the South "the criterion for who and what is Jewish is more visceral than rational." Lipson-Walker believes that southern Judaism is a mix of "loyalties, historical memories, beliefs, and cultural expressions," and chief among those cultural expressions is food.[32] Although Delta Jews share the same religious heritage as urban Jews in the Northeast, they are bound to their gentile Delta neighbors by fried chicken, cornbread, and field peas.

Eli Evans, the unofficial dean of the Jewish South, grew up in Durham, North Carolina, where his father, E. J. "Mutt" Evans was the first Jewish mayor in the 1950s. Eli Evans became the first Jewish student-body president at the University of North Carolina at Chapel Hill in 1958. In his personal biography of growing up Jewish in the South, *The Provincials,* Evans writes about the complicated negotiation of regional and religious identity:

> I am not certain what it means to be both a Jew and a Southerner—to have inherited the Jewish longing for a homeland while being raised with the Southerner's sense of home. The conflict is deep in me—the Jew's involvement in history, his deep roots in the drama of man's struggle to understand deity and creation. But I respond to the Southerner's commitment to place, his loyalty to the land, to his own tortured history, to the strange bond beyond color that Southern blacks and whites discover when they come to know one another.[33] Evans's words eloquently capture the spirit of Jewish life in the Delta. Delta Jews value their own expression of religion and ethnicity, yet their world is defined by the region's rules of race, class, intermarriage, strong family ties, social activities, deep sense of place, intimate ties to Gentile white and black neighbors, and the agricultural economy. They are also defined by a sense of Jewish self-sufficiency and by the inventiveness required to obtain Jewish foods, supplies, and educational and cultural resources for their Jewish community. The rich cultural world of the Delta that is expressed in the region's music and food is an equally important part of the region's Jewish life. Delta Jews are southerners, and this allegiance to region profoundly influences their Judaism. "I love the South. I can't imagine living anywhere besides the South," said Fred Miller of Anguilla. "We believe in our Jewish heritage for sure, but I think that there's no one who was born in this area who doesn't feel a real kinship with the South—and with the history of the South. Right or wrong, we are and were part of it."[34]

Notes

I would like to thank Dr. Stuart Rockoff, director, history department, Goldring/Woldenberg Institute of Southern Jewish Life, Jackson, Mississippi, for his review of earlier versions of this article. I am indebted to Mike DeWitt for his interviews of Jewish southerners in the Delta.

1. Interview with Stuart Rockoff, director, history department, Goldring/Woldenberg Institute of Southern Jewish Life, Jackson, Mississippi, 3 September 2003.

2. See David Goldfield's theory of social "place" in "A Sense of Place: Jews, Blacks, and White Gentiles in the American South," *Southern Cultures* 3.1(1997): 58.

3. Craig Claiborne, *A Feast Made for Laughter* (Double Day and Co., Inc., 1982) 47, 31.

4. David W. Blight, "Southerners Don't Lie; They Just Remember Big," *Where These Memories Grow: History, Memory, and Southern Identity,* ed. W. Fitzhugh Brundage (University of North Carolina Press, 2000) 348–49; W. Fitzhugh Brundage, "No Deed but Memory," *Ibid.,* 2, 7.

5. Joan Nathan, *Jewish Cooking in America* (Alfred A. Knopf, 1994), 3, 4.

6. See Frederik Barth, *Ethnic Groups and Boundaries: The Social Organization of Culture Difference* (1969; Waveland Press, Inc., 1998), 15; Mary Douglas, *Implicit Meanings: Selected Essays in Anthropology* (1975; Routledge, 1999), 231–51; Claude Levi-Strauss, "The Culinary Triangle," *Food and Culture: A Reader,* ed. Carole Counihan and Penny Van Esterik (Routledge, 1997), 28; Sidney W. Mintz, *Tasting Food, Tasting Freedom: Excursions into Eating, Culture, and the Past* (Beacon Press, 1996), 7. See also Susan Kalcik, "Ethnic Foodways in America: Symbol and the Performance of Identity," *Ethnic and Regional Foodways in the United States: The Performance of Group Identity,* ed. Linda Keller Brown and Kay Mussell (University of Tennessee Press, 1984), 37–65.

7. Blu Greenberg, *How to Run a Traditional Jewish Household* (Simon and Schuster, 1983), 95.

8. Jenna Weissman Joselit, *The Wonders of America: Reinventing Jewish Culture, 1880–1950* (Hill and Wang, 1994), 171, 293–94; see also Barbara Kirshenblatt-Gimblett's article, "Kitchen Judaism," *Getting Comfortable in New York: The American Jewish Home, 1880–1950,* ed. Susan Braunstein and Jenna Weissman Joselit (The Jewish Museum, 1990), 77, for a discussion of the term "kitchen Judaism."

9. Sylvia Klumok Goodman, email to the author, 4 June 2001.

10. "Kosher-style," explains historian Jenna Joselit, was an American invention that allowed Jews to ignore the rigor of the Jewish dietary laws by choosing which rules of kashrut they wished to observe and which chose to ignore. Jenna Weissman Joselit, *The Wonders of America,* 173–74.

11. Betty G. Lamensdorf, interview with Marcie C. Ferris, Cary, Mississippi, 28 June 2001; Betty G. Lamensdorf, telephone conversation with Marcie C. Ferris, Cary, Mississippi, 21 October 2003.

12. Ben Lamensdorf, Cary, Mississippi, *Delta Jews,* dir. Mike DeWitt, 1999, Mike DeWitt Productions.

13. Betty G. Lamensdorf, interview.

14. Cliff Taulbert, *Delta Jews,* dir. DeWitt.

15. Leonard Rogoff, "Is the Jew White? The Racial Place of the Southern Jew," *American Jewish History* 85.3 (September 1997): 195; see also Jennifer Stollman, "Building up a House of Israel in a 'Land of Christ': Jewish Women in the Antebellum and Civil War South," (Ph.D. diss., Michigan State University, 2001), 275. Jack Nelson, *Terror in the Night: The Klan's Campaign Against the Jews* (Simon and Schuster, 1993), 41.

16. Ann G. Gerache, interview with Marcie C. Ferris, Vicksburg, Mississippi, 27 June 2001; see Jacqueline Jones, *Labor of Love, Labor of Sorrow: Black Women, Work, and the Family, from Slavery to the Present* (Vintage Books, 1985) 127–30, 325, for a discussion of the daily lives of African American female domestic workers and what she describes as the "double day."

17. Ann G. Gerache, interview.

18. Betty G. Lamensdorf, interview; Hortense Powdermaker, *After Freedom: A Cultural Study in the Deep South* (1939; Atheneum, 1968), 118, 31–32.

19. Ann G. Gerache, interview.

20. Ann G. Gerache, interview.

21. Ann G. Gerache, Vicksburg, Mississippi, Southern Jewish Foodways Survey, 3 October 1998.

22. James C. Cobb, *The Mississippi Delta and the World: The Memoirs of David L. Cohn* (Louisiana State University Press, 1995), xii, 171.

23. Ann G. Gerache, interview.

24. Joe Erber, Greenwood, Mississippi, *Delta Jews,* dir. DeWitt.

25. Cecile Gudelsky, email to author, 17 July 2001.

26. Segal's Kosher Delicatessen advertisement, *The Hebrew Watchman,* Memphis, Tennessee, 30 March 1928; Halpern's Kosher Snack Shop advertisement, *The Hebrew Watchman,* Memphis, Tennessee, 12 December 1946; Rosen's Kosher Delicatessen; advertisements for Dalsheimer's Brothers, Albert Seessel and Son, *The Jewish Spectator,* Memphis, Tennessee, 1908, 23rd Anniversary Edition, Temple Israel Archives, Memphis, Tennessee; Gilbert Halpern, interview with Marcie C. Ferris, Memphis, Tennessee, 20 December 2001.

27. Bess Seligman, interview with Marcie C. Ferris, Shaw, Mississippi, April 1991, Museum of the Southern Jewish Experience, Jackson, Mississippi; Sylvia Klumok Goodman, email to author, 25 May 2001, 25 August 2003.

28. Ibid.

29. Jennifer Stollman, "We're Still Here: Delta Jewish Women in the Twentieth Century," lecture, Southern Jewish Historical Society Annual Conference, 1 November 2003, Memphis, Tennessee.

30. James C. Cobb, *The Most Southern Place on Earth: The Mississippi Delta and the Roots of Regional Identity* (Oxford University Press, 1992), 138.

31. LeMaster, *A Corner of the Tapestry,* 255.

32. Lipson-Walker, "Shalom Y'all," 43–44.

33. Eli N. Evans, *The Provincials: A Personal History of Jews in the South* (1973; Free Press Paperbacks, 1997), 22.

34. Fred Miller, Anguilla, Mississippi, *Delta Jews,* dir. DeWitt.

CHAPTER 11
BOY SCOUTS AND THE MANLY ART OF COOKING
Jay Mechling

I was something of snob when it came to cooking dinners on the weekend campouts my Boy Scout troop would take in various South Florida locations in the late 1950s and early 1960s. Around the time I was twelve or so, my parents bought a bar. My father had been a bartender all of his adult life, and every bartender's dream in that generation, I suppose, was to own a bar. The fantasy quickly turned into the money, time, and energy pit small business owners know all too well, and my parents had to devote increasing amounts of their time to running the bar through my junior high school years and into high school. In my own memory, I can't quite sort out whether my interest in cooking began in the Boy Scouts and served me well when I was increasingly responsible for family meals at home, or whether the necessity of cooking for myself and my overtired parents just happened to coincide with my learning to cook in Scouting. Either way, as an only child with increasing responsibility for a share of the cooking, I came to enjoy planning, preparing, and serving meals.

[...]

In the mid-1970s, I began fieldwork, studying the annual summer encampment of a Boy Scout troop in California; several years later, that work culminated in my book on the Boy Scout experience.[1] One of the matters that I touch upon briefly in that book concerns the potential for the Boy Scout experience to produce adult men who are comfortable performing tasks and roles the society normally considers feminine, as "women's work." At Scout camp, boys cook, clean pots and pans, launder clothes, nurse injuries, and even do some of the emotional work (like comforting a homesick boy), all gender work typically reserved for women. Does this socialization setting, I wondered, work somehow to create boys who, as men, will hold less rigid notions about gender arrangements, or is the Boy Scout camp experience so easily framed by the boys and young men as "not everyday" that they can return home, hand a bag full of dirty laundry to Mom, and ask "what's for dinner?"

I did not answer that question then because both outcomes seemed equally likely to me. There are so many variables in the equation that each boy probably responds differently. And yet, the question seems too important to drop, so I return to it here under the rubric of a meditation on "Boy Scouts and the Manly Art of Cooking," with those larger questions in mind.

After all, the Boy Scout experience is exceptional in expecting every boy to learn to cook for others and to be able to perform other domestic chores. In the long history of home economics classes in school, pity the boy who chose cooking over shop crafts. No other youth movements for boys—not the YMCA, not the 4-H, not the Future Farmers of America—trained the boy in the full range of domestic skills, from cooking and sewing to home gardening. What's more, the Boy Scouts was founded in 1910, in large part, as a response to the perceived "feminization" of American boys. White, middle-class, native-born heterosexual men were

Jay Mechling, 'Boy Scouts and the Manly Art of Cooking', *Food and Foodways* 13 (2005), 67–89. (Excerpt printed here: 67, 68, 69–78, 78–80, 81–82, 85, 86–88. Omitted text is indicated by ellipses.) Reprinted by permission of the publisher (Taylor & Francis Ltd, http://www.tandfonline.com).

experiencing a "masculinity crisis" in the waning decades of the nineteenth century, largely due to unnerving economic cycles, shifting occupational patterns, increasing urbanization, waves of immigrants, and the entry of women into the workplace (albeit as poorly trained clerks and the like).[2]

Just as Lord Robert Baden-Powell, founder of the Boy Scouts in Great Britain in 1908, created his movement to toughen up boys made soft by civilization, so the founders of the Boy Scouts of America (the BSA) had a strong sense that mothers and female teachers were having a deleterious effect on boys, and that an outdoor-based youth movement for boys, ages eleven through seventeen, would do much to revitalize American manhood.

The paradox I aim to explore in this article lies in the Scouting program's apparent philosophy that teaching the boy domestic skills can actually enhance his masculinity. From a feminist perspective, boys' everyday experiences with cooking and eating are formative in the boys' understanding of caring and being cared for, of serving and being served, and therefore, of naturalized patterns of gender dominance and submission.[3] Yet, under certain circumstances, boys can be urged by men and other boys to cook and serve, to nurture others, without surrendering male privilege. The Boy Scout movement has always had selfless "service to others" as a key element in its program, but, at the same time, the BSA has had to construct this service, caring, and nurturing as distinctly masculine, as not feminine.

The evidence I have at hand consists of the published materials created by the BSA and by commercial food companies for the boys and adult male leaders. These handbooks and pamphlets provided boys concrete instructions in preparing and serving food, but they also provided narrative strategies meant to frame cooking and caring for others as a legitimate kind of masculine performance. The prescribed activities themselves are also important, as a great many boys learn better by doing than by reading. The structures of those activities are as important as the words in the manuals. I also turn to my own fieldwork with a California Boy Scout troop over a nearly twenty-five year span. Only in fieldwork can the researcher get a glimpse of whether and how real boys follow the adult script for cooking and caring. These are American teenage boys, after all, so we should not be surprised to learn that they work to make cooking and caring a part of their autonomous, sometimes rebellious, male folk cultures.[4]

Cooking, caring, and masculinity

Object-relations theory and other psychoanalytic ideas at the root of most prevalent theories about the social construction of masculinity assume that the performance of masculinity is a fragile accomplishment always at risk. In patriarchal societies, such as ours, where mothers are the primary caretakers of children, the usual "solution" to the Oedipal drama is for the boy to separate and distinguish himself from his mother, identifying with the father. This calls for a radical rejection of the feminine.[5] Because masculinity is defined by a "negative," that is, as "not feminine," the boy and man always must "prove" himself.[6] Misogyny and homophobia are common symptoms of this separation of the boy from the feminine, even from his own feminine side. Boys practice a culture of shame in order to keep each other in line, on the right track for adult heterosexual masculinity; they police the borders of masculinity, using jokes, taunts, and insults to attack anything vaguely feminine in another boy's appearance or behavior. Cooking food, serving it to others, and cleaning up the mess are acts that have great potential for feminizing the boy or man, so associated with the feminine are these behaviors in our society. In all male institutions, like a Scout camp or a hunting camp or a military boarding school or a firehouse or a military unit, where boys or men work, eat, and sleep together in full cycles of days and weeks, boys and men necessarily perform tasks normally considered "women's work." The male friendship culture in these all-male settings must frame the potentially feminine behavior as masculine; the work does not make the man feminine, the man makes the otherwise feminine work masculine somehow in his performance of the work, even if (as is so often the case) joking about the man's incompetent performance of a domestic chore is what makes it seem masculine. So how did the BSA manage to turn something feminine into something masculine? How has the BSA manage to define an ethic of caring, especially as expressed through feeding others, as appropriate to boys headed for lives as masculine, heterosexual men? That is the story I pursue here.

"Cooking is a man-sized job . . ."

My first *Handbook for Boys* helped me camp out in my imagination even before I pitched my first tent and built my first cooking fire. I made the easy transition from Cub Scouts (aged 8–10–1/2) to Boy Scouts and hunkered down with that new *Handbook,* the 1955 printing of the fifth edition, initially published in 1948. I can't tell you how much of that handbook I read by flashlight, but it was plenty. I still have that copy, and as I open its curled pages to Chapter 17, "Camp Cooking," I see the text begins with this statement: "Cooking is a man-sized job, and every good outdoorsman knows how to do it. He has to. . . . A Patrol cooking its own meals is playing one of the most fascinating games in Scouting."[7] The chapter recommends that the boy begin his learning how to cook at home, guessing the ingredients of a dish, watching his mother cook, and trying some recipes and techniques at home before taking them into the field. The *Handbook* advises the boy about how to assemble his "cook kit," how to plan a menu, how to create a balanced meal from the "Basic 7" food groups, and how to get organized before cooking. Then come fifteen pages of recipes. This all depends on the previous chapter on "Fire Building," which has elaborate instructions (with drawings) on the differences between campfires and cooking fires and, beyond that, types of cooking fires.

Cooking in the Boy Scouts is not just a matter of feeding oneself and others on hikes and campouts. The core of the educational program is "advancement," the earning of badges and ranks within the organization. The boy begins as a "Tenderfoot," but the Second Class and First Class ranks require ever-more-elaborate cooking on campouts. The very first *Handbook for Boys,* published in 1911, established that the Second Class Scout had to "prove ability to build a fire in the open, using not more than two matches," and "cook a quarter of a pound of meat and two potatoes in the open without the ordinary kitchen cooking utensils." The requirements for First Class Scout increased the challenge, asking the boy to "prepare and cook satisfactorily, in the open, without regular kitchen utensils, two of the following articles as may be directed. Eggs, bacon, hunter's stew, fish, fowl, game, pancakes, hoe-cake, biscuits, hardtack or a 'twist,' baked on a stick; explain to another boy the methods followed."[8] Some version of these cooking requirements have remained for the ranks of Second and First Class Scout to the present.[9] The boy has to know how to build a fire in the open, he must know how to fashion from native materials any cooking "utensils" he needs, he must cook and serve a complete meal for a small group (patrols are the smaller groups of six-to-eight boys that make up the larger troop), and he must teach another boy these skills.

Having older boys teach younger boys the Scouting skills lies at the center of the instructional strategy in the Boy Scouts. The *Third Handbook for Scoutmasters* (1937) impresses upon the adult leaders the importance of planning well for feeding boys at camp, suggesting that that the troop might need to enlist the help of a volunteer or even a paid professional cook to train the boys. "At the same time," reminds the writer, "it must be remembered that the Scout method involves learning by doing . . . ." The goal is to "banish the professional cook (or for that matter the adult cook) from the camp."[10] As far as the *Handbook for Scoutmasters* authors are concerned, there is no question that cooking is a manly "art." They quote the Chief Scout Executive, James E. West, on the aesthetic pleasures of this manly art. "When you get to the point where you can have your juicy steak broiling sweetly over a bed of coals," wrote West, "your corn on the cob steaming in the kettle, while you slice the red-ripe tomatoes and prepare the fruit, happy and cool and unconcerned—my boy, you're a man."[11]

That *Handbook* stresses training the boys at home even before taking the troop on a campout. "Secure the aid of the mothers in training their boys," advise the authors. "There are certain things which may be more readily learned in the family kitchen than in camp, such things as: the consistency of pancake batter and biscuit dough, how to test to see if potatoes, stringbeans and other vegetables are done, and making gravy."[12] Today, reading this 1937 *Handbook* written for the adult male leaders, we might detect that the authors recognized the paradox of the moment. They assume in the passage quoted above that it is the mothers who will be in the home kitchen training the boys, but they also had to know that if the Scouting program was successful, then boys and the men they became would be as comfortable in the kitchen as were women. The notion that mothers would teach their sons, not just their daughters, how to cook reveals changing gender roles in the homes in the 1930s, changes brought about partly by women's movements but probably more forcefully by economic conditions in the Great Depression, conditions that disrupted normative gender roles.[13] Judging from this *Handbook,* it seems likely that a good many adult men and women in the late 1930s saw themselves as living on the cusp of some fundamental changes in gender arrangements, and the BSA was willing to be a partner in forging those changes, creating boys and men far more comfortable than their fathers were with cooking, sewing, and other domestic skills.

The 1937 *Handbook's* rhetoric is all the more remarkable, because that language disappears in later handbooks. The fifth edition (1959) of the *Scoutmaster's Handbook,* for example, deals with camp cooking in a rather straightforward way, advising careful planning, menus, and equipment to bring along on the campout. Gone are the aesthetic and gender comments, including who might teach the boy cooking at home, perhaps because those matters were taken for granted in the 1950s. I suspect, though, that what we see in this contrast is the way the 1950s returned to a separation of spheres, where men cooked outdoors and girls cooked indoors.

To follow the paper trail on Scouting's thoughts about teaching boys how to cook, we also must look at the successive pamphlets for the Cooking merit badge. The Cooking merit badge requirements outlined in the first *Handbook for Boys* (1911) add even more sorts of dishes beyond the First Class requirements, including baking bread in an oven and demonstrating knowledge of how to "carve properly and serve correctly to people at the table."[14] By the 1930s the BSA was publishing separate merit badge pamphlets, one for each badge. The 1939 "Cooking" pamphlet, for example, takes 36 pages to explain every step in building a cooking fire and cooking a complete meal for the boy's patrol. The pamphlet's opening paragraph places the boy's cooking skills in a larger context:

> The Merit Badge in Cooking is a test of ability to do the things that a Scout should be able to do if he is "prepared" beyond the rank and file of Scouts who have completed only the Second and First Class requirements. Naturally most of the Scout's cooking is done in camp and on hikes, but he may find it necessary also to know how to cook at home or even in a hotel kitchen, if the emergency should arise.[15]

I am not sure what to make of the hotel kitchen emergency scenario, but clearly the anonymous authors of this pamphlet envisioned the preparedness of the boy to help with the cooking at home. The authors portray cooking as a skill a normal boy and man should have. Just a bit further in the introductory paragraphs, the authors point to even more possibilities, imagining that their pamphlet "points the way for those who are ambitious to go beyond the beginner's stage to expert cooking, either as a hobby or as a profession."[16]

The rest of the pamphlet's instruction and information is pretty straightforward, until we get to the section addressing the badge's requirement that the boy demonstrate how to carve meat at the patrol or family table. Although its makes better sense to carve in the kitchen and serve the carved meat at the table, the authors lapse into very interesting commentary about gender roles in the 1930s. The "older practice" of carving at the table will survive, observe the authors, because "many a father of the family would rebel against being deprived of his right to practice this ancient art." "Now and again," continue the authors,

> mother does the carving, either because she likes to, or because she can do it better than father can, or because father is too lazy to do it. Of course, if she likes the job, it may be considered the part of gallantry for father to resign in her favor. Or, if she is actually a better carver than he is, he may yield to her, if his pride will let him admit that she can beat him at a game in which it should be his pride to excel. Of the head of a household who doesn't carve because he is too lazy to learn to do a good job, perhaps the less said the better.[17]

What an interesting, conflicted paragraph to appear in a Boy Scout merit badge pamphlet in 1939. Again, as noted above, the impact of the Great Depression on gender roles in the home and the ways employment of mothers outside the home forced home cooking duties on children and adolescents, including boys. The continuing employment of mothers outside the home during World War II would have extended those domestic cooking duties well into the 1940s.

This paragraph reflects the strains in the changing gender roles of the 1930s. On the one hand, the paragraph contains some references to traditional male pride, gallantry, and (though not using this word) duty. Yet, the paragraph seems to offer the notion that abilities and desires to perform certain tasks, not traditional gender role expectations, should be the basis for a family member's assuming certain domestic activities. This paragraph hints at the possibilities for radical gender work rearrangements in the 1940s, a potential lost when the American middle class returned to the "normalcy" of traditional separation of the work world into the female domestic sphere and the male dominance of the workplace outside the home.[18] This 1939 pamphlet, including the interesting paragraph on carving new gender relations, went through many reprintings, including the one I used to earn the badge in the late 1950s.

The evidence from over ninety years' worth of Boy Scout publication on cooking suggests that it was only in the 1930s and immediately after the Second World War (in 1948 Fifth Edition of the *Handbook for Boys* I first knew) that there was much explicit talk linking cooking and masculinity. The earlier handbooks from 1911 to 1927 take it for granted that a man should learn how to cook as a fundamental survival skill in the woods; the continuity between a Scout's skills and pioneer woodsman skills affirms that such cooking for oneself was masculine. No doubt the felt crisis in masculinity brought on by the Great Depression influenced the language of the 1939 pamphlet. Similarly, the 1948 *Handbook* reasserts the manliness of cooking as part of the postwar return to separate spheres.

In contrast, the Sixth Edition of the *Boy Scout Handbook,* first published in November of 1959, presents the cooking instruction very matter-of-factly, with no romanticizing of food preparation and serving and with no language asserting how manly it was to cook outdoors. It was not until 1967 that the "Cooking" merit badge pamphlet was revised with a tone and approach a bit more enthusiastic about cooking and food than is the 1959 *Handbook.* In fact, the 1967 pamphlet opens with an announcement that the reader should "prepare for an adventure in cooking" and a lasting interest in food. That introductory page closes with this paragraph extolling the pleasures of feeding others:

> Cooking for others will show you things about your fellow humans as clearly as any of life's experiences. While serving tasty meals to a hungry gang, you'll see a pattern beginning with nagging impatience, moving toward a more peaceful time, and finally the pleasant after-effect of cheerful, quiet, and contented companionship.[19]

Along the way, the 1967 pamphlet also encourages the boy cook to develop an "intuition" or "imagination" that will give him the confidence to improvise with recipes and menus. The Boy Scout program promotes the improvisational frame of mind in camping altogether, showing boys how to cook in the woods using sticks, rocks, tin cans, and wire to create any cooking utensil needed, but in the 1967 pamphlet, the improvisational style extends to the food itself, for the first time recommending that the boy experiment with an assortment of herbs to bring "the gourmet touch" to his cooking.[20] In this pamphlet, cooking is more than an instrumental skill; it is an expressive skill with social bonding functions. The bonding in this case was boys with boys, but implicit was the notion that cooking for others—possibly even the family at home—was a noble activity. To the degree that the readers of these handbooks would normally associate the expressive, social bonding functions of cooking and eating with female values, the Scout program of teaching boys how to cook seems to have carried great potential for creating men more flexible in their thinking about ways to perform their masculine identities.

By the latest revision of the "Cooking" merit badge pamphlet in 2001, the authors declare an easy and natural continuity between cooking for other boys in the field and cooking for the family at home. "Cooking is a skill that you can use and enjoy for a lifetime," begin the authors, assuring the boy that

> There is a certain satisfaction in preparing food for yourself and your friends and family that can't compare with anything else. It is no small accomplishment to turn an assortment of everyday ingredients into a delicious, nourishing meal. Learning to cook gives you a new respect for those who prepared meals for you. Best of all, cooking is fun.[21]

All the science and technology of cooking shows up in this pamphlet, as cooking over fires in the wilderness recedes in importance and food preparation with modern utensils and heat sources garner more attention. The requirements for the badge now ask the boy to learn about vocational possibilities in professional cooking, and the pamphlet discusses that career option.

The trajectory of the nearly-one-hundred-year history of cooking rhetoric in the Boy Scout publications and programs, then, suggests in some ways the increasing "feminization" of the cooking boy. Whereas the *Handbooks* and other materials for the first few decades stressed the "manliness" of wilderness survival skills like cooking, by mid-century, the boy cook looked more and more like he was playing the mother's or sister's role in cooking for the domestic group. This domestication of boy cooking continued through the remainder of the 20th century. This "feminization" thesis parallels what scholars of play and games have found—namely, that in the last hundred years or so, boys' play and games have come to resemble girls' play and games.[22]

On second look, though, I think "feminization" is the wrong term to use to describe what has happened in the Boy Scouts. There always has been a strong ethic of selfless "service to others" in the organization. While it is true that the dominant image of the boy cook has evolved from the lone wilderness Scout to the Scout cook in the context of a more domestic male culture and then in the context of a domestic family culture, Scouting has maintained across its entire history a rhetoric identifying "caring for others" as suitable for masculine boys and men. Despite some very masculine rhetoric in the first few decades of the movement, an equally common rhetoric in these BSA publications portrays what I would call a "relaxed androgyny," seen to characterize an ideal Scout who combines the best qualities of the masculine and feminine, as our society defines those qualities.[23] So rather than a clear trajectory toward feminization, which is true in some respects, I think the better way to understand this history is to see how in any historical moment the felt tensions between traditional masculinity and a non-feminine masculinity of care and service played out in the rhetoric.

I argued in *On My Honor* that one really does not understand the Boy Scout experience by looking only at the official organizations and its publications. Boys and men experience the Boy Scout movement in a concrete folk group (the "troop" and its smaller "patrols") of men and boys, and the only way to get at the Boy Scout experiences as they are actually performed is through ethnographic fieldwork with a troop. The same warning applies to my look at the official publications of the BSA in the matter of cooking and feeding others. Despite the organization's rhetorical strategies for constructing boy cooking as masculine, what is really happening when boys cook at Scout camp? I can draw on my ethnographic work to examine three issues in the Boy Scout's performance of masculinity through cooking—process versus product, eating with male friends, and playing with food.

Cooking outdoors: Process vs. product

It is significant that Boy Scout cooking at camp happens outdoors. A boy cannot satisfy the cooking requirements for Second and First Class Scout by cooking a meal indoors in a kitchen. Similarly, the Cooking Merit Badge requires outdoor cooking, though the requirement to carve meat "properly" and serve it "correctly" could be met by doing this at the family table instead of at the patrol campout.

Although I want to look at actual performances in approaching this issue, it is noteworthy that the BSA rhetoric has made much of the distinction between process and product. A Boy Scout Service Library pamphlet published in 1935, "Camp Fires and Cooking," makes clear the importance of outdoor cooking in the Scouting program. Written by Charles F. Smith of Columbia University Teachers College, the pamphlet explains the philosophy of teaching cooking. "The expert indoor cook without experience in outdoor cooking," writes Smith, "has much to learn. The science of cooking is the same, regardless of where the operation is performed, but the application must be modified to fit very different conditions."[24] Reflected here is the growing sense that domestic skills required a scientific approach, one suited to "home economics"; but calling cooking a "science" also helped legitimate it as a masculine pursuit.

One of the "different conditions" in the field, of course, was the control of heat when cooking over a fire. "Cooking cannot be taught intelligently outdoors as a separate subject," continues Smith.

> Boys would not be interested in outdoor cooking if they were supplied with gas stoves. Their interest is divided between cooking, fire building, use of knife and ax, construction of rustic devices, gathering of wild materials and wood, and finally eating. Of these interests, eating sometimes seems least important in view of the food they sometimes eat and seem to enjoy.[25]

The genius of the Scouting program is that it recognized from the start that boys at certain ages are more focused on physical doing rather than talking. So cooking was always seen in the broader context of a connected chain of skills and activities the boys would value for their own sakes. This approach to outdoor cooking takes advantage of boys' fascination with fire, which has many explanations, including a psychoanalytic one.[26] It also takes advantage of boys' fascination with knives and larger woodcutting tools. The boys learn about different woods, about safe uses of sharp tools, and the published Scouting materials describe and picture things boys can make for cooking projects, such as turning a No. 10 tin can and a wire coat hanger into a cooking pot with handle and carving a stick or lashing together sticks to create an apparatus for hanging the can over the fire.

An old set of ideas grounds the emphasis on process and construction in the Boy Scout cooking requirements. Already I have noted how the founding of the BSA in 1910 was, in large part, a reaction to a felt "crisis" in white, middle-class masculinity in the 1890s and early 1900s. The BSA also adopted the anti-modern ideology that was reaching a crescendo at the turn of the century. These anti-modern sentiments were one common reaction to the increasing industrialization, urbanization, and bureaucratization of Western societies.[27] The Arts and Crafts Movement in England and the United States, for example, amounted to a broad aesthetic reaction to the machine-made commodities increasingly common in everyday lives.[28] An ideology valuing the unique, "handmade" object spread through the white middle-classes, who felt the greatest anxiety about the transition to modernity; we have to see the BSA's emphasis on handcrafts and campcraft as part of this return to the virtues thought to arise out of those crafts. The modern, machine-based production of goods and even of art in this period focused on the material product—the commodity—that was the end-state of production. The anti-modernists, in contrast, attempted to recapture the folk, pre-modern emphasis on "process."

Understanding this ideological background, we can appreciate why the Boy Scout program emphasizes slow process in its cooking requirements. Not unlike the recent "Slow Food movement," Scouting approaches cooking and eating as something that should be appreciated for its process. This approach to cooking from 1910 on, moreover, works against the more popular view that cooking conveniences were to be welcomed as signs of progress. Nothing is hurried in the official Scout instructions on cooking. Gathering the firewood, digging the firepit, carefully cutting and stacking the wood, the preparation of kindling, and the sheer wait for the fire to burn down to glowing coals before cooking was a valued process that taught skills and such virtues as patience and the aesthetic sense of a job well done.

[...]

A peculiar paradox lies in Scouting's distancing its cooking requirements from technological advances in cooking, at least for its cooking rituals, as opposed to the routine cooking aimed at getting nourishing food into boys and their adult leaders. While we tend to associate technology with masculinity, in this case, the technology of easy, fast cooking seems more likely to be associated with women, who are said to be willing to adopt whatever technology makes their domestic work easier.[29] In this case, then, rejecting the "easier way" offered by technology also rejects, by association, the women's way of doing things.

We should note the possibility that the Boy Scout's focus on process is totally an artifact of the exceptional, almost ritual (as opposed to routine) act of a boy's cooking and of the wilderness frame for the activity. At home, a boys' approach to preparing a meal might lapse into the routine that worries more about product— just getting a meal on the table—than on the process.[30] The "slow food" approach relies on certain privileges of time and economic circumstances, so it is hard to sort the effects of the ideology from these other factors. Still, the anti-modern impulse drives this instruction for boys.

[...]

Conclusion

[...]

Certainly, everything I have presented here should convince us that the Boy Scouts, in seeking to make men less dependent on women by teaching men domestic skills traditionally thought to be women's work, actually embarked on a social experiment bound to change the performances of masculinity by hundreds of thousands of boys and young men. The official rhetoric of the movement has always seen cooking and feeding others as part of a complete masculinity and as, in fact, one of the best ways to show other boys and men that you care about them. The actual performances of cooking in the field support this rhetoric, elevating cooking for others as a difficult-to-master, noble gesture of affection and brotherhood. The open question is whether something more fundamental will be changed if boys and men come to see that cooking for and serving women in domestic settings does not "feminize" the males.

[…]

Notes

1. Jay Mechling, *On My Honor: Boy Scouts and the Making of American Youth* (Chicago: University of Chicago Press, 2001).

2. See, for example, the history of these decades as recounted in E. Anthomy Rotundo, *American Manhood* (New York: Basic Books, 1993), Michael Kimmel, *Manhood in America* (New York: Free Press, 1995), and Gail Bederman, *Manliness and Civilization: A Cultural History of Gender and Race in the United States, 1880–1917* (Chicago: University of Chicago Press, 1995).

3. See Marjorie L. DeVault, *Feeding the Family: The Social Organization of Caring as Gendered Work* (Chicago: University of Chicago Press, 1991). The gendering of cooking and feeding need not be a matter of coercion, of course; women willingly serve these caring functions in the family because they have learned the gender codes and they see virtue in the caring behavior. DeVault pays some attention to how mothers teach their daughters how to cook and feed the family, and she certainly picks up on the ways men come to expect this gender arrangement of caring, but she apparently saw no case of mothers or fathers teaching sons how to cook. Some sons doubtlessly learn how to cook in the home, from mothers or fathers or both (maybe even from grandparents or other adults in the home). But this seems a largely invisible and, one would guess from the scholarship on feeding the family, insignificant phenomenon.

4. In thinking about the significance of the Scouting experience for boys, we need to remember that the BSA has been mainly a white, middle-class movement.

5. See, for example, Stephen Frosh, *Sexual Difference: Masculinity and Psychoanalysis* (London: Routledge, 1994).

6. See, for example, Timothy Beneke, *Proving Manhood: Reflections on Men and Sexism* (Berkeley: University of California Press, 1997).

7. Boy Scouts of America, *Handbook for Boys* (5th ed.; New Brunswick, NJ: Boy Scouts of America, 1948), p. 305.

8. Boy Scouts of America, *Handbook for Boys* (Garden City, NY: Doubleday, Page & Company, 1911), p. 17.

9. Boy Scouts of America, *Boy Scout Requirements 2002* (Irving, TX: Boy Scouts of America, 2002).

10. Boy Scouts of America, *Handbook for Scoutmasters* (3rd ed.; New York: Boy Scouts of America, 1937), vol. 2, p. 744.

11. West quoted in the *Handbook for Scoutmasters* (3rd ed.; New York: Boy Scouts of America, 1937), vol. 2, p. 731.

12. *Handbook for Scoutmasters* (1937), p. 732.

13. Still the best study of the ways the Great Depression realigned gender roles is Glen H. Elder, Jr., *Children of the Great Depression: Social Change in the Life Experience* (Chicago: University of Chicago Press, 1974).

14. *Handbook for Boys* (1911), p. 31.

15. Boy Scouts of America, *Cooking* (New York: Boy Scouts of America, 1939), p. 1.

16. *Cooking* (1939), p. 1.

17. *Cooking* (1939), pp. 27–28.

18. World War II, of course, interrupted all kinds of traditional gender arrangements, and opened briefly some radically new gender arrangements. See, for example, John Ibson's *Picturing Men: A Century of Male Relationships in Everyday American Photography* (Washington, DC: Smithsonian Institution Press, 2002), esp. Chapter 7: "Men Set Free: World War II and the Shifting Boundaries of Male Association." As Ibson shows, the end of the war brought a sudden end to the public exploration through everyday photography of the new gender relationships between men.

On the effects of the war on families and children, see William M. Tuttle, Jr., *"Daddy's Gone to War": The Second World War in the Lives of America's Children* (New York: Oxford University Press, 1993).

19. Boy Scouts of America, *Cooking* (New Brunswick, NJ: Boy Scouts of America, 1967), p. 7.

20. *Cooking* (1967), pp. 64–65.

21. Boy Scouts of America, *Cooking* (Irving, TX: Boy Scouts of America, 2001), p. 9.

22. On this feminization of boys' play and games, see various essays in *Children's Folklore: A Source Book,* ed. by Brian Sutton-Smith, Jay Mechling, Thomas W. Johnson, and Felicia R. McMahon (Logan, UT: Utah State University Press, 1999).

23. I discuss this androgyny—including the androgynous figure of the American Indian so revered by Ernest Thompson Seton, one of the founders of the BSA—in *On My Honor,* esp. the chapter on "The 'Problem' of Gays and Girls in the Boy Scouts."

24. Charles F. Smith, *Camp Fires and Cooking* (New York: Boy Scouts of America, 1935), p. 29.

25. Smith, p. 29.

26. For more detail on the psychoanalytic understandings of the campfire, see Jay Mechling, "The Magic of the Boy Scout Campfire," *Journal of American Folklore* 93 (Jan.–March, 1980), pp. 35–56.

27. Still the best intellectual and cultural history of this antimodern movement is T. J.Jackson Lears, *No Place of Grace: Antimodernism and the Transformation of American Culture, 1880–1920* (New York: Pantheon Books. 1981).

28. For a comprehensive look at the philosophy and productions of the Arts and Crafts Movement, see Wendy Kaplan et al., *"The Art that Is Life": The Arts and Crafts Movement in America, 1875–1920* (Boston: Museum of Fine Arts & Little, Brown and Company, 1987).

29. Of course, as historians like Ruth Schwartz Cowan show, these technological "advances" in domestic work more often than not create extra work. See her *More Work for Mother: The Ironies of Household Technology from the Open Hearth to the Microwave* (New York: Basic Books, 1983).

30. I wish to thank Jon Wagner for this and several other observations in response to earlier drafts of my essay. Comments from my colleague Carolyn Thomas de la Peña and from two anonymous reviewers helped me get clearer on what I wanted to say and, in some cases, not say.

PART III
FOOD AS ART, SYMBOL, AND RITUAL

INTRODUCTION TO PART THREE

Art and aesthetics

European folklife studies initially treated food as a component of the material culture of a community, documenting tools used for planting and harvesting, containers for preservation, cookware and cooking implements, dishes, table coverings, kitchen lay-outs along with skills needed to produce and prepare food, and regional variations in ingredients and recipes. This data demonstrated the craftsmanship involved in foodways and could be used for comparison and identifying geographic distribution. They also studied beliefs and ritual customs attached to food.

As folklorists began broadening their definitions of "folk" and "lore" in the early to mid-1900s, they began recognizing the aesthetic qualities of folk objects and practices.[1] Folk art became defined as art that both came out of a specific community and spoke of that community. As with the "formal" or "fine arts," folk art is also "a conscious attempt on the part of an individual to produce an aesthetically pleasing expression in a form recognized by society," (Toelken 1979: 181), but, unlike them, folk art is not exclusive, exceptional to the everyday, or requiring formal training to execute or appreciate. It also can be utilitarian, and the intent of the artist can be to produce an object that is both artistic and functional.[2] It contrasts with "high art" in that the evaluation of the object is by community consensus rather than by a group of artistic "elites."

These ideas were then applied to understanding food, particularly to everyday foodways and the foods associated with ethnic and regional folk groups.[3] Folklorists now approach foodways as both art (ornamental) and craft (utilitarian) that demand skillful competence of techniques and specialized knowledge as well as individual creativity. They therefore study the elements of form and style, the techniques and skills needed to execute those competently, the ways in which producers learn those skills, and the ways of expressing judgment considered appropriate in that community. By identifying the artistic ("poetic" or "ethno-poetic") patterns in those foods, they discover the criteria qualifying them as "good" to the communities that produce and consume them. Those criteria define the community aesthetic and reflect the historical forces that have created and shaped that aesthetic.

The role of communal consensus in identifying folk art leads to two other fundamental concepts within folkloristics: cultural relativism and genre. Cultural relativism is the notion that each culture should be understood within its own belief system, values, and practices. Rather than measuring folk arts against what were considered "high" and elite arts, they should be evaluated according to the standards and expectations of their community. Furthermore, every community and culture has its own ideas of what is artistic, reflecting an oftentimes unarticulated aesthetic philosophy and system for evaluation. Resources, circumstances, beliefs, values, and histories shape those ideas, and in order to fully understand how and why art functions the way it does, we need to understand the background of that community. The goal of the folklorist, then, is not to evaluate or affirm the artistic merit of a product using elite criteria, but to identify and describe the community's aesthetic system for evaluation.[4]

Applying the idea of relativism to food calls for identifying the aesthetic system of the group appreciating it. Studying food through this lens does not require denying one's own tastes and value system, but recognizes that using one's own system as the standard is not useful in assessing the aesthetic value of specific foodways from a different food culture. Individual tastes are a combination of cultural, social, and personal construction, and individuals within the same culture can have different food preferences reflecting their own beliefs, experiences, situations, and personality.

Genres are categories that carry their own set of expectations and values. Most often used in reference to literature and music, genre theory observes that we need to identify the expectations for each category in order to evaluate how "good" an individual piece is. For example, a musical piece composed in the genre of jazz might be judged excellent according to its genre but would fail miserably in another, such as opera. Folklorist Dan Ben-Amos suggested the term "ethnic or native genres" for the categories actually in use within a folk group (1969). These genres might not be articulated by the community, so part of the role of folklore scholarship is to identify and describe the patterns, ornaments, and aesthetic expectations—the "ethnopoetics"—of that genre.

Genre is a useful concept for evaluating aesthetics in foodways. The kinds of expectations that we have from "fast food" are different than those from a home-cooked meal or a meal in a fine-dining establishment, and we judge these food experiences differently. The taste of a dish can be satisfying and fulfilling within its own genre but might not be evaluated favorably in another genre. Everyday meal, celebration food, gourmet restaurant dinner, diner menus, breakfast, snack, and so on, can all be considered foodways genres, calling for different criteria for evaluation.

Also significant within folklore scholarship on folk art is the recognition that each artist produces variations, and that these variations, while working within the communal aesthetic and definition of that art, demonstrate personal artistry whether or not that is intentional. This challenges common notions of tradition as a static force constraining individuality and innovation. Instead it is dynamic, offering resources and guidelines reflecting the communal ethos and aesthetic but allowing for individuals to express their own tastes and circumstances and even experiment with new ideas, techniques, mediums, and forms. Folklorists then explore how individuals work within a particular tradition, balancing personal expression with a sense of belonging to that community. Similarly, a study of an individual cook, farmer, or other foodways participant can help us to better understand these processes, demonstrating how people oftentimes use food to ground themselves in a past or a place, but also experiment with the new or unknown.

Folklorists also recognize that folk art is a creative process that draws from many sources, including mass-produced and commercial ones. These products are then adapted or used in ways that fit within the communal aesthetic. In foodways, store-bought ingredients, Internet recipe sites, and fast food or chain restaurants can all be used in creative ways and adapted into the foodways repertoire of an individual or community for artistic expression. Also, individuals can exercise artistry and creativity in foodways by arranging various elements, not only in the creation from raw ingredients.[5] Few of us have the complete control over the entirety of the process and materials used in cooking, that was the case with peasant cultures.

A significant implication of folklore theories of art for studying food is that understanding the skills needed to produce that art is important in understanding it as an aesthetic experience. That is, we need to actually cook in order to understand the aesthetics of it. Similarly, we need to consume food, experience the hustle and bustle of a marketplace, or sweat with the labor of farming or chopping vegetables to fully appreciate the role of creativity in these activities.

Symbols

Food as art is closely related to food as symbol. As a cultural, social, and personal construction, however, its symbolic meanings are not universal. Folklorist Gerald Pocius's statement about art is true of food as well: "Art is a universal phenomenon, yet at the same time it is culturally specific." (Pocius 2003: 43). Drawing from the field of semiotics,[6] folklorists approach symbols as social constructions that can be used to wield power as well as to communicate relationships, status, and identity. They are dynamic and fluid, with changing meanings, functions, and impacts.

An important principle in understanding symbols is that those meanings are not intrinsic to the symbol itself. Meaning is socially constructed through usage and communal consent, but can also be invented and purposefully assigned, as in marketing or in creating an identity for a group. The meaning of a sign, then, is not found in itself, but in relationship with other signs within a system. This has several implications. First, symbols are polysemic: they can have multiple meanings and can be interpreted differently by different people or even at different times by the same person. Secondly, the intended meaning by the user of that symbol is not necessarily understood by the receiver, resulting in "misinterpretation." Third, the meaning depends on what is going on around it, its social, historical, and cultural context.

Symbols also have affective power. Like art, they can evoke emotional associations that give meaning to them. This means that responses to a symbol can be a visceral one, in which the meaning is "felt" rather than intellectually recognized. Fried chicken and watermelon, for example, were historically (and sometimes in the present) used in derogatory portrayals of African Americans as being primitive, unintelligent, dishonest, and childlike. Although these foods are now commonly consumed throughout the United States, they still carry those stereotypes and can stir feelings of discomfort and humiliation among individuals with African American heritage.

This last example illustrates another characteristic: symbols are political in that who gets to do the constructing and interpreting of meaning is a matter of power. Part of the reason watermelon is so emotionally charged as a symbol is that economic, social, and cultural opportunities in the United States were historically shaped by race. Individuals "of color" could not define themselves and their traditions in the way they wanted to, but had those definitions imposed upon them, and watermelon became a symbol of that lack of power.

While meanings are not intrinsic, symbols can carry meanings with them, transferring them to—and possibly changing the meaning of—a new action, context, or event.[7] A food associated with one celebration, for example, can imply some of those meanings or emotions in a different context. Similarly, symbols have the power to tell us what to expect in a social event and how to interpret the other actions and other artifacts in that event. "Food has a tendency to transform itself into situation," stated French cultural theorist Roland Barthes, observing that specific dish or type of food carries certain associations for behaviors and thus defining for us the situation in which it occurs.[8] People frequently unknowingly enact Barthes's concept in creating social events. For example, Americans might signal relaxing and informal social eating by serving barbecue or hot dogs on paper plates. Similarly, offering chocolate or dining by candlelight signals a romantic evening, setting the atmosphere for such an event.

Rituals

Folklore scholarship utilizes these understandings of symbol in the studies of food rituals, defining rituals as intentionally symbolic recurring actions, behaviors, or events that reference something beyond their immediate function. Rituals can be sacred, that is associated with spiritual concepts or beliefs and usually occurring in designated contexts set aside from the ordinary and everyday, or they can be secular, referring to nonspiritual beliefs, such as patriotism, family, and the importance of group. Rituals are complex events, which are oftentimes composed of multiple smaller rituals, with multiple meanings and functions. They can transform relationships, individuals, and groups and can also be used to construct, affirm, and challenge them. Rituals, in this sense, can be powerful tools for social and cultural change. Furthermore, both symbols and rituals reflect the existence of power hierarchies in the struggle for who gets to define them and their meanings.

Rituals are usually categorized according to what they reference: season, passage, unity, affirmation, intensification, spectacle and excess, and reversal.[9] Food frequently play a large role in rituals, not only as a symbolic object but also in the acts of preparing, sharing, or consuming it. We can all think of instances in which our participation in a meal means much more than simply satisfying hunger. Food rituals can be interpreted in multiple ways, misinterpreted, or even not recognized as carrying meaning. "Breaking bread," for example, is frequently seen as a way to demonstrate and even create harmony between individuals or groups, but the symbolic meanings of that bread might not be shared or agreed upon.[10]

A single ritual can have more than one theme. For example, Thanksgiving dinner celebrates national unity, but it also celebrates the harvest season, unity of the family, abundance of resources or even the wealth and status of an individual or a group.[11] Each participant may emphasize something different; the same dinner can mean different things to different people. Also, events frequently contain more than one ritual, and certain rituals, especially reversal, can be components of other rituals. Holidays tend to be celebrated with a variety of rituals, allowing for a range of emotions to be experienced, and enriching the meaningfulness of the holiday to the individuals participating.

Folklorists also examine the ways in which rituals actually function within society and are used by individuals or groups. They are frequently social in that they can bring people together, but in doing so, they can also set people apart. One of the intended functions of many rituals is to create a sense of belonging and a feeling that every individual is equally significant and important (nonhierarchical) within a group, a concept of "communitas" suggested by Anthropologist Victor Turner (1969). While sharing of food is a frequent means of bringing people together and creating groups and relationships, it can disrupt relationships and dismantle groups. Also, gift exchanges, as in the giving of food, have long been studied by anthropologists and folklorists and are frequently a way to establish a higher social status or power over another person (Shuman 2000).

Rituals can have a teleological function in that they connect individuals with the larger cycles of nature, birth and death. Religious rituals often officially have this function, but other institutions may aspire to it. Patriotic rituals celebrate the larger ideals and purposes of the nation, reminding people that they are part of the history and future of the country. Similarly, seasonal celebrations help individuals feel connected to nature and to the universal passing of time. Consuming foods just harvested at an autumn supper, for example, celebrates the hard work that went into producing those foods, but it also reminds us of the winter to come and the ongoing changing of the seasons.

Rituals also celebrate, affirm, or challenge cultural identity, and food oftentimes plays a significant symbolic role. The Fourth of July, for example, is celebrated in the United States with outdoor picnics and stereotypic "American" foods, such as hot dogs, hamburgers, and steaks that are frequently grilled, celebrating both the meat-centered food culture and the notions of masculinity and domesticity prevalent in the American society.

Rituals serve a psychological function in that they can provide times of release, personal re-assessment, and escapist fun. Food is oftentimes a medium for such release. "Party foods" tend to be those that emphasize taste over nutritional value; require little stress in preparation; and can be eaten with a minimum of formal etiquette. Conversely, many holiday food traditions require a large amount of labor and skill, but the continuity of including such traditions gives a comforting stability and "completeness" to the celebration.

Rituals can develop organically from within a group, growing out of activities or behaviors that the group might already be participating in. For example, a group of students taking a class together grab a bite to eat after that class because it ends at lunchtime. At the end of the semester, the students realize they enjoy the friendship and decide to meet regularly for lunch. That lunch meeting may then turn into a ritual. Rituals can also be purposely created to convey specific meanings and functions. Such "invented traditions" (Hobsbawm and Ranger 1984) may then be adopted and adapted by a group, becoming a meaningful ritual for them.

This background on symbols and rituals helps us to understand the role of food in festivals and holidays. Holidays are times officially set aside for public cultural performances and rituals. They most frequently celebrate religious or national ideas, but many also are based on the cycles of nature (the seasons, the cycles of the moon and the sun). Festivals are similar to holidays, but are specific celebrations in a specific time and place. They also tend to be complex events with multiple rituals and layers of meaning. Foodways activities are central to both holidays and festivals and are frequently used symbolically and ritualistically. Since these "times out of time" are occasions for reflection, participants are encouraged to think about the meanings of the foods selected, and the public spaces of many festivals and holiday celebrations also allow for food symbols and rituals to be intentionally and self-consciously constructed and negotiated. Folklorists therefore find holiday celebrations and festivals to be ideal settings for documenting foodways traditions.

Articles in *Reader*

In "Bread and the Artistic Process: Hand-Shaping by Heart," Annie Hauck-Lawson and Sean Galvin draw from fieldwork with five bread makers in Brooklyn, New York, to examine the artistic process, the constraints upon that process, and how the individual bakers demonstrate creativity and innovation. They also address the interplay between baking as an art and baking as a business and the ways in which religious and cultural values are promoted through the bread making.

Gary Alan Fine explores the aesthetic and expressive aspects of production in his article, "The Culture of Production: Aesthetic Choices and Constraints in Culinary Work." Using ethnographies that he conducted in restaurants, he demonstrates that professional cooks make aesthetic choices, negotiating those within the social and economic constraints of the occupational context.

Mass-produced foods as well as homemade ones can become meaningful foodways traditions. In "Green Bean Casserole and Midwestern Identity: A Regional Foodways Aesthetic and Ethos," Lucy Long explores the historical conditions for taste and the cultural logic behind the adoption of a nationally distributed commercial food as a meaningful regional family tradition.

Personal innovation and creativity can also be applied to commercial foods, enabling them to become meaningful expressions of an individual's aesthetics and identity. In "Ramen Noodles & Spam: Popular Foods, Significant Tastes," using a group not usually thought of as folk—college students—So Jin Kim and Mark Livengood demonstrate that such foods, even when eaten out of necessity rather than choice, can be varied in creative ways to become aesthetically satisfying dishes.

Not all foodways traditions are pleasant or tasty. In "Paradox of Pride and Loathing," Simon Bronner critiques the limitations of conventional fieldwork methodologies through an analysis of his own work on the "turtle-soup complex," a tradition of hunting turtles and preparing turtle soup in southwestern Indiana. He explores the apparent contradiction that some participants expressed distaste for the soup itself but an appreciation for the tradition and what it represents. He points out, though, that such contradictory attitudes should not be seen by researchers as needing resolution, but as reflecting the complexities of human behavior. It is a reminder that there can be multiple and competing motivations for individuals participating in a tradition, and that aesthetic responses can similarly range from positive to negative.

Renee Valeri also explores distaste in "A Preserve Gone Bad or Just Another Beloved Delicacy? Surstromming and Gravlax." After examining the two different traditions of fermenting and salting fish in Sweden, he concludes that the resulting "unpleasant" flavor and smell become part of the appeal of those foods.

In "Playing to the Senses: Food as a Performance Medium," Barbara Kirshenblatt-Gimblett explores the opportunities and constraints posed by the convergence of food and performance art. Proposing that "perform" can be broken into three types of activities—to do, to behave, and to show—she looks at similarities between food as art and food in everyday life. She also argues that the selected performance pieces have the potential to change the way audiences perceive the food system and even spur them to make corresponding changes in their own food habits.[12]

Food as symbol is investigated by Patricia Lysaght in "Milk, Magic, and Women in Ireland." She describes the significant place of milk and butter in historic and modern Irish foodways and economy which then explains the wealth of rituals and customs surrounding the need to protect milk's quantity and quality. Many of these beliefs reflected gender roles as well as social hierarchies within the local community.

In "Thanksgiving in the U.S.A. The Meal as Medium and Message," Jay Allan Anderson examines the meanings of a ritual meal. Tackling the largest and most significant food ritual of the United States, he identifies themes within the pilgrim narrative and demonstrates that the meal communicates—and thus celebrates—a particular perspective on heritage.

In "When Producers Became Consumers: Cultural Processes in Daily Life," Yrsa Lindqvist discusses how changes in Finnish food habits over the last hundred years represent a shift from most individuals producing their own food to most consuming what others have produced. Information and knowledge about food used to come from family and community, but now they come from mass media, symbolizing an expansion of the local.

A community expression of values is explored by Luisa Del Guidici, in "Rituals of Charity and Abundance: Sicilian St. Joseph's Tables and Feeding the Poor in Los Angeles," in her analysis of display tables created for a religious holiday celebration. She describes the foods included on these tables and the ways in which the tables themselves symbolize hospitality and redistribution of wealth.

Discussion questions

I. Food as art

1. Explore the aesthetics (poetics) of an everyday food (such as peanut butter and jelly sandwich, pizza, and coffee). Identify the criteria for evaluating form, texture, taste, content, size, shape, etc. (What makes a "good" sandwich?) Who sets that criteria? Does your personal taste differ from the general pattern? How much can you vary it before it is no longer "good" or represents that genre? What skills are needed in order to make that food and how are those skills acquired?

2. Can you observe aesthetics in other aspects of foodways—in the way people load their dishwasher, arrange cans in the cupboard, ornament their kitchen table, select dishware for serving food, arrange their food on their plate, etc.? Even something that is as seemingly mundane as eating a cookie can be done in different aesthetic styles.

3. Do you ever "personalize" or "traditionalize" mass-produced and processed foods? Describe the adaptations, variations, and arrangements you make to them and why.

4. Identify the different food genres in your own life (such as home-cooking, school food, party food, and comfort food). Discuss your expectations for each genre. What makes each of them good? How does the context for eating these foods shape expectations?

II. Symbol

1. Identify the symbolism of some of the foods you eat. How did they acquire those meanings?

2. Think of foods representing different aspects of identity—family, race, ethnicity, class, gender, occupation, age, religion. In what contexts do those foods appear? What images do they carry? How did those meanings become attached to that food?

3. Select a single food or dish. Explore the multiple meanings it has across time and place (throughout history and across cultures) as well as the emotions and memories it evokes for different people in your own culture. Do you see a difference between meaning and meaningfulness?

III. Ritual

1. Can you identify any foodways rituals in your everyday life? Discuss the difference between mundane routines, such as purchasing coffee on the way to class, and activities that you consciously think of as rituals, such as meeting with friends for coffee, purchasing a specific food every weekend (pizza on Friday night, for example), or consuming a particular meal certain times of the year (visits home, holidays, etc.).

2. Are there special foods for special occasions in your life? How did those foods become associated with those occasions?

3. Identify holiday foods that are tied to your family. Do they represent your ethnic, regional, or religious background in any way?

4. The American Thanksgiving dinner meal carries multiple meanings and functions. Describe the menu your family commonly has and discuss the different references possible for each dish in that menu. How does the meal itself function as a ritual for you and your family?

Notes

1. This recognition challenged the fundamental Western notions of art, specifically that it is transcendent to and separate from everyday life, produced by exceptional people with exceptional gifts and training, and that it represents the best of a culture and its concept of beauty and goodness. The dualism prevalent in Western thought did not work in instances of folk art in which objects were both utilitarian or functional and ornamental or decorative. Folklorists, in contrast, recognized that the creation of these homemade and hand-made objects took skill, discipline, and creativity and were judged by aesthetic standards as well as by how well they functioned.

2. A significant concept here is that of the individual artist being able to be creative within the boundaries of tradition, which was frequently seen as a constraint on innovation and individuality. Much of the folklore scholarship in the 1970s and 1980s addressed the issue of how an individual could demonstrate both personal creativity and belonging to a collective. Barre Tolkien formulated one approach by looking at what he called the twin laws of folklore—dynamism and conservatism—in which every individual negotiates between change and stability, the old and the new, the community expectations and their own innovations (Barre Toelken, *The Dynamics of Folklore* [Boston: Houghton Mifflin, 1979]).

3. There has historically been a tendency in the Western world to view everyday cooking and eating as a necessary domestic chore rather than a medium for creative expression. "Gourmet" cooking and eating, on the other hand, emphasized creativity, innovation, and personal self-expression, but also carried status, so that possessing and demonstrating knowledge of it was "cultural capital."

4. The idea of cultural relativism is most often applied cuisines of "other" cultures, but it is also useful for understanding the foodways of different groups within a culture. Class, race, ethnicity, gender, ethnicity, and religion or ethics all offer commonalities that can form sub-cultures or folk groups. These groups may then develop their own food culture, their own foodways with its own aesthetic system. From this perspective, there are multiple foodways circles within a single society, each with their own culinary culture.

5. The notion of assemblage is useful here as a grouping of items that put together takes on new meanings and new aesthetic properties. The concept was developed by Jack Santino in reference to the dynamic character of material artifacts in holiday rituals ("The Folk Assemblage of Autumn: Tradition and Creativity in Halloween Folk Art," in *Folk Art and Art Worlds*, ed. John Michael Vlach and Simon J. Bronner [Ann Arbor, MI: UMI Research Press, 1986], 151–70).

6. Semiotics (called semiology in Europe) was developed at the turn of the 1900s by an American philosopher and physicist, Charles Sanders Peirce, and a Swiss linguist, Ferdinand de Saussure.

7. A useful exploration of how objects take on meaning is Barbara Kirshenblatt-Gimblett's discussion of "objects of memory," in which she explores the aesthetics behind "kitsch" displays in the homes of older women (1989). Her concepts are applicable to food.

8. Roland Barthes, "Toward a Psychosociology of Contemporary Food Consumption," in *Food and Culture: A Reader*, ed. Carole Counihan and Penny Van Esterik (New York: Routledge, 1997), 26 (originally published in 1961).

9. For more details on the different types, characteristics, and functions of rituals, particularly in relation to folklore, see Falassi (1986), Turner (1969, 1982), Stoeltje (1983), and Van Gennep (1960).

10. For an example, see Long (2014) for a discussion on the multiple meanings of Irish soda bread and the relationship of those meanings to political alliances.

11. For more readings on the history and meanings of the Thanksgiving meal, see James W. Baker, "Thanksgiving," in *Encyclopedia of American Holidays and National Days*, Vol. 2, ed. Len Travers (Westport, CT: Greenwood, 2006), 436–65; James Deetz and Jay Anderson, "The Ethnogastronomy of Thanksgiving," *Saturday Review of Science* (November 25, 1972): 29–38; Janet Siskind, "The Invention of Thanksgiving: A Ritual of American Nationality," in *Food in the USA: A Reader*, ed. Carole M. Counihan (New York: Routledge, 2002), 41–58; and Jennifer Jensen Wallach, *How America Eats: A Social History of U.S. Food and Culture* (Lanham: Rowman & Littlefield, 2013).

12. Kirshenblatt-Gimblett has also written on the history of the place of food and eating in theatrical performances (2006).

References

Abrahams, Roger. 1984. Equal Opportunity Eating: A Structural Excursus on Things of the Mouth. In *Ethnic and Regional Foodways in the United States: The Performance of Group Identity*, ed. Linda Keller Brown and Kay Mussell, pp. 19-36. Knoxville: The U of Tennessee Press.

Adema, Pauline. *Garlic Capital of the World: Gilroy, Garlic, and the Making of a Festive Foodscape*. Jackson: University of Mississippi, 2009.

Adler, Elizabeth Moxby. 1983. Creative eating: The Oreo Syndrome. In *Foodways and Eating Habits: Directions for Research*, ed. Michael Owen Jones, Bruce Giuliano and Roberta Krell, pp. 4-10. Los Angeles: California Folklore Society.

Armstrong, Robert Plant. *The Affecting Presence: An Essay in Humanistic Anthropology*. Urbana: University of Illinois Press, 1971.

Barthes, Roland. "Toward a Psychosociology of Contemporary Food Consumption." In *Food and Culture: A Reader*, edited by Carole Counihan and Penny Van Esterik, 26. New York: Routledge, 1997 (originally published in 1961).

Bell, Michael J. "Tending Bar at Brown's: Occupation Role as Artistic Performance." *Western Folklore* 35, no. 2 (1976): 93-107.

Ben-Amos, Dan. "Analytical Categories and Ethnic Genres." *Genre* 2 (1969): 275-301.

Boas, Franz. 1995 [1972]. *Primitive Art*. New York: Dover.

Bronner, Simon J. *Grasping Things: Folk Material Culture and Mass Society in America*. Lexington, KY: University of Kentucky, 1986.

Bronner, Simon J. "The Paradox of Pride and Loathing and Other Problems." *Western Folklore* 40, no. 1 (1981): 115–24.

Bronner, Simon J. and W. F. H. Nicolaisen, eds. *Creativity and Tradition in Folklore: New Directions*. Logan, UT: Utah State University Press, 1992.

Di Giovine, Michael I. "La Vigilia Italo-Americana: Revitalzing the Italian-American Family Through the Christmas Eve 'Feast of the Seven Fishes'." *Food and Foodways* 18, no. 4 (2010): 181–208.

Douglas, Mary. 1972. Deciphering a Meal. *Daedalus* 101 (Winter): 54-72.

Douglas, Mary. "Deciphering a Meal." *Daedalus*, Winter, 1972. [Reprinted in *Implicit Meanings: Essays in Anthropology*. Ed. Mary Douglas, 249–75. London: Routledge & Paul, 1975.]

Douglas, Mary. *Implicit Meanings: Essays in Anthropology*. London: Routledge & Paul, 1975.

Falassi, Allessandro, ed. *Time Out of Time: Essays on the Festival*. Albuquerque: University of New Mexico Press, 1986.

Glassie, Henry. "Folk Art." In *Folklore and Folklife: An Introduction*, edited by Richard M. Dorson, 253–80. Chicago: University of Chicago Press, 1972.

Gutiérrez, Ramón A. and Geneviève Fabre, eds. *Feasts and Celebrations in North American Ethnic Communities*. Albuquerque: University of New Mexico, 1995.

Hagstrom, Christine. 1992. Let Them Eat Top Ramen: Pay Hikes Show Contempt for Students. *Los Angeles Times*, 24.

Harris-Lopez, Trudier. "Genre." In *Eight Words for the Study of Expressive Culture*, edited by Burt Feintuch, 99–120. Urbana: University of Illinois, 2003.

Humphrey, Theodore C. and Lin T. Humphrey, eds. *We Gather Together: Food and Festival in American Life*. Ann Arbor: UMI Research Press, 1988.

Jones, Michael Owen. 1991. Afterword: Discovering the Symbolism of Food Customs and Events. In '*We Gather Together': Food and Festival in American Life*, ed. Theodore C. Humphrey and Lin T. Humphrey, pp. 235-45. Logan: Utah State Univ. Press.

Jones, Michael Owen. *Exploring Folk Art: Twenty Years of Thought on Craft, Work, and Aesthetics*. Ann Arbor, MI: UMI Research, 1987.

Jones, Michael Owen. "Food Choice, Symbolism, and Identity: Bread-and-Butter Issues for Folkloristics and Nutrition Studies." *Journal of American Folklore* 120, no. 476 (2007): 129–77.

Jones, Michael Owen. *The Hand Made Object and Its Maker*. Berkeley: University of California, 1975.

Jones, Michael Owen. "What's Disgusting, Why, and What Does It Matter?" *Journal of Folklore Research* 37 (2000): 53–71.

_____. 1993. Aesthetic Attitude, Judgment, and Response: Definitions and Distinctions. In *Exploring Folk Art: Twenty Years of Thought on Craft, Work, and Aesthetics*, pp. 161=75. Logan: Utah State Univ. Press.

Kirshenblatt-Gimblett, Barbara. "Making Sense of Food in Performance: The Table and The Stage." In *The Senses in Performance*, edited by Sally Banes and Andre Lepecki, 71–90. New York and London: Routledge, 2006.

Kirshenblatt-Gimblett, Barbara. "Objects of Memory: Material Culture as Life Review." In *Folk Groups and Folklore Genres: A Reader*, edited by Elliott Oring, 329–38. Logan: Utah State University Press, 1989.

Korsmeyer, Carolyn. 2005. *The Taste Culture Reader: Experiencing Food and Drink*. Oxford: Berg.

LeBesco Kathleen and Peter Naccarato, eds. 2008. "Introduction." *Edible Ideologies: Representing Food & Meaning*. Albany: SUNY Press.

Long, Lucy M. "Breaking Bread in Northern Ireland: Soda Farls, Implicit Meanings, and Gastropolitics." In *Political Meals*, edited by Regina F. Bendix and Michaela Fenske, 287–306. Berlin: Lit Verlag, 2014.

Long, Lucy M. "Food As Symbol." In *Encyclopedia of Food and Culture*, edited by Solomon H. Katz and William Woys Weaver. Vol. 3, 376–78. New York: Scribner, 2003.

Long, Lucy M. "Holiday Meals: Rituals of Family Tradition." In *Dimensions of the Meal: The Science, Culture, Business, and Art of Eating*, edited by Herbert L. Meiselman, 143–59. Gaithersburg, MD: Aspen, 2000.

Manning, Frank E. "Carnival in Canada: The Politics of Celebration." In *Folk Groups and Folklore Genres: A Reader*, edited by Elliott Oring, 78–86. Logan, UT: Utah State University Press, 1989.

Manning, Frank E. *The Celebration of Society: Perspectives on Contemporary Cultural Performance*. Bowling Green, OH: Bowling Green University Popular, 1983.

Mickler, Ernest Matthew. 1986. *White Trash Cooking*. Berkeley: Ten Speed Press.

Newton, Sarah E. 1992. "The Jell-O Syndrome": Investigating Popular Culture/Foodways. *Western Folklore* 51: 249-68.

Neustadt, Kathy. *Clambake: A History and Celebration of An American Tradition*. Amherst: University of Massachusetts, 1992.

Pocius, Gerald L. "Art." In *Eight Words for the Study of Expressive Culture*, edited by Burt Feintuch, 42–68. Urbana: University of Illinois, 2003.

Prose, Francine. 1992. Cocktail Hour at the Snake Blood Bar: On the Persistence of Taboo. *Antaeus* 68: 112-19.

Prosterman, Leslie. *Ordinary Life, Festival Days: Aesthetics in the Midwestern County Fair*. Washiington, DC: Smithsonian Institution Press, 1995.

Rappaport, R. A. "Ritual." In *Folklore, Cultural Performances, and Popular Entertainments: A Communications-centered Handbook*, edited by Richard Bauman, 249–60. New York: Oxford University Press, 1992.

Santino, Jack. *All around the Year: Holidays and Celebrations in American Life*. Urbana: University of Illinois, 1994.

Santino, Jack, ed. *Halloween and Other Festivals of Death and Life*. Knoxville: University of Tennessee, 1994.

Santino, Jack. *New Old-fashioned Ways: Holidays and Popular Culture*. Knoxville: University of Tennessee, 1996.

Sanchez, Jesus. 1988. Dishing up the Ramen: Los Angeles is Now the Oriental Noodle-Making Capital of the U.S. *Los Angeles Times*, 4 July: 119.

Shermon, Sharon R. 1988. "The Passover Seder: Ritual Dynamics Foodways, and family Folklore." In *We Gather Together: Food and Festival in American Life*, edited by Theodore C. Humphrey and Lin T. Humphrey, 27–42. Ann Arbor: UMI Research Press.

Shuman, Amy. "Food gifts: Ritual Exchange and the Production of Excess Meaning." *The Journal of American Folklore* 113, no. 450 (2000): 495–508.

Smith, Robert J. "Festivals and Celebrations." In *Folklore and Folklife, an Introduction*, edited by Richard M. Dorson, 159–72. Chicago: University of Chicago, 1972.

Stoeltje, Beverly J. "Festival in America." In *Handbook of American folklore*, edited by Richard M. dorson, 239–46. Blommngton: Indiana university Press, 1983.

Theophano, Janet S. 1991. "I Gave Him a Cake": An Interpretation of Two Italian-American Weddings. In *Creative Ethnicity: Symbols and Strategies of Contemporary Ethnic Life*, ed. Stephen Stern and John Allan Cicala, pp. 44-54. Logan: Utah State Univ. Press.

Toelken, Barre. *The Dynamics of Folklore*. Boston: Houghton Mifflin, 1979.

Tsing Loh, Sandra. 1991. L.A. on $20 a day: Roommates and Ramen: A Guide for Bohemians. *Los Angeles Times*, 12 November: S19.

Turner, Victor W. *Celebration: Studies in festivity and Ritual*. Washington, DC: Smithsonian Institution Press, 1982.

Turner, Victor W. *The Ritual Process: Structure and Anti-Structure*. Ithaca: Cornell University Press, 1969.

Van Gennep, Arnold. *The Rites of Passage*. Chicago: University of Chicago Press, 1960.

Vlach, John Michael and Simon J. Bronner, eds. *Folk Art and Art Worlds*. Ann Arbor, MI: UMI Research Press, 1986.

Wyman, Carolyn. 1993. *I'm a Spam Fan: America's Best-Loved Foods*. Stamford, CT: Longmeadow Press.

Yoder, Don. *Discovering American Folklife: Studies in Ethnic, Religious, and Regional Culture*. Ann Arbor, MI: UMI Research, 1990.

Yoder, Don. 1972. Folk Cookery. In *Folklore and Folklife: An Introduction*, ed. Richard M. Dorson, pp. 325-50. Chicago: Univ. of Chicago Press.

CHAPTER 12

BREAD AND THE ARTISTIC PROCESS: HAND-SHAPING BY HEART

Seán Galvin and Annie Hauck-Lawson

Introduction

Breadmakers and their artistic products continue to hold a place of importance and respect in many contemporary communities. This is especially true in Brooklyn, New York, one of the most densely populated areas of the United States. For a recent feature length videotape proposal we chose to examine breadmakers from five culture areas: Western Europe (Italian), Hispanic (Mexican), Middle East (Syrian), Jewish (primarily Ashkenazim), and Caribbean (specifically St. Vincent). Each of these groups is present in significant numbers in the borough of Brooklyn, and each has one or more clearly defined neighborhoods which are unquestionably demarcated spatially and visually. We intended to discuss the means by which these breadmakers promote the continuity of traditional religious and community values in ritual, celebratory, and everyday settings. Using the breadmakers, their bakeries, and their neighborhoods as focal points, our fieldwork examined the similarities between breadmaking techniques, the community's sense of the role of the breadmaker as a modern-day "town crier" who announces the onset of a season or a festival, and, ultimately, the breadmaker's sense of himself as artist and community member. The proposed videotape title, "'Our Daily Bread': Breadmaking as Artistic Process in Five Brooklyn Neighborhoods," conveys our own wonderment at the simplicity of bread and its manifest import to almost every known celebratory interaction.

Foodways may perhaps be one of the most obvious indicators of ethnic identity, but it may also be the most problematic in a cross-cultural analysis. Breadmaking, for example, no longer retains the place of importance it once held in the home. The village or neighborhood bakery which replaced the domestic, individual production of bread is itself being quickly replaced by supermarkets, sophisticated frozen food techniques, and automated production lines with elaborate distribution patterns. Although a daily feature in the cuisine of most households, bread holds more than everyday significance in its relationship to the ritual, celebratory, and sacred traditions of these communities.

The bakers are themselves practicing artisans and community members who must conform to requirements set by the calendar, the community, and their own aesthetic. For this reason, bakeries and the people who create the bread are perfect points of entry into the inner workings of an artistic process within the neighborhoods. Here, we understand "artistic process" to mean the specific means by which neighborhood bakers continue to thrive by promoting cultural values above and beyond the everyday in an environment which does not readily favor individual artistic achievement for something as commonplace as bread.

Seán Galvin and Annie Hauck-Lawson, 'Bread and the Artistic Process: Hand-Shaping by Heart' in *Digest: An Interdisciplinary Study of Food and Foodways* (1991), 5–10.

Reprinted with permission from *Digest*.

The study of foodways as artistic process concerns adaptation and continuity: it involves changes in environment, availability of foodstuffs, and evolving kitchen technologies. Artisan-bakers, as community spokespersons, creatively reaffirm old traditions in new ways by continuing to serve the needs of that community as they successfully incorporate these changes. The unique blend of ethnic enclaves and a rootedness in traditional religious and cultural values makes the neighborhoods of Brooklyn unique expressions of continuity and change over time, where the dynamic tensions of old world vs. new and recent immigrant vs. third- and fourth-generation ethnic meet on the streets, in the religious centers, and at the local bakeries. The communities who support these bakeries are not exclusive in their tastes, however, and there is a tremendous amount of "crossover" between neighborhoods. Members of any community may indiscriminately eat breads such as *babka, pita, challah,* or *papadum* for everyday consumption but will tend to be very discriminating when the time comes for ritual or celebratory foodways behavior. For these and many other reasons, we discovered that the study of foodways, and particularly breadmaking in a multi-ethnic setting, presents formidable challenges and interesting questions which require elucidation, if not evocation. It is to these ends that our proposed videotape addresses itself.

Methodology

This study evolved from the above-mentioned video proposal. We were looking for a video project that was foodways- and occupation-oriented and that lent itself to a visual and spatial ethnographic study. Because of the diversity of ethnic and cultural representation in Brooklyn's neighborhoods, the idea of something as simple as bread, in its everydayness, struck us as an engaging subject for study. Although there have been studies on Hispanic breads, Greek holiday breads, and Italian bread, such as Tony Denono's film, *It's All in the Hands,* there is no evidence of a cross-cultural study of bread, either on the bakers or on their products.

Our research design encompasses some generalizations, both about Brooklyn and about the study of ethnic foodways. For example, the proposed ethnic divisions were chosen to represent major bread types: *hardo, challah, pita,* etc. But in a 1990 study by the Brooklyn Historical Society (Marks 1990:10), it was reported that the Spanish-speaking population of Brooklyn constitutes forty percent of the population of the borough. According to the 1980 census, Puerto Ricans rank first in number with 71.3 percent of the Hispanic population, and Dominicans are second, with the general designation "Central and Latin American" as a distant but growing third part of the Hispanic population. We sought the advice of several folklorists on the matter of representing Hispanic bread. As we visited "Hispanic" bakeries, we found that there was not one bread, but several, and that Hispanic, as an overarching "ethnic" category, was especially problematic.

When we went back to our community contacts, we found that the tortillas we had originally rejected as being "too Mexican" are indeed consumed, according to informant Fernando Sanchez, in a fair number of other Hispanic households, particularly in light of the huge influx of recent immigrants from Central and South America. Tortillas, therefore, although not universally consumed by Hispanic-Brooklynites, will stand as the functional and representative "bread" of choice for our study and are included in references to bread and bakeries. In addition, we found that how to represent Jewish bread was also one of the questions that proved both challenging and problematic. Not all Jews, for example, observe *Shabbos* and, for that reason, one could argue that *challah* is not necessarily the bread of choice for practicing Jews. Other considerations included deciding whether a bakery had a neighborhood following or reputation, or whether it had been around long enough to be "worthy" of inclusion.

An ethnographic primer on bread

Bread is a basic foodstuff, common to most of the culture groups of the world in one form or another, and serves a role in ritual, celebratory, and festival occasions as well. It is clearly a marker of ethnic identity, for some to a greater degree than for others, but nonetheless important to the setting of a table or the planning of a function, whether it be a funeral or a wedding. The crux of the project's rationale rests in the assumption that the people who make the bread in a community, and the kinds of breads they make, are guided by a combination of personal and community aesthetics that inform their choices about size, quantity, ingredients, packaging, and whatever other concerns there are to making bread. Secondly, we found that the members of that community, who share this aesthetic and have helped mold it over time, understand the baker to have a responsibility both to himself, as artist, and to the community, as fellow participant, to promote and maintain ethnic, religious, or cultural markers in the form of a single food item endemic to their ethnic identity.

Our first concentration of interest was the interplay between the advances in food and equipment technology, market demands, and our baker's artistic philosophy. The working paradigm that we developed in this project concerned the bakers with whom we worked: the individual conception of how big or little they wanted to become determined the degree of technological sophistication that they embraced. Further, their individual philosophy determined the degree of artistic sophistication they employed in the breadmaking process. These two concepts worked simultaneously in each of our chosen settings. Although our data are extensive, it would be helpful to present brief profiles of the origins of our five establishments and community responses to them. Our bakers began making their products solely by hand and, with time, their businesses evolved to the point where they needed to keep up with increased customer demands and new technology. Each was an immigrant and started with a handmade product and basic equipment.

Ben Togati, an Italian baker, apprenticed with a cousin twenty-seven years ago in Brooklyn. Now in his Bensonhurst neighborhood, he and his two sons hand make daily 1500–2000 loaves of bread which are baked in his coal-fired brick oven. Ben feels that the neighborhood is his best friend. He feeds them and they feed him. Since he opened on this site fourteen years ago, his business has increased seventy percent and two competitors have left the neighborhood. He says, "I have no rivals. Mine is perfection. I'm very confident in my work."

Pita, according to one of our informants, first came to the United States in the 1930s. Hassan Halaby was the first documented Syrian breadmaker in the United States. He started Damascus Bakery on Atlantic Avenue in the 1930s as a response to the pan-Arabic influx to this neighborhood. His *pita* was hand-mixed, hand-rolled, shaped, and baked, emerging from the oven with a golden brown surface, spongy texture, and characteristic "pocket" that his customers still talk about today. They say it was the "best bread. His was a craftsman's product, handmade." That *pita* built the Damascus reputation.

Korn's Bakery has become an institution in the Boro Park section of Brooklyn with five outlets and numerous trucks delivering warm *challahs* to points around the greater New York area. Mr. Korn, Sr., one of two Holocaust survivors in his family, followed a traditional immigrant pattern and established a storefront bakery, first on the Lower East Side of Manhattan and then in Boro Park. His son set himself up with a wholesale bakery in Williamsburg, Brooklyn, in 1950. Dispirited because this business had not thrived, he confided in his rabbi during Purim, 1952. The rabbi related the story of Haman's turning point and auspiciously wished Mr. Korn good luck. With renewed confidence, Korn Jr. moved to Boro Park in 1955 and bought his father's operation. The center of their business and the centerpiece of the *Shabbos* table is *challah,* because "every good Jewish woman will light candles and put two braided loaves on the table." Each handmade loaf is crafted from six pieces of dough. Two braided loaves together represent the intermarriage of the twelve tribes of Israel.

"Tortillas made by hand are more fresh. When you see your wife making them, rolling [the *masa* on] the *metate,* clapping them to form, you say 'My wife is making my tortillas for me, for my sons.' You're filled with a good feeling. You're in your home. Here, people are just making tortillas. It's not family. It's nothing." So says Fernando Sanchez, who is representative of a typical recent immigrant story. He came from his home in Piaxtla, Mexico, to work in a series of New York City restaurant kitchens as do so many of the Latin American immigrants who have come to New York to earn money. He then went to work for his cousin who ran a *tortillaria* in Passaic, New Jersey. After seven years of working every end of that operation, Sanchez decided to go off on his own. He imported an oven, mixer, and refrigerator from Los Angeles and opened his own *tortillaria* in Bushwick in 1986. From an initial outlay of $10,000 for that single setup, he has since expanded the business to the point where he produces over 500,000 tortillas each twenty-four hours.

Another relatively recent immigrant, Allan Smith, came to Brooklyn from the island of St. Vincent. Baking was his hobby. After a day at his factory job, he baked and sold breads and sweet buns. In 1968, he opened a bakery in Crown Heights, the heart of Brooklyn's Caribbean population which comprises the single largest group of foreign-born residents in Brooklyn. Allan produced baked goods for the tastes of the local Caribbean community. He quickly developed a loyal following for his hand-shaped breads and rolls, *hardo,* milk, light sweet, and tennis, due in part to his commitment to the use of high quality ingredients.

Quantity vs. quality: A conundrum

It should be clear from the above that these five establishments are solidly integrated into their respective neighborhoods. They gained success on the reputation of their handmade products. Over time, some of the businesses were passed on to sons, daughters, and in-laws. In any event, each of the proprietors came to a crossroad. They arrived at a point where the interplay between technological advances and artistic license forced a decision which perhaps favored a greater production level at the expense of the handmade artistic input.

What to do? Some continued in the belief that the greater market share should be the overriding concern. To bring our story to the present, one of Hassan Halaby's grandsons has taken over the retail storefront of the Damascus concern, and another grandson is running the *pita* factory that was started by their fathers. Edward Mafoud, who is now the president of the Damascus *Pita* Factory, would love to see his bread in every supermarket in the country. Working with the notion that a ten-fold expansion in ten years is a reasonable goal, he is stretching the technological capacity of his operation to introduce more and new products, such as garlic, onion, whole wheat, and oat bran *pita,* to name a few. Consequently, his operation is far removed from the handmade process. As it presently stands, only two people handle the raw dough throughout the baking process. Ninety percent of the labor force is involved in bagging, boxing, and shipping.

Dennis Halaby, the other grandson, has successfully maintained the Damascus storefront operation and his cousin supplies him with fresh *pita* daily. However, he is not entirely satisfied with this new, technologically advanced product. He wants to return to his grandfather's golden brown, spongy-textured, pocketed *pita*. Dennis feels so strongly about returning to his grandfather's aesthetic of bread that he will support his venture with a secondary, more profitable item, namely spinach pies, which he will also hand make in-house, and will slowly begin to bake his own handmade *pita* again.

Fernando Sanchez came to his crossroads as a result of a price war with his former employer and cousin, a now-jealous rival for the same tortilla market. The only way Sanchez could survive was to increase his output. Did his artistry suffer? No. He has been able to maintain the same level of input by hand and still increase productivity by adding an identical fourth oven.

Ben Togati is our saint. He stays where he is. He and his sons continue to produce their fully handmade loaves, inserting them into the coal-fired brick oven with long-handled bread shovels. Ben's personal philosophy is intertwined with his operation. Twenty-seven years ago he found baking to be his conformity with God. He says, "it's a grace to be able to bake bread."

The Korn family operation, now almost a Boro Park dynasty, has been passed to the Korn daughters and is managed by the sons-in-law. Their original business was based on three breads: pumpernickel, rye, and *challah*, with *challah* taking the lion's share of the total. Although sixteen types of bread are now baked at the factory, the handmade *challah* is still the backbone of Korn's business. But in order to meet the staggering weekly demands of 30,000 *Shabbos* loaves, they have installed a series of huge walk-in freezers which allow them to freeze the hand-shaped dough early in the week. Some of these are delivered to local supermarkets and the rest are baked in-house on Thursday and Friday. Does the handmade *challah* suffer? Not according to Mr. Korn's son-in-law, Mordechai Berkovits, who feels that freezing "ages" the *challah*, rendering the baked product even more desirable. Further, the availability of Korn's frozen *challah* in the supermarket gives the sense of homemade to the housewife who bakes it herself on Friday afternoon.

The operating ethos which guides Allan's Bakery lies somewhere in between Ben's and Korn's. He will not freeze his bread. In fact, he will make only as much as he can sell hot. In the same vein, his customers will happily wait to get the hot loaf and are even willing to pay more if the market demands that Allan increase his prices. Allan continues to use 2.2 pounds of dough to make his *hardo* bread. When the costs of ingredients and labor go up, the customer pays more to get the same bread, because Allan will not make concessions to the marketplace. With the help of his son Terry, Allan's Bakery has become a model of a successful minority-owned business in a neighborhood where the small business turnover rate is very high.

We have shown how the question of how to respond to technological advances in food technology and where the response will lead a small breadmaking concern are of paramount importance to each of our groups. The most astute business persons cannot foresee all of the variables of fluctuations in market prices or in geopolitical concerns over which they have no control. Because breadmaking has such a low profit margin, our participants, with the exception of Ben, have expressed their constant fear that one unwise decision could affect all of their operations. Risk is an everyday factor in their businesses.

Adherence to Kosher dietary law prohibiting the use or consumption of leavening at Passover is strictly observed at Korn's. Four years ago, a miscalculation in production caused Korn's to sacrifice 3,000 loaves of frozen dough. The response from Berkovits was that it was criminal to waste, but in the same breath he accepted this financial loss in light of his religiosity, obviously a governing principle in the Korn family operation.

Certainly there are other examples that we could relate from our interviews with these five very different family businesses. What we were most impressed with, however, was the ease with which they shared their stories and agreed to go on record, should the project go forward as planned.

As we have maintained from the beginning, this fieldwork represents a year-and-a-half of work-in-progress and is by no means complete. For example, we have yet to accomplish one of our preliminary goals, which is to follow the hot bread home from the bakery. Not only was this conceived as an interesting and necessary ethnographic portion of the proposed video, but it would also serve to confirm the ideas and impressions we had gathered from the interview process. Secondly, seeing people in their home environment would not only allow them a chance to be themselves in familiar surroundings, but really establish the contextual backdrop to support our leitmotif, "Our Daily Bread."

This project began with certain assumptions, both about the research design and the groups we would use as examples. We got into the field and found out that many of these assumptions required modification. However, we can honestly say that every time we had a problem or a question, the community itself supplied the answer. What our model has suggested, to us at least, is that many of the esoteric/exoteric markers of ethnic identity we thought would be obvious were deeply embedded in the breadmaker's personal philosophy regarding the artistry and creativity involved in a business enterprise. The personal experience narratives collected indicate that tremendous cross-cultural data will be gained by pursuing this dialogue further. None of these participants ever suggested that the machine-made product could supplant the "real thing," and several were genuinely sorry that the product they offered was not the same as their grandfathers had made.

Amidst their wistful recollections of how it was then, they also spoke to the realities of free market enterprise, the growing trend of health-conscious and calorie- or cholesterol-wise consumers, and the fact that they had to pay the rent at the end of the month just like anyone else. The reality is that bread is actually a high volume, low profit item. Although the hours are long and the work can be repetitive, most of the participants were happy in their work and pleased with their choice of occupation. Their work is their life by choice. To each of them, baking is a way of earning a livelihood in the new country while simultaneously earning the prestige of being in business for himself and fitting into an established community. All of the businesses we studied are family concerns; several of the participants apprenticed themselves to other family members before going out on their own; all plan to keep the businesses within their family through sons, in-laws, or cousins.

Summary conclusions

Can we truly say that bread of any type is a genuine ethnic marker? The answer is yes, within the context of these particular neighborhoods vis-à-vis our focus on the producers themselves. Each of the individuals with whom we spoke agreed that the handmade product is the best. In spite of increased leisure time, necessary expansions to compete with supermarkets, or changes in taste or neighborhood profiles, the breadmaker would like to continue his artistry according to his individual aesthetic, but he is bound by marketing and productivity prerogatives which, in most cases, require a compromise in the level or degree of handmade or artistic input. The consumers, on the other hand, especially in light of the proliferation of media and medical reports encouraging low-fat diets, are sophisticated shoppers. They will go to the baker to get what they consider the best approximation of the handmade product with a complete willingness to buy into the more advanced technology because they are unwilling to bake it themselves.

In the same vein, from the point of view of the baker (whom we have chosen to call artist), this process of making bread (what we are calling the creative expression) serves several functions:

1. confirming his ethnic identity;
2. establishing him in the community as artist and as community member;
3. promoting and maintaining what he conceives to be primary and exemplary products of his ethnic roots in the belief that the maintenance of these markers will promote community coherence.

Why five groups? As we maintained in the beginning, Brooklyn's long history as entry point and place of acculturation for hundreds of different ethnic groups lends itself to this type of study. In fact, we were surprised that no one else has attempted a cross-cultural study of bakeries and their breads to date. Again, these five groups, very loosely referred to as Italian, Jewish, Hispanic, Caribbean, and Arabic, are concatenations of recent immigrants and established ethnics, of families of mixed ethnic backgrounds, and of individuals of vastly differing religious practices. We cannot assume to speak for an entire ethnic population. For example, we have confined ourselves to the Orthodox Jewish population of the Boro Park section of Brooklyn, so we have not even considered the conservative or reformed sectors of Jewish Brooklyn. In point of fact, the borough of Brooklyn, which is one-fifth of the City of New York, is said to have a Jewish population of 552,000, or more people than Tel Aviv.

Our method of selecting research sites was not random, however, and by choosing these particular businesses and their neighborhood communities we have endeavored to show a cross-section of the foodways of ethnic groups with the hope that we can later extrapolate some meaningful cross-cultural inferences that may or may not hold up under closer examination in a San Antonio, Texas, or a Knoxville, Tennessee. As a result, we can begin to see some of the most important consequences of conducting research on bread and breadmakers through their personal philosophies on style, technique, and creativity. We can witness how the handmade product is still alive and well, despite the supermarket chains—although it is often buoyed by secondary, but perhaps more profitable, items. We encounter the artist-cum-religious figure when he signals the beginning of a religious holiday such as Easter, or Passover, or the Day of the Dead, by putting a specific bread in the storefront window. We can judge how the decisions made by his predecessors at the crossroads between technology and artistry continue to affect him, and how he, in this generation, has also made artistic and processual decisions based on what he conceives to be the changes in community aesthetic combined with ever-changing food technology.

We can also see how he is already making sure that everything is in place for the future generation, hoping that they will preserve the same cultural and ethnic markers and enjoy the same status in the community that he has worked so hard to maintain. Throughout all of this there is only one constant—bread—made with flour, water, heat…love, and the conscious artistry of the people who give us the stuff of life, Our Daily Bread.

Notes

Portions of this paper were presented at the American Folklore Society Annual Meeting, Oakland, California, 1990, and at the monthly meeting of the Culinary Historians of New York, February, 1991.

References

Marks, Morton, ed. 1989. From *Colonias* to Communities: Brooklyn's Hispanic Neighborhoods, pp. 9–10. In *Brooklyn's Hispanic Communities*. Brooklyn, NY: The Brooklyn Historical Society.

CHAPTER 13

THE CULTURE OF PRODUCTION: AESTHETIC CHOICES AND CONSTRAINTS IN CULINARY WORK[1]

Gary Alan Fine

The creation of objects of "aesthetic value" is not merely a topic of philosophical speculation, but is a distinctly sociological activity. Each occupation maintains a sense of superior production (an "occupational aesthetic") that is not reducible to organizational demands. This perspective extends the production of culture approach that sees art as being like all work, suggesting, in contrast, that all work is like art. An aesthetic component to work is reflected in the desire to produce objects (or perform tasks) so as to demonstrate the competence of the worker, as exemplified in a case study of work in four restaurant kitchens. The production of quality is not unbounded, as client demands, organizational efficiency, and the organization's resource base have effects. The centrality of an aesthetic orientation depends upon the market niche of one's organization, career stage in the occupation, and the nature of the work task.

De gustibus non disputandum. [Latin proverb]

How is "good" work possible, given demands for autonomy and organizational constraints on that autonomy? Unfortunately sociologists of work have been little concerned with how work gets done, as that doing relates to questions of style and form: the aesthetics of work. We have lost sight of the conditions that produce "quality," while emphasizing the technical, functional, and goal-directed doings of workers and how workers attempt to undercut authority in the workplace. This choice means that we often examine work worlds from the outside, little realizing that what is useful to the consumer may (or may not) be elegant to the worker. We do not examine ways in which organizations facilitate and restrain occupational aesthetics. This lack of theoretical interest in form and content may be excused in studies of occupations we label "industrial" or "professional," but it is curious that this deemphasis on the sensory components of work occurs in studies of occupations that involve aesthetic production.

Extending a "production of culture" approach (Peterson 1979; Becker 1974; Hirsch 1972), which analyzes cultural production by the same tools as industrial work, I argue that (1) issues of quality are central to production and that process involves "aesthetic choices," (2) aesthetic choices are a form of organizational decisions, are capable of being negotiated, and are not fully reducible to organization demands, (3) organizational features encourage, channel, and limit explicitly aesthetic choices, and (4) organizations can define their own aesthetics, given their placement within a market niche and clients' definitions. There has been a tendency in sociology of culture (see Wolff 1983) to downplay aesthetic choices, effects, and constraints. My goal is to demonstrate how options and constraints produce the expressive form of work products: what we might term

Gary Alan Fine, 'The Culture of Production: Aesthetic Choices and Constraints in Culinary Work', *American Journal of Sociology* 97 (1992), 1268–1294. (Excerpt printed here: 1268–1271, 1272–1285, 1288, 1291–1294. Omitted text is indicated by ellipses.)

© 1992. Reprinted with permission from the University of Chicago Press.

the *culture of production*. I hope to demonstrate how organizational, market, and client constraints affect the qualities of work products.

In speaking of the expressive side of production, I select the slippery term "aesthetics" to refer to the sensory component of production.[2] Why aesthetics? This concept is the broadest of a cluster of terms that involve the sensory qualities of experience and objects: beauty, creativity, elegance, goodness, and the like. For purposes of this analysis, an aesthetic object (or act) is defined as an object (or act) that is intended to produce a sensory response in an audience (e.g., Shepard 1987; Wolff 1983). No special brief other than its utility and general reasonableness exists for this definition. It captures the cognitive (satisfaction) and affective (sensory) components of aesthetic judgments, and also includes the intentional quality of human action. Aesthetics reminds us that these choices are distinct from purely instrumental and efficient choices: workers care about "style," and not only about technical quality. Although form and function are typically intertwined, aesthetics refers specifically to the production of form, not only to function. Attempts to produce "good work" often involve an intimate linkage between form and function, and functionally perfect objects may be seen as having perfect form. Judgments of quality adhere to both form and function, although the focus here is on the former. In cooking, and other work arenas, the sensory characteristics of objects (and services) have a special standing in appreciation both among workers and publics.[3]

Sociologists recognize that the practical creation of industrial objects is a fundamentally social enterprise, constructed through interaction and organizational constraint.[4] Yet, the feeling for form or creative impulse, as well as its limitations, needs to be emphasized in theorizing on the structure of work and occupations. Not doing so gives a distorted picture of the workplace, making it alternatively seem too instrumental (denying a sense of identity and craft to workers) or too filled with conflict (emphasizing how workers are separated from their work and their supervisors). Work matters to workers, and workers have craft standards by which they judge work products and performance that transcend the narrow goals of producing things with efficiency and to bureaucratic specification. This connection between the worker and the work is central to the occupational identity of workers. Craft is a part of all work life.

I examine a single occupation, professional cooking, hoping to demonstrate four things. First, cooking, like all occupations, involves an aesthetic concern, which takes its form in decisions about the sensory components of food. Second, the practical doing of cooking is an everyday accomplishment and must be negotiated in practice by workers. Third, culinary production is channeled by social and economic constraints and by occupational segmentation. Finally, this argument is generalized to other occupations, suggesting an integration of the sociologies of work and culture.

The world of restaurants

Whatever cooks may wish to think of their own work, restaurant managers often refer to this economic segment as "the hospitality industry." This phrase reminds us that restaurants are industrial organizations operated for profit by capitalists. Although food must look, smell, taste, and feel good to maintain an audience, this is not sufficient. Food must be priced to be profitable and must be produced consistently and efficiently. Among the techniques used by restaurant managers to achieve profit are paying low wages, hiring few employees, and procuring inexpensive raw materials and equipment. Food services are caught between the demands of aesthetic creation and the viselike grip of free-market capitalism.

Cooks suffer the strains of a set of conflicting ideologies that push them to be artists, professionals, businessmen, and manual laborers (Fine 1982). Because professional cooking is situated amid demands for aesthetic choices, consistency, efficiency, autonomy, and highly skilled technical work (Hall 1975, pp. 188–200), it provides a challenging site from which to examine the development, conflicts, and negotiations of sensory judgments at work. Whyte (1948; Gross 1958) notes that restaurants are both production and service units, providing the cook with two separate "authorities"—managers and customers—adding further strains. Whereas factory workers, beauticians, and sculptors do not have the same balance of concerns, some of the same dilemmas are also present in these work worlds—all occupations combine expressive and instrumental demands, personal freedom, and organizational control in varying degrees.

I conducted participant observation in four restaurants in the Twin Cities metropolitan area (St. Paul/ Minneapolis and their surrounding suburbs), spending a month observing and taking notes in the kitchen of each restaurant during all periods in which the restaurant was open.[5] In each restaurant I interviewed all full-time cooks—a total of 30 interviews. Interviews lasted approximately 90 minutes, with some over three hours long. Field notes and interviews from this material are identified throughout the text.

[…]

Doing aesthetics

All work is socially situated and constrained environmentally and organizationally. No matter how idealistic the goals of the worker, ultimately these goals are embedded in the negotiated compromises of work. Howard Becker, discussing art as work, claims that aesthetics is ultimately activity rather than a doctrine (Becker 1982, p. 131)—it is an everyday accomplishment. Theory only flickers around the edges of the consciousness of workers. It follows from this that most workers are not explicit about (or even conscious of) their aesthetic decisions.[6] They desire to produce objects or services that are pleasing sensually, but typically the basis on which they realize this is vague. For example, a hotel cook told me: "When I make my soup . . . I try to make it look as nice as possible, and to taste. I feel I take a lot of pride in it. When other people make soup it doesn't always look like mine" (field notes, Blakemore Hotel). This worker has a generalized sense of "niceness" that includes looks and taste, but analysis does not transcend this partially inarticulate sentiment (Fine 1987).

The content of this sensibility varies by cook and restaurant and is further complicated by the realization that cooking involves situated choices. Still, all cooks hope to present what they consider appealing dishes of which they are proud—food that will appeal to their customers' senses, not merely food that will satiate them or make them healthy (the functional characteristics of food). This culinary evaluation involves numerous senses. The head chef at La Pomme de Terre responded when I asked what he liked best about cooking:

> Making something that I think is just the greatest. I did a bouillabaisse . . . and I thought it was just the greatest. . . . It had a lot of seafood in it, a lot of shellfish, shrimp, lobster, mussels, clams, and about six other seafood items in it, and the sauce was a somewhat thin, primarily lobster-based sauce, lots of butter, and very, very rich, and the thing that was best about it was everything was made to where, typically if you have bouillabaisse, you have to hold onto something with the tongs and dig meat out of the shell and stuff like that, but I prepared it so that everything was done for you. . . . It was not only tasty and unusually fantastic as far as flavor, smell, and sight; it was easy to eat. (Interview, La Pomme de Terre)

The range of senses is implicated in this cook's sense of his culinary triumph.[7] Lest one believe that this sensory concern applies only to those finer restaurants (where some might claim the cooks really are artists), it applies to the steakhouse as well. The chef at the steakhouse responded to my question about what a piece of baked salmon should be: "It should be just very lightly, you should see a tinge of brown on the outside, but it shouldn't be overcooked. It should be just done. Nice and moist" (interview, Stan's). Again, a range of sensory modalities affects the evaluation of food, even where one might assume that such interest is limited.

Evaluation need not only involve the production of sensory appealing products, but may also adhere in the sense of doing—an experience that we might liken to that of "flow" (Csikszentmihalyi 1975). Here the doing is the end. Some cooks speak of themselves in terms of their actions (Clark 1975, p. 33), making cooking into a performance art:

> It's very much like an actor preparing to go on stage and go into work and start in a quiet pace and figure what you're going to be doing; you get your equipment ready, sharpen knives, cut meats, trim your fish, and make your vegetables and make your sauces and get everything set up and it gets a little bit hotter; people start talking more and the waiters start coming in, and this is going on over here, and by the time everything starts coming together, it's like you're ready to go onstage. It's there. . . . Once the curtain goes up, everyone knows exactly what they're supposed to do. (Interview, La Pomme de Terre)

For some, the criteria for quality labor are primarily in the product (the sight, feel, taste, or smell), for others they are in the performance, but for each, the work has a style, a sense of form, an aesthetic.

Ideally this evaluation should be grounded within the occupation—although products are typically also judged by clients and on occasion performance is as well (as in the proliferating demonstration kitchens). The evaluation of production is not only a function of demands of customers and managers; cooks see themselves as having independent standards of judgment. Certainly these independent standards cannot radically vary from the demands of their customers, even for elite chefs (Kimball 1985, p. 18), and there are critical situations in which clients' demands take precedence, but cooks have their own judgments that are not reducible to organizational requirements. Management and customers do demand aesthetic production, and, so are in sympathy with the goals of the cooks, but the constraints that they demand and their standards of aesthetics may limit what cooks are able to produce. All parties want good work, but the meanings and the external considerations differ.

The salience of evaluations by cooks is evident when workers are creating "unique" items. This follows from the observation that the more special the product and the less routine the task, the less an organization can rely on formal rules, and the greater the autonomy that must be given to workers (e.g., Woodward 1965; Faulkner 1971; Coser, Kadushin, and Powell 1982). Individualized production technologies lead to choices, but can also simultaneously (as I shall describe later) lead to a recognition of the lack of autonomy from constraints. When cooks can create without pressure, they do, and are proud of the results. For example, one cook, preparing a wedding dinner, carved a pair of birds of paradise from apples and sent them to the bride and groom as *his* gift for their marriage (personal communication, Robert Pankin, 1987). Likewise, after making a chocolate cake, the pastry chef at La Pomme de Terre added four raspberries and drizzled chocolate sauce over them, commenting, "I'll put some fruit on here so it looks a little more abstract" (field notes, La Pomme de Terre). Her touch was not a result of management policy (although she was expected to make "beautiful" desserts); rather, the standards and techniques she used developed out of her sense of what it meant to be a competent pastry chef.

Although cooks have some measure of control over the sensory characteristics of the food they prepare, the doing of this aesthetic work is an everyday achievement; it is not merely grounded in theoretical choices. The production of "high quality" items, as defined by cooks, depends on a balance of culinary ideals (e.g., using natural ingredients) and production constraints. The ends direct production choices, as in two separate discussions of the color of a sauce:

> The head chef at the Owl's Nest pours a considerable amount of Gravy Bouquet in his Brown Sauce to make it "richer." He then adds white pepper and stirs the sauce. He tells me that: "Black pepper shows up and looks like mouse turds. Little black specks. So I use white pepper." White pepper is also added to the restaurant's mashed potatoes. (Field notes, Owl's Nest)

> The head day cook is preparing cheese sauce, using powdered cheese. He adds a capful of orange food color to the pot, saying that this makes the sauce look more like cheese, and, if you were actually to add cheese, "it gets too sandy." (Field notes, Owl's Nest)

These cooks are making decisions in practice. They believe, certainly correctly, that the visual appeal of the food, the first thing that both cooks and customers notice, affects the way the dish tastes—sensory realms are interconnected (e.g., Moir 1936; Pangborn 1960).[8]

Cooks can be admiring or critical toward what they prepare, based on their evaluation of the outcomes, both instrumentally (success in sales and customer appreciation) and in terms of their occupational standards. This evaluation implies a realm of objects that are considered lacking in these components that other objects have. No occupational world can long survive if participants judge everything equal to everything else.

For collective judgment, differentiation in the evaluation of produced objects is essential.[9] In cooking this judgment may involve any of the relevant senses. For example, one cook criticized a bunch of grapes as having "bad lines." An outsider might be confused how grapes can have bad lines, until it is learned that the ideal of a bunch of grapes is a pyramid and that other bunches meet this criterion better. Crepes can be described as "lopsided," implying agreement that crepes should be circular. A more detailed example is the condemnation of a particular dish that "doesn't work":

> Howie and Tim taste the beet fettucini that they had planned to serve with a tomato sauce—an orange-red sauce on top of a crimson pasta. Tim says to Howie: "There's something that didn't work. It looks like puke." Howie adds: "It tastes like Chef Boyardee. It tastes like Spaghetti O's. It tastes like snot rag." They decide not to add the sauce. (Field notes, La Pomme de Terre)

This judgment is predicated on their view of what constitutes proper food presentation—which colors go together and what the taste and texture of a properly made sauce should be. Such standards, while based within the occupation, must be echoed by at least some customers. Although the judgments of cooks are never far from their sense of the customers in their market niche, when being creative they use themselves as guides:

> You have the idea in your mind of how something should come out and you have to use your hands and eyes and taste and nose. You have to make it come out the way . . . you want it. (Interview, Stan's)

> The thing is to just have the guts to go in and do it. Just try it. Not worry about is this thing going to work or not. . . . It's color, flavor, texture, smell. It's all those things put together and somehow I have a sense of organizing these things and putting them together. (Interview, La Pomme de Terre)

Cooks do not discuss these judgments in terms of their customers, but in terms of what they believe works, even if they lack a formal theory of what they are doing (Sclafani 1979). There is a set of aesthetic conventions that are based on occupational standards (Becker 1982), separable from organizational demands, but which must be fitted into the constraints imposed (or believed to be imposed) by external sources and by the structure of the occupation itself. Occupations struggle to gain control over criteria for judgment from regulators, employers, and clients. Although the recognition of this struggle has been a staple of the analysis of "professions" and other occupations, it applies equally to the control of the aesthetic choices in work.

Constraints and negotiations

Given claims of independence within an occupation, on the one hand, and structural limits, on the other, how do workers produce objects that they consider satisfying and of high quality? What are the dimensions that channel how workers do good work? In order to examine this question, I describe three forces external to occupational autonomy that constrain production choices and show how workers cope with these constraints. In cooking, as elsewhere, organizational constraints not only determine the products but ultimately shape the values of workers. On some occasions, cooks chafe under the restrictions of the workplace, but often these restrictions are taken for granted and treated as merely a reality of the occupation.

Cooking, like all occupations, as Anselm Strauss (1978) emphasizes, is grounded in negotiations and compromises. Cooks strive to control the means and circumstances of production, both to make their own day passably pleasant and to permit them to be satisfied with what they produce.[10] The proximal source of constraints is a restaurant management that depends on the loyalty of its customers, and this pressure is filtered through the head chef who is given an annual or monthly budget with which to work. The irony is that for the same reason management also supports and encourages aesthetic presentations, as long as this good work remains profitable. To satisfy management the chef must manipulate the staff to make a profit and to produce good food. At three of the restaurants studied, the chef received a bonus if he operated within the budget. This control is furthered through the internalized acceptance of these economic and temporal constraints by most cooks.

The ultimate dilemma for cooks is the recognition that often they must serve "bad food"—food that they believe is not up to their own standards of quality, but they have no choice.[11] It is difficult to propose rules for when "poorly prepared" food will be recooked—the etcetera rule, which suggests that no complete set of rules can be formulated, is too prominent (Garfinkel 1967)—but the cost of the food, the time for cooking, the pressure in the kitchen, the status of the customer, the conscientiousness and mood of the cooks, what is wrong (and if it can be partially corrected without recooking), and the status of the restaurant all affect the decision. These decisions can be negotiated among the kitchen staff and with management on the spot, but all cooks must recognize that they must serve food that they know is not up to their standards. Cooks shrug when they send substandard food to unknowing customers and respond sarcastically when, at times, servers announce that they were complimented on these dishes.

One cook described her frustration with a rack of lamb: "I've racked some lamb . . . that was just an abortion. It was just awful; I rolled the pastry too thin and the lamb was overcooked and . . . it came out looking not like it was supposed to. That makes me feel bad, even though that's fine and you have to use it. You can't throw it away, but I feel really bad" (interview, La Pomme de Terre).

Cooks are dismayed when serving food of poor quality, and like so many workers, they deny that they really care by turning the offensive food into a sick joke, engraving role distance in their performances:

The watercress sauce, created for the salmon appetizer, has separated. Tim (the Head Chef) says sarcastically: "Oh, well, they all look like shit. We don't have to worry." Gerry, his co-worker, jokes: "The room's dark." (Field notes, La Pomme de Terre)

Such joking is legitimate in that cooks have other occupational rhetorics than that of artist to rely upon; for that moment they can constitute themselves as manual laborers, as alienated as any. In occupations, such as cooking, that can draw upon several occupational rhetorics,[12] workers can strategically employ these to preserve their self-integrity. They project themselves into the food that they produce, seeing inner qualities in the outcome. When the food does not meet their standards, they must use techniques for backing away from the equation of self and product. The strategic use of rhetoric is one way of coping with the personal tensions of presentation of self. Switching the available metaphors of their work can serve important ends in preserving role distance and in indicating their control (Fine 1982).

Having demonstrated that cooks are limited in their ability to produce dishes they consider of high quality, I turn to three forces that prevent their achieving their occupational ideals: customer taste (client demands), time (organizational efficiency), and the economics of the restaurant industry (the resource base of the occupation). These three factors cause cooks to compromise their own taste. Through the constraints of production the production of culture model fits into an analysis of aesthetic choices. To be considered problematic, production depends on a recognition of aesthetic options for constraints.

Client demands

The restaurant cook prepares food for an audience that does not belong to his or her occupation—an audience that may not have the same standards or even be aware of the existence of standards. Yet, both cooks and customers agree that restaurant food should be aesthetic, whether or not they agree on these expressive dimensions.

Because of the power of the market, autonomy is given up to the expectations of one's audience (Arian 1971). As a result of the loss of autonomy, workers may resent those they work for who do not have their standards of quality and competence—not just bosses, whose sin is cynicism, but also clients, who are seen as culpably ignorant.

Unlike such occupations as beauticians, plastic surgeons, and house-painters in which workers negotiate directly with those who ultimately judge them, cooks must rely on their typification of their audience, given their understanding of the restaurant's market niche.[13] Their evaluation is mediated through managers and servers. Those standing beyond the output boundary are not easily known (see Hirsch 1972; Dimaggio 1977). Dishes are cooked for typifications, not persons; yet, it is persons who have the options to complain. Customers can judge the dish, whereas cooks have difficulty judging the customer.

As a consequence, cooks have developed techniques for dealing with the vagaries of customer taste. At the steakhouse and the continental restaurant it was standard procedure to undercook beef slightly. This allowed for correction if the customer wanted the meat more thoroughly cooked. Steaks can never be cooked less. Still, these cooks became annoyed when customers insisted on having their steaks well done. One Friday night at Stan's, a large number of steaks were sent back, to the cooks' frustration:

> One waitress says to the head chef, referring to the customers: "Are those steaks burnt up enough?" The chef responds: "I hope so. I don't want them." Later another cook comments about the evening: "Bunch of assholes out there. They don't know what they want." He means that they don't want what he wishes to serve them. (Field notes, Stan's)

The problem is equally relevant at La Pomme de Terre where the canons of nouvelle cuisine emphasize not overcooking the food and spoiling its "natural" taste. These cooks, too, became annoyed when their "perfectly" cooked dishes (pink duck breast, translucent fish) are returned for additional work. Not only is the cook's ability questioned by the customer, but cooks believe that by accepting the motto, "The customer is always right," they are prostituting themselves,[14] even though they hope that they may eventually educate their customers (see Becker 1963, pp. 79–100). By pleasing the customer, they deny the validity of their standards. The legitimacy of their aesthetic standards is being invalidated by external demands.

Spices and condiments pose a similar problem. The head chef at the Owl's Nest notes: "You season things, but not completely seasoned. The first thing the customer does is see the salt and sprinkle it on, pepper and et cetera. Takes a bite and puts it down and says this has too much salt on it, and take it back. He was the one who put the salt on it; we didn't. So we underseason things. You have to think for the customer. . . . You have to think of everybody's taste" (interview, Owl's Nest). Even if cooks feel that some foods are unappetizing, they must serve them to customers who enjoy them. Further, even though they personally feel that some foods taste "bad" (e.g., fried liver, spinach), they must learn how to cook them in such a way that the customer who likes them will know that they are cooked correctly, that they represent the best professional practice. They must role-play the standards of their clients. This concern for customer taste (and its limits on cooks) is evident at La Pomme de Terre in the selection of fish specials:

I ask Tim how they select the two fish specials each night. Tim tells me: "We try to have variety. If we have an unusual one, like with peach, we'll have a conventional one, like the monkfish." (Field notes, La Pomme de Terre)

Customer taste is always taken into account, often explicitly, by cooks. This differentiates them from the higher reaches of the fine arts where, rhetorically at least, obeisance to client demands is considered subversive to an artist's occupational standing.

Organizational efficiency

Organizations are expected to produce a certain number of products or services in a set time period (Lauer 1981). As a result, temporal demands constrain production decisions in restaurant kitchens (Fine 1990). Customers will wait only so long for any dish to be prepared, and cooks have limited time in which they can prepare for dinner, given the size of the staff, affecting what can be served. These temporal constraints suggest why, discomfiting as it may be, when food falls on a dirty counter or floor after being cooked, cooks will wipe or rinse it, and then serve it, with the customer none the wiser. The illusion of quality demands hidden affronts. Since cooking is a backstage occupation, innumerable depredations to the foodstuffs are possible (e.g., Orwell 1933, pp. 80–81). A steak that takes 30 minutes to cook must be served because of customers' temporal expectations; customers would never wait for a "second try." Likewise, if a fillet of fish breaks while being removed from the pan to the plate, the cook will rearrange it as nicely as possible, but still serve it. The production features of the kitchen and, ironically, the demands of the client, permit no alternative.

Time also affects specific tasks in the kitchen, which, although they would make the food more appealing, cannot be tried because of time constraints. One cook explained that he wishes to do a "French cut" on a rack of lamb, but adds "I'd never have the time to do it" (interview, Blakemore Hotel). Likewise, cooks do not have the time to improve poor quality produce:

Martha (the day cook) says to Doug (the head chef): "The radishes are bad, but I don't have time to clean them up. . . . These look awful." They are dirty, discolored, and misshapen. Doug sorts through them, and throws out a few of the worst ones, and they serve the others. (Field notes, Stan's)

The problem of timing is particularly acute at Stan's Steakhouse, which, of the four, serves the largest number of customers. Often plates are not wiped off if sauce spills. As one cook joked on a busy evening: "I'm going for numbers, not for quality." Although this is not entirely true, it is truer than it might be under ideal circumstances. *Quality* production is a luxury; production is a necessity.

Time constraints apply not only to particular dishes, but to the creation of more elaborate food presentations. As one cook remarked: "To be creative you need time. You can't always have a deadline behind you. Because when you do, you're in a rush. And then when you're in a rush you tend to fail with the creativity. 'I need this by such and such a time,' and then you start getting out the same old thing" (interview, Blakemore Hotel). The head chef at La Pomme de Terre learned the day before that he must prepare a large press party for his employer. The chef confides to me that despite an impressive menu (sole turban, smoked goose breast with port wine and fruit, goose liver mousse, and duck galantine): "It's not going to be as good as I'd like. I only learned about it today. I'd like to make a grandiose first impression. . . . It's a matter of pride. The artist's pride is at stake" (field notes, La Pomme de Terre).

Ideas for a large display with fresh lobsters and a lobster mousse had to be shelved for lack of time. Although the owner felt that the party was a great success, the head chef was disappointed because it did not measure up to the quality of which he felt they were capable. While the organization was technically efficient—it did produce *something*—it was not sufficiently aesthetically productive, given the aesthetic standards of the chef.

Resource base

The final constraint is the cost of materials. Cooks must remind themselves that ultimately they are part of corporate capitalism—what Blau (1984, p. 10), studying architects, terms "professional practice." Indeed, in few other market segments does a truly free market operate as clearly as in the restaurant industry.

Price and quality combine together to determine restaurant success, as judged by external publics. Restaurants are known directly by clients who learn about them through advertising, experience, word of mouth, the publicity of managers, and institutionalized gatekeepers, such as critics and journalists. On some fundamental level, price and quality conflict, and the manager and head chef must decide to which market niche to appeal, given their perception of the organizational ecology. The head chef at the Owl's Nest recognized these economic trade-offs: "We always have variables. The compromise in your mind is using the best you can use, and still putting it into an affordable level for the average customer" (interview, Owl's Nest). As decisions are locally situated, this trade-off involves specific decisions about particular products, rather than an absolute rule of thumb:

> In theory the head chef of the Owl's Nest believes in using the best that is available. He explains: "The customer may not be able to tell in the finished product. The finished product might taste the same, but it should be made that way." However, when I ask later why he adds cheap American cooking wine to sauces, rather than expensive French wine, he claims: "People can't tell the difference." (Field notes, Owl's Nest)

Of course, the question is best for what? Imported truffles, beluga caviar, and Chateau Margaux add enormously to the cost, but only slightly to the taste. For this chef the possibility of adding these other expensive ingredients is not even a part of his consideration, until a sociologist brings them up. The economic reality of food preparation affects his aesthetic vision.

According to the staff at La Pomme de Terre, what distinguishes them from elite American restaurants is not the quality of the preparations, but "the touches"—those extra garnishes that restaurants can afford to add if they have a large staff and a loyal clientele. They compare their restaurant to others of which they are aware, and find themselves wanting:

> The owner confides to me that one of the Twin Cities restaurant critics said that La Pomme de Terre was the best restaurant in the Twin Cities, but not as good as Le Perroquet (Chicago) or Lutece (New York). He explains: "I asked him why. He said, 'The touches.' . . . They have more people in the kitchen. The difference is volume. They can count on being sold-out every night of the week. We can't." (Field notes, La Pomme de Terre)

Timing, customer taste, and resources merge to prevent this restaurant from reaching its potential, as filtered through the owner's estimation of the Twin Cities restaurant market. A year later, this man opened a restaurant that was more expensive and formal than La Pomme de Terre, and included "the touches." It failed; the market was not there. Cultural products have different price elasticity, even within particular niches. Some food prices are simply considered "obscene." There is an obdurate reality that prevents unconstrained aesthetic activity.

As a consequence, cost must be considered by decision makers. The staff at La Pomme de Terre experimented with different blends of coffee to find a mix that had the richness of expensive coffee with as much inexpensive coffee as possible. Likewise, the pastry chef commented about a raspberry-lemon gateau: "It's called, 'Let's be creative using the leftovers'" (field notes, La Pomme de Terre).

The skill in running a profitable organization is to provide goods or services that clients desire and that appear to be worth more than they cost to provide. Some foods seem expensive, but are not. When the head chef at La Pomme de Terre created Saffron Pasta with Lobster Sauce, he noted that the food cost "is not all that high." Likewise, the head chef at the Blakemore Hotel explains that salami horns filled with cream cheese look elegant, but are inexpensive.

An ability to compromise on quality when one's judgments conflict with the economics of the organization is crucial for advancement. The head chef at La Pomme de Terre had planned to promote his head day cook to sous (assistant) chef, but decided against it:

> Because he's such a renegade. I can't rely on him to do what I want him to do. . . . As an example, last week he's been doing that veal special that he came up with and it's a real beautiful dish. He takes the veal roulade and he puts prosciutto ham and goat's cheese with herbs and folds it over and sautés it, and serves it with tomato sauce. It's a good dish. He had a couple in there that were getting a little bit dark. The veal starts to get a sort of grey when it gets old, but they were fine; they were just starting to turn grey. I looked at them, and I said they're fine . . . and he was putting up a couple of veal specials, and I went in the walk-in and those suckers were sitting there . . . I called him in, and said, "What is that, for your mother or what? Come on and get moving. This is a restaurant." He's got such a paranoid pride over being criticized for something that he just took it upon himself to do it. . . . He doesn't have the concept that we're in business. He just thinks it's one big happy deal. (Interview, La Pomme de Terre)

This cook placed his standards of quality (standards with which in theory his head chef would agree) above the production needs of the organization, and, being unwilling to negotiate, lost his opportunity for promotion.[15] Cooks must keep one eye on the stove and the other on the marketplace, balancing their sensibilities with what the hospitality industry will permit. While chefs and cooks negotiate with each other, and chefs negotiate with managers as to the boundaries of their decision making and their commitment to quantity and quality (e.g., the number of scallops to serve or the time at which food begins to be "off"), an economic imperative channels the ability to produce.

The segmentation of aesthetic work

Although each occupation reveals concern with the expressive quality of production, comparative analysis would demonstrate that this concern is variable, not absolute; it certainly is expressed in different forms that may be more or less central to the doing of work. I have argued above that some outcomes and performances are seen by workers as having more value than others. Further, a determination of what constitutes quality is not absolute within an occupation or art world. There is no single aesthetic sense or unified set of conventions. Painters do not paint alike, and they do not believe that they should. Even the task influences one's orientation to work and the role that aesthetic or sensory concerns should have in production. Every occupation is socially segmented (Bucher 1962), and it is the effect of this segmentation that I wish to explore. Cooking is segmented on several dimensions; three of the most prominent are the restaurant's status, the cook's career stage, and the work task—reflecting differences among organizations, actors, and events.

[…]

The concern with the sensory qualities of products is a variable characteristic of occupations. While aesthetics is always present, its form and prominence differs. The status and market niche of an organization, the stage of one's career, and the particular task that must be completed, each influences how workers address their aesthetic concerns. These choices cannot be reduced to organizational demands, but they are channeled and specified by organizational and occupational characteristics.

[…]

The culture of production

Management and labor are in firm agreement that work quality is crucial. Aesthetic production should be consistent with organizational goals, not subversive of them. Yet, the intersection of the expression of quality may produce friction. Workers wish that they had more time (implying they need more co-workers) and more resources, so they can produce in an unhurried fashion. Management is likely to emphasize greater efficiency. Good work is profitable to a point, and this point is connected to market niche and price elasticity. Management has the direct problem of profitability, whereas for workers, profitability is only an indirect concern. As a result, value consensus may devolve into conflict or frustration in actual practice.

To the extent that workers have and can maintain a craft orientation, they can extend their zone of discretion in production decisions. To the extent that they are connected into a bureaucratic organization, management makes the choices, solidified into rules and procedures, that workers carry out. A strain exists between the craft organization of work, which vests authority with the members of the occupation, and the bureaucratic organization of work, where decisions are a result of authority hierarchies and formal procedures. Occupations in which each object is uniquely prepared reinforce the craft orientation; jobs that emphasize consistency and efficiency tend to be found in bureaucratic organizations (Stinchcombe 1959). Even in the latter arenas, management may tolerate, even encourage, some worker discretion if, although it does not maximize profits, it reduces labor discontent and allows for a predictable flow of production (Burawoy 1979). The role of discretion is indicated by the willingness of management to permit cooks to take extended breaks, shift positions, and choose which dishes to recook. The effects of this light hand are seen in cooks' willingness to work overtime (or to come in early), fill in for absent others, and make special dishes for important customers—each beyond the limits of formal job requirements. Furthermore, when worker aesthetics are congruent with that of management, some flexibility on material and labor costs may be tolerated, and passed on to the customer as the inevitable expense of quality.

Producers, consumers, and managers all value good work within imperatives of monetary or psychic costs. When the system is working, each is willing to accede at critical points. The challenge for management, especially evident at La Pomme de Terre, the most explicitly artistic of the sites, is to have workers accept management's vision of material constraints as a given, and to work within those constraints. Since there is a trade-off in quality and cost, mediated by customer evaluation, the choices are not objective. Organizational success in expressive production involves a moving dynamic: to be good enough *and* cheap enough that one's targeted customers will return and recruit others.

This analysis suggests the importance of transcending the commonplace that art is like all work, but it also shows where, when, and how aesthetic autonomy and social control interpenetrate and how they are negotiated. Under which circumstances do workers have concerns about the sensory quality of their products and services and when are they permitted control over this quality? The answer is shaped by the situated reality of workplace negotiation and by the reality and the typification of the market.

The sociological treatment of the expressive side of production remains largely unmapped. A single case can only provide outlines for others to fill. Specifically the causes of particular aesthetic choices have been ignored. How do workers derive an understanding of what is right and valued? What dimensions—instrumental and expressive—determine quality of production? How is cultural capital generated in work? Under what circumstances is elegant simplicity valued? When is self-conscious creation of the beautiful crucial? Issues of the aesthetics of performance and the aesthetics of products need to be differentiated. Finally, comparative research on numerous occupations avoids a haziness of the description of aesthetic choices.

The emphasis on and expression of aesthetic choices depends on the work environment, the standing of the worker, and the particular work task. Workers' orientations to the expressive side of production are grounded in the core sociological concepts of contention, autonomy, and community; management's limitations are equally sociological, based on demands for control and efficiency deriving from instrumental requirements. Work is a minuet between (expressive) form and (instrumental) function. In this dance, as in others, he who pays the piper ultimately calls the tune.

Notes

1. I wish to thank Therese Baker, Howard S. Becker, Harold Bershady, Jacqueline Boles, Charles Bosk, Priscilla Clark, Terry Clark, George Dickie, William Finlay, Wendy Griswold, Larry Gross, Hans Haferkamp, Sherryl Kleinman, Michal McCall, Charles Stevens, Gerald Suttles, Doris Taub, Richard Taub, and, especially, Robert Faulkner for comments and critiques on earlier versions of this material. Correspondence should be addressed to Gary Alan Fine, Department of Sociology, University of Georgia, Athens, Georgia 30602.

2. The study of aesthetics has been filled with conflicting assumptions and opinions. Philosophers rarely choose to examine situations in which aesthetic decisions are made in the messy reality of everyday life and suggest that aesthetic judgments transcend the production of an aesthetic object and its socially situated character (e.g., Diffey 1984; Hincks 1984). These explanations, focusing on qualities of mind (Aldrich 1966; Stolnitz 1960) or the qualities of an object (Beardsley 1958) that produce the recognition that one has had an aesthetic experience (Wolff 1983; Shepard 1987), downplay the sociological interest in the interactional, relational, or institutional features of aesthetic evaluation (see Dickie 1974; Danto 1981).

3. In this article I bracket the origin of aesthetic choices, wishing to see how such choices are constrained and utilized. My concern is not to trace the dynamics by which particular judgments come to be seen as aesthetic

(see Fine 1989), but only those choices that have been accepted by a group of workers. Nor am I concerned with the qualities of the object involved. Griswold (1986) argues that the aesthetic involves both elegance (simplicity) and beauty (amplitude) to produce a response. While I use Griswold's distinction to focus on the characteristics of objects, my definition emphasizes the relationship between actors and objects.

4. Sociologists of aesthetics interested in comparative research must confront two basic presuppositions: (1) that all occupations have aesthetic components, that is, that sensory issues are a part of all work, and (2) that occupations vary on the self-consciousness and centrality of these aesthetic issues to the work. Because this research is grounded on a single occupational case study, I can do no more than suggest the plausibility of these claims.

5. This constituted approximately 75–100 hours per restaurant.

6. Although all cooks have aesthetic orientations, most do not fit in that category of workers that we describe as artists. For an occupation to be an art world, it requires (1) that a group of persons be working toward a common end. The group should be aware of each other and should have social and professional contacts; (2) that the group have an artistic theory to guide them and to demonstrate their shared commitment. A theory of art is essential (see Danto 1964, p. 581); and (3) that there be a set of recognized institutional gatekeepers and gatekeeping organizations that choose candidates for ascension into the canons of art—what Dickie (1974) refers to as the "institution of art." Cooks in the Twin Cities lack tight networks, a widely held aesthetic theory, and acceptance by artistic gatekeepers. While one might discover a culinary art world in small sectors of the hospitality industry in New York, New Orleans, or San Francisco, throughout most of the rest of the country, cooks just cook.

7. "Occupational triumphs" consist of occasions in which workers feel that they have operated to the limits of their jobs—they are "pushing the envelope." Working within the rules, they have transcended them, demonstrating in their own minds at least that they are not mere workers, but true artists, true professionals, or the like. They have produced not just an object but a memory that they can narrate to convince others of their virtues, even given constraints and normal operating procedures.

8. For a more extensive analysis of aesthetic ideologies in food preparation see Fine (1985). In practice, cooks negotiate which sensory realm is most significant for particular dishes, but the visual appeal of a dish is typically given greatest weight. This may be because the visual realm is the first encountered or because it is in this sensory domain that schoolchildren are more extensively trained—art classes typically lack stoves or perfume atomizers.

9. My argument is that Kant's idea of free judgments of taste is unlikely to be made in most practical aesthetic worlds; rather, aesthetic judgments have a relational character. We judge things in relationship or in comparison with other objects. At some level we are deciding, not whether something is good, but whether it is good of its kind (Kant 1952; Shepard 1987).

10. Some workers at the hotel kitchen would come in an hour early (without overtime) in order to set themselves up, feeling that the volunteered time would be worthwhile in improving the quality of their production and permitting them a less hassled day.

11. Comparative data indicate that this is not unique to this scene, as Walker and Guest (1952, p. 60) describe similar attitudes of autoworkers.

12. I have spoken of cooks as drawing from the rhetorics of business, art, manual labor, and professionalism to define their work and protect their selves (Fine 1982). Other rhetorics such as craft or sales might affect this occupation on certain occasions.

13. Market niches are in part a function of conscious decisions by managers and chefs to capture audiences. In this they create an establishment that will provide an experience that appeals to a potential pool of clients (e.g., Finkelstein 1989; Shelton 1990). In contrast, niches are occasionally carved by customers who discover establishments; then managers must ensure that they continue to meet the desires of these clients.

14. This is a problem that is faced by portrait painters who give up their artistic autonomy to the client. The client feels that he or she has the right to determine his or her personal likeness (see Stewart 1988).

15. This is a story for those with a sentimental attachment to a happy ending: within a few years this young man had become head chef at an outstanding, creative restaurant in the Twin Cities. By then he had learned to control his employer's costs.

References

Aldrich, Virgil. 1966. *Philosophy of Art.* Englewood Cliffs, N.J.: Prentice-Hall.

Arian, Edward. 1971. *Bach, Beethoven, and Bureaucracy.* University: University of Alabama Press.

Beardsley, M. C. 1958. *Aesthetics: Problems in the Philosophy of Criticism.* New York: Harcourt Brace.

Becker, Howard S. 1963. *Outsiders.* New York: Free Press.

—. 1974. "Art as Collective Action." *American Sociological Review* 39:767–76.

—. 1982. *Art Worlds.* Berkeley: University of California Press.

Blau, Judith. 1984. *Architects and Firms.* Cambridge, Mass.: MIT Press.

Bucher, Rue. 1962. "Pathology: A Study of Social Movements within a Profession." *Social Problems* 10:40–51.

Burawoy, Michael. 1979. *Manufacturing Consent.* Chicago: University of Chicago Press.

Clark, Priscilla. 1975. "Thoughts for Food I: French Cuisine and French Culture." *French Review* 49:32–41.

Coser, Lewis, Charles Kadushin, and Walter Powell. 1982. *Books.* New York: Basic.

Csikszentmihalyi, Mihalyi. 1975. *Beyond Boredom and Anxiety.* San Francisco: Jossey-Bass.

Danto, Arthur. 1964. "The Artworld." *Journal of Philosophy* 61:571–84.

—. 1981. *The Transfiguration of the Commonplace.* Cambridge, Mass.: Harvard University Press.

Dickie, George. 1974. *Art and the Aesthetic.* Ithaca, N.Y.: Cornell University Press.

Diffey, T. J. 1984. "The Sociological Challenge to Aesthetics." *British Journal of Aesthetics* 24:168–71.

Dimaggio, Paul. 1977. "Market Structure, the Creative Process, and Popular Culture." *Journal of Popular Culture* 11:436–52.

Faulkner, Robert. 1971. *Hollywood Studio Musicians.* Chicago: Aldine.

Fine, Gary Alan. 1979. "Small Groups and Cultural Creation: The Idioculture of Little League Baseball Teams." *American Sociological Review* 44:733–45.

—. 1982. "Multiple Socialization: The Rhetorics of Professional Cooking." Paper presented to the American Educational Research Association, New York.

—. 1985. "Occupational Aesthetics: How Trade School Students Learn to Cook." *Urban Life* 14:3–32.

—. 1987. "Working Cooks: The Dynamics of Professional Kitchens." Pp. 141–58 in *Current Research on Occupations and Professions,* edited by Helena Z. Lopata. Greenwich, Conn: JAI.

—. 1989. "Wittgenstein in the Kitchen: The Creation of Meanings of Talk." Paper presented to the Midwest Sociological Society, St. Louis.

—. 1990. "Organizational Time: The Temporal Experience of Restaurant Kitchens." *Social Forces* 69:95–114.

Finkelstein, Joanne. 1989. *Dining Out: A Sociology of Manners.* New York: New York University Press.

Garfinkel, Harold. 1967. *Studies in Ethnomethodology.* Englewood Cliffs, N.J.: Prentice-Hall.

Griswold, Wendy. 1986. *Renaissance Revivals.* Chicago: University of Chicago Press.

Gross, Edward. 1958. *Work and Society.* New York: Crowell.

Hall, Richard H. 1975. *Occupations and the Social Structure,* 2d ed. Englewood Cliffs, N.J.: Prentice-Hall.

Hincks, Tony. 1984. "Aesthetics and the Sociology of Art: A Critical Commentary on the Writings of Janet Wolff." *British Journal of Aesthetics* 24:341–54.

Hirsch, Paul M. 1972. "Processing Fads and Fashions: An Organization-Set Analysis of Cultural Industry Systems." *American Journal of Sociology* 77:639–59.

Kant, Immanuel. 1952. *Critique of Aesthetic Judgment.* Oxford: Oxford University Press.

Kimball, Christopher. 1985. "The *Cook's* Interview: Jeremiah Tower." *The Cook's Magazine* (Jan./Feb.):18–19.

Kleinman, Sherryl. 1984. *Equals before God.* Chicago: University of Chicago Press.

Lauer, Robert H. 1981. *Temporal Man.* New York: Praeger.

Moir, H. C. 1936. "Some Observations on the Appreciation of Flavour in Foodstuffs." *Chemistry and Industry* 55:145–48.

Orwell, George. 1933. *Down and Out in Paris and London.* New York: Harcourt Brace.

Pangborn, R. M. 1960. "Taste Interrelationships." *Food Research* 25:245–56.

Peterson, Richard A. 1979. "Revitalizing the Culture Concept." *Annual Review of Sociology* 5:137–66.

Sclafani, Richard J. 1979. "Artworks, Art Theory, and the Artworld." *Theoria* 39:18–34.

Shepard, Anne. 1987. *Aesthetics.* Oxford: Oxford University Press.

Shelton, Allen. 1990. "A Theater for Eating, Looking, and Thinking: The Restaurant as Symbolic Space." *Sociological Spectrum* 10:507–26.

Stewart, Doug. 1988. "For a Portraitist, Making Faces Is a Hard Day's Fight." *Smithsonian* (July): 43–50.

Stolnitz, Jerome. 1960. *Aesthetics and Philosophy of Art Criticism*. Boston: Houghton Mifflin.

Stinchcombe, Arthur. 1959. "Bureaucratic and Craft Administration of Production: A Comparative Study." *Administrative Science Quarterly* 4:168–87.

Strauss, Anselm. 1978. *Negotiations*. San Francisco: Jossey-Bass.

Walker, Charles R., and Robert H. Guest. 1952. *The Man on the Assembly Line*. Cambridge, Mass.: Harvard University Press.

Whyte, William Foote. 1948. *Human Relations in the Restaurant Industry*. New York: McGraw Hill.

Wolff, Janet. 1983. *Aesthetics and the Sociology of Art*. Boston: Allen & Unwin.

Woodward, Joan. 1965. *Industrial Organization: Theory and Practice*. London: Oxford University Press.

CHAPTER 14

GREEN BEAN CASSEROLE AND MIDWESTERN IDENTITY: A REGIONAL FOODWAYS AESTHETIC AND ETHOS

Lucy M. Long

Introduction

Mass-produced, factory-processed, commercial foods have been a significant part of American food culture since industrialization allowed their development in the 1800s.[1] Many of these foods have been incorporated into family, community, and national traditions: for example, ramen noodles, Rice Krispies treats, gelatin salads, popcorn and Cracker Jacks, candy canes at Christmas and marshmallow bunnies at Easter.[2] Adoption of such foods is frequently interpreted as resulting from skillful marketing, capitalist hegemony, class envy, ignorance, or poor taste.[3] Regardless of the motivations behind their initial acceptance, however, such foods can become surprisingly meaningful carriers of identity and memory. An exploration of these food traditions raises questions about the nature of food and identity: Why do we eat what we eat?[4] How do some foods take on special meanings for particular cultures, individuals, or meals? Furthermore, some of these commercial foods also seem to represent regional identities and appear to reflect an attachment to place, for example, Spam in Hawaii, Cincinnati chili, California or Chicago pizza, and hot dogs and hamburgers throughout the nation. In some cases, the food originated in a place and spread nationally from there; in others, the food was commercially distributed but became localized, taking on local ingredients, forms, uses, or meanings.[5] What does it then say about a region to have such foods as a significant part of its identity?

Much contemporary exploration of regional foods focuses on the presence of *terroir*—the French concept of the "taste of the soil," also translated as "taste of place"—embodied through food. For example, the crops grown, the animals raised in a particular locale have a distinctive flavor and quality due to the physical characteristics of that place—the type of soil, the quantity of rainfall, the types of flora and fauna, and so on. The food, then, literally represents place and is intrinsically attached to place as an objective reality. Commercial mass-produced and mass-distributed foods defy such geographic boundaries and blur the distinctions between regions. Do regions that embrace those foods call into question their own attachment to place?

Green bean casserole is an example of such a food. Officially a baked mixture of green beans, cream of mushroom soup, and canned fried onions or some substitute that adds "crunch" to the dish,[6] it was invented in 1955 by the Campbell Soup Company. Since then it has been marketed nationally with the recipe printed on the labels of its canned ingredients; the recipe has been reproduced in women's magazines and, today, on the Internet. The dish is the epitome of a mass-produced, processed, commercial food, yet it seems to have become a common, even expected, part of family meals, community potlucks, and holiday dinners throughout the nation.

Lucy Long, 'Green Bean Casserole and Midwestern Identity: A Regional Foodways Aesthetic and Ethos', *Midwestern Folklore* 33 (1) (2007), 29–44.

Reprinted with permission from the author and *Midwestern Folklore*.

The dish seems to hold a special place in foodways of the Midwest. Judging from informal ethnographic research I have conducted in northwest Ohio, an area representative of the larger region, green bean casserole is ubiquitous there, showing up in public and private, in everyday as well as celebratory meals, crossing ethnic, religious, and socioeconomic differences. Every November local supermarkets display cans of fried onions, mushroom soup, and green beans in a sort of holiday assemblage,[7] foreshadowing the Thanksgiving meal and suggesting that this dish is part of the "proper" national meal. The typical regional attitude is expressed in the tagline with which one middle-aged woman ended her response to a query about her Thanksgiving dinner menu: "And, of course, green bean casserole!" This area of the Midwest seems to have embraced the dish wholeheartedly and enthusiastically. Considering the strong, ongoing agricultural heritage of the area and its emphasis on family values, why is this so? And how does a recipe that involves little more culinary skill than opening cans purchased from any food retailer make sense in the context of the down-home, Mom-and-apple-pie image of midwestern cooking?

As anyone who has grown up in the Midwest knows, the common answer to these questions in the midwestern context would be a humorous and self-deprecating comment on the lack of taste and culinary refinement stereotypical of the region. However, such foods have a logic specific to the culture using them, and they reflect an aesthetic and ethos essential to that culture's foodways. "Foodways aesthetic" refers to the system for evaluating the quality, the pleasingness (or tastiness) of a food and the activities surrounding the preparation and consumption of that food, while "foodways ethos" refers to the moral and social values attached to food and eating.[8] The term "foodways" rather than "food" emphasizes that food is more than just "stuff we eat." Borrowing from folklorist Don Yoder's definition of foodways as "the total cookery complex, including attitudes, taboos, and meal systems—the whole range of cookery and food habits in a society . . ." (Yoder 1972:325), I use the concept to refer to the network of activities, habits, and conceptualizations surrounding food and eating (Long 1999:33). As a concept, foodways emphasizes the systemic nature of food activities as well as the ways in which memories and meanings get attached to food, oftentimes through seemingly trivial activities.[9] "Foodways" also implies that identity is expressed through food; that the choices we make concerning food activities are performances negotiating our pasts with our present identities and contexts. Although some eating occasions and foods are intentional articulations of identity, many are not. We choose foods out of hunger, curiosity, social etiquette, health concerns, and for many other reasons. Identity seeps through anyway.[10] Green bean casserole in the Midwest seems to be in many contexts an unintentional performance of identity, but at other times a very purposeful expression of local identity. If we extend Pierre Bourdieu's observation that "the style of a meal people offer is a good indication of the image they wish to give or avoid giving to others" (quoted in Bentley 2002:179) to particular foods, then what exactly is the image intended by serving and eating green bean casserole? And since the Midwest tends to be a region defined by a historical connection to the land, does that identity have any connection to region or place?

Green bean casserole in northwest Ohio

I first realized that green bean casserole holds a special place in midwestern foodways when I noticed that it frequently showed up in menus of family dinners, particularly Thanksgiving meals, that I collected from my students at a state university in northwestern Ohio, an area that seems to typify midwestern physical and cultural landscapes. Most of these students were middle-class to lower-middle-class, with a number coming from blue-collar backgrounds and the first in their families to enter college. Farming was also in the heritage and experiences of many of them.[11] Coming from a different regional heritage and from a family that emphasized homegrown and homemade foods, I was struck that something so commercial, so easy to make, and so everyday was a significant part of holiday meals and family traditions. Initially I wondered if it represented a generation that is characterized by a family life disrupted by extracurricular activities and career obligations, with food being eaten on the go and valued for efficiency, low price, homogeneity, and quantity over quality.

I then began informally surveying people from the local community, asking them whether or not green bean casserole was a part of their own family traditions, and asking their own response to the dish.[12] I found that it was a well-known favorite not only at many everyday family meals but also at potlucks and holiday meals, including Thanksgiving dinner. In many cases, it seemed to be the very characteristics that could be considered as diminishing its culinary and cultural value that were being praised in its favor: it was inexpensive and quick to make, it always turned out as expected, and it was easy to transport. It was a dependable dish, one that cooks could rely upon and that consumers almost always liked.

Personal reactions to the casserole varied. In many families it was the favorite dish, the one item that was never turned into leftovers. In some cases, it was a favorite of an individual family member. For example, during one interchange I had with local residents, a wife discovered that her husband liked green bean casserole. After listening to her describe her mother's recipe, he asked: "Why don't we have that? I like it. At church potlucks, it's always the first thing I get." She responded in surprise: "Really? I guess we'll have it at Thanksgiving then!"

Those who liked the dish pointed to its aesthetic qualities. They liked the saltiness of the canned soup and the crunchiness of the onions. Thick and fattening, it reminded them of home, "Mom's cooking," and comforting, familiar tastes.

Not everyone I interviewed appreciated green bean casserole, and reasons ranged from personal aesthetics and taste to health concerns, as seen in some of these representative responses:

We always have green beans—fresh green beans. But green bean casserole? My mother used to . . . it just doesn't seem healthy—all the salt in the canned stuff . . . [Fortyish woman, midwestern born and bred]

He's always hated that canned soup [he interjected, "glop"], so I never made it, but I remember it in my family. [Thirtyish woman, midwestern born and bred, who usually purchases organic foods]

Well, I never really liked green beans . . . [Forty-year-old man, a newcomer to northwest Ohio]

Green bean casserole? Yuck. It always looked gross, kind of congealed, with things sticking out of it, [Fifty-year-old man, midwestern born and bred]

Even if they did not eat the food themselves, these individuals recognized it as a part of their local culinary universe. Green bean casserole was considered a normal, standard component of both everyday and ritual meals. Many people were aware of its commercial origins, but that did not deter its integration into family foodways. In fact, the dish was often mentioned with affectionate irony because of its commercial character. Most individuals, however, had never thought about the dish and assumed it was just one of those foods that, as one person stated, "had always been there." They did not think of it as a tradition because they did not consciously and intentionally prepare and consume it as an expression of identity or heritage.

The midwest as region, northwest Ohio as subregion

Like every region, the Midwest is both a physical, objective space and a cultural mindset, an imagined community (Anderson 1983) of shared values, experiences, and expressive forms. Ranging from Ohio in the east westward and north to Minnesota and Wisconsin, it also includes Michigan, Indiana, Illinois, Iowa, and Missouri. It represents both the Hinterland, a backwater of social conservatism and pragmatism, and the Heartland, the physical, land center of America as well as the bastion of the nation's "family values" and pioneer spirit (Lee 2004:xvii–xxvi; Fertig 2003). Although there is wide diversity within the region, particularly in urban centers such as Cleveland, St. Louis, St. Paul, Minneapolis, and Chicago, there tend to be overarching cultural patterns that are recognizable to both insiders and outsiders. Several university towns—Ann Arbor, Michigan; Madison, Wisconsin; and Antioch and Oberlin in Ohio—stand out as oases of artistic creativity, social progressivism, and political liberalism—demonstrating by contrast a recognizable midwestern identity. Frequently, residents think of themselves as representing a mythical Middle America with straightforward, all-American cultural traditions. Ironically, this also translates into a perception of lacking a specific regional identity.

Analyses of the region's foodways affirm that representation of Middle America. Geographer Richard Pillsbury states that "the cuisine of the Midwest is mostly a product of the Industrial Revolution" and that "the region's consumption patterns clearly reflect the conservative character of the population" (1998:220, 221). Other scholars have described midwestern food as "plain and straightforward, hearty and wholesome, food that sticks to your ribs to get you through the day" (Long 2004:281; see also Prosterman 2005 and Shortridge 2003). The public image of midwestern food is meat and potatoes, home cooking, basic ingredients, and few spices or surprises. Other than a few ethnic dishes, it is not seen as having an actual cuisine, the perception being that people just cook and eat traditional, wholesome American food without thinking too much about it.

My research focused on the northwest corner of Ohio, solidly within the physical and cultural boundaries of the Midwest. Encompassing an area known as the Great Black Swamp, this subregion of the Midwest is on the eastern edge of the Great Plains, so is defined by a flat landscape, and what used to be swamps and oak forests before drainage systems were developed and the trees were cut for lumber in the mid-1800s. The earliest settlers tended to be Anglo-Americans and German immigrants looking for farmland. Nestled at the southern tip of Lake Erie, the largest city, Toledo, was anticipated in the mid-1800s to become one of the great interior ports and conduits for trade; highly urban and industrial, Toledo attracted immigrants to its factories, while the rest of the area remained agricultural. Bowling Green, where I teach, is a city of approximately thirty thousand (with another twenty thousand students); home to a state university, Bowling Green is surrounded by farmland and small towns. Since the mid-1990s, the farmland has been rapidly turning into housing developments, and the area between Bowling Green and Toledo is now full of bedroom communities for commuters.

Northwest Ohio's population today is a mix of urban and rural. It has wide variation in socioeconomic class and is largely European, with pockets of African American and Hispanic settlement. Although seemingly homogeneous, the subregion has wide diversity in that there are numerous European ancestries represented, from descendents of early Anglo-American colonists to nineteenth-century Germans and Irish to later immigrants from eastern Europe.

The culture tends to be a pragmatic and practical one, with a conservatism shaped by a trust in hands-on experience. Its people generally do not romanticize the past or nature. The past is to be learned from, and nature is there to be tamed and made useful—or at least, not dangerous—to humans. It also tends to be economically conservative, fully supportive of capitalism and commercialization. At the same time, it has always embraced technology, concentrating on developing machinery to improve work and living conditions.[13] Outside of Toledo, northwest Ohio is agricultural, but the agriculture is a highly industrialized and commercialized one. Along with large corporate farms producing corn and soybeans, the area is home to major processing plants and canning factories, including such well-established national companies as Heinz and Campbell Soup.

Within this cultural context, food is fuel and is often evaluated by its energy-giving qualities rather than by aesthetic ones related to refined tastes. Heavy on carbohydrates and starches, local foodways also reflect the German and British settlement heritage, as seen in dishes such as roast beef, potatoes, meat loaf, sausages, cream sauces, blends of sweet and sour flavors, and a heavy use of sugar. Even though most families raised garden vegetables, these tended to be preserved by canning, so that using canned goods, albeit commercially processed ones, is a part of traditional preparation methods. Tastes have been trained to accommodate the preserved and processed foods. This is a culture, then, that accepts commercial and processed foods as the normal and "right" way for food to be. Consistent with this ethos, the recipe for green bean casserole—open cans, mix, bake—can be read as a celebration of technology.

Green bean casserole: The corporate identity

The green bean casserole's commercial identity is well established and its origination in the food industry is in no way hidden. Campbell Soup's official histories and promotional materials proudly claim it as its own invention, stating that the green bean casserole is both one of the company's "top ranked" and "most recommended" recipes.

The official recipe, as given on the company's Web site, begins as follows:

Green Bean Casserole

From: Campbell's Kitchen
Prep Time: 10 minutes
Bake Time: 30 minutes
Serves: 6

Ingredients:
1 can (10 3/4 oz.) Campbell's® Condensed Cream of Mushroom Soup OR Campbell's® Condensed
    98% Fat Free Cream of Mushroom Soup
1/2 cup milk
1 tsp. soy sauce
dash ground black pepper
4 cups cooked cut green beans
1 1/3 cups French's® French Fried Onions

(Campbell Soup Company 2005a)

Campbell's claims of the popularity of the casserole are not hyperbole, as is proven by the inclusion of the recipe in most popular American cookbooks and by references to it in the mass media. It is marketed nationally for Thanksgiving meals and seems to have become an accepted part of the holiday within mass-mediated culture. For example, in a *Cincinnati Post* column in 2001, a food reviewer gave these suggestions for a successful Thanksgiving: "First, there's Green Bean Bake, which is made of canned cream-of-mushroom soup and canned French-fried onions. Countless families count on this particular dish being among the dishes of stuffing, cranberries, mashed potatoes and turkey gravy." She presented the recipe, "in case it's not embedded in your brain," and contrasted the recipe from Durkee with that of Campbell's Soup, the differences being minor: the amount of milk, pepper (one-eighth teaspoon as opposed to a "dash"), and the inclusion of soy sauce by Campbell's. Another Web site lists a recipe for green bean casserole, asking, "What would the fall season be without the traditional American favorite?" (Chiff Directory 2007). The site also includes links to "Thanksgiving Recipes" and "Delicious Casserole Recipes for your Holiday Season." Other Web sites and published recipes describe the casserole as "classic," "traditional," "a Thanksgiving standard." These references in popular culture both assume and affirm the place of green bean casserole in the public consciousness as a traditional dish and as a traditional component of Thanksgiving dinner.[14]

Part of this sense of traditionality attached to the dish may come from the long history of the company that invented it and from that organization's place in American popular culture. According to its Web site, the Campbell Soup Company was founded in 1869 in New Jersey by Joseph Campbell, a "fruit merchant," and Abraham Anderson, an "icebox manufacturer." In 1897, the company invented condensed soups, selling them for a dime for a ten-ounce can. This condensed soup was displayed at the Paris Exhibition of 1900, where it won a gold medal—an image of which is still shown today on the can labels. In 1916, the company published a cookbook, *Helps for the Hostess,* that suggested ways to incorporate condensed soups into cooking. In 1931, they began radio ads, including the saying "M'm! M'm! Good!" which then entered into popular culture. In 1934, cream of mushroom soup was invented and was the first of Campbell's soups to be promoted as a sauce as well as a soup. In 1955, the green bean casserole was invented by "Campbell home economists." Today, more than one million cans of soup are used everyday and the green bean casserole is "one of the most popular and most requested recipes" from the company (Campbell Soup Company 2005b).

Originally, the Campbell Soup Company demonstrated modernity through its factory production, marketing, and emphasis on convenience. Its products, however, have been incorporated into the home cooking of many families to the point that their use has become traditional. The canned soups have been attached to people's memories of their childhood and to family lunches.[15] Canned tomato soup and a grilled cheese sandwich, for example, is still a popular lunch for wintry days.

Casseroles in American culture

Another factor in understanding the acceptance of the green bean casserole into tradition is its categorization as a casserole. Casseroles have a special place in American identity. They connote communal eating, sharing, and generosity. At office potlucks, church suppers, and community picnics, casseroles are a staple. This is partly due to their convenience—they are easy to transport, their ingredients are readily available and relatively inexpensive, and they are quick to prepare—but it is also due to their dependability—they require little culinary skill. Referred to as "hot dishes" in the upper Midwest or "bakes" in northwest Ohio, casseroles actually represent a departure from the usual British-based *A+2B* meal structure (featuring a piece of meat with two accompaniments) that underlies the American meal. In fact, nutritionists originally discouraged such mixing of ingredients since it was considered an obstacle to digestion (Bentley 2002:179). According to Sarah Rath, however, the casserole became integrated into American foodways during the depressions of the 1890s and the 1930s, when "the economical casserole provided a welcome way to stretch meat, fish, and poultry." Rationing during World War I required cooks to rely on leftovers, often recycling them into casseroles. Rath also points out that casseroles originally "denoted culinary sophistication to American cooks, but immigrants brought their own casserole recipes to the New World in the nineteenth century, and favorite ethnic and regional classics evolved" (2004:194).

Like many foods that started out as high-class, then, the casserole filtered down to the middle and lower classes. According to Jack Goody (1997), this process occurred throughout Europe, where the adoption of new foods was a search for status, a form of social climbing by emulating the eating habits of the upper classes.

In the United States, the process may have taken a different turn in that the casserole seems to have been adopted out of convenience rather than status-seeking. It was then democratized, used for everyday as well as festive meals, and turned into a familiar comfort food.

Ironically, the green bean casserole does not satisfy the definition of the standard casserole, which is a mixture of a protein source—meat or fish—with a starch and, usually, some chopped vegetables, all bound together with a sauce. The tuna-noodle casserole, also invented by the Campbell Company (in 1934), better fits the expectation. (Like the green bean bake, the tuna-noodle casserole uses a can of cream of mushroom soup and was invented purposely to expand the market for Campbell's soups; at the same time, it modernized the American casserole more generally by specifying a topping of potato chips rather than the more traditional breadcrumbs.) Although the green bean concoction is not, strictly speaking, a casserole, the fact that Campbell's marketed it as one in 1955 suggests that the images of casseroles as traditional and homey were already implanted in the national American consciousness.

Variations on the recipe

One of the primary ways in which new materials, whether mass-produced or handmade, are incorporated into existing cultural systems is through variations. These variations represent performances of identities and circumstances of the individuals and communities adapting those materials. This process of folklorization (Dégh: 1994:23), akin to traditionalization (Hymes 1975), then allows new materials to carry memories and meanings specific to those performers. While this is a naturally occurring process, successful marketing recognizes its usefulness and nudges consumers to feel that they are personalizing a recipe through variations.

The current Web site for Campbell Soup includes a number of alternatives to the original, basic recipe. For example, a can of "Condensed 98% Fat Free Cream of Mushroom Soup" can replace the regular soup. The basic recipe then uses one-half cup of milk flavored with one teaspoon of soy sauce and a "dash" of ground black pepper. Four cups of "cooked cut green beans" are called for, but the type of cut is not specified. In a list of preparation tips, variations on the beans are suggested: frozen green beans (one bag or two packages), canned green beans (two sixteen-ounce cans), or fresh green beans (one and one-half pounds). It is interesting to note these as variations, since many cooks would consider them obvious substitutions rather than creative alternatives. French's french-fried onions are also said to be essential. Everything except half of the onions is mixed together and baked for twenty-five minutes in a 350-degree oven. The remaining onions are then sprinkled over the top, and the casserole is baked for five more minutes. Campbell's tips suggest variations "for a change of pace," "for a creative twist," "for a festive touch," and "for a heartier mushroom flavor." Again these variations seem minor: substituting "broccoli flowerets" for green beans, substituting "Campbell's Condensed Golden Mushroom Soup" for "Cream of Mushroom Soup," and adding chopped red pepper (the assumption being that this is red sweet pepper, not red chili pepper). A note from a Web site member states that she used slivered almonds to replace the fried onions since she is allergic to onions—"and it tastes really good" (Campbell Soup Company 2005a).

Campbell's recipe is written in such a way as to make it sound more sophisticated and requiring a bit more skill than the recipe in oral tradition, which, to quote an informant, is: "Open a can a mushroom soup, two cans of green beans, and a can of fried onions, mix together in a pan, and bake in the oven."

Although suggesting the personalization of commercial products is a common marketing strategy, it is also a way of encouraging individuals to attach their own identities to the product, which can result in developing individual meanings. It encourages people to participate in recipe alteration, thus creating a sense of ownership of the resulting variant recipe. That personal variations fit into the standard practices of cooks and meet the artistic needs of individuals to experiment is suggested by the numerous alternative recipes given in magazines and cookbooks. For example, in a column for the *Cincinnati Post* in 2001, the writer offered her own variations for green bean casserole:

> I can't resist an addition or two, such as chopped water chestnuts or diced jicama for more crunch than the fried onions give; a cupful of fresh mushrooms sliced and sautéed over high heat to make the mushroom soup more mushroom; fresh green beans, well cooked, in place of canned or frozen french-cut beans; sour cream and a tot of dry sherry to jazz up the soupy sauce.

While particular brands of ingredients are frequently specified by cookbooks and published recipes—such as Campbell's soup or French's (previously Durkee) french-fried onions—in actual practice any number of variations are possible. None of them challenge the basic paradigm. The beans can be fresh or frozen; they can be french-cut (i.e., in thin strips) or regular. The soup can be replaced with a homemade white sauce (very daring!) and sautéed fresh mushrooms; the canned onions can be substituted with potato sticks, crumbled potato chips, or toasted slivered almonds. These variations give individual cooks the sense of personal ownership of the recipe, and in fact, people discussing the casserole frequently refer to the recipes of specific individuals.

Similarly, in my research I found that people in my area of the Midwest often discussed the variations of the casserole, arguing, for instance, the merits of toasted slivered almonds over those of canned fried onions, the "best" amounts of salt and pepper or of soy sauce, or the use of frozen green beans rather than canned ones (or home canned rather than commercially canned). Interestingly, there did not seem to be variations that were unique to northwest Ohio—a regional oikotype of green bean casserole, so to speak.[16] However, the variant ingredients often carried personalized memories. For example, the canned green beans had been bought at the favorite grocery store, or the home canned ones had been canned by a relative. Similarly, the arrangement and presentation of the ingredients were often personalized. One family had a white ceramic dish that was always the green bean casserole dish. Another had to have the fried onions sprinkled on top in a particular pattern.

This critiquing of variations suggests, first of all, the existence of an aesthetic system, a system for the evaluation of tastiness and satisfaction. In my research sample, it was common for individuals to have a favorite version of the recipe or to prefer one maker—usually a grandmother—over another. The evaluation also frequently included the merits of different brands of commercial goods, and there tended to be a high degree of brand loyalty. Ironically, the ingredients were not specific to the Midwest, but attention to the identity of commercial products seemed to be common. It may represent a local ethos that embraces the industrial, incorporating it into personal tradition. Brand loyalty was evident in other dishes—chili had to be made with a certain brand of beans and sauce; and hot chicken sandwiches, another local tradition, had to be made with Roots canned shredded chicken.

Familiarity and ritual

One point that repondents consistently bought up as an advantage of green bean casserole was its familiarity. Midwesterners, particularly, find the ingredients, preparation, and form of the casserole familiar. One woman, in describing its success, suggested: "It's at every potluck and it's always popular. It's so quick to make—perfect for the office potluck—and I guess people like the familiar."

This aura of familiarity seemed to lend itself to the dish being perceived as common and "normal." Its presence was assumed at group events, and while that presence usually wasn't celebrated, the casserole's absence would be noticed and commented upon. Furthermore, the casserole may appeal by virtue of its ability to neatly synthesize apparent oppositions. It represents the familiar, mundane, and everyday in that it is thought of as an everyday convenience food, yet it also represents the festive in that it is closely associated with potlucks and holiday meals. Those festive events can be both semipublic, involving members of occupational, recreational, or religious communities, and private, within the family. At such events, the casserole acts as a bridge between two realms, connecting public and private domains, making coworkers like family, and making family relationships somewhat more formal and ceremonial than they might otherwise be.

Green bean casserole also utilizes ingredients that are generally familiar, but in a more "worked" fashion that can connote festivity.[17] In northwest Ohio, green beans are a common vegetable, often cooked and canned and served alongside meat and potatoes; they are also made into a salad with a sweet-and-sour dressing. Casseroles are a familiar form here, connoting comforting sociability, and canned cream soups are common for lunchtime meals. Dressing up familiar foods like these for holiday and special occasion meals lends itself to ritualization. A recurring symbolic event (Santino 1994:11), the special dinner relies on stable components to ground it in people's experiences as a ritual celebration. Highlighting components that are familiar allows for more individuals to participate in the ritual and to create a greater sense of unity through it. In my study, I found that this sense that green bean casserole had been ritualized was part of what people seemed to like about it. Like the turkey, dressing, and mashed potatoes for Thanksgiving dinner, the casserole appeared every year, comforting in its reliability and consistency, and connoting family tradition and stability. The fact that it was also found at other festive occasions and was not exclusive to Thanksgiving underscored its air of familiarity.

I also found a ludic or playful quality to many discussions of green bean casserole. Most of the individuals with whom I spoke were aware of the stereotypes of midwestern culture and cuisine, and the ways in which the casserole fed into those stereotypes. They discussed the dish with a trace of sarcasm in their voices, laughingly recounting the recipe: Open cans, mix, and bake. They also recognized the apparent irony of this highly processed food being a family tradition. One informant describing her family's traditional dinner rolled her eyes and recalled:

> Well, let me tell you how my mother made it. She opened a can of Campbell's mushroom soup, and a can of Del Monte's green beans [her husband interjected, "and those onion things"]. Yeah, canned fried onions, but she used potato sticks . . . I think that's the way . . . Sometimes she used almonds, slivered almonds.

Such playfulness suggests that, for at least some individuals, the casserole was a ritual turning-upside-down of more elite assumptions about festive food and good food. The dish defies the usual qualities of fine cuisine and gourmet cooking and eating. By celebrating such food, the culture surrounding it is also celebrated and affirmed.[18]

The meanings of green bean casserole

The meanings surrounding green bean casserole in northwest Ohio are multiple and surprisingly complex, often representing conflicting oppositions. These meanings are an interplay of public, commercially motivated meanings presented through marketing and advertising, and private meanings developed through informal use and experiences with the dish. On one hand, the casserole seems to represent the traditional, but it also represents the modern, an embracing of technology and corporate America. It represents the familiar and mundane, yet also represents the festive and celebratory. Likewise the casserole is simultaneously "fancy," in that green beans have been "worked" into a more cultural product, and "plain," in that the ingredients are familiar and available and the techniques for preparation are minimal, requiring no culinary skills other than wielding a can opener. Artistry, however, can be displayed in the casserole's presentation—as in the choice of a casserole dish and the arrangement of the onions on top—and personal taste and identity can be expressed through variations in ingredients and preparation. Finally, the casserole is simultaneously national and regional. While it is perceived as common across the U.S., it seems to resonate with midwestern eaters, logically fitting into their family and community traditions.

The casserole, then, suggests a regional foodways aesthetic in several ways: a reliance on canned, processed foods; a lack of spices other than pepper (the salt is built into the canned soup and onions); an emphasis on hearty and filling foods; a conservative approach to new tastes and ingredients; and a pride in well-crafted, functional dishes that are economical and efficient. Green bean casserole embodies and celebrates that aesthetic.

These meanings of the casserole also suggest a regional foodways ethos, a system for valuing food and the activities surrounding it. Dishes such as the green bean casserole lend themselves to *communitas,* the feeling of belonging to a community in which members are bound in nonhierarchical relationships (Turner 1969). No one is superior; no one is more of a gourmet. In a sense the dish cuts across class, in that it is available to all and draws from national rather than elite culture, although it would probably be scorned at gourmet meals. For those concerned with status, however, it is easily available for manipulation to perform class. Homemade white sauce, fresh green beans, almonds instead of canned fried onions, and the addition of little extras—capers, pimento, green pepper—can all denote wealth and more refined tastes. In fact, the ingredients and preparation methods of this dish are accessible to all regardless of class, race, gender, and ethnicity. The cans of green beans, cream of mushroom soup, and french-fried onions are distributed nationally; they are inexpensive and available at almost any grocery store. We can all enjoy green bean casserole and we can even develop a connoisseurship of the subtle variations available.

The meanings associated with the casserole suggest that, in midwestern culture, food functions not so much as cultural capital but as social capital (Bourdieu 1984). It is used to build and affirm relationships in the family or community rather than to demonstrate status. In this culture, valued foods and valued eating experiences are those that bring people together and that erase the social distinctions of class, gourmet tastes, and individualistic preferences. Green bean casserole does just that.

Corresponding with this finding, personal taste seems to play a secondary role to the inclusionary function of the dish. In some of the families I interviewed, the casserole was an obligatory, ritual part of a ritual meal, a dish that had to be included but that no one actually liked or ate.[19] In some cases, it was the contribution of an extended family member, and it was considered more important to accept the contribution—and by implication the family member—than it was to have all the foods be well liked.

Conclusions

The folklorization, traditionalization, and ritualization of green bean casserole suggest that it is possible for a commercial, processed food to be broadly representational and also to carry the emotional attachment that a group may have to its region, an attachment that geographer Yi-Fu Tuan refers to as local patriotism (1974:101). Such patriotism might well be displayed throughout the Midwest whenever green bean casserole is served.

Green bean casserole, then, rather than reflecting a lack of taste, a lack of culinary skill and sophistication, or, perhaps worse, a passive acceptance of mass-produced, commercial foods and meanings, represents a regional foodways aesthetic and ethos. The popular stereotype of the Midwest as having no distinctive identity is well known by midwesterners and comes into play whenever the region is discussed. Their awareness suggests that their playfulness with green bean casserole is a rhetorical strategy acknowledging and celebrating this representation of midwestern identity (see also Kalcik 1984). Furthermore, the dish is used by its midwestern consumers, in their own understanding of their region, as a performative discourse (Bourdieu 1991:223) that not only claims the Midwest as an identity but also helps to construct a sense of the character of that identity. Such performativity was evident in many of the interviews and informal discussions of green bean casserole. Initially, individuals responding to my questions about the casserole often displayed surprise at the idea that this dish could be taken seriously as a food and as a tradition. They often considered it a tasty food and a part of their family customs, but since it did not qualify as "fine cuisine" or as publicly celebrated symbol, they did not associate a meaningful significance with it.[20] That surprise then turned to acknowledgment, almost a sense of discovery, that there is indeed a distinctive midwestern regional identity and that foods having commercial origins can hold meaningful places in individuals' memories and foodways. The very qualities of green bean casserole that might seem to work against it as a meaningful regional tradition—mass-production and factory-processing of ingredients, ease of preparation, mundaneness, heaviness in calories and carbohydrates—are the very ones that make it a logical representation of local identity.

Notes

1. For more discussions of the history of the industrialization of food in the U.S., see Levenstein 1988 and 2003; Grabaccia 1998; Pillsbury 1998; and Counihan 2002. Scathing critiques of the impact of industrialization of food on American eating habits are offered by Nestle 2002 and Pollan 2006. For the acceptance, by women in particular, of "progress" in cooking, see Inness 2001 and Shapiro 2004.

2. For a discussion of the adoption of commercially produced, mass-mediated products into contemporary tradition, see Santino 1996.

3. Most analyses of contemporary American food habits conclude that Americans lack an appreciation for refined cooking because our national culture has emphasized quantity over quality, packaging over content, and speed and size as measures of value. Capitalism is usually blamed, and while I agree that the capitalist system has encouraged such values, I think we also need to look at the ethos and historical conditions that allowed Americans to embrace such a worldview. An excellent analysis of the philosophical foundations of Western thought can be found in Barndt 2004, which explores how the reductionist philosophy of Descartes and the anti-nature theologizing of Bacon created a mindset that allowed North Americans (she includes Canadians in her indictment) to sever their connections with nature and the natural through food.

4. I am not looking here at why people think something tastes good or at how particular tastes develop. The psychology of taste is a field in itself and addresses the biological, physiological, and psychological factors in taste. My focus is on how a dish comes to "make sense" as part of a meal to a group of people. For psychological approaches, see Macbeth 1997. Taste as a philosophical issue is discussed in Korsmeyer 1999 and Curtin and Heldke 1992.

5. I could also use "glocalized" here, since the spread of dishes such as green bean casserole is due partially to successful marketing as well as to a hegemonic power of such companies as Campbell Soup to define what is considered the norm of American food. The term glocalization comes from sociologist Roland Robertson (1992). For a comprehensive discussion of theories of the relationship of food to place, see Bell and Valentine 1997.

6. Roland Barthes identified "crisp" as a basic American food aesthetic and as the binary opposite of "sweet" ([1961]1997:23).

7. In a holiday assemblage various items are artfully arranged to signify the holiday. The individual items may have publicly established symbolism—such as a pumpkin carved into a jack-o'-lantern or a baby in a manger—but the items may also have either no or too many meanings on their own: in this case, a can of cream of mushroom soup does not represent Thanksgiving until it is juxtaposed with a can of fried onions and cans of green beans. For holiday assemblage, see Santino 1994:34–41.

8. These are my own terms, although the ideas are explored and discussed by philosophers and anthropologists of food, for example, Deane Curtin and Lisa Heldke (1992). My use of the word foodways is specific to folklore in that it refers to a network of activities and meanings surrounding food.

9. For more explanation of "foodways," see Yoder 1972 and Long 1999.

10. For more discussion of identity being expressed in food, see articles in the volume edited by Linda Keller Brown and Kay Mussell, particularly one by Susan Kalcik (1984). My own approach to the expression of identity through food draws heavily from performance theory in folklore, as articulated by Richard Bauman ([1977] 1984) and Dell Hymes (1974): see Long 1999:33–35.

11. This collecting was not done as a statistical survey, although that kind of information would be helpful. The focus in these classes was on the basic concepts of how food traditions carry and construct identity. I also collected information from graduate students, but they tended to have more varied backgrounds and were not representative of the region.

12. While this ethnography was not systematic, I did make sure that I talked to both longtime residents of the area and newcomers. Social distinctions in this area tend to be along occupational and political lines rather than racial, ethnic, or socioeconomic ones, so I attended potlucks at community events, observed reactions to a "culinary expo" at a local mall, and gave workshops and talks in the area on a variety of food-related topics. Judging from responses to my tentative conclusions, I feel that I accurately assessed the uses and meanings of green bean casserole across town-gown lines as well as the spectrum of political beliefs.

13. In the late 1980s, I conducted fieldwork for an exhibit on folk art in this region. Instead of the expected paintings, sculptures, and textile arts, I found that the artistic impulse tended to be expressed through pragmatic forms, such as farm implements and machinery, neatly aligned tree rows and yards, and well-organized larders (Long 1990).

14. A recent advertisement suggesting green bean casserole for Easter plays upon this idea, stating that the dish is not only for Thanksgiving anymore. The advertisement, which was copyrighted in 2006, has appeared in women's magazines such as *Family Circle*.

15. Longtime Bowling Green resident Tom McLaughlin recalled that the local diners and hamburger joints served canned soups in the 1940s and 1950s. When soup was ordered, the cook would simply open a can of Campbell's soup (interview, 6/26/2007).

16. "Oikotype" is more commonly used to refer to narrative variants that are found in a particular locale and that display some aspect of local culture (Brunvand 1998:197).

17. Claude Lévi-Strauss suggests that humans have to act upon the raw ingredients in order to turn them into a cultural item known as food ([1968] 1997).

18. Such rites of reversal are significant ways in which dominated cultures maintain a sense of identity as well as vent anger at oppression. While the American Midwest is in no way an oppressed culture, its residents often express frustration at the lack of awareness and appreciation of their region by other areas of the country, particularly the coasts.

19. Cranberry sauce held a similar place, particularly in its canned, jellied form. Students expressed disgust with both these qualities and wondered why such sauce was part of the national paradigm.

20. This reflects common misperceptions of the nature of these phenomena, rather than a lack of meaning of green bean casserole itself. Dishes to be celebrated tend to be thought of as either gourmet (representing evidence of the mastery of specific culinary arts and usually displaying a higher socioeconomic status) or as having a long history, even though that history may be a mythical one (e.g., turkey for Thanksgiving, apple pie, or certain ethnic dishes). Similarly, many informants seemed to think of the casserole's ritual place in their family as due to inertia and lack of curiosity, so that it could be a tradition, but not one to be celebrated, (See Pillsbury 1998, pp. 11–13, for a discussion of tradition as inertia.) In either case, informants did not consider themselves arbiters of what defines Food and Tradition.

References

Anderson, Benedict R. 1983. *Imagined Communities: Reflections on the Origin and Spread of Nationalism.* London: Verso.

Barndt, Deborah. 2004. *Tangled Routes: Women, Work, and Globalization on the Tomato Trail.* Lanham, Md.: Rowman and Littlefield.

Barthes, Roland. 1997. Toward a Psychosociology of Contemporary Food Consumption. In *Food and Culture: A Reader,* ed. Carole Counihan and Penny Van Esterik, pp. 20–27 (reprinted from 1961). New York: Routledge.

Bauman, Richard. (1977) 1984. *Verbal Art as Performance.* Prospect Heights, Ill.: Waveland.

Bell, David, and Gill Valentine. 1997. *Consuming Geographies: We Are Where We Eat.* New York: Routledge.

Bentley, Amy. 2002. Islands of Serenity: Gender, Race, and Ordered Meals during World War II. In *Food in the USA: A Reader,* ed. Carole M. Counihan, pp. 171–192.

Bourdieu, Pierre. 1984. *Distinction: A Social Critique of the Judgement of Taste.* Trans. Richard Nice. Cambridge, Mass.: Harvard University Press.

—. 1991. *Language and Symbolic Power.* Cambridge: Polity.

Brunvand, Jan Harold. 1998. The Study of American Folklore: An Introduction. New York: W. W. Norton & Company.

Campbell Soup Company. 2005a. http://www.campbellkitchen.com/recipedetail.aspx?recipeID=24099; accessed 9/15/2006.

—. 2005b. http//www.campbellsoupcompany.com/history.asp; accessed 9/15/2006.

Chiff Directory. 2007. http://www.chiff.com/a/green-bean-casserole.htm; accessed 9/15/2006.

Cincinnati Post. 2001. Food review.

Counihan, Carole M., ed. 2002. *Food in the USA: A Reader.* New York: Routledge.

Curtin, Deane W., and Lisa M. Heldke, eds. 1992. *Cooking, Eating, Thinking: Transformative Philosophies of Food.* Bloomington: Indiana University Press.

Dégh, Linda. 1994. *American Folklore and the Mass Media.* Bloomington: Indiana University Press.

Fertig, Judith M. 2003. The Midwest. In *Encyclopedia of Food and Culture,* ed. Solomon H. Katz, pp. 454–457. New York: Charles Scribner's Sons.

Gabaccia, Donna R. 1998. *We Are What We Eat: Ethnic Food and the Making of Americans.* Cambridge, Mass.: Harvard University Press.

Goody, Jack. 1997. Industrial Food: Towards the Development of a World Cuisine. In *Food and Culture: A Reader,* ed. Carole Counihan and Penny Van Esterik, pp. 357–369. New York: Routledge.

Hymes, Dell. 1974. Ways of Speaking. In *Explorations in the Ethnography of Speaking,* ed. Richard Bauman and Joel Sherzer, pp. 433–452. Cambridge: Cambridge University Press.

—. 1975. Breakthrough into Performance. In *Folklore: Performance and Communication,* ed. Dan Ben-Amos and Kenneth S. Goldstein, pp. 11–74. The Hague: Mouton.

Inness, Sherrie A. 2001. *Dinner Roles: American Women and Culinary Culture.* Iowa City: University of Iowa Press.

Kalcik, Susan. 1984. Ethnic Foodways in America: Symbol and the Performance of Identity. In *Ethnic and Regional Foods in the United States: The Performance of Group Identity,* ed. Linda Keller Brown and Kay Mussell, pp. 37–65. Knoxville: University of Tennessee Press.

Korsmeyer, Carolyn. 1999. *Making Sense of Taste: Food and Philosophy.* Ithaca, N.Y.: Cornell University Press.

Lee, Judith Yaross. 2004. Introduction. In *The Midwest,* ed. Joseph W. Slade and Judith Yaross Lee, pp. xvii–xxx. Westport, Conn.: Greenwood.

Levenstein, Harvey. 1988. *Revolution at the Table: The Transformation of the American Diet.* Cambridge: Oxford University Press.

—. 2003. *Paradox of Plenty: A Social History of Eating in Modern America.* Los Angeles: University of California Press.

Lévi-Strauss, Claude. 1997. The Culinary Triangle. In *Food and Culture: A Reader,* ed. Carole Counihan and Penny Van Esterik, pp. 28–35 (reprinted from 1968). New York: Routledge.

Long, Lucy. 1990. *Folk Arts of The Great Black Swamp.* Exhibit Catalogue. Bowling Green, Ohio: Bowling Green State University.

—. 1999. Foodways: Using Food to Teach Folklore Theories and Methods. *Digest: An Interdisciplinary Study of Food and Foodways* 19:32–36.

—. 2004. Food. In *The Midwest,* ed. Joseph W. Slade and Judith Yaross Lee, pp. 281–322. Westport, Conn.: Greenwood.

Macbeth, Helen, ed. 1997. *Food Preferences and Taste: Continuity and Change.* Providence, R.I.: Berghahn.

Nestle, Marion. 2002. *Food Politics: How the Food Industry Influences Nutrition and Health.* Los Angeles: University of California Press.

Pillsbury, Richard. 1998. *No Foreign Food: The American Diet in Time and Place.* Boulder, Colo.: Westview.

Pollan, Michael. 2006. *The Omnivore's Dilemma: A Natural History of Four Meals.* New York: Penguin.

Prosterman, Leslie. 1995. *Ordinary Life, Festival Days: Aesthetics in the Midwestern County Fair.* Washington, D.C.: Smithsonian University Press.

Rath, Sarah. 2004. Casseroles. In *The Oxford Encyclopedia of Food and Drink in America,* ed. Andrew F. Smith, pp. 194–195. Cambridge: Oxford University Press.

Robertson, Roland. 1992. *Globalization: Social Theory and Global Culture.* London: Sage.

Santino, Jack. 1994. *All Around the Year: Holidays and Celebrations in American Life.* Urbana: University of Illinois Press.

—. 1996. *New Old-Fashioned Ways: Holidays and Popular Culture.* Knoxville: University of Tennessee Press.

Shapiro, Laura. 2004. *Something from the Oven: Reinventing Dinner in 1950s America.* New York: Penguin.

Shortridge, Barbara G. 2003. Not Just Jello and Hot Dishes: Representative Foods of Minnesota. *Journal of Cultural Geography* 21(1):71–94.

Tuan, Yi-Fu. 1974. *Topophilia: A Study of Environmental Perception, Attitudes, and Values.* Englewood Cliffs, N.J.: Prentice-Hall.

Turner, Victor. 1969. *The Ritual Process: Structure and Anti-Structure.* Ithaca: Cornell University Press.

Yoder, Don. 1972. Folk Cookery. In *Folklore and Folklife: An Introduction,* ed. Richard M. Dorson, pp. 325–350. Chicago: University of Chicago Press.

CHAPTER 15
RAMEN NOODLES AND SPAM: POPULAR FOODS, SIGNIFICANT TASTES

Sojin Kim and R. Mark Livengood

We begin with the notion that if folklorists are to more fully understand the role of food in culture, they need to consider the significance of mass-produced, commercial foods—items which have been largely neglected by researchers. Two such foods are ramen noodles and Spam. While these products have engendered humorous and often derisive associations, they are frequently eaten with pleasure and even celebrated. By exploring various dimensions of ramen noodles and Spam, we intend to illustrate the necessary inclusion of mass-produced foods in the study of foodways.

In his article "Folk Cookery," regarded as an initial call to the study of foodways by folklorists, Don Yoder closes his essay by noting the changes in domestic cookery brought about by the production of "ready-made" foods. Writing in 1972, Yoder asks: "Whether we are better off with our 'enriched' bread and our often flavorless frozen foods is a question that the historian and the folklife scholar as well as the nutritionist and public health official can help to answer" (1972:347). While we are not certain that the foods we eat today are necessarily "better" than those of the early 1970s, we would argue that the comestibles resulting from mass-production are increasingly more central to our lives in the late twentieth century. Mass-production, however, has not led to the homo-genization of the American diet nor to the demise of culinary ingenuity; the preparation, consumption, and even celebration of mass-produced foods are projects undertaken in an array of meaningful and imaginative manners.

Several folklorists have addressed mass-produced foods. Elizabeth Mosby Adler briefly discusses ways of eating the Oreo cookie, in addition to fried eggs, corn-on-the-cob, and layer cake, in her examination of the creative manipulations involved in and sensory experiences characteristic to the act of eating (1983). In a more recent article, Sarah E. Newton suggests that "the study of popular commercial food products can have value to the folklorist, as well as the student of American culture, in uncovering the intimate, important, and sometimes symbolic relationships people develop between themselves, their world, and the foods they eat" (1992:266). Newton surveys the "cultural and folkloric implications" of another mass-produced food, Jell-O, outlining the narratives, jokes, and other forms of expressive behavior that emerge around this food. Our study complements Newton's by demonstrating how the preparation and consumption of mass-produced products by individuals or groups may be anchored within a complex of personal aesthetics, memories of significant social relationships, and/or ethnic identification.

Ramen noodles

In 1972, after years of production in Japan, Nissin Foods began manufacturing ramen noodles in Gardena, California. Since ramen's introduction in the United States, the small blocks and Styrofoam cups of dehydrated

Sojin Kim and R. Mark Livengood, 'Ramen Noodles and Spam: Popular Noodles, Significant Tastes', *Digest: An Interdisciplinary Study of Food and Foodways* 15 (1995), 2–11.

Reprinted with permission from *Digest*.

noodles have become ubiquitous. In 1988, Nissin expected domestic sales totalling $85 million—a substantial sum considering that in Los Angeles today the noodles can sell for as low as nineteen cents a package (Sanchez 1988:10). Ramen is now available in a variety of flavors, ranging in price up to $1.50 for "gourmet" noodles. According to one writer, Los Angeles "has become the Oriental noodle-making capital of the United States, with at least six companies in the region" (Sanchez 1988:1). Of course, this says nothing of the many restaurants that serve steaming bowls of homemade noodles throughout the city.

Ramen noodles piqued our research interests when we enrolled in a seminar on foodways in the UCLA Folklore Program. By focusing on this product with which many students are familiar, we hoped to articulate some of the issues folklorists often consider in analyzing eating behaviors while positioning our discussions in the immediate contexts of students' lives. Therefore, many of the participants in our study were, and in some cases still are, undergraduate and graduate students at UCLA. According to one marketing survey, many people get their first taste of ramen noodles while in college (Shapiro 1989:D1). Indeed, students seem to be one of the populations targeted by the Nissin Corporation. A quotation from the company's brochure suggests how the corporation conceptualizes its market:

> The America of the 1980s found young families working harder than ever but unable to afford homes, even as double income households proliferated. People had less time for personal enjoyment, and still struggled to support themselves. The dollar tumbled in both international and domestic value. The college generation faced downward mobility.
>
> These factors all contributed to a hectic pace across the nation. People demanded that what free time and money they did have was to be spent on quality activities and products. Nissin Foods' instant oriental noodle (ramen) products fit perfectly into that environment. [Nissin Foods Corporation 1989]

Our research corroborates the product's pragmatic appeal suggested by this statement. Students often describe ramen as an inexpensive, convenient, and last-resort staple food. Indeed, one person stated, "It's usually like, 'Oh I don't have any time this week, so I better get some ramen,' or 'Wednesday I'm going to be really busy, so I better get some so I can whip it off real quick.'" Although people offer such explanations, some individuals prepare the product in aesthetically satisfying ways that may be evocative of meaningful past experiences.

The relative ease of preparation—boiling the noodles for three minutes and mixing in the flavor powder from the enclosed tin foil packet—is highlighted by efforts to make the mass-produced product sensorially pleasurable (see Jones 1991:235). People indicated ingredients, utensils, and procedures necessary for the creation of a visually and gustatorily pleasing dish. For example, one person stated that the essential ingredient, pink fishcake, or *kamaboko,* adds color to the dish. She said, "All the different stuff, the existing stuff that we add on, makes it look good—color and that it just looks cooked, and mostly color." Another commented upon the way her addition of certain ingredients contributed to a more appealing dish: "You can see with the hot dogs and you can see the color the cheese made it . . . sort of a yellow instead of that nasty puce color. And it looks a lot more edible and it tastes better anyway." Still another described his use of two different kinds of noodles as a means of making the dish "prettier." These statements indicate that cooks make aesthetic judgments about the appearance of ramen (see Jones 1993).

For one preparer of ramen, who adds very little to what is provided in the package—soy sauce and sometimes an egg—the utensils with which he eats ramen contribute to pleasant sensory experiences. He said, "You've got to cook this with chopsticks. You can't do it with a fork. The fork gets too hot, plus that metallic taste on the mouth isn't good. I always eat them with chopsticks. Never with a fork. It just doesn't taste the same for some reason." This person further indicated that he customarily eats ramen out of a white bowl, or *chow won*, with a blue design because of the agreeable color contrast with the brown noodles. Upon pouring his noodles into this bowl, he held it up and remarked that no vegetables were needed as there was already "enough color."

Furthermore, preparation procedures may be very deliberate. One person who methodically sautes vegetables before adding them to the noodles commented that he did so because he did not want the dish to be like "the slop like on old Western movies" or "jailhouse food." Another cook discussed his detailed method of mixing the powder with other spices and sauces in order to obtain the optimum flavor:

> I like to use a lot of curry . . . . I like to stir it up until it's all absorbed into the nut butter. I like to have my curry powder suspended in this nut butter because some of the biochemicals that give these spices their flavor are only alcohol or oil soluble and they're not water soluble. And so if you have a soup broth that has water and no oil in it, then it's harder to taste these biochemicals from these spices. They just won't taste, the curry powder, won't taste right because these biochemicals won't be released as freely as they would be.

Recalling Franz Boas's oft-cited edict that "[all] human activities may assume forms that give them esthetic values" (1955 [1927]:9), such elaborate procedures turn three-minute boil-and-serve operations into half-hour culinary endeavors that create possibilities for pleasurable gustatory experiences. Thus, as various ingredients are added and procedures are enacted, the possible aesthetic aspects of ramen preparation and consumption complement, if not supersede, the product's use as cheap and quick sustenance.

The preparation and consumption of single-serving ramen also may be imprinted with memories of meaningful relationships, thus connecting the maker with past social contexts. For one individual, the social interactions she associated with eating ramen occurred in the context of her eating the noodles with friends in college. She explained that this is where she first began to eat ramen and where she learned to prepare it in the manner in which she still eats it. Asked what memories she had of eating instant ramen noodles, this woman, a graduate student at UCLA from Huntington Beach, California, and a particularly dynamic storyteller, related the following narrative to the researchers who videotaped the storytelling while the woman cooked:

> One night I went to visit a friend and she actually served top ramen—my friend Stephanie; I'll never forget that night. We were there and we ended up talking into the wee hours of the morning so maybe it's about 2:30. And I decided to go home; I'm driving through this really bad neighborhood in San Diego to get to my other apartment from hers. I had a great Italian sports car called a Lancia at the time and the thing decided to basically blow up at the time. It was just not such a good night [throws arms in air]. So the thing's smoking and it's dark, and I'm in a very horrible neighborhood. So I go running to this phone. And I'm dialing my apartment and dialing my apartment, and the answering machine keeps picking up and I knew my roommate Leila was home—she said she wasn't going out that night. And I'm freaking out, "Oh my God, she's dead. There must be a reason she's not answering the phone." And then like some drug creature from the street comes up and started bothering me and pulling at my clothes and things. So I was just freaking out. I didn't know what to do. I'm scared to death. And a police car drives up. I'm like "Yea!" This person melts into the woodwork, I go running to the police car, and I'm like "Oh please help me, help me, help me. I don't know what to do. My car broke down." He looks at me and goes, "Oh call Triple A in the morning." And then he drives away. I'm so upset. I'm crying. I'm hysterical. So I go back to the phone and I'm dialing, dialing, dialing. Finally my roommate picks

it up. She starts screaming at me what a horrible person I am to interrupt her beauty sleep and all this. So, I was not thrilled to say the least. And so I said, "fine, I hate you" and hung up the phone. And then I called the friend whose house I had just come from. She came and picked me up. And I went home. I was so upset, I never talked to my roommate again until she moved out a couple months later. That was really fun. But the whole point of the thing is that I got home and I was hungry. Not hungry [but] like a nervous kind of hungry you know—there's something that you need to do. And I made myself some top ramen and sat there and ate it [laughs] for like an hour. I just sat there watching TV and eating ramen because I was too upset to think of anything else.

And this was like comfort food.

The content of this story reasserts the important role narrative plays in foodways research. Objects and experiences with objects generate narratives, and narratives in turn become attached to objects. Very often, potential meanings of food and eating are communicated in story form. Foodways researchers, therefore, should be attentive to narrating about food, eating, and cooking, and should consciously document such narrations. Furthermore, this woman's use of the term "comfort food" is an example of culinary cant which suggests a unique category of foods while implying a basic need to have a positive aesthetic experience in daily life, particularly in juxtaposition to the less-than-ideal circumstances she characterizes in the story. For this narrator, ramen recalls a significant, albeit negative, social experience.

Another person associated the dish with communal family eating experiences as a child growing up in Hawaii and now attempts to recreate those experiences by preparing commercially-packaged ramen with her adult siblings who live in the Los Angeles area. Another links the addition of an egg to his ramen with recollections of his grandmother. He said, "I think I learned to do the egg thing from my grandmother, she used to do that sometimes when she used to cook for me. Also when she made seaweed soup. And what she would do when you came home late, she would yell from the back room, 'drop an egg in there, drop an egg in there.'" In this sense, the simple procedure of adding an egg to a mass-produced comestible becomes mnemonic and metonymic, prompting the reconstruction of memorable experiences. In these cases, the preparation and consumption of the mass-produced ramen suggests the veracity of Mary Douglas's assertion that "each meal carries something of the meaning of the other meals" (1972:69). The making and eating of ramen, therefore, may encode memories and associations, both positive and negative, of past culinary experiences.

In addition to sensations and memories, wrapped up in ramen is the complex issue of ethnicity. As packaging and advertising suggest, the origin of the "Oriental" instant noodles is in Asia. In its corporate brochure, Nissin attempts to establish the traditional nature of the mass-produced noodles by outlining the evolution of noodles through time. This effort was underscored by a marketing campaign in 1986 which emphasized ramen's Japanese background and promised customers a means by which to "get authentic oriental taste without spending centuries at the stove" (Nissin Foods Corporation 1989). Interestingly, this discourse attempts to establish the historic continuity and thus the traditionality and authenticity of a mass-produced food item.

Nissin's commercial campaigns have now been expanded to suggest other constituencies via flavors of ramen, such as Picante Shrimp, and recipes which the Nissin company distributes, such as Top Ramen Knockwurst and Veggie Skillet and Rio Ramen. Furthermore, a manager of Maruchan, another noodle manufacturer, was quoted in the *Los Angeles Times* as saying, "It's [ramen] definitely an American staple. We feel it's as American as a hot dog" (Sanchez 1988:1). Recent scholarship in folklore and related cultural studies has demonstrated the problems in assuming a straightforward and obvious connection between a particular item and its ethnic association in any given situation (see Theophano 1991). Similarly, our research has revealed how a mass-produced comestible's original ethnic markings are often shed or reinterpreted within individual domestic contexts.

Some people prepared ramen as if it were a Japanese or "Oriental" noodle dish, adding ingredients to it according to their conceptions of what is appropriate to such an ethnic dish. For instance, one cook added what he referred to as a "Chinese trilogy"—ginger, garlic, and soy sauce or oyster sauce. For others the noodles became more a generic starch bed—like rice, bread, or spaghetti—around which individuals created dishes with other ethnic or altogether different models in mind. One person, while acknowledging the Japanese derivation of ramen noodles and her transgression of Kosher laws, adds Hebrew National hot dogs, the kind she "grew up on," and Kraft cheese singles in her preparation of the product. Another person refers to the dish he prepares as *namyun* and explains that this is the way *ramen* is pronounced in Korean. The dish he commonly fixes, however, is a conscious departure from the manner in which noodles are prepared in Korean tradition; he adds almond butter, tahini butter, curry, and avocado. The case of this individual broaches an important question, for the manner in which he linguistically tags the product and the ingredients with which he prepares ramen do not correspond. Therefore, how ramen may function as an ethnic marker for this person remains ambiguous.

Our informants from Hawaii demonstrated through the ingredients they added to their dish that the model for their preparation was the way in which *saimen* noodles are commonly prepared in Hawaii. They identified certain ingredients as "ethnic" and indicated that they were always included in the *saimen* served in Hawaii, not only in the *saimen* shops, but even at McDonald's. On the mainland they still prepare ramen according to the Hawaiian model. In this instance, ingredients in conjunction with naming suggest ramen is a marker of ethnicity. The particular ingredients these people highlighted were *shoyu, kamaboko,* and Spam. This last ingredient presents another example of the unexpected emergence of an ethnic association with a mass-produced food—Hormel's "miracle meat in a can."

Spam

According to Carolyn Wyman, author of a history of popular foods, *I'm a Spam Fan,* "Americans consume 3.8 cans of Spam every second, or 122 million cans a year" and it is served in nearly thirty percent of American households (1993:64). The meat was developed in 1937. Originally consisting of pork shoulder, ham, and spices, this product was marketed as "Hormel's Spiced Ham," until the name was contracted to the more catchy "Spam." During World War II, Spam became a staple of U.S. service men who reportedly grew to loathe it, yet upon their return to the states created a market that raised and maintained the food's popularity and sales. For many Americans today, Spam often evokes the eating patterns of people of a certain socioeconomic status. Residents of Hawaii, however, as well as those who live in areas of the mainland with concentrations of relocated Hawaiians, are aware that the people of that state consume more Spam per capita than any other state in the union. Indeed, many people from Hawaii living in Los Angeles will readily offer statistics confirming the popular place of Spam in the diets of those living on the islands. For example, one person suggested that "20,000 cans of Spam are consumed daily in Hawaii." Another pointed out that "the state of Hawaii consumes half of the nationwide consumption of Spam" (see Chin 1991).

In Hawaii, Spam is consumed in both domestic and commercial realms. McDonald's has been savvy about incorporating items from local cuisine into the menus of regional franchises, and in Hawaii the restaurant offers Spam along side Big Macs and Quarter Pounders. Spam dishes are offered at Hawaiian-Japanese cafes in Los Angeles. And Bess Press of Honolulu publishes a Spam Cookbook (1987). The ubiquity of Spam in Hawaii may be partially explained as the legacy of World War II meat shortages and the presence of U.S. military bases on the islands; the continuing popularity of Spam in South Korea and Guam is another American military legacy.

The Hawaiian Community Center Association's second annual Spam Cookoff Picnic held 3 July 1993 in Torrance, California, provides an interesting context in which to explore the cultural significance of Spam. An all day affair advertised in the *Los Angeles Times, LA Weekly,* and Japanese-American newspapers, the event was covered by television and newspaper reporters. The public celebration at the Hawaiian Community Center suggests the complexity of associations that can be affixed to a mass-produced food item.

The Spam Cookoff showcased aspects of contemporary Hawaiian culture. Spatially, the Torrance Community Center was composed of roughly three interior rooms and an outdoor courtyard. In the largest interior space, vendors sold items such as *batiks* and other handmade textiles. At the end of the room was a window through which food was sold. Two of the dishes contained Spam; another food served was a large bun filled with a mixture of barbecued pork called *manapua*. In the entry-way interior space stood a main reception table laden with information about the sponsoring organization, a stack of records by a Hawaiian artist that were being distributed gratis, and a variety of "Spam items" for sale; for example, aprons, banks, and T-shirts. The third interior space contained the table on which were set the competing final Spam dishes before judging, as well as an area relegated to craft activities. Children were especially encouraged to participate in printing on textiles as well as making *leis* from fresh flowers.

The exterior space contained tables and chairs, a stage for music and dance entertainment, a booth at which beverages and Hawaiian shaved ice were sold, and the preparation areas of the eight Cookoff contestants. Sitting at the tables, festival-goers could watch the entertainment, including hula dancing, guitar and ukelele bands, and an occasional rendition of the festival's theme song "Spam on the Range," sung to the tune of "Home on the Range." Most patrons took at least some time to inspect the tables of the contestants, watch the food preparation, and chat about Spam.

The eight contestants competed for first place prizes, giant baskets filled with Spam-related products, in two food categories—main dish and *pupu* (appetizer). All of the contestants were either from Hawaii or had relatives from the islands, and indicated that they consumed Spam in their daily lives in the past and/ or currently. The recipes for entrees were culled from relatives, cookbooks, and last minute inspiration and improvisation, as well as from the cooks' existing repertoires. Competing for the main dish prize were: "Al Chang's House Special," a mix of mushrooms, asparagus, and Spam on a bed of rice; "Spam Fried Rice," Spam, canned corn, scallions, cilantro, and rice; "Sweet Soup Spam," a soupy sauce containing Spam poured over rice. Competing for the *pupu* were: "Bitter Melon Spam," a chunky mixture of baby shrimp, fishcake, Spam, scallions stuffed into one-inch wide slices of bitter melon; "Hawaii Sweet Islands," a variant of "pigs in a blanket" consisting of Spam, dijon mustard, and water chestnuts rolled in a Pillsbury biscuit; "S'potato," baked potatoes stuffed with a mixture of brown sugar, hot mustard, green onions, mayonnaise, and Spam topped with melted cheese; and "The Fruity Spam Cup," hollowed out, deep-fried slices of Spam filled with cream cheese and topped with canned fruit.

Ostensibly created as a charity function, the Spam Cookoff created a context for members of the Hawaiian Community Center Association to highlight various aspects of their expressive culture—dance, crafts, music, and different foods. The public face of ethnicity is a complicated and compelling subject. In public demonstrations of ethnicity, people often attempt to create an impression of their uniqueness by highlighting "colorful" and "exotic" features, while remaining somehow familiar or unthreatening. At festivals and ethnic food restaurants, "traditional" ethnic dishes are highlighted, altered, or even elided in accordance with conceptions about consumer expectation and preference. That Spam emerged as the central component of a festival celebrating contemporary Hawaiian culture justifiably prompted one person to ask, "Why did they choose Spam when they have thousands of years of traditions to choose from?"

The organizers of the Hawaiian Community Center Association's Spam Cookoff indicated that their benefit event was organized around Spam predominantly because for many people from Hawaii, eating Spam is evocative of the years they lived on the islands and is symbolic of Hawaiian culture. One of the cookoff contestants stated, "Spam is still our tradition since the baby boomer time." She further compared Spam to *poi,* a dish prepared from tarot, an ingredient indigenous to the islands, thus metaphorically linking Spam and *poi* as traditional foods. Many of the organizers of the Cookoff relayed nostalgic anecdotes about family or childhood memories of eating Spam when they still lived in Hawaii. One organizer stated that the Cookoff provided people who were from the Islands the opportunity to learn and trade different ways of cooking Spam.

It is also important to consider the more ignoble associations Spam engenders in a large number of people when discussing Spam as a potential symbol of identity for people from Hawaii. For instance, several people from Hawaii expressed: "It's embarrassing to buy Spam. Americans don't eat Spam. You know how they are; they go, 'eeeuww—you eat Spam!'" Interestingly, this person clearly draws a distinction between "Americans" and "Hawaiians," a division which, for this person, is reflected in eating behaviors. Another person who made the geographic distinction between people "up here," on the mainland, stated: "Whenever I tell them about it, they'll really cringe, they'll crinkle their nose, they'll say it's gross, why do you eat it . . . stuff like that. But I tell them if you prepare it right . . . . They think it's sick, I guess. They associate it with hot dogs where it's just a bunch of junk meat thrown together and compressed into a cube."

These statements which draw distinctions between constituencies based on reactions and eating behaviors related to Spam contrast with other, more positive, comments. At the Spam Cookoff, one woman went so far as to suggest that "Spam is our heritage. And we call it our Hawaiian steak back home. If you go anyplace, they'll ask you, 'would you like me to bring some Hawaiian steak?' And if you didn't know what it was you would get the shock of your life." Another person said, "You know in Hawaii they sell more Spam than they do anywhere else because everyone in Hawaii eats Spam. That's staple for us. Spam—everything is Spam for us. We use Spam everywhere. It's our cheap version of ham." Similarly, when a festival-goer expressed perplexity to one of the judges about the number of times Spam dishes showed up on menus in Hawaii, the judge replied with joking indignation, "Hey, that's Hawaiian steak you're talking about. We eat Spam three times a day."

Although Spam is the central organizing component of the festival, it is one component of a complex of forms and activities consciously displayed to the public as representative of Hawaiian culture. The crafts, costume, and performances included in this event are part of the conventional popular imagining of Hawaiian culture, and they purportedly refer to the culture that is indigenous to the islands. While Spam is not a vestige of the pre-territorial era, and while it is a processed food that was imported to Hawaii during World War II, its inclusion in the public display of Hawaiian culture is not merely hyperbolic or insincere. The public celebration of Spam for the Hawaiian community, as these voices suggest, was a playful performance that also conveyed a sense of cultural pride. The event resonated with the humorous and derisive attitudes directed toward Spam in a hospitable festival context. The Cookoff was at once a conscious inversion of the mainstream disdain of the product while an affirmation of the positive associations of a familiar, indeed traditional, food for the Hawaiian community. Significantly, as the recipes suggested, the festival also highlighted the unexpected and innovative use of this product by a subset of this public.

Conclusions

Both ramen noodles and Spam point to a larger issue of foods becoming circumscribed with the status of "poverty foods" or "economy foods." "Poverty foods," like "comfort foods," constitutes a distinguishable category of eating behaviors which are constructed in the minds of individuals and which potentially become codified in a culture at large. Clearly, both ramen noodles and Spam have been considered poverty foods. They were initially developed and distributed during periods of economic distress: ramen in post-World War II Japan; Spam during the depression in the United States. As the quotation from the Nissin corporate brochure reveals, a major appeal of ramen in the United States has been its economic value. Indeed, ramen has been often associated with the status of being a student—a time when, arguably, many do not have sizeable disposable incomes. For example, an editorial by a UCLA student criticizing the salary increases of university administrators at the time when students were being subjected to tuition hikes was titled "Let them eat top ramen: Pay hikes show contempt for students" (Hagstrom 1992:M3). In an article in the *Los Angeles Times Magazine,* the author wryly describes how it is possible to subsist in L.A. for twenty dollars a day. When it comes to eating, the author suggests, "Those packets of ramen noodles and broth can run as low as 19 cents each; two or three will easily dull the desire for food" (Tsing Loh 1991:S19). Spam is often regarded as a cheap substitute for "real meat." One of the organizers of the Spam Cookoff explained his ideas about the economic reason behind the popularity of Spam in Hawaii: "Grass roots people can't afford prime rib . . . . You can feed a whole family on a can of Spam and two heads of cabbage." Similarly, another Hawaiian speculated on the mainstream public's negative attitude towards Spam: "People up here think it's whatever—welfare, depression food. Someone told me that they associated it with the depression up here, which is why people up here look down on Spam I guess."

Essayist Francine Prose has characterized well the regard different social groups assign to certain foods:

> Often, the poor and the working class distrust the weird foods of the rich and ethnic: the brains, the sweetbreads, the snails, the bloody duck breast, the nasturtiums and edible flowers . . . . Meanwhile, the rich, who flatter themselves that nothing humanly edible is foreign to them, do in fact draw the line at the pitiful, unesthetic, unsavory food of the poor: the white bread, the processed spreads, the rat-tail-pink luncheon meat and the sugary, carnival-colored cereals. [1992:118–19]

Furthermore, Ernest Matthew Mickler's recipe book *White Trash Cooking* is a reverent and humorous reflection on a much maligned category of eating behavior (1986). Mickler's introductory remarks project his empathy and admiration for the people from whom he collected his recipes, instead of the common disdain reflected in the qualifier "white trash." Similarly, ethnic and immigrant groups have been derisively described or labeled by means of referring to their eating habits (e.g., beaner, kraut, watermelon). Eating is such a central aspect of human behavior that folklorist Roger Abrahams, among others, has pointed out that to negatively comment upon what others ingest is to negatively assess their civility: that is, no sane or civilized person would consider eating that (1984).

Similarly, one may also note the negative manner in which popular thought often considers or derides those who subsist regularly on mass-produced foods, which are neither home-cooked nor gourmet. Assumptions do not concern simply the economic necessity or time constraints of the consumers; such a diet is often considered as the result of lack of food preparation skills, unhealthy lifestyles, or an undiscriminating palette (bad taste), all qualities which reflect the consumer's culinary/dietary ignorance or ineptitude. One person with whom we spoke about his ramen preparation indicated that his past social involvements have left him with an association of ramen as the food preferred by "stoners and fuckups," people lacking the ability to prepare more complex foods:

> I was anxious to try to do things that would allow me to see myself in a good light. So for that reason I thought I could eat ramen only for breakfast because that was different. If I made it for lunch and dinner

that would mean that I was too lazy to cook another meal. I didn't want that and I couldn't live with myself presumably if I did that. But if I ate ramen for breakfast, that was an adequate excuse because breakfast is supposed to be quick.

Another person relayed a rumor he heard at Utah State University in which a "foreign" student is rushed to the hospital after he collapses from malnutrition brought about by his misguided attempt to subsist solely on packaged ramen noodles.

What we have learned in our forays into private kitchens and a public celebration is that many people who rely on such food products do so with ingenuity and much culinary know-how. People from Hawaii repeatedly emphasized the fact that while many Americans are repulsed by Spam and the way it tastes, this is because "they don't know how to cook it <u>right</u>." Several people indicated that their children expressed disdain for Spam, considering it unappetizing and unhealthy. These individuals dismissed the sincerity of such remarks, however, noting that disdain was engendered because the "younger generation" simply did not know the proper way to cook Spam and despite all their negative comments, they would always eat it when prepared well and served to them. Furthermore, the criteria used in judging dishes at the Hawaiian Community Center Association's Spam Cookoff emphasized the imaginative and convenient aspects of the mass-produced food. These criteria were how the dish tasted, how it was presented visually, and how long it took to prepare.

Ramen and Spam are items that many people regularly pick up on their trips to the supermarket and that share cupboard space with tuna fish, "instant" macaroni and cheese, and bags of rice or pasta. They belong to a class of food whose currency lies in its cheapness, convenience in preparation, and most of all its flexibility. A Spam press release claims: "Spam has endured because of its convenience and versatility. You can eat it hot or cold. You can slice, dice or cube it. You can eat it for breakfast, lunch, dinner or snacks. In fact the only thing that limits your use of Spam is your imagination" (quoted in Chin 1991).

Our research has consistently suggested the ways in which dishes created with little money and/or little time are done so with imagination, taste, and culinary finesse. In those many instances in which the preparer of ramen or "instant" macaroni and cheese utilizes whatever ingredients are at hand, or adds tuna or Spam to enliven an entree, a sense of improvisation characterizes the gastronomic enterprise. This use of ingredients at hand, or "left-overs," and the low price of the products, enable and encourage the repeated preparation of dishes using these products. These repeated experiences, in turn, potentiate the accumulation of associations and memories of social involvements.

By illustrating the places of two mass-produced food items, ramen noodles and Spam, in the individual and collective lives of people, we have attempted to demonstrate the need to more consciously include these types of foods in examinations of food and culture. What we have found interesting in our research is the ways in which individuals, aware of these products' reputations as bland, unhealthy, and/or "poverty foods," create tactics for eating and displaying them in manners that are innovative, personally evocative, and satisfying. What begins as a mass-produced uniform product can serve as a window into a complex network of sociocultural behaviors.

References

Abrahams, Roger. 1984. Equal Opportunity Eating: A Structural Excursus on Things of the Mouth. In *Ethnic and Regional Foodways in the United States: The Performance of Group Identity*, ed. Linda Keller Brown and Kay Mussell, pp. 19–36. Knoxville: The U of Tennessee Press.

Adler, Elizabeth Moxby. 1983. Creative Eating: The Oreo Syndrome. In *Foodways and Eating Habits: Directions for Research*, ed. Michael Owen Jones, Bruce Giuliano and Roberta Krell, pp. 4–10. Los Angeles: California Folklore Society.

Boas, Franz. 1995 [1972]. *Primitive Art*. New York: Dover.

Douglas, Mary. 1972. Deciphering a Meal. *Daedalus* 101 (Winter): 54–72.

Hagstrom, Christine. 1992. Let Them Eat Top Ramen: Pay Hikes Show Contempt for Students. *Los Angeles Times*, 24.

Jones, Michael Owen. 1991. Afterword: Discovering the Symbolism of Food Customs and Events. In *"We Gather Together": Food and Festival in American Life*, ed. Theodore C. Humphrey and Lin T. Humphrey, pp. 235–45. Logan: Utah State Univ. Press.

—. 1993. Aesthetic Attitude, Judgment, and Response: Definitions and Distinctions. In *Exploring Folk Art: Twenty Years of Thought on Craft, Work, and Aesthetics*, pp. 161–75. Logan: Utah State Univ. Press.

Mickler, Ernest Matthew. 1986. *White Trash Cooking*. Berkeley: Ten Speed Press.

Newton, Sarah E. 1992. "The Jell-O Syndrome": Investigating Popular Culture/Foodways. *Western Folklore* 51: 249–68.

Prose, Francine. 1992. Cocktail Hour at the Snake Blood Bar: On the Persistence of Taboo. *Antaeus* 68: 112–19.

Sanchez, Jesus. 1988. Dishing up the Ramen: Los Angeles is Now the Oriental Noodle-Making Capital of the U.S. *Los Angeles Times*, July 4: 119.

Theophano, Janet S. 1991. "I Gave Him a Cake": An Interpretation of Two Italian-American Weddings. In *Creative Ethnicity: Symbols and Strategies of Contemporary Ethnic Life*, ed. Stephen Stern and John Allan Cicala, pp. 44–54. Logan: Utah State Univ. Press.

Tsing Loh, Sandra. 1991. L.A. on $20 a day: Roommates and Ramen: A Guide for Bohemians. *Los Angeles Times*, November 12: S19.

Wyman, Carolyn. 1993. *I'm a Spam Fan: America's Best-Loved Foods*. Stamford, CT: Longmeadow Press.

Yoder, Don. 1972. Folk Cookery. In *Folklore and Folklife: An Introduction*, ed. Richard M. Dorson, pp. 325–50. Chicago: Univ. of Chicago Press.

CHAPTER 16

THE PARADOX OF PRIDE AND LOATHING, AND OTHER PROBLEMS

Simon J. Bronner

"This is fieldwork," another folklorist said to me, grinning, as I consumed a bowl of homemade turtle soup at a church picnic in Fulda, Indiana. "Yes," I replied, "but most people would call it eating." True, I had been told by my colleagues that I had "experienced the artifact," or had been a "participant observer"—orientations which seemed to make my lunch more ethnographic. Underlying these jests, however, is a notion that present methods of collecting and analyzing foodways data are inadequate for an understanding of the complexities of food-related behavior, and a notion perhaps that food researchers are more interested in consuming exotic foods than in explaining food-related behavior. Indeed, too often the literature on foodways merely identifies the completed product rather than elucidating the behaviors associated with that product, and too many researchers seem to adapt their field methods to this literature. Actually, I had not traveled to southwestern Indiana with the intent to undertake a study of turtle consumption or to challenge some conventions in foodways study. But in an effort to document various activities in local communities, I was drawn to the turtle-food complex because it seemed to relate to some basic aspects of human behavior having far-reaching ramifications. The comments on my experience that follow are intended to suggest a few of the limitations of conventional methods in foodways research that I became aware of through my own work and to outline directions for developing new interpretations of food-related behavior.

My previous encounters with interview schedules and questionnaires for the Archive of New York State Folklife had sowed the seeds of dissatisfaction, because I was convinced that such methods treat individuals as one-dimensional, passive recorders of bits of information, rather than as complex, even sometimes capricious, beings who have many options of behavior available to them. Reflection on our own foodways, I realized, should make us aware that behavior and thought are not as static and seemingly ordered as regional food studies based on questionnaires assume or imply.

Nonetheless, as I finished my lunch that day in Fulda, I was still uncertain as to whether I could fully investigate turtle consumption, let alone figure out the best way to proceed. Later, however, while I was exploring a log house in Huntingburg, I saw two men up the road butchering turtles on their front lawn and asked them a few questions. Edwin Englert, a 76-year-old former blacksmith, and his 46-year-old son, Gene, carried on a lively conversation with me regarding their butchering techniques. They also revealed some of their attitudes and feelings towards turtles, personal information that is often neglected in foodways research. It appeared to be a propitious beginning. In subsequent visits to the homes of the Englerts and other turtle butchers, I entered a "directed-interview situation" focusing on these individuals and the specifics of what they said and did. This seemed to solve the problem of how to proceed with the inquiry. Certainly these encounters led me to amass the usual information on the tools and techniques of turtle butchering in southwestern Indiana, which I have reported elsewhere.[1]

Simon J. Bronner, 'The Paradox of Pride and Loathing, and Other Problems', *Western Folklore* 40 (1), Foodways and Eating Habits: Directions for Research (1981), 115–124.

© Western States Folklore Society.

But my observations of the processes involved in the turtle-soup complex, useful as they were in one respect, led to yet other problems—seeming behavioral paradoxes—which needed to be addressed. Two enigmas concerned the eating of turtle soup especially. One problem, created early in the course of my interviews, is that while residents of a small area within southwestern Indiana continue to butcher and regularly to consume turtles at church picnics, few of the people I talked to reported actually liking the taste of turtle meat or even recognizing it (the soup often is confused with vegetable soup), and even fewer enjoyed the work required to hunt, butcher, and prepare the turtles. A second and related problem, which arose while I was trying to answer the first question, is why an individual—not a "community"—often expresses apparently contradictory opinions about the compelling and repulsive qualities of a food or its preparation, such as turtle soup.

If many people do not enjoy the gore of butchering turtles, or the effort to prepare the soup, or the flavor of turtle meat, I asked myself, then why is turtle soup featured so often and so prominently at social events? Neither this nor the second, related question is limited to turtle soup but is relevant to other instances of food-related behavior. For example, some people who raise their own livestock and enjoy the meat consumed at the table, sometimes wonder whether the ends justify the means. Other people refer to dishes composed of an animal's organs euphemistically or with terms that disguise or direct attention away from the object. Certain ethnic dishes, especially strong-smelling or unusual-tasting ones, served and eaten on special occasions, similarly produce conflicting feelings in people. Chitterlings, for instance, are both a symbol of racial pride and a source of embarrassment for many blacks who continue to prepare and eat the food despite the laborious process of preparation. Many restaurants serve headless fish in order to alleviate the discomfort of customers who have to face the creatures eye-to-eye. When they receive the fish, some customers drown the meat in lemon or sauce to remove the "fishy" taste, precisely the flavor intrinsic to the product. The same dual attitude was displayed by my fellow researchers who admitted to being repelled by, but still curious, and therefore attracted to my examination of turtle butchering. The point to be made is that the questions regarding turtle consumption and the methods appropriate to answering these questions pertain as well to other instances of approach-avoidance conflicts in food-related behavior. What might be hypothesized to explain the preparation of turtle soup in a community (even though preparing and eating this soup is met with mixed feelings)? What inferences drawn from foodways research in the past might help illuminate paradoxes regarding other foodstuffs besides turtle soup?

A historical precedent exists, certainly, for eating turtle soup. The Dubois County area in southwestern Indiana has always been predominantly German-Catholic; the restriction by the Catholic Church against eating meat on Fridays did not prohibit the eating of turtle flesh. Nonetheless, this conventional explanation of historical precedent as the sole or principal determinant is questionable because turtle butchering and consumption are not limited to Catholics. Moreover, no informants cited historical precedent as an explanation of their behavior. The paradox of seeming pride and loathing therefore remains unresolved, though obviously turtle soup would not be prepared so often if turtles were not plentiful and the butchering of them acceptable. In fact, however, butchers must often travel as far as southern Illinois to obtain aesthetically pleasing and numerically sufficient quantities of turtles.

Is the preparation and consumption of turtle soup regionally determined, a type of boosterism? This is another solution often proposed in foodways research to explain the popularity of other foods. But it is fraught with inconsistencies and uncertainties. George Blume, an ex-turtle hunter, told me that the people of the neighboring communities of Mariah Hill and St. Henry both "thought they made the best soup even though the turtles came from the same people, and often, the same folks prepared it." People who buy five- and ten-gallon jugs of the soup support through their purchases the claim of some local church members to the best soup available. This fact and George Blume's remark indicate simultaneous *sub*-regional identifications as well as associations with the general "turtle soup area." To complicate matters, informants also had different reasons for eating turtle soup. Several expressed a denial of conformity to a region. And some defended turtle soup consumption by proclaiming simply, "Hell, I've always eaten it." Thus, turtle soup may or may not be a regional symbol. And even if it does sometimes serve as a symbol for some people, a direct connection between the vague concept of regionality in the minds of residents and the persistence of turtle consumption in the world of actual experience is difficult to show.

Perhaps the social significance of turtle soup consumption overrides the loathing felt by some individuals, for at church picnics turtle soup preparation is a labor-intensive endeavor requiring the cooperative effort of many individuals. Men gather in groups while the cooking goes on, and women interact while making preparations for the soup—preparations which may start many days before the picnic. In these situations, turtle soup has perhaps become a ceremonial food that defines the community, maintains social relationships, reinforces loyalty to the church, and provides a framework for interaction essential to the stability of the group. One social aspect of the soup preparation which is particularly pronounced is the sexual division of labor. The men are the hunters and butchers; women are the preparers and preservers. In addition, men assume Sunday cooking and supervisory duties, a pattern not uncommon in America.[2] Some of the men I spoke to at the Mariah Hill picnic did not think of their cooking as a usually feminine task, but rather thought of it as the assumption of a ceremonial function. "Guys always cooked the turtle for special occasions," one informant explained; another said, "Keeps you coming back to the church." This is not to suggest, however, that such functions are causal; they are more properly effects of the tradition. In addition, turtle soup preparation can be an expression of family or individual volition, open to human vagaries, and not just community action, as evidenced by the Englerts' selecting turtle butchering as a role for themselves apart from church picnics and as a foodway in their homes. The functioning of turtle preparation and consumption for social maintenance, then, seems to be an overstatement, ignoring individual motivation and behavior in deference to the a priori model of sociocultural equilibrium. This interpretation insists on homogeneity of behavior and attitude, single-mindedness within a community, and unity of spirit; yet firsthand observations reveal diversity and capriciousness, contrary to what might be expected.

Could turtle soup consumption have an ecological justification? To the Englerts, one of turtle soup's appealing features is its ability to absorb a great variety of food substances common to the area. The desirability of mixing together various vegetables and meat in a soup—the "everything in the garden" sentiment expressed by the Englerts—is echoed by others with whom I spoke. Indeed, people in many areas often have recipes that prevent food waste by calling for a "gumbo" style inclusion of a diversity of food substances. Furthermore, eliminating food discards by feeding them to turtles before butchering offers a convenient disposal system. In this way turtle butchers, like hog butchers, take advantage of the natural ecologic system by manipulating the life-food cycle. The turtle soup tradition supports the butchering of turtles, and conversely, the turtle butchering tradition encourages turtle soup preparation. Yet why would not the ecological justification for hog butchering (which is similar to turtle butchering) and stew (which is similar to the concept of turtle soup) preclude the additional need for turtle butchering and turtle soup? The ecological function, as others cited above, is more likely to be the effect of a phenomenon and not necessarily its cause.

Maybe the pride felt for the success of specialists contributes to the continuance of turtle-butchering and soup-making traditions. Attainment of personal status through turtle specialization is a motivation that could be achieved by individuals who excel at hunting and butchering turtles. Some interviewees expressed great respect for successful hunters and butchers, because of the central role these men play in the church picnics and because they independently follow an "older," rural model of behavior; but informants also recognized that these figures are often peripheral to the community. The Englerts, for example, live on the extreme northern edge of their town on a road officially known as Cour de Lane but commonly, and perhaps revealingly, called

Pig Turd Alley. Thus while personal status achievement is one element in reconciling the paradox of turtle butchering, such achievement also reinforces the conflict by highlighting the singularity of behavior.

Another argument might claim that socially derived and shared food aesthetics and tastes support the continuance of the turtle soup complex by placing turtle consumption in a cognitive category of acceptable meats. Edwin Englert will butcher hogs and turtles, but not cattle—"I don't have the stomach for it," he said. But individuals often defy area standards, proclaiming either their preference for or dislike of turtle butchering in order to establish their individuality or to imply an identification with or against selected others. Personal motivation, then, might actually weaken the tradition of turtle butchering. And the extreme individuality of many tastes, preferences, and aesthetics makes it difficult to establish connections to large aggregates of behavior and makes less defensible in this instance an aesthetic or motivational explanation.

What I have proposed thus far are interpretations suggested by conventional approaches in the study of foodways and eating habits. Each interpretation seems defensible to some extent, but each also appears to be inadequate to the task of solving any of several problems regarding what people eat and why they consume these things. It might even be contended that the seeming paradox of pride and loathing—on the level of abstraction of "community"—results from the very existence of these kinds of explanations in the literature and from their effects on researchers, who confront contradictory evidence while making firsthand observations. For a researcher familiar with the trends and preoccupations in the food-ways literature is likely to assume that the community as a whole perpetuates the tradition of turtle soup (or some other food substance) and that the community simultaneously objects to the continuation of turtle butchering. In fact, however, while turtle soup appears at weekly church picnics during the summer, the turtles are hunted, cared for, and butchered by only a few men; the soup is not prepared or countenanced by everyone; and those who eat the soup are not necessarily of the same mind as to its taste and aesthetics. Thus, disparities as well as continuities in individual behavior and thought must be significant to the analysis of food-ways. And in the search for consistencies in aggregates of human beings, the singular nature of eating and acting should not be neglected in favor of attention to similarities.

It is apparent also that conventional explanations are based on the assumption that paradoxes and the conflicts they manifest need to be resolved; yet the reconciling by the researcher of seemingly conflicting behaviors, such as those that pivot around turtle butchering and consumption, might be presumptuous in light of the coexistence of opposing impulses in the minds of the people they study. Contrary to the usual assumption, attitudes towards foods are not mutually exclusive nor are they static or tangible. It is not uncommon for an individual to entertain—virtually simultaneously—attitudes, beliefs, and preferences that when isolated and examined in the deceiving glare of logic are seemingly incompatible and irreconcilable. The existence of opposing impulses, however, does not necessitate anxiety or dissolution. Indeed, some analysts like Michael Kammen have shown that tensions may stiffen a particular character, provide a strong motivation for action, or supply decision-making options.[3] Often individuals are compelled to approach exotic foods but simultaneously avoid or compromise their approach because of risks sensed in attempting the unprecedented. Yet, this approach-avoidance affects behavioral variations, attitudes, and options in personal food habits—options which change in subsequent food encounters. Human behavior and thought involve processes which allow for a variety of orientations—polarities so to speak—which are comprised of elements one of which may become prominent momentarily while others recede only to give way to those temporarily ignored or suppressed. Individuals thinking these opposing thoughts may or may not recognize the paradox. They may resolve it temporarily in various ways, or they may leave it unresolved, perhaps to trouble themselves occasionally at other times.

Cognitive ideas in the literature on food traditions tend to appear absolute and complete. Yet it must be realized that while models of food-related behavior are available to people, these people make choices and alterations on the basis of their own orientations, the demands of certain situations, and personal assessments of the balance of polarities. The biformity of eating behavior—social activity/singular act—is paralleled by the biformity of social behavior: human beings conform to societal models yet strive to retain an individual identity. Researchers often isolate the societal models without recognizing or appreciating the importance of the individual identities. Hence, all the explanations cited above—separately or in combination—may be relevant depending on particular individuals' attitudes at any given moment. But while some explanations may indicate that harmony exists, one should not be misled into supposing that discord does not exist; for discord is a natural part of the human condition. Thus, many reasons might be given generally as to why some people in southwestern Indiana butcher turtles or eat turtle soup: historic, religious, sociocultural, geographic, and so forth. None, however, is the only explanation or necessarily pertains to any particular individual. Each suits the bias of a discipline, but does not satisfy everyone. And all of them together, when offered as an eclectic explanation, simply underscore but do not account for the disparities in human behavior. We must reconcile ourselves to the fact that human beings are not consistent in their behavior, however disconcerting that fact might be to our analytical egos.

Assuming for a moment that an individual is aware of and distressed by the existence of a paradox in attitude or a conflict between attitude and action, then how does he or she cope with this dilemma? Several mechanisms prevail. Some people express their dislike for the "turtle taste" of turtle soup jokingly, in the form of "nervous laughter," to make their dislike less threatening or less offensive. Others compensate for conflict by reacting in a way contrary to existing standards. That is, an individual may take pride in what others claim to loathe, thus making this person different and presumably superior to those who reject the attitude or activity. Though he himself might not always relish the butchering of a turtle, one of the aspects of frying turtles sometimes appealing to Edwin Englert is watching his wife "squeal" when the turtle's feet "scratch and squirm" as if it were alive in the pan. Still others who butcher turtles, or eat the soup, seem to be aware that not everyone does so and that perhaps the activity is abhorrent to some; perhaps this very fact is a source of justification. Another mechanism for dealing with the conflict is to erect mental blocks to, and to establish "psychic distance" from, the disturbing activity or object. In this way one need not confront the image of the creature whose flesh is being eaten or admit to participating in its destruction (particularly if someone else is required to do the preparation and if the product "masks" the taste or image of the creature). Similarly, an individual may also construct a mental image that redirects the supposed, intended use of an object for consumption (the eating of turtles for their nutritional value) to some other use that might be more acceptable—for example, to allowing people to support the church or to interact with others of a similar regional, ethnic, or religious identity. In the end, however, such mechanisms actually preserve rather than resolve paradoxes by contributing to the persistence of tradition.

In sum, an apparent paradox arising out of observable behaviors may exist largely because of presuppositions in the literature with which researchers are familiar and which affect their conceptions of what to expect; when the expectations are not met but are in fact contradicted, then a dilemma is created. In this instance, turtle butchering and soup preparation seem to be simultaneously encouraged and rejected by the community; however, only some people—and not the "community"—butcher turtles or eat the soup, despite expectations to the contrary. Further, a paradox may actually exist in the thoughts or actions of an individual, a dilemma that might never be resolved by that person or one which can continue because of external factors and internal motivations. Finally, turtle butchering and consumption serve as reminders of a number of matters usually ignored. Aggregates of behavior display disparities as well as continuities; conflicts are inherent in the transmission of models of food-related behavior to which people are exposed; polarities in behavior and thought often are preserved and not always resolved; food and attitudes are dynamic, complex reflections of fundamental thought processes; and food-related behavior must be analyzed in terms of individual options first and foremost. These observations indicate the need for a reorientation in study that will illuminate more fully the complexities of human activities. And they suggest that many specific reasons, rather than a single general one, explain why individuals consume the foods they do—even if or when they eat these things with mixed feelings of pride and loathing.

Notes

1. The technical details and manual procedures of turtle butchering are described in my article "Turtle and All the Trappings," *Center for Southern Folklore Magazine* 3 (1980): 11.

2. See Thomas A. Adler, "Making Pancakes on Sunday: The Male Cook in Family Tradition," in this issue.

3. See his *People of Paradox: An Inquiry Concerning the Origins of American Civilization* (New York, 1972), especially his chapter "Biformity: A Frame of Reference." For other treatments of this concept or something analogous to it, see Margaret Clark and Barbara Gallatin Anderson, *Culture and Aging: An Anthropological Study of Older Americans* (Springfield, Illinois, 1967); John M. Roberts and Michael L. Forman, "Riddles: Expressive Models of Interrogation," *Ethnology* 10 (1971): 509–33; Hasan M. El-Shamy, "Folkloric Behavior: A Theory for the Study of the Dynamics of Traditional Culture" (Ph.D. dissertation, Indiana University, 1967); Michael Owen Jones, *The Hand Made Object and Its Maker* (Los Angeles and Berkeley, 1975), especially 140–67; Simon J. Bronner, "Investigating Identity and Expression in Folk Art," *Winterthur Portfolio* 16 (1981), in press; Milton Sapirstein, *Paradoxes of Everyday Life* (Greenwich, Connecticut, 1955); and Anthony Storr, *The Dynamics of Creation* (New York, 1972).

CHAPTER 17
A PRESERVE GONE BAD OR JUST ANOTHER BELOVED DELICACY? SURSTRÖMMING AND GRAVLAX

Renée Valeri

In the modern world, we demand that methods of preservation should not change the taste and the aspect of foods – perhaps a consequence of freezing becoming more common than other techniques. On the other hand, there are instances where it might be precisely the changes in taste which have contributed to keeping certain preserving methods in existence.

For some foods such as fish, however, postponing consumption is considerably more difficult than for others. All over northern Europe, herring from the North Sea has long been a staple for survival and, for many, the salted version was indeed the epitome of everyday food. However, in the northern part of Sweden, drying and salting were less suitable than they were further south – the former technique for climatic reasons, the latter for financial ones, as salt had to be bought from far away.

In the area of the northern Baltic, using only a small amount of salt, thereby producing fermentation of the fish, has long been a common technique for preserving fish, especially herring, which prepared in this way is called *surströmming* (literal translation: sour, fermented Baltic herring). As in many fermented foods, the result is a long shelf-life and a complex taste. An important side-effect of this fermentation is the strong smell, which many will associate with a food gone bad or one that is rotting.

Another fish that was in great supply in this area in the past was salmon, which gave rise to another rather special preparation, *gravlax* (literal translation: pit salmon). This is to most people a more accessible food, close to raw fish, a quickly made preserve pickled with some salt, sugar, and dill, often eaten with a sauce made with oil, vinegar, mustard and dill.

The first technique (*surströmming*) is interesting for several reasons, one being that fish is an unusual object for preservation other than in its dried, salted and/or smoked state. Even more intriguing, however, is the fact that in research on taste it is striking how most of the food literature has been concerned with what is good and delicious food – and how few examples one will find in the field of food history of writing about 'bad' taste. Today's vast food literature is brimming with suggestions for delicious foods, but few or no examples are given of what is perceived as disgusting – and why.

Still, with the growing interest in the different foods and techniques of preparation typical of other countries or cultures, finding comments and opinions on food from early travellers in this area – as well as more recent ones – could shed some light on the boundaries of taste in different societies or periods of time. Fish is a good subject for a food-mapping of Sweden, since both the surrounding seas and the many lakes and rivers have supplied the population with everyday foods, as well as more recherché ones, throughout history. This paper will focus on just one in each category.

Renée Valeri, 'A Preserve Gone Bad or Just Another Beloved Delicacy? *Surströmming and Gravlax*', in Helen Saberi (ed.), *Cured, Fermented and Smoked Foods: Proceedings of the Oxford Symposium on Food and Cookery 2010* (Totnes: Prospect Books, 2011), pp. 343–352.

Reprinted with permission from author and Prospect Books.

As for the herring, which was historically a most common everyday food all over northern Europe, there is a clear difference between the herring species found in the Atlantic and in the Baltic (Davidson 1989: 26, 29). The latter (called *strömming*) is smaller and less fat than the one from Sweden's west and south coast (*sill*). Whereas there are many local ways of preserving the herring catch (salting, smoking, pickling, drying, etc.), *surströmming* has been the preferred one in the northern Baltic.

Several factors have contributed to the different food habits and preservation techniques in the northern part of the country. Until quite recently, this area was sparsely populated. The long and severe winters accentuated the great distances between villages and towns, especially away from the coast, affecting both trading patterns and other interactions. The original Sami population inland, moving with their herds of reindeer, and the Swedish settlers who lived mostly along the coast, have coexisted there for centuries, but with very different lifestyles.

In spite of good supplies of game, the early descriptions of the life in this area stress that fish was a mainstay of the diet, both fish from the Baltic and freshwater varieties from the numerous rivers and lakes. However, the distances between home and fishing waters, combined with long periods of snow, ice, lack of daylight, and the fact that roads were often not passable during the long spring thaws, necessitated methods of preserving the catch away from home for later retrieval and consumption. Wrapping it in birch bark and burying it in the ground with a little salt was a theory put forward by earlier researchers (Berg 1962: 49ff.) to explain names like *gravlax* ('grav' meaning a place dug in the ground) and the older and more general name for fish preserved like the *surströmming*, i.e. *gravfisk*. The oldest mention is from the province of Jämtland in 1348, where a man called Olafur Graflax changes a fishing allotment.

Another name for this same type of preserved fish was *lundsfisk,* a term used by Carl von Linné during his travels in Dalarna, where he encountered it on August 4, 1737 in the village of Lima: 'They also have lundsfisk here, put in birch bark or other bark, kept in ravines and cold holes, smelled bad, was red by the bones, and said to be delicious for those who liked it' (C. von Linné 1889/1984).

In his sixteenth-century work on many different aspects of the life of Nordic people, the Swedish Archbishop Olaus Magnus points out that salt was not easy to obtain for his Swedish contemporaries (O. Magnus 1555/1976, book 13: 43, on difficulties of importing salt into Nordic countries). This might have been the origin and *raison d'être* of *surströmming*. After the catch in the spawning season in May–June, and as a consequence of only a light salting, the fish starts to ferment in the summer, changing the taste – and adding the smell.

More recently, the *strömming* was put (and sold) in small wooden barrels, and for the last 100 years it has been preserved in metal cans. The prevailing technique is still in two stages: a preliminary light salting, starting the fermentation, followed by a transfer to a second, saltier brine, where the fish is kept for a longer period, ranging from a couple of months to over a year.

The sealed tin cans with today's *surströmming* will not reveal the state of their contents by the smell (as did the wooden kegs), but perhaps by bulging, as long as they are not opened. However, when pierced and opened, the smell of the contents will invariably provoke powerful spontaneous reactions from people nearby, ranging from 'this makes me hungry!' (a 22-year-old student who grew up in the north), to 'this is smell terrorism!' (a 40-year-old woman who had grown up in the south, passing by a *surströmming* dinner).

Although fermentation is fairly widespread as a method of preserving in various parts of the world (*choucroute*, pickles, etc.), not all of them share the contradictory characteristics of offensive smell and good taste. What is interesting in such foods (e.g. the French cheese Époisses, the Roman sauce *garum*, a similar present-day paste called *belatjan* in south-east Asia, and the fruit in the latter area named durian) is that if one is able to overcome the initial adverse reaction to the smell and try them, the taste is quite different – and beloved by its fans. Today, most of the population along the northern Baltic, as well as many *surströmming* converts in the rest of Sweden, celebrate the start of its season in late August with a *surströmming* party or feast.

A threat to the continued enjoyment of this speciality is a ban coming from the EU, caused by today's dioxin-content of Baltic fish. The current exemption ends in 2011, a great concern for many fans. Not surprisingly though, the paradox between smell and taste in *surströmming*, and concern about its health consequences, was actually studied (and put to rest) as early as the late nineteenth century by Carl Th. Mörner, a medical doctor in Uppsala, who in 1895 published a very serious article about *surströmming*. He began by saying that:

> In certain parts of Northern Sweden, there is an odd custom of preserving fish, preparing so-called *surfisk* (sour fish), a collective name covering products prepared from different species of fish and by methods that vary in detail.
>
> Characteristic of all kinds of sour fish is, however, that they are only lightly salted and that the final product has an intense smell, which causes a person unfamiliar with it to involuntarily pull back. The smell of this sour fish is, however, not in a strict sense sour or acidulous, nor does its taste have this quality . . . but it is probably in the meaning of slightly putrid that it has become synonymous with sour fish and related names, such as *surströmming, sursik* [*sik* means whitefish]. Practically unknown south of the river Dalälven (i.e. 60° N), sour fish has a not-insignificant place in the food of the lower classes, and this has probably been the case for a very long time.

The *surströmming* is usually eaten either raw or pan-fried, together with potatoes or bread, and Mörner comments: 'Concerning a food with such an exquisite smell taste like *surströmming*, it is natural that the subjective opinion regarding its taste or palatability goes in two opposite directions; many individuals – and in the regions where *surströmming* is not a common food, these represent the greater number – look on *surströmming* with disgust, whereas others see it as a great delicacy, although it must be admitted, that they usually have come to this conclusion through a shorter or longer period of training.'

Mörner realized, of course, that the reason for the very particular character of *surströmming* is to be found in a chemical alteration of the fresh fish and the impact of certain bacteria, but its nature was not known at the time, since it had not at that point been subjected to scientific enquiry. Naturally, the first question was what exactly gave the *surströmming* its notorious smell and Mörner's research provided an answer. The mixture of gases that emanate when you open a keg of *surströmming* is sufficient to noticeably 'perfume' an entire room in a couple of seconds. Apart from carbon dioxide and hydrogen sulphide (the latter being well-known for its unpleasant smell), another substance, methyl mercaptan (CH_3SH), is a 'primus inter pares' in affecting our olfactory organ, its smell being comparable to rotten cabbage (which incidentally is a comparison also used by the Dutch botanist Rumphius in 1747 when describing the experience of another of the foods mentioned earlier, the south-east Asian fruit durian, *Durio zibethinus*). Since the latter gas is very volatile, and although it is quite noticeable if the *surströmming* is raw, it will almost completely disappear when *surströmming* is grilled, leaving room for other transient smells, such as butyric acid.

So, should *surströmming* be considered a putrid product or not? Mörner's answer is no, basically because of the two-stage process of light salting followed by immersion in a saline solution, which excludes all air. In the first stage, the putrefactive bacteria are modified and, in the second, completely annihilated. In short, there is nothing to indicate that *surströmming* is a foodstuff which is harmful or unsuitable from a health point of view (Mörner 1895–96). Considering that for several centuries it has been eaten by large numbers of people in northern Sweden and Finland, this is reassuring. Whether, however, this also goes for other fermented fish preserves in the Nordic countries, which are more properly defined as 'buried fish' (cf. *gravlax*, above), is difficult to say. They include: shark on Iceland (buried in the gravel just by the water on the shore and eaten raw); the *rakörret* (salmon trout) made sour in Norway; and the tallow buried in the Faeroe Islands that was first allowed to rot slightly, then finely chopped and kneaded into big chunks, which were buried in damp ground and left there for a long period, until it ended up by smelling like old cheese (Bergius, 1780/1960, p. 64).

As mentioned above, the method still in use to produce *surströmming* was earlier used for several kinds of fish, both from the Baltic's brackish water and from inland lakes – the point being not which variety of fish was at hand, but the fact that a surplus catch needed to be preserved in order to serve as a food supply during the winter months. To illustrate this, I provide translations of a couple of answers to a list of questions on *surfisk, gravfisk,* pickled fish, *lutfisk* and similar preparations sent out by the Uppsala Institute for Dialectology and Folklore Research in 1956.

Twenty-seven answers were received from eleven Swedish provinces, mostly north of Stockholm:

For a period, *surströmming* fell into disuse; people did not want to eat 'rotten fish'. Some people 'spoiled' it by making *surströmming au gratin* with breadcrumbs on top. But, after a while, it came back in use again. Now, eating *surströmming* is almost one of the year's rituals. Many want to have a real *surströmming* feast, some eat it with the family – but often they want to have a party and invite some friends – naturally other *surströmming* consumers. Offering them *surströmming au gratin* would be considered cheating, and opening the tins outside would not be acceptable to 'real' *surströmming* consumers. The hosts would provide the *tunnbröd* (thin, flat, unleavened, soft bread) and schnapps. The guests sit down, full of expectation, the tin is opened, the smell spreads and the guests help themselves directly out of the tin. After having eaten a couple directly from the tin, the guests help themselves to *mandelpotatis* (a small kind of almond-shaped potato grown in northern Sweden), and roll the *surströmming* into the *tunnbröd,* accompanied by schnapps (and/or beer). They say real *surströmming* lovers eat up to twenty in one evening.

Both *strömming* and salmon were pickled raw. Preparing such fish was (and still is) considered a great art. Fish was, to a great extent, a poor man's food, except for herring, which was considered good for you and healthy.

(ULMA 219, Gästrikland 29063, 1973)

In the north-western province of Dalarna it was mostly freshwater fish such as roach (*mört*), ide (*id*) and bleak (*löja*) which were preserved with salt as *surfisk* (or *gamtfisk*). Spawning fish were preferred and could be caught in larger quantities. The roe of *mört* and *id* was eaten in different ways, for instance, spread on *tunnbröd*. The bones were removed from larger fish, after which the remainder could more easily be spread on the bread.

The *surfisk* can be saved for years as long as it is kept in a cool place after fermentation is completed, if it is well covered by the brine, and the stone weight is heavy enough to press out all the brine. As such, it is a good complement to potatoes and bread. The blood by the backbone is left, as it colours the brine and thus the fish.

The spawning fish caught from mid-May until around midsummer was not ready for consumption as *surfisk* until the end of September. Had it been kept in a warm place, however, it would be ready much earlier, although it should not be in large containers. This type of preparation still exists.

There is a big difference in taste between *surfisk* and *surströmming*. To us the preparation of *surströmming* is a secret. The fish prepared in one of the ways above is called *surfisk* or *gamtfisk*.

The *surfisk* was poor man's food, but even the rich liked it. Spring or autumn fish is the tastiest. Properly cooked and prepared fish is considered healthy.

To 25–30 kg fish one should use a little more than 1 kg crushed coarse-grained salt (fish salt). After salting, the container should be left untouched for three days, so the salt will dissolve, and the brine cover the fish. The temperature during this time should be 15°C, after which a weight (of no more than 10 kg) is placed on the fish to ensure that the brine covers it. The same temperature should be maintained afterwards, if possible. After a month, or at most six weeks, the fish will be ready as *surfisk*, and one can start consuming it – but when some has been taken out, the stones must be replaced.

(ULMA 23669, Dalarna, 1957)

Early Swedish sources rarely go into detail on everyday food preparation among the common people. However, even at that time there was obviously a difference between those who were offered *gravlax* and those who would encounter the fermented *surströmming*. Messire Aubéry du Maurier, visiting the Swedish Chancellor Axel Oxenstierna at the Swedish court in 1637, says in his *Mémoires* that he often ate there and one of the dishes offered was 'sundried salmon, in Sweden called *Lacs*, with a sauce made of oil, vinegar and pepper; and he told me one day that he found this *Lacs* better than he did the Bisques that had been served to him by the Cardinal de Richelieu & to confirm this, he cut a slice of this dried salmon, and ate it, after having dipped it in the sauce, with the best appetite in the world.'

In the seventeenth and eighteenth centuries, a number of foreign travellers came to visit Sweden and wrote accounts of their experiences in what was then quite an exotic country – partly since those who actually went beyond the court in Stockholm often made for Lapland and the Sami people in the far north. Since the latter lived a very different life from the settlers on the coast, food descriptions would naturally focus on reindeer products, and occasionally on venison, berries, etc., depending on the season (and they did not use salt, nor consume *surströmming*). However, some travellers also provided interesting descriptions of huge salmon traps in the rivers (Acerbi 1802).

In the same period, we find a surge of topographical sources, a number of which mention the existence of *surströmming* (sometimes under local names) as well as *gravlax*. Carl von Linné, on his early travels to investigate Sweden's economy, makes passing notes about it in the province of Dalarna and some years later in his travel account of Lapland – although that was on his return through Finland (at that time part of Sweden, not becoming independent until 1809).

In the early nineteenth century, a new type of traveller appeared, more like the travel journalists or tourists of today. One example is the Scotsman Samuel Laing (1839), who described the *strömming* fishery in Hudiksvall:

The stromming is about the size of a sprat, but is a much more delicate fish. They are cured like herrings; and a barrel of salted stromming is as necessary in every household on this side of the peninsula, as the barrel of herrings on the other. They are also used extensively over all Finland and the north of Russia. In these countries, salt is a scarce commodity in the interior. The sea affords none, and all that is used must come from Spain, France, or England. Salted fish seems to be the cheapest form in which salt can be carried into the interior; and from some natural craving of the constitution for salt as a condiment, people here relish, in a way we who are abundantly supplied with salt cannot understand, a dish once or twice a week of salted herrings. A herring or stromming raw out of the pickle, and bread with soup of milk or beer, make a favourite repast even in families of condition.

Laing also comments on salmon, a fish which was very common indeed in Swedish rivers in the past, and therefore a likely object for preservation. There are examples of work contracts from the west coast of Sweden, stipulating that the employees would not have to eat salmon more than a couple of days each week. With the expansion of various Swedish riverside industries in modern times, the quantity of domestic salmon has been reduced, and most of what is consumed today is the imported and cultivated variety, prepared in a very different way. Today's *gravlax* is a short-term preserve, closer to raw fish: the fleshy side of two equally sized pieces of fish are rubbed with salt, sugar and crushed pepper, liberally strewn with chopped fresh dill, and put together in the form of a sandwich. They are chilled for a couple of days with a heavy weight on top. The fish is eaten in thin slices, preferably with a dill-mustard sauce and has a very delicate taste. This version has been exported to restaurant menus in various countries – a fate which will hardly befall *surströmming*.

Laing also experienced eating *gravlax* (in Umeå):

> There is nothing of Lapland here, except perhaps in the food. I had seen graf lax . . . raw salmon, on the carte of a restaurateur in Stockholm; and seeing other people eat it with relish, I called for a portion too, but could not bring myself to swallow a slice of raw fish. Here it was put down for breakfast along with slices of smoked salmon, and slices of smoked reindeer flesh, but none of these articles had ever been on the fire. The two German shipmasters breakfasted at the same time, but could make nothing of these raw materials. I determined to try, since such is the food of the country – and I must live like the people of the country, to know how they live – and with oil, vinegar, and pimento, which is used here instead of black pepper, I found graf lax not a bad thing. The meat, however, of these fresh-water salmon (. . .) is of a finer texture, and is not oily or stringy; which I suspect a raw slice of a Tweed salmon would be.

Another traveller, Friedrich Wilhelm von Schubert, professor of theology in Greifswald, who travelled in Sweden in 1817, describes the fishing of salmon in a river much further south, near Gävle, and comments that,

> the salmon is here prepared in the same way as in the north of Sweden, i.e. it is salted like in other areas, boiled, fried, smoked, but it is also prepared as so-called Gravlax, and this is mostly the habit in Norrland, but it is also supposedly common in Scotland. To prepare gravlax, the fresh raw salmon is cut in pieces, which are strewn with salt and some sugar, and left so covered for a shorter or longer period of time, preferably two or three days. This way the salmon keeps for a rather long time, mostly so if it is salted twice, which is the custom in some places. With oil, vinegar, and sugar the gravlax is a tastier preparation than boiled or smoked. A necessary condition for this preparation is that it takes place as soon as possible after the catch. Only fifteen minutes later the salmon is edible, but the taste is still better if it has been in the salt for a couple of hours or for a day. . . . Gravlax is quite different from the salmon which has been salted in the usual stronger way. The latter will keep for several years, whereas the smoked one soon will be tough and be of no use, a reason why salmon smoking is in use in few places in Norrland, where the salmon fishery is such an important industry. By adding flour or grain people also make salmon soup, called salmon gruel.

Admittedly, *gravlax,* in spite of its unusual seasoning (salt, sugar, pepper and dill) and the fact that some people will hesitate because of its close relation to raw fish, is much easier to accept as food than its 'cousin' *surströmming.* The latter is indeed an odd preserve, which to newcomers invariably raises the question of why it was ever invented.

One answer is the history of salt in the north. Unlike Norway, Sweden had no natural salt deposits. Many attempts to extract salt on the west (North Sea) coast failed, and earlier the Swedes had no need to do so, since they bought their salt from the Dutch and German ships coming from Spanish, French and British ports who sold it at a reasonable price (O. Magnus). The weak point in this trade was, of course, that in wartime, such as during the sixteenth century, the salt trade becomes a political issue, affecting the Swedish national economy. Shrinking supplies of salt affected the food stores of settlers and fishermen in northern Sweden, already dependent on barter for their subsistence (O. Magnus 1555/1976, Book 13, chapter 43–44; for a more detailed account of salt in Sweden, see Bonge-Bergengren, 1989).

Nature was generous in supplying fish for subsistence, but in order to store the catch of spawning herring (or other fish) for winter needs, salt was necessary. The different techniques used traditionally have been well described in the answers to questionnaires above, sent out by the Swedish institutes of ethnology. Comparing these answers, stretching back to the mid-eighteenth century, with descriptions and comments in printed and archival sources of the past, we find that the technique of *surströmming* has been an acquired taste in the north. But looking at the contemporary situation, with comments on the internet and interviews with *surströmming*-converts in the very south of Sweden (born and raised with very different food and taste habits), the acceptance of this food is no longer learned, but a matter of personal choice.

Dr Mörner's research, quoted in the beginning of this article, was no doubt a relief to many *surströmming* consumers at the time, although a large number of them had come to similar results through personal empirical research. At his time (the end of the nineteenth century), an 'export' of *surströmming* was already taking place to people in the area north of Stockholm. Indeed, the consumption is still spreading to parts of the country well beyond the northern regions. Today *surströmming* is sold to, and consumed by people originating from the very south of the country, albeit on a smaller scale than in the north. There is even a health-food based on it . . .

It is probably no coincidence that Mörner's research was published about the same time as an interest in culinary matters, of French origin, became noticeable in Sweden. Another man combining a medical profession with a great interest in and knowledge of the art of cooking was Charles Emil Hagdahl, author of *Kok-Konsten som vetenskap och konst* (The Art of Cookery, as a Science and an Art), the 'Swedish Brillat-Savarin', clearly also inspired by A. Dumas. He describes *surströmming* in the following manner:

> *Surströmming* is an old preparation, which nature itself has always taken care of ever since the creation of the world. Our first parents caught the scent of it just outside the gates of Paradise, and it was a well-known smell from earliest times, beside all the *kjökkenmöddingar* (kitchen middens) and the *pålhyddor* (pile-huts), as well as for the Greeks and Romans, for everyone knew what rotten fish meant; but the taste for it was not yet as developed as it is now – people did not yet know *haut goût*. *Surströmming* is eaten only by the initiated, *au naturel*, without any other sauce than that the mouth waters. They consider it a delicacy of the most sublime kind; but it will never become a festive food, unless the host prefers to eat alone, or maybe chooses guests who have no nose.

Although Hagdahl has been proved wrong in predicting the *surströmming*'s role today, the question might now be more one of why the new adepts (addicts?) have adopted a dish which has such a bad reputation, and which is socially exclusive in shared housing situations. For today's mobile population, one answer might lie in our desire to expand the boundaries of taste – be they geographical or physical, or both. The closely related preserve *gravlax* has had a less controversial history. Made in a couple of days, it is eaten practically raw, although this to some people can also be repugnant. Here the boundary is maybe more one of nature/culture, which can be difficult for some civilized individuals.

Thus, in the final analysis, both preparations mentioned are interesting through their place on the outer margins of food habits. *Surströmming* questions our sense of smell, which since ancestral times is supposed to have been basic for selecting what is safe to eat or what should be avoided. *Gravlax* challenges our idea of defining ourselves as civilized persons, who should eat cooked meat or fish (cf. Lévi-Strauss, *Le Cru et le cuit*), a concept which has been loosened through travel and food-custom exchanges (cf. sushi) in recent years. One young woman travelling to the north and trying *surströmming* for the first time with some trepidation, commented that just after the meal she thought that it was fun to try, but once was enough. But thinking back, a few weeks later, she would definitely sit down for some more – just as she had with sushi. Maybe that is how taste is acquired.

References

Andersson, Sten. *Matens roller.* Almqvist & Wiksell Förlag AB, 1980.

Acerbi, Joseph, *Travels through Sweden, Finland and Lapland, in the years 1798–1799.* London, 1802.

Aubéry du Maurier, Louis, *Memoires de Hambourg, de Lubeck et de Holstein, de Dannemarck, de Suede et de Pologne.* Amsterdam, 1736.

Berg, Gösta, 'Gravlax och surströmming', in *Gastronomisk Kalender.* Stockholm, 1962.

Bergius, Bengt, Tal om läckerheter både i sig själva sådana och för sådana ansedda genom Folkslags bruk och inbillning [Speech at the meeting of the Royal Academy of Sciences on May 3, 1780: About delicacies, both those being so in themselves and those considered as such through people's usage and imagination]. Printed by Victor Pettersons Bokindustri AB, Stockholm, 1960.

Bonge-Bergengren, Inge, *Den nödvändiga sältan.* Fataburen, 1989, pp. 123–141.

Bonnefon, Paul. *Mémoires de Louis-Henri de Loménie Comte de Brienne,* dit Le Jeune Brienne, Paris, 1916.

Consett, Matthew, *A tour through Sweden, Swedish Lapland, Finland and Denmark. . .* London, 1789.

Davidson, Alan, *North Atlantic Seafood.* New York: Harper & Row (Perennial Library edn), 1989.

—, *The Oxford Companion to Food.* Oxford: Oxford University Press, 1999.

—, *Sea Food: a connoisseur's guide and cookbook.* London: Mitchell Beazley, 1989.

Hagdahl, Charles Emil: *Kok-konsten som vetenskap och konst* (The art of cookery as science and art), 2nd revised edn. Stockholm, 1896.

Hogguer, Daniel von. *Reise nach Lappland und dem nördlichen Schweden.* G. Reimer: Berlin, 1841.

Keyland, Nils, *Svensk Allmogekost.* Carlsson Bokförlag in co-operation with the Inst. f. Folklivsforskning och Nordiska Muséet, 1989.

Linnaeus, Carl, *Dalaresan/Iter Dalecarlia, Natur och Kultur* 1889/1984.

—, *Lappländska resan/Iter Lapponicum 1732,* edited by Magnus von Platen & Carl-Otto von Sydow. Wahlström och Widstrand, 1957.

Mat i Västerbotten, Västerbottens Museum och Två Förläggare Bokförlag, Umeå 1985.

Mörner, Carl Th. 'Meddelande om surströmming', in *Uppsala läkareförenings "Förhandlingar"* 1895–96, pp. 365–373.

Olaus Magnus, *Historia om de Nordiska Folken,* Roma 1555 (1976, second edition, together with Inst. för folklivsforskning vid Nordiska muséet. Kommentar av prof. John Granlund).

Outhier, Reginaud. *Journal d'un voyage au Nord en 1736 & 1737.* Paris, 1744.

Scheller, Johann Gerhard. *Reisebeschreibung nach Lappland und Bothnien.* Jena, 1713.

Schubert, Friedrich Wilhelm von. *Reise durch Schweden, Norwegen, Lappland, Finnland und Ingermanland in den Jahren 1817, 1818 und 1820.* Bd 1–3. Leipzig 1823–24.

Seigneur A de la. *Motrayes resor 1711–1725* (facsimile edition by Rediviva 1988, from the 1912 edition).

Talve, Ilmar. *Folkligt kosthåll i Finland en översikt.* Gleerup, 1977.

Archival sources

DAUM: Institute of Language and Folklore research in Umeå

ULMA: Uppsala Institute for Dialectology and Folklore Research

Nordiska Muséet: Collection of excerpts by Prof. Gösta Berg concerning surströmming and gravlax.

CHAPTER 18
PLAYING TO THE SENSES: FOOD AS
A PERFORMANCE MEDIUM

Barbara Kirshenblatt-Gimblett

Points of Contact: Performance, Food and Cookery, a conference organized by the Centre for Performance Research in Cardiff (13–16 January 1994) was a food event in its own right. We heard papers on everything from 'Banquets as Gesamtkunstwerk' and 'The archeology of the trifle' to 'How the French played with their food: Carême and the *pièce montée*'. We sampled durian, a large tropical fruit with a horny peel and creamy lobes of flesh – it exudes a penetrating aroma of vanilla, rotten eggs, almonds, turpentine and old shoes. We saw the East Coast Artists' *Faust/Gastronome*, directed by Richard Schechner, violate the boundaries of the body when performers passed chewed food from mouth to mouth. Bobby Baker performed *Drawing on a Mother's Experience,* in which she recited the painful story of her life, while flinging onto a white sheet the contents of her shopping bags – cold roast beef, tomato chutney, sponge fingers, brandy, black treacle, sugar, eggs, Guinness, flour, skimmed milk, tinned black currants, frozen fish pie, and Greek strained sheep's-milk yogurt – finally rolling herself up in the sheet.[1] We feasted at Happy Gathering, a nearby Chinese restaurant, sampled Welsh cheeses, and alternated roasted meats and rounds of polyphony at a Georgian banquet in a local church. We watched an instructional video on how to slaughter and butcher a pig and another of a street vendor in Thailand tossing morning glory (water convolvulus) in a glorious arc from his fiery wok to a plate held by a waiter across the street. We cooked our own Welsh breakfasts of sausage, laver-bread (seaweed) and eggs in iron skillets on stoves brought into the conference space for the purpose – preceded by a lecture-demonstration, of course. We 'harvested' our lunch in the edible greenhouse, entitled *A Temperate Menu*, created by Alicia Rios.

Attentive to what is performative about food, we looked at the most ordinary and the most extraordinary food events and not only at domestic and professional cooks, but also at artists who work with food. Since cooking techniques, culinary codes, eating protocols and gastronomic discourses are already so highly elaborated, what is there left for professional artists who choose to work with food as subject or medium to do? Food, and all that is associated with it, is already larger than life. It is already highly charged with meaning and affect. It is already performative and theatrical. An art of the concrete, food, like performance, is alive, fugitive and sensory.

Food and performance converge conceptually at three junctures. First, *to perform is to do,* to execute, to carry out to completion, to discharge a duty – in other words, all that governs the production, presentation and disposal of food. To perform in this sense is to make food, to serve food. It is about materials, tools, techniques, procedures, actions. It is about getting something done. It is in this sense, first and foremost, that we can speak of the performing kitchen.

Barbara Kirschenblatt-Gimblett, 'Playing to the Senses: Food as a Performance Medium', *Performance Research* 4 (1) (1999), 1–30. (Excerpt printed here: 1–3, 6–7, 8, 11–15, 16–17, 18–19, 20, 21–24, 25–30. Omitted text is indicated by ellipses.) Reprinted by permission of the publisher (Taylor & Francis Ltd, http://www.tandfonline.com).

Second, *to perform is to behave*. This is what Erving Goffman calls the performance in everyday life. Whether a matter of habit, custom, or law, the divine etiquette of ritual, codifications of social grace, the laws governing cabarets and liquor licenses, or the health and sanitation codes, performance encompasses the social practices that are part and parcel of what Pierre Bourdieu calls *habitus*.[2] To perform in this sense is to behave appropriately in relation to food at any point in its production, consumption, or disposal, each of which may be subject to precise protocols or taboos. Jewish and Hindu laws of ritual purity and formal etiquette stipulate the requirements in exquisite detail. They involve the performance of precepts, as well as precepts of performance.[3]

Third, *to perform is to show*. When doing and behaving are displayed, when they arc shown, when participants are invited to exercise discernment, evaluation and appreciation, food events move towards the theatrical and, more specifically, towards the spectacular. It is here that taste as a sensory experience and taste as an aesthetic faculty converge. The conflation of the two meanings of taste can be found in Enlightenment aesthetics and in the Hindu concept of *rasa* alike.[4]

During the Enlightenment, aesthetics was realigned from 'a science of sensory knowledge' to a philosophy of beauty in relation to sensory experience.[5] The sensory roots of aesthetic response were, however, preserved. While taste as an aesthetic faculty lacks a dedicated organ, Enlightenment aesthetics thought of it as *'le sens interne du beau'* or the 'sixth sense within us, whose organs we cannot see'.[6] Moreover, gastronomic metaphors for aesthetic response inflected the visual with the gustatory (Voltaire compared the taste for beauty in all the arts with the ability of the tongue and palate to discern food) and the tactile (Voltaire wrote that 'Taste is not content with seeing, with knowing the beauty of a work; it has to feel it, to be touched by it').[7] Touch in this context both concretizes emotional response, and speaks to what el-Khoury calls the 'tactility of taste'.[8] Given that gastronomy and eroticism share not only touch but also appetite and oral pleasure, Enlightenment thought associated the two, particularly in the figure of the libertine and the orgy.

As a sensory experience, taste operates in multiple modalities – not only by way of the mouth and nose, but also the eye, ear and skin. How does food perform to the sensory modalities unique to it? A key to this question is a series of dissociations. While we eat to satisfy hunger and nourish our bodies, some of the most radical effects occur precisely when food is dissociated from eating and eating from nourishment. Such dissociations produce eating disorders, religious experiences, culinary feats, sensory epiphanies, and art.

Sensory dissociations

The distinction of the senses is arbitrary.

(Marinetti)

Food that is dissociated from eating bypasses the nose and mouth. Such food may well be subject to extreme visual, and for that matter tactile and verbal, elaboration. The showpieces in culinary olympics and exhibitions of pastry and confectionery are exhibited, but they arc not generally eaten (with the exception of hot entries). Eat them at their freshest and there would be nothing to exhibit. Wait till after the exhibition and they are not worth eating. They are literally a feast for the eye and they are called *showpieces*. Food stylists produce a toxic cuisine that may well look more edible and delicious than real food, particularly under hot studio lights. Featured in images that sell food, magazines and cookbooks, dishes fashioned from substances never destined for the mouth 'look good enough to eat'. They are a case of inedible spectacle.

The task of the stylist is to 'show' sensory experiences that are invisible, or more accurately, to provide visual cues that we associate with particular tastes and smells, even in the absence of gustatory and olfactory stimuli. In this regard, the art of studio food is at once mimetic (the dish prepared for the camera must look as if it could grace the table) and indexical (the visual details must index qualities that we can know only from other sensory modalities). From color, steam rising, gloss and texture, we infer taste, smell and feel, as well as whether the food in question is supposed to have been fried, roasted, baked, steamed, or grilled, and whether it is hot or cold. Taste is something we anticipate and infer from how things look, feel to the hand, smell (outside the mouth), and sound. We use these sensory experiences to tell, before putting something into the mouth, if it is fresh, ripe, or rotten, if it is raw or cooked, if it is properly prepared. Our survival, both biological and social, depends on such cues. So does our pleasure.

Our eyes let us 'taste' food at a distance by activating the sense memories of taste and smell. Even a feast for the eyes only will engage the other senses imaginatively, for to see is not only to taste, but also to eat. The chef's maxim, 'A dish well presented is already half eaten', recognizes that eating begins (and may even end) before food enters the body.[9] The cookery shows seen on television – there are now channels devoted entirely to food – are a way of eating it with the eyes by watching others prepare, present and consume food, without either cooking or eating it oneself. Cookbooks, now more than ever, are a way of eating by reading recipes and looking at photographs. Those books may never see the kitchen. Indeed, experienced readers can sightread a recipe the way a musician sightreads a score. They can 'play' the recipe in their mind's eye.

While not unique to the experience of food, visual aspects of food are no less essential to it. First, the eyes play a critical role in stimulating appetite. Visual appeal literally makes the mouth water, gets the juices going, starts the stomach rumbling – in other words, sets the autonomic reflexes associated with digestion in motion. These responses – salivation, secretion of gastric juices, hunger pangs – are involuntary, spontaneous, instinctive, though the cues are ones that we learn. Second, the eyes are bigger than the stomach. This is not only a reason not to shop for food when hungry, but also an incentive to feast with the eyes. Visual interest can be sustained long after the desire to taste and smell has abated and appetite has been sated. Perhaps for this reason, the most spectacular displays are likely to come at the end of the meal.

[…]

While taste is an analytic sense – we can clearly distinguish sweet, salt, sour, and bitter – smell is widely held to be a holistic sense. To discriminate its many components (the olfactory system can sense thousands of different molecules), it seems to be necessary to encode the olfactory verbally in memory.[10] This is what the language of wine-tasting is about. Michael Broadbent's account of a 1981 red Bordeaux (Chateau Pétrus) reads like a description of a musical performance in a delicatessen:

Five notes: Black; dumbness, concealing depth of fruit; full, fleshy, rich, complete – sort of puppy fat a year after the vintage. Next, in magnum, at Frericks' Pétrus tasting in 1986; medium-deep, plummy, spicy bouquet developing, meaty, calf's foot jelly. At the 'Stockholm' Group blind vertical tasting in 1990, one of the few vintages I got right. Maturing; a bit hard at first but opened up. Crisp fruit; rather leathery texture, acidity noticeable. Most recently decanted in the office, laste, then taken to the Penning-Rowsells'. Four hours later, opulent, mulberry-like fruit; seemed sweeter, full of fruit flavour though blunt.[11]

Broadbent last tasted this wine in 1990, a year before he published this account, and no doubt will keep tasting it to the year 2005, the last year he recommends for it.

Wine is alive. It matures over the years and changes in even a few hours. It is an event. Even a single taste can be like an Act in a play that is as long as the life of the vintage. The succession and duration of sensations in that single mouthful is what Roland Barthes calls tiering in his commentary on Brillat-Savarin's *Physiology of Taste*. After noting the movement from excitement to stupefaction that Brillat-Savarin attributes to champagne and Barthes to whisky, Barthes describes taste as the sense that 'experiences and practices multiple and successive apprehensions – beginnings, recurrences, overlappings, a whole counterpoint of sensation: to the arrayed arrangement of the sense of sight (in great panoramic delights) corresponds the *tiering of taste*'.[12] Indeed, he says of the gustatory sensation that when submitted to time it can 'develop somewhat in the manner of a narrative, or of a language'.[13] It could be said that a particular wine is inferred from these sensations, which themselves tell the story of the climate, the soil, the grape, the cultivation, the processing, the pre-phylloxera years, the barrel – by a process of learned associations and inferences, aided by language.

A key to this process is olfaction, which stands in a special relationship to memory. While difficult to recall, once an aroma registers and the next time it is experienced, it can call up vivid memories of its previous contexts. Indeed, its ability to do so is involuntary and it is through disciplined attention and verbal description that wine tasters develop the ability to remember and identify tastes. Smell is the 'most interior' and 'least informative' of the senses, according to Kant.[14] This is one reason why wine-tasters use language to exteriorize the information they derive from sensory experience. As Hans Ruin notes in his essay on the phenomenology of smell:

> The paradoxical objectivity of smell is that it is more intruding, more immediate, than any other sensation, and at the same lime essentially fleeting and elusive. Its presence is never permanent. Not even when that which emits it is present in its materiality is it possible to remain attentive to the smell. . . . Smell does not permit the continuous examination and enrichment of the first impression which we take for granted, when it comes to the other senses. . . . The nose must continue to act incessantly, without being able to store the impression. The impression does not become more dense, it is not solidified as when we concentrate on a tone or a color. If is always evaporating.[15]

[...]

Along the alimentary canal

All my experiences are visceral.

(Dali)

There is another body of work that takes as its site the alimentary canal proper, from the mouth into the viscera and out through the anus. While experiences associated with the inside of the mouth, the throat, where there are also taste receptors, and the nasal cavity have been aestheticized through cuisine, wine and gastronomy, experiences of food inside the body cavity have been understood largely in terms of science, medicine and religion, and specific practices associated with them – dissection, surgery, spiritual discipline, and moral order. When artists enter the alimentary canal, what do they do? They visualize the inside of the body, they externalize it by presenting substances suggestive of it, and they project photographs and videos of the body's interior. Some artists literally make the insides perform by activating the entire alimentary canal through the process of eating or by violently disrupting the normal operation of the digestive tract by inducing vomiting, pissing, or shitting.

[...]

Art/life

> . . . nonart is more art than Art art,

> (Allan Kaprow)

The materiality of food, its dynamic and unstable character, its precarious position between sustenance and garbage, its relationship to the mouth and the rest of the body, particularly the female body, and its importance to community, make it a powerful performance medium. Indeed, it could be said that food and the processes associated with it are performance art *avant la lettre*. This presents an obstacle and an opportunity to artists. Food's already artfulness is an obstacle to those working in the gap and across the boundary between art and life, for the life they value is precisely that which is not (or not yet) art until their intervention makes it so. Through extreme attentiveness, contextualization, framing, arbitrary rules and chance operations, these artists are attracted to the phenomenal, towards raw experience, or towards the social as the basis for a participatory art practice, or towards process, rather than a permanent work that can enter the art market. They gravitate towards materials not usually associated with a fine art practice and attend to the particularity of those materials. They are likely to produce actions (which may or may not be events) and to leave documents, relics, souvenirs, detritus, and other evidence of those actions.

In contrast, those for whom food's already artfulness is an opportunity look to the arts of everyday life for a resource that they work on right where it is, taking the life world itself as their site of operation, or they divert it into the art world, or make the two converge. Recognizing what is already artful in life, they may curate it or they may collaborate with ordinary people. In either case, this is an aesthetics other than that of Hegel. It takes its cue from the already total performance of the life world.

It is precisely in opposition to the notion of art as an autonomous object, in prescribed media and spaces, that the historical avant-garde and postwar experimental performance proceed. Food offers them a performance medium on the boundaries and at the intersections of the life world and the art world. While considerable attention has been accorded food as image, theme, or symbol, less is understood about food as a performance medium and the particular ways in which food and the settings and events associated with it engage the senses. While many historical examples of table and stage inspiring each other could be cited, experimental performance during the twentieth century, especially after the Second World War, offers a particularly rich array of possibilities.

Reviewing the role of food in performance art, Linda Montano classified what she had found prior to 1981 as follows:

> Artists have used food as *political statement* (Martha Rosier, the Waitresses, Nancy Buchanan, Suzanne Lacy), as a *conceptual device* (Eleanor Antin, Howard Fried, Bonnie Sherk, Vito Acconci), as *life principle* (Tom Marioni, Les Levine), as *sculptural material* (Paul McCarthy, Joseph Beuys, Kipper Kids, Terry Fox, Carolee Schneemann, Motion, Bob & Bob), for *nurturance and ritual* (Barbara Smith), for *props and irony* (Allan Kaprow), as a *scare tactic* (Hermann Nitsch), in *autobiography* (Rachel Rosenthal), as *feminist statement* (Suzanne Lacy, Judy Chicago, Womanhouse), in *humor* (Susan Mogul), for *survival* (Leslie Labowitz).[16]

While useful, these categories are not commensurate with one another, however accurately they differentiate the work. Consider instead how these and other artists insert themselves into the food system, work with and against it, or produce work about or outside of it.

All three senses of performance – to do, to behave, to show – operate all through the food system, but vary according to which sense of performance is focal, elaborated, or suppressed, For the purposes of this analysis, the food system may be segmented into five processes (the order may vary and one process may and generally does occur more than once): procuring and producing (hunting, gathering, cultivation); storage, distribution and exchange; processing and preparation; consumption; and disposal. These processes have been elaborated (or simplified) in historically and culturally specific ways so that they are at once repetitive tasks and customary practices. Ritual protects the hunter, increases the crop, governs tithes, and surrounds the eating of first fruits. Balinese temple festivals are like a systemic clock in the way that they time and regulate the flow of water into rice paddies along terraces.[17] Work songs synchronize the movements of grinding or pounding and make repetitive tasks less boring. Rules of reciprocity and laws of ritual purity govern who may accept food from whom, while etiquette stipulates how those who cat together must behave. The tools and techniques for brewing and baking, roasting and steaming, cutting and mashing may be staged as performances in their own right. On a small scale, patrons can see into restaurant kitchens. On a large scale, entire events are organized around the boiling and baking of a 900-lb (400-kg) bagel or the frying of a gigantic omelet – 70,000 eggs and 200 lb (90 kg) of truffles.[18] Highly staged feasts are overtly theatrical. Depending on who touched them, leftovers are sacred or polluting. They are discarded or recirculated or recycled.

Performing the food cycle

When the durians come down, the sarongs go up.

(Malay proverb)

Production

Two archetypes, the Garden of Eden and the Last Supper, inform the work of several performance artists working with food, whether explicitly or implicitly. Gardens, with their long histories, are prime examples of multi-sensory environments and an art form in their own right, whether formally designed by professional landscape architects or vernacular expressions of local knowledge. Adam Purple's 'Garden of Eden', created from the detritus of abandoned buildings on the Lower East Side during the economic downturn in New York City in the 1970s, was an indictment of a city government that had allowed the urban fabric to disintegrate. Laid out in relation to a cosmic plan visible from outer space and cultivated using the gardener's own nightsoil, the 'Garden of Eden' was first and foremost a life work, though many considered it an art work. During an economic upturn, the city destroyed the garden and built public housing on the plot.[19]

Farming dictated by values other than maximizing profit has many of the qualities valued by performance artists. Intentional societies such as the Amish eschew what they deem to be unnecessary technologies. Alternative communities such as the biodynamic followers of Austrian philosopher Rudolf Steiner (1861–1925), whose anthroposophy offered a new science of cosmic influences, work from a kind of cookbook of 'biodynamic preparations': 'Naturally occurring plant and animal materials arc combined in specific recipes in certain seasons of the year and then placed in compost piles. These preparations bear concentrated forces within them and are used to *organize* the chaotic elements within the compost piles. When the process is complete, the resulting Preparations are *medicines* for the Earth which draw new forces from the cosmos.'[20]

While advocates of biodynamic farming cite scientific verification of the efficacy of their methods, they are guided in the first instance by spiritual values. They envision the farm as a self-sufficient entity in harmony with the Earth, consistent with the principles enunciated by Steiner in a series of lectures that he delivered in

1924, toward the end of his life. In 'Spiritual foundations for the renewal of agriculture', he imagines the farm in corporeal terms – the soil is a diaphragm and 'planetary forces [are] active in the "head" (below ground) and in the "belly" (above ground).'[21] He accords smell importance in developing a personal relationship to farming, and in particular to manure and composting. Cows-horns filled with manure to collect forces beneficial to crops are ritually inserted into the ground. Inspired by Christian and Eastern mysticism, Steiner was a prodigious lecturer and author and produced, in addition to his farming manual and series of lectures on bees, books on performance dealing with such topics as eurhythm as visible speech and song, creative speech, and the art of acting. Steiner spawned a movement, complete with schools, a philosophy of art, and farms.

In contrast with these idiosyncratic and programmatic projects, but certainly in keeping with their spirit, local communities use local knowledge to sustain a culturally based biodiversity. In the Big Coal River region of West Virginia during the early spring, people gather ramps (*allium tricoccum*), or wild leeks, and eat them at ramp suppers and festivals that double as fundraisers for local causes.[22] As Mary Hufford notes in her evocative account, these practices and the knowledge associated with them (and with other wild greens, and morels), 'interweave biodiversity and community life.' This is a deeply rooted and committed set of relations among people tied by kinship and friendship.

Ramps are what artists would understand as a material with strong presence,[23] particularly because of their smell, which has prompted the Menominee Indians to call it 'the skunk.' The stink of ramps is integral to their character as a restorative that operates on both the body and the spirit: 'Some have seen in this practice of restoring the body while emitting a sulphurous odor a rite of death and resurrection, serendipitously coinciding with Easter', though as Mary Hufford notes, 'Actually, with ramps the motif appears to be breath and insurrection.'[24] So much so, that children who had eaten ramps were sent home from school because of the overpowering odor that emanated from them. One ramp supper announced itself by its smell in the *West Virginia Hillbilly* – ramp juice had been added to the printer's ink. The Postmaster General reprimanded the publisher.

Ramps, the places where they grow, and the larger named and known landscape of which they are part, are activated through collaborative knowledge, practices and memory. In this way, a community sustains itself and its way of life – 'Stories of plying the seasonal round, of gathering ramps, molly moochers [morels], fishing bait, and ginseng, are like beacons lighting up Hazy's coves, benches, walk paths, historic ruins, and camp rocks', as ramp gatherers make their way to and from the 'de facto commons' in the hills.[25] This is their way of laying claim to a place under pressure to yield to 'progress' and in particular to a form of mining that involves mountaintop removal and reclamation. This is also a prime case of performance art *avant la lettre*, though it is not likely to be written in the history of performance.[26] The envy of many an artist, such complexes do not have to work across the gap between art and life because there is no gap. Moreover, what we have here is not a one-time action or project of limited duration but a seasonal ritual that is part of a sustained way of life and a committed set of attachments to people and places. Foraging for wild greens, traditionally a woman's role, is part of an 'alternative, rural economy that enables survival outside the mainstream' and that includes gardening, bartering, and other tactics for making do.

[...]

Provisioning

The market has historically been a crossroads and vibrant site of food, conviviality and performance, from the street cries and banter designed to sell goods to the formal Punch and Judy shows and myriad street performers, Above all, in city markets like the Mercado de Antón Martín in Madrid, Makhane Yehuda in Jerusalem, the Fulton Fish Market in Manhattan, the former Les Halles in Paris, the food emporia in department store basements in Tokyo, and other markets in cities and towns around the world, the star is the food, its presentation, and the transactions they engender.

From November 1995 until November 1997, Annie Lanzillotto undertook *The Arthur Avenue Retail Market Project* in a once vibrant Italian neighborhood in the Bronx.[27] Like the 'Garden of Eden', *The Farm* and *Flood*, this project was sited in a location that was vulnerable and therefore more accessible (though not necessarily receptive at first) to artistic intervention. In part, such projects insert themselves into existing communities, and in part, they create communities around themselves. Unlike these projects, however, Lanzillotto gave herself the same challenge she says she gives all artists: '"Go home." Challenge yourself to go home and do your work. Work with the mentalities that you fled in your development.'[28] For her this raised such questions as 'Can I work with the close-minded Eurocentric anti-intellectual working-class Bronx Italian-Americans I grew up with?' She had no patience for 'middle-class white artists who worked in the most marginalized communities they could imagine, easy prey for all their projections.' Rather than 'dabble in prison work', they should make a video of the communities they come from and can gain access to, like the women on Park Avenue – 'I'd like to see that', she quips. In choosing to work at the Arthur Avenue market, Lanzillotto was 'rebelling against the value system of the downtown artist communities. The glorification of sexy urban detritus as a stage set. The values that discourage "working" with family', the commercialism of the art world and the 'anesthetized audience.'

Basically, Lanzillotto set up shop in the market for two years with the following intention: 'to make an opera in the market, and highlight the opera that is already there, daily.' Unlike the jaded art world that she rejects, 'At the market, the butchers pound their cleavers when the tenor misses a note. The patrons shout like a sports audience.' 'I like that', she says, and adds that 'The fourth wall is not even a remote possibility. A performer must communicate, for these merchants arc the best performers and storytellers in the world. And their countertops – the best stages.' Through a series of 'over-the-countertop interviews', Lanzillotto gradually gained the trust of the eighteen butchers, fishmongers, cheese purveyors, and fruit and vegetable merchants.[29] Lanzillotto and her team entered into the life of the market, attending merchant meetings, going with the merchants early in the morning to Hunts Point Terminal Market for produce, and talking with them about the problems they face. The project reached out beyond the market to the community park, senior citizen center, and outlying neighborhood.

[…]

Preparation

Culture is a kitchen, if we are to take Lévi-Strauss's culinary triangle to heart: 'Adapting itself to the exigencies of the body, and determined in its modes by the way man's insertion in nature operates in different parts of the world, placed then between nature and culture, cooking represents their necessary articulation. It partakes of both domains, and projects this duality on each of its manifestations.'[30] The Chinese word *shu* means both 'knowing something well' and 'ripe, mature, or cooked.'[31] The raw and the cooked are conceptual categories. Thus, in the case of sashimi, the knife, not the fire, has 'cooked' the 'raw' fish by transforming it from nature to culture within a culinary system. One man's culture (sashimi) is another man's nature (raw fish). A Japanese delicacy that I experienced during a local festival in Himeji in 1983 is dancing shrimp. Quivering little blue shrimp are downed more or less whole and intact so that their movement can be felt 'dancing' in the stomach. Reversing the terms, the cooked can be treated as raw in recipes that call for prepared packaged foods: the Pink Champagne Cake calls for white cake mix, instant pistachio pudding, club soda, a jar of red cherries, a tin of crushed pineapple, margarine, cream cheese, and, for added color, bottled red and green cherries.[32]

Substance At the heart of preparation is the notion of substance with strong presence, to use Stiles's felicitous phrase. Meat, as already suggested in Jana Sterbak's flesh dress, has particularly strong presence and figures in the work of various performance artists, often in relation to death, sex, and affinities between animal and human flesh. Meat, the flesh of sentient beings, is central to the history of sacrifice. Antoine's use of an actual carcase on the stage of 'The Butchers' was a sensation (literally) not only because it was 'the real thing', but also because it was real meat.

Luxury foods have strong presence (truffles, caviar), as do foods with a penetrating odor, such as fermented fish and aged cheese. One of the most vivid examples is durian, a fruit about the size of a basketball and covered with a thick and spiky rind. It is popular in Malaysia and other parts of southeast Asia. Notorious for its relentless smell, appetizing to some and disgusting to others, durian is not allowed in public enclosed spaces like hotel rooms or airplanes. In durian season, lovers of durian will drive out to the orchards at night, when it is cool and the aroma suffuses the air, and eat them at a roadside stand. They are freshly gathered by men who know how to dodge the ripe ones, attached by only a thin stem, as they fall from a height of 30–120 feet (9–36.5m) Durian is considered yang and an aphrodisiac, no doubt because of its funky smell. According to a Malay proverb, 'When the durians come down, the sarongs go up.'[33] According to a guide to Singapore food, 'Animals esteem the durian equally as much as humans – tapirs, tigers, pigs, flying foxes, rhinos and monkeys are known to eat them voraciously, and elephants often swallow them whole. Protected by their horny shell, they emerge from the elephant's digestive tract intact. Indeed, this specially "processed" variety is coveted above all others by the natives of northern Malaya.'[34] The staples of life – rice and bread, among others – are among the foods with the strongest presence, as evidenced in their role as sacramental food, the consecrated host being a prime example.[35]

[…]

Instructions Instructions for doing something are subject to their own poetics. According to André Viard, however eloquent poets and prose writers might wax on the subject of food, 'what can they say that is worth the precise rules followed by an adept, and which are the true poetics of culinary arts.'[36] Paul Schmidt, the late poet, actor, and translator of Russian literature, takes up this theme in his appropriately titled essay '"As if a cookbook had anything to do with writing," – Alice B. Toklas', which appeared in 1974. In this astute discussion of four American women (Julia Child, Adelle Davis, Alice B. Toklas, and M. F. K. Fisher) he distinguishes two traditions of culinary writing and traces them to Brillat-Savarin's *La Physiologie du Goût* (1825) and Auguste Escoffier's *Le Guide Culinaire* (1903) respectively. Whereas Brillat-Savarin wrote that 'I soon saw, as I considered every aspect of the pleasures of the table, that something better than a cookbook should be written about them', it is precisely the definitive cookbook that Escoffier set out to create.[37] Yet, as Schmidt notes, that textbook 'unwittingly provides possibilities for the imagination to run riot. . . . Simply to list and describe 114 recipes for sole unleashes the mind, and what is intended as a most precise kind of inventory becomes glittering caprice. The names slide from the pages – *Sole au Chambertin, Sole Montgolfier, Sole Meunière à l'orange. Filets de sole Chauchat, Filets de sole Mary Stuart, Filets de sole "Otéro"* – names, colors, balloons, queens, and courtesans – and a wave of fantasy overwhelms us.'[38] Consistent with the principles that Kaprow espouses, Schmidt notes that 'Any speculation upon the art of cooking – upon an esthetics of eating – must cope very soon with a non-esthetic dimension. To speak primarily of art where food is concerned is somehow to ignore life; but when we consider food at any length at all, life bursts incredibly and awfully upon our speculation.'[39] Finally, there are dirty dishes and kitchen garbage and the toilet bowl – 'Ici tombent en ruines toutes les merveilles de la cuisine.'[40]

[…]

The principles governing the nature of the recipe in these examples – a set of instructions for action (Kaprow), a gift in the form of a coded message that holds the keys to the inner life of someone's kitchen (Miralda), a substitute for substance, in the fullest sense of the word (the women of Terezín), and as the very substance for which it provides the instructions – also govern the actions (preparing food) and events (eating food) that emanate from them. Some of these actions and events are formal exercises in doing, others are intensely social and symbolic, sometimes moving toward the theatrical, while still others focus on substance, its materiality and sensory qualities.

Actions If a recipe can be thought about as a composition in the form of instructions, then those instructions could be said to be performed even as enunciations (written, spoken) and, of course, as actions on substance to produce a culinary result or performance in its own right. Those actions are themselves the basis for demonstration – television cooking shows are watched in and of themselves, quite apart from their instructional value – as well as performance in the sense that one realizes the recipe, just as one performs a musical composition (transforms written notations into sounds).

The theatrical nature of the cooking demonstration, not unlike the poetics of even a highly technical recipe, inspired *Bon Appétit!*, a musical monologue starring Jean Stapleton as Julia Child. Performed in 1989 at the Terrace Theater at the John F. Kennedy Center for the Performing Arts in Washington, DC, the one-woman show also traveled to Long Beach, California, and Santa Fe, New Mexico. It was based on Julia Child's 1961 television cooking shows; Stapleton mimes Child's actions, which are legendary for their robust gestural style, and sings the recipes – 'It was Mrs. Child's theatricality' that sparked the idea for the production.[41]

Kaprow and artists inspired by the kind of work he represents focus on the action and try to avoid the theatrical, even in the presence of an audience. Some projects are documentary in their conception and execution, while others are live actions in real time which may or may not leave some material trace or record. From 1970 to 1980, Nancy Barber made 'videos of twenty or twenty-five people cooking in their homes. They put them on Channel C Cable TV.'[42] What interested Barber was the chance to talk with people in their homes, 'not for aesthetic reasons but for the bigger experience.'[43] More recently, *The Starving Artists' Cookbook* (1991) by Paul and Melissa Eidia is a verité video and book project consisting of short segments documenting many artists cooking in their everyday contexts. What emerges from their work is the intensely social nature of what is at one level a set of actions applied to substance.

[…]

The form of food events lends itself to performance, because not only are those forms well known but also they are easily staged – or perhaps it would be more accurate to say restaged. As Knowles explains, 'I made those early performances as real experiences which weren't disguised as anything else. I wasn't making salad to glorify a concept or eating a sandwich in the IDENTICAL LUNCH to make music. It was merely the experience itself that interested me although I did it to happen in the context of a concert hall.'[44] Making a salad in a concert hall for many people and making it at home in her kitchen is the same, she explains, because 'food preparation has always been a meditation for me.'[45] Knowles never loses sight of food as 'a substance which nourishes. When we see it being used as art we examine it more intensely. We enrich our lives because we encounter this food again in life. The nonverbal energy that happens when

I perform with food interests me.'[46] Knowles has also done pieces with beans and eggs. Since then other artists have done their own salad-making pieces, among them Susan Mogel's *Design for Living* (1980), a frantic performance of an out-of-control salad.[47]

Consumption

Events The world made edible makes for unusual meals. Those who came to see the gallery installation of Allan Kaprow's *Persian Rug* were invited to 'eat your way through the designs, right across the room, making new ones behind you as you went along.' When visitors partook less fully than he had hoped, Kaprow surmised that gallery spaces could not provide the right atmosphere for his kind of interactive work.[48]

In contrast, guests attending the 1971 wedding of Alicia Rios and Francisco Garcia de Paredes took part in an act of vegetarian anthropophagy: 'We designed a savory man to scale, a portrait of Paco [the groom], and a sweet woman, whose breasts were pies; her belt, a rectangular tart; and the skirt, flowers, fruits, sweets of all types; and around the whole thing an aura of flowers. Then came the act of cannibalism. Paco disappeared first, and then Alicia. The left-over sweets were carried away for the people who didn't come.'[49] In the absence of plates and containers, guests ate directly from the table. There to witness and celebrate the union of two people, they commingled the two into one within themselves. This was fully in the spirit of the role of feasts in rites of passage. In Van Gennep's classic book on the subject, rites of passage move through three stages – separation, transition, incorporation. Feasts are prominent in rites of incorporation, where commensality, the act of eating together, is an archetype of union.[50]

The challenges to commensality include, first, today's fractured and blended families, which have produced the most complex genealogies and kinship arrangements, and, second, the proliferation of individualized dietary regimens: even if it were possible to gather everyone to eat together in the same place at the same time, it might well be just as difficult to get them to eat the same food. The solution is either to prepare several different meals (lowfat, vegetarian, kosher, allergenic, etc.) or to offer the most restrictive diet, which is finally the most inclusive. As people cease to be guided by traditional proscriptions and prescriptions, they follow other rules and regulations and individualize them. Even if they are at the same table, they are not eating the same food. The restaurant menu (or eating *à la carte* all the time) becomes the norm.

In this context, the dinner party takes on special significance and has attracted artists who find rich possibilities in its event structure and in particular in its commensal nature. In contrast with Barbara Smith's dark *Ritual Dinner* and Bonnie Sherk's *Public Lunch* at the zoo are Judy Chicago's massive set table, which celebrates individual women, Suzanne Lacy's many dinner projects to honor women, and most recently the Foundry Theater's *A Conversation on Hope* (1998), which was held in part over a carefully staged dinner in Lower Manhattan. Feminist artists find in the dinner party, an arena for women's creativity, the possibility of creating new forms of commensality and of resignifying what it means to eat together. The dinner party is a particularly charged event, not only because the women responsible for preparing food on a daily basis often feel undervalued, but also because the artists attracted to food have struggled with serious food anxieties.

[...]

What would theater history look like were it written backwards from the Futurist banquets and Dali dinners and performance art? Canonical histories of theater take as their point of departure that which counts as theater in the modern period – namely, theater as an autonomous art form – and search for its 'origins' in fused art forms of the past. Thus, Oscar G. Brockett's *History of the Theater* is a history of drama and its performance: it does not view courtly banquets, tournaments, royal entries, and street pageants as performance genres in their own right but as occasions for plays and playlets. Such histories attend not to the fusion of *opera gastronomica,* the Renaissance musical banquet, conceived from the outset to play to all the senses, but to the seeds of what would become an independent art form.[51] A history of the theater in relation to the senses – and specifically the interplay of table and stage, the staging of food as theatre, and the theatrical uses of food – remains to be written.

Suffice it to say that it has taken considerable cultural work to isolate the senses, create genres of art specific to each, insist on their autonomy and cultivate modes of attentiveness that give some senses priority over others. To produce the separate and independent arts that we know today, it was necessary to break apart fused forms such as the banquet and to disarticulate the sensory modalities associated with them. Not until the various components of such events (music, dance, drama, food, sculpture, painting) were separated and specialized did they become sense-specific art forms in dedicated spaces (theater, auditorium, museum, gallery), with distinct protocols for structuring attention and perception. It was at this point that food disappeared from musical and theatrical performances. No food or drink is allowed in the theater, concert hall, museum, or library. In the process, new kinds of sociality supported sensory discernment specific to gustation, the literary practice of gastronomy, and increasing culinary refinement. Food became a sense-specific art form in its own right, as Marinetti's *Futurist Cookbook* so vividly demonstrates.

Performance artists working on the line between art and life – denying the line, crossing it, bringing art into life and life into art – are particularly attentive to the phenomenal, one might even say phenomenological, nature of food and the processes associated with it. For those interested in raw experience, it is a particular kind of attention that 'cooks' the raw, making it both edible as food and recognizable as art, without ceasing to be life.

Notes

1. See Baldwyn 1996.
2. See Bourdieu 1977.
3. See Kirshenblatt-Gimblett 1990.
4. See el-Khoury 1997 and Pinard 1991.
5. Inwood 1993: 98.
6. el-Khoury 1997: 50.
7. el-Khoury 1997: 51.
8. el-Khoury 1997: 52.
9. 'Un plat bien presenté est un moitié mangé.' Roger Fessaguet, personal communication, 1989.
10. Duffy and Bartoshuk 1996: 146.
11. Broadbent 1991: 111.
12. Barthes 1985: 61.
13. Barthes 1985: 61.
14. Quoted in Ruin 1991: 139.
15. Ruin 1991: 140.
16. Montano 1981–2: 45.
17. See Lansing 1983.
18. Anon. 1989: 25. This omelet was prepared in Bédoin, a town in southern France, to raise money for health care for the poor.

19. See Kirshenblatt-Gimblett 1996. See also Klein 1993 for a discussion of garden plots in an immigrant suburb of Stockholm.

20. Wildfeur 1995. The following discussion of biodynamic farming is inspired by Bartlett 1998.

21. Steiner [1924]. See Steiner 1993.

22. This account is based on Hufford 1998.

23. See Stiles 1998: 146.

24. Hufford 1998: 5.

25. Hufford 1998: 10.

26. To her credit, Linda Montano, who edited the 'Food and Art' section in a special issue of *High Performance* (1981–2), does include an essay by anthropologist Diane Rothenberg on food among the Seneca. Rothenberg, who lived on the Seneca Indian reservation in western New York from July 1972 to August 1974 while doing field work for her dissertation, is, together with Jerome Rothenberg, part of an experimental poetry scene.

27. The project was commissioned by 'Dancing on the Streets' On SITE/NYC Fund.

28. Lanzillotto 1997a: 61. All the quotations are from this page.

29. Lanzillotto 1997b.

30. Lévi-Strauss 1978.

31. Chow, in press.

32. http://www.joyofbaking.com/wwwboard/messages/226.html

33. Oey 1980: 14.

34. Oey 1980: 14.

35. See Feeley-Harnik 1981 and Camporesi 1989 on the consecrated host.

36. Quoted by Bonnet 1997: 158. More recently, Susan J. Leonardi's article about the recipe as a literary form surprised the readers of the esteemed *Publications of the Modern Language Association*, when it appeared in 1989.

37. Schmidt 1974: 182–3. At the same time, Julia Child and Alice B. Toklas can be classified as 'Epicureans, philosophers of the here-and-now – hedonists even' and Adelle Davis and M. F. K. Fisher as 'Platonists, philosophers of a world beyond this one' (1974: 199).

38. Schmidt 1974: 183.

39. Schmidt 1974: 184–5.

40. Schmidt 1974: 185.

41. Gussow 1989.

42. Montano 1981–2: 47.

43. Montano 1981–2: 47.

44. Montano 1981–2: 46.

45. Montano 1981–2: 46.

46. Montano 1981–2: 46.

47. Banes 1980 and Montano 1981–2, 51–2.

48. Kaprow quoted by Stiles 1998: 282.

49. Kirshenblatt-Gimblett 1997: 110.

50. Gennep 1960. See also Turner 1969.

51. Nevile 1990: 128. According to Graham Pont, the term *opera gastronomica* 'was first used in the title of the musical banquet, *Les goûts réunis* or *Apollo in the Antipodes: opera gastronomica in tre atti.* This was the celebration which concluded the Fourth David Nichol Smith Memorial Seminar in Eighteenth Century Studies and the First National Conference of the Musicological Society of Australia, held at University House, Canberra, 31 August, 1976.' Pont 1990: 123–4.

References

Anon. (1989) 'It's no small truffling matter', *Daily News* (4 April), 25.

Antin, Eleanor (1981–2) 'Carving: a traditional sculpture', *High Performance* 4(4): 62.

Bakhtin, Mikhail (1968) 'Banquet imagery in Rabelais', in *Rabelais and His World,* trans. Helene Iswolsky, Cambridge, MA: MIT Press, 278–302.

Baldwyn, Lucy (1996) 'Blending in: the immaterial art of Bobby Baker's culinary events', *The Drama Review* 40(4) (T152): 37–55.

Banes, Sally (1980) 'Consciousness razing', *Village Voice* (1–7 October), 110.

Barthes, Roland (1985) 'Reading Brillat-Savarin', in Marshall Blonsky (ed.) *On Signs,* Baltimore, MD: Johns Hopkins University Press, 61–75.

Bartlett, Lisbeth (1998) 'Biodynamic agriculture and community supported farming: the performative interaction of food production, with nutritional/spiritual healing.' Unpublished paper.

'Biodynamics: home page of the biodynamic association of America' [Web Page] (5 December 1998). Accessed 19 January 1999. Available at http://www.biodynamics.com/

Bonnet, Jean-Claude (1997) 'Carême, or the last sparks of decorative cuisine', in Allen S. Weiss (ed.) *Taste and Nostalgia,* New York: Lusitania Press, 155–82.

Bourdieu, Pierre (1977) *Outline of a Theory of Practice,* trans. Richard Nice, Cambridge: Cambridge University Press.

Brillat-Savarin, Jean A. (1971) *The Physiology of Taste; or, Meditations on Transcendental Gastronomy,* trans. M. F. K. Fisher, New York: Knopf.

Broadbent, Michael (1991) *The New Great Vintage Wine Book,* New York: Knopf.

Brockett, Oscar G. and Findlay, Robert R. (1973) *Century of Innovation: A History of European and American Theater and Drama Since 1870,* Englewood Cliffs, NJ: Prentice-Hall.

Camporesi, Piero (1989) 'The consecrated host: a wondrous excess', in Michel Feher, with Ramona Nadaff, and Nadia Tazi (eds) *Fragments for A History of the Human Body,* volume 1, New York: ZONE, 221–37.

Carr, C. (1986) 'Unspeakable practices, unnatural acts: the taboo art of Karen Finley', *Village Voice* 31(25): 17 ff.

Chicago, Judy (1979–80) *The Complete Dinner Party,* 2 vols, New York: Anchor/Doubleday.

Chow, Rey (in press) 'Consumption and eccentric writing: notes on two Hong Kong authors', *Communal/Plural: Journal for Transnational and Multicultural Studies.*

Dali, Salvador (1973) *Les Diners de Gala,* trans. J. P. Moore, New York: Felice.

Duffy, Valerie B. and Linda M. Bartoshuk (1996) 'Sensory factors in feeding,' in Elizabeth Capaldi (ed.) Why We Eat What We Eat: The Psychology of Eating, Washington, DC: American Psychological Association, 145–172.

Eidia, Paul and Eidia, Melissa (1991) *The Starving Artists' Cookbook,* New York: Eidia (idea) Books.

el-Khoury, Rodolphe (1997) 'Delectable decoration: taste and spectacle in Jean François De Bastide's La Petite Maison', in Allen S. Weiss (ed.) *Taste and Nostalgia,* New York: Lusitania Press, 49–62.

Epstein, Marcy J. (1996) 'Consuming performances: eating acts and feminist embodiment', *The Drama Review* 40(4) (T152): 20–36.

Feeley-Harnik, Gillian (1981) *The Lord's Table: the Meaning of Food in Early Judaism and Christianity,* Washington, DC: Smithsonian Institution Press.

Gennep, Arnold van (1960) *The Rites of Passage,* trans. Monika B. Vizedom and Gabrielle L. C. Caffe, Chicago: University of Chicago Press.

Goffman, Erving (1959) *The Performance of Self in Everyday Life,* Garden City, NY: Doubleday.

Gussow, Mel (1991) 'Jean Stapleton playing Julia Child set to music', *New York Times* (26 September), C18.

Hufford, Mary (1998) 'Tending the commons: rampsuppers, biodiversity, and the integrity of the mountains', *Folklife Center News* 20(4): 3–11.

Inwood, Michael, ed. (1993) 'Commentary', in Georg Wilhelm Friedrich Hegel, *Introductory Lectures on Aesthetics,* London: Penguin.

Jacob, Mary J., Brenson, Michael and Olson, Eva M. (1995) *Culture in Action: a Public Art Program of Sculpture Chicago,* Seattle, WA: Bay Press.

Jones, Amelia (ed.) (1996) *Sexual Politics: Judy Chicago's Dinner Party in Feminist Art History,* Los Angeles: University of California Press, with UCLA at the Armond Hammer Museum of Art and Cultural Center.

Kaprow, Allan [1966] *Assemblage, Environments & Happenings,* New York: H. N. Abram.

Kaprow, Allan (1993) *Essays on the Blurring of Art and Life*, ed. Jeff Kelley, Berkeley: University of California Press.

Kirshenblatt-Gimblett, Barbara (1989) 'Edible art', *Artforum* (November): 20–3.

Kirshenblatt-Gimblett, Barbara (1990) 'Performance of precepts/precepts of performance: Hasidic celebrations of Purim in Brooklyn', in Richard Schechner and Willa Appel (eds) *By Means of Performance: Intercultural Studies of Theatre and Ritual,* Cambridge: Cambridge University Press, 109–17.

Kirshenblatt-Gimblett, Barbara (1996) 'Ordinary people/everyday life', in Georg Gmelch and Walter P. Zenner (eds) *Urban Life: Readings in Urban Authropology,* 3rd ed., Prospect Heights, Illinois: Waveland Press, Inc., 548–62.

Kirshenblatt-Gimblett, Barbara (1997) 'Alicia Rios, tailor of the body's interior: an interview', *The Drama Review* 41(2) (T154): 90–110.

Lansing, John Stephen (1983) *The Three Worlds of Bali,* New York: Praegner.

Lanzillotto, Annie (1997a) 'The fall and decline of Ancient the Bronx', *Art Journal* (Special Issue: *Performance Art*) 56(4): 59–61.

Lanzillotto, Annie (1997b) 'a'Schapett!' Final report [Arthur Avenue Retail Market Project] to The Rockefeller Foundation and 'Dancing in the Streets' Inc.

Leonard, Roy (1997) 'Blue Man Group, feature review', *Roy Leonard's Going Out Guide* (October). Accessed 29 January 1999. Available at http://www.blueman.com/revs/rev4a.html

Lévi-Strauss, Claude (1978) 'The culinary triangle', in *The Origin of Table Manners: Introduction to a Science of Mythology,* Vol. 3, trans. Peter Brooks, New York: Harper & Row, 471–95.

Marcus, Ivan G. (1996) *Rituals of Childhood: Jewish Acculturation in Medieval Europe,* New Haven, CT: Yale University Press.

Marinetti, Fillippo T. (1989) *The Futurist Cookbook,* trans. Suzanne Brill, San Francisco: Bedford Arts.

Miralda, Antoni (1994) *Menus/Miralda,* Bareelona: Area de Cultura: Sa Nostra, Obra Social i Cultural.

Miralda, Antoni (1995) *Miralda: Obras 1965-1995,* Barcelona and Valencia: Fundacion 'La Caixa' and IVAM, Centre Julio Gonzalez.

Miralda, Antoni (1998) 'The source of . . . Nutrition Pavilion' [Web Page]. Accessed 21 January 1999. Available at http://www.mlink.net/~foodcult/eng/home.html

Montano, Linda (1981–2) 'Interviews', *High Performance* 4(4): 46–55.

Nadotti, Maria (1989) 'Karen Finley's poisoned meatloaf', *Artforum* 27 (7 March): 113–16.

Nemiroff, Diana (1991) *Jana Sterbak: States of Being = Corps à Corps,* Ottawa: National Gallery of Canada.

Nevile, Jenny (1990) 'The musical banquet in Italian quattrocento festivities', in Anthony Cornnes, Graham Pont and Barbara Santich (eds) *Food in Festivity: Proceedings of the Fourth Symposium of Australian Gastronomy,* Sydney: Symposium of Australian Gastronomy, 125–35.

Oey, Eric M. (1980) *Singapore Feasts,* Singapore: APA Productions.

Philadelphia Museum of Art and Educational Management Group (EMG) (1998) 'Rirkrit Tiravanija, Untitled 1998 (On the road with Jiew Jeaw Jieb Sri and Moo)' [Web Page]. Accessed 17 January 1999. Available at http://www.philamuseum.org/exhibits/ontheroad/menu.htm

Pinard, Sylvia (1991) 'A taste of India: on the role of gustation in the Hindu sensorium', in David Howes (ed.) *The Varieties of Sensory Experience: A Sourcebook in the Anthropology of the Senses,* Toronto: University of Toronto Press, 221–230.

Pont, Graham (1990) 'In search of the *Opera Gastronomica'*, in Anthony Corones, Graham Pont and Barbara Santich (eds) *Food in Festivity: Proceedings of the Fourth Symposium of Australian Gastronomy,* Sydney; Symposium of Australian Gastronomy, 115–24.

Rietbergen, Peter (1983) 'Prince Eckembergh comes to dinner: food and political propaganda in the seventeenth century', *Petits Propos Culinaires* 15: 45–54.

Ruin, Hans (1991) 'Smell – notes for a phenomenology of olfaction', *Kris*: 43–44.

Sandford, Mariellen R. (ed.) (1994) *Happenings and Other Acts,* London: Routledge.

Sausser, Gail (1986) *Lesbian Etiquette: Humorous Essays,* Trumansburg, NY: Crossing Press.

Schimmel, Paul (ed.) (1998) *Out of Actions: Between Performance and the Object, 1949–1979,* Los Angeles and London: Museum of Contemporary Art and Thames & Hudson.

Schmidt, Paul (1974) '"As if a cookbook had anything to do with writing", – Alice B. Toklas', *Prose* no. 8: 179–203.

Steiner, Rudolf [1924] 'Spiritual foundations for the renewal of agriculture' [Web Page]. Accessed 1 April 1999. Available at http://www.angelfire.com/id/biobaby/contentslist.html

Steiner, Rudolf (1993) *Spiritual Foundations for the Renewal of Agriculture: a Course of Lectures Held at Koberwitz, Silesia, June 7 to June 16, 1924,* ed. Malcolm Gardner, trans. Catherine E. Creeger and Malcolm Gardner, Kimberton, PA: Bio-Dynamic Farming and Gardening Association.

Stiles, Kristine (1998) 'Uncorrupted joy: international art actions', in Paul Schimmel (ed.) *Out of Action: Between Performance and the Object, 1949–1979,* Los Angeles, California, and New York: Museum of Contemporary Art and Thames and Hudson, 227–329.

Synnott, Anthony (1991) 'Puzzling over the senses; from Plato to Marx', in David Howes (ed.) *The Varieties of Sensory Experience: a Sourcebook in the Anthropology of the Senses,* Toronto: University of Toronto Press, 61–76.

Turner, Victor (1969) *The Ritual Process: Structure and Anti-Structure,* Ithaca, NY: Cornell University Press.

Wildfeur, Sherry [1995] 'What is biodynamics?' [Web page]. Accessed 19 January 1999. Available at http://www.biodynamics.com/bd/def.html

CHAPTER 19

WOMEN, MILK AND MAGIC AT THE BOUNDARY FESTIVAL OF MAY

Patricia Lysaght

[...]

And he made peace for the sake of his cows and his people (*do righne síth dar ceann a bhó 7 a mhuinntire*).

(*Annals of Connacht for the year 1125 A.D.*)[1]

So far, evidence has been adduced to show the importance of milk and milk products in the early, medieval and modern Irish diet and economy. For the early period this consists mainly of textual references to the predominance of cattle, particularly milch cows, in the economy, and to a wide variety of milk preparations and products. The testimony of foreign observers of the Irish scene provide valuable evidence for the medieval period, and recent historical works and official data help to fill in the picture for the late medieval and modern periods. But the importance of cows, milk and milk products in the diet and economy of the Irish people from ancient to modem times may also be assessed in another way—in mythological terms. There is no shortage of source material to support such an assessment, though of course the data, which becomes more apparent from the sixteenth century, really becomes abundant from the nineteenth century onwards, as we shall now see.

Bealtaine: The boundary festival

Indicative also of the importance of milk and milk products in the ancient and medieval Irish economy and diet, are the numerous literary references to the sensitivity of cows to mystical and occult forces, benign or malign, an idea which has, with some variations, persisted into modern times. From about the twelfth century we get glimpses of a belief system—not unfamiliar to a twentieth century Irish country person—concerned *inter alia* with the susceptibility of milch cows to good and evil influences, particularly at *Bealtaine,* the boundary festival of May, which heralds the beginning of summer, and thus also the commencement of the milking season in Ireland.[2] For the duration of May eve (*Oíche Bhealtaine*) and May day (*Lá Bealtaine*)—the period of transition between the winter and summer seasons of the year—one's dairying luck was felt to be very precariously balanced, and could be either lost, maintained or promoted during this ambiguous time. That fears in relation to the loss of milk and butter luck predominated at this time is evident from the rich corpus of beliefs, customs, rituals and legends concerning milk and milk-'profit' theft, and in particular, the measures taken to protect one's milk and butter luck, or to recover one's stolen 'profit', as the case may be.[3]

Patricia Lysaght, 'Women, Milk and Magic at the Boundary Festival of May' in Patricia Lysaght (ed.), *Milk and Milk Products: From Medieval to Modern Times*, (Edinburgh: Canongate, 1994), pp. 208–228. (Excerpt printed here: 211–228. Omitted text is indicated by ellipses.)

Reprinted with permission from the author.

The main repository of relevant primary source material, which is both quantitatively and qualitatively suitable for a full-scale study of Irish attitudes to milk and dairy produce at the boundary festival of May for at least a century, is the archive of the Department of Irish Folklore, University College Dublin. Most of the material in relation to *Bealtaine* in the archive, including a questionnaire on the topic issued in 1947, has not yet been fully analysed or published.[4] This article is based mainly on that questionnaire material, and on the author's fieldwork in relation to the festival of May undertaken in recent years in the Irish countryside.

It is immediately obvious from an analysis of this material that in Ireland in the nineteen forties, some people still firmly believed that their milk 'profit' could be stolen during the festival of May. A correspondent from Co. Laois, in the midlands of Ireland, stated that although belief in milk and butter stealing had almost died out in the area, nevertheless, for some it was still a firmly held belief, and she adds:

> Miss Moran, a poultry and dairy instructess for Co. Laois for nearly forty years, told me she had been consulted on several occasions a bout getting back butter that had been *taken* . . .[5]

It is also evident that the milk stealing activities, and the vast majority of the protective measures taken to guard against 'profit' theft (both usually referred to as *piseoga*), were regarded as acts of magic, but not, it seems, involving a diabolical pact. The 'profit' thief was almost invariably believed to be a woman—a farmer's wife, or an independent woman farmer seeking to increase her own dairy produce at the expense of that of her neighbour's, and usually a neighbour or even a relative.[6] Protective rites began on May eve when the festival of May properly began, and continued until noon on May day, while rites connected with taking milk or milk profit were usually performed around sunrise on May morning—though some might take place between May eve and noon on May day. Both sets of rites could be performed either in the wild landscape—at particularly magical spots such as at the confluence of three rivers, or at the meeting point of three townlands or farms, or in the domesticated landscape—on the family farm, at wells, in the farmyard, outhouses or in the dwelling-house, though of course some rites might be performed in both landscapes. We shall now consider aspects of both 'profit' stealing and the protective rites in more detail.

Stealing the milk 'profit'

Measures to protect one's milk luck were taken throughout the milking season, and indeed throughout the year: on any occasion when milk was given away, a pinch of salt was usually added to it, and salt was also sprinkled on butter destined for the market before it left the farm. But it is evident from the source material that it was undoubtedly during the festival of May that peoples' fears were greatest in relation to interference, not just with milk quantity, but especially with milk quality, and the usual protective measures were intensified and special ones introduced at this time. Occasionally clearly expressed, but more often implied in the numerous references to the loss of *sochar an bhainne* or 'milk profit', or in those reports which state that the butter had been 'taken', is, that the milk quality i.e. the butter fat or cream content, has been meddled with. This is evident in those accounts which tell of churnings producing only froth and a foul or sour-tasting liquid.

Interference with milk quality is also emphasised in narratives detailing unproductive or difficult churning situations believed to have resulted from the May morning theft of substances symbolic of cream (often referred to as the 'top of the milk'), such as the dew on the grass, the surface water of the well or 'the top of the well', or water from a stream or river constituting a territorial boundary of some sort. Dew could be collected by a would-be butter thief in a number of ways. Simply walking across other peoples' land was considered sufficient as the thief involved could be walking off the dew and hence the milk luck.[7] Consequently, people all over Ireland intensely disliked seeing others, especially strangers and women, walking through their land on May Eve or May Day. A Co. Galway correspondent who wrote in 1947 that 'people who went into other peoples' land on May Day were still thought to be up to no good . . . to be trying to work evil magic', succinctly sums up the general reaction typical of the archival material.[8] Indeed, around the same period a Co. Cork farmer was quite unequivocal in his response to a query about this matter. The questionnaire correspondent who spoke to him wrote as follows:

> Some people will not allow any person to walk their land for any purpose on May Day. A man living about four miles from my own village of Knocknagree makes no secret of it that he would shoot any man or woman he'd catch walking through his land on May morning. He says 'what would bring them there, don't they know it is May Day, and don't they know what is said about such things on May Day? If they have no bad intention they won't be found doing it, and if they come with a bad intention don't they deserve to be shot? And the man that would shoot such a person would be doing a good act for the neighbours.[9]

Generally it is an object intimately associated with milk production that is used to gather the dew. What is most commonly employed is the cow-spancel or *buarach* (< *bó* 'cow', *árach* 'fetter'), usually a short piece of rope used to bind the cow's hind legs together during milking in order to immobilize her. Traditionally in Ireland milking has been regarded as a woman's job, and the spancel the *vade mecum* of the milker. Thus in view of the close sympathetic association between the woman and the spancel, and also between the cow and the spancel, especially since it was often made of a short two-ply rope twisted from the long tail hairs of cows, its use as a medium for milk-stealing is understandable.[10] Where a rope is employed to gather dew, the implication is that it is a spancel which is being used, and the following Co. Fermanagh account gives a fairly typical description of the May morning dew-gathering activity:

> A [man] on May morning, saw two women (neighbours) in his field dragging a rope across the field. It was very early, so he went to them and he recognised them as two women who lived alone a few miles away and who were infamous for these sort of activities.[11]

Further evidence of the vigour of the belief that the May morning dew on a neighbour's land represented his milk profit, and that this profit could be magically stolen from him through the appropriation of the dew by dragging, for example, a spancel, a rope, a cloth, or even a briar as we shall see below, along the dew-laden grass, is the following version of a legend common in Ireland. This version from south-west Donegal, tells of a priest going on a sick call who accidentally becomes a party to a magical milk-stealing rite being performed by a woman, who is 'gathering the dew with a cloth. The legend also underlines the probable butter loss which any farmer in these circumstances might sustain by emphasizing the huge butter gains to the 'thief':

> . . . There was a priest in Ardara long ago, and early one May Day morning he was going on a sick call out west to Luachros point. He saw an old Protestant woman drawing a piece of cloth after her through the dew and calling out that all the milk belonging to certain people should come to her. He called out that two-thirds of it were to come to him.
>
> Well and good. He went on and attended the sick person and when he returned home, his barn was filled with butter and milk. Next Sunday he announced from the altar that anyone who had lost his butter or milk should come to him and that it was all to be got in his barn. They came, and so he got all the butter and milk back to the people of Luachros point who had lost it.[12]

Indeed a farmer could put his own milk and butter supply at risk on May morning as the following legend from Co. Westmeath warns. In this narrative, the woman of the house is shown to have accidentally collected the May morning dew of the farm, and thus the farm's milk profit, by inadvertently trailing a briar along the grass causing it to become a medium for milk theft, which was then appropriated by an outsider thus putting her milk and butter-supply for the season at risk:

> A woman milked her cows in a field and was bringing the milk home along a road where a man happened to be fencing [i.e. constructing a fence]. A long briar which got attached to the lady's skirt trailed after her. As she passed, the man noticed the briar and cut it with the spade. The milk at once poured out over the pail tops and was lost on the road. The woman at once threw herself on her knees, cursed the man and threatened to steep a sheaf for him.[13]

For a traditional farming audience the woman's immediate and powerful reaction portrayed in the narrative—involving cursing and a threat of black magic[14]—confirms belief in, and a fear of milk stealing.

Other methods of milk stealing are also mentioned in the sources. Spancels might be used not only for gathering dew, but might also be placed in boundary water for the purposes of stealing the milk and butter of the cow herd which drank there. Women seen at boundary water on May morning were believed to be 'gathering butter', and the following legend from Co. Kerry tells how the *buarach* might be used in boundary water for that purpose. The collector reports:

> One woman told me (she is about 81 years old) that her father drove the cows to the water of three boundaries one May Morning. The cows began to bellow loudly and seemed much agitated. He examined the hole of water and noticed a rope made of cow's hair in the water with a stone on either end of it. He took it out and the cows ceased to bellow and drank quietly. He brought the rope home and thought no more about it. From that day on, whenever they churned they had a very large quantity of butter and hardly any buttermilk. After churning a few times and wondering at all the butter, he remembered the rope. He searched for it, found it and threw it into the fire where it burned with loud crackling. He was uneasy and went to the priest and told him his story. The priest told him that he should not have burned the rope, that he was only getting back the butter that had been stolen from him, and as soon as he had got his right, the churn would only yield the normal amount of butter.[15]

It was also commonly believed throughout Ireland that well water could be used for butter stealing purposes, and the cream skimmer was often used to skim the surface of a communal well, or a neighbour's well, on May morning. The first water taken from the well on May morning was regarded as being potent for the purposes of good or evil. Thus, whoever was first to skim the well was believed to have milk and butter luck for the coming year, including also perhaps, that of his neighbour, (or neighbours), if a communal well had been skimmed. People therefore tried to ensure that a member of their own family drew water from their well on May Morning before any other person did so. We hear of wells, particularly those privately owned, being physically guarded from sunset on May Eve to sunrise on May Morning, a custom which was particularly common in the rich dairying areas of the South and East of Ireland. But it was also practised on smaller farms, and the following account from south Co. Clare—apart from detailing the commercial aspect of even small-scale butter-making—shows the context in which belief in butter theft by means of magical interference with the family's water supply could be actualized:

> My father was a farmer's son. His father's farm . . . carried about twelve cows, and in addition to the farm proper they had a large tract of mountain. One year they utterly failed to make any butter. The cream

was skimmed off the pans as was the custom then, and put into the barrel- or hand-churn. They then made an effort to churn it into butter as usual, but without a satisfactory result. The cream, with all the churning, turned into a gaseous frothy mass. Everyone in the house took a hand with the churning, but all their combined efforts effected no change in the cream. Eventually it was given to animals.

Now, at that time and for years after, the custom was that 'partners' filled firkins of butter. That meant that the farmers' wives churned once a week, and each brought her quantity of butter, small or big, to our house for that week. There the whole quantity of butter was put into a tub and mixed, and eventually put into the firkin for conveyance to the market. Small farmers with three or four, or even five cows in bad land, never had more than one firkin for the market. Larger farmers had two, while a farmer able to market three firkins of butter together was very snug indeed. When the firkin or firkins were filled the visitors were entertained to tea, and after a little delay for gossip, then left for home with their empty butter vessels.

Now during this period under review my grandparents had no butter to give, and consequently no butter to get. A small farmer of four cows lived near them. Very frequently he passed over my father's 'street'[16] on the way to the market with *two* firkins of butter on the car, and his wife perched up on the seat as proud as punch. This fact gave rise to thought. One May morning my grandfather hid near a spring well in his land. About four o'clock he saw the woman approaching the well. On peeping out stealthily he found she was [the woman who had] the two firkins for the market out of the small farm. She approached the well and started the incantations. My grandfather didn't let her proceed far when he appeared. There was a scene of course. He got her to admit that she stole, and was then making an effort to steal, his butter. When he threatened exposure and publicity, she vowed to give up the practice on condition that he kept her secret. His butter-making came alright after that. This is a perfectly true fact.[17]

Communal wells presented a particular danger to those who used them, but in some areas the person on whose land the well was situated had the right to take the first water from the well on May morning.[18] Such wells, like those privately owned, might also be guarded as the following account from Co. Waterford shows:

At Mooneire, at the well used by the people of the hamlet of Seskin, the local farmers used to watch together. [A man] told me recently that his father, [and a number of other men] were watching, and getting thirsty agreed to go for a drink. [One of the men] tried to skim the well on the sly, but [another man] caught him at it and knocked him into the well with his ashplant.[19]

In the foregoing account it is, as far as the material to hand shows, atypically, a man who tries to skim the well. Generally speaking, however, the material points to women as the milk thieves, and some families had even a reputation for milk stealing, the power being passed on from mother to daughter one such family in Co. Leitrim was nicknamed 'pull the rope'!). In a narrative from the rich dairying Golden Vale area of Munster about a woman attempting to set charms at a neighbour's well on May morning, the woman's daughter is also said to have been involved in milk-stealing activities, which she engaged in in hare-form:

A daughter of this woman . . . was, on another occasion, the subject of *piseoga*. On May eve a dog chased a hare and the hare ran towards this woman's house, and was jumping through the window, when the dog caught her and bit her. The woman wore the mark of the bite ever after.[20]

The foregoing is a version of a migratory legend found throughout Ireland which substantiates the belief— articulated already in the Irish context by Giraldus Cambrensis in the twelfth century[21]—that some women were capable of shape-shifting and could transform themselves into a hare in order to suck the milk of their neighbour's cows. The following version is from Co. Clare:

> Some people would milk their neighbour's cows on May morning. One such woman was shot at here when she was milking. She turned herself into a hare. She was fired on as such and hit. She was tracked by blood and found bleeding in bed beside her husband.[22]

In other versions of the legend the 'hare' is forced to regain human female shape when attacked by a jet black hound (i.e. 'without one single white hair'), as in the following example from Co. Longford in the midlands of Ireland:

Milking Hare

> A story is told of a hare that used to be seen milking cows—I don't know was it on May morn or was it a frequent occurrence. She was chased by hounds on many occasions but always got away. A strange travelling woman told that the hare could be caught only by a black greyhound—completely black without even one white hair. Such a dog was found after a long search, the hare was waited for, arrived, and the chase commenced. All the other dogs in the district—of every breed and class—took part, but as the hunt was a long and fast one, all dropped out or were left behind except the black one who was closing in on his quarry. The hare, being pressed, made towards a little house where an old woman . . . lived alone, and was escaping through the window when the black greyhound snapped at her and took a piece of flesh off her hind leg. There was no other exit except the door which was closed. The hunters were in view of the window, and on arrival barred it up, and entered the house to search for the hare. The old woman was spinning in the corner and could give no information. After searching fruitlessly some of the hunters became suspicious, and on examination, found a wound on the woman's leg still bleeding and exactly corresponding with the piece of flesh the dog had torn off. It is not recorded what became of her but a family is still [nick] named *Girreys* [< It. *giorria,* 'hare'].[23]

So far, milk stealing rites at boundary water, in pastures, or at household or communal wells, have been considered. But a whole range of milk and butter-stealing rites are also linked to the farmyard and the dwelling-house. Opening all the farmyard doors and gates was a way of letting the farmer's luck escape according to a Co. Carlow correspondent writing in 1947:

> Another belief is that the luck is taken by a person coming during the night of May eve and opening all the doors and gates of the farmyard. I am reliably informed by a local that he saw the opening performed once, and could not know what it meant until some older people made him wise.[24]

The charm-setter might also use sympathetic magic to take milk and butter luck. This was done by appropriating dairying objects or utensils belonging to the farm, or by taking cow hairs, mud from the cloven foot, cow droppings, or especially the spancel from the byre. Spancels so stolen might be used for mock or symbolic milking in order to take a neighbour's profit, as the following account from Co. Fermanagh shows:

> There are also stories of milking the rope. An old hag who lived at Coragh was spied upon, and was seen with a rope suspended from a beam at the end of the churn and she milking it. She too was noted for the amount of butter she sold in relation to the number of cows she had.[25]

Appropriating, or obtaining by means of a trick, milk, butter or a milk vessel from a house on May morning could also put the family's butter supply for the coming year in jeopardy, according to popular belief. This was particularly so if a May morning visitor did not help with the churning while it was in progress. Indeed so great was the fear of being blamed if the churning failed that people were very reluctant to visit, or be seen near, their neighbour's house on May Day. It was also strongly believed throughout Ireland that a person could steal a household's butter by taking fire—symbolic of the household's luck, which on May Day centres on milk and dairy produce—out of the house on that day. Thus, even a frequent pipe-smoking caller to the house would be refused a live cinder to 'redden' his tobacco pipe on May Day, and indeed he would be expected not to ask for it. The following legend, while hinting at the carelessness of the housewife who left her churn unattended, tells how a tailor foiled the attempts of a butter thief attempting to steal butter by means of a live coal from the household fire:

> A travelling tailor was one May day engaged in a certain farmhouse. The woman of the house was churning, and once while she left the house a strange woman entered and took the coal from the fire. No sooner did the tailor see this than he picked up a coal and dropped it into a pail of water. It seems that this had the effect of quenching the coal the woman had taken because she presently returned and took another glowing coal. The same operation performed by the tailor resulted in her returning again. Her next attempt also failed, and by this time she understood that some power greater than her own was at work, and so she departed, but through the sharpness of the little tailor, without the butter she intended to bring.[26]

Even the smoke from the kitchen fire could represent cream, and the household's butter could be stolen by the charm-setter who recited *im an deataigh sin ar mo chuid bainne-se*, 'the butter of that smoke on my own milk', while reversing into her own house. Consequently people were reluctant to be the first household in their townland to light a fire on May morning for fear of drawing the attention of charmsetters. *Codladh Bealtaine* ('May morning sleep') was an expression applied to late rising on May morning in parts of Connacht, and indeed a Co. Galway correspondent tells us that:

> The women of south Conamara (along the seashore) would not light a fire on May morn until they saw smoke from the houses in Co. Clare, because they were afraid that the Clarewomen would take the butter from them across the sea.[27]

Thus people tended to do outdoor work such as hedging in sight of each other's homes on May Morning in order to keep watch for smoke rising from houses, and this activity is the basis of the remark 'he is May morning hedging', to describe a person who is spying on his neighbours.[28]

Protecting the milk profit

In view of such a strong belief that milk and milk products were seriously at risk during the festival of May, it is to be expected that people would take measures to protect them, and it is quite clear from the source material that a wide variety of protective measures were known and practised during the festival for that very purpose. Some of these derived from official religion, such as having a Mass said in the family home, sprinkling holy water and especially Easter water on the farm, on the farm animals, and on the milking and churning utensils, or hanging religious medals or other sacred artifacts in the cow byre. But it is also clear that these measures were not always considered to be sufficient to counteract the perceived threat to dairy produce at Maytime, and thus recourse was had to other, or additional measures of an a-Christian nature, for protective purposes. These measures had the sanction of tradition, and even though they were recognised as acts of magic, people felt justified in performing them in order to protect milk and butter which were a vital food resource, and perhaps also, a source of income.

Only a small sample of the extensive catalogue of protective measures detailed in the source material can be mentioned here.[29] Included among them are attempts to protect boundary water and well water by the application of iron (often in the form of horseshoe nails) and salt. Twigs of the quicken or rowan tree were placed at the four cardinal points on the farm, or a more formal redefining of the farm boundary might take place.[30] Cows were driven through fire, or a small fire of furze bushes might be lighted in a field near the farmhouse. At the farmyard, all gates and shed doors, especially those of cow-byres, were securely fastened or locked, and milking and churning vessels were protected with twigs of the rowan tree. Care was also taken not to allow any such vessels out of the farmyard on May day, or to give away milk or butter, and also to prevent people from taking live coals or cinders from the household fire on that day. In addition, in the eastern and southern parts of Ireland in particular, a variety of protective domestic verdure symbols including May flowers, the May bough and the May bush were used in farmyard or dwelling house, or at the well, during the festival of May. The May flowers—usually yellow flowers such as marigolds, cowslips, buttercups and furze blossoms—were normally picked on May eve and placed over the kitchen and byre doors, on the thresholds and window sills and perhaps also at the well. The May bough—typical of the province of Munster—was brought into the house and put in a place conspicuous to any would-be milk thief, while the May bush—common in the southeast and north-midlands, and often a whitethorn bush decorated with yellow flowers and eggshells—was placed before the kitchen door or at the farmyard gate. These verdure symbols, placed at liminal points about the farmyard and house, were intended to protect and promote the household's seasonal luck and prosperity concerned with milch cows, pasturage and dairy produce.[31]

If, however, in spite of, or due to a lack of, protective measures, the milk profit was believed to be stolen, further measures could, and should be immediately taken to recover the butter. In the case of repeated failures to make any butter, or a reasonable quantity of it, recourse was often had to the parish priest to bless the dairy and farm utensils, or to say a 'May Mass' the house or church for the recovery of the milk profit.[32] For an unexpected churning failure on May morning more traditional methods may be used such as putting hairs from a cow's tail on the churn dash, as the following account from Co. Clare indicates:

[A] family were unable to make a churn until [an old woman came in. She took a *dreas* [a turn at churning] and was unable to make progress. She went out, made a ring [of cow hair and put it on the dash of the churn] and all was well.[33]

The heating of iron—especially ploughing irons—in a strict ritual process intended to reinforce boundaries was very common. This was designed to reveal the identity of the butter thief and thus recover the butter, as outlined in the following legend from Co. Westmeath:

To get back your butter: bolt the door tight, close the window, put salt in the milk, and put the coulter and plough chains into the red fire, and then start churning. As the irons become red you'll hear someone at the door, but keep churning. Then the person who took your butter will screech to you and beg of you to let her in. But take no notice until your churning is done and you get the butter. After that this person will have no power over the milk.[34]

Conclusion

The perception that both the knowledge and performance of milk-stealing and protective magic belong essentially to women, is evident from the traditional source material. Men on the other hand are shown to be involved in the theft of milk profit only in exceptional or accidental circumstances, and, as is pointed out in some of the legends quoted above, they are said to take steps to 'return' the 'stolen' milk profit. Indeed a male informant from Co. Cork claims that 'It was never heard of that a man was found trying to steal the produce of a neighbour's herd',[35] and a mid-nineteenth century account from Co. Derry states that a husband died of shame after his wife had been found guilty by the local church minister of milk theft by means of acts of magic.[36] Men's role in relation to the protection of milk and butter luck is concerned mainly with situations in which their physical strength or force is required, such as at the guarding of wells, hunting the milk-stealing hare, or preventing women from gathering the dew. Indeed the use of physical force against women—or at least the threat of it—is a recurring feature in traditions about milk luck protection at Maytime where men are involved.[37] This may reflect prevailing social prejudices which consider women to be more prone to magic than men, with the added effect of shielding men from community criticism.[38] But on balance, the main reason that society has viewed women as milk 'thieves', is undoubtedly linked to the fact that traditionally, it was the women or women of the household, who had responsibility for milking, butter-making and associated utensils, as well as the care of milch cows especially after calving, and the calves too. In the Irish context there is abundant evidence of the importance of the woman's role in the production of dairy produce, ranging from the ancient law tracts of about the eighth century, to the personal experiences of some Irish farmers' wives in modem times.[39] It was the woman's responsibility to ensure that there was a plentiful supply of milk and dairy produce, both for household use and, also, perhaps for the market. To achieve this it was necessary to have not only the required technical skills in relation to milk and butter production and the care of cows, but also to have knowledge of the performance and effects of milk magic and counter-magic.

Since milk and butter production were the responsibility of the women of the community, and since they no doubt wished to be as successful as possible in this vital undertaking, they were, of course, in competitions with each other. However, it was important not to be arrogant about one's butter luck, or to appear too successful. As we have seen in some of the material presented above, if the quantity of butter produced on a farm was considered disproportionate to the number of cows it supported or the size or quality of the holding, the woman could be suspected of milk-stealing, especially if a neighbouring farmer in ostensibly better circumstances was unable to produce a reasonable quantity of butter. For example, a certain old woman farming bogland in Co. Laois, with a couple of what appeared to be poorly fed cows, who yet had big baskets of butter for sale despite having a family to provide for, was considered to be a butter thief.[40]

But it would also seem that it was not just the marginal location or status of farm holdings which might give rise to suspicions of butter-stealing on the part of some women. While any woman in the neighbourhood was felt to be a potential butter thief at the boundary festival of May—even one' most obliging and friendly next-door neighbour[41]—it is evident that some women in particular were considered a threat at this time. The extra-categorical status of some of the women farmers seems to be a particularly relevant factor. It is evident from the descriptions of milk 'thieves' in the source material—only a small proportion of which is presented here—that many of these women were old, or ugly, and in this connection a Co. Monaghan informant states: 'It is said still of any ugly woman that she was like one 'who would be sweeping the dew'.[42] Others were women who were widowed, unmarried, or independent women farmers living alone, or women of the Protestant faith living amongst old Catholic stock—all thus lacking supportive social ties and, therefore, potentially culpable and easy scapegoats.[43]

Accordingly, there can hardly be any doubt that some farming women became community scapegoats, as a result of attempts by their neighbours to account for variations in the expected return from their milch cows, due perhaps to changes in environmental conditions, fluctuations in milk quality, or mismanagement. From the point of view of those households which had suffered churning failures or a substantial reduction in butter quantity, for whatever reasons, the general belief in the possibility (or indeed, probability) of women stealing butter by magic during the boundary festival of May, enabled them to shift the responsibility for such a situation onto other members of the community—who were almost invariably women. Thus, the ineffectual farmer could escape criticism, and the housewife who had failed in her responsibility to provide a sufficient quantity of butter for the household or market, could de-emphasize her own inefficiency in butter production by placing the blame for her failure on other neighbouring women, some of whom were clearly more competent and prosperous than she, but also, unfortunately, socially disadvantaged.

The festival of May was a time of considerable reorganisation on the farm especially in relation to cattle. The cow herd which had been kept indoors over the winter and spring seasons was now turned out of doors into nearby pastures, or sent to the mountain or moorland *buaile* for the duration of the milking season, if transhumance was still practised. The women's daily routine was also altered to cope with the summer supply of milk, and the substantial and labour intensive butter-making task. As Mayday was considered the beginning of the milking season, it was a time of heightened competition between neighbouring milk producers, when women in general, but some women in particular, were under suspicion both by men and women, as potential milk-profit thieves. It was a time of latent hostility—or even obvious aggression—towards one's neighbours, as people sought to safeguard their livelihood during the dangerous transition period between spring and summer—the boundary festival of May.

Note: IFC—Irish Folklore Collection in the archive of the Department of Irish Folklore, University College Dublin, which includes the questionnaire entitled May Eve and May Day circulated by the Irish Folklore Commission in 1947. Because of the extensiveness of the material it has only been possible in this short paper to give the most pertinent references. Individual and family names as well as some place-names have been omitted from the IFC texts.

Notes

1. A. T. Lucas, *Cattle in Ancient Ireland*, Kilkenny 1989, 3, and note 3, p. 250. For a textual example of the sentence, see M. Freeman (ed.), *Annála Connacht. The Annals of Connacht, (A.D. 1224–1544)*, Dublin 1944, 19, par. 26, I. 4–'... 7 *doronsatur sith dar cend a mbo 7 a muintire* ('... and they concluded peace for the sake of their cattle and their people').

2. The belief that old women in the form of hares sucked milk from cows is mentioned by Giraldus Cambrensis towards the end of the twelfth century—see note 55 below. An account from the middle of the sixteenth century links this belief to May Day and mentions other May Day beliefs well known in modern times in Ireland—in this connection, see K. Danaher, *The Year in Ireland*, Cork/Dublin, 1972, 109–110.

3. For the festival of May see Danaher 1972, 86–127; C. Ó Danachair, 'The Quarter Days in Irish Tradition', *Arv* 15, (1959), 49–50, 53–55; R. Buchanan, 'Calendar Custom', *Ulster Folklife*, 1962, 24–30; E. E. Evans, *Irish Folk Ways*, London 1957, 272–4; P. Lysaght, 'Maytime Verdure Customs and their Distribution in Ireland', *International Falklore Review*, London 1991, 75–82; P. Lysaght, Bealtaine: 'Irish Maytime Customs and the Reaffirmation of Boundaries', in H. E. Davidson (ed.), *Boundaries and Thresholds*, Woodchester, 1992, 28–43; P. Lysaght, *Féile na Bealtaine in Iarthar agus Iar-Dheisceart Thír Chonaill* ('The May Festival in West and Southwest Donegal'), forthcoming in B. Almqvist (ed.), *An Chéad Céad. The First Hundred. Festschrift for Séamus Ó Catháin*, Department of Irish Folklore, Dublin, 27–41. *See also* H. Glassie, *Passing the Time*, Dublin 1982, 778, note 1, and A. and B. Rees, *Celtic Heritage*, London 1961, Ch. 3.

4. Cf. Lysaght 1991, 76–77, 1992, 31. Although a large body of material was collected as a result the questionnaire about May Eve and May Day in 1947, a few collectors experienced difficulties because of some peoples' reluctance to admit familiarity with the Maytime magical rites for fear of being thought to practise them (IFC 1095: 280, Co. Tipperary).

5. IFC 1097: 185.

6. While strangers might occasionally be blamed for butter theft, the weight of the evidence is that it was envious neighbours who were believed to be involved. A relative is specifically mentioned in IFC 1095:145, Lismore, Co. Waterford, for example. The belief that women were involved in milk profit theft by means of magic acts is also found in other cultures as is evident from the proceedings of witch trials. For the situation in the Nordic countries cf. J. Wall, *Tjuomjölkande väsen*, I, Studia Ethnologica Upsaliena III, Ch. 4.

7. IFC 1096: 83 Co. Mayo.

8. IFC 1096: 8. (*Ceaptaí (agus ceaptar í gcónaí) gur droch-fhuadar a bheadh faoin duine a rachfadh ar talamh duine eile Lá Bealtaine i.e. chun piseoga a chur ag obair.*).

9. IFC 1095: 114—115.

10. For the composition and construction of the *buarach,* see Lucas 1989, 44. Lucas has also presented a wide-ranging survey of early and medieval Irish literary texts to show that from earliest times milking was regarded as woman's work, and that the spancel was regarded as her indispensable accessory in that task.

11. IFC 1096: 341. Cf. Lysaght 1993, 32–33.

12. Translation of Irish text from the bilingual collection of legends: S. Ó hEochaidh M. Ní Néill, S. Ó Catháin. *Síscéalta Ó Thír Chonaill/Fairy Legends from Donegal* Dublin, 1977, No. 25. This legend expresses the common idea that alien population groups—and in this case with an alien faith—had occult powers. For a further version of this legend from southwest Donegal expressing a similar view of Protestant women, see IFC 1096:407–8.

13. IFC 1097: 81; it would seem as if virtually any object could become a medium for magical milk-stealing on May morning provided it was used in the prescribed manner.

14. The reference to black magic is contained in the threat 'to steep the sheaf' or 'to bury the sheaf' as the magical activity is more usually called. The sheaf represented the intended victim, and pins might be stuck in the joints of the straw wisps in order to give a painful death. The sheaf was buried (or thrown into water in an inaccessible place such as a boghole), and as it decayed, the person it represented was also believed to fade away. This custom was strong in the eastern midlands of Ireland settled by English colonists, including Co. Westmeath, from where the legend cited comes. For an analysis of this phenomenon, see N. McLaughlin, *Burying the Sheaf. A Form of Murder by Magic,* student essay in the Department of Irish Folklore, 1977.

15. IFC 1095: 35.

16. 'Street' is the yard in front of the farmhouse in west-Co. Clare.

17. IFC 1095: 236–7. Cf. Lysaght, 1993, 33–34.

18. IFC 1196: 407, Ardara, Co. Donegal.

19. IFC 1095: 335.

20. IFC 1095: 278 Tipperary.

21. *Giraldi Cambrensis Opera,* Vol. V. ed. James F. Dimock, London 1867, 106; 'Item, vetulas quasdam, tam in Wallia quam Hibernia et Scotia, se in leporinam transmutare formam, ut adulterina sub specie ubera sugendo, lac alienum occultius surripiant, vetus quidem et adhuc frequens querela est.' For a mid-sixteenth century reference to the belief that old women in hare-form sucked milk from cows on May Day, see the section entitled 'Ireland and the Smaller Ilands in the British Ocean', in W. Camden, *Brittania,* London, 1610, 146: '. . . If they finde an hare amongst their heards of cattaile on the said May daie; they kill her, for, they suppose she is some old trot, that would filch away their butter . . .'; also quoted in Danaher 1972, 109–110. For nineteenth and twentieth century references see T. Crofton Croker, *Researches in the South of Ireland,* London 1824, 94 (Also facsimile edition, Shannon, 1969, 94), and S. O Duilearga, *Leabhar Sheáin Í Chonaill,* (Baile Átha Cliath 1948, 1971), 437/*Seán Ó Conaill's Book,* Dublin 1981, 399–400; P. Lysaght, 'A Tradition Bearer in Contemporary Ireland', in L. Röhrich/S. Wienker-Piepho (eds.), *Storytelling in Contemporary Societies,* Tübingen 1990, 208.

22. IFC 1095: 199.

23. IFC 1097: 151. For a Nordic perspective on milk-stealing creatures, see J. Wall, *Tjuvmjölkande väsen*, 1, 2, Studia Ethnologica Upsalienia III, 5, 1977, 1978.

24. IFC 1097: 214.

25. IFC 1096: 341, 337; see also a Co. Waterford account of an old woman milking a *buarach* placed across the fire crane into a bucket (IFC 1095: 317).

26. IFC 1095: 227–8. See also Ó Duilearga, *op. cit.,* 1948, 1971, 310–311, 437; 1981, 272, 400.

27. IFC 70: 57.

28. IFC 1096: 341.

29. See Danaher 1972, 109–119; Lysaght 1992, 37–42.

30. For a formal redefining of boundaries described in a nineteenth century source, see Ó Danachair 1972, 116–117.

31. Danaher 1972, 88–9; Lysaght 1991, 77–82; 1992, 39–41.

32. For example IFC 1095: 90, Co. Cork.

33. IFC 1095:200.

34. IFC 1097: 66.

35. IFC 1095: 134: Cf. Lysaght 1993, 36–37.

36. Danazher 1972, 115–116.

37. Indicative of this is the following remark allegedly made by a missioner at the Parish mission in Cappawhite, Co. Tipperary in 1936, and reported in IFC 407: 286: Missioner: 'I'm told that the man who fired on the woman who was taking his butter by *piseoga* only wounded her—more's the pity!'. In addition, a Co. Tipperary questionnaire correspondent wrote in 1947, that there had been a law case in Cashel a few years previously brought by a woman who was assaulted by a neighbour at the well on May Morning (IFC 1095: 269). Also from Co. Tipperary it was reported that a man who encountered a woman in the field on. May morning 'taking' milk with a *buarach*, took the *buarach* from her and flogged her with it (IFC 1095–254).

38. According to Marcel Mauss, women, because of society's attitude to them, are everywhere considered more prone to magic than men: M. Mauss, *General Theory of Magic,* (trans. R. Brain), London, 1972, 28. (Engl. edn.).

39. See note 44 above, and O Corráin, *op. cit.,* 9, who writes in reference to the value of the law tracts as ethnological evidence: 'The legal tracts incidentally provide first class evidence of the importance of a woman's role (as manager and worker) in the rural economy—in dairying, in the production of woollen and linen garments, in caring for farmyard animals (especially the fattening of stall-fed beasts for the table), and in organising the ploughing and reaping of corn, (and, no doubt, the feeding of the labourers)'. The gender-based bias in favour of women as milkers still persists to some extent in Ireland in farms where the number of cows is small, or where a milking machine has not been installed.

40. IFC 1097: 186, (1947). Families living in marginal or remote locations who were successful butter producers might become suspect, like a family on. Inniskeen Island, Co. Fermanagh, about whom the questionnaire correspondent commented: 'I myself remember the last members of this family and they were certainly queer' (IFC 1096:337).

41. IFC: 1096:419–22.

42. IFC 1096: 367, (1947). Cf. in this connection, C. Lamer, *Enemies of God. The Witch-hunt in Scotland,* Oxford, 1981, 9: 'The witch is old, ugly, and female in most societies.'

43. R. P. Jenkins, 'Witches and fairies: Supernatural Aggression and Deviance', in P. Narváez (ed.), *The Good People: New Fairylore Essays,* London/New York, 326–7. This is evident from a number of the extracts from the archival material presented in this paper. It is also evident from the sources that some of these women had a general had reputation and they would be specially watched on occasions like the May festival. (IFC 1097: 199, Co. Laois). A correspondent also states that some of them were blamed without foundation (IFC 1095: 170, Co. Cork).

CHAPTER 20
THANKSGIVING IN THE USA: THE MEAL AS MEDIUM AND MESSAGE
Jay Allan Anderson

History

Thanksgiving Day is the last Thursday in November. Every year, two hundred million people in the United States sit down to a basic meal of roast turkey, stuffing, cranberry sauce, sweet potatoes, mashed white potatoes and gravy, creamed onions, a green vegetable, and pumpkin and mince pie. Beverages are water, milk, and coffee. The majority will stay at home — Thanksgiving being a family feast. The meal will take place sometime in the afternoon. Throughout the weekend that follows, families will relax together, watching sports events and special programs on television, chatting before an open fire, all the while eating turkey soup and sandwiches and cold leftovers. The dominant mood is familial and nostalgic: talk centers on the family's recent activities and the good old days. Controversial subjects such as sex, politics, and religion are bypassed. It is a time for quiet pleasures and the giving of thanks for the many real blessings that living in America still brings.

Outside the home, the feast is given national recognition. The government declares the day a holiday, schools are shut, churches hold special services and stores feature traditional foods and in some large cities sponsor parades. The mass media offers a variety of special »uplifting» articles and programs ranging from scholarly pieces such as Saturday Review's »Ethnogastronomy of Thanksgiving» to Walt Disney's T.V. cartoon »The Mouse that Came Over on the Mayflower». Little attempt is made to exploit the feast commercially as are Christmas and Easter the other major holidays. Gifts are not given, nor greeting cards sent. Restaurants and hotels do compeat for the business of those who cannot or prefer not to eat at home. Apart from this, Thanksgiving still belongs to the people — and tradition.

Our modern Thanksgiving is a combination of two very different and very old holidays: 1) the Harvest Home feast celebrated when the main crops were harvested and 2) the formal day of thanksgiving proclaimed by a community's authorities to focus attention on a particular event, such as a military victory, or the need for rain.

The first group to celebrate both a Harvest Home and a Day of Thanksgiving were the settlers in Plymouth, now commonly known as Pilgrims. They were the first group of families to settle the eastern United States. One third of them were religious refugees from England who had spent ten years in exile in Holland before obtaining permission to found a colony in America. The other twothirds were farmers and craftsmen seeking a better life. They numbered about 100 and sailed in 1620 from England on the Mayflower. Upon their arrival in America, they declared a Day of Thanksgiving to give thanks for their safe voyage. The more religious held a church service, the others just feasted on the ship's stores: dried beef, cheese, biscuits, and beer. During the winter half the colonists died, but the others with the help of Samoset and Squanto, two Indians who had lived in England, managed to plant and harvest a good crop of maize, beans, and squashes. When these crops had

Jay Allan Anderson, 'Thanksgiving in the USA: The Meal as Medium and Message' in Nilo Valonen and Juhani Lehtonen (eds), *Ethnologische Nahrungsforschung: Ethnological Food Research: Reports from the Second International Symposium for Ethnological Research*, 1973. (Helsinki, 1975), pp. 9–14. Reprinted with permission from the author.

been gathered, they held a week long Harvest Home feast. There were no church services — just parading, sports, eating, and drinking. Ninety Wampanoags Indians, who enjoyed feasting, joined them for part of the week and contributed five deer.

For almost the next two hundred and fifty years, these two kinds of »thanksgiving» remained quite distinct. Very few formal »days of thanksgiving» coincided with harvest. They were proclaimed at various times in all regions of the English colonies and were popular. No special foods became associated with them. During the same period (1620–1870) harvest home feasts also flourished. The menues of these feasts differed along regional and ethnic lines. The harvest supper of the Germans in Pennsylvania, the Dutch in New York, the Scotch-Irish in Appalachia, the African Americans in the South, and the English in New England: all were unique. Because these regional ethnic cultures remained isolated and autonomous, their harvest home and thanksgiving day feasts continued to be local and provincial in character.

During and after the Revolutionary War (1775–83), a desire for national rather than local holidays developed and an attempt was made to combine harvest home with the formal day of thanksgiving. George Washington noted in his orderly book on October 31, 1777, »Tomorrow being the day set apart by the honorable Congress for Public Thanksgiving and praise, and duty calling us devoutly to express our grateful acknowledgements to God for the manifold blessings he has granted us . . .». Later in 1789 as President, he appointed the last Thursday in November as a national thanksgiving day. Regional feeling was, however, still too strong for the feast to be accepted nationally. But regionalism began to crumble in the nineteenth century as mass communications and transportation evolved. Hard surfaced highways, canals, and railways helped a national market develope. An industrial revolution began, cities expanded, and tens of millions of immigrants flooded in from Europe. A nationalistic spirit developed and pressure was put on both regional and immigrant ethnic cultures to adopt the new national, popular culture. Compulsory education in public schools insured a measure of common enculturation. The story of the Pilgrims became an ideal medium for fostering »Americanism». Regionalism's last attempt to thwart this nationalism came in 1861 when the southern slave owning states seceded, setting off Civil War. During the worst of the fighting, President Lincoln in an attempt to bolster unionist spirit, appointed the last Thursday in November as an annual national Thanksgiving holiday. Soon afterwards, the northern regions won the war and the union was preserved. As regionalism quickly faded, the tradition of a combined harvest home and thanksgiving day feast celebrated nationally was accepted. The »new» holiday featured all the characteristics common today: a church service in the morning, followed by an afternoon's feast and a weekend of sports. The menu centered around roast turkey, stuffing, cranberry sauce, numerous vegetables, and pumpkin pie — the main dishes of the New England harvest home feast. Many of these foods had gained popularity because of their supposed connection to the Pilgrims. Thanksgiving as a national cultural event is now just about a century old and still relatively unchanged. In a nation of continual and rapid change, it remains surprisingly vital.

Analysis

Thanksgiving is a complex folkloric event that plays an important role in American culture. By means of the two central elements in the festival: the narrative of the Pilgrims and their »first» Thanksgiving and the meal itself (both believed by most people to be very old) Americans reinforce with varying degrees of consciousness their image of themselves as a unique people with a special history. The feast, then, is the medium by which Americans share a message which they believe is of great importance.

Although days of thanksgiving and harvest home feasts are clearly older than the nation, the meal as a national event of importance is a product of the nineteenth century when a national culture was being forged out of the various regions and ethnic groups. The country needed a new folklore to bind together its heterogeneous population. The story of the Pilgrims and their feast helped fill this need and was widely diffused throughout the population especially in the newly created public schools. Longfellow's poem, »The Courtship of Miles Standish», (1858) was virtually required reading for every child and established the Pilgrims at the very center of the new national mythology. (The secular »trinity» is the Pilgrim Fathers, Washington, and Lincoln — all closely associated with the feast). The Pilgrim story is still emphasized in schools and homes. Five motifs in the narrative have been and are still being stressed by parents and teachers. Each reinforces a particular belief Americans have of themselves and their history.

1. Americans believe that they are an idealistic people, descendents of European immigrants who — like the Pilgrims — came to America to obtain religious and political freedom. There is a tendency to picture Europe at least as it was in the Pilgrim's day, as an intolerant and dictatorial place, and in strong contrast to an America which offered all men »life, liberty, and the pursuit of happiness». Because the Pilgrims were the first families to come to this »brave new world» they are considered everyone's ancestors and Plymouth, »home town USA».

2. Americans believe that their national culture is a »melting pot» of diverse regional and ethnic cultures, each of which willingly became part of the whole. »Un-americanisms» have been fiercely attacked as threats to the national »American way of life». The Pilgrims are cited as good Americans for they too were worried during their exile in Holland about the Dutch »foreign» culture influencing their children.

3. Americans believe that they are a hardworking people, like the Pilgrims, who have had to endure periods of economic hardship before achieving success. It is said that »when the going gets tough, the tough gets going».

4. Americans believe that God helps those who help themselves — and retain their faith. The Pilgrim's devoutness and confidence was rewarded by the virtual miracle of help from two English speaking Indians. They were taught how to farm successfully using Indian crops and methods and thus kept from starving.

5. Finally, Americans still believe that the United States is the best country in the world to live in and therefore they should be thankful and generous to others less fortunate. The Pilgrims are cited for their understanding of this, even after one year in the new world, and their Thanksgiving feast and kindness toward the Indians.

In short, the Pilgrims are considered the first true Americans: idealistic, unified, hardworking, confident, thankful and generous. They have become heroes, the »Fathers». Because they lived so long ago, they escaped most of the later controversial aspects of American history. Their story offends none (except the Indians) and can be easily identified with. It helped shape the national culture and now comes to its defence. In this contemporary world of »future shock», Americans can escape into the mythic golden age of Plymouth 1621 and vicariously become Pilgrims. The experience is profoundly reassuring.

The other central element in Thanksgiving, the feast, strongly reinforces this escape into a better, simpler, and more genuinely 'American' past. Because eating is a total sensory activity, food has extraordinary symbolic potential. Thanksgiving is a good example. The basic menu of roast turkey, stuffing, cranberry sauce, sweet potatoes, mashed white potatoes, and pumpkin pie as a unit is thought by the people who eat it to be very old, very rural, and more »natural» than ordinary fare. It is like Plymouth in 1621, better, simpler, and somehow more American. It elicits strong nostalgic feelings and a yearning for the good »folk» life. Few Americans, of course, would or could put these feelings into words, or even bother to formulate the question »What does this food mean to you?» in the first place. They simply eat and compliment the housewife and tradition for setting such a good table. Still, the attitudes and feelings are there as the advertizing men are well aware. When Thanksgiving food is marketed, primarily in magazines and newspapers, it is usually surrounded by images that suggest the »good old days on the farm — once upon a time». The exceptions reverse the image and sell a particularly convenient way to cook the traditional food. But they, too, reinforce the tradition by suggesting ways traditional proscriptions can be met (the right meal cooked in the right way in the right place at the right time) more easily. They understand that Thanksgiving is a kind of secular, nationalistic »mass» where people eat symbols of their folk history, thereby regaining some of the qualities they believed their ancestors possessed. And they are clever enough not to tamper with this. When changes in the meal are suggested — it is usually the addition of side dishes that also symbolize the past (wholemeal bread, maple syrup, etc) or more historic recipes.

Thanksgiving is an excellent example of the significance of traditional food habits to the people of a modern industrial state. The recent extraordinary rise in the demand for and production of »natural organic» food further emphasizes that the symbolic importance of food is a force to be taken into consideration by the food industry. Already food scientists have discovered that markets exist within mass cultures like the United States for special lines of food that particular groups have selected as their »culinary» totems. Thus, the average American today has a far greater range of foods to choose from than he ever did before. And he is using this freedom to select foods that serve to compliment his image of himself in the subculture of which he is a part. A modern equivalent to the old regional and ethnic group is evolving and food is playing an important part in its development. Thanksgiving is but one of the first of many coming examples of the utilization of food and meals as medium and message.

CHAPTER 21
WHEN PRODUCERS BECAME CONSUMERS: CULTURAL PROCESSES IN DAILY LIFE

Yrsa Lindqvist

In 2009 I published a book about the changes that had occurred in Finnish food culture during the twentieth century. In less than one hundred years society, technology and materiality had developed faster than ever before, with resultant changes in daily life in Finland, including in the areas of food production and eating habits. As a specialist in the areas of food, work practices and methods, at an archive of Folk Culture, with collections dating from, the late nineteenth century to the present, it is obvious that the older material, including photographs, interviews, recipes and all kind of notes related to these subject areas, have become essentially documents concerning a way of life that has definitely passed when compared to the present situation.

Two aspects, which a study of the archival material concerning food brings into focus, deserve attention. Such a study shows, first of all, how ethnological research has changed overtime. The early ethnologists were focusing on rural life and were documenting buildings, the sowing and harvesting of crops, animal slaughtering, fishing methods, and so on. It would seem, from this material, that daily life was mainly about the production and preservation of food. In Finland, where the vast majority of the population lived in rural areas, the production of food was, for most people, what life was actually about. In the early twentieth century, ethnologists tended not to document people's attitudes to the food which they ate, or why it was customary to serve certain dishes on festive occasions, or how a cook worked on a wedding feast in which the whole village would participate. The discipline, at that time, required facts, documenting, for example, recipes, menus, and the order in which people sat at table. The recording work that was carried out was regarded as a rescue mission with the aim of saving evidence of an existing lifestyle in a changing world. An ethnologist of today, in seeking to effectively use this older material, must endeavour to read between the lines, so to speak, in order to connect diverse sources to a context. Atmosphere, for example, is seldom described in the older ethnological notes, but photographs in archival collections can be good sources of information in this regard, as arranged pictures can show status through symbols, and snapshots can capture a moment of happiness or sadness in a face.

The second aspect, which a study of the archival material highlights, concerns cultural processes. In contrast to how food was viewed at a time when it was necessary to be self-sufficient in the area of nutrition, food today has many associated implications concerning, for example, the areas of ecology, ethics, health, lifestyle, weekend hobbies, and socialising with friends. These are all aspects of ethnological food research nowadays. In this paper, I will present three aspects of change with regard to food, ranging from the time when matters of production were paramount, to nowadays, when food is concerned more and more with consumption and the choosing of a lifestyle.

Yrsa Lindqvist, 'When Producers Became Consumers: Cultural Processes in Daily Life' in Patricia Lysgaht (ed.), *Time for Food: Proceedings of the Eighteenth Conference of the International Commission for Ethnological Food Research, Abo Akademi University, Turku, Finland, 2010.* (Abo, 2012), pp. 57–67.

Reprinted with permission from the author.

Welfare by gardening

In the late nineteenth century, Finland was still part of the Russian empire, but the search for a national identity was intense at that time, and there was also grave concern about the general level of education of the people, and thus about the nation's welfare. Many families lived in very simple conditions and their food consisted mainly of potatoes, salted fish or meat, porridge, milk and bread. It is a well-known fact today that one of the best ways of achieving improvement in living conditions in developing countries, is to educate the women folk of these regions. That is also what happened in Finland within the last one hundred years, when, in 1899, a women's organisation, called the Martha Association, was founded, This organisation aimed to make women the fosterers of coming generations in Finland; it also sought to increase their awareness of the political situation in the country, to increase their self-confidence, and to improve their knowledge and skill in housekeeping and family matters. Just a few years later, the first housekeeping schools, with the aim of improving women's cooking skills and of establishing new eating habits, in order to achieve a healthier life for their families, were established.

It was decided that one way of achieving the above aim was by teaching women how to grow vegetables, berries and fruit, and how to use them as part of a balanced diet. It was also considered to be economically beneficial to grow vegetables, both from a national and a family perspective. Nowadays, gardening is regarded as being a relaxing hobby with an associated therapeutic dimension, but this same idea was evident in the Martha project, as gardening was meant to provide women with a private space outside the inner household. For the children, vegetable gardening, working with plants and the soil, was seen as a way in which to learn responsibility and, in a moral sense, as a means by which to feel connected to home, to one's native district and, by extension, to the nation. In the cities, allotment gardens where established for industrial workers and others who did not have the opportunity of visiting the countryside during the summer months. The economic aspect, arising from the possibility of being able to grow some of the household's food requirements, was, perhaps, an even bigger incentive for citizens who tilled allotments. And, as regards the moral issue, allotments were to provide city workers with a healthier way of life.

The Martha organisation also considered it important to teach housewives how to preserve berries and vegetables for home use. The Association arranged exhibitions of, and competition for, preserved fruit, and for the finest products from the vegetable garden. The prizes to be won were usually seeds or fruit trees as an encouragement to keep up the good work.

Very little information about this early kitchen-gardening activity among the peasantry is to be found in the archival material because, until that time, gardening had been essentially an upper-class activity. The collectors in the field did not pay much attention to the gardening activity of the peasant as it was a new idea and activity which was be disseminated through organisations, schools, and experts, and was thus seen as an agent of change affecting old lifestyles and eating habits. Since the ethnologists' mission was to collect and preserve a disappearing rural culture, contemporary change was seldom documented. Some evidences of kitchen gardens call, however, be found in site plans of farmyards, and in family photos.

Nevertheless, kitchen gardening was a common activity in the Finnish countryside in the twentieth century. During the war years - 1939–1942 - it was necessary to grow potatoes, vegetables, apples, and so on, even in cities, if access could be had even to the smallest piece of ground, even in public parks. In the course of the 1960s and 1970s, however, the economic aspects of kitchen gardens diminished and they came to be seen, more and more, as something which older people did, or as something which some people just continued to do as part of an 'old tradition'. I believe that, by the 1970s, many adults who had the experiences of being, more or less, compelled to participate in kitchen gardening as a child, or in collecting wild berries, wanted to spare their own children this kind of work, since it was no longer necessary: from an economic point of view.

This, combined with a strong movement from rural areas to cities, and to a more urban style of life, meant that the natural know-how concerning the organisation and tilling of a kitchen garden was no longer being transmitted between generations.

Today, kitchen gardening is back, and, as was the case in the beginning, it is once more connected to an ideology, to some extent, at least. The younger generations have discovered that it is possible to grow one's own food, and older people have also taken up gardening as a hobby. There is, indeed, an economic aspect to this new phenomenon, but of primary importance is an ethical dimension. There is a constant flow of information about the extent to which pesticides are used in farming, and how vegetables and fruit are transported all over the world by airplanes, and how workers from the third world, employed just for the harvest period, are badly paid and live in poor conditions. The ecological issues are, perhaps, of most concern to people today – we no longer only count calories out of concern for our own bodies; we also count how much pollution the production and availability of our food produces, thus contributing to global warming. Our consciousness has extended from a sense of responsibility for our own health to the welfare of the earth.

Several movements have taken up gardening as a protest against, or as alternative to, the on-going consumer society. The Slow Food movement started in 1989 as a protest against fast-food eating habits, and its remit has been extended to include not only time to cook and eat, but also time to grow one's own food. In many cities, people have organised themselves into growing communities and have started to cultivate gardens in urban milieus. The Guerrilla gardening movement started in London in 2004, and in several cities in Finland, city-growers have organised themselves under the name Dodo. Even Michelle Obama has given a good example by starting a fruit and vegetable garden at the White house.

However, the environmental awareness shown here is still the concern of only a very small group of people. Its primary aim is to show that, although being brought up as a consumer in the western world, the production of food can be very exciting, ideologically challenging, and have a revolutionary tinge to it – even if it was a normal procedure for the majority of the population only two or three generations ago. In that sense, these new organisations resemble, to some extent the aim of the Martha Association which started one hundred and twenty years ago- that is, to again enlighten people about healthier food. But, instead of a salty and an unbalanced diet, as was often the case in the past, the enemy today is too much of everything, as well as food containing additives, azo dyes, flavourings, and so on.

The food industry needs authenticity

My second example of household change concerns cooking. Women are supposed to know how to cook, and one's mother is supposed to serve the tastiest of dishes. Informer times, cooking skills were usually learnt by a daughter from her mother, or by a daughter-in-law from her mother-in-law. In middle- and upper-class families, servants took care of the household and many newly-married young women did not have much knowledge of kitchen management. Cookbooks where not very common then, and in the eighteenth and nineteenth centuries, they still mainly contained recipes for so-called finer dishes. Young women usually collected recipes from family members, relatives and acquaintances, before marriage. By writing down the recipes in booklets, they made their own cookbooks. These usually consisted not only of food recipes but also of recipes for dying textiles and for fruit and vegetable preservation, as well as for household remedies for all kinds of illnesses and complaints of the period. The recipes often have remarks or titles concerning those who provided or created them, and it is possible thereby to follow the kinds of networks which women had at that time.

The idea of being educated in gardening and cooking activities went hand-in-hand with the social project of introducing healthier food habits to the Finnish people through household schools. For example, menus were introduced in which every dish had a side dish of some sort of vegetables, and a dessert – usually some kind of fruit-syrup cream – was also recommended.

As society modernised in the 1950s and 1960s, the Finnish food industry also expanded. As a result of industrial expansion and urbanisation, women were needed in the work force, and young girls, who had formerly worked as domestic servants, got better-paid jobs in the cities and industries. Society had changed. From then on it was necessary for most women to be able to quickly feed the family at the end of a working day. Convenience, or ready-to-eat, food was the answer. What followed over time is well known. Some got stuck in the ready-to-eat pattern and after a couple of generations it was said that people no longer knew how to use primary products or how to cook In the 1990s, during a serious economic depression in Finland, the Martha Association- which was still in existence- started up cooking courses once more. On this occasion, however, the purpose of the courses was mainly to teach people how to save money by cooking at home rather than by using ready-made food. This was followed by reports on how much salt, fat, preservatives and other additives which oven-ready food contained, and the dangers which these posed to one's health Thus, the only way to avoid the health risks involved was by using primary products and by cooking at home, like people used to do in the past.

This growing sense of awareness about food content, created by books, articles and other forms of documentation, caused the food industry to realise that, by now, a lot of people feel uncomfortable about eating mass-produced foodstuffs. To counteract this, food companies started to use the terms 'old-time' and 'home-made' in advertising, but since home-made cannot actually be used for industrially-produced food, a Finnish food company is, quite ingeniously, marketing their products as being made by mothers. The idea here is to imply that the dish is like what one's own mother would make.

A brochure, for ready-to-eat foodstuffs which I have seen, is dearly influenced in terms of appearance, layout, and content, by a traditional kind of handwritten recipe-booklet that women traditionally used to keep. It lists what to eat for lunch, what to eat between meals, and what to eat for supper, day-by-day, and is nicely illustrated by photos of the products. By appealing to mothers, and having the appearance of an old-time recipe booklet, the food acquires a more genuine touch. Even if the food is new, the values presented in this instance are traditional.

The kitchen, a place of lifestyle symbols

My third example deals with living conditions and lifestyle issues. It was mainly the very poor living conditions in Finland which the Martha Association, among others, sought to improve for the betterment of households. There was actually nothing called a kitchen in Finnish houses, just a stove that gave both light and warmth in a room in which a variety of activities took place. Food supplies were kept in different buildings, the water which was needed for the household was kept in a tub inside the door, and a chair was the only surface on which utensils and foodstuffs needed during cooking could be placed. Daily cooking was just about the feeding of the family.

Again I choose to point out three factors that led to change in household management in the late nineteenth and twentieth centuries. The iron-stove was an innovation that required change with regard to the kitchen utensils, recipes and eating habits of the family. The cooking of food in a pot over an open fire did not allow much scope for creativity, and the household oven itself was large, and was mainly used for the baking of bread, which took place twice a year. With the introduction of the efficient iron stove it was possible to fry food and to bake more easily, and also to save firewood. Secondly ergonomics became an important issue. No one had previously counted all the steps a housewife took in a totally unplanned cooking environment, until the 1920s and 1930s when women's housework was viewed in terms of convenience, saving time, and hygiene. In the 1960s, although the standard of living was rising, improvements carried out in many household were more pragmatic than aesthetical, and while the iron stove was still common in country houses, a gas or electric cooker was often placed beside it and used in addition to it when cooking. Later on, in the 1970s, as modernity and practical solutions dominated, everything reminiscent of the old times tended to be also associated with poverty. Every housewife's dream, when living in an old country house, was to rebuild at least the kitchen, without nostalgia.

The third revolution happened when men started to participate in cooking. Now the kitchen became a more interesting place for the whole family, and it was no longer built as a small separate room with doors which locked in the smell of cooking. Today, houses are built in open-plan style; the kitchen is often a part of the living room with matching interior fixtures. And even when it is a separate room, it is spacious and representative. The kitchen can actually be the most expensive part of the house, and it is probable that it is men's interest in cooking that has led to the improved technical level of kitchen fittings. It is not that women would not also have planned the kitchen solutions and wanted the new technology, but men nowadays use kitchen materials and machines as evidence of family's lifestyle and standard of living, and are ready to invest in an elaborate and technologically advanced kitchen, just as they would in a fine car. In purchasing a kitchen today, one is also buying into a dream of togetherness and of happy family life, since food and eating are nowadays first and foremost regarded as acts act of socialisation. This is so, at least in the dream, since, in reality, many fine kitchens are not used that much on an ongoing basis. There is also an advertising slogan which says something like 'Show me your kitchen and I can tell you who you are'. Today, country-style stands for romantic values, for something' cosy, for harmony and nostalgia – perhaps, also for family values. On the other hand, there are also kitchens that are rigidly structured and sterile-looking, but they, too, can be regarded as being exclusive and can also signify success.

Food patterns change

My three examples – the kitchen-garden project providing an incentive for people to grow and consume vegetables and fruit, the food industry requiring a connection to something real, such as mother, and the kitchen as a 'showroom' for ideals- are taking place in food studies. They are examples of how traditional subjects can be reshaped in anew context in modem times. For me, as someone who works at an archive, it is interesting and natural to compare the way of life portrayed in historical documents with modem life. Things change, but few things are completely new; they acquire new meanings in a different context. The discipline of ethnology, with its historical and contemporary dimensions, enables us analyse contemporary society while keeping the historical perspective in mind.

Today, the media are an important channel for both the provision and the acquisition of information. The flow of information, concerning all aspects of life, is also very fast. It is easy to get information on the Internet and especially in the social media, like Facebook, and friends are influenced by each other. I have read many comments in the social media provided by people making jam and syrup and this serves to inspire others to do the same. There are plenty of blogs where people publish recipes, home-style hints, and so on. We are subject to many influences and we are increasingly expected to take a stand, choose how to live, and how to consume. The consuming patterns of today are also questions of conscience. In the Western world, food is no longer just a question of nutrition; it is about choosing a lifestyle, and, in recent times, it is also concerned with discovering old traditions in order to provide useful skills in a new context. Even if consumers of conscience still only represent a marginal group of people, they are part of a growing trend. A new change is taking place-this time in the consumer society. And I think that we, as researchers, should be aware of the saying 'food patterns are hard to change, yet they change often and rapidly'.

CHAPTER 22
SICILIAN ST. JOSEPH'S TABLES IN LOS ANGELES, CALIFORNIA[1]

Luisa Del Giudice

In memory of Virginia Buscemi Carlson

(Villafranca Sicula, July 9, 1935 – Downey, Calif., Jan. 28, 2007)

This essay considers the mid-Lenten *Tavola di San Giuseppe* (St. Joseph's Table) in Los Angeles, a predominantly Sicilian custom of preparing food altars or tables in honor of St. Joseph which has at its core: a propitiatory sharing of abundance, a practice of hospitality and *caritas,* and in its diaspora manifestations, also a symbolic representation of the migration narrative itself.

Description of Los Angeles tables

St. Joseph's feast day is March 19 but often lasts from one to three days. St. Joseph's Tables include a devotional altar with a statue (or image) of Joseph holding the infant Jesus rising up, or separate from, a table. The table is blessed by a priest before the foods are consumed. Closest to (or on) the altar are placed sacred objects and foods, such as the large traditional ritual braided breads (Sic. *cucciddati*), weighing from three to seven kilograms and dedicated to the Holy Family. These large votive breads represent: a cross or crown for Christ, a palm frond for Mary, and a staff for St. Joseph. Implements of the Passion (e.g., ladder, tongs) are sometimes present, as are emblemata of Joseph the Carpenter's trade (saw, nails, plane). The table is laden with elaborate food displays and randomly distributed smaller and fanciful, zoomorphic and phytomorphic breads, e.g., birds, flowers, animals, fish, fruit, grapes, wheat. These smaller breads also hang among verdant festoons of foliage (in Sicily laurel, myrtle, and here citrus).[2] Because it falls within the meatless season of Lent, the tables feature vegetables, fried or stuffed—cauliflower, artichokes, zucchini, eggplant, peppers, cardoons, *frittate* [omelettes] of every sort—fava bean, asparagus, peas, peppers), literally and symbolically prominent fish, fruit (the season's finest first fruits — *primizie* — in baskets or cornucopias of plenty), and sweets: e.g., *persiche* (cream-filled pastries made to look like peaches), *cassadini/cassadeddi* (sweet ricotta filled ravioli or panzerotti), *sfinci* (cream-filled puffs with cheese, chocolate, and orange zest), *cannoli, cucciddati* (also referring to fig and nut-filled cookies; cf. Piccitto 1977), *cuddureddi* (*ciambelle* or donut-shaped cookies, but also referring to round breads with a hole in the middle, variant: see Varvaro and Sornicola 1986), and increasingly today, commercial baker's cakes, and even store-bought biscotti or *panettone* (an Italian Christmas specialty). In order to have traditional Sicilian sweets and breads for the table, one has traditionally relied on home bakers who know their family traditions and contribute to the tables, although their numbers are waning.[3]

An earlier version of this article appeared as 'Rituals of Charity and Abundance: Sicilian St. Joseph's Tables and Feeding the Poor in Los Angeles', *California Italian Studies* 1 (2010), 1–30. Revised and excerpted by the author for this publication.

Although the votive breads are the key ingredient on the table, breads are increasingly giving way to cakes and cookies. Do we attribute this to an acquired American taste for sugar (cf. Del Giudice 2001a)? Actually, Sicilians themselves seem to have the sweetest tooth of all regional Italians and have a long tradition of artistic marzipan confections, ritual cakes, and cookies and a particular genius for creating faux fruit (and fish: e.g., *pesce d'uova*; *pesci di funghi*),[4] along with candied figurines (*i pupi*) of lambs, human figures, horses; sweet bones (for the dead, *i Morti*), or eyes (for St. Lucy).[5] This penchant for sweets may have been formed, in part, by the Arab presence on that island centuries ago. Note that the Italian word for "sugar" (*zucchero*) comes via Sicilian, derived from the Arabic *"sùkkar"* (Caracausi 1983: 407).

The tradition also features a pageant of the Holy Family (*i santi*), who process from door to door, are twice turned away, and are ultimately welcomed by the family sponsoring the table. Private tables are given by a devotee, with the assistance of family, friends, neighbors, and business associates who donate labor, food and money to the host-family. Public celebrations in multiethnic environments such as Los Angeles frequently also become "ethnic display events" (e.g., with flags, ethnic costumes, banners). One of the most fully-articulated celebrations occurs at Mary Star of the Sea Church in San Pedro. A procession with saint's niche borne by men is accompanied by women of the St. Joseph Society, rallying to the traditional cry of: "Viva Gesù, Maria, Giuseppe, evviva!," followed by children in ethnic costumes, a marching band, guilds, societies, and confraternities carrying banners, and ending in a large banquet including e.g., *pasta e ceci* (a chickpea soup with small noodles) and seafood salad (or fried calamari), courtesy of the fishermen of this port city. This was the parish church of two Italian island fishing communities—Sicilians and Ischians (Ischia is an island off the coast of Naples) — as well as Croat fishermen. The church has its own St. Joseph Society, founded by Sicilian women, whose yearly task it is to organize the public charity event and feed hundreds from the church kitchen. In Sicily, confraternities played a large role in the public celebrations. In 1998, when we curated the UCLA Hammer Museum table, the Society was celebrating its 25th anniversary and was present to sing novenas. Indeed, along with elaborate foodways, a significant number of Sicilian oral expressions (songs, orations) dedicated to St. Joseph, have also been maintained among local Sicilian women.[6]

A brief history of the cult of St. Joseph

Under prominently Spanish leadership, Counter-Reformation theology carefully guided "Josephine" iconography and continued to shape folk religious traditions around the patron feast day of St. Joseph in Italy. The carefully crafted image of St. Joseph as the patriarchal *paterfamilias* — of the Holy Family and the Universal Church — promoted not only the veneration of fatherhood in Joseph, but of male authority within the Catholic Church and in the heart of all Catholic families. This patriarchal narrative was likely conceived as a counterbalance to the far more ancient and ingrained veneration of the feminine divine in the form of the Madonna. In *Creating the Cult of St. Joseph*, UCLA art historian Charlene Villaseñor Black (2006) masterfully demonstrates the theology and politics behind the cult of St. Joseph. At its most extreme, the image of Father and Son attempts to displace (literally to dethrone) the iconography upon which it was closely modeled, that of Madonna and Child. At its most benevolent, the image of Joseph as a "mothering father" (cradling, embracing, and teaching his son a trade) fostered new discourses around masculinity in Hispanic society.[7] Alongside Joseph's image as the nurturing "foster father" of Jesus, were equally compelling images of the worker saint (Joseph the Carpenter) and the Holy Family's *Flight into Egypt* (Joseph as migrant) — all images amply repeated throughout the Catholic world, Old and New.[8]

Thanks in part to Spanish hegemony in Southern Italy (i.e., Aragonese as Viceroys, and as direct rulers in Naples as late as 1816), Joseph became deeply rooted in Sicilian soil, where the cult was likely appropriated and popularized. Mary, however, resurfaces in the pageant that accompanies the Sicilian tables, reaffirming the Earthly Trinity in the Holy Family triad. She is also hailed, along with Joseph and son, in the ritual calls of the devoted.

Joseph has been invoked by multiple categories of supplicants, a fact which points to his *de facto* versatility and the range of meanings his narrative embodies. His diverse attributes (e.g., Joseph the Worker, Joseph the Carpenter, A Just Man, Joseph the Patriarch, Joseph and the Good Death) have earned him a great number of confraternities, professions, social groups, and even nations that have adopted him as their patron saint. As an old and slightly comical figure, he was even considered the patron saint of drunks, as well as the patron of cuckolds (in medieval times). As a saint always accompanied by his (flowering) walking staff, and as the journeying saint, I would posit that he makes an ideal patron saint of migrants. Attesting to the popularity of the saint is the ubiquity of the name *Giuseppe* throughout the Italian peninsula from Trento to Palermo. *Giuseppe* is the most popular name given males (paired with *Maria* for women), judging by the study of 1982 telephone directories. In Palermo, for example, *Giuseppe* numbered 14,303, *Salvatore* 9,408, and *Pietro* only 3,570 (De Felice 1982: 91, 332f).

Sermons, both historic (cf. Villaseñor Black 2006) and contemporary (e.g., in conjunction with St. Joseph Tables in Los Angeles, cf. IOHI Collections), give us a good indication of how Joseph is to be "officially" interpreted. These tend to focus on Joseph's special and intimate relationship with his son, since he raised, guided, provided for, and taught the future savior of humanity, making Joseph critical to the Salvation and Redemption narrative. Joseph is always a faithful and obedient servant of God, accepting his role as good husband to Mary and as father to Jesus — an ideal family man, in other words. As a "virgin" father, he provides the ideal complement to the "virgin" mother Mary. In Sicily, in fact, the costumed threesome of the St. Joseph day pageant, are alternatively referred to as *i santi* or as *i virgineddi* (even when they were not played by children).

Geographic distribution of St. Joseph food altars in Southern Italy

The St. Joseph's Table was widely diffused throughout Sicily (see: *Feste patronali in Sicilia*, 1900; as cited in Uccello 1976: 75), and regional variants can be found throughout the Italian South besides (although, for the most part, not as elaborately articulated): e.g., Abruzzo/Molise,[9] Lucania, and notably in the Salento (Puglia).[10] In Sicily, it appears to be strongest in the west, especially in the provinces of Palermo, Trapani, Salemi, Enna, Agrigento, but is also found in Ragusa, Catania, Siracusa, and the Egadi Islands. St. Joseph Tables throughout the U.S. have been almost exclusively associated with Sicilian Americans.

In Los Angeles, the custom of preparing St. Joseph's Tables may be considered one of the major folk celebrations of the Italian community today — thanks, in part, to the efforts of the Italian Catholic Federation.[11] Not long ago, it was estimated that as many as 100 (between private/public) tables were given each year. The tables reported in the Los Angeles area are represented by immigrants from: Trappeto, Terrasini, Piana degli Albanesi (Palermo), Favignana (Trapani), Villafranca Sicula (Agrigento), Valguarnera Caropepe (Enna). I found that Sicilians, for a variety of reasons, seemed particularly committed to preserving their cultural heritage. As Sicilian-American Virginia Buscemi Carlson, passionately affirmed: "Without our traditions, there would be nothing left; we would be just like everyone else." In 1998, with Virginia and the Sicilian community in Los Angeles, I co-curated a St. Joseph's Table at UCLA's Armand Hammer Museum, right next to the visiting exhibition: "The Invisible Made Visible: Angels from the Vatican." The juxtaposition of an abundant food altar of local folk tradition next to the imposing paintings and sculptures from Rome was curiously moving. In more ways than one, the local community (and not just the Vatican angels) were overcoming invisibility.

Sicilian St. Joseph Tables in the diaspora (e.g., New Orleans, Los Angeles)

Anecdotal and documentary evidence suggests that tables are to be found all over North America, as well as in other places to which Sicilians emigrated.[12] For example, a Campanian colleague, Giuseppe Colitti, reports (via e-mail communication) that in the late 1990's he had found a long list of the *"pietanze rituali"* prepared for the feast of St. Joseph at the Museo dell'Emigrante in São Paolo, Brasil.

Further, besides crossing Italian regional lines, the custom has even crossed ethnic boundaries. In New Orleans, where a high percentage of its Italian community originates in Sicily, the St. Joseph table has crossed into the African American community as well,[13] notably African-American Spiritualist churches where Haitian Vodou is practiced. The syncretic nature of Vodou allows for a stratification of deities where indigenous and Christian saints share identities (cf. Cosentino 1995). These African Americans not only have adopted St. Joseph Tables, but have assimilated St. Joseph into their own pantheon of deities. Chupa reports that in her New Orleans research on Damballah, this African spirit came to be associated with St. Patrick and with Moses, and she also saw frequent references to St. Joseph (http://www.houstonculture.org/laproject/stjo.html). Saxon notes that the attraction among Louisiana African Americans is toward the figure of St. Joseph the Worker and is invoked especially for his assistance in finding work or shelter. We speculate that the tradition may also have inherently appealed for a variety of other reasons: the spectacular food displays, the pageantry of costumed dramatizations, the focus on the poor and marginalized, and obviously the "symbolic value" of St. Joseph himself as a defender of the humble, the hard working, and the defenseless. The Mardi Gras spirit of Louisiana Creoles seems to have had a profound effect on the tradition, marrying St. Joseph to the grand ball tradition. African Americans frequently donned their Mardi Gras costumes on St. Joseph's night. In its Sicilian origins, St. Joseph, despite the occasional merrymaking around bonfires, was more Lenten and less Carnivalesque in spirit.

Interpreting the tradition: Table, altar, banquet

Within the St. Joseph's Table tradition several convergences and morphologic synchretisms appear to have occurred over time. Such layering may also be discerned in the variation in nomenclature: is it a table (*tavolata*, *tavola*) or an altar? That is, although the terms "altar" and "table" seem to be used almost interchangeably, they more likely represent a blurring of two historically superimposed worldviews, Antique/Classical and Christian, roughly corresponding to Table and Altar. Tables indeed range from the pared to the extravagant. The sacramental breads on the altar, of course, forming the minimal "table" are still the norm in private settings, where the food may instead be spread out in an altogether separate room (perhaps also due to space constraints). Public tables instead seem to revel in visual and gastronomic excess.

But where does the abundant table end and the sacred altar begin? Where is the ancient rite of Spring located, as distinct from the more sober Christian ritual? While the focus of the St. Joseph tradition is on the saint himself and associated ritual breads, i.e., on Christian *agape* in the form of a communal meal, clearly the table lends itself to displays of gastronomic abundance. The collective meal provided to the poor is a basic, simple meal; the foods taken away by visitors are minimal (bread roll, orange, fava bean); while the foods found on the table and served to the saints are varied, rich, special foods. The latter are frequently destined for some honored group: guests of friends and family, priests of the congregation, the Holy Family itself — and no longer the poor. The non-perishable foods collected for the occasion (dry pasta, oil, packaged foods) are given to retirement homes and orphanages or distributed to the visiting needy. In the Sicilian tradition and its diaspora reenactments, all forms ranging from minimal to maximal altars and tables are present. On or near the altar are those items most readily associable with Christianity: bread, wine, oranges, whereas "profane" foods are more distant from it. But it is not clear if those partaking perceive a subtle division between table and sacred altar.

Bread in Italian culture

As I have written elsewhere (i.e., 1997), the primal role of bread in Italian culture and in the Christian rite accounts for the central place of bread on the Sicilian (and Apulian) St. Joseph's Tables. Bread forms one of the sacramental foci of Christianity, along with wine — both southern Mediterranean legacies. And Southern Italy's is a quintessentially Mediterranean food culture. Bread is the staff of life and for centuries was the stuff which barely kept the masses this side of starvation in the South (cf. polenta in the North). Direst poverty was known as *"miseria di pane"* "bread poverty" — that is, when even the minimal meal was not possible. The most elemental form of charity, in fact, was giving bread to the poor. It is the basic food and hence is sacred, never wasted nor disrespected. It represents the embodied divine, e.g., the body of Christ. The primal activity of baking bread is also the symbol of hearth and home. It is a moral touchstone. How many dialects sum up the honest and generous as *buono come il pane* (as good as bread)? Close friends broke bread together as "companions" < COMPANIONE (Latin) < CUM + PANEM (cf. It. *companatico* which suggests that bread is the mainstay for which other foods — cheese, olives, vegetables — formed only an accompaniment). The preparation and consumption of bread is always an act of devotion,[14] a daily ritual, and in Sicily besides, the variety of ritual breads is rich.

Dramatization of migrant journeys: Into Egypt and out of Sicily

The dramatization of the Holy Family's migrant journey is an integral part of the tradition. Joseph, carrying his wayfarer's staff, is a seeker, a migrant, in search of food and shelter for his family. In the pageant, the saints ritually knock on three doors and ask to be let in; they are twice turned away and then given hospitality (cf. the Mexican Nativity tradition of *Las Posadas*). It was three of the poorest of the village, including orphans, who were traditionally dressed as Mary (a young girl), Joseph (an old man), Jesus (a small child)—although today, they are normally a young couple, and the roles are largely honorific (i.e., no longer enacted by the poor). The saints were then seated directly at the table and served a substantial meal (a taste of every item of blessed food or sometimes a ritual three).

After the saints have eaten, all are invited to a communal banquet where typically a "poor man's meal" — either a bean soup (*pasta e ceci*) or a *"Milanisa"* (pasta with fresh sardines, fennel, pine nuts, and raisins, topped with sweetened and toasted breadcrumbs, to replicate sawdust from a carpenter's workshop), or even Trapanese couscous—all depending on Sicilian provenance—as well as bread and fruit, are served. No one is turned away. In Sicily, often an olive branch or palm frond over the door signaled to the village that a family had opened its doors to the community. After supper, guests are given blessed foods, a bread roll, perhaps an orange or lemon, and a fava bean to take home. Bits of the blessed bread have historically been used as talismans, to keep away storms or hunger. In the African community of New Orleans, fava beans (also known as "lucky beans") were also used as good luck charms. The statue of St. Joseph itself brings luck: e.g., he is supposed to assist home buyers or sellers, if buried upside down in the yard.[15]

St. Joseph may be particularly attractive to Italian Americans, in part, because of his close association with migration[16] — fleeing into Egypt, a stranger in a strange land, at the mercy of a foreign and historically hostile people. For migrant Sicilians too, the welcome was not always warm, not in foreign lands, not in other parts of Italy (at times, just as foreign). For peoples with a long history of migrations, wayfaring Mediterranean peoples understood the ideal (and absolute necessity) of practicing hospitality. Lodging the traveler and feeding the stranger were key cultural values throughout the Mediterranean world, from ancient times to modern. In Christian hagiographic narratives (e.g., St. Christopher, St. Martin), assisting the stranger often translated into welcoming into one's midst the divine presence disguised in human form. The motif of "entertaining angels unawares" was also known (e.g., the story of Abraham just before the destruction of Sodom and Gomorrah; Elijah the Prophet tales). Hospitality is a sacred duty.

Emigration, for the most part, was not a matter of choice but of necessity. Poverty, under-development, famine, and natural catastrophes, caused millions to flee Italy during the nineteenth and twentieth centuries in a mass migration that had had no equal. One of the most commonly shared "foundation" legends as the basis of the St. Joseph's Table tradition is found almost exclusively in diaspora written and oral sources. It involves variations of the following:

> The tradition of building the altar to St. Joseph began as far back as the Middle Ages [sic] in gratitude to St. Joseph for answering prayers for deliverance from famine. The families of farmers and fisherman built altars in their homes to share their good fortune with others in need.[17]

The tables do in fact symbolically focus on the poor, but the *festa* also discretely: a) dramatizes the story of immigrant success, b) celebrates the work ethic, and c) affirms the patriarchal family — pillars of the Italian immigrant ethos. In fact, opulent tables are possible *as a result of* material success and therefore, may also be a form of tribute to family businesses (often food-related), which heavily sponsor them. As such, the tables can inadvertently become monuments to immigrant triumph. Food — its production and distribution — has indeed sustained numerous Italian immigrants in America. Therefore, what better way to enshrine the source of many an immigrant fortune than in food for the table? Vast quantities of cheese, pasta, oil, and wine are donated to the tables each year, to be consumed, sold or distributed. Wealth and its redistribution therefore, are often twin items on the St. Joseph's Tables.

Private vs. public tables

In Sicilian village settings even a "private" table was open to all. In earlier Los Angeles neighborhoods too, more ethnically homogeneous and compact, this lack of strict demarcation appeared to obtain (Speroni 1940), as streets continued to function as extensions of "private" space.[18] It is attested that in Sicily, in fact, the more archaic tradition was to place the altar/table outside the home (e.g., in the courtyard or outside one's front door), while today instead it is prepared in larger inside locations (e.g., a grocer's warehouse)—a shift likely attributable to modern and urban uses of private/public space.

In the early 1990s, Los Angeles presented a full range of celebrations along the private/public axis existed: from modest private tables meant primarily for the enjoyment of family and friends (e.g., Vaccaro, Buscemi, També, Grammatico, Russo, Mistretta tables); to semi-public spaces such as restaurants (e.g., the early tables of Perricone) and social clubs; and increasingly as public charitable events, sponsored by corporate groups (the ICF, a saint's society or church guild), connected to specific parishes or cultural centers (e.g., Casa Italiana, Mary Star of the Sea). Father Pisano seems to have played a key role in this shift of focus toward public table (n. 11).

Many though continue to be private devotional tables prepared as an *ex voto* for the saint, either to secure his favor or in response to a petition which has been granted (*per grazia ricevuta*), to celebrate one's name sake, or as a devotion to one's favorite saint. In the literature and in oral narration, one finds a variety of stories of sick children cured, sons returning from war unharmed, husbands saved from a serious accident, and so forth. But tables may also be given for the simple pleasure of inviting guests to a celebration, as an act of heritage preservation, as a "Sicilian Thanksgiving." In any case, although a table may represent the outcome of a personal vow (normally expressed by a woman),[19] the execution and production of the actual altar includes a devotee's spouse, family, *comari/compari,* and *paesani* for no one person could possibly accomplish such a culinary *tour de force.* St. Joseph's Tables therefore are always something of a cooperative, communal event.

Rituals of abundance: Pre-Christian and new world re-visitations

The variant forms of St. Joseph celebrations may well result from syntheses of historically-layered, anthropological, and ethnographic convergences. This semantic accumulation is present, if latent, in the various forms of his feast day in the communities that celebrate him. Food altars seem to replicate rituals of abundance at the heart of key calendrical occurrences in agrarian societies — anticipating the harvest in spring, celebrating the harvest in summer and fall. Several features in the contemporary St. Joseph tradition seem to identify aspects of such rites in the "tables of plenty." E.g., the tables feature the season's first fruits, including ripe shafts of wheat (or pasta), as well as freshly germinated wheat buds (the so-called *"giardini di Adone"*, cf. "Gardens of Adonis" for the feast of Aphrodite and Adonis in ancient Greece). The cult of Demeter, the goddess of grain, was particularly strong in the Sicilian interior and a major ritual celebration in her honor occurred mid-March (cf. St. Joseph day, March 19). The pagan cult of Ceres (> cereal or grain) centered on Enna where in Roman times a sanctuary to the goddess became the focus of agrarian fertility rites. Even today, the overall effect of a beautiful table is to represent the Earth's bounty in an endless variety of dishes — an *"orgia elementare"* as Giallombardo puts it — and to collectively celebrate and share that abundance in the form of a communal banquet.

The naturalistic shape of the breads (birds, flowers, animals, fruits), the presence of fava beans, and the building of bonfires, also recall practices linked to the world of the ancients—although bonfires are normally associated with the Summer Solstice, they here occur during the Spring Equinox. Further, in all of Italy, the sweets most closely associated with Joseph are not bread, but fritters of all sorts, the empty and filled variants. *"San Giuseppe frittellaro"* is responsible for *frittelle* in Latium, for *zeppole* in Naples, or *sfinci* (filled cream puffs) in Sicily— apparently both of Arabic derivation: *zalabiyah* and *sfang* (both forms of fried pastry). In ancient Roman times, such sweets were prepared for *Liberalia,* a festival held on March 17 in honor of Bacchus and Silenus in proximity of their temples (Field 1997: 399)

And so, just as elsewhere on the Christian ritual calendar (e.g., Easter, Christmas), the non-Christian and Christian ideologies form a connubium, so too it would appear for St. Joseph's Tables. In any case, there seems to be little awareness of any ideological conflict, for altars and tables are frequently found together. The profusion of dishes that dominate public spectacle produces a visual cornucopia that overwhelms and delights, reproducing a *Cuccagna* festive paradigm even here in a Lenten context (cf. Del Giudice 2001a).

Social justice, "Sabbath Economics" and feeding the poor in Los Angeles

The Christian narrative, particularly in diaspora contexts, seems to be equally strong in this ritual of abundance and hospitality. E.g., one welcomes the Holy Family and thereafter all pilgrims into one's home, sheltering and feeding them. It is important to remember that the *questua,* or begging ritual, is a key component of giving a table and of the pageant itself. This ritual begging of food, humbling oneself before friends, family, and even strangers, is a necessary aspect of giving a table and cannot be delegated. (It was originally performed barefoot or in stocking feet, as a symbolic act of humility.) This seems to create an embodied experience of poverty, fostering empathy for the actual poor: until one has begged for food or lived on the streets, one cannot fully understand or care for those who must do this every day. Indeed, it has become the daily reality of growing numbers in Los Angeles today — for the unemployed poor, the homeless, and the migrant (often one and the same).

The focus of the tradition, of course, is always on the table and on feeding community (whether family and friends, a neighborhood, or a village), whether truly needy or not. The pageant seems to have become secondary or sometimes eliminated altogether. Food is gathered and then shared. Alternatively funds are collected, either by selling or auctioning food, requesting a donation for the meal, or for viewing the table. Candles, figurines, prayer cards, and other artifacts may be sold, or paper money pinned directly to the saint's sashes. Formerly in Sicily, significant funds could be raised by auctioning off St. Joseph's beard, which then might be given directly to Jesus, Mary, Joseph (i.e., the poorest members of the village). In Sicily, a direct form of wealth redistribution was arranged (at a time of year when food stores were low), by actually feeding the poor. Today, tables generally help raise funds for charities of various sorts.

Through the tables, the community, in fact, feeds itself in the form of a communal meal for rich and poor, thereby somewhat leveling the division between charity givers and receivers, and mitigating the stigma attached to hunger. The shared banquet enshrines the value of hospitality as a social and religious rite. It also seems to remind the collectivity that at any given moment the one may become the "other" — as the wheel of fortune is constantly in motion. The recent recession in our midst is reviving a consciousness of the topsy-turvy world, as those who had never previously been subjected to the indignities of bread lines or soup kitchens are now being forced to rely on them. Of course, for many Sicilians, the begging ritual, as well as the pageant, also powerfully commemorate early family history, while ritualizing the immigrant experience per se: wandering and "knocking on doors," searching for food, lodging, and work (see Del Giudice 2009b, 2010a). Its message of hospitality and the injunction to open one's doors to the stranger, is especially poignant.

The fact is that the poor are no longer Sicilians (once so abundant), nor even Italians, and it is now we who must welcome the stranger, the migrant, the "other," and feed the poor among us. The community we serve may now be interethnic and interfaith. How does one reconcile cultural preservation of specific customs in a multiethnic society? Strategies to deal with these questions have at times been creative and generous. Facing the dilemma over ethnicity versus the mandate to actually feed the poor, Sam Perricone resolved the debate in favor of the latter. In fact, to my mind, few have taken the "feeding of the poor" more literally,[20] or accomplished it with more grace. In 1989 and 1990, I attended Sam and his friend Virginia Buscemi Carlson's tables at St. Joseph's Church (a poor, largely Latino parish, in East Los Angeles, at 12th and Los Angeles St.). It was a symbiotic relationship. Virginia (a repository of many Sicilian traditions), along with many members of Arba Sicula ("Sicilian Dawn," a cultural association) decided to "reclaim" the feast to ensure its authenticity and organized a table (largely using the resources of Sam). During the two-day period, over 1,500 people were fed a lavish (not a poor man's) meal of: pasta, grilled swordfish, fennel salad, fruit, traditional sweets, bread, and even wine ("let them enjoy themselves," he insisted). Sam refused to cut corners (e.g., costly swordfish, extra virgin olive oil). Although not all may have appreciated the swordfish or the fennel (perhaps acquired tastes), Sam nourished the community in the best way he could and did so in a spirit of joy rather than duty, despite the evidence of discarded swordfish (offensive to some of his Sicilian friends). For Sam and his family, food had been the focus of professional life (Sam Perricone Citrus, Inc.). Many business associates (a large number of them Jewish, in fact) contributed over the years to his patron saint's celebration. Further (according to Virginia), although a second-generation Sicilian, he never forgot his roots nor his early poverty. When he became prosperous and returned to Sicily during a St. Joseph celebration one year, he was inspired to make a table of his own — first in his restaurant, "Salvatore" (at Olympic and Soto) for many years (sending the proceeds to St. Joseph's Church), then at the church itself.

Opportunities for public education and intercultural understanding are always available. One apologist (Sicilian actor Lou Cutrell) warmly addressed the largely Latino of the congregation, stating that "you don't need to be Sicilian to have a table." Both the St. Joseph mass and the explanation of the legend and food altar custom preceding the communal banquet were translated into Spanish. At the banquet itself, gratitude came in many languages and forms. One Native American danced his gratitude for those giving the table. Virginia hoped to plant the seed and to have the tradition continue in the parish, even in the absence of Sicilians, although this proved not to be the case.

The impulse to share traditions across ethnic and socio-economic boundaries, as well as the call to engage in social action in a contemporary world, is not unique to the St. Joseph's custom. Many are the instances of folklore practices encouraging compassionate action and addressing real-life, current social, economic, and political issues. My own thinking on "ethnography as spiritual practice" has redirected many of my own efforts toward social advocacy: e.g., St. Joseph's Tables vis-à-vis food justice and poverty, migrations, and development, in the Watts Towers Common Ground Initiative (Del Giudice 2014). "Sabbath Economics"— the periodic redistribution of wealth, the pardoning of debts, the dismantling of patterns of hierarchy, wealth and power— are urgently relevant today. And thus, this ethnically-specific ritual of food redistribution, the St. Joseph's Table, has again become a "feast for our times."

How do we, in practice, both affirm and preserve our own cultural practices and ethnicities while addressing local and global wellbeing? And how can we academics overcome our seemingly constitutional aversion to utopian discourse and action (although we may be adept at analyzing them from a safe distance), and engage such ethical obligations? We can all, I believe, creatively imagine ways to harness our own best traditions and identify indigenous practices that work — to better to preserve and share them (cf. Del Giudice 2009a) for the benefit of all. And we, as scholars, mediators, and presenters of such cultural traditions, can assist in these effort. At times, the inherent humanity and beauty of a cultural tradition will make it infinitely adaptable and acceptable to others. In our case, for instance, given their creative food genius and cult of abundance, their heightened aesthetic sense and varied food practices, and the generous spirit with which hospitality is practiced, Italians stand to accomplish what mere soup kitchen do not and cannot do.

Notes

1. This essay excerpts my own: "Rituals of Charity and Abundance: Sicilian St. Joseph's Tables and Feeding the Poor in Los Angeles" (Del Giudice 2010), soon to be republished in: *In Search of Abundance: Mountains of Cheese, Rivers of Wine and Other Gastronomic Utopias*, New York: Bordighera Press.

2. E.g., in Salemi, entire chapels *"sono rivestite interamente di mirto, alloro e adorne di pani, arance e limoni"* ['are entirely festooned in myrtle, laurel, and covered with breads, oranges and lemons'] (Giallombardo 1990 [1981]: 24).

3. Virginia recalled the huge personal energy invested in these activities on the part of the women involved. E.g., she herself worked on her table for two months, making all the breads for display and for distribution. She had three freezers set up for this purpose and gave away 150 kilos of bread and nearly "killed herself" in the effort.

4. Given the Sicilian genius for creating *trompe l'oeil* foods of one sort and another, it is interesting to note that bread and breadcrumbs, mixed with vegetables, frequently are modeled to imitate fish (another sacred symbol of the St. Joseph Table) — e.g., *pesce d'uova* (fish made of egg); *pesci di funghi* (fish made of mushrooms)—continuing in savory dishes the delight of sweet marzipan faux foods (cf. *frutta di Mortarana*). Cf. Field 1997: 395.

5. Uccello's 1976 seminal work on Sicilian breads and sweets includes many beautiful photographs of Martorana fruits, Easter and Christmas hearts, jellied candies, bones of the dead for All Souls day, eyes of St. Lucy and many others for a variety of nature and life-cycle occasions. Another valuable and exhaustive study, including visual documentation of Easter ritual breads can be found in Ruffino 1995, which features: Easter wreaths concealing eggs in a variety of fanciful shapes: e.g., doves, pineapple, baskets, donkey, horse and cart, etc.

6. A novena dedicated to St. Joseph hinges on *"Lu viaggiu di san Giuseppi"* (The Voyage of St. Joseph) and was sung by blind *cantastorie* (street performers) in Sicily, with the accompaniment of organ and violin (Giallombardo 1990 [1981]: 21). For oral expressions recorded in Los Angeles, see materials in the IOHI Collections. A "St. Joseph Rosary and Song Book" assembled by Rosalia Manzella Orlando (and dedicated to her mother Paolina Manzella and to Giuseppa LaFata) for the St. Joseph Society of Mary Star of the Sea Church, San Pedro, lists 11 songs and prayers for St. Joseph and 2 for the Madonna. One of the St. Joseph's songs is in Sicilian (p. 7):

Canzoncina a San Giuseppe

Dio vi salvi Giuseppi
Cu Cristu e cu Maria
Sta bedda cumpagnia
A vui fu data (2 times)

A vui fu cunsignata
Maria la virginedda
Tutta pura e tutta bedda
A vui tuccau (2 times)

Di li santi fustivu elettu
Di Diu fustivu amatu
Fedeli miu avvocatu
E prutitturi (2 times)

Li santi pi vui l'amuri
L'affettu e lu piaciri
Unn'aiu chi vi riri
Aiu vita e morti (2 times)

Morti vurria la sorte
D'avirivi l'assistenti
Gesù Maria e Giuseppi
Eternamenti (2 times)

Cantari vurria sempre
Maria di l'auri santi
St'armuzza mia si impigna
E si ni va cuntenti (2 times)

7. The Josephine cult indeed is considered to be largely the product of Spain, with its most noted example in the Chapel of St. Joseph in Toledo, where the El Greco painting of the saint once resided (see: *"Giuseppe: padre putativo di Gesù"*). For a detailed consideration of this cult, see especially: Villaseñor Black 2006. See also Stramare for the contemporary cult.

8. Despite concerted efforts to promote such gendered imagery in New Spain, colonials reverted to a more indigenous veneration of the Mexican Madonna, i.e., la Virgen de Guadalupe (Villaseñor Black 2006: 157 f.).

9. Although, Giuseppe Colitti notes that, during a recent visit to the Museo da Migracao in Sao Paolo, Brazil on June 21, 1998, he transcribed the elaborate list of dishes for the St. Joseph's table to be thirteen (sometimes nineteen) in the tradition of the Molise region, and that besides the Holy Family and angel, twelve guests were normally invited to play the role the Apostles—all taking precisely assigned places at the table, and that after the recitation of prayers, the woman of the house served them in stocking feet, beginning with St. Joseph (personal communication). See www.giuseppecolitti.it and the Web site of the Research Center he directs: www.centrostudivallodidiano.it.

10. The Salentine tables, judging from available images, seem to be distinctive in the even replicability of the plates laid out. They are all the same (although in odd numbers and ready to be served to the saints). In Uggiano, it is the head of the household, as St. Joseph, with his *bastone*, who signals the beginning of the meal and strikes the ground with his staff at the successive eating rounds until the ritual meal, shared with his other saint/guests, is over. As with Sicilian tables, here too the tables can be viewed by pilgrims on the eve of March 19 and throughout the next day. Frequently a small table is set at the entrance of the home where the *"pacino"* (small bread), *lambascioni* (wild onion), and fried dough sweets can be taken away by visiting pilgrims. On March 19 instead, St. Joseph and the other saints (a minimum of three and a maximum of thirteen — again always an odd number), eat precisely the same things.

11. The primary sites for viewing St. Joseph's Tables in Los Angeles are: Casa Italiana, the social hall adjacent to St. Peter's Italian Church (the only national parish in the Southland); Mary Star of the Sea Church (the home parish of the original fishing communities, Sicilian and Ischian, in San Pedro, Los Angeles' port city); and some years at Villa Scalabrini (the Scalabrinian retirement home in Sun Valley). Today, they are largely affiliated with churches within the Italian Catholic Federation (ICF). It was Father Pisano (of Pugliese provenance), himself a devotee of St. Joseph, who was instrumental in diffusing the *public* table tradition via the ICF throughout Southern California. According to Pisano the first table given publicly in a church was at Mary Star of the Sea Church in San Pedro in 1958. Previously, tables had been prepared exclusively in private homes (cf. Speroni 1940, for early tables in southern California). Pisano's personal view of such folk traditions is that they are good for the faith; that, while the Bible is primary, traditions form an important corollary, as a "source of truth." Traditions are, in his view, a living *proof* of faith, and in fact, in those for whom faith is weak, folklore seems to reinforce religious observance through devotional practice. Pisano concedes that no group prepares the tables with more devotion or splendor than the Sicilians.

12. And they are likely present elsewhere, despite the lack of formal documentation. Chupa, Anna Maria, n.d., in her "St. Joseph's Day Altars" ("Louisiana Project: Land, Environment, Culture," Houston Institute for Culture: http://www.houstonculture.org/laproject/stjo.html), also reports researching the tables in Gretna, Louisiana, and Starkville, Mississippi. Tables have been reported in Texas as well (see Sturm 2007).

13. The "Virtual St. Joseph's Altar" provides much useful information regarding altars in Louisiana (http://www.thankevann.com/stjoseph/. It reports that the 2008 altar (its tenth) had 4,000 visitors and over 224 offerings. Members of The Greater New Orleans Italian Cultural Society (GNOICS) built their first *public* altar in 1967 "on the front steps of the St. Joseph church on Tulane Avenue." In 1978, the altar location was moved to the Piazza D'Italia, due to inclement weather in previous years (Chupa: 98). Private tables however had likely been given among Sicilians from their earliest years in Louisiana.

14. Note the variety of sacred symbols which were frequently imprinted on bread or the many rituals of devotion which accompanied its preparation and consumption (kissing the loaf of bread, making the sign of the cross over it, the taboo against turning it upside down or dropping it on the floor, etc.). In part, this reverence also reflected the understanding that it *physically* represented the body of Christ and therefore should be handled with care and awe.

15. A recent *Los Angeles Times* article ("3 BR, 2 BA, plastic saint buried in yard," April 19, 2009) reports on the marked increase in the practice of burying the statue upside down to sell property (and removing it when the sale is made) during the current recession as homeowners are desperate to make sales in a sagging market. Philip Cates, a Modesto, California-based mortgage banker and owner of www.StJosephStatue.com has sold more than a quarter million do-it-yourself kits since he launched the mail-order company in 1990. And it is not only Italian Catholics who are buying them. On the Virtual St. Joseph Web site, this practice is attributed to St. Teresa of Avila who was assisted in the opening of Carmelite Convents throughout Europe by her traveling statue of St. Joseph! See: "Devotion to St. Joseph to Sell your house" (http://www.thankevann.com/stjoseph/sellhome.html).

16. Indeed this was the narrative followed by Fr. Pisano in his sermon at the Mistretta altar in 1998 and by Fr. Provenzano at Mary Star of the Sea Church, in San Pedro, in 2009.

17. E.g., The Virtual St. Joseph Altar, http://www.thankevann.com/stjoseph/. These are especially evident in local publications, many of them apparently relying on an oral tradition. They provide a good indication of the narrative as it widely circulates. There are a plethora of such "how to" guides for creating St. Joseph's Tables. I cite merely one example: *Viva San Giuseppe: A guide for Saint Joseph Altars.* n.d. Sisters of St. Joseph, St. Joseph Guild, New Orleans, Louisiana.

18. Cf. Sciorra's research on yard shrines [1993] and *presepi* [2001] in New York.

19. For a consideration of how the Sicilian St. Joseph tradition plays with gender roles and gendered work, cf. Turner/ Seriff. The tables observed in Los Angeles cannot be said to strictly adhere to a gendered division of labor, for men cooked the pasta, stirred sauce, baked the bread (as professional bakers) alongside women. And men were as much "givers" of tables (e.g., També, Perricone) as were women (e.g., Buscemi Carlson, Vaccaro). The *majority* of the cooking and baking, the singing of novenas, and especially the intimate knowledge of culinary traditions, were clearly in the woman's domain, however. On Texan traditions, see also: *Texas Tavola*, 2007.

20. Father Giovanni Bizzotto (a Scalabrinian), formerly at St. Peter's Italian Church on N. Broadway in Chinatown, is another example of this fervor for feeding the poor from the Casa Italiana kitchen, as the Church under his direction became a focal point in the neighborhood for the feeding of the homeless and migrants.

Works cited

Caracaus, Girolamo. 1983. *Arabismi medievali di Sicilia*. Palermo: Centro di Studi Filologici e Linguistici Siciliani. Supplementi al Bollettino 5.

Chupa, Anna Maria, n.d. "St. Joseph's Day Altars." *Louisiana Project: Land, Environment, Culture*. Houston Institute for Culture http://www.houstonculture.org/laproject/stjo.html

Cosentino, Donald. 1995. "Imagine Heaven," in *Sacred Arts of Haitian Vodou*, eds. Donald Cosentino, et al. Berkeley: University of California Press.

Del Giudice, Luisa. Forthcoming. *In Search of Abundance: Mountains of Cheese, Rivers of Wine and Other Gastronomic Utopias*. New York: Bordighera.

—. 2014. "Feeding the Poor – Welcoming the Stranger: The Watts Towers Common Ground Initiative and St. Joseph's Communal Tables in Watts." In Regina Bendix and Michaela Fenske (eds.), *Political Meals* (*Politische Mahlzeit*). *Wissenschaftsforum Kulinaristik* (Forum Culinaristics), Lit-Verlag.

—. 2010. "Rituals of Charity and Abundance: Sicilian St. Joseph's Tables and Feeding the Poor in Los Angeles," in *California Italian Studies*, ed. Lucia Re, Claudio Fogu, Regina Longo, 2010. http://escholarship.org/uc/item/56h4b2s2.

—. 2009a. "Ethnography and Spiritual Direction: Varieties of Listening," in *Rethinking the Sacred*, Proceedings of the Ninth SIEF Conference in Derry 2008, ed. by Ulrika Wolf-Knuts, Department of Comparative Religion, Åbo Akademi University (series: Religionsvetenskapliga skrifter), 2009: 9–23. Forthcoming in LDG, *Ethnography as Spiritual Practice*.

—. 2007. "Ischian Cultural Sites on the San Pedro, California Map" ('Siti culturali ischitani sulla mappa di San Pedro, California'). In *Pe' terre assaje luntane: L'emigrazione ischitana verso le Americhe*. Ischia.

—. 2001a. "*Paesi di Cuccagna* and other Gastronomic Utopias," in *Imagined States: National Identity, Utopia, and Longing in Oral Cultures*, ed. Luisa Del Giudice and Gerald Porter, 11–63. Logan: Utah State University Press.

—. 1997. "Tomie de Paola and the Writing/Illustrating of Italian Folk Culture." in *Italian Americana* 15:1 (1997) 22–30.

Estes, David C. 1986–87. "St. Joseph's Day in New Orleans: Contemporary Urban Varieties of an Ethnic Festival." *Louisiana Folklore Miscellany*. 6:2 (1986–87) 35–43.

—. 1987. "Across Ethnic Boundaries: St. Joseph's Day in a New Orleans Afro-American Spiritual Church." *Mississippi Folklore Register*. 21:1–2 (1987) 9–22.

Field, Carol. 1997. *Celebrating Italy: The Tastes and Traditions of Italy as Revealed Through its Feasts, Festivals, and Sumptuous Foods*. ("San Giuseppe," 392–407.) New York: Harper-Collins.

Giallombardo, Fatima. 1990 [1981]. *La festa di San Giuseppe in Sicilia*. Vol. 2. Folkstudio, 1990 [In, *Archivio delle tradizioni popolari siciliane*, No. 5, Palermo 1981].

Giompaolo, Vincenzo. 1995. *Feste del Popolo Siciliano*, Vol. I, Ragusa: Iblea Grafica.

—. 2006. *San Giuseppe in Sicilia, altari, cene, tavolate*. Chiaramonte Gulfi: Utopia Edizioni.

Huffstutter, P.J. 2009. "3 BR, 2 BA, plastic saint buried in yard." *Los Angeles Times*, April 19, 2009 (section A5).

Piccitto, Giorgio, Ed. 1977. *Vocabolario siciliano*. Centro di Studi Filologici e Linguistici Siciliani. Opera del Vocabolario Siciliano. Catania – Palermo.

Ruffino, Giovanni. 1995. *I pani di Pasqua in Sicilia. Un saggio di geografia linguistica e ethnografica*. Palermo: Centro di Studi Filologici e Linguistici Siciliani (Istituto di Filologia e Linguistica, Facoltà di Lettere e Filosofia). Vols. 1 and 2.

Sciorra. Joseph. 1989. "Yard Shrines and Sidewalk Altars of New York's Italian Americans." In *Perspectives in Vernacular Architecture, III*, edited by Thomas Carter and Bernard L. Herman, 185–98. Columbia: University of Missouri Press.

Speroni, Charles. 1940. "The Observance of Saint Joseph's Day Among the Sicilians of Southern California." In *Southern Folklore Quarterly*, 4:3 (1940) 135–9.

Stramare, Tarcisio. 1993. *San Giuseppe (nella Storia della Salvezza)*. Torino: Editrice Elle Di Ci.

Sturm and Lewis 2007. *Texas Tavola: A Taste of Sicily in the Lone Star State*, 2007, 34 min., directed by Circe Sturm and Randolph Lewis.

Turner, Kay and Suzanne Seriff. 1987. "'Giving an Altar': The Ideology of Reproduction in a St. Joseph's Day Feast." *Journal of American Folklore*. 100:398 (1987) 446–60.

Uccello, Antonino. 1976. "La cena di San Giuseppe," 73–81. *Pani e dolci di Sicilia*. Palermo: Sellerio.

"Un paese in festa (Valguarnera)." http://www.festasangiuseppe.it/(accessed February 6, 2009).

Varvaro, Alberto and Rosanna Sornicola. 1986. *Vocabolario etimologico siciliano*. Palermo.

Villaseñor Black, Charlene. 2006. *Creating the Cult of St. Joseph: Art and Gender in the Spanish Empire*. Princeton and Oxford: Princeton University Press.

The Virtual St. Joseph Altar. http://www.thankevann.com/stjoseph/(accessed February 6, 2009).

Viva San Giuseppe: A guide for Saint Joseph Altars. n.d. Sisters of St. Joseph, St. Joseph Guild. New Orleans, Louisiana.

PART IV
FOOD AS COMMUNICATION, PERFORMANCE, AND POWER

INTRODUCTION TO PART FOUR

Communication

Folklorists, like most scholars of culture, see food as a system of communication, and in Arjun Appadurai's words, "a condensed social fact" that reflects underlying worldviews and cultural processes (1981).[1] As a biological necessity for life, it does reflect the universality of human existence, but, like any aspect of culture, its meanings are invested by and specific to the people using it. Foodways practices reflect cultural beliefs and histories and express group and individual identities, concerns, values, and creativity. Contrary to popular sayings, though, food is not a universal language. It "speaks" differently to different people at different times.[2] It does give voice to individuals and groups, and speaks in its own voice as well,[3] but how does it actually communicate?

Contemporary understandings of folklore see it as a communicative system. Although it has been much refined, Ben-Amos's definition of folklore as "artistic communication in small groups" emphasizes approaching folklore "not [as] an aggregate of things, but a process—a communicative process, to be exact (1971:7)." He elaborates on this, observing that folkloric communication requires both the producer and audience to share a situation and a reference group, enabling "the tellers [to] know their audience and relate specifically to them, and the listeners know the performer and react to his particular way of presentation (1971:13)." In this way, the tale, song, or whatever is produced reflects those individuals, embodying their identities, concerns, and histories. Variations in folklore, then, demonstrate that that product is a living, viable tradition among those groups that "not only results from communication, but is a form of communication (Ben-Amos 1971: 13)."

This perspective suggests that food—as an aspect of folklore—communicates cultural worldviews, values, and histories through its structure, and individual and community experiences, preferences, and creativity through the variations on that structure. For example, hamburgers (a cooked meat patty between two pieces of bread in the form of a bun) are quintessential icons of contemporary American food culture. The meat is traditionally beef, which is representative of US history of frontier life, cattle ranching, and "manliness" as well as the relatively secure economic status of the nation in its reliance on an ingredient—beef—elsewhere considered a delicacy. Furthermore, meat and bread are the basic structure to American meals, reflecting the historical foundation of British and German food cultures. The optional addition of a cheese slice similarly illustrates the significant role of dairy products, while vegetables (lettuce, tomato, onion, pickle) are used to add crunch, color, nutritional value, and flavor, but are not essential. There can then be innumerable variations on hamburgers within that framework, each representing the individuals and groups producing them. For example, one town in the Midwest advertises "pork-a-leans," a local version with a patty made of pork instead of beef, reflecting the strong German heritage of the area. Similarly, veggie burgers, made of a variety of meat substitutes, are now available commercially, even at fast food restaurants, and can represent an individual's ethical choice to be a vegetarian as well as factors such as taste or health concerns.

Such variations express something about the individuals creating them, but expression alone is not communication. Communication involves both a performer and an audience with the audience's responses (or a lack thereof) shaping the variation. For example, if an individual usually eats hamburgers with beef patties, one might switch to veggie ones in a group of vegetarians—out of respect for them or, perhaps, because that is all that is offered. In either case, the variation reflects the situation, and the meanings of the communication can only be understood within that context.[4]

Performance

Communication is related to another key folklore concept, that of performance. Popular usage of the term refers to presentations of an artistic piece as well as to a self-conscious, intentional, dramatic presentation of the self, but it is used by folklore scholars to examine how meaning is generated and communicated. Drawing from the work of Swiss linguist Ferdinand de Saussure, they use the term, within folklore studies, to refer to two fundamental concepts: each instance of speaking or other activity ("speech act") enacts an individual's history, identity as well as the cultural and the immediate contexts, and such enactments include an aesthetic dimension that sets it apart from ordinary acts.

The first concept observes that each of us has a pool of resources (language, grammar, vocabulary) for expressing our thoughts. These resources have been shaped by the forces in our past and present, such as our culture, family, ethnicity, race, class, gender, religion, region, occupation, and personality. We then draw upon them when we are looking for words to use and ways to put them together. Our choices, though, are also shaped by the immediate context in which we are speaking—the people we are speaking to, the setting in which we are speaking, the purpose of our speaking, and so on. This context then shapes what words we select from our pool of resources, so that the actual "speech act" has meaning specific to these contexts. Also, it is always original, personal, and situationally contingent, although the larger culture creates the framework of rules and tools for performing and interpreting it.

Food "acts" in the same way (Camp 1978, 1979; Theophano 1984), suggesting an "ethnography of eating" drawn from Dell Hyme's ethnography of speaking model (1962). Every choice made in foodways represents an enactment of the individual's history and identity responding to the specific context in which the choice is made. The meaning of that choice is then contingent on the situation. For example, selecting tofu for lunch can have a variety of meanings: the eater is in a Chinese restaurant and wants to try an "authentic" dish; the eater is a vegan; tofu is the only food left in the refrigerator; etc. To understand what that "food event" means to that particular individual, it needs to be placed within the contexts of the pool of options available, the immediate setting and situation, and the individual acting. Only then can we accurately interpret the meanings of that choice.

Individuals making choices, however, are not always aware of the contexts shaping those choices, so that their choice is not necessarily a self-conscious and intentional expression of identity. It is more likely that they are cognizant of the immediate contexts rather than the larger social, cultural, and political ones. Anthropologist Mary Douglas uses the phrase "implicit meanings" to refer to those unspoken—and oftentimes, unexamined—assumptions that reflect the larger contexts.[5] These contrast with the explicit meanings that are articulated and consciously acknowledged. Part of the work of ethnography is to uncover and identify those implicit meanings. Folklore studies contribute an additional perspective by attending to the emotional and aesthetic aspects of meaning and the processes by which choices become personally meaningful to an individual.[6]

An example of the implicit meaning in relation to food is the word "supper," which, for many Americans, means an evening meal, usually less formal than "dinner." In Ireland, however, supper can be anytime between dusk and dawn, and is oftentimes a social meal of comfort foods, such as fried eggs, soda bread, rashers of bacon, and broiled tomatoes. Church suppers after evening events could include baked potatoes and chili and scones, while supper after dances might be in the "wee hours" of the morning. Without realizing these distinctions, Irishness is being performed through these events. Inviting an American visitor to supper, however, would highlight that an entirely different set of expectations are being offered and that the individuals are operating within a larger cultural context. Furthermore, Irish-Americans might choose to use the word "supper" for a "midnight snack" in order to highlight—and to perform—the ethnicity of the event. The context changes the meanings attached to it.

Folklorists also emphasize the creative and aesthetic nature of performance, not only in rituals and celebrations, but also in everyday life, in settings not always thought of as artistic or on public display, where individuals are not intentionally and self-consciously aware of performing. Although performance occurs in routine activities, it is different from routine behavior in that it somehow calls for an evaluation of the competence, skill, and creativity with which it is delivered. Richard Bauman points out that performance is "marked as subject to evaluation for the way it is done, for the relative skill and effectiveness of performer's display of competence (Bauman 1984: 11)." For example, an individual frying an egg might turn an otherwise mundane activity into a performance by adding a flourish when one flips the egg over, by attempting to produce crispy edges to the whites of the egg, or by presenting it on special dishware. All of these may mark the activity as one in which the individual's abilities as a cook or hostess can then be evaluated. Also, performances are usually framed in such a way that audiences know the activity is now a performance rather than the usual routine. Back to the individual cooking an egg, he or she might state, "Look at this perfect egg," or "These are my grandmother's plates," in order to call attention to the aesthetic qualities involved. Framing can occur in more subtle ways, too, such as tying on an apron, clearing the counter, bringing out the ingredients, or setting the table. These activities can all mark that a performance is about to occur; a food event is about to happen. Similarly, the windows in the restaurants that allow consumers to view the cooks at work act as literal frames for viewing that cooking as a performance.

Performance further enhances an experience by engaging the senses and calling for attention to its aesthetic qualities. It heightens awareness and encourages the individuals watching it to bring the full force of their attention to it. It also encourages participation in the event, eliciting emotions and personal interpretations of the meanings of the actions. This can be seen in a variety of foodways activities. Fine dining experiences, in which the food is expected to be evaluated, are the most obvious. The décor, table setting, servers' skills, financial transactions, and overall ambience all enhance the taste and consumption of the food and are also evaluated for how well they do these functions.

Everyday and routine activities can become a performance when individuals recognize the aesthetic quality of those actions. Dell Hymes discusses this shifting of attention as "breakthrough into performance" (Hymes 1975).[7] Cooking and other foodways activities supply ample occasions for this shift: an individual arranging cans on a shelf realizes that there is a visually pleasing pattern of colors; a gardener steps back and views with satisfaction the straight rows of growing vegetables; an eater rearranges food on one's plate or the dishes on the table to be symmetrical. In these instances, the viewer has moved from emphasizing the functional aspect of foodways to appreciating its ornamental, decorative, sensually pleasing qualities. The activity has become an aesthetic one and is evaluated as such.

This brings up another idea, that of performativity. An identity, concept, belief becomes reality through being performed (Austin 1962, 1970; Searle 1979; Parker and Sedgewick 1995). "You are what you eat" takes on a new meaning from this perspective. By eating proper foods, one becomes a proper person; by growing one's own food, one sustains the earth and becomes part of a social movement surrounding sustainability; by bringing out a birthday cake, an individual turns a year older. In the last example, the individual obviously ages regardless of the presence of the cake, but the cake makes them feel and acknowledge that passing of time. Similar to Barthe's notion of "food is situation (1961/1997)," performativity suggests that individuals construct not only meanings for food, but also identities, boundaries, and events through foodways.

Power

Recognition of the role of power in shaping communication and performance is fundamental to folklore scholarship. As de Saussure stated, "all social behavior is political in that it reflects some personal or group interest (1916)." "Political," in this sense, refers to the role of power in defining cultural forms, selecting images, and interpreting actions. Some individuals or groups rather than others are given the authority, whether officially or informally by social consensus, to make those decisions. Performances, therefore, are shaped by the external forces that in some way constrain, limit, or define the choices that an individual can make. They reflect the larger distributions of power, which are oftentimes inequitable.

Folkloristics as a discipline tends to approach power issues by focusing on individuals and the ways in which they deal with external forces, recognizing personal agency within culture in general. Furthermore, since every individual lives within larger structures, each of us, even the ones having economic, political, or social power, has his or her choices defined by those structures. None of us are completely free to perform ourselves in whatever way we might like; we are all constrained in some way by the cultural and immediate contexts surrounding us. Folklore emerges from the negotiating and balancing of individual agency and imposing structures.

This perspective applies to the understanding of food and foodways. Both the past and the present are defined by power structures external to that individual, but within those structures, each individual can make one's own choices about participation in and interpretation of foodways activities and events. For example, those with African American heritage growing up in the South, particularly if they are female, may feel hesitant to eat fried chicken in public due to historically racist stereotypes (Williams-Forson 2006). It is their choice, however, to go ahead and do so, perhaps dismissing the stereotypes as out-dated or reinterpreting the choice as one of personal taste. Racism is still present in the meanings attached to that food act, but the eater has personal agency in how they interpret that act and respond to those meanings.

Furthermore, contemporary scholarship sees folklore in general as being subversive to authoritative, dominating structures. Folk traditions are not simply entertaining pastimes. They are unofficial cultural forms transmitted through informal means, the expressions of the realities of the individuals' lives and of their hopes and fears. As such, they not only critique a larger world that frequently dismisses, rejects, or somehow devalues us as individuals, but also offer possibilities for finding meaningfulness within that world. Tapping into one's folkore (and remember, we all have folklore), then, gives strategies and strength for survival.[8]

This power of folklore results partly from the nature of the folk group. A communication or performance is considered folkloric when, among other things, the performer and audience share a common frame of reference, so that there is an assumption of understanding between them. Through folklore, individuals within a group can express opinions, values, or preferences that might not be well received outside that group, giving it a subversive quality. Although the expression might not intentionally challenge the status quo, it is recognized by others sharing that reference group and becomes a communication among them. Such communication often occurs among groups that experience some type of discrimination or oppression, but it can occur anytime a perspective clashes with the views dominating that context and therefore cannot be expressed openly.

Food and foodways are frequently used to communicate in this way. Political or moral statements can be made through choices of types of food or where to shop. Gardening can be pleasant way to have fresh tomatoes, but growing one's own food can also be a way of subverting the capitalist economic system, and attending a farmers market can be a way of "recoupling the food chain" by bypassing the usual links of processor, packager, marketer, and distributor between producer and consumer. Children attempt to assert their autonomy by not eating according to their parents' wishes, and we all assert our individuality through our food choices. Social movements around food, such as Slow Food, critique society and culture, challenging the industrial agricultural system, while others defend their position within the mainstream by aggressively making choices for those foods that have become symbolic, such as beef or gmo produce. Similarly, ethnic groups affirm the value and worth of their situational and differential identity by eating specific foods and maintaining their foodways traditions. Participation in foodways, then, while ostensibly a matter of taste or convenience, also communicates personal agency within the larger structures.

These communications are not always obvious, particularly to people outside the group in which they occur. Folklorist Joanne Radnor refers to these "hidden" communications in folklore as "coding," defining it as "an unintentional critique or expression of dissatisfaction that is "read" and interpreted correctly only by other members of that particular group (1993:3)." Radnor's scholarship on "feminist messages" is applicable to understanding how food can be used to communicate, especially since food frequently overlaps with women's culture, and both are oftentimes dismissed. Her identification of strategies of coding (trivialization, appropriation, distraction, juxtaposition, indirection, incompetence) offers insights into some of the ways in which food can be used to obtain and exert power without drawing attention to itself.

Aside from its potential for subversiveness and personal agency, food intersects with power on a number of levels, including public policy and global economic and military politics, as well as within social and cultural arenas. To distinguish between these levels of power, a number of terms are used, although these are not always clearly defined. Folklorists have tended to address the cultural and commensal politics of food, but are beginning to contribute scholarship to the first two levels also.

Food Politics—Issues of power concerning the access and distribution of food. For example: Who decides where to locate supermarkets? Who decides how to stock and price the campus store? Who makes the laws controlling farm subsidies and trade agreements around food? (The phrase "food security," refers to people having a stable supply of enough nutritious, affordable, and safe food, is relevant here.[9])

Gastro-politics—food is the medium and message of conflict (a condensed which social fact). Arjun Appadurai, who coined the term, uses it to explore how food was used in South India to both bring together people and divide them to construct a political unity.[10]

Cultural politics—Issues of power concerning the representation of food traditions and the representation of cultural identity through food.[11] Who has the authority to say that Midwesterners eat meat and potatoes? How did the tourism industry acquire the power to symbolize Maine with lobsters when these are harvested only on the coast?[12] How did barbecue and grits become the iconic foods of the American South or the taco and margarita symbols of Mexican cuisine?

Commensal politics—Issues of power concerning eating together. Who gets to choose the menu for Thanksgiving dinner? Who gets to choose the restaurant? Who has to set the table? Who has to clean up? and who gets served first, etc.?[13] (Most parents can relate well to this level of politics!)

Food clearly is a powerful medium through which we communicate with each other and perform our selves, our communities, and our nations. Its power is used in daily life as well as in rituals and celebrations throughout the world. If we can better understand the processes and dynamics of power in foodways, we can better understand how to channel it toward developing solutions and creating a more equitable and just world.

Articles in *Reader*

Janet Theophano's work on Italian American foodways explored frameworks for studying the meanings of food and was based on performance theory.[14] Her article, "'I Gave Him Cake': An Interpretation of Two Italian-American Weddings," examines how food communicates through specific rituals surrounding a particular food item. Her analysis of food in two weddings discloses the layers of meaning attached to those items and the rituals connected to them, and highlights the importance of studying the context in order to understand the meaning. She also discusses food as a marker of ethnicity and how food itself demonstrates the fluidity of ethnic identity and community.

The portioning out of food can be a way to communicate social relationships, something every child with siblings knows. Amy Shuman explores such communication in her article "The Rhetoric of Portions." While rules of etiquette have historically shaped the ways in which food is portioned, these rules can be manipulated, and thus communicate attitudes toward the food itself as well as toward hospitality, the situation, and the individuals involved. The last piece of food oftentimes carries particular meaning, and the choosing of it is oftentimes a ritual. Shuman points out that both portion sizes and the acts of choosing and serving portions are arenas for displaying power.

In "Foodscapes: The Culinary Landscapes of Russian-Jewish New York," Eve Jochnowitz examines the ways in which food reflects as well as performs place. Jewish cuisine in the Soviet Union was tied to the physical environment. Jochnowitz found that when it was moved to a new place, New York City, innovation and retention of tradition occurred at various sites of performance within the foodways system—the mouth, the body, kitchen, table, and street. Cultural perceptions of the body, health, fat, cooking, and eating are enacted in the new space, creating not only new patterns of behavior, but also a new culinary landscape. Food is used in this landscape to delineate public and private spaces and who may participate in those spaces. A new facet of the public space is culinary walking tours, which she explores as pilgrimages in which the participants are seeking a deeper and more authentic experiencing of food.

In "Fruitcake Always Makes Me Think of Grandma": Food and Memory in L. M. Montgomery's Creation of Female Landscapes, Diane Tye looks at the use of food in a literary work and the journals of the author of that work, applying scholarship on food and memory and the ways in which everyday and ritual eating are connected. Tye discusses how Montgomery uses food to evoke a sense of place and to represent characters' personalities as well as to mark the seasons and the passing of time. Food communicates these ideas and also reflects the role of gender in the expectations created around the use and the meaning of food.

Issues of power are addressed by Mario Montano in his article, "Appropriation and Counterhegemony in South Texas: Food Slurs, Offal Meats, and Blood," in which he explores how food is used to stigmatize a group, but also ways in which it is used to fight back. He identifies strategies of resistance, including turning stigmatized foods into an object of celebration. Consumption of that dish can then empower and strengthen the community. The appropriation of a food by a more powerful group can strip it of its original meanings, but it can also be re-appropriated and given additional meanings.

Luanne Roth also looks at how food is used to challenge and negotiate power structures. In her article, "Beyond Communitas: Cinematic Food Events and the Negotiation of Power, Belonging, and Exclusion," she examines the ways in which several mainstream films use food to move the narrative or as motifs and metaphors, frequently representing groups as different, foreign, and distasteful. The films reflect current social concerns but also provide a medium through with audiences can work through issues represented by food.

Patricia Turner turns attention to rumors and urban legends as sites similar to films in representing fears held by certain populations. In "Churches Fried Chicken and the Klan: A Rhetorical Analysis of Rumor in the Black Community," she explores a rumor about a fast food chicken restaurant being owned by the Ku Klux Klan and serving chicken that would cause sterility in black consumers, illuminating how food can represent social divisions and conflicts as well as concerns about physical well-being. Mostly told among black male college students, the rumor reflects the history of race conflict in the United States and the legacy of fear, particularly among this demographic. Applying rhetorical analysis adapted by folklorist Roger Abrahams from Kenneth Burke, Turner demonstrates that the context of these rumors is important for understanding how they are interpreted, an important point in the paradigm shift in folklore studies in the 1970s.

Issues of power are also addressed by Rayna Green in "Mother Corn and the Dixie Pig: Native Food in the Native South," (2008) in which she asks why Native American foodways are usually left out of any popular, professional, or academic discussion of foodways in the American South. She points out that Native foodways are being revitalized in the service of new trends toward slow, local, organic, and seasonal food elsewhere in the United States, and some native communities are even finding ways to participate in these trends. In the South, however, discussions of race have focused primarily on Black and White relationships, and Native Americans have been largely ignored. The significant role of Native foodways, particularly corn, in Southern history, culture, and cuisine should be recognized, and opportunities made for inclusion in current food discussions.

Discussion questions

Communication

1. Are there any foodways activities that you use to "say something" to someone else?
2. Think of a dish that is commonly eaten. Do you vary it in any ways that express your individual history, values, or taste? How does it function as a food voice for you?

Performance

1. Using the ethnography of eating concept, how have your foodways choices been defined by external factors in your past and present? Do you choose different foods depending on who you are eating with, the time of day, the place, or other contexts for eating?
2. Identify a "food event" (any instance of participation in foodways). Describe the context of that event, the options available to the individuals participating, and possible reasons for their choices. If possible, ask them why they made those choices? How do their answers compare with your assumptions? Does your perspective on the larger context give any insights into individual participation?

Power

1. Think about your own childhood and the present. Does seating at a table have an impact on your participation in a meal, in your relationships with the other eaters, and in your sense of agency or power to make your own choices?

2. What foods are meaningful to you (carry significant memories, reflect your identity)? Are there stereotypes of those foods that you disagree with or find offensive? Who has the power to define their meanings and how did they acquire that power?

Notes

1. Folklorists draw from foundational anthropological and social theory in order to understand how food and other cultural products express fundamental worldviews and social structures, such as Claude Levi-Strauss's analysis of "the raw and the cooked" as a manifestation of the binary nature of human thought (1997). First published in 1968, his culinary triangle suggests the process in which culture develops out of a synthesis of two oppositions. Folklorists also found useful Mary Douglas's critique of Levi-Strauss, observing that the structure of meals reflected the structure of specific societies and that interpretation needed to be "located" specifically within each context (1975). Also relevant is Roland Barthes's 1961 work on food as a communicative system (1997).

2. It is also important to recognize that food is an aesthetic domain and that, as such, what it communicates cannot always be put into words. As Charles Seeger stated in reference to studying music, "Sometimes we can only music about music." Charles Seeger, Speech Music and Speech about Music, in his *Studies in Musicology, 1935-1975* (Berkeley: University of California Press, 1977), 16–30.

3. The concept of "voice" is a common one in folklore and anthropology and usually refers to ethnographic research and presentation as enabling individuals and groups to speak for themselves and to present their own perspectives of cultural events and productions. The anthropologist Mary Douglas, for example, used it in her 1982 collection of essay, *In the Active Voice* (Routledge & K. Paul). The concept has been used in relation to food by a number of scholars, particularly in the context of presenting stories about food and interpretations of them by the individuals being studied rather than the scholar. Carole Counihan and Penny van Esterik, for example, use it in their *Food and Culture: A Reader* for a section on interpreting food, "Food, Meaning, and Voice," (1997), and Counihan uses it again in her essay, "Food as Women's Voice in the San Luis Valley of Colorado," in *Food in the USA: A Reader*, ed. Carole M. Counihan (NY: Routledge, 2002), 295–304. Meredith E. Abarca uses it similarly, but also recognizing the role of power in being able to present one's opinions in her *Voices in the Kitchen: Views of Food and the World from Working-class Mexican and Mexican American Women* (College Station: Texas A & M University Press, 2006).

    Of particular significance is Annie Hauck-Lawson, who explored the concept in her dissertation and introduced the phrase "food voice" to food studies discourses as early as 1992 in one of the first scholarly journals devoted to food: "Hearing the Food Voice: An Epiphany for a Researcher," *Digest* 12, no. 1 and 2: 6–1. She has developed the concept further through panels at conferences, special issues of journals (*Food Culture, and Society* 7, no. 1 (Spring 2004)) and books (editor with Jonathan Deutsch. *Gastropolis: Food and New York City*, New York: Columbia University Press, 2009). The last includes several essays specifically using food voice to refer to stories from individuals and groups about their lives around and through food. Lucy Long has also used the concept and phrase in her work on interpreting the meanings and meaningfulness of food and developing frameworks for the systematic study of those concepts. See for example, her essays, "Food Demonstrations in the Classroom: Practicing Ethnography and the Complexities of Identity with Tamales in Northwest Ohio," *Digest* 19 (1999) (2005): 46–52 and "Learning to Listen to the Food Voice: Recipes as Expressions of Identity and Carriers of Memory (Class assignment)," *Food, Culture, and Society* 7, no. 1 (Spring 2004): 118–22.

4. Mary Douglas's work has been foundational to understanding food as a communicative domain, and she has continued to influence folklore scholarship. See for example, her essay "Food as a System of Communication," in *In The Active Voice*, ed. Mary Douglas (London: Routledge & K. Paul, 1982). Scholars in other fields have also explored food as communication. For example, see Cramer, Janet Muriel, Carlnita P. Greene, and Lynn Walters (eds), *Food as Communication, Communication as Food* (New York: Peter Lang, 2011).

5. See her classic essay, "Deciphering a Meal." *Daedalus*, Winter 1972 [Reprinted in *Implicit Meanings: Essays in Anthropology*, ed. Mary Douglas (London: Routledge & Paul, 1975), 249–75]. The latter volume explores the concepts of implicit and explicit much further.

6. For a longer discussion of researching meaning, see Lucy M. Long, "Meaning Centered Research in Food Studies," in *Research Methods in the Anthropology of Food and Nutrition,* ed. John A. Brett and Janet Chrzan.

7. For an example of this concept within storytelling and conversation, see Richard Bauman, "The La Have Island General Store: Sociability to Verbal Art in a Nova Scotia Community," *Journal of American Folklore*, vol. 85, 1972.

8. This understanding of folklore as challenging the status quo is a thread throughout much of contemporary folkloristics, but its potential relevance to food has been perhaps best explored and articulated in feminist folklore scholarship. A foundational publication was *Women's Folklore, Women's Culture*, ed. Rosan A. Jordan and Susan J. Kalcik (Philadelphia, University of Pennsylvania, 1985), which includes the essay, "Burning Dinners: Feminist Subversions of Domesticity," ed. Susan S. Lanser (36–53). Also, a section of the American Folklore Society, New Directions in Folklore, addresses contemporary examples of the use of folklore in the modern world as well as new means of transmission and new types of communities. Their on-line journal, *New Directions in Folklore* (http://scholarworks.iu.edu/journals/index.php/ndif), is a useful resource.

9. These types of issues have not been addressed in the past in folklore scholarship, but have recently gained a great deal of attention from numerous disciplines. Several publications draw from theoretical constructs shared with folklore, in particular, Carole Counihan and Valeria Siniscalchi (eds), *Food Activism: Agency, Democracy and Economy* (London: Bloomsbury, 2014); and Allison Caruth, *Global Appetites: American Power and the Literature of Food* (Cambridge University Press, 2013). The section on Public and Applied Folklore in this Reader discusses this area further.

10. The phrase "political gastronomy" is used by Michael A. Lacombe in his study of *Food and Authority in the English Atlantic World* (2012).

11. While numerous folklore scholars have explored the role of power in folk cultures, the work of American studies scholar David Whisnant was particularly significant in introducing the "politics of culture" into scholarship and debates through his analysis of folk schools and documentation of folklore in the southern Appalachian mountain region. See David E. Whisnant, *All That Is Native & Fine: The Politics of Culture in an American Region* (Chapel Hill: University of North Carolina, 1983). For an insightful look at power in the interpretation of food, see Holly Everett, Vernacular Moralities and Culinary Tourism in Newfoundland and Labrador, *Journal of American Folklore 2009* 122, no. 483: 28–52.

12. Lobster was chosen to represent Maine on its license plates, much to the dismay of residents of the state who lived in-land and did not have access to lobster and usually could not afford to purchase it. See George H. Lewis, "The Maine Lobster as Regional Icon: Competing Images Over Time and Social Class," in *The Taste of American Place: A Reader on Regional and Ethnic Foods*, ed. Barbara G. Shortridge and James R. Shortridge (Lanham, MD: Rowman and Littlefield, 1998), 65–84. Crawfish have similarly been contested, but accepted, as a symbol of Cajun foodways. See C. Paige Gutierrez, Cajuns and Crawfish, in the same publication, 139–44.

13. See Julier (2013), Long (2014), and Shuman (1981).

14. Theophano frequently published with other scholars, and is perhaps best known for an essay that explores meals as patterned events: J. Goode, J. Theophano, and Karen Curtis, "A framework for the analysis of continuity and change in shared sociocultural rules for food use: The Italian-American pattern," in *Ethnic an Regional Foodways in the United States: The Performance of Group Identity*, ed. L. K. Brown and K. Mussel (University of Tennessee Press, 1984), 66–88.

References

Abrahams, Roger D. "Shouting Match at the Border: The Folklore of Display Events." In *'And Other Neighborly Names': Social Process and Cultural Image in Texas Folklore*, edited by Richard Bauman and Roger D. Abrahams, 303–22. Austin: University of Texas, 1981.

Appadurai, Arjun. "Gastro-politics in Hindu South Asia." *American Ethnologist* 8, no. 3 (1981): 494–511.

Austin, Joel L. *How To Do Things With Words*. Oxford: Clarendon, 1962.

Barthes, Roland. "Toward a Psychosociology of Contemporary Food Consumption." In *Food and Culture: A Reader*, edited by Carole Counihan and Penny Van Estrik, 20–7. New York: Routledge, 1997.

Bauman, Richard. *Verbal Art as Performance*. Ect Heights, Ill: Waveland, 1977.

Bauman, Richard and Joel Sherzer, eds. *Explorations in the Ethnography of Speaking*. London: Cambridge University Press, 1974.

Ben-Amos, Dan. "Toward a Definition of Folklore in Context." *Journal of American Folklore* 84, no. 1 (1971): 3–15.

Ben-Amos, Dan and Kenneth S. Goldstein, eds. *Folklore: Performance and Communication*. The Hague: Mouton, 1975.

Brown, Linda Keller and Kay Mussell. "Introduction: Part 1: Food in the Performance of Ethnic Identity: Theoretical Considerations." In *Ethnic and Regional Foodways in the United States: The Performance of Group Identity*, edited by Linda Keller Brown and Kay Mussell, 3–18. Knoxville: University of Tennessee, 1984.

Camp, Charles. "The Food Event." In *American Foodways: What, When, Why and How We Eat in America*, edited by Charles Camp, 55–81. Little Rock: August House, 1989.

Cramer, Janet Muriel, Carlnita P. Greene, and Lynn Walters, eds. *Food as Communication, Communication as Food*. New York, NY: Peter Lang, 2011.

Douglas, Mary. "Food as a System of Communication." In *The Active Voice*, edited by Mary Douglas , 82–104. London: Routledge & K. Paul, 1982.

Ellis, Bill. "Whispers in an Ice cream Parlor: Culinary Tourism, Contemporary Legends, and the Urban Interzone." *Journal of American Folklore* 122, no. 483 (2009): 53–74.

Goody, Jack. *Cooking, Cuisine, and Class: A Study in Comparative Sociology*. Cambridge: Cambridge University Press, 1982.

Hymes, Dell H. "Breakthrough Into Performance." In *Folklore: Performance and Communication*, edited by Dan Ben-Amos and Kenneth S. Goldstein, 11–77. The Hague: Mouton, 1975.

Hymes, Dell H. *Foundations in Sociolinguistics; an Ethnographic Approach*. Philadelphia: University of Pennsylvania, 1974.

Julier, Alice P. *Eating Together: Food, Friendship, and Inequality*. Chicago: University of Illinois, 2013.

Lanser, Susan S. "Burning Dinners: Feminist Subversions of Domesticity." In *Feminist Messages: Coding in Women's Folk Culture*, edited by Joan Newlon Radner, 36–53. Urbana: University of Illinois, 1993.

Levi-Strauss, Claude. "The Culinary Triangle." In *Food and Culture: A Reader*, edited by Carole Counihan and Penny Van Esterik, 28–35. New York: Routledge, 1997.

Lien, Marianne E. and Brigitte Nerlich. *The Politics of Food*. Oxford: Berg, 2004.

Lewis, George H. "The Maine Lobster as Regional Icon: Competing Images over Time and Social Class." In *The Taste of American Place: A Reader on Regional and Ethnic Foods*, edited by Barbara G. Shortridge and James R. Shortridge, 65–84. Lanham, MD: Rowman & Littlefield, 1998.

Long, Lucy M. "Breaking Bread in Northern Ireland: Soda Farls, Implicit Meanings and Gastropolitics." In *Political Meals*, edited by Regina F. Bendix and Michaela Fenske, 287–306. Berlin: Lit Verlag, 2014.

Mintz, Sidney W. *Sweetness and Power: The Place of Sugar in Modern History*. New York: Penquin, 1985.

Nabhan, Gary P. *Coming Home to Eat: The Pleasures and Politics of Local Food*. New York: W.W. Norton & Company, 2002.

Naccarato, Peter and Kathleen LeBesco. *Culinary Capital*. London; New York: Berg, 2012.

Naccarata, Peter and Kathleen LeBesco, eds. *Edible Ideologies*. Albany: State University of New York Press, 2008.

Parker, Andrew and Eve Kosofsky Sedgwick, eds. *Performativity and Performance*. New York: Routledge, 1995.

Gough, Richard, ed. "Special issue: On Cooking." *Performance Research: A Journal of Performing Arts* (vol. 4 issue 1, 1999).

Radner, Joan Newlon, ed. *Feminist Messages: Coding in Women's Folk Culture*. Urbana: University of Illinois, 1993.

Searle, John R. *Expression and Meaning: Studies in the Theory of Speech Acts*. Cambridge: Cambridge University Press, 1979.

Turgeon, Laurier and Madeleine. Pastinelli. "'Eat the World': Postcolonial Encounters in Quebec City's Ethnic Restaurants." *Journal of American Folklore* 115, no. 456 (Spring 2002): 247–68.

Watson, James L. and Melissa L. Caldwell. *The Cultural Politics of Food and Eating: A Reader*. Malden, MA: Blackwell Pub, 2005.

Williams-Forson, Psyche. *Building Houses Out of Chicken Legs: Black Women, Food, and Power*. Chapel Hill: University of North Carolina Press, 2006.

CHAPTER 23

"I GAVE HIM A CAKE": AN INTERPRETATION OF TWO ITALIAN-AMERICAN WEDDINGS*

Janet S. Theophano

In the study of American ethnic groups, food has been viewed, like language, as an indicator of the degree to which the group has retained or shed its culture of origin.[1] In fact, it has been argued that food is one of the last aspects of culture to be discarded, that food is particularly resistant to change.[2] In this view, the presence or absence of a food item, dish, or recipe on a particular occasion may indicate the continuity of culture or its breach. Conversely, the presence of an item of food from the so-called dominant culture seems an intrusion.[3]

This account of two Italian-American weddings departs from these perspectives in several ways. The study sought to discover not only patterns of food use, but the principles by which meals and events are constructed in the organization of one family. This view therefore moves away from *food items* as the focus of study to the system of beliefs, values, and ideas about food and social life that organize any event.[4]

These life-cycle events were not studied in isolation; rather, I observed the whole fabric of everyday life in which these rituals were embedded.

Together, both ritual and mundane enter into the family's food system, and it is only through knowledge of both that either can be understood. I could not have interpreted the significance of the two occasions I describe had I not participated in the everyday life of the family.[5]

The interpretations I provide are my own. I derive them from stories and conversations that occurred before and after the events I portray. Wherever possible, I use the words of the women and their families or, at the least, paraphrases of statements and conversations about their activities. Because of the continuity of my relationship with members of the community, my analyses have been read and sometimes changed by corrections they have made. But in the final analysis, this interpretation is based on delicately balancing conscious statements and beliefs with the additional desires, fears, or concerns that I infer motivated family members' actions. In the words of Janice Radway, who has constructed an analysis of women's reading of romance novels, I moved back and forth "between the readers' perceptions of themselves and their activities and a more distant view of them that makes an effort to include the unseen cultural ground or set of assumptions upon which they stand."[6]

Though the food patterns of a wider network were observed and recorded, this account focuses on one woman, Marcella Fiore. It is, after all, *individuals* who create, change, and continue a culture. A woman in her fifties now, Marcella has thick, wavy, silver-colored hair framing large brown eyes. Her brows have never been thinned and are dark, setting off her expressive, lively face. Her features are generous in proportion, her smile wide. She had dieted on and off for years, but is, by her own account, still somewhat overweight.

Janet S. Theophano, '"I Gave Him a Cake": An Interpretation of Two Italian-American Weddings' in Stephen Stern and John Allan Cicala (eds), *Creative Ethnicity: Symbols and Strategies of Contemporary Ethnic Life*, (Logan: Utah State University Press, 1991), pp. 44–54. Reproduced with permission of Utah State University Press in the format 'Republish in a book' via Copyright Clearance Center.

Marcella is a prominent member of the Italian-American community of Maryton, a small suburban town in the northeastern United States. At the turn of the century, residents of Maida, Calabria, in southern Italy were imported to the town, which was then inhabited primarily by people of English and Welsh background. The Italians' task was to work the stone quarry and do construction for one man who owned a large asbestos plant. The industrialist so controlled the town that the Italians were not permitted to live near the original residents. Instead, they were segregated by the railroad tracks, forced to live in poor housing, often without indoor plumbing. For two generations they were required to remain apart.

Finally the industrialist lost power, and the Italians who had previously lived on the margins of the town were able to move to other, more desirable locations—yet they chose to live, again, close to other Italian families. At the time of their arrival, their propinquity to one another had been imposed, yet there is little doubt that much of their interaction was voluntary, for it afforded companionship in a strange world. Later, when mobility might have encouraged separation, they chose, once again, to remain close to one another spatially and socially.

This community is the center of Marcella's world. It is no coincidence that Marcella herself stands at the center of a large network of family and friends. These range from the mayor to the sisters at the convent and include local merchants, fellow choir members, and bingo and "girls' club" friends. She is also one of six siblings, each of whom is married with children and grandchildren. In addition, many cousins, aunts, and uncles live nearby.

Marcella has a widespread reputation as a traditional cook. Many people in the Italian community rely on Marcella's expertise and knowledge of traditional cooking, and she uses food as gifts and as payment in an unending bond of reciprocity. Over the years the Italian residents of Maryton have developed, among other cultural forms, a shared food system, which though changing is still perpetuated. Basically there are two components to the system: an Italian meal called "gravy" composed of macaroni and tomato sauce combined in many forms, and an American "platter" or serving of meat, starch, and vegetable. This dual meal system has been elaborated into several festive formats which are considered appropriate celebratory meals for calendrical and life-cycle events.[7]

Life-cycle events are usually celebrated with a "buffet" consisting of multiple dishes from the American and the Italian repertoires. A typical buffet might present meatballs in "gravy" (red sauce), American and Italian cold cuts, Italian bread, potato salad, coleslaw, Jello molds, and an assortment of desserts.

An exception to this pairing of buffet format and life-cycle event is the wedding. Since it is the most formal of the occasions, the wedding requires a "sit-down dinner" for all of the guests. The content of the celebratory meals may vary from occasion to occasion and from family to family, but the expectation of the appropriate mode of celebration remains.

Because of these shared expectations, even the most subtle changes in the presentation of the food are statements about what is going on. As I reviewed the circumstances of each of the weddings of Marcella's daughters, which had at first seemed unusual, I began to see the significance of the food choices and the meaning of these events for Marcella and her family, the messages she conveyed to them through food.

Like other cultural idioms, food is multivalent; only in particular contexts does meaning emerge.[8] Though it may carry the symbolic load of ethnicity, food may also be a vehicle for expressing other issues and concerns, such as the nature of relationships within the ethnic group. In these cases, food was used by Marcella to signify her changing roles, her relationships to her family and community, and her identity as a woman in an Italian-American family.

Marcella and Pat Fiore have three daughters. Within a three-year period, the middle child, Jeanette, and the eldest, Roxanne, both married. But during this period, the family underwent several dramatic changes. Marcella expressed the nature of these social transformations in the mode for which she is noted—food.

Jeanette, the first to marry, had an Italian wedding. Only Italian foods prepared by Marcella and her sisters appeared at the wedding meal. Sandwiches made with provolone and pepperoni, baccala (dried cod) salad, and Italian salads were served with Italian bread and rolls. Three years later Roxanne was married. Her formal dinner featured "English" foods:[9] veal cordon bleu, green beans with almonds, and baked potatoes. As with the first wedding, Marcella's choices were deliberate and meaningful. Why did Marcella want an all-Italian meal for her middle daughter's wedding but an "English" meal for the eldest's marriage? I was especially puzzled when I remembered Marcella's comment that Roxanne's husband wanted to marry, in his words, "an old-fashioned Italian girl," and they had been introduced on that basis. Knowing Marcella's life situation provided me with some clues. I felt the answers could be found in the interpersonal dynamics of the family and Marcella's relationships with her daughters and her husband, who in the years between the two marriages had asked for a divorce.

On a Saturday in November 1976, Jeanette Fiore married John Peterson. She was then eighteen years old. She chose a young man, a non-Italian, who was regarded as irresponsible. Marcella said: "He won't be any kind of husband to Jeanette, or a father to her children." Many in the Italian community were skeptical about the match, but Jeanette was adamant. She said, "We love each other and we want to marry." Since the marriage was not sanctioned by Pat or Marcella, the wedding itself became a matter of controversy. Despite this, the family and community wished to demonstrate their support and provide a joyous celebration for the couple. They hoped for the best.

They decided to have the wedding reception at home. It would be small: about a hundred people were invited. The ceremony would take place in the chapel at church with only family members present.

Further, Marcella was adamant about the wedding meal. She decided that she would serve nothing but Italian foods. "I wanted to have all Italian, no American or English food." She prepared the wedding meal herself with the help of her sisters and presented it in the old-fashioned way.

The reception took place in the Fiore home in the late afternoon. Marcella served provolone and pepperoni sandwiches, without mayonnaise,[10] presented in clothes baskets in the traditional way. Accompanying the sandwiches were baccala salad, antipasto, tossed Italian salad, and Italian bread and rolls. No potato, macaroni salad, or coleslaw was served. There was a "bar" with wine, beer, and mixed drinks. A tray of cookies bought from a well-known Italian bakery in Philadelphia provided dessert. Such trays include pizzelles,[11] pepper cookies, fruit-filled cookies, and macaroons, among others, and are served at all significant life-cycle and calendrical events.

The wedding thus featured traditional foods, but the format was a marked departure from that of most wedding celebrations in the community. The wedding meal was pointedly not a sit-down dinner, which is requisite to this life-cycle event and indicates its importance.

In contrast to Jeanette's wedding, the marriage of Roxanne to Robert D'Amico provides an illuminating comparison. In May of 1979, Roxanne married a young Italian policeman whose home is in Philadelphia. Their courtship began when Robert asked a friend if he knew any "old-fashioned Italian girls." He was introduced to Roxanne. The two soon became engaged and plans were made for their wedding during the engagement period, which lasted a full year. By this time Jeanette's marriage had ended, and she was struggling to earn a livelihood and care for her young son. Marcella's twenty-five-year marriage to Pat had also ended. She had been stunned by his abandonment of her and their family.

The full financial responsibility for the family fell to Marcella. The economic stress was complicated by Jeanette's situation. Nonetheless, Marcella decided that her eldest daughter would have an elegant wedding; every aspect of it would be the best it could be. The groom's father, with whom the newly married couple would live, offered financial assistance to Marcella. She refused. Though she had no idea how she would pay for the wedding, she felt it her responsibility to assume the financial burden. Often she said, "I'm doing this wedding the American way, where the bride's family pays for it. The Italian way is to have each family pay for half."

Eventually Marcella accepted Mr. D'Amico's offer to help with some of the costs of invitations and other paraphernalia. The rest of the wedding expense was hers.

Formal invitations were mailed to almost two hundred people. The marriage ceremony was a High Mass followed by a reception at an elegant, expensive, nearby country club. The bride and bridesmaids were dressed in fashionable and elaborate gowns and carried bouquets of silk flowers. Nearly everyone who was invited attended.

For weeks before the wedding, friends and family prepared dozens and dozens of cookies. Marcella had decided that the customary "two large trays of cookies on either side of the wedding cake" was not a good idea. The reason she offered was that in such situations not everyone had a choice of the best cookies. Especially if the cookies were bought at a bakery, the finest cookies were only a single layer on top of the inexpensive variety. People had a habit of selecting the best and leaving the remains for those who followed. She wanted everyone to have a choice of all the cookies, and so decided that a tray of cookies would be placed at each table. Family and friends worked for three days to assemble the cookie trays, which were decorated with sugar-coated almonds and silver thread.

The wedding cake was an elaborate confectionery. A local bakery prepared the alternating layers of Italian cream cake and chocolate-chip pound cake. The groom had wanted the first, the bride the latter. The cake consisted of three pedestals, each with three tiers. The three sections were joined by a plastic ramp which held miniature figures of the wedding party. Underneath the central section was a fountain which splashed pink liquid.

The cake was reminiscent of the elaborateness of the ice sculptures of the formal dinners of another era. Importantly, the cake was decorated by Jeanette, who had learned the art of cake decorating at the local bakery. It took five hours to decorate and assemble it the night before the wedding.

The banquet room of the country club was the site of the wedding meal. The dining tables were arranged in a large circle to leave the center of the room free for dancing. The head table was placed in front of a large window overlooking the grounds. In front of the head table was the cake. The groom's family was seated to the right; the bride's family to the left. The menu, chosen by Marcella, included veal cordon bleu, accompanied by green beans with almonds and "scooped baked potatoes with cheese." A fruit cup would begin the meal, followed by a Caesar salad. Dessert was a strawberry parfait. The meal was not atypical of that offered and served by many catering establishments.

Marcella's reasoning was that veal was expensive and elegant and that the dish itself was unusual. One of the tacit rules of eating behavior in this community is that "eating out" is something special, and choices made on those occasions are of dishes that are not served in the home. The groom would have preferred an Italian meal. Marcella was resolute that if she were paying for the meal then she would select an exotic menu.

While the bride and groom received the guests, there was an "open bar" and cheese and crackers were served. Following the wedding dinner, the guests were able to select drinks of any variety. Once again the emphasis was on extravagance. Marcella was careful about her decisions; the primary criterion was quality; cost was disregarded. Pat Fiore was involved only in that he "walked his daughter down the aisle." He was not invited to the wedding dinner. Members of his family were invited, although many of them did not attend.

At the wedding, people said, "This is Marcella's wedding." And it was. In many senses, this was the beginning of a new life for Marcella. She was no longer married. For her, this was a disillusionment and a personal tragedy but simultaneously what she considered freedom from the tyranny of marriage. In her efforts to provide the finest wedding she could, she was also acknowledging her new status. Further, Marcella was communicating something to her husband and the community. The wedding was a matter of pride. As she put it, "I can make it on my own. I don't need help from Pat. God has always taken care of me and He will provide now." After mourning the loss of her husband and their marriage, her bitterness now emerged as hope. She submerged her own disappointments with marriage and glorified the occasion in order to show that she had not lost her faith, her hope, or her belief in the cultural values with which she had been raised.

One of the central themes of both weddings had to do with the threat to traditional values that each situation engendered. Though the weddings stand in marked contrast to one another, they share a common concern with the stability of the community and the continuity of a way of life.

Superficially, the weddings seem to have different meanings. One might even interpret the variation between the two events as signifying the loss of ethnic identity. One might assume that Marcella and her family had somehow relinquished the values of their parents in favor of "American culture." At the first wedding, the meal and the presentation of the food were "traditional." Three years later the Italian fare seemed rejected for an American menu and a standardized caterer's format.

Viewing the two weddings as members of a single class of events might engender such an interpretation, but a closer look suggests otherwise. Only in contrasting the two weddings do Marcella's food choices become meaningful.

In the first case, Jeanette married a non-Italian. By itself, this choice—in today's world—was not significant. However, her choice of a mate was not approved. Family and friends were concerned that the marriage would not last. John's behavior was perceived as that of a child. He was not responsible. And he would not be responsible in the ways which Marcella felt were important. He would not be a good husband or father. To Marcella, marriage signifies the acceptance of responsibility of adult life. Her daughter's happiness was important, her well-being a concern. Marcella expressed those concerns through her choice of foods and the structure of the occasion.

Not only was her family threatened by the intrusion of a "stranger," but her family's relationship to the group and the group's values were threatened as well. By selecting Italian foods in a situation of potential embarrassment and vulnerability, she was affirming the very values which were threatened. Her refusal to permit anything "English" to be used in the celebration of her daughter's wedding was an attempt to shun and reject not only the male who violated her family's honor and boundaries, but the culture with which he was identified. By drawing her family into an intimate and bounded group at this time, she protected the sanctity of the family domain. Only the family would witness the marriage itself; only close friends would be invited to celebrate the occasion.

The format which Marcella chose, the buffet—"the old way"—was both an affirmation of a way of life and, simultaneously, a marker of the lower status accorded to this event, given the format usually reserved for the wedding meal: "the sit-down dinner."

A "sit-down dinner" for a large number of guests is a prestigious and expensive occasion. In some ways it is an American ideal, both the creation of caterers' institutions and an ideal conception of the American way of life. It signifies wealth, success, and achievement as well as communion. Without a meal of such prestige, Jeanette's wedding was glossed as hurried, unplanned, and lacking the joyousness of this event, which theoretically should be the pinnacle of a young man's and woman's life.

Jeanette's wedding took on added importance at another level; it was a celebration of traditional values and an affirmation of continuity for the celebrants. Marcella protected her world by circumscribing the boundaries clearly, marking them with the food that represented her world, the culture of her parents' generation.

Roxanne's marriage responded to a violation of another sort, one from within. It was the dissolution of her own marriage that Marcella confronted in the wedding of her eldest daughter.

Roxanne married an Italian, who had himself articulated in his search for a woman his respect for "traditional" values. Their lives were to be guided by Robert's father. The bride and groom were an approved match.

Roxanne's and Robert's wedding celebration marked the beginning of that union and the end of another, that of Pat and Marcella. Marcella's choice of the prestigious and normative "sit-down dinner" at an elegant location outside of the home was an acknowledgment that her eldest daughter had married with her approval and married well. Her choice of the expensive and elaborate meal, though "English," was not an expression of distance from Italian culture, but a statement of her independence and pride. In conforming to the standard format of such occasions, and in choosing the finest meal available, she showed the community that she could and would continue to care for herself and her family without the support of a husband. No breach would occur in their lives because of his leaving. She would give him no satisfaction watching her struggle.

For the rest, the marriage was as it should be. With no threat to the community or its values, there was no need to mark the boundaries of the group. Adherence to the shared community pattern affirmed the appropriateness of this occasion and the choices Marcella had made.

The weddings of both Jeanette and Roxanne Fiore dealt with the issues of male abrogation of responsibility and the threat to the values and membership of the culture group. In the first case, the violation was perpetrated by an "outsider"; in the second case the dishonor came from within. In both instances Marcella expressed her concerns and those voiced by the community through her manipulation of the food system. She used common understandings of the meanings of foods and the structure of events to underscore and amplify the community's knowledge of these events and her feelings about them.

The use of food in these two contrastive but similar occasions suggests that food contributes to the creation of meaningful social discourse. Clifford Geertz has said that "cultural forms can be treated as texts, as imaginative works built out of social materials."[12] Food is one of culture's most redundant and pervasive materials. It has the capacity to communicate, in any one event, many layers of meaning. The particular interpretations given to such cultural texts are dependent upon the "readers," in this case the participants in these ritual events.

What was being expressed in these weddings had not only to do with weddings and the institution of marriage, or even with Italian weddings and marriages, but with the affirmation and acceptance of one woman's changing relationship to her family and society. There is an expression in the Italian community which means that someone got his dues, his comeuppance. Marcella felt that both Pat Fiore and John Peterson got what they deserved: she "gave them a cake."

Notes

* I would like to thank Karen Curtis for the historical data in the paper, which is the result of her thorough and meticulous documentation of the history and development of the community. I am deeply grateful to Jeffrey Shultz for his careful, lucid, critical comments; without him the paper would not have this form. Michael Owen Jones also read and commented on the paper. His wise suggestions have been incorporated and gratefully so.

1. This perspective assumes that immigrant or ethnic groups are stable, bounded, and homogeneous enclaves living in relation to a dominant society. It also presumes that culture change is unidirectional and irrevocable; that groups of people will eventually merge with the cultural mainstream. See, for instance, Milton M. Gordon, *Assimilation in American Life* (New York: Oxford University Press, 1964). The influence of these ideas is apparent in Nathan Glazer and Daniel P. Moynihan's *Ethnicity: Theory and Experience* (Cambridge: Harvard University Press, 1975).

2. Melford Spiro, "The Acculturation of American Ethnic Groups," *American Anthropologist* 57 (1955): 1240–52.

3. Concurrent with these foci has been the assumption that the meaning of the food inheres within the item itself. For example, spaghetti with tomato sauce is accepted as part of the Italian diet. According to this perspective, then,

the serving and eating of this dish by Italians signifies an identification with Italian culture. This view assumes not only that food carries meaning intrinsically, but that it carries one primary meaning, that of continuity for the culture group.

4. McKim Marriott, "Caste Ranking and Food Transactions" in *Structure and Change in Indian Society,* edited by Milton Singer and Abner Cohen (Chicago: Aldine-Atherton, 1968).

5. Fieldwork was carried out jointly with Karen Curtis, Department of Anthropology, Temple University. The principal investigator was Dr. Judith G. Goode, Chairman, Department of Urban Studies and Associate Professor, Anthropology Department, Temple University. Funding was provided by the Russell Sage Foundation, New York, under the directorship of Dr. Mary Douglas. The research was conducted from December until June 1979. Four families were observed, each for a period of one or two months. We spent from morning until bedtime, each day, observing and recording the food and eating behavior of the families. This involved participating in shopping, visiting, mealtimes, and special occasions. The fieldwork experience gave us the opportunity to observe domestic life in all its facets; we asked questions and were asked many in return. We observed, recorded, and talked about daily occurrences and, in particular, the role that food played in the lives of the people with whom we stayed. Pseudonyms have been used for the name of the town and for the names of family members.

6. Janice A. Radway, *Reading the Romance: Women, Patriarchy, and Popular Literature* (Chapel Hill: University of North Carolina Press, 1984), 10.

7. Janet S. Theophano, "It's Really Tomato Sauce, but We Call It Gravy," unpublished doctoral dissertation, Department of Folklore and Folklife, University of Pennsylvania, 1982, contains a more detailed account of these issues.

8. Arjun Appadurai, "Gastro-Politics in Hindu South Asia," *American Ethnologist* 8 (1981), 494–511.

9. Although the food served at Roxanne's wedding could best be described as "continental" or "French," it is referred to here as "English" or "American," the terms used interchangeably by Marcella and others in the community to refer to non-Italian foods.

10. Mayonnaise is considered American or English food. Newly immigrated Italians reportedly refuse to eat it.

11. A pizzelle is a type of Italian cookie. In Italian, the word is pluralized as "pizzelli" or "pisselli," but in this community the plural is Anglicized and pronounced "pizzelles."

12. Clifford Geertz, *The Interpretation of Cultures* (New York: Basic Books, 1973).

CHAPTER 24
THE RHETORIC OF PORTIONS
Amy Shuman

The Ginsbergs always ask for small slices. You can ask them if they wouldn't like just a bit more or if they're sure that's enough, and they always say with great certainty, "I really only want a tiny slice." But then a few minutes later, one of them is bound to ask for another small piece. And it's one round of tiny slices after another. That's what we call the "Ginsberg portion."[1]

Now a part of family folklore, this narrative indicates some of the ways in which the apportionment of food and its acceptance may constitute a kind of communication. Whether food is served in a family setting or between a host or hostess and a guest, it can embody roles, expectations, and identities; and the behavior which accompanies the service may be interpreted as an expression of the feelings, attitudes, and sensitivities of the participants. If quantities of food were infinite and appetites always hearty, if the service of food and the resultant acceptance or refusal of it were never a part of larger social events, and if food itself were never symbolic, then the apportioning of food might be a more simple and straightforward matter. But rarely is that so. For food apportionment is almost always embellished with questions of etiquette, perceptions of social hierarchy, and a variety of rules of conduct about which there is not always agreement, even among members of the same family.

This preliminary study of the social negotiations of food allocation relies on various sources of information and is intended as an introduction to the study of a neglected area of behavior. It focuses on no single time or social unit. Although geographically and historically disparate, the sources reveal that the division of portions is often a serious endeavor with significant implications for social relationships. The accommodation of an unexpected guest, an offer to share food, or the delegation of the last piece of food on a serving dish are all social acts. The offering of portions as a part of foodsharing may be intended, and often is taken to be, an act of communication; hence, the "rhetoric of portions." Often, indeed, food is apportioned and accepted not according to a person's wants or needs, but as a means of expressing relationships or in accordance with one's assessment of an event and its participants. Considerable effort may be expended on intricate negotiations, people might be embarrassed or offended or unaccountably pleased, and relationships may be made, broken, reinforced, or strained. The tacit assumption that people who are allied in one way or another should be able to eat together pleasantly and peacefully may be undermined by misunderstandings and conflicting habits, attitudes, and interpretations of acts. In sum, then, the matter of portions often requires tact and diplomacy and necessitates delicacy in the monitoring, interpreting, and assessing of behavior.

In Western civilization, the apportionment of food has generally corresponded to trends both in the style of food service and in the use of certain types of vessels and cutlery. In the Middle Ages, all of the food for a meal was placed on the table at once.[2] Guests served themselves on "trenchers"—thick slices of stale bread—and often they brought their own knives and spoons.[3] The central matters of food etiquette were whether one ate directly from a serving dish or from the trencher and whether one sampled all of the foods or ate only

Amy Shuman, 'The Rhetoric of Portions', *Western Folklore* 40 (1981), 72–80.
© Western States Folklore Society.

one delicacy. Nothing edible was allocated to the individual, although loaves of bread to be cut into trenchers were in some instances distributed to the diners,[4] so it was not the responsibility of the host to insure that each person received an appropriate share. But the seventeenth century saw a change from the earlier form of distribution to the neat arrangement of dishes and a sequence of courses. The bread trenchers were replaced with pewter or wooden trenchers. The shape of the dining table was changed from a U-shaped table with guests seated on only one side to a rectangular table with guests seated on both sides facing each other. The historical record contains little information about the apportionment of food to individuals, but Lorna Sass's study of dining habits in Tudor England indicates that attention was certainly paid to drink:

> These sculptures of sparkling glass remained on the cupboard until, at mealtime, a diner called for a drink. When the cupful was brought, a guest never drank all of its contents, for that was considered rude; nor was it polite to request the cup more than twice during an ordinary meal.[5]

In the eighteenth and nineteenth centuries, new forms of table service emerged and with them new attitudes toward the individual guest. By the end of the nineteenth century, in many instances the host apparently took the responsibility for serving food and apportioning it to guests.

Thus, the record concerning European dining customs indicates a shift from the presentation of food in great variety and abundance for all to help themselves, to an offering of food in a particular sequence with more ceremony accorded to the serving and eating of specific types of dishes. Among those of wealth and status, both modes required the help of servants and sometimes the children of the household to distribute the food.[6] No doubt in households lacking servants a more immediate relationship existed between host and guest; in these households the host showed as much discretion and propriety in the careful apportionment of food according to status as did the host at state dinners. At the state dinners, the distribution of food was accomplished indirectly, through the mediation of servants, while in other situations hosts and hostesses would present food directly to guests. In either case, inappropriate portions might be understood as an insult to a guest.

The obligations of the host to a guest are historically related to the obligations of the head of a household to provide food for dependents. The words "lord" and "lady," in fact, refer to the position of those in charge of the bread to be distributed to their households. "Lord" has been traced by etymologists to "hlafweard" [hlaf (loaf) + weard (keeper)], and "lady" derives from the Anglo-Saxon "hlafdia" [hlaf (loaf) + dia (to knead)].[7] The obligation to provide food for children, elderly parents, priests, or other dependents is sometimes explicitly designated by a society and may be fixed to exact amounts. For example, R. J. Bernard has shown that specific food pensions for aged parents were included in eighteenth century marriage contracts and wills.[8] In contrast, however, the portion accorded a guest is more often negotiable and is rarely formalized into written law.[9] Hence, the host and hostess must accommodate the needs of the guests. In addition, they must satisfy the social demands of the occasion.

As in any communication, however, food service and food apportionment may create conflict. The expectations of the guests, for example, may not match the readiness of the providers. But etiquette requires that the parties collaborate silently to disguise the discrepancies and mitigate their effects. Some families explicitly recognize this by developing signals as part of a collusive communication designed to prevent guests from recognizing discrepancies. For instance, a family might develop a code language in which "F. H. B." means "Family Hold Back," so the guests will have more to eat; "L. K. F." means "Lick and Keep Forks," so there will be enough flatware for everyone; and "M. I. K." designates "More in Kitchen."[10] The accommodation of unexpected guests often requires similarly surreptitious moves to extend the amount of food prepared. Simon Lichman describes such a situation in Marshfield, England:

One Sunday when we were having our elevenses at Jesse's, he asked his wife Gladys, "Do you think you can stretch it then?" She said, "Oh, I expect so." We didn't know what it meant then, but we saw the twinkle in their eyes and got persuaded to stay for lunch. Afterwards we discovered that "stretching it" meant adding a couple of extra potatoes and slicing the roast thinner.[11]

A central concern in food apportionment is for the host and hostess to appear generous and to present their offering with no apparent strings attached. Similarly, the guest must not seem to be exclusively interested in the food and yet must pay the proper compliments to the providers. These concerns echo Marcel Mauss's remarks characterizing gift exchanges in general as, "presentations which are in theory voluntary, disinterested and spontaneous, but are in fact obligatory and interested."[12] A host or hostess who monitors a guest's plate appears too interested. A guest who attends only to the food and not to the conversation appears to be a glutton.[13]

The importance of not seeming overly concerned with the food on one's plate is interestingly demonstrated in the camp game of "Pig." At a summer camp in Canada, the game may be started when one camper puts his finger on his nose. As soon as others notice, they put their fingers on their noses, and so on until only one camper remains, unobservant and still eating. The other campers point to him and shout, "Pig!"[14]

Monitoring eating behavior is rarely as simple as attending to another's needs. Especially in situations in which host or hostess and guest are of very different backgrounds (or for other reasons have different expectations and interpret events in different ways), relationships may be strained in the apportionment and the acceptance or refusal of food.[15] Systems for acceptance and refusal often clash. For example, Ana Cara Walker tells about the first meeting of her maternal grandmother from Czechoslovakia, and her paternal grandmother, from Argentina, in the home of the Czech grandmother. They met during the courtship of their respective offspring. The Czech woman was not aware that in Argentina it is the custom among some to refuse the first three offers of food. The hostess may or may not offer a fourth time; this gives her the chance to be hospitable even if she does not have any food to offer, and it provides the guest the opportunity to decline the first offers as a gesture of modesty.[16] The Argentine woman did not know that many Czechs observe a different etiquette in which food is offered only once; people are not required to accept food, but when they do, they are expected to eat everything given to them. According to the story, the Czech grandmother offered some beautiful pastries to the Argentine grandmother, who, of course, refused. To her surprise, the pastries were whisked away to the kitchen not to be offered a second time, much less a third or fourth. The Czech hostess thought that her Argentine guest was either not hungry or did not find the pastries appealing; otherwise she would have accepted some. At the same time, the Argentine woman was greatly distressed by the Czech's apparent rudeness. Because both parties felt the other lacked proper manners, the relationship between the in-laws was in jeopardy for a short while.

Such errors of interpretation are not uncommon in situations of food sharing, and they always create a dilemma for the participants in the exchange. Should they accept the awkwardness of the situation, overlooking faux pas, or should they call attention to the matter, thus risking further indiscretion?

Similar problems sometimes arise when delicacies are presented.[17] While the offering of a comparatively small quantity of a food may be thought by host and hostess to signal that the dish is a delicacy, they may not always make this signal explicit; further, what seems to them a delicacy may not seem one to their guests. Serving a small portion, then, might seem to a guest to be an affront; eating too much of a certain food may be taken by the hosts to be a mark of rudeness. In addition, while the well-mannered host or hostess should monitor the guest's behavior in order graciously to offer more food when appropriate, for some the act of observing must be done surreptitiously.[18] In at least one upper class American home, it is reported that one never asks guests if they want "more" of something, for that would indicate that one had noticed how much they had eaten. Instead, the host or hostess asks, "Would you like some of. . .," a certain food. (And a guest who wishes to refuse is expected to say something like, "No, thank you; it's very good, I'm sure.")[19]

Food hospitality, then, is a matter of appearances. Large portions are commonly perceived to be a sign of abundance. However, when food supplies are thought to be limited, restraint from taking more than one's share may be seen as a test of appropriate social behavior.

A major point of contrast in notions of food hospitality concerns whether or not people leave food on their plates and how the last piece of food is managed.[20] Finishing food can be a compliment to the cook. Elenore Smith Bowen provides an example in her autobiographical ethnography, *Return to Laughter*:

> The cook had boned the chicken and stuffed it superbly. Even after I had eaten all I wished of it, my sense of duty obliged me to eat on. Such labor should not go unappreciated. And, judging by the murmurs from the kitchen as Monday bore out the almost empty platter, the cook was gratified. I had left little room for anything else. Eating had become a duty. Guest to my own staff, I approached the remainder of the meal with the reluctant appetite of one who does not wish to insult his hostess.[21]

In some situations, eating all the food offered may be understood as a sign that the amount was insufficient. Or, when only one piece of food remains on a serving dish, this last piece can become the subject of elaborate negotiations. Sometimes diners have monitored each other's consumption to determine who has not had a fair share and thus deserves the last piece. In other cases, someone may offer to divide the last piece, and it may be continually divided until too insignificant to divide further. Even so, some people are reluctant to take the last crumb for fear of appearing hungry at the end of the meal. The last piece, sometimes known as the "old maid," is rarely taken without notice and may involve complicated moves, as in the following incident reported by a member of a communal student household:

> Just before dinner, three welcome, but unexpected, friends showed up, and after inviting them to stay I was faced with the problem of extending twelve meatballs to feed eight people. I cut the meatballs in half, and when I served them, announced that there was enough for everyone to have three meatballs (and unspecified quantities of other foods). That was my big mistake. Each person took only two meatballs and politely said that someone else could have the third. We ended up dividing the meatballs in half again.

The last piece of food is thus heavily laden with significance. It calls into question the abundance of the food available, the modesty of the guests, and the equality of the portions.[22]

The apportionment of food often has significance beyond the immediate dining situation. Since the rules for appropriate conduct regarding the apportionment of food are unstated, violations are easily committed, and may vary with the company. The following story, told to a child as a lesson of what not to do, describes a mother-in-law whose attempts to be helpful created an awkward situation:

> Did I ever tell you the story of Martha's mother? Well, Martha and her husband, Oliver, had invited Oliver's boss for dinner, and Martha's mother was living with them at the time, so they were all going to have dinner together. Oliver, the boss, and Martha's mother were sitting at the dining room table, and Martha was bringing in the main course which was already served onto plates. She brought in two plates and gave one to her mother and one to the boss. While she was getting the other plates, her mother noticed that her own portion was bigger than the boss's portion, so she switched the plates and said, "Here, you have this one." When Martha brought in the other plates, her mother again saw a portion bigger than that on the boss's plate and made another switch. Oliver was just about to take a bite when

Martha's mother attempted another switch, but it was stopped as Oliver stood up and shouted, "For God's sake, it doesn't make any difference! Let's eat!"

Of course, the incident did make a difference. The fact that the son-in-law protested indicates that the interaction had reached the limits of his tolerance. The mother-in-law's well-intentioned concern that the special guest receive the largest portion might not be out of place in some social settings, but on this more formal occasion the concern, so often repeated, had become an irritation or even an embarrassment.

The foregoing examples and discussion, then, demonstrate that food apportionment, while often viewed as an incidental dimension of social life, can have important social consequences. In some cases, hosts and hostesses may attempt to neutralize the potential significance of portions by providing equal shares to all. In other instances, portions may be used to discriminate explicitly between categories of guests. The assessment of the intended significance of an offer or presentation of food is complicated by both unstated rules and the pretended insignificance of the food. Tact demands that diners not appear over-interested in the food, for eating is rarely the sole purpose of a gathering. At the same time, participants must discreetly monitor each other's behavior to know what is expected of them. The rhetoric of portions requires the covert cooperation of all parties to turn situations with limited resources and a priori expectations into the appearance of unqualified generosity and appreciation.

Notes

1. Ed Hirsch, personal communication, 1977.

2. Reay Tannahill, *Food in History* (New York, 1973), 225.

3. Gerard Brett, *Dinner Is Served: A Study in Manners* (Hamden, Conn., 1969), 61.

4. Ibid., 60.

5. Lorna Sass, *To the Queen's Taste* (New York, 1976), 17.

6. Ibid., 18.

7. See *Oxford English Dictionary.*

8. R. J. Bernard, "Peasant Diet in Eighteenth-Century Gevaudan," in *European Diet from Pre-Industrial to Modern Times,* ed. Elborg and Robert Forster (New York, 1975), 19–46.

9. For a discussion of obligations to provide food to kinsmen and to strangers, see Audrey I. Richards, *Hunger and Work in a Savage Tribe* (Cleveland, 1964), 81–82.

10. These examples were collected at the Smithsonian Festival of American Folklore, Family Folklore Area.

11. Simon Lichman, forthcoming doctoral dissertation, "The Marshfield Paper Boys Mumming Tradition," University of Pennsylvania.

12. Marcel Mauss, *The Gift* (New York, 1967), 1.

13. In Taiwan, the word "glutton" literally means to give too much attention to eating. Maxine Miska, personal communication.

14. Shelley Posen, personal communication, 1980.

15. See, for example, Jacques Dournes, "Time and Menu," in *The Anthropologists' Cookbook,* ed. Jessica Kuper (London, 1977), 163.

16. See Erving Goffman's discussion of "negative bargaining" in Erving Goffman, "On Facework" in *Interaction Ritual* (New York, 1967), 31.

17. See the example in Abraham Hay ward, *The Art of Dining: or Gastronomy and Gastronomers* (London, 1852), 105 (cited in Tannahill, 340).

18. For a description of surreptitious monitoring, see Israel Zangwill, *Children of the Ghetto* (Leicester, 1977), 120–126.

19. Sam Walker, personal communication.

20. Contrast the remarks to children reported in James H. S. Bossard, "Family Table Talk—An Area for Sociological Study," *American Sociological Review* 8 (1943): 300, with those reported in Vera Y. N. Hsu and Francis L. K. Hsu "Modern China, North" in *Food in Chinese Culture: An Anthropological and Historical Perspective,* ed. K. C. Chang (New Haven, 1977), 305. See also Frances R. Horwich, "The Last Pancake" in *Miss Frances' Story Book of Manners* (New York, 1955), 52–54.

21. Elenore Smith Bowen, *Return to Laughter* (Garden City, New York, 1964), 242–243.

22. Sheldon Posen discusses coaxing in his forthcoming doctoral dissertation, University of Pennsylvania.

CHAPTER 25

FOODSCAPES: THE CULINARY LANDSCAPES OF RUSSIAN-JEWISH NEW YORK

Eve Jochnowitz

The influence of landscape on cuisine has long been a subject of study for ethnographers, food scholars, and ideologues of every stripe. The French famously cite *le goût du terroir,* "the irreplaceable flavor of the soil" or "the taste of place" as being an essential component in the flavor of local foods.[1]

This chapter will address the influence of food on a landscape. I will argue that the foods and foodways of a culture form a landscape of their own. Food makes place. Jews of the former Soviet Union, in bringing their foods and food practices to new homes, have created new places. This culinary landscape, or foodscape, is not just the foods alone; it also includes the traditions of display and performance associated with the food. It includes deliberately and intentionally created aesthetic productions as well as incidental culinary "noise."

For the concept of a foodscape, I am primarily indebted to the musicologist R. Murray Schafer, whose concept of soundscape included deliberately produced "aesthetic sounds" as well as incidental sounds such as overheard conversations, weather, roadwork, and so on.[2] Schaffer's model is particularly useful because of his understanding of the many, possibly infinite, components that combine to create a perceived sensory experience. A foodscape differs from a soundscape in that all senses, rather than just the sense of hearing, are engaged, and in that all these sensory perceptions are related to the ultimate edibility (or inedibility) of the food perceived. I am indebted as well to Jeffrey Shandler, whose definition of a virtual "Yiddishland" provides many useful tools for thinking about how performance creates space and how space itself performs.[3] Work by the geographers David Bell and Gill Valentine on food and space is particularly valuable to anyone seeking to understand the interactions of landscape and eating, and my five-part definition of the foodscape follows their seven-part hierarchy of the geographies of consumption. Bell and Valentine's findings demonstrate that food habits shape one's experience of spatial scale.[4]

Nation and nationalism are central to the French concept of *terroir,* and to the regional foodways of other European countries, but neither Russian nor Jewish nationalism quite fit into the framework of nationalism in the European sense. Russian nationalism is anomalous because Russian nationhood is connected with the multilingual and multi-textured histories of the Soviet Union and before that, the Russian Empire of the Czars. Jewish nationalism, oddly enough, is parallel to Russian Nationalism in this sense, even while the Jewish situation could not be more different from that of an empire. While Jews and Russians may feel deep connection to a place, and powerful impulses toward nationalism, it is not the same phenomenon as the nineteenth century romantic European notion of a consanguineous people united in a contiguous place.

As a diasporic people, Jews are connected culturally, linguistically, and gastronomically to many places, yet are connected to one another by a shared set of dietary laws and a shared liturgical language. Jewish culinary performance, in this sense, can be understood as a medium that provides a virtual presence for

Eve Jochnowitz, 'Foodscapes: The Culinary Landscapes of Russian-Jewish New York' in Julia Brauch, Anna Lipphardt and Alexandra Nocke (eds), *Jewish Topographies: Visions of Space, Traditions of Place,* (Aldershot: Ashgate, 2008) pp. 294–308.

© 'Foodscapes: The Culinary Landscapes of Russian-Jewish New York', Eve Jochnowitz, 2008, Ashgate.

people separated in space but proximate in practice. As Barbara Kirshenblatt-Gimblett has argued, the dispersion associated with diaspora, long understood as a pathological condition of displacement from a central or privileged origin, is only half of the diasporic condition. The other half, the production of the local by a rearticulated population in a space of dispersal, is the element of diaspora too frequently neglected in the study of immigrant communities.[5] The commonly voiced concerns about the inauthenticity of the cultural and religious practices of Jews from the former Soviet Union illustrate Kirshenblatt-Gimblett's point. The foods Russophonic Jews are creating in New York are worthy of study. It may be valid to question whether particular innovations, such as "Russian sushi" or whole-wheat versions of traditional breads, are sound or unsound within the context in which one makes them, or to interrogate the reasons for which some home cooks and retailers embrace some innovations while shunning others, but it is irrelevant to argue whether or not they are "authentically Russian" or "authentically Jewish." These phenomena are better understood as an expression of the "independence and stubborn resistance" of what John Bodner calls the "children of capitalism."[6]

The foodscape

I define a foodscape as consisting of these five separate and partly nested personal sites: the mouth, the body, the kitchen, the table, and the street. My paper will examine each of these culinary landscapes in relation to the ways in which Jews understand and create space, the geographies of Russophonic Jewish New York, and in particular the culinary and place-making practices of the Jews of the former Soviet Union. An examination of Jewish place-making practices, such as the traditions of eruvin and pilgrimage, provide illustrations for understanding the connections of food and space in a larger Jewish context.

This chapter will begin to explain what happens when a phenomenon as inextricably linked to a place as a cuisine continues its existence in a new place entirely. Stemming from Eastern Europe, Georgia, the Caucasus, and Central Asia, the Jewish communities I studied use food to articulate an intense and intimate connection with place, both the place left behind and the place created through sensory and social practices. The cuisines of uprooted and rearticulated Jewish communities selectively retain traditions and innovate at each point in the food system.

The mouth

All of culture passes through the mouth.[7] As a liminal zone, neither outside nor inside, the mouth is a particularly contested cultural landscape. The mouth is the space within the Jewish tradition that accepts the physical nourishment of food and the spiritual nourishment of Torah. Joel Hecker has found that the mouth has mystical significance in rabbinic culture as the point of entry for both nourishment and Torah.[8] In the Jewish communities of North Africa, a Torah pointer is a teething toy for a child, especially a male child, so that the object that has touched every letter in the Torah can transmit the sacred text to the child when he puts it in his mouth, giving literal meaning to the expression "*Torah she be-al pe*" or "oral law."[9]

The palate is part of the mouth but is also understood as a socially constructed site; that is geographically specific, and possibly even gender- and class-specific. The landscape of one's own mouth, physiological and cultural, determines how all other foodscapes will be perceived. I agree in this case with Amy Trubek's argument that the taste of a place is very much an acclimatization of the palate, and as the agrarian landscape has changed, the landscape of the palate has changed.[10]

While I am not suggesting that there is any difference between a Russian mouth and a mouth belonging to a person from anywhere else, I do feel that I can safely make a case that different groups use and view their mouths differently, or that the mouth occupies a variety of social spaces. Tasting and smelling, chewing and swallowing, speaking, smoking, and spitting are all performances that distinguish the mouthscapes of a culture.[11] Within the community of recent Russian immigrants, smoking is widely considered acceptable among males. Almost no restaurants enforce the city's smoking prohibitions and it is common for men to smoke even while food is being served.

The body

That food creates the landscape of the body is obvious. All the physical material of one's body and the energy to keep the body functional is made out of food that body has consumed; but one's cells and tendons are not the only components of the body's foodscape. The body, or more precisely, the way in which people see their bodies as needing nourishment (in the form of good food) and protection from harm (through avoidance of bad food) is a culinary landscape that might seem to be unchanged by relocation. In fact, one's body and one's understanding of one's body are socially determined phenomena. Historian Mark Swislocki has noted that a new eating system involves a new concept of what the body is and how it works.[12] In China, for instance, people who adopted the western biomedical understanding of the body and nutrition found themselves inhabiting new bodies. Adopting a new system, however, does not necessarily mean one discards the old. A diner familiar with Chinese food theory can approach a meal and see it both as containing calories, fiber, vitamins, and other elements of food as understood in western medicine, and also as occupying a position on the heating-cooling (Yang-Yin) spectrum, and having various proportions of the five elements as understood by Chinese philosophy. Swislocki describes the people who participate in two eating systems as being "bi-corporal."

"In Russian there is no cholesterol," one restaurateur told me. He was partly joking, of course, but in fact it is no joke. There is a very different Russian body, which requires what it requires according to an internally consistent system. Cholesterol is not one of the components a Russian body encounters when evaluating a food. A popular Russian proverb reminds us that "you can't spoil kasha with butter."[13] While one's Russian body needs fat to be healthy, one's western body needs to avoid it. "Who ever heard there about cholesterol, saturated fats, free radicals, or anything in that vein?" asked one recent immigrant. Similarly, the dieting and health practices that many women commonly followed in the former Soviet Union, such as fasting once a week, or "separated eating" seem alarmingly ineffective and even dangerous to someone familiar with the western biomedical model of the body.[14]

Many instances of bi-corporality exist within the Russian-Jewish foodscapes of New York. The most salient example is that of the social space occupied by fat. This space is very different in Russia, both with regard to fat as an ingredient, something wholesome, delicate, and expensive in the Russian context, unhealthy, cheap, and greasy in the West, and with regard to fat on the human body. Socialist realist art of the Soviet era shows attractive women as being powerful, sturdy, or even plump, while by no means overweight. Within the context of the revolutionary ideal, the valorization of the fuller figure may be related to the primacy given to a woman's work or to the difficulty of maintaining such a figure in times of scarcity, or both. One immigrant ruefully reported: "In Russia we did not have enough to eat because of shortages; here we do not have enough to eat because of calories. What was the point of emigrating?"[15]

Annie Hauck-Lawson has found that women who immigrated to the Americas from Poland have experienced what she calls going "from under-nutrition to over-nutrition." Since emigrating and facing the bewildering choices of a new foodscape, these women find themselves reaching sizes with which they are uncomfortable.[16] Women from Russian-speaking lands face the same difficulty. Their discomfort is due not only to their weight gain, but to the fact that having adopted the bi-corporal model, they are judging themselves against much harsher standards of thinness. Vera Kishinevsky encountered a young woman who can only be understood as bicorporal—her American body was too fat (the young woman herself reported), while her Russian body was too thin. Her grandmother objected to her weight loss: "You have only your nose left!"[17]

Modern Western Europeans, faced with the prospect of Jewish emancipation and citizenship, imagined a pathologized Jewish body created, at least in part, by Jewish food.[18] This "Jew's Body" was broken, incomplete, incapable of military service, and lacking the productive capacity for full citizenship. To become emancipated, the Jews of eighteenth- and nineteenth century Europe became bicorporal. Judah Leib Gordon's famous prescription is that one ought to be "a Jew in one's home and a man outside," but in some sense a Jew had to understand himself as occupying two bodies both at home and in the street in order to function as an emancipated citizen. Russian popular culture before the revolution also associated Jewish eating, and particularly Jewish consumption of garlic, with the pathology of the Jewish body. Emancipation, however, was not an issue within the Russian empire because no one in Russia, whether Jewish or not, had such an option.

The kitchen

Culture itself is a kitchen, transforming the "raw," the untamed phenomena of the natural world into the "cooked," the domesticated, the civilized, the cultured. The landscape of the kitchen sees the creation of order out of chaos, and the very creation of this order can reduce the kitchen landscape itself to chaos. For my understanding of the landscape of the kitchen, I follow geographer Maria Elisa Christie, who defines "kitchenspace" as the complex of spaces, both indoors and out, involved in the preparation of food. Activities and relationships, according to Christie, delineate kitchenspace as much as do physical structures.[19] It is in the performances associated with provisioning, food preparation, and cleaning up that the foodscape of a kitchen is created. Deidre Sklar suggests that women (and men as well) perform according to a specific "choreography of the kitchen" when they cook and that this choreography infuses the foods prepared with meaning. Her performance ethnography of the fiesta of Tortugas examines the back-region of the kitchen as well as the front-regions of sacred space.[20]

While perhaps not as intimate as the landscape of one's own body, for many cooks a kitchen is a crucially personal place. For Russian Jewish immigrant women, the kitchen is the seat of one's power and a safe venue to play out one's enthusiasm for innovation while also choosing at times to resist change. One young woman observed, "We try new things we find here and then we make it in our Russian way."

For those old enough to remember the social upheaval that occurred during the middle years of the twentieth century, when the Soviet Union attempted to revolutionize domestic space and work, autonomy in one's own kitchen is not to be taken for granted. The Soviet model of equality for women in the workforce and home required the abolition of the private kitchen entirely.[21]

The crisis that prompted the Soviet Union to attempt to abolish domestic cooking and housekeeping had the opposite effect in the United States, where the work of American housewives in their kitchens was idealized as patriotic, especially in wartime.[22] No one in the former Soviet Union had the choice of working full-time as a homemaker, and women's movements took very different forms from those of the West, where feminism's second wave, heralded by *The Feminine Mystique*, valorized work outside the home as a means to liberation. The modernization of the Soviet kitchen did not lead to less division of labor between the sexes in domestic housekeeping. If anything, males from the Russophonic communities are even more bewildered by the world of cooking than their counterparts in the west.

The kitchen in an urban apartment in Russian-Jewish New York is primarily functional. While many Russophonic immigrants have delightedly adopted ultramodern décor for the rest of the house, they have not followed the Italian-American or the Italian-Canadian practice, noted recently by food scholars and journalists, of outfitting the kitchen so lavishly that any actual cooking and eating has to occur somewhere else, usually a makeshift kitchen and dining room set up in a basement or garage.[23] The Russian kitchen remains a back-region, while the Western kitchen has been moving toward the front of the dwelling since the beginning of the twentieth century, and in the twenty-first century has become the most displayed room in many houses.

The table

The table is a particularly resonant Jewish landscape. The phrase "the set table" (*shulhan arukh*), is the synecdoche within Jewish practice for the entire complex of Jewish observance. "*Shulhan Arukh*" is best known as the title of the sixteenth-century work that codified Jewish practice, but the term is much older.[24] "A set table" has become a common Jewish vernacular expression describing everyday practice, both sacred and profane.

How the table is to be laid is culturally relevant for Jews of the Former Soviet Union. Non-Russophones frequently remark on the abundance with which Russians set tables at home and in public venues. One Russian-born woman commented: "My husband could not understand why they put more food on the tables than anyone could possibly eat. My father had to explain that you need to feed the eyes—the eyes need to eat as well."[25]

For this woman's Western-born husband, a table laid *à la Russe* is itself an unfamiliar landscape—uncharted territory that is difficult for an explorer to navigate. Her father's comment that "the eyes need to eat as well" illustrates the different geography of the Russian table.

Anthropologist Barbara Myerhoff found performance of precepts rooted in normative Judaism to shape the behavior of the Jews with whom she worked in their struggles and celebrations. A lady Myerhoff called Basha explained that she begins each meal she eats alone in her tiny apartment by laying the table with linen and saying the blessings before eating. "This [what] my mother taught me to do. No matter how poor we would eat off white linen and say the prayers before touching anything to the mouth." Myerhoff argues that Basha is part of a hidden aristocracy. She dines more splendidly on chicken feet than most do on far finer fare. Basha gives an example of acting Jewish that involves both specifically ordained religious actions—in this case, saying the blessing—and the gestural household traditions she learned from her mother. For Basha, the two performances are inseparable and indispensable for a Jewish table.[26]

Within the Ashkenazic context in particular a table thrums with ritual and cultural significance. The *tish*, or "table" is the central event of Hasidic gathering. A *rebe* (Hasidic Rabbi) is said to "preside at a table" (*firn a tish*), when he interacts with his *khsidim*.[27] A *tish* involves food, both real and symbolic, as well as prayer, paraliturgical song, and conversation. On the Jewish holiday of Purim, the table itself becomes the stage on which the Hasidim perform a *pirimshpiyl* (Purim play).[28] "*Es tut zikh oyf tish un oyf benk*" is a common Yiddish expression meaning "Things are really happening." Within Jewish tradition the table is a stage for eating and meal related ritual.

In Russian, the word *stolichny,* or "of the table" can indicate both that a given food or drink is ordinary and that it is indispensable. The preparation of potatoes, meats and vegetables in a matrix of mayonnaise known as *Salat stolichnii,* or *salat Olivier* unites all communities with any connection to the former Soviet Union. The salad itself functions as a matrix, almost a kind of cultural mayonnaise, in the way it binds together peoples separated by language, cuisine and physical distance. *Vodka Stolichnaya,* Russia's most popular vodka, was the most familiar product from the Soviet Union available in the United States during the Cold War years.

The street

Street food, fast food, cafés, restaurants, and grocery stores comprise a culinary streetscape. When the architect Louis Kahn famously noted, "A street is a room by agreement," he had in mind the synergy created by buildings, businesses, pedestrians, and other travelers and their means of communication. In the neighborhoods of New York, the culinary streetscape engages all senses to bring a walker into a food-world.

In any urban context the street is a significant theater, and in the Jewish context particularly, the street is where observers can most clearly discern the patterns and communications of a neighborhood. The phrase *"di yidishe gas"* (The Jewish street) means not just the street itself, but what is going on inside the homes and even inside the minds of a Jewish community. The expression *"Shikt dayne oyern in di gasn"* or "Send your ears into the streets" means be aware, or find out what is really going on. The many greengrocers' produce spills out onto the streets. *Gastronom* shops, that provide specialty imported foods as well as locally-made pickles and smoked fish, tempt passersby and lure them in with colorful window displays and briny fragrances. Pushcarts sell fried pastries and the many coffeehouses welcome busy pedestrians.

Delis and grocers provide immigrant communities with familiar foods and with safe venues to connect with people from the old country as well. Medical sociologist Larissa Remennick has found that it is food businesses in particular that function as social and cultural centers for shoppers seeking more than physical sustenance.[29]

Russian food stores, carrying a wide assortment of familiar groceries, also serve as places of social encounter and information exchange. Many women in my sample said they found work, housing or caretakers for their elderly (if they could afford it) via Russian grocery or bookstores.[30]

In some cases, the imported items are identical to local versions, at least to my untrained eye, but shoppers will choose to select familiar packages.

Jewish food, Jewish space

The most essential and indispensable concept in understanding the Jewish approach to space is the unique place making practice of the *eruv.* The word 'eruv', in its most common usage, refers to a boundary between public and private space.[31] Within traditional Jewish practice, the eruv is an important concept in the understanding of space and the creation of place. The Talmud defines three kinds of *Eruvin,* all of them intimately connected to food: the *Eruv hatseroth,* or eruv of courtyards; the *Eruv tavshilin,* or eruv of cooking; and the *Eruv thummim,* or eruv of distance.[32] All three types of eruv require the assembly of various foods. In common usage, the word 'eruv' refers almost exclusively to the *Eruv hatseroth,* which symbolically separates an inner or "private" space from an outer or "public" space. While it has become a convention to use the word 'eruv' to refer to a physical barrier, or a symbolic physical barrier which serves to unite everything that lies within and distinguish this space from the outside, in fact, the word 'eruv' literally means "mixture," and refers to the foods that the residents of an area assemble to unite themselves symbolically as one courtyard. In cases where it might become necessary for a group of householders to define their separate residences and the yards and all the areas between them as one symbolic domain for the purposes of carrying on the Sabbath, neighbors will agree to establish an eruv. It is food that is the essential element for this most Jewish idea of creating space, even while the food collected for the eruv stays in a synagogue or other central location, and is not consumed. As Charlotte E. Fonrobert, a scholar of Talmudic and early modern Jewish culture, has noted:

> The *Eruv* community is first and foremost established by a collection of food. It is food, though not a meal per se that forms the center of the entire ritual system. The food collected is not consumed, but deposited in a suitable location within the confines of the neighborhood. Thus, the point is not actual commensality but a symbolic representation thereof. Indeed, I would venture to suggest that the food operates as a symbolic representation of the community itself. As such, the food serves the purpose of unification and integration of the neighborhood.[33]

The foods that constitute the eruv are defined in the Talmud as being anything other than water and salt, but later commentators make it clear that bread, and only a whole loaf, is the ideal. It is vital to note that the assembly of symbolic foods unites neighbors ritually just as the assembly of actual foods unites them in fact. Whether or not a given Jewish community participates in the establishment of an eruv, the traditional Jewish connection of food to the relationship with one's home and one's neighbors continues to resonate. Neighbors who engage with the foodscape of a place, by buying produce, by adapting their cooking, and by dining out and inviting others in, are creating what I would argue is a secular eruv, an invisible barrier between the public and private, between the sacred and the profane. The foodscape is the territory of the secular eruv.

Foodscapes: The pilgrimage

Within the Jewish context, food and pilgrimage are first connected in the passages in the Hebrew bible, which prescribe three pilgrimage festivals in the course of a year (Exodus 23:17 and Deuteronomy 16:16). The adult male Israelites who participated in the pilgrimage brought grain, fruit, and meat on the hoof to Jerusalem, where they would subject each foodstuff to the required ritual. They would then eat the food they had brought, minus the portion given to the priests working in the Temple.[34] In the ancient Near East, these pilgrimages served to unite tribes that were geographically scattered and possibly ethnically diverse by creating what Victor Turner understands as "communitas," or a deeply felt bond that transcends the official or formal connections people might have with one another.[35] As in the case of eruvin, pilgrimage unites people by uniting their food.

For the pilgrim, the journey can be as important as the sacred site that is its goal. The novelty of the terrain, including the experience of unfamiliar foods, pleasurable or unpleasant, is part of the process that transports and transforms the traveler: As the pilgrim moves away from his structural involvements at home his route becomes increasingly sacralized at one level and increasingly secularized at another. He meets with more shrines and sacred objects as he advances, but he also encounters more real dangers (. . .). But all these things are more contractual, more associational, more volitional, more replete with the novel and the unexpected, fuller of possibilities of communitas as secular fellowship and comradeship and sacred communion, than anything he has known at home.[36]

In the modern world, Hasidic tradition ties the concept of biblical pilgrimages to the modern Hasidic custom of making a pilgrimage to a *rebe*. "*Kayn kotsk fort men nisht; kayn kotsk geyt men; vayl kotsk iz dokh bimkoym hamikdesh, un kayn kotsk darf men oyle regel zayn."* The words of a well-known Hasidic hymn explain "you do not travel to Kock, you walk to Kock, because Kock fulfils the place of the Temple, and pilgrimage to Kock must be made on foot." Journeys on foot, as it happens, are an important element of culinary pilgrimages to Russian-Jewish New York: the culinary walking tours.

Culinary pilgrimage: The walking tour phenomenon

Walking tours of New York City became popular in the wake of the city's fiscal crisis of 1975–76, when a shared sense of emergency and grievance stirred New Yorkers with local patriotism.[37] One consequence of the civic pride provoked by the crisis was a renewed interest in and curiosity about the city's history and culture among all sorts of laymen for the following thirty years. Culinary walking tours began to multiply shortly afterward. Myra Alperson, who has been leading culinary walking tours and bicycle tours since 1983, reports that people of all ages and backgrounds attend the tours and many repeat their favorite tours several times.[38]

Seth Kamil, who began leading walking tours in 1990, and founded New York's "Big Onion Walking Tours" in 1991, emphasizes the role of the tour in providing broader historical context for a visitor's understanding of a neighborhood while on the other hand providing what he calls a "micro-history" in contrast to the macro-history of text.[39]

Several years ago, in answer to a call from the New School University, I agreed to lead culinary walking tours of New York's Jewish neighborhoods, including "Queensistan," the Central Asian Jewish enclave, located in the Rego Park section of Queens.

The Rego Park tour begins in front of the oldest synagogue in the area with a discussion of the history of the development of the neighborhood and the influence of the New York World's Fair of 1939–1940. Our first stop is a bakery where students sample such treats as walnut *halwa*, fried noodles in honey, *lipeshka* (pronounced lipyoshka), a bialy-shaped *naan* (frequently spelled "non") and *roti-toki*, or shelf-bread, so-named because of its keeping qualities, a matzo-like wafer baked in the shape of a bowl. I have found it is best to schedule eating early and often throughout the tour so that students do not become fatigued and so that they have the feeling of being repeatedly surprised and delighted. After restoring ourselves at the bakery, we take a long walk to 108th Street, Rego Park's central Jewish shopping street. I use the walking time to discuss the history of the Bukharan Jews, how they came to settle Central Asia after leaving what is now Iraq and Iran, and subsequent Muslim and then Soviet domination of the area. On 108th street we visit a Hungarian bakery (a layer of the culinary landscape from a previous wave of Jewish immigration), a *gastronom* (deli/supermarket) and a tableware store and then proceed to lunch.

I was intrigued to learn that my tour is one of scores of well-attended culinary walking tours of New York City neighborhoods. The appeal of a guided tour that puts the culinary in context is clearly widespread among many elements of the population. Pilgrims of all ages and backgrounds enjoy the tours for their safe introduction to a new food-world. They want to sample the flavors of another group, but they do not want to venture alone into an unknown environment. They also do not want to "miss" anything. Ideally, trusted friends introduce one another to new culinary and cultural territory. One student told me, "In New York, I want someone else to tell me what's good." A tour guide in these cases plays the role of a friend from another community. In fact, almost all of the guides leading culinary tours, myself included, are outsiders in all the Jewish communities in which we conduct tours. Seth Kamil suggests that it may even be preferable to have an outsider as a tour guide, because outsiders can provide passion for a neighborhood without the emotional attachment that comes from feeling personally threatened by a neighborhood's changes.[40]

These visitors are seeking more than just a good meal. Folklorist Lucy Long has found that culinary pilgrims seek a deeper and more personal understanding of foodways that are in some way more authentic than those of their everyday lives. Within the Jewish context, the cuisines of the former Soviet Union evoke both places and times of heightened significance. In many cases, the pilgrims' quest is as much for more authentic Judaisms as it is for more authentic foods. Culinary pilgrims to Rego Park are likely to be unfamiliar with the flavors of Bukharan cuisine, and to have no familial connections to central Asia, but for them as well, the tour is a kind of homecoming because they identify with the journey that this new group of New Yorkers has made, recapitulating the phylogeny of the Jewish immigrant experience to the Americas.

Cuisine as cultural performance

Cultural performances are the occasions in which as a culture or society we reflect upon and define ourselves.[41] Food is at the center of some of this community's most important events, where collective history and memory are dramatized. Food, in its many manifestations, can be viewed as the prism that refracts all-important cultural concerns into their elemental components. In an unfamiliar setting, as Bell and Valentine have noted, a familiar meal "helps fight off the panics of disorientation."[42]

Even *terroir* itself performs. Gustavo Esteva and Madhu Suri Prakash give us an opportunity to think of virtual *terroir* with the concept of "cultural soil," the virtual soil in which people's experiences are rooted.[43] The imagined rootedness of populations, along with its metaphors, is useful in understanding how people experience food, region, and place. In the case of a population in transition, or to use the titles of two landmark histories of immigration, *The Uprooted* and *The Transplanted,* the food practices of a community throw into relief all of their cultural practices.[44] Taken together, the studies in this article make a clear case that food makes place at least to the same extent that place makes food.

Notes

1. The term *terroir* originally referred to the typical taste of a specific wine region such as Burgundy, Alsace, Bordeaux etc., the French, however, understand *terroir* also in a broader sense encompassing not only the geographical characteristics of a specific wine region and the specific agricultural techniques applied in this area, but also the regional foodways and cuisine. The concept of *terroir* thus integrates a cultural dimension and is tied to regional identity and the European understanding of regionalism.

2. R. Murray Schafer, *The Tuning of the World,* 1st ed. (New York: Knopf, 1977). I am grateful to Lucy Long for bringing this work to my attention.

3. Jeffrey Shandler, *Adventures in Yiddishland: Postvernacular Language and Culture* (Berkeley: University of California Press, 2005).

4. David Bell and Gill Valentine, *Consuming Geographies: We Are Where We Eat* (London, New York: Routledge, 1997).

5. Barbara Kirshenblatt-Gimblett, "Spaces of Dispersal," *Cultural Anthropology* 9, no. 3 (1994): 339–44; here 342.

6. John E. Bodnar, *The Transplanted: A History of Immigrants in Urban America, Interdisciplinary Studies in History* (Bloomington: Indiana University Press, 1985), 216.

7. Susanne Skubal, *Word of Mouth: Food and Fiction after Freud* (New York: Routledge, 2002), 43. Skubal, a literary theorist, finds that the mouth unites "nature and culture, biology and mythology, art and science."

8. Joel Hecker, *Mystical Bodies, Mystical Meals: Eating and Embodiment in Medieval Kabbalah,* Raphael Patai Series in Jewish Folklore and Anthropology (Detroit: Wayne State University Press, 2005).

9. Harvey E. Goldberg, "Torah and Children: Symbolic Aspects of the Reproduction of Jews and Judaism," in *Judaism Viewed from within and from Without,* ed. Harvey E. Goldberg, Suny Series in Anthropology and Judiac Studies (Albany: State University of New York Press, 1987), 107–30; here 114–15.

10. Amy B. Trubek, "Tasting Wisconsin," in *The Restaurants Book: Ethnographies of Where We Eat* (Oxford: Berg Publishers, 2005), 20.

11. Most relevant smelling takes place *inside* the mouth. See Linda Bartoshuk, "The Biological Basis of Food Perception and Acceptance," *Food Quality and Preference* 4 (1993): 21–32.

12. Mark Steven Swislocki, "Feast and Famine in Republican Shanghai: Urban Food Culture, Nutrition, and the State (China)" (PhD diss., Stanford University, 2002).

13. Vladimir Ivanovich Dal', *Poslovitsy Russkogo Naroda: V Dvukh Tomakh* [Proverbs of the Russian people], 2 vols. (Moskva: Khudozh. lit-ra, 1984), quoted in Robert A. Rothstein and Halina Rothstein, "Food in Yiddish and Slavic Folk Culture: A Comparative/Contrastive View," in *Yiddish Language and Culture: Then and Now,* ed. Leonard Jay Greenspoon, Studies in Jewish Civilization (Omaha: Creighton University Press, 1998), 305–28.

14. Vera Kishinevsky, "Survival in the Land of Glamor: The Experience of Three Generations of Women Who Emigrated from the Former Soviet Union (Acculturation in the United States and Its Influence on Their Perceptions and Lifestyles)" (PhD thesis, New York University, School of Education, 2001), 324.

15. Ibid.

16. Annie Hauck-Lawson, "Foodways of Three Polish-American Families in New York" (PhD diss., New York University School of Education, Health, Nursing, and Arts Professions, 1991).

17. Kishinevsky, "Survival in the Land of Glamor," 292.

18. Sander L. Gilman, *The Jew's Body* (New York: Routledge, 1991).

19. Maria Elisa Christie, "Kitchenspace: Gendered Spaces for Cultural Reproduction, or, Nature in the Everyday Lives of Ordinary Women in Central Mexico" (PhD diss., University of Texas, 2003).

20. Deidre Sklar, *Dancing with the Virgin: Body and Faith in the Fiesta of Tortugas, New Mexico* (Berkeley, Calif.: University of California Press, 2001), 78.

21. Musya Glants and Joyce Toomre, *Food in Russian History and Culture* (Bloomington: Indiana University Press, 1997).

22. Cindy J. Dorfman, "The Garden of Eating: The Carnal Kitchen in Contemporary American Culture," *Feminist Issues* 12, no. 1 (1992): 21–38; here 28.

23. Lara Pascali, "Two Stoves, Two Refrigerators, Due Cucine: The Interplay of Public and Private Spheres in Italian Canadian Homes" (paper presented at the American Folklore Society, Salt Lake City, Utah, October 14, 2004).

24. The code of Jewish law entitled *Shulhan Arukh* by Joseph Caro was published in 1565. A supplement by Moses Isserles (the Remu) covering Ashkenazic practice entitled *Ha-mapah* [The tablecloth] was first included in a published edition of the *Shulhan Arukh* in 1571.

25. Audience member attending the panel "Unorthodox Expressions: Jewish Self-Assertion in Russian Popular and Material Culture" at the Association for Jewish Studies Boston, MA December 21, 2003.

26. Barbara Myerhoff, *Number Our Days: A Triumph of Continuity and Culture among Old People in an Urban Ghetto* (New York: Simon & Schuster, 1980), 22.

27. The term *firn a tish* literally means to "lead a table."

28. Shifra Epstein, "Drama on a Table: The Bobover Hasidim "Piremshpyil," in *Judaism Viewed from within and from Without,* ed. Harvey E. Goldberg (Albany: State University of New York Press, 1987), 195–217.

29. For a detailed discussion of kosher delis and grocery stores in suburban Toronto, see Etan Diamond's article in this volume.

30. Larissa I. Remennick, "All My Life Is One Big Nursing Home": Russian Immigrant Women in Israel Speak About Double Caregiver Stress," *Women's Studies International Forum* 24, no. 6 (2001): 685–700; here 696.

31. For a detailed discussion of the *eruv,* see Manuel Herz's article in this volume.

32. The *Eruv tavshilin* is a plate of two kinds of cooked food prepared before a holiday. The *Eruv thummim* extends the distance a person may walk on the Sabbath.

33. Charlotte Elisheva Fonrobert, "The Political Symbolism of the Eruv," Jewish Conceptions and Practices of Space, *Jewish Social Studies* 11, no.3 (2005): 9–35; here 12.

34. Eleven chapters in the book of Leviticus detail the requirements involved with the ritual offerings, most frequently translated as "sacrifices." While historians differ on whether or not the Israelites did in fact carry out the ritual sacrifices in the manner prescribed in the Pentateuch, the idea of uniting people and food through pilgrimage was clearly the ideal.

35. Victor Witter Turner, *Dramas, Fields, and Metaphors: Symbolic Action in Human Society* (Ithaca: Cornell University Press, 1974).

36. Ibid., 182–83.

37. The front page headline of the New York *Daily News* for October 30, 1975 screamed "Ford to City: 'Drop Dead!'" Milton Glasser's famous and widely imitated "I ♥ NY" logo became ubiquitous shortly thereafter.

38. Myra Alperson, "Welcome to Nosh Walks" (2004); available from http://noshwalks.com (accessed August 8, 2007).

39. Seth Kamil, "Tripping Down Memory Lane: Walking Tours of the Lower East Side," in *Remembering the Lower East Side,* eds. Hasia Diner, Jeffrey Shandler, and Beth Wenger, *The Modern Jewish Experience* (Bloomington: University of Indiana Press, 2000), 226–40; here 232. Interestingly, while Alperson stresses that a walking tour spares the traveler the "hassle" of overseas travel, Kamil points out that a walking tour is more challenging "without the protective walls of a bus or the comfort of watching a videotape at home." (ibid., 230)

40. Ibid.

41. Milton B. Singer, *Semiotics of Cities, Selves, and Cultures: Explorations in Semiotic Anthropology, Approaches to Semiotics* (Berlin: Mouton de Gruyter, 1991).

42. Bell and Valentine, *Consuming Geographies: We Are Where We Eat,* 19.

43. Gustavo Esteva and Madhu Suri Prakash, *Grassroots Post-Modernism: Remaking the Soil of Cultures* (London: Zed Books, 1998), 192.

44. See, for instance, Oscar Handlin, *The Uprooted,* second and enl. ed. (Boston: Little, Brown, 1973) and Bodnar, *The Transplanted.*

CHAPTER 26

"A FRUITCAKE ALWAYS MAKES ME THINK OF GRANDMA": FOOD AND MEMORY IN L. M. MONTGOMERY'S CREATION OF FEMALE LANDSCAPES

Diane Tye

I made a big fruit cake today – quite a job, especially the baking of it, which is half the trick in a fruit cake. But I think it turned out pretty well. Somehow, making fruit cake always makes me think of Grandma. Once a year, in the fall, Grandma made a big fruit cake, which always lasted the year out. It was quite an event. The evening before the fruit was prepared, Grandma washed the currants and I proudly stoned the raising – for there were no 'seeded' raisins for the buying in those days. Next morning 'we' concocted the cake. Grandma brought out the spare-room washbasin, washed and scalded it very carefully and used it to mix the cake in with her bare hand – which is really the only way to mix a fruit cake properly. I helped best the eggs and hovered around watching everything with fascinated eye. When it was mixed completely the big pan with the peak up the middle was brought out, lined with greased brown paper and filled with the mixture. Invariably two little 'patty pans' were also filled – 'to see what the cake would be like' – but they were always given to me to eat as soon as they were cooked. [...] I have never been very food of fruit cake except when eaten with soda crackers to take its richness off. But it is always a comfort to my soul to know there is a great juicy, plummy, spicy fruit cake in my cellar box lest 'unexpected company' come. My last fruit cake lasted three years and was even better at the end than at the beginning

(*The Selected Journals of L. M. Montgomery*, vol. III, pp. 394–5)

This 1929 journal entry reveals L. M. Montgomery relying on food memories to evoke the past as she moves from her day's work of baking a fruitcake, to recalling her grandmother and her childhood, and then back to the present as she muses on the benefits of having a fruitcake on hand. [...] Although food is not an emphasis in Montgomery's work (she rarely includes long descriptions of meals), it nonetheless emerges as a grounding, if sometimes oppressive, force for the author as well as an important means through which she develops character and creates convincing female fictional worlds. Building on recent literature on food and gender (see for example, Theophano [2002], Shapiro [2001], Inness [2001]; DeVault [1994]; Cline [1990]) and food and memory (see Jochnowitz [2004], Sutton [2001]; Bardenstein [2000]; Berkeley[2000]), I engage in a project of 'literary folklore' as I reflect on the importance of food and memory in Montgomery's work. Much of the discussion that follows is sparked by David Sutton's insightful exploration of the relationship between food and memory on the Greek island of Kalymnos (2001). Specifically, I adapt two food-related

Diane Tye, "'A Fruitcake Always Makes Me Think of Grandma": Food and Memory in L. M. Montgomery's Creation of Female Landscapes', *CREArTA: Journal of the Centre for Research and Education in the Arts* 5, Special issue: 'L. M. Montgomery's Interior and Exterior Landscapes', edited by Rosemary Ross Johnston (2005), 112–24. (Excerpts printed here. Omitted text is indicated by ellipses.)

Reprinted with permission from CREArTA.

aspects highlighted in Sutton's study: food ritual and food exchange. In examining how food structures life on Kalymnos, both through daily routines and more long term rhythms represented by seasonal harvests, feasts and fasts, and life-cycle markers, Sutton emphasizes that 'ritual and everyday contexts of eating echo and mutually reinforce each other' (2001, p. 16). As a first approach to what he calls the food-ritual-memory complex, Sutton considers how the role of food acts as a mnemonic for the passing of time and the seasonal cycles. Here, he argues, the gaze is not altogether backwards in that: '...food production and consumption not only structures time through providing repetitive markers annually across the years. It is equally important that these food-related events are looked forward to from the point of view of the experience of the passing of the year (intra-annually)' (2001, p. 31). Another dimension – food exchange – is also central to Kalymnos islanders' construction of self, for as Sutton writes, 'Exchange is about social relations, yes, but social relations are about identity construction as much as they are some calculus of future gain/material obligation' (2001, p. 50). Food exchanges, then, are key indicators of social character. In Montgomery's stories the food-ritual-memory complex and food exchanges are central to the shaping and interpreting of particular fictional worlds. In her journal entries they are integral to the author's own self constructions of wife and mother.

Ritual

As Anne Murcott (1982) reminds us, 'Food is a cultural affair, a product and reflection of the norms and values characteristic of the society' (p. 678) and Montgomery's fiction reveals food's centrality to culture in multifaceted ways. Importantly, food, memory and ritual represent means by which she evokes a sense of place. The restrictiveness of Montgomery's fictional worlds take form in the pattern and structure of meals while characters' responses to that world are symbolized through the withholding or bestowing of food or in the enjoyment of a crisp apple.

In Montgomery's fiction, as well as her journal writing, seasons are marked by the picking of strawberries, the canning of pears, the making of a fruitcake. In *The Golden Road*, rhubarb pie signals the arrival of spring (p. 135) while the harvesting of apples marks the coming of fall (p. 220). Montgomery's own summer work that included berry picking that then led to the creation of pies and other desserts, canning, and the making of preserves, jellies, and wine is mirrored by the women in her fiction. For example, Jane in *Jane of Lantern Hill* takes pride in her full pantry of jam made from berries she has picked (p. 105, p. 137). In Montgomery's fiction, calendar days are celebrated with special foods. For example, Christmas brings plum pudding (*Anne of Windy Poplars*, p. 163); mincemeat (*The Golden Rood*, p. 15); and mince pie (*GR*, p. 36). Similarly, in her journals, Montgomery describes her own Christmas preparations that include the preparation of turkey, cranberry sauce, pudding (*SJ*, vol. II, p. 140); doughnuts (*SJ*, vol. II, p. 39); and 'Lemon Bread Pudding' from Park Corner (*SJ*, vol. III, p. 31).

Life events are marked with special foods as well. Montgomery describes preparing and serving a supper for twenty-five people following her Aunt Annie's funeral: 'They enjoyed the supper and I had seen that it was a good one – cold chicken aplenty, biscuits, preserves, pies, cakes galore. Even Aunt Annie herself would have accorded it her approval I think' (*SJ*, vol. II, p. 194). Weddings were even more elaborate affairs as this description of her own wedding supper attests:

That dinner made history in Park Corner I believe. 'Gad, they never had the like of this at Government House', gasped old William Ramsay to Stell. It was certainly a memorable repast. Frede was just home from Household Science at Macdonald and she 'did herself proud' to produce a menu that should reflect lustre on her college, and training. Not that the Park Corner cuisine could not stand on its own merits. But Frede had all the latest frills of decoration and serving and it was the smartest repast I have seen anywhere.

(*SJ*, vol. II, p. 67)

[…] In *Emily's Quest*, Emily's aunts contribute wedding-cakes, creams, jellies and salads as well as hams and chickens to the marriage supper of their neighbour, Dr Burnley (p. 209).

The specialness of these food events parallels the significance of corresponding moments in the calendar year (as with Christmas) or in the lives of individuals and their families (as in the case of funerals and weddings). However, as Mary Douglas (1971) points out in her classic work, 'Deciphering a meal', ceremonial meals are significant in part because they replicate the structure of other ordinary meals. In Montgomery's writing, it is the ordinary, everyday meals that are more frequently remembered, described and reflected upon. In her books, characters routinely consume a substantial breakfast: toast (*Emily Climbs*, p. 235), sometimes a poached or boiled egg (*Anne of the Island*, p. 18) and often porridge… something children may struggle to finish (*AIs*, p. 18; *Anne of Avonlea*, p. 165). Dinner is a cooked dinner and, in *The Story Girl*, Felicity demonstrates her female competency when she takes care to reproduce this type of meal for the family in her mother's absence. With the help of the other children she peels turnips and potatoes, shells peas and makes a 'roly-poly pudding' (p. 93). Supper or tea shows more variation from an elaborate 'spread' when company comes to call (*Emily of New Moon*, pp. 86–7) to a light meal made from food on hand: a cold ham bone (*AA*, p. 226); canned chicken and sponge cake (*Anne of Windy Poplars*, p. 99) or two little oatcakes and a glass of milk (*ENM*, pp. 54–5). Characters distinguish between good suppers and bad based on the quality; whereas Emily declares that one dish, New Moon sausages, 'were the last word in sausages' (*ENM*, p. 173), she is less enthusiastic when given bread and an egg for her evening meal: 'The bread was soggy and her egg was underdone' (*ENM*, p. 3).

While this narrow pattern that underlines meals in all of Montgomery's fiction probably derives most heavily from her youth in Cavendish, it does not veer too far from the meal structure of her adult life. Montgomery's journals and published recipes certainly reflect more variety than what her fictional characters enjoy; but as a minister's wife visiting her husband's parishioners, Montgomery finds that supper, or tea, varies in composition, quantity and quality of preparation from household to household. At one point she complains about a 'sweet supper' – 'consisting of nothing but jam, pie and several kinds of poorly made cake… no wonder they are dull and depressing when they live on such stuff' (*SJ*, vol. II, p. 353).

While tea may present the family's public face, the day's fourth meal – a bedtime lunch – is more important to the family's reconstitution. Montgomery's fictional world is divided between those who enjoy food before bed and those who do not. Unsympathetic characters withhold food at bedtime. In *Emily of New Moon*, housekeeper Ellen Greene does not often permit Emily to eat anything before going to bed, and when she does 'it meant that for some reason or other she wanted to confer a special favor' (p. 2). Later in the book, Aunt Laura is presented as the kind aunt who ensures that even animals go to bed with a full stomach; she gives the cat, 'Saucy Sal a whole cupful of strippings' and Emily 'a big plummy cooky' and kisses (p. 116). Characters' attitudes toward their bedtime lunch may also be the source of humor, as in the case of Old Robert Scobie and his half-sister, who had lived together without quarreling for thirty years, until she took the last doughnut that he had intended for his bedtime lunch and he threw her out of the house (*EC*, p. 24). […]

Montgomery herself takes pleasure in lunch. Housekeeper Lily Meyers recalls how in the evenings 'she would make a quick fire in the cookstove to warm themselves and to get something warm to eat before going to bed. Their favourite bedtime snack was warm milk, toast and a fried egg' (Anonymous, p. 14). […]

Unlike the many social obligations that fill her life, lunch has no demands. Usually constructed from food on hand, it requires little preparation and carries with it few expectations. It brings together like-minded people – family members or friends – in a food event that signals release from the day's work and social obligations:

> Frede and I work all day cleaning and disinfecting the house; then at night, when Aunt Annie and Ella are safe in bed out of hearing, we shut ourselves up in the cosy sitting room, devour snacks, and talk and laugh at our pleasure…as for our snacks – well, we are good foragers. Frede and I have, neither of us, over been indifferent to the charms of a 'good bite'. […] The Park Corner chicken-bones and ham-slices have lost none of their old-time flavor and savor and delight. (*SJ*, vol. II, p. 273)

For Montgomery the freedom of the lunch is particularly welcome. She frequently complains about the strain she feels in fulfilling her roles as minister's wife and Canadian author. The pleasant social face she presents to the world does not reflect her boredom and impatience with the teas and socials she feels obligated to support. Amidst a busy life in Ontario full of what she considers to be meaningless social commitments, memories of late night lunches at Park Comer sustain Montgomery: '…that famous pantry, stored with good things, into which it was our habit to crowd at bedtime and gnaw bones, crunch fruitcake and scream with laughter. That pantry is historical' (*SJ*, vol. I, p. 257).

Like lunch, certain foods hold special significance in Montgomery's world: for example, plums, peppermints, and perhaps above all apples convey symbolic or iconic meanings. The first two foods seem to have singular meanings: plums signify richness and quality in home cooking (eg. *The Story Girl*, p. 120; *AWP*, p. 162; *AA*, p. 77, p. 129; *AIs*, p. 213) while peppermints generally represent the opposite: cheaply manufactured candy that well-intentioned adults bestow on children who do not really like them (*AIs*, p. 158; *GR*, p. 55). Apples, on the other hand, are more complex. In Montgomery's assertion that 'I spent my childhood and girlhood in an old-fashioned Cavendish farmhouse, surrounded by apple orchards' (*The Alpine Path*, p. 19), she links apples to her youth and to an old-fashioned time. It was another time. When Montgomery reflects on the beginning of a long-time friendship, she indicates how apples were a commodity that made her special:

> Mollie began to go to school. It was always thought a great thing among the older scholars to have a new pupil sit with them. Pensie and Emma Stuart had corralled Mollie and kept her for two days. I was sitting alone in the seat just ahead. I offered Pensie and Emma four big sweet apples if they would let Amanda sit with me. We had almost the only orchard in C. at that time and I was a power in the school because of this. Apples would purchase almost anything, from 'chews' of gum up to 'new girls.' They bought me Mollie. Pensie and Emma took the apples and Mollie was transferred chattel-wise from their seat to mine. We were never again separated from that day until we left school last summer. Mollie and I sat together through thick and thin, through evil report and good report. It was not a bad bargain for four apples! (*SJ*, vol. I, p. 50)

Like the release of the bedtime lunch, the specialness of apples was a rarity in the life of a young girl brought up by stern grandparents and surrounded by relatives who more often than not made no effort to make her feel special. The pleasure of eating apples was something she enjoyed throughout her adult life, on occasion describing in her journal having spent a pleasant evening at home reading and eating a plate of russet apples (SJ, vol. II, pp. 280–1). And, on her last trip to Cavendish, when she visits the site of her old home, one of the only tangible aspects of her former life there are apples. Amidst a black fox ranch erected by her Uncle John in what had been the front orchard,

I found the old apple tree still there. It was just as it is now when I was a girl. It must be close on to a hundred years old. And it is still bearing apples. I brought them home and tasted them. I never dreamed of eating an apple off that tree again. And they tasted good. They were sweet apples, but they had a nice nutty flavor – quite different from the insipid sweetness of the 'sweet apples' in the back orchard. (*SJ*, vol. IV, p. 11)

All that remains of the homestead and her youth is the taste of an apple.

Montgomery makes frequent use of these associations in her fiction. [...] Throughout the novels, characters read apple varieties as part of a familiar landscape: Yellow Duchess trees bear apples that are great for pies (*AA*, p. 275) while 'Strawberry apples' are best for eating (*Anne of Green Gables*, p. 143). Apples add interest and sweetness to life without much victual variety. Emily tells her fortune by counting the seeds in the big 'sweet' (*ENM*, p. 134). But their power can be transformative. The hardened Katherine Brooke is awakened to the joys in life though the fun of finding sweet apples stored in the cellar in December (*AWP*, p. 163). And, apples embody the pleasures of being 'home'. Montgomery provides many passages throughout her novels where apples bring comfort to the characters who surrender to their pleasures: 'But even a storm at Green Gables had charms of its own. It was cozy to sit by the stove and dreamily watch the firelight flickering over the ceiling while you munched apples and candy' (*AWP*, p. 166).

In her own life, Montgomery relies on the food-ritual-memory complex as part of identity construction for her family and herself. The everyday routines of which daily meals are part and the repetition of particular foods builds a familiarity that can be key to children's sense of security and of family (DeVault 1994, p. 39; Murcott 1982, p. 693). According to Mary Rubio (1996), Montgomery 'understood very well how much human pleasure comes from good food' and Rubio describes how Stuart Macdonald treasured childhood memories of his mother's mock cherry pie. For him, this ordinary food held symbolic value (see: Kelly 2001, pp. 30–1) and until the end of his life he associated it with his mother and her nurturing (Rubio 1996, p. vii).

Food exchanges

Many of the food references in Montgomery's journals and stories describe food exchanges. This is not surprising given that food is more important to social exchanges than any other commodity and therefore subject to strong prescriptions of sharing across most cultures (see Sahlins 1972, p. 215). Reading her journals, one is struck by the extent to which Montgomery's life was, in fact, governed by food exchanges. In turn, she draws her experiences and memories of these interactions to shape the characters and communities of her novels. Montgomery describes endless social functions. These events introduce variety and sociability, lifting the community out of the ordinary as they bring together members and often raise needed funds for school and church, literacy programmes and community improvement initiatives. Despite such positive elements, however, they represent what the author sometimes personally experiences as an almost unbearable burden: 'I spent the forenoon making sandwiches and putting quilts in the frames in the church. This afternoon we had the quilting and served tea. It was a rather hard day and it can't be said I enjoyed any part of it' (*SJ*, vol. III, p. 243).

In her journal, Montgomery documents her ongoing struggle to run a household, maintain a writing career, as well as produce baked goods for the latest Sunday School picnic or meeting of church session. In one congregation in which her husband served, initiation and organization of church events often fell largely to her. In writing of the Norval women, she complains: 'It never worried them if they saw they were not going to raise their allocation. It was I who had to scurry round and get up a "pie social" or something of the sort – at which I admit they worked valiantly – to raise the deficit' (*SJ*, vol. IV, p. 289).

Outside of more special food events, like church socials or garden parties, Montgomery's social obligations are played out in daily food exchanges expressed through the hospitality she extends to others and that which she accepts, largely in her role as a minister's wife. In these exchanges food generosity is key and is a key determinant in a family's reputation. Families like the Alberts are renown for the 'banquets' they offer guests (*SJ*, vol. III, p. 391). Others are considered 'close' because of the sparseness of their offerings:

> We spent Monday night at Streetville with the McKays. The traditions of the pantry seem to be lean as ever in that ménage. I cannot understand how people can invite people to visit them, be, or appear to be, glad to see them, and then literally starve them. Seven of us sat down to a table whereon was just about enough food to supply three…
>
> (*SJ*, vol. III, pp. 59–60)

David Sutton (2001) writes that 'exchange itself is an attempt to create potential future memories through the destruction of material objects' (pp. 16–7) and Montgomery sometimes looks both backward and forward, as when drying meat for the first time after her cousin Frede's death:

> Today when I was hanging up my beef hams to dry I broke down and cried because Frede could never come to taste them. 'Maud,' she used to say, 'I love you but even if I hated you I would come to see you for the sake of getting some of your beef ham'
>
> (*SJ*, vol. II, pp. 301–2)

At other times Montgomery expresses a self conscious desire to indebt her guests. Years after the fact, Montgomery is able to recall in great specificity her friend Fan's failed attempt at food generosity. She describes arriving at Fan's house after a long journey to be greeted with '[a] cup of lukewarm tea. Three very small very dry half slices of bread. A bit of butter. And two stale shrunken pieces of what looked like to be gingerbread dating back to the reign of Ramese I!!' The lengthy journal entry recounts an entire visit of inadequate meals (*SJ*, vol. IV, p. 4). When Fan returns the visit years after, Montgomery writes:

> I was determined that I would have extra good meals while Fan was here for I have never forgotten those awful days of starvation at 'Heart's Desire.' I like Fan immensely as I always have done, and it comes natural to me to put up a good bite for my guests. And I just wanted to heap coals of fire on her head!
>
> (*SJ*, vol. IV, p. 2)

As this journal entry indicates, Montgomery judges her friends and others, like Fan, who are miserly in their food exchanges harshly; at the same time she prides herself on providing her own guests with well cooked meals and ample servings. As she says, she 'keeps a good table' (*SJ*, vol. II, p. 364). She sees it as a part of her Montgomery lineage and a way by which she expresses her family identity and upholds the family name. Showing guests food generosity is what Montgomerys do. […]

Like Montgomery, the characters in her books uphold family traditions of hospitality. Emily in *Emily of New Moon* is given rare praise by her Aunt Elizabeth when, left home alone, a dreadful thing happens, as she puts it, that had 'never happened before in the annals of New Moon': company arrives and there is no cake in the house.

Emily rises to the occasion by making cake to serve to the visitors and Elizabeth tells her she 'has some Murray in her' (p. 177). Little Fellow remarks in *Anne of Windy Poplars,* 'You ought to see the rice puddings [my father] makes… There's nothing mean about my dad' (p. 109). Conversely, others are criticised when they fail to show generosity, even to children. Davy, a young boy in *Anne of Avonlea,* describes Mrs Boulter as 'real mean' when she does not offer him any preserves or cake at a tea where even the bread was scarce (p. 288). In *Anne of Avonlea,* a character is regarded negatively when she locks up all the cake, cheese and preserves, guarding against the possibility that others might offer too much to company if it arrived in her absence (p. 208).

Being able to reproduce food and meals to the quality and quantity of acceptable family and/or community standards is particularly important to the construction of female identity (see Theophano 2002; DeVault 1994). Repeatedly young girls in Montgomery's books are carefully taught the feminine skills of cooking and baking by older kin. Mastering the complexities of cake making or pickling according to old and sometimes secret family recipes marks their rite of passage into womanhood. They objectify concern for others through food. In *Jane of Lantern Hill,* Jane learns to cook in order to keep house properly for her father and, as a parting gesture before returning to Toronto for the winter, she teaches him to fry steak and boil potatoes (p. 137). In *The Story Girl,* Felicity argues that while her mother is not physically demonstrative, she does serve the family pie with every meal (p. 44). Reproduction of dainty food for teas and social occasions is vital to a woman's reputation in the community and a means by which they prove themselves capable (see Inness 2001, pp. 52–70; Shapiro 2001). Yet, economy is also highly valued in Montgomery's fictional worlds and consistent displays of lavish hospitality or even daily excess are frowned upon as Anne communicates to Davy in her distinguishing for him the difference between economy and stinginess in Marilla's use of jam (*AA,* p. 198). The community looks for balance.

Exchange of informal knowledge underlies successful food exchanges and Montgomery expresses her own valuing of female traditional culture when she records in her journal a recipe for her favourite 'Lemon Pudding' 'so that it may not be lost from earth.' (*SJ,* vol. III, p. 338). In *Jane of Lantern Hill,* Jane relies on neighbouring women to mentor her in the art of making bread, pie crusts and doughnuts and in other novels young girls learn to create designs in pickle jars (*EC,* p. 213) and appreciate the art of making mincemeat (*GR,* p. 14). There is often an importance associated with these tasks, particularly with the reproduction of old family recipes for dishes for special days such as Christmas. While some like Jane are born cooks, others are expected never to succeed, no matter what their training. Sara Stanley in *The Story Girl* is contrasted with Felicity throughout the book; whereas Felicity is recognized as an accomplished cook, Sara Stanley is very much the amateur, often foiling her attempts in the kitchen as when she puts sawdust in a pudding (p. 127).

Culinary disasters add humour to the *The Story Girl,* as they do throughout Montgomery's writing: The children in *The Golden Road* mistakenly use tooth powder in place of baking powder (p. 51); Jane adds icing sugar rather than salt to an Irish stew (*Jane of Lantern Hill,* p. 95) and Anne bakes a cake with liniment instead of vanilla when the minister and his wife come to tea (*AGG,* pp. 182–7). These incidents, or at least the mistaken use of liniment, are based on real-life incidents which became lively narratives in Montgomery's repertoire (*AP,* p. 75). The events, and stories recounting them, support Sutton's assertion: 'Acts of food exchange do not work to create memories on their own…They must be reinforced by *narratives* of generosity past, of failed generosity or of the false generosity of others' (Sutton 2001, pp. 16–7). He continues, 'The fact, that hospitality, to strangers or to kin, has to be narrated and re-narrated, then, reflects the reality that it is an important part of the construction of an honorable personal, local or national identity' (Sutton 2001, p. 51). Montgomery uses accounts of food generosity and stinginess as well as food mishaps to vividly create what Sidney Mintz (1996) describes as 'a shared food community'.

Sensory memory and the construction of female worlds

As seen in the recollection of fruitcake that opens this paper, Montgomery's food memories are multifaceted, often weaving together the present and the past through memories of smells, tastes, and food events themselves. Reading her journals, one is struck by how variously these memories are evoked. For example, watching a woman pour tea in cups before grace one day brings back thoughts of Mrs Wm. Mcneill who used to do this:

> Instantly I was back thirty or thirty-five years ago. …I saw the dish of raspberry preserve, the little pat of butter on a small plate, the little cubes of cheese, the glass plateful of small squares of fruit cake and the invariable round thin cookies which completed the unchanging menu of a supper there – and always tasted good, too.

> (*SJ*, vol. III, p. 46)

After her cousin Frede dies, Montgomery finds that reading a recipe or preparing a dish involuntarily evokes intense memories of her cousin:

> Have been haunted all day by thoughts of Frede. Some days are more like this than others. This house is so full of her. I can't even make a cake without a stab of agony for my recipe book is full of the Macdonald College recipes she gave me.

> (*SJ*, vol. I, p. 308).

[…]

At other times the associations are more positive. Weeding parsnips reminds her of a joke she shared with her cousin Clara at Park Corner many years earlier (*SJ*, vol. IV, p. 22) and picking wild strawberries immediately transports her to youth (*SJ*, vol. IV, p. 271). For Montgomery these memories are powerful, and made all the more real when she records them in her diary or shapes them into a narrative. In her fictional worlds Montgomery transforms specific memories of smells, tastes, and experiences to create vivid pictures for her readers. For example, in *Emily's Quest,* Emily echoes Montgomery's own feeling about berry picking when she declares, 'I love picking strawberries. The occupation has in it something of perpetual youth' (p. 104).

In her journal entries, one can see Montgomery relying on memories of food – rituals and exchanges – to 'return to the whole' (Fernandez 1982; see also Sutton 2001, p. 75). In his 1982 work, James Fernadez describes how integrity is restored through a remembered coherence, or structural repetition between domains. This occurs because a food event evokes a whole world of family, agricultural association, place names and other 'local knowledge' (Sutton 2001, p. 83). Montgomery's housekeeper. Lily Meyers recalls that: 'All things from the Island were loved by Mrs Macdonald, and every fall, red potatoes and two kegs of salt mackerel were shipped up for their use' (*L. M. Montgomery as Mrs Ewan MacDonald of Leaskdale Manor*, p. 6).

In PEI potatoes and in the recipes passed down through generations of her family, Montgomery brought together her remembered life on the island with her present one; but, this is not to say her multiple identities – PEI expatriate and Ontario resident, minister's wife and Canadian author, and nineteenth century farm girl and modern woman – never collided. Food can carry hegemonic identities through its very ability to connect the mundane with the pleasurable and the necessity (Sutton 2001, p. 4; see also DeVault 1994) and there emerges in Montgomery's writing an understanding that while food should be enjoyed, to revel in it too much is a guilty pleasure. She often confesses her own love for a 'tasty bite' (*SJ*, vol. II, p. 364), yet notes such an admission is unfashionable. Together Montgomery's fiction and non-fiction reinforce the patriarchal views of her day that food generosity was expected; that it was women's work to provide it and the skills to produce this generosity were a mainstay of successful female identity. An undercurrent as well is that the needs of the body often run counter to the needs of the artistic soul. Certainly the author's life contained many examples of when her social obligations of minister's wife conflicted with those of her writing career (see Buchanan 1999). Montgomery's characters who concern themselves overly with food production, like young Felicity in *The Story Girl*, are appreciated but they also may be made fun of or chastised. On the other hand, Sara Stanley's incompetence in the kitchen is remarked on, but these skills are valued less highly by her friends than her storytelling ability. As Felix says to her, 'there's lots of folks can make bread. But there isn't many who can tell a story like you' (p. 98). Her writing re-enforces western notions that food is not conducive to thought. [...]

However, despite these conflicts and limitations, and maybe because of them, food memories offer Montgomery a means by which she could occasionally achieve a synergy among her subject positions and between her life and her writing. And in drawing on memories of fruitcake, apples, bed-time lunches, and both successful and falled displays of food generosity, she creates convincing fictional characters and lasting female landscapes.

References

Bardenstein, C. 2000, 'Transmission interrupted: Reconfiguring food, memory, and gender in the cookbook-memoirs of Middle Eastern exiles', *Signs. Journal of Women in Culture and Society*, vol. 28, pp. 353–88.

Berkeley, E. P. (ed) 2000, *At Grandmother's Table: Women Write about Food, Life and the Enduring Bond Between Grandmothers and Granddaughters*, Fairview Press, Minneapolis, MN.

Buchanan, R. 1999, "I wrote two hours this morning and put up grape juice in the afternoon": The conflict between woman and writer in L. M. Montgomery's Journals', *L. M. Montgomery and Canadian Culture*, eds I Gammel & E. Epperly, University of Toronto Press, Toronto, pp. 153–8.

Cline, S. 1990, *Just Desserts: Women and Food*, Deutsch, London.

DeVault, M. L. 1994, *Feeding the Family: The Social Organisation of Caring as Gendered Work*, University of Chicago Press, Chicago.

Douglas, M. 1971. 'Deciphering a meal', in *Myth, Symbol and Culture*, ed C. Geertz, Norton, New York, pp. 61–82.

Fenandez, J. 1982, *Bwiti: An Ethnography of the Religious Imagination in Africa*, Princeton University Press, Princeton, NJ.

Inness, S. A. 2001, *Dinner Roles: American Women and Culinary Culture*, University of Iowa Press, Iowa City, 1A.

Jochnowitz, E. 2004, 'Flavors of memory: Jewish food as culinary tourism in Poland', in *Culinary Tourism*, ed. L. M. Long, University of Kentucky Press, Lexington, KY.

Kelly, T. M. 2001, "'If I were a voodoo priestess": Women's culinary autobiographies', in *Kitchen Culture in America: Popular Representations of Food, Gender and Race*, ed. S. A. Inness, University of Pennsylvania Press, Philadelphia, pp. 251–69.

L. M. Montgomery as Mrs Ewan Macdonald of the Leaskdale Manse 1911-1926, 1965, n.p. Leaskdale, ON.

Mintz, S. 1996, *Tasting Food: Tasting Freedom*, Beacon Press, Boston.

Montgomery, L. M. n.d. (1917), *The Alpine Path*, Fitzhenry & Whiteside, Toronto.

Montgomery, L. M. 1964 (1908), *Anne of Green Gables*, Ryerson, Toronto.

Montgomery, L. M. 1979 (1909), *Anne of Avonlea*, McGraw-Hill Ryerson, Toronto.

Montgomery, L. M. 1983 (1927), *Emily's Quest*, McClelland-Bantam Seal Books, Toronto.

Montgomery, L. M. 1984 (1925), *Emily Climbs*, McClelland-Bantam Seal Books, Toronto.

Montgomery, L. M. 1985a (1925), *Emily of New Moon*, McClelland-Bantam Seal Books, Toronto.

Montgomery, L. M. 1985b, *The Selected Journals of L. M. Montgomery, Volume I: 1889-1910*, eds M. Rubio & E. Waterston, Oxford University Press, Toronto.

Montgomery, L. M. 1987a (1915), *Anne of the Island*, McClelland-Bantam Seal Books, Toronto.

Montgomery, L. M. 1987b, *The Selected Journals of L. M. Montgomery, Volume II: 1910-1921*, eds M. Rubio & E. Waterston, Oxford University Press, Toronto.

Montgomery, L. M. 1987c (1944), *The Story Girl*, McClelland-Bantam Seal Books, Toronto.

Montgomery, L. M. 1989a (1936), Anne of Windy Poplars, McClelland & Stewart, Toronto.

Montgomery, L. M. 1989b (1910), *The Golden Road*, McClelland-Bantam Seal Books, Toronto.

Montgomery, L. M. 1989c (1937), *Jane of Lantern Hill*, McClelland-Bantam Seal Books, Toronto.

Montgomery, L. M. 1992, *The Selected Journals of L. M. Montgomery, Volume III: 1921-1929*, eds M. Rubio & E. Waterston, Oxford University Press, Toronto.

Montgomery, L. M. 1998, *The Selected Journals of L. M. Montgomery Volume IV: 1929-1935*, eds M. Rubio & E. Waterston, Oxford University Press, Toronto.

Murcott, A. 1982, 'On the social significance of the "cooked dinner" in South Wales', *Social Science Information*, vol. 21, no. 4/5, pp. 677–96.

Rubio, M. H. 1996, 'Preface', *Aunt Maud's Recipe Book*, eds E. Crawford & K. Crawford, Moulin, Norval, ON, pp. vii–xi.

Sahlins, M. 1972, *Stone Age Economics*, Aldine, Hawthorne, New York.

Shapiro, L. 2001, *Perfection Salad: Women and Cooking at the Turn of the Century*, Modern Library, New York.

Sutton, D. E. 2001, *Remembrance of Repasts: An Anthropology of Food and Memory*, Berg. Oxford.

Theophano, J. 2002, *Eat My Words: Reading Women's Lives through the Cookbooks they Wrote*, Palgrave, New York.

CHAPTER 27

APPROPRIATION AND COUNTERHEGEMONY IN SOUTH TEXAS: FOOD SLURS, OFFAL MEATS, AND BLOOD

Mario Montaño

The literature of foodways includes numerous examples of how people use food to stigmatize social and cultural groups. Typically, after a "dominant" culture conquers a "subordinate" one, the victor labels the defeated group as biologically, morally, and gastronomically defective. Such was the case during the period 1836–1950, when Anglos militarily and politically conquered the Mexican people of South Texas. Texas Anglos considered the Mexicans inferior in many ways and communicated this belief through a vast array of behaviors, ranging from outright violence to racist attitudes symbolically dispersed in food slurs. This essay addresses the social and cultural history of Mexican folk foodways in the lower Rio Grande border region. In doing so, it provides an understanding of how the dominant culture appropriated and redefined the local foodways and imposed a selective Mexican cuisine in the United States.[1]

Greaser, Chili, and Frijole Guzzler: Mexican food slurs

Since the beginning of their contact, Anglo Texans viewed Mexicans as biologically, culturally, and morally defective. Their racist attitudes have been traced to a mental framework imported from England, to negative reports of Mexicans in newspapers, and to the outcome of warfare.[2] Anglo losses during the Texas Revolution helped to justify their bitter emotions toward Mexicans. According to Américo Paredes, "The truth seems to be that the old war propaganda concerning the Alamo, Goliad, and Mier later provided a convenient justification for outrages committed on the Border by Texans of certain types, so convenient an excuse that it was artificially prolonged for a century."[3] In the 1860s, an Anglo writer provided a view of Mexicans' alleged racial impurity: "They are of the mongrel blood the Aztec predominating. . . . These degraded creatures are mere pilferers, scavengers, and vagabonds, downright barbarians but a single remove above the Digger Indians, hanging like vermin on the skirts of civilization—a complete pest to humanity."[4] In sum, Mexicans were perceived as a detestable human race, untouchable and repulsive.

In considering Mexicans a contaminated race, Texas Anglos noted particularly that their food was flavored with strong spices and that their diet consisted of poor quality ingredients. Mexican food was considered unhealthy and unfit for human consumption. Because it was unpalatable, very spicy, and irritating to the Anglo stomach, said Anglo Texans, coyotes and buzzards passed up the dead bodies of Mexicans to feed instead on the bodies of horses and Texans. According to one account, wild animals passed over Mexican corpses during the Mexican War because they were full of red pepper. The scavengers' disdain was "attributed to the nature of their food, it being antiseptic."[5]

Mario Montaño, 'Appropriation and Counterhegemony in South Texas: Food Slurs, Offal Meats, and Blood' in Tad Tuleja (ed.), *Useable Pasts: Traditions and Group Expressions in North America*, (Logan: Utah State University Press, 1997) pp. 50–67. Reproduced with permission of Utah State University Press in the format 'Republish in a book' via Copyright Clearance Center.

In general, Mexican food symbolized everything that was degenerate and despicable about the conquered Mexican population. The red pepper, or chile, in particular, was used extensively to refer to Mexicans in a derogatory manner. For example, a nineteenth-century farmer, in trying to convey his feelings about Mexicans, said, "The chilis are Creatures somewhere in between a burro and a human being."[6] Mexican food was thought to be not only dirty, but also greasy. As a result, Mexicans were referred to as "greasers." The ethnic slur "greaser" has also been associated with what was thought to be the dirty appearance of Mexicans, but the food connotation was a common one.[7] Américo Paredes, in addressing the use of food slurs among Texas Anglos, wrote that "the Mexican diet has been a much richer source of derogatory names, among them 'pepper belly,' 'taco choker,' 'frijole guzzler,' 'chili picker,' and (of a woman) 'hot tamale.' Aside from diet, no other aspect of Mexican culture seems to have caught the fancy of the Anglo coiner of derogatory terms for Mexicans."[8]

The psychological function of slurs, according to José Limón, is to "reduce, dehumanize, and shape our conduct toward the object of the slur."[9] Without a doubt, then, Texas Anglos viewed both Mexicans and their food as dirty, contaminated, and unhygienic. Food, which conveniently encoded their racist attitudes, was employed symbolically to denigrate the entire group and its culture. Sidney Mintz summarizes this particular role of food by saying that it can serve to encode racial and class relations. As a result, says Mintz, we sometimes think of people who eat different foods or eat them differently as being less than human.[10]

In recent years, however, Mexican food has been enjoying such popularity that it is considered by many food writers to be the most popular ethnic food in the United States. This is, to say the least, ironic. How can a food considered repulsive, unfit for human consumption, and associated with the working-class poor reach such a level of acceptance by the dominant culture? The answer lies not in the alleged enlightenment of the dominant culture in appreciating the exotic, but in the concept of cultural hegemony, especially as it has been defined by Raymond Williams.[11]

The American food industry, enacting the principles of cultural hegemony, has effectively incorporated and reinterpreted the food practices of Mexicans in the lower Rio Grande border region, relabeling them "Tex Mex" and further using that term to describe any Mexican or Spanish food that is consumed by Anglos. Although Mexicans in this region do not refer to their food as Tex Mex, and indeed often consider the term derogatory, the dominant culture has redefined the local cuisine as "earthy food, festive food, happy food, celebration. It is peasant food raised to the level of high and sophisticated art."[12]

The identification with celebration is not entirely off the mark, for what Anglos now call Tex Mex food was indeed associated with festive occasions in its original communities. The typical communit of South Texas in the late nineteenth century, according to Américo Paredes, was the "ranch or ranching village" populated by "small tightly knit groups whose social structure was the family or the clan."[13] Mexican settlers in these *ranchos* relied extensively on a sufficiency economy based on fruits, vegetables, and livestock. Among the meals that animals provided, special significance was given to those prepared from offal meats and blood. Organ meats, intestines, and glands were part of a food system typically associated with festive occasions.

Along the lower Rio Grande, many of these meats continue to be associated with celebration. During the Christmas season, for example, people along the border still slaughter animals, or have them slaughtered, to prepare *morcilla* (pig's blood sausage), *tamales, chicharrones* (pork rinds), *chorizo, menudo* (tripe stew), *patagordilla* (organ meats and blood stew), *mollejas* (thymus glands), *barbacoa de cabeza* (cow's head barbecue), and *fajitas* (beef skirts). All of these special foods evoke strong images of animal slaughtering and of the festive food events of working-class families.

But at least two of them, menudo and fajita, have also been appropriated by Anglo culture and infused with different meanings. These two folk foods comprise the focus of the following discussion.

Menudo: From offal to cook-off food

Menudo is a tripe stew: the name refers to the use of calf's stomach, the honeycomb beef tripe.[14] It is prepared with aromatic herbs (oregano, cilantro, marjoram) and spices (ground dried chiles, black pepper, salt, and garlic). Cut into squares or wedges, the tripe is usually braised or boiled, simmered for several hours, and then served in bowls garnished with lime wedges, chopped onions, chopped chile serrano, and chopped cilantro. This is the basic method of preparation, although many other versions of menudo exist throughout the border region and Mexico. Local variations, such as menudo that includes hominy, pork, or calf's feet, or menudo spiced with red or green chile, reflect regional influences such as the availability of ingredients and local cultural rules. Whatever the variations, however, menudo is embedded with a rich history and folklore. In addition, it is widely viewed as an "acceptable" Mexican folk food by the dominant culture throughout the Southwest.

In South Texas, Mexicans prefer their menudo to be fresh, preferably from a recently slaughtered cow. When I interviewed Don Perfecto Mancha, a folk food specialist from Maverick County, he told me that as a child, working at the local slaughterhouse in the barrio de San Lusito, he would go from house to house selling livers, esophagi, lungs, hearts, and stomachs for menudo.[15] However, today it is very difficult to find fresh menudo because sanitation laws prohibit slaughtering animals in one's backyard. As a result, most of the menudo is bought frozen at border grocery stores. According to some vendors, the meat packing and freezing process significantly reduces the quality of the meat. Don Salome, a third-generation Laredo food vendor, complained about the quality of today's menudo: "Well, before, we made menudo during the week and all that. But it was less expensive, the merchandise. Today it is more expensive. You can find it because sometimes the menudo sold today, well, the menudo coming out of the packing company is not that good. . . . Because when you cook it and it ends up, imagine an onion skin, paper thin. Well, twenty-five pounds, well, I believe that in a small pan, all of it fits in. Nothing left of it."[16] Although he has never met Don Salome, "Chaco" Rodriguez, a second-generation butcher from my home town of Eagle Pass, agrees with this assessment. In one of our conversations, Chaco provided a glimpse of how tripe used to be processed at the Uvalde, Texas, slaughterhouse where he worked for several years: "Well, back then, the menudo was given away with the feet until it went up in price a lot, and left a lot of profit. . . . It is cleaned with water and calcium or with some kind of chemical that is used so it will clean faster. But the drawback is that the menudo that they kill today, then it is frozen in a freezer for tomorrow, instead of selling it right away, hanging fresh. They put it in boxes and freeze it for three or four months until it reaches the store and until they sell it to you."[17] Don Salome and Chaco, like many others in this region, agree that the quality of tripe has declined due to the health laws and packing companies' processing procedures. To them, much menudo is not worth selling, and Don Salome himself has actually stopped selling it because of its high cost and low quality.

The preparation and consumption of menudo embody strong elements of folklore and social practice. As a specialty dish of the border region, it continues to be prepared in households, restaurants, and by street food vendors. In some border towns and urban centers with large Mexican populations, it is a weekend food prepared and sold in neighborhood stores. Although it is consumed at all times of the day and night, it retains strong associations with festive events and is often a party food. For example, it is the custom after a wedding reception to assemble at an in-law's house for the *torna boda* (postwedding party) to eat menudo. After a drinking binge, it is customary to have a hot bowl of menudo in the belief that it will soften the effects of the hangover. Menudo, in short, is still a celebratory folk food.

It is also a food, however, that has gained wide acceptance among Anglos, is sold in Mexican restaurants throughout the border region, and has even made its way into the popular culture of South Texas. It is sold in cans in grocery stores and commemorated on t-shirts with the inscription MENUDO, THE BREAKFAST

OF CHAMPIONS. Almost every Mexican cookbook produced in the United States has at least one menudo recipe as though to lend credibility and authenticity to the volume. Menudo has also been incorporated into corporate and business sponsored Mexican cook-off festivals. As early as 1970, these festivals began to proliferate in South Texas in much the same way as chili cook-offs glut the nation today.[18]

These menudo cook-off contests, like the chili cook-offs, have stirred extensive joking and mockery among Mexicans in the border region. I asked a respected folk cookery specialist in Maverick County why he did not participate in these contests. He responded, "Bueno, Mario, para comenzar, tienes que estar panzon, barbon, vigoton, y tienes que ser un 'redneck' para poder ganar." (Well, Mario, to start off, you have to be fat, bearded, mustached, and you have to be a redneck in order to win.)[19] The results of these contests bear him out. Many menudo cook-off champions are indeed members of the dominant culture, leading even some working-class Mexicans to believe that Texas Anglos now know how to cook Mexican food better than the Mexicans. In addition, women, who traditionally prepare menudo in border households, are usually excluded from participating in the contests—providing a gender as well as a racial bias. Thus, even though menudo continues to occupy a special position in the popular culture and folk food system of Mexicans in South Texas, its appropriation by Anglo entrepreneurs has also invested it with a culturally dominating effect.

Fajitas: The appropriation process of a folk food

Fajita is the folk name Mexicans in the lower Rio Grande border region give to the cut of meat known as skirt steak; the cut itself is actually the cow's diaphragm muscle. There are two parts to the skirt steak. The inside part is the less desirable because it is tougher and leaner. The outside steak is preferred by fajita cooks because it is thicker and marbled with fat. Since the early 1970s, this cut of meat has been enjoying national popularity, making its way from humble beginnings to some of the most distinguished restaurants in the country. Along the way it has become surrounded with culinary legends. To distinguish them from the facts, it is necessary to provide some historical background.

Among Mexicans in the lower Rio Grande border region, fajitas are typically served with tortillas (either flour or corn) as well as guacamole, beans, and rice. In preparing the dish, the meat is first grilled and sliced in strips. Then the strips are placed into a folded tortilla and garnished with the guacamole and *salsa fresca* (ground fresh chile sauce of tomatoes, garlic, onions, and cilantro) or *pico de gallo* (a relish of fresh diced chile serrano, scallions, tomatoes, cilantro, olive oil, and beer).

Other terms used along the border also refer to fajitas. When I was a boy in Eagle Pass, my parents referred to this cut of meat as *arracherras*. This term appeared in a 1944 cookbook written by Elena Zelayeta, one of the persons responsible for making Mexican food popular in California, and it is still used today in conversations and on restaurant menus.[20] However, this term, although it refers to the same cut of meat, has a slightly different connotation, evoking a different preparation process. In my house, as in other houses in this region, arracherras were broiled or steam-baked in the kitchen oven along with onions, tomatoes, and chile serrano.[21] Today, in many restaurants along the Rio Grande, arracherras are sold by weight as *arracherras asadas* (grilled arracherras), not as fajitas. Another word that often gets confused with fajitas and arracherras is *aldilla*, which means "flank steak." Yet, fajita remains the most common term used to refer to the cut of meat known as skirt steak.

Along with the different words used, correctly or incorrectly, for fajitas, there are culinary legends that proliferate in news stories attempting to define the dish, locate its origin, and describe its history. Most of these legends describe the same supposedly typical social pattern. First, the lowly and despised food is thrown away by members of the upper class and picked up by hungry poor people. Then, the upper class reappropriates and "improves" it so that it becomes "civilized" and socially acceptable. Finally, the food enjoys the status of a delicacy that is legitimized and enjoyed by members of the upper class.

In trying to account for the origin of fajitas, newspaper food writers usually attribute the dish to South Texas Anglo cowboys. One story quotes a Texan from the Rio Grande Valley: "They used to be dirt cheap. They used to almost throw them away, like junk."[22] In another story, fajitas are associated with vaqueros. "Fajitas actually originated in South Texas along the border. They were first used by Mexican cowboys along the border in the 1900s. . . . For a long time . . . fajitas remained a secret among Mexican cowboys in San Antonio and South Texas."[23] In a third article, fajitas are associated with the more general class of ranch hands. "According to legend, it was once the thrown away cut of meat that South Texas ranchers gave to their hands when they slaughtered a carcass."[24]

The folk term fajitas in these newspaper legends takes on the role of different characters or personas. In one, the meat acquires a fairytale persona: "This is a Cinderella story for the skirt steak, a cut of meat once as neglected as the fairytale heroine."[25] In another, the fajita becomes an undocumented worker: "Fajitas crept across the border about a decade ago and in the past three years have swept through the state."[26] All of these newspaper legends rely on non-Mexicans to legitimate the origin of fajitas, associating it with the general culture of South Texas.

Some native Mexicans of this region agree on South Texas as the dish's first home. However, they usually localize it to a certain town or region. Many of the people with whom I discussed fajitas said that they started in the Rio Grande Valley. Some of my friends from Eagle Pass who attended Texas A&I University in Kingsville told me that it was there they were first exposed to the term. My brother, who lives in Mission, Texas, introduced them to our household in 1970, having discovered fajitas himself at a *carne asada* (cook-out) in Madero, which is close to the Rio Grande River. Chaco Rodriguez, a fellow native of Eagle Pass, describes the origin of fajitas in this way: "The fajita is a border name. Started like in the seventies, started over by Laredo, Brownsville, and Harlingen. Started over by the valley, fajitas this and fajitas that. That was not the name used here. The Mexican name is arracherras and the old name that was around was aldilla."[27] Hence, the origin of fajitas has been well documented to have been somewhere in the South Texas border region. However, the cultural meaning of the word has been a source of conflict between the dominant United States culture and Mexicans of South Texas.

Initially an offal meat consumed by working-class Mexicans, the fajita has become a delicacy associated with almost *any* kind of grilled meat consumed by upwardly mobile urban dwellers. In most restaurants, the term refers to any grilled beef served with the side dishes that define the Mexican meal: frijoles, rice, pico de gallo, guacamole, and tortillas. Many restaurants do not use the traditional skirt steak but instead serve chuck, T-bone, round, or flank steak.[28] Some restaurants, moreover, do not even use beef. "Fajita" is now often used to signify the grilling of any kind of meat, from "chicken fajitas" to "shrimp fajitas." One self-styled "Fajita King," Sonny Falcon, reacts adamantly against such innovations, stating that "only the fajita cut makes a fajita. . . . If you put anything else in a flour tortilla, you have a taco al carbon or maybe carne asada, but not a fajita."[29] But this traditional definition is widely ignored by Anglo restaurant owners.

Through these examples, we see that the meaning of the folk food fajita has been changed to signify the grilling process and not the cut of meat—a change that effectively obscures the fajita's origin as an offal meat. To further "sanitize" the dish, restaurants provide menus where the term is spelled phonetically (fah-HEAT-uhs) and where instructions are provided on how to eat a "fajita taco." Restaurants have also altered the traditional presentation of the dish, bringing it to the table sizzling hot in a pancake griddle or iron skillet. This style of presentation, according to one writer, lends "authenticity" to the folk dish: "If they do not come to the table sizzling from the grill, they are not fit to be called fajitas."[30]

This is a particularly vivid example of class appropriation and distortion, for the original eaters of fajitas had no such "tradition." In the border, region, fajitas are still served, both in backyards and in restaurants, without any fanfare or theatrics. Mexicans recognize the sizzling griddle as a promotional gimmick that bears no relation to the original culinary frame.

As the level of consumer income rises, the preparation of fajitas becomes more sophisticated and is accompanied by highly charged status ingredients. In a national newspaper column, two food writers state that fajitas are "the ideal food for yuppie grazers. They are packed with flavor and are easy and fun to eat. The meat—chicken, beef, or pork—is first marinated, then grilled and served with guacamole and pico de gallo." The writers continue by presenting an innovative fajita recipe to cater to yuppie taste. "We've used an avocado relish in place of guacamole because the raw green flavor of mashed avocado can be a problem with wine. To counteract this, we used a Chardonnay in the relish and added the drained juices from the tomato salsa." As an accompaniment, they recommend that the best wine matches are a 1983 Pouilly Fumé and a 1983 Beaujolais Village.[31] At this level, the preparation of what was once seen as a "junk" meal assumes a radically altered social significance. It is unlikely that many Mexicans of the border region would take eagerly to an avocado "relish" made with Chardonnay.

Nor, of course, would they be able to afford it, and here we see most blatantly the class distinction that separates the backyard fajita from its upscale cousins. One of the unwelcome, but entirely predictable, side effects to the cultural appropriation of this folk food is that its price has risen dramatically—so dramatically, in fact, that it is now beyond the means of its Mexican originators. The process that George Lewis documents later in this volume with regard to the Maine lobster is just as clearly evident in the case of fajitas. In Manhattan, for example, skirt steak was going for $3.50 a pound in 1984 and over three times that—$10.98 a pound—in 1989. Expensive restaurants buy huge quantities of the meat, and fajita parties have proliferated in urban centers, many of them catered by fajita "specialists." In annual newspaper ratings of Austin, Texas, restaurants, the "Best Fajita" award routinely goes not to any of the city's many Mexican restaurants, but to the sizzling griddle productions of the Hyatt Regency Hotel.[32]

In view of this upscaling of a once working-class food item, many Mexican people in South Texas have reacted by modifying the traditional fare. So intense has been the appropriation process that they have in a sense redefined the fajita according to their own economic needs. In backyard "carne asada" events, many now avoid the high-priced fajita cut entirely and have turned to using the more affordable seven-bone chuck steak known as "El Siete."[33]

Resistance and the unincorporable

This switch to a less expensive meat, moreover, is only one example of how the appropriation process has encountered resistance. As Williams understood, hegemony is never complete or all encompassing. Its dominance is constantly challenged by oppositional cultural forms. This has clearly been the case in South Texas, where folk foods other than menudo and fajitas have signalled resistance to the upscaling process, being almost totally ignored or consciously excluded from Anglo tables. This is true of *morcilla* (pork blood sausage), *fritada* (goat blood stew), *machitos* (offal meat and marrow), *cabezitas* (goat's head), *tripas* (chitlins), and *barbacoa de cabeza* (cow's head barbecue). These folk foods involve using freshly killed animals, and they rely on organ meats, innards, or blood. As a result, they possess what might be called counterhegemonic qualities, which make them unusually resistant to incorporation. Let me explain with some ethnographic detail from Eagle Pass.

In the case of morcilla and fritada, the main ingredient is fresh blood from a recently slaughtered pig or goat. So, slaughtering is part of the production process—a part that violates the dominant culture's laws. The use of blood for cooking has been outlawed by various legislatures, since blood is considered an "unsanitary" or "uncivilized" element of cuisine. Despite legal restrictions, however, in the confines of their own backyards, Mexicans still slaughter their own animals, keeping the blood to be used in the preparation process. In other cases, they get the blood from the local butcher. When I interviewed Chaco Rodriguez, the son of an Eagle Pass butcher, he recalled, "We slaughtered a lot there in the home for ourselves, and friends would say, 'Ah, we want some blood or something else. Well, just don't tell anybody.' We only did this because it was not sold. Only to relatives and some family members. Mom would give it to them, always to close friends."[34] Today in Eagle Pass, these outlawed folk foods are prepared by vendors who avoid peddling them in the streets because of the health and tax restrictions. These underground food vendors do not sell to the general public, only to select customers. For example, Doña Noemi Herrera recalled her occasional business with a morcilla seller. "This man does it often," she told me. "He comes by and tells me he is going to have morcilla or he comes looking for the ingredients to make morcilla. And I ask him, 'Are you going to make morcilla?' And he says, 'Yes, and I will sell you some.'"[35]

Underground food vendors are not limited to Eagle Pass. Throughout the lower Rio Grande border region I have met food vendors operating without a license and without health certificates. Many of them sell these folk foods to supplement their incomes. They use local plants and animals to prepare items such as *ceviche de matalote* (carp cooked in lime) and *miel de mesquite* (mesquite syrup); they use mesquite wood as fuel in the cooking process; and they make imaginative use of recycled or discarded items such as utensils, cooking pots, and mayonnaise jars. In some cases, this semiclandestine activity involves several families and neighbors who have known each other for generations.

Thus the production process itself, along with the finished products, are intimately linked to nonalienated labor and the rejection of commodity fetishism.[36] At the same time, the production of these foods is an aesthetic and symbolic political act—a subversive act that brings friends and relatives together to express who they are, where they come from, and where they stand in relation to the larger world. The production of unappropriated food items becomes a significant expression of Mexican border identity—an expression that confirms Limón's observation that in the "very aesthetic act of performance may be found the inherent oppositional quality of all folklore."[37]

Conclusion

The concept of cultural hegemony provides insight into the process of appropriation with regard to the food practices of Mexicans in the lower Rio Grande border region. In incorporating folk foods, the dominant culture can succeed in neutralizing, reinterpreting, and setting boundaries that separate "acceptable" foods from those perceived as disreputable or threatening. Many Mexican foods have been appropriated successfully with such strategies. Restauranteurs and food promoters have labeled their versions of Mexican food "Tex Mex," resulting in some of the most alien and adulterated Mexican food forms imaginable; among some natives of the Rio Grande region, these are considered merely another form of ethnic slur.

After twenty years of "Tex Mex" (and "Nouveau Hispano") food popularity, some restauranteurs have recently gone even further, distancing themselves from the cuisine of northern Mexico in favor of more "exotic" cuisines further south. In search of status and of the elusive and ambiguous concept of authenticity, many owners have begun to explore the gastronomy of central Mexico, adding new twists to *its* traditional cuisine. In many urban restaurants, the food is consciously classified as "ethnic," providing customers another opportunity of experiencing a foreign culture without having to deal with its people. These restaurants have become commercialized centers of "staged authenticity" and "internal tourism."[38] So rapid and fierce is the competition to present the latest fashionable "tradition" that what some people consider traditional Mexican food has in fact been around for only a couple of years.

In contrast to these yuppified enclaves of invented tradition, border Mexicans themselves, like the people of other rural cultures, do not consider their cuisine to be exotically "ethnic." Working-class Mexicans eat carne asada because it is what they have eaten for generations, not—as is the case with many middle-class, -urban Mexicans—because it is a way to stress their "Mexicanness." Their relation to culinary tradition, in other words, is one of natural, rather than manufactured, group identity. Within this relationship, food can be viewed not only as a source of nourishment, but as what Baudrillard refers to as a "witness object," that is, as a social text embedded with cultural meaning.[39] That meaning is inevitably defined not by the dominant culture, but by the people whose social identity, the cuisine encapsulates.

As I hope this case study has shown, the study of folk food preparation and consumption can enable us to go beyond mere description to address issues of cultural outlook and symbolic ethnicity. Oral texts in particular can reveal counterhegemonic discourses surrounding foods that contest the values and beliefs of the dominant culture. Thus the study of folk cuisine can provide concrete evidence of durable social realities that the "official" record ignores. In particular, native discourse about culinary events can expand our understanding of food as expression and its vital link to the "performance of group identity."[40]

Notes

For their help in the preparation of this essay, I would like to thank Richard Flores, José Limón, Victor Nelson-Cisneros, Olga Rubio, Tad Tuleja, and Bill Westerman.

1. The *Handbook of Middle American Indians*, vol. 12 (Austin: University of Texas Press, 1972) identifies four culture areas of northern Mexico: Baja California; the northwest from Sonora south to Nayarit; the north central area including Chihuaha, Durango, and parts of Coahuila; and the border area from Acuña to Del Rio. My research focusses on this last area, which Américo Paredes calls "the lower Rio Grande border" and which falls between the Nueces and Rio Grande Rivers. Also known as South Texas, it is the area where I was born and grew up.

2. Arnoldo De León, *They Called Them Greasers: Anglo Attitudes toward Mexicans in Texas, 1821–1900* (Austin: University of Texas Press, 1983), 10.

3. Américo Paredes, "The Problem of Identity in a Changing Culture: Popular Expressions of Culture Conflict along the Lower Rio Grande Border," in *Views across the Border: The U.S. and Mexico,* ed. Stanley Ross (Albuquerque: University of New Mexico Press, 1978), 19.

4. Cited in De León, *They Called Them Greasers*, 5.

5. Ibid., 67–68.

6. Cited in David Montejano, *Anglos and Mexicans in the Making of Texas, 1886–1986* (Austin: University of Texas Press, 1987), 187.

7. For discussion of the word "greaser," see Américo Paredes, "On Gringo, 'Greaser,' and Other Neighborly Names," in *Singers and Storytellers,* ed. Mody Moatright et al. (Dallas: Southern Methodist University Press, 1961); Paredes, "The Problem of Identity," 79; and De León, *They Called Them Greasers*, 16.

8. Paredes, "The Problem of Identity," 79.

9. José Limón, "Folklore, Social Conflict, and the United States–Mexico Border," in *Handbook of American Folklore,* ed. Richard Dorson (Bloomington: Indiana University Press, 1986), 218.

10. Sidney W. Mintz, *Sweetness and Power: The Place of Sugar in Modern History* (New York: Penguin, 1985), 3.

11. My views on hegemony are based on Raymond Williams, *Marxism and Literature* (Oxford: Oxford University Press, 1977). For a good discussion of the historical development of the concept of hegemony, see M. J. Weismantel, *Food, Gender, and Poverty in the Ecuadorian Andes* (Philadelphia: University of Pennsylvania, 1988), 34–37.

12. This description, by food critic Craig Claiborne, can be found on the back cover of Diana Kennedy, *Cuisines of Mexico* (New York: Harper & Row, 1978).

13. For good descriptions of the typical ranching community, see Jovita Gonzalez, "Social Life in Cameron, Star, and Zapata Counties" (master's thesis, University of Texas, 1930), and Fermina Guerra, "Mexicans and Spanish Folklore Incidents in Southwest Texas" (master's thesis, University of Texas, 1941).

14. The ultimate authority on French cuisine, the *Larousse Gastronomique* (New York: Crown, 1988), refers to tripe as the stomach of ruminants (especially ox, calf, and sheep) used as food. The volume provides a history of tripe as prepared in the *haute cuisine* of French regions.

15. My interview with Don Perfecto took place at his home on July 22, 1982.

16. I interviewed Don Salome in Laredo on June 3, 1983.

17. Rodriguez is a butcher with twenty-five years' experience. I interviewed him on July 7, 1982, in San Antonio.

18. For useful questions about the role of Mexican cook-offs in Anglo society, see Limón, "Folklore and Social Conflict," 219.

19. Jacinto Ramirez, an Eagle Pass native, made this statement in the summer of 1983. Ramirez is what might be called a folk caterer. He sometimes provides free barbecue to wedding parties as a gift to the bride and groom.

20. Elena Zelayeta is mentioned in Barbara Hansen, "The Hot New Sensation from Texas," *Philadelphia Inquirer,* June 14, 1985.

21. Doña Consuela Escontrias, a resident of Eagle Pass and a native of the Coahuila village of Jimenez, told me that as a child she remembers preparing arracherras in the oven and not on the grill.

22. Hansen, "Hot New Sensation." Compare George Lewis's discussion in this volume of the original "junk" character of Maine lobster.

23. Jacque Crouse, "Feasting on San Antonio History," *San Antonio Express,* March 13, 1986, D1.

24. Kitty Crider, "Austin Fajita Chefs Skirt Issue on Meat That Meets Taste Test," *Austin American-Statesman,* June 8, 1989, p. El.

25. Hansen, "Hot New Sensation."

26. Carol Sugarman, "Fajita Fad Drives up Skirt Steak Price," *Boston Globe,* June 27, 1986.

27. From my interview with Rodriguez on July 7, 1982, at his home outside of San Antonio.

28. Several top-rated restaurants in Austin, Texas, admit that they do not use the beef skirt for their fajitas. Rich Cortese, food and beverage director of the Hyatt Hotel, says of his establishment's fajitas, "It's a corporate secret, but it is not skirt. It is a high quality meat and it is not marinated." Mike Ravago, owner of Fonda San Miguel, uses pork. Bobbie Covey, owner of the Salsa Mexican Restaurant, uses beef flap, the institutional cut of meat that comes from the end of a T-bone steak. See Crider, "Fajita Chefs Skirt Issue," El.

29. Ibid.

30. Hansen, "Hot New Sensation."

31. The yuppie fajitas are described in Anne Linsey Greer and Michael Bauer, "With Tex-Mex, Try a Pouilly Fumé," *Philadelphia Inquirer,* October 30, 1985.

32. Restaurant ratings appear in the *Austin Chronicle.*

33. During "carne asadas" in Eagle Pass, most men in their forties and above seem to prefer the "El Siete" steaks over fajitas. It was common to see these men grilling "siete steaks" behind the Sunset Inn and El Tropico Inn. The hotels' customers would often eat the steaks with beer while they were watching the game of the week on television. For an ethnography of eating fajitas and other organ meats, see José Limón, "Carne, Carnales, and the Carnivalesque: Bakhtinian Batos, Disorder, and Narrative Discourse," *American Ethnologist* 16 (August 1989): 471–86.

34. From an interview at his San Antonio home, July 15, 1982.

35. From an interview at her Eagle Pass store, El Barrio Loma Bonita, June 28, 1981.

36. For the importance of the production process and its link to the oppositional qualities of folklore, see José Limón, "Western Marxism and Folklore: A Critical Introduction," *Journal of American Folklore* 96 (1983): 34–52.

37. Ibid., 50.

38. See Pierre Van den Berghe, "Ethnic Cuisine: Culture in Nature," *Ethnic and Racial Studies* 7 (July 1984): 387–97.

39. Jean Baudrillard, *For a Critique of the Political Economy of the Sign,* trans. Charles Levin (St. Louis: Telos Press, 1981), 37. Other articles that approach food as a medium of communication include Mary Douglas, "Food as a System of Communication," in *In the Active Voice* (London: Routledge, Kegan, Paul, 1982); Arjun Appadurai, "Gastro-Politics: In Hindu South Asia," *American Ethnoloqy* 8 (1981): 494–511; and B. S. Turner, "The Discourse of Diet," *Theory and Culture and Society* 1 (1982): 23–32.

40. Linda Keller Brown and Kay Mussell, eds., *Ethnic and Regional Foodways in the United States: The Performance of Group Identity* (Knoxville: University of Tennessee Press, 1984). Other books that address the relationship of cuisine to cultural outlook include Michael Owen Jones, Bruce Giuliano, and Roberta Krell, eds., *Foodways and Eating Habits: Direction for Research* (California Folklore Society, 1981); Theodore C. Humphrey and Lin T. Humphrey, eds., *"We Gather Together": Food and Festival in American Life* (Ann Arbor: UMI Research Press, 1988); and Charles Camp, *American Foodways: What, When, Why, and How We Eat in America* (Little Rock, Ark.: August House, 1989).

CHAPTER 28

BEYOND *COMMUNITAS*: CINEMATIC FOOD EVENTS AND THE NEGOTIATION OF POWER, BELONGING, AND EXCLUSION

Luanne Roth

Many classic studies of foodways by folklorists and other scholars have effectively shown the sophisticated ways in which food functions to foster a heightened sense of group cohesion. Owing to the ethnographic tradition of representing cultures in a decidedly celebratory manner, as well as the tendency for individuals and groups to self-consciously perform, it follows that most depictions of food within communities fall in line with this paradigm of "communitas" (*cf.* Humphrey and Humphrey 1988). Recently, a few studies have moved beyond this positive function of food behavior to consider how food may be employed simultaneously to reinforce hegemonic or patriarchal structures, as well as to punish, cajole, or otherwise negotiate power relations.

Looking at cinematic portrayals of food events may be particularly revealing in this regard because, as mimetic devices, they represent aspects of food behavior not generally included in extant ethnographic and auto-ethnographic representations of foodways. As a matter of fact, "scenes which suggest happiness, comfort, or fulfillment are exceptional among Hollywood productions," observes film critic Parley Ann Boswell. "In American movies, food and dining are most often associated with crisis, frustration, conflict, or emptiness. No matter what the food, or what the meal being presented to us, Hollywood shows us not how Americans celebrate an abundance of food, but how this very abundance of food exposes other yearnings and other needs of American culture" (1993:9). As such, I approach popular American films through an ethnographic lens, relying on folkloristic, feminist, psychoanalytic, and postcolonial theories for insight. Moving beyond the obvious examples of food films, those employing food as a central thematic device, I examine mainstream popular films for the brief, subtle, yet powerfully resonant moments when food functions to symbolize *Western Folklore* 64:3&4 (Summer & Fall 2005):163–87. Copyright © 2006, Western States Folklore Society racial and cultural identity and, more significantly, to negotiate power, belonging, and exclusion.[1]

In this schema, the foreign "other"—like the "disgusting" foods the other is presumed to eat—manifests as the "abject." Presented cinematically as defiled and polluting, the other must be expelled, a process painfully evident in Tony Kaye's *American History X* (1998). In this and other films, there exists a simultaneous desire to consume the other. A negotiation of this conflict is exemplified in Joel Zwick's *My Big Fat Greek Wedding* (2002) and John Hamburg's *Along Came Polly* (2004) where the other is confronted (and confined) safely at the ethnic restaurant—a mediating site that, in the final analysis, serves to reinforce colonialism and complicate traditional approaches to foodways.

Luanne Roth, 'Beyond *Communitas*: Cinematic Food Events and the Negotiation of Power, Belonging and Exclusion', *Western Folklore* 64 (3/4) (2005), 163–187. (Excerpts printed here. Omitted text is indicated by ellipses.)

© Western States Folklore Society.

Abjecting the other in *American History X*

People being equated with the food they eat, of course, is not a new idea. In light of the worn adage, "we are what we eat," most people can quickly rattle off a number of foods associated with their own families and communities; food in this sense clearly functions to create "an" ethnic identity. The flip side of creating communitas through food is that it often does so by defining alterity—what is outside, what is foreign—we are what we don't eat. Hence, people can also, if asked, recall stereotypes about the food of other groups, the juiciest being reserved for "foreigners" (Kalcik 1984).

Historically, food has been one of the primary ways in which the other is posited as inferior, and it constituted an integral part of the social construction of race during the early Colonial period. Africans, for example, were seen first and foremost as bodies, and perceived bodily functions were used to differentiate the traveler from the native (see, for example, Fanon [1952] 1967:111–14; Pratt [1992] 1998:52; Spurr 1993:22; Turner 1993:2–32). The construction of the other, above all, as a body, positions the other as an embodiment of filth, something that needs to be abjected. The more "foreign" a group of people are taken to be, the more likely their food behavior will be taken to be repulsive, immoral, or barbaric. The reverse is also true: the more a group's food is perceived to be repulsive, immoral, or barbaric, the more likely the people who eat (or are presumed to eat) that food will be perceived as repulsive, immoral, or barbaric. Whether it involves rumors about "man-eating" Africans (e.g., Fanon 1952; Turner 1993) or endogamic cannibalistic Asian-American immigrants (Kalcik 1984), real or imagined food behavior has been used to justify the colonization of many nations and cultures and to otherwise express racism and hatred.

Several processes of the other via food and the mouth are exposed in *American History X*, a powerful and stirring film that reveals the world of Derek Vinyard (Edward Norton), who is trying to salvage his ruptured family after serving a three-year prison term for involuntary manslaughter. The film traces the ripple effects of Derek's racism and the tangled web of the neo-Nazi movement in Venice, California, which has now been spawned in his younger brother, Danny (Edward Furlong). The movie begins with the sound of a sorrowful trumpet playing over a sunset beach, then it rapidly transitions to a brief image of Danny sleeping and cuts to a graphic sex scene between a barely-of-age white woman and Derek, his swastika tattoo displayed prominently. Outside the window three black men conspire to steal Derek's pickup truck. Derek shoots, killing one and wounding another. After a digression, the film returns to Danny's memory of this pivotal incident. The brutal manner in which Derek murders the already wounded man (Antonio David Lyons) is significant to this analysis. By gunpoint, he orders the man to place his open mouth—the oral cavity that becomes a preoccupation in later scenes—on the curb's edge. "Now say *goodnight*," Derek says, as his boot comes stomping down on the man's head. We hear a smashing/ripping sound as the camera cuts to Danny's horrified reaction and then back to Derek, who spits in disgust on the dead man and walks away. "The sound of the kid's head splitting open on the curb went right through me," writes Danny at his computer, framed by multiple swastikas, portraits of Hitler, and other symbols of white supremacy.

Most of the film's story, in fact, unfolds via either Danny's recollections, shown in black-and-white flashbacks, or via events happening in the present. Assigned by as a consequence for submitting a history paper that argued for Adolf Hitler as a civil rights hero, Danny's new paper assignment—"American History X"—calls for him to analyze and interpret the events surrounding his brother's incarceration. Through a stream-of-consciousness process, Danny recalls several food-related moments. For example, at a basketball game on Venice beach—between the white guys and the black guys—a black player (Antonio David Lyons) plays the dozens on a morbidly obese white supremacist player, Seth Ryan (Ethan Suplee), calling him a "fat, pale, pasty, pastrami-eating, cracker mother-fucker." The same player later knocks Derek down during the game, giving him a bloody lip. A scene in the Vinyard family living room appears shortly thereafter, where

Seth crashes in a chair, complaining loudly about "starving" as he reaches for handfuls of jellybeans, throwing a black one, as if repulsive, onto the floor. These scenes, though brief, draw attention to connections between food and race.

In her analysis of the competing discourses surrounding soul food, Doris Witt confronts "the discrepancy between filthy 'matter' and filthy 'actions'" (1998:260), theorizing where the "disorder" of non-whiteness is situated in terms of food. Is it in the person (who eats the food), in the act (of eating), or in the object of action (the food itself)? (265). Exploring key ontologies of blackness, Witt finds that those stigmatized elements "have been thought to reside not in black bodies but instead in foods said to nourish those bodies" (260). This problem of where filth and foreignness are located manifests itself several times in *American History X*.

Accounting for how Derek became *the* Skinhead, a scene shows a black-and-white flashback of him holding a pep rally for his white followers in a parking lot across from the old neighborhood supermarket, now owned by "some fucking Korean." Calling immigrants "social parasites," "criminals," and "border-jumpers," the charismatic leader preaches about how "they" have taken over "our" country and "our" jobs, giving "decent, hard-working Americans [. . .] the shaft." The supermarket becomes the battlefield. The terrorist group, wearing stocking and ski masks as disguises, rushes into the market, shouting and smashing everything in sight, including the workers (who appear to be Latino) and food, with baseball bats, fists, and feet. Forty-pound bags of pinto beans, as if they were human bodies, are slashed open with knives ("like a fucking piñata"), the gutted bags pouring their contents onto the floor—a symbolic display threatening further brutal acts.

A dark-skinned woman worker (Francine Morris) cowers behind the cash register as the vandals tear apart the place. When they discover her, three masked men hoist her screaming and struggling body onto the counter, separating her legs and otherwise positioning her as if to gang rape her. One of the men says soothingly, "It's okay, sweetheart . . . I'm not going to hurt you." We hear the other men saying things such as, "This bitch stinks," "Get some cleaning products on her," and "She smells like fish and chips and guacamole." The camera cuts quickly back and forth between the scenes of food items being destroyed and the men's degrading treatment of the woman. The men force what we take to be Mexican food items (hot sauce and salsa) into her mouth, followed by what appears to be applesauce and cow's milk, which they also smear over her face. The camera lingers uncomfortably on the viscous whiteness dripping out of the woman's mouth and off of her face in slow motion, and then cuts to Seth standing at the door, clutching a night stick in one hand and what appears to be a large plastic hamburger in the other, while the gang runs out of the store.

This rape-by-food scene is ripe for analysis. In addition to the willful destruction of the other's food, as a symbol of destroying the other, is the suggestion that the consumption of certain *stinky* foods is associated, however erroneously, with *foreignness*. Following Joel Kovel ([1970] 1988), Richard Dyer writes: "Non-white people are associated in various ways with the dirt that comes out of the body, notably in the repeated racist perception that they smell [. . .] that their food smells, that they eat dirty foods—offal, dogs, snakes—and that they slaughter it in direct and bloody forms. Obsessive control of faeces and identification of them as the nadir of human dirt both characterize Western culture: to be white is to be well potty-trained" (1997:75–6). Focusing on the connection between the color of excrement and of skin, Kovel explains "the central symbol of dirt throughout the world is faeces, known by that profane word with which the emotion of disgust is expressed: shit . . . when contrasted with the light colour of the body of the Caucasian person, the dark colour of faeces reinforces, from the infancy of the individual in the culture of the West, the connotation of blackness with badness" ([1970] 1988:87).

The men's insults to the female grocery story clerk draw upon food names, particularly those deemed "smelly" and disgusting. Taken to eat disgusting cultural foods, the woman becomes disgusting herself and must be purified before she can be safely approached. Threatening to pour cleaning products on her (we do not see whether they actually do so), the men force into her mouth first Mexican foods and then various *white* foods, smearing them on her face. We hear the attackers saying, as they rub in the liquids, "Hey, this is a great color on you," "You could get a white woman's job, bitch," and "Moving up in the world, huh?" Such comments reveal their attempt to make her more white and graphically illustrate how the other's "stinkiness," "filthiness," and "badness" may be countered, symbolically at least, with pale/white/American foods, because: "To be white is to have expunged all dirt, faecal or otherwise, from oneself: to look white is to look clean" (Dyer 1997:76).

Of the handful of male workers attacked, the woman is the only one violated on such a personal and degrading level. In the sad reality of war, women are raped and sexually abused by members of the conquering group as a symbol of their dominance. Even in the postwar period, women often are used to symbolize the West's penetration of foreign markets. Traise Yamamoto argues, for instance, that the "unstated structure of heterosexual mastery reveals itself if we look at what are frequent descriptions of the present economical need to '*penetrate* the Japanese market'" (1999:22; emphasis in original). Common American phrases, such as *the opening of Japan,* contain images of *forced penetration* that are repeatedly utilized in such American institutions as the military, government, and the media, all of which draw upon the "language of rape in the postwar period" (23). On the battlefield of the supermarket, therefore, the men penetrate the *foreign* woman through her oral cavity as a way of expressing anger and hatred over the nonwhites in America. And if the connection to rape is still elusive to the viewer at this point, the inescapable allusion to male ejaculation is underscored as the white fluids drip out of the screaming, gagging woman's mouth.

Like the food on which the woman in the supermarket gags, this scene is hard to swallow. What makes it particularly intriguing to me are the attackers' statements of the need to "clean" the victim. The more I reflect on this scene, the more I cannot escape Kristeva's theory of abjection as an analytical tool. Abjection is the primary form of repression, according to Kristeva, that occurs prior to ego development. Before abjection, the infant exists in a state of "chora," where the child "experiences itself . . . as being one with all" (1982:13). Abjection is the moment that makes the dichotomy between the ego and the object possible. It is the infant subject's initial attempt to establish a corporeal schema separate from the maternal body, first enacted by the infant spitting out the mother's milk. This moment is "a violent, clumsy breaking away" from the state of undifferentiated "chora" with the maternal prior to the constitution of the "I" (1982:13). Having established the self via this expulsion, the abject then comes to threaten the "clean and proper body" and thereby becomes loathsome and disgusting. The process is complicated, though, by the concomitant experience of dread and attraction. If we could just expel the abject and "get it over with," that would be one matter. But because we must continually live with the abject, because we cannot escape it completely, "the abject is fascinating, bringing out an obsessed attraction" at the same time it creates "dread of the unnamable" (Young 1990:145).

While the primal other for Kristeva is the maternal, her theory has room for positing the foreigner (or racialized other) as abject, as others have done, for "defilement is what is jettisoned from the symbolic system" (Kristeva 1982:65).[2] Kristeva argues, by implication, that the constitution of western hegemonic identity, the "symbolic order," requires abjection in some form. Something must be othered in the construction of the hegemony's identity. If, as Kristeva claims, "abjection is coextensive with social and symbolic order," then wherever a social system exists, we can expect to find abjection (1982:68), and we see this idea illustrated in *American History X* through the murder-by-mouth scene and two rape-by-food scenes. Like the primal abjection Kristeva describes, the threat of the foreign other's presence, with the possible disintegration of the boundaries of the nation-state self, is experienced as frightening. The supermarket no longer offers comfort as the white gang's "neighborhood" store because "foreigners" now own it. While the foreigner is recognized as a threat to the borders of subjectivity, s/he is simultaneously desired and feared, and necessary for the constitution of the nation-state self.

It is no accident that, in films such as *American History X,* this process of abjection manifests itself so frequently via alimentary images, considering that "food loathing is perhaps the most elementary and most archaic form of abjection" (Kristeva 1982:2). Although the abject is associated with filth and disgust, Kristeva reminds us, "It is . . . not lack of cleanliness . . . that causes abjection but what disturbs identity, system, order. What does not respect borders, positions, rules. The in-between, the ambiguous, the composite" (1982:4)—like the border-jumping, foreign woman in the grocery store. Hence, the woman is rendered the abject—desired by the men, yet standing outside the white colonial system, making that desire disturbing. To survive this psychological crisis, the men transform her into filth, allowing them to clean her, so that they can then consume her without risk of becoming themselves defiled.

This rape-by-food scenario becomes especially poignant when a similar one occurs in the following scene, taking place over a family meal. Thanks to food scholars, we understand how the family meal—a microcosm of family dynamics—serves to socialize, educate, express, and play out relational and power dynamics. James Bossard suggested long ago that the family meal is the family "at ease" (1948). Just as often, though, it is the family battlefield (Belasco 1989; Roth 2005). As a symbolically charged occasion, the family meal manages to operate—like other family dynamics—largely unselfconsciously, that is, until a change is introduced. Boswell challenges the assumption that "In American films [. . .] home cooking should tell us that all is well in these American homes." This is rarely the case, she notes, "When we see entire families sitting around a table eating a home-cooked meal, we are almost never made to feel comfortable. In Hollywood productions of the last 20 years, home-cooked food and family dining scenes have been used to highlight unhealthy aspects of the American family" (1993:17).

In this particular disrupted family meal at the Vinyard home, the attending family members include the recently widowed mother (Beverly D'Angelo), oldest brother Derek, middle sister Davina (Jennifer Lien), and younger brother Danny. They sit around a formal dining room table the evening before Derek commits murder. Joining the family are two non-family members: the mother's new boyfriend, Murray (Elliot Gould) (who, we quickly learn, is Jewish), and Stacey (Fairuza Balk), Derek's skinhead girlfriend. Consider how the family meal serves as a judicial court where people evaluate and judge each other, debate contemporary issues, make important decisions, and negotiate relationships. The already tense table conversation quickly becomes heated with the highly charged issue of race—the Rodney King case—being debated. We see Derek expressing his racist doctrine, to which his sycophantic girlfriend cheers her approval, Davina becoming increasingly shocked and frustrated at the racist attitudes being expressed, and newcomer Murray trying to be the mediating voice of reason, but clearly disturbed by the direction of the conversation. As the tension between the liberals and the racists rises, the mother touches Murray's hand several times in comfort, but then she explodes briefly, slamming her open hand on the table and saying, "Can we just drop this Rodney King thing?" She pauses, takes a deep breath, then forces a smile and says sweetly, "Who'd like some dessert?"

But the arguing resumes immediately. When it becomes heated again, with Stacey beginning to rant, Davina interrupts to ask desperately, "Can I please be excused?" to which her mother quickly answers, "Yes," to forestall further escalation. But Derek, having stepped into his deceased father's shoes, immediately overrides his mother, asserting his presumed patriarchal dominance over her. "No, you cannot" [be excused], he declares to Davina, "You need to stay until you learn some fucking manners!" "Who the hell do you think you are?" Davina retorts back to him and stands to leave. Derek physically blocks Davina; when she attempts to get around him, he grabs her by the hair, yanking her back and forth. Grabbing a handful of roast beef from the serving dish on the table, he shoves it into her mouth, yelling, "You need to learn some fucking manners," until she cries and chokes, gasping for breath.

After this explosion, Derek turns triumphantly to Murray, ripping off his shirt to expose his white power tattoos and yelling:

> My family . . . my family [. . .]. You're not a part of it and you never will be [. . .]. You don't think I see what you're trying to do here? You think I'm gonna sit here and smile while some fucking kike tries to fuck my mother? It's never going to happen, Murray, fucking forget it, not on my watch, not while I'm in this family. I will fucking cut your shylock nose off and stick it up your ass before I'll let that happen. Coming in here and "poisoning my family's dinner" with your Jewish, nigger-loving, hippie-bullshit. Fuck you, fuck you, asshole. Fucking Kabala-reading motherfucker. Get the fuck out of my house! (emphasis added)

Like the black jellybean and the "foreign" supermarket workers, the Jewish boyfriend threatens the "clean and proper" body of the Caucasian-American family and is considered, therefore, to be filthy and disgusting. The "foreign" boyfriend is abjected from the sanctity of the family, just as the "foreign" woman and African-American man were abjected in the prior scenes. Family systems theorists Michael Nichols and Richard Schwartz explain: "Family structure involves a set of covert rules that govern transactions in the family . . . altering the basic structure will have ripple effects on all family transactions . . . . Whatever the chosen pattern, it tends to be self-perpetuating and resistant to change" (1998:244). If one group member shifts within the family structure (in this case, because of the father's death), the others fill in the absent space and/or pressure deviating members to return to their earlier roles—hence, Derek steps into the space left by his father. Note, for instance, that after this violent eruption, Derek stops calling his mother Ma and begins calling her Doris instead. The change in family roles also affects Davina. When she does not listen to Derek's orders, he asserts his patriarchal authority by disciplining her. With physical force, and with food, he teaches her manners. Dyer explains: "There are special anxieties surrounding the whiteness of white women *vis-à-vis* sexuality. As the literal bearers of children, and because they are held primarily responsible for their initial raising, women are the indispensable means by which the group—the race—is in every sense reproduced" (1997:29). A significant point of Derek attacking his sister is to prove his dominance not just to Davina, but to Murray, and Derek's verbal attack on his mother, "How could you bring him to my father's table? [. . .] You disgust me" follows suit.

Significantly, it is roast beef that Derek uses to choke his sister, instead of green beans, dinner rolls, or dessert. Recently, feminist scholars have addressed the more than metaphorical connection between the killing of animals and the raping of women (at least in Western cultures). As several scholars have argued, meat eating inherently involves sexual politics—meat being identified with maleness, masculinity, virility, and strength (see Adams 1994; Twigg 1983). Meat manifests as a symbol of male dominance in this cinematic scene, a celebration of patriarchy itself. And in light of Dyer's observation about white women reproducing "the race," it is no accident that Derek penetrates his sister/daughter's mouth with meat—a hyper masculine symbol that powerfully communicates his dominance. That he exerts his power by penetrating her oral cavity is also not accidental. Near the end of this scene, the mother, in despair, crouches down to the curb in front of the house—foreshadowing the place where Derek will enact the brutal murder-by-mouth later that night.

Mary Douglas has discussed how the oral cavity is believed to be highly vulnerable, especially during times of stress. Explaining why certain groups of people approach foods more cautiously than others, she suggests that people with minority status are more likely to be suspicious of food cooked by outsiders and more protective of the orifices of the body. "Food is not likely to be polluting at all," in fact, "unless the external boundaries of the social system are under pressure" (1966:126; see also Angyal 1941; Turner 1987, 1993). Moving beyond the either/or of Douglas's model, in *American History X* we see members of the minority being violated, but also members of the dominant group (white males) experiencing themselves as being threatened, fearing defilement and poisoning by nonwhite outsiders. By tying together these three parallel incidents of people being violated through the oral cavity, Tony Kaye's *American History X* blatantly portrays how this perceived vulnerability of the mouth relates to processes of othering and abjection. As I will show, these dynamics are worked out in other films as well.

Othering, abjecting, and continuing colonialism in *My Big Fat Greek Wedding* and *Along Came Polly*

Beyond the explicitness of American History X's depiction of race relations, abjection and processes of othering are played out in other examples of recent popular film, albeit in less extreme forms. I turn next to Joel Zwick's My Big Fat Greek Wedding and John Hamburg's Along Came Polly, both romantic comedies in which food functions as the main vehicle for the expression of difference (and otherness). However, if the other's food is initially viewed with suspicion, it is eventually embraced in ritual spaces (i.e., ethnic restaurants) as a sign of adventurousness and cultural capital.[3]

[...]

Food in the comedies *My Big Fat Greek Wedding* and *Along Came Polly,* as with the drama of *American History X,* functions to express distrust about other cultures and fear of being contaminated/soiled, while revealing the simultaneous impulse to consume the other. Because food events in such popular cultural "texts" function to negotiate gender, culture, and race, as well as familial relationship dynamics, we can employ film to work out theories—showing how processes of "othering," "abjecting," and "colonizing" may be enacted over food traditions. Such analyses of food behavior forge promising new directions for further research into the interrelationship between food, identity, and power dynamics in ways that move beyond food traditions creating communitas, toward a theory of how food behavior and ideology also function to negotiate power, belonging, and exclusion.

Notes

1. See the website, www.lib.berkeley.edu/MRC/foodmovies.html, for a fairly recent filmography and bibliography of food in the movies.

2. See hooks 1998; McAfee 1993; Moruzzi 1993; Witt 1998; and Young 1990.

3. Turgeon and Pastinelli's definition of ethnic restaurants as "a restaurant whose sign board or publicity clearly promises the national or regional cuisine of another land" (2002:252) suggests that the label is applied by the ethnic other. Ethnic restaurants are not simply places to eat, but become symbolically and politically charged: "The term *ethnic* refers to outsiders, people who come from far away and who are foreign to the mainstream culture. Groups in control are never ethnicities; they use ethnic distinctions to organize social and spatial marginalities . . . and to legitimize a sort of negative integration of minority groups" (252). Hence, restaurants such as Denny's, Country Kitchen, Cracker Barrel, Perkins, McDonald's, and so forth, are presumed to be unproblematic, "all-American-style" restaurants in a paradigm where they are not marked as Anglo or *ethnic* in any way (see Dyer 1997). That ethnic distinction is almost invariably reserved for the category of other, usually of nonwhite groups of people. My emphasis of the word ethnic WFJ uses italics, not quotes, for emphasis herein is a small attempt to address this problem.

Filmography

Along Came Polly (2004), 91min. John Hamburg.
American History X (1998), 119 min. Tony Kaye.
My Big Fat Greek Wedding (2002), 95 min. Joel Zwick.

References

Adams, Carol J. 1994. The Sexual Politics of Meat. In *Living with Contradictions: Controversies in Feminist Social Ethics,* ed. Alison M. Jaggar, 548–57. Boulder, Colorado: Westview Press.

Angyal, A. 1941. Disgust and Related Aversions. *Journal of Abnormal and Social Psychology* 36:393–412.

Belasco, Warren. 1989. *Appetite for Change: How the Counterculture Took on the Food Industry, 1966–1988.* New York: Pantheon Books.

Bossard, James H. 1943. Family Table Talk—An Area for Sociological Study. *American Sociological Review* 18:295–301.

Boswell, Parley Ann. 1993. Hungry in the Land of Plenty: Food in Hollywood Films. In *Beyond the Stars III: The Material World in American Popular Film,* ed. Paul Loukides and Linda K. Fuller, 7–23. Bowling Green, Ohio: Popular Press.

Douglas, Mary. 1966. *Purity and Danger: An Analysis of Concepts of Pollution and Taboo.* London: Routledge.

Dyer, Richard. 1997. *White.* New York: Routledge.

Fanon, Frantz. (1952) 1967. The Fact of Blackness. In *Black Skin, White Masks.* Trans. Charles Lam Markmann, 109–40. New York: Grove Press.

hooks, bell. Eating the Other: Desire and Resistance. In *Eating Culture,* ed. Ron Scapp and Brian Seitz, 181–200. Albany: State University of New York Press.

Humphrey, Theodore C., and Lin T. Humphrey, eds. 1988. *"We Gather Together": Food and Festival in American Life.* Logan: Utah State University Press.

International Movie Database. 2005. http://www.IMDB.com, accessed July 19, 2005.

Kovel, Joel. (1970) 1988. *White Racism: A Psychohistory.* London: Free Association Books.

Kristeva, Julia. 1982. *Powers of Horror: An Essay on Abjection.* New York: Columbia University Press.

—. 1991. *Strangers to Ourselves.* Trans. Leon S. Roudiez. New York: Columbia University Press.

McAfee, Nöelle. 1993. Abject Strangers: Towards an Ethics of Respect. In *Ethics, Politics, and Difference in Julia Kristeva's Writing,* ed. Kelly Oliver, 116–34. New York: Routledge.

Mintz, Sidney W. 2002. Food and Eating: Some Persisting Questions. In *Food Nations: Selling Taste in Consumer Societies,* ed. Warren Belasco and Philip Scranton, 24–32. New York: Routledge.

Moruzzi, Norma Claire. 1993. National Abjects: Julia Kristeva on the Process of Political Self-Identification. In *Ethics, Politics, and Difference in Julia Kristeva's Writing,* ed. Kelly Oliver, 135–49. New York: Routledge.

Nichols, Michael P., and Richard C. Schwartz. (1984) 1998. *Family Therapy: Concepts and Methods.* Allyn and Bacon: Boston.

Pratt, Mary Louise. (1992) 1998. *Imperial Eyes: Travel Writing and Transculturation.* London: Routledge.

Roth, LuAnne. (in press). "Beef. It's what's for dinner": Vegetarians, Meat-Eaters, and the Negotiation of Familial Relationships. *Food, Culture, and Society* 8(2), 32 page MSS.

Spurr, David. 1993. *The Rhetoric of Empire: Colonial Discourse in Journalism, Travel Writing, and Imperial Administration.* Durham, N.C.: Duke University Press.

Todorov, Tzvetan. 1984. *The Conquest of America: The Question of the Other.* Trans. Richard Howard. New York: Harper and Row.

Turgeon, Laurier, and Madeleine Pastinelli. 2002. "Eat the World": Postcolonial Encounters in Quebec City's Ethnic Restaurants. *Journal of American Folklore* 115(456): 247–68.

Turner, Patricia A. 1987. Church's Fried Chicken and The Klan: A Rhetorical Analysis of Rumor in the Black Community. *Western Folklore* 46:294–306.

—. 1993. Cannibalism: "They Doe Eat Each Other Alive." In *I Heard It Through the Grapevine: Rumor in African-American Culture,* 9–32. Berkeley: University of California Press.

Twigg, Julia. 1983. Vegetarianism and the Meanings of Meat. In *The Sociology of Food and Eating: Essays on the Sociological Significance of Food,* ed. Anne Murcott, 18–30. England: Gower Publishing Company Ltd.

Witt, Doris. 1998. Soul Food: Where the Chitterlings Hits the (Primal) Pan. In *Eating Culture,* ed. Ron Scapp and Brian Seitz, 258–87.

Yamamoto, Traise. 1999. Masking Selves, Making Subjects: Japanese-American Women, Identity, and the Body. *Modern Fiction Studies* 46(4): 1045–7.

Young, Iris Marion. 1990. *Justice and the Politics of Difference.* New Jersey: Princeton University Press.

CHAPTER 29

CHURCH'S FRIED CHICKEN AND THE KLAN: A RHETORICAL ANALYSIS OF RUMOR IN THE BLACK COMMUNITY

Patricia A. Turner

Few genres of oral discourse more tellingly reveal racial anxieties than do rumor and legend.[1] While many studies have focused on the ways in which these genres reflect white anxiety about potential black hostility, folklorists have paid little attention to the rumors and legends that reflect black uneasiness about potential white enmity. Yet the centuries-old conflict between the races still generates mistrust, fears, and suspicions that are most conspicuous in the ostensibly true stories about whites that circulate among blacks. Since the early 1980s, blacks have been sharing one particularly provocative story with each other. The tellers allege that the Church's Fried Chicken Corporation is owned by the Ku Klux Klan, and that the white supremacist organization is contaminating the chicken so that eating it will cause sterility in black male consumers. In many versions the tellers "authenticate" the story by claiming that a friend saw a television news magazine exposé on the plot. The perpetuation of such an item demonstrates that blacks, like whites, articulate their racial fears in folkloric forms.

Before examining the context within which the Church's item emerged, it would be worthwhile to clarify the issue of genre. The item quite clearly exhibits features of both legend and rumor.[2] At first glance, the story seems strikingly similar to the urban legends about fast food contamination and conspiracies that have been quite prominent in the latter part of the twentieth century. However, the form of the Church's item, unlike that of these urban legends, lacks a distinctly narrative element; tellers relate it as an ongoing occurrence, rather than as a specific incident. None of the versions I have collected contains any element of closure—other than a personal observation along the lines of "so I am not going to eat there anymore." While some informants mention specific locations where they have purchased a meal, no one has attributed this plot to only one franchise operation. A black male who eats in any Church's was and is in danger. Since these non-narrative formal features are those most often characteristic of rumors, I will use this designation for the item; when discussions of the rumor's content can be enhanced by references to urban legend scholarship, I will make use of the appropriate material.

In what follows I use this story as a case study of one rumor's popularity among a fairly significant segment of the black community. By exploring its possible origins, profiling the audience most convinced of the story's veracity, comparing and contrasting it to other contemporary urban legends and rumors, and examining its distinctive features from an essentially rhetorical perspective, we can discover in this folk text the suspicions and doubts many blacks maintain about white desires for racial parity.

I first encountered the Church's rumor in the winter of 1986 in a black literature class at the University of Massachusetts at Boston. After I had referred briefly to several contemporary urban legends, a black male

Patricia A. Turner, 'Church's Fried Chicken and the Klan: A Rhetorical Analysis of Rumor in the Black Community', *Western Folklore* 46 (4) (1987), 294–306.

© Western States Folklore Society.

student compared these items to a "fact" about the Church's Fried Chicken franchise.[3] He told the class that Church's was owned by the Ku Klux Klan and that they were putting something in the chicken that would cause sterility in black male customers. He claimed that he knew this was true because a friend of his had seen a story about it on *60 Minutes*. Other black members of the class verified the first student's information. Of the students in the class unfamiliar with the rumor, the black ones expressed almost immediate belief in the item, while the white ones raised questions about the item's veracity.

The Church's rumor has not been well-documented in print. In his 1985 book *Rumor in the Marketplace: The Social Psychology of Commercial Hearsay,* Tulane University social psychologist Fred Koenig includes a brief reference to the Church's rumor in his chapter on contamination rumors.[4] According to Koenig's research, the rumor had circulated in New Jersey in 1982 and was conspicuous again in southern California in 1984. Alarmed by his constituents' concerns in this matter, San Diego representative Jim Bates arranged for the Food and Drug Administration to use gas chromatography and mass spectrometry to test the chicken. After finding no evidence of foreign materials, an assistant of Bates and two West Coast Church's officials held a press conference to share their research findings with the public. Professor Koenig reveals his own naiveté about the nature of oral tradition when he concludes, "Following the press conference, the rumor simply ceased to exist."[5] Since the rumor was well-known to my Boston-based black students in 1986 and 1987, it is clear that Koenig underestimated this particular rumor's potency.

Indeed, between February of 1986 and June of 1987 I was able to collect over one hundred versions of this rumor. Although about half of the versions were collected in the greater Boston area, I was able to gather several from other parts of the country, namely Washington, D.C.; Newark, New Jersey; College Park, Maryland, and San Francisco, California. My fieldwork, along with the information supplied to my by J. David Bamberger, Chairman of the Board of the Church's Chicken Corporation, leads me to conclude that the rumor surfaces in most communities that have both a Church's franchise and a black community. I had very little success in collecting versions from white informants. The few versions I managed to solicit came from whites whose family or work situations put them daily contact with the black community. This suggests that blacks do not share the rumor with whites with whom they have only casual encounters; obviously a degree of trust must be established before a black will share this information with a white.

While most of my black informants are students, I am convinced that this is because young people are the prime movers of this rumor, not because I restricted my collecting to this population. My informants range in age from seventeen to fifty. In Washington, D.C., I had very little success when I tried collecting the rumor from federal employees on their lunch breaks in the Smithsonian mall area. However one woman told me that she had heard the rumor from her daughter, a Howard University student. At Howard, a predominantly black college located in Washington, the rumor is very much in evidence. Given the liminal status of black college students, it is easy to see they would be the most susceptible to a rumor that plays so deeply on their vulnerability.

The rumor was as easy to collect from black females as it was from black males. Not surprisingly, black males were more vehement in their hostility toward the product. In his analysis of the Kentucky Fried Rat legend, Gary Alan Fine suggested that fast food rumors and legends frequently reflect an anti-feminist impulse.[6] After noting that the alleged victims of the Kentucky Fried Rat are most often female, he claims "the woman as victim is symbolically proper. The woman by neglecting her traditional role as food preparer helps to destroy the family by permitting the transfer of control from the home to amoral profit-making corporations."[7] Even though the supposed victims in versions of the Church's rumor are male, Fine's comments still seem applicable. One informant put it particularly well. After claiming that the rumor led him to stop patronizing Church's, he said that he didn't miss it and that he didn't really care for chicken. After I expressed surprise at someone's disliking fried chicken, he assured me that he enjoyed fried chicken "if my mother makes it or something like that, you know, real fried chicken, but I don't care about that other stuff." This sentiment is evident in the testimony of other informants and suggests that black males, like white, resent the flexibility that fast food restaurants afford to modern households.

Anyone familiar with the study of urban lore recognizes many aspects of the Church's rumor. Virtually each of the motifs contained can be identified with contemporary urban legends. The manner in which these familiar components emerge in the Church's rumor reveals a great deal about the evolution and transmission of rumor in the black community.

The most dominant and common motif in the versions that I have collected is that the Ku Klux Klan owns Church's chicken. Each informant questioned who "knew" the rumor attributed ownership of this particular franchise to this particular white supremacist group. No one blamed the John Birchers or Lyndon LaRouche or the Moral Majority—each informant identified the Klan. In this sense the rumor is very much like the conspiracy rumors that have plagued many large American corporations, such as Proctor and Gamble, McDonalds, and Entenmanns. Koenig describes conspiracy rumors as "those in which the allegation connects a political, religious or ideological movement with a visible target: a successful commercial enterprise. The carriers of the rumor are members of a population who feel that the movement is undesirable and threatening."[8]

Certainly no movement is more notoriously anti-black in its philosophy than the Ku Klux Klan. In her seminal study of Klan-related lore, Gladys-Marie Fry notes that "the humor that is clearly present in Black Testimony concerning the patrollers is almost totally absent in discussions of the Klansmen. There was nothing funny about Klan terrorism, either in its supernatural manifestations or in its physical brutality."[9] In a personal conversation on contemporary black perceptions of the Klan, she agreed with me that the group's potency in the mind of the black community no doubt exceeds its actual power.[10] My informants had no trouble believing that the Klan was capable of devising a conspiracy of this magnitude. When I asked one black female student informant if she didn't think that the Food and Drug Administration would have tried to stop the Klan from doing this, she speculated that the Klan would have no problem gaining control of the FDA. Another female informant believed Klan infiltration was rampant in all phases of American life.

All but one informant identified the Church's chain. This informant though that she might have heard the rumor associated with Kentucky Fried Chicken but was more confident of the Church's attribution. This particular motif seems to violate one of the "laws of urban folklore." In enumerating these laws, Fine claims that "The frequency of attachment of an urban legend to the largest company or corporation is so common as to be considered a law of urban folklore."[11] Church's is not the largest corporation in the fast food chicken market, but it is the one most committed to the black community.[12] This suggests that if a smaller company serves a particular ethnic group, it will be the one most likely to generate folklore from that group.

Understanding the unique relationship that has developed between the Church's company and black communities throughout the United States requires a brief examination of the company's origins, development and corporate philosophy. The Church's Chicken Corporation has been publicly owned since April of 1965. The company was started by George Church, a former chicken incubator salesman. In 1952 he opened the chain's first store, actually a chicken stand not far from a poor Spanish section of San Antonio, Texas. Shortly thereafter he opened another five stores in Texas. His son, George Junior, took over in 1963. He also built more stores in Texas as well as out of state.

On the surface at least, the Church's company has done nothing to "earn" this association with the Ku Klux Klan. But several aspects of the company's philosophy and, perhaps, the name, location and product of the company itself could have contributed to the item's popularity. Koenig cites Larry Varney, a Church's public relations representative who speculated about a news story in which the Ku Klux Klan was connected with churches in their efforts. Varney thinks that it is at least possible that some people incorrectly understood that to mean the fast food company instead of the religious institutions.

Perhaps this can be carried one step further. In giving his company his name, George Church paved the way for the public to associate it with houses of worship. The notion that "Church's" could be responsible for such destructive behavior has a perverse, ironic, antithetical appeal. None of my informants who expressed belief in the item knew that the company's corporate headquarters and place of origin is San Antonio, Texas. Most informants who were familiar with the company, whether believers or non-believers of the rumor, associated the company with "the South." Some claimed Alabama, some Georgia, but no one thought that the company was northern. Given the fact that the company concentrated its initial efforts on the south, this association should come as no surprise. The Ku Klux Klan is also perceived by most people as a southern-based enterprise. It seems reasonable to assume that a southern company is more likely than a northern one to suffer guilt by association.

Just as the company's location and name may indirectly support this rumor, so may their philosophy and product. The Church's menu boasts a wide selection of foods not unlike those available at a soul food restaurant—okra, corn on the cob, catfish dinners, rolls, and southern fried chicken. If a white supremacist organization were going to use a fast food chain to infiltrate the black community, Church's would be "made to order." Another observation frequently made by informant/believers related to the location of the Church's stores. Asked what kind of substance would affect only black males, informants would counter by claiming that that was why Church's were always located in inner-city black areas where whites would be unlikely to venture.

There is some truth in this comment. According to a 1984 *Business Week* article, Church's was one of the last fast food companies to begin using mall and suburban locations.[13] The company has tended to locate in the kind of inner city locations mentioned by my informants. In the greater Boston area, for example, the stores are located in Dudley Square, right in the heart of Roxbury; in Central Square, the black part of Cambridge; on Dorchester Avenue, a thoroughfare that criss-crosses the white and black sections of Dorchester; and on Blue Hill Avenue, another thoroughfare in the largely black suburb of Mattapan. In the persistently racially conscious Boston, these are the kind of areas traditionally avoided by whites.

One other dimension of Church's corporate persona tends to lend credence to the rumor. Unlike most fast food franchises, Church's does not like to advertise. In 1978, Church's ad budget was one of the lowest in the industry. In that year Chairman George W. Church, Jr., maintained that other fast-food chains have often relied too much on new products and slogans. He claimed that these devices are "a trap executives can get into to save themselves instead of solving the real problems of their operations."[14] Its lack of advertising has contributed to the company's low visibility. Many white Bostonians not only were not familiar with the rumor, they had never heard of the company. In an age where most fast food companies bombard us nightly with their televised pitches, a company with little or no advertising becomes conspicuous through its anonymity. Perhaps the folk assumption is that a company that doesn't boast about its product has something to hide.

In trying to cope with the rumor's impact, the company has maintained the same close-mouthed approach. According to Chairman of the Board J. David Bamberger, "Our policy in this rumor is to let our record in minority relations and hiring speak for itself. We don't wish to dignify such a malicious rumor."[15] Bamberger is obviously quite proud of his company's efforts to effect integration. He claims:

From its very humble beginning, one of our ideas for growth incorporated the idea of "making big people out of little people.". . . Today we have approximately 17,000 people in the company. Eighty-four percent of these are minority! This extends from our stores through the Board Room. Seventy-two percent of our store managers and fifty percent of our Board are minority people and this hasn't happened overnight because of a crisis, but rather over the years because of a philosophy.[16]

Bamberger's response to my initial inquiry also contained a separate sheet identified as "references." It listed fourteen minority individuals and companies who would purportedly vouch for the company's integrity. The list was headed by Benjamin Hooks, executive director of the NAACP. Nonetheless, the company's good intentions and notable contacts have not alleviated the rumor's impact. Bamberger candidly acknowledges that "There is no question but that it hurts our business and our employees."[17]

From the company's point of view, the rumor represents an unearned assault from a community it has endeavored to embrace. From the black community's point of view, the rumor represents a plausible explanation for the Church's company's commitment to this community.

The second most common folk idea in this rumor is that Church's is putting something in the chicken to make black men sterile. Exactly one half of my informants claimed that Church's goal was to put something (spices, drugs) in the chicken (batter, flour, injections into the chicken) that would cause sterility in black men. So the rumor is as much about contamination as about conspiracy. In most conspiracy rumors and legends, the group's goal is to use a profitable company to make money for their cause. Contamination rumors and legends traditionally are associated either with instances of accidental, incidental contamination (e.g., the Kentucky Fried Rat, the mouse in the Coke bottle) or with premeditated food substitution, ostensibly for the purpose of decreasing the company's cost (e.g., wormburgers, use of dog food on pizza). In the latter case, the company is not trying to hurt its customers, but rather to use "distasteful" but essentially safe products to save money. In the Church's rumor, greed is not a strong factor. Although seven informants provided versions that lacked any contamination motif (they merely maintained that the Klan owned Church's), not a single informant speculated on how much money the Klan could make through its ownership of the Church's chain. The Klan's attributed motive was to decrease the black population.

Sterilization and castration motifs are not new in folklore. In the past thirty years the age-old "mutilated boy motif" has appeared often in urban legends and other genres.[18] As Brunvand points out, the Choking Doberman can certainly be construed as a castration legend targetting the black male population.[19] Rumors that the army is tampering with the male G.I.s' food in order to decrease the sex drive also emerge from time to time.[20]

Black men are apt to be even more alert to castration motifs due to the publicity that accompanied the disclosure of the syphilis experiments conducted by the white medical establishment at the Tuskegee Institute. Told merely that they had "bad blood," black men from the rural south participated in an experiment through which the effects of untreated syphilis were measured on them long after effective treatment could have mitigated their suffering.[21] Black men and women have also grown accustomed to hearing whites decry the black birth rate. In a controversial television series Bill Moyers highlighted this "social problem," and on an April 6, 1986, *60 Minutes* feature story on the problem of teenage pregnancy, every male and female teenager interviewed was black. Bemoaning this attention, Harvard sociologist Charles Willy noted on January 30, 1986, that the whites are obsessed with blacks having babies. Given all of this attention, it is not surprising that a certain paranoia would emerge over black fertility.

In the other half of the texts collected, it is the entire black population that is the intended victim of Church's conspiracy. Several informants suggested that the Klan's goals were to "make blacks infertile." Thus both men and women have something to fear. One black female informant claimed that eating the chicken "makes something go wrong with pregnant black women so that their children come out retarded."

The third common element in the Church's rumor is that the teller heard it from a friend who saw it on *60 Minutes*. Several of the students cite the television news magazine as the source of their information, and the chain store managers I have interviewed also cite the program as the source of their problem. Brunvand, perhaps with his tongue in his cheek, has offered "rip" as a shorthand designation for accounts that "verify" their story by saying "I read it in the paper."[22] The fact that none of my informants claimed to have read this item in the paper, while several cited CBS's *60 Minutes* and a handful attributed it to ABC's *20/20,* seems to suggest television referents may soon replace print ones. In response to my phone call to CBS News, a *60 Minutes* staffer claimed that although she personally had heard the rumor, she knew that the program had never done a feature on the chain or the Klan's connection to black religious institutions. In an effort to help its franchise managers cope with the problem, the Church's company included in a packet of information sent to all of its franchises a letter from a *60 Minutes* representative disclaiming any story. Unfortunately, the Boston area managers whom I have interviewed refused to show me any of this information. In discussing the negative effect the rumor has had on his business, the manager of the Dorchester Avenue Church's assured me that the rumor had to be false because "my wife just had a baby."

The context within which this rumor is performed infuses it with potency and establishes its credibility. Indeed credibility is a key feature of all urban legends and rumors. The "successful" ones—such as the cat in the microwave, the choking doberman, the Kentucky fried rat—all remain in folk tradition because people who believe them or find them plausible transmit them to others. Urban legends and rumors are inherently persuasive. The people who believe the choking doberman legend, however, may not be the same ones who believe the Church's rumor. The more a particular rumor or legend reminds a person of his or her vulnerability, the more apt a person is to accept the item. When a person hears a rumor or legend that doesn't trigger any insecurities for that person, then he or she will focus on the item's weakest features. When the Church's rumor was explained to whites, they were astonished by its existence and by the fact that anyone could be taken in by it. Probably the most frequently asked question was, "how is this mysterious substance supposed to differentiate between white and black eaters?" A close second was, "how could anyone think that the Klan get away with it?" Whites just couldn't understand and almost refused to believe that educated blacks take this rumor seriously. Whites' skepticism reflects the distance between the races in their perception of threatening possibilities inherent in contemporary American society.

Rhetorical theory, with its emphasis on the persuasive strategies embedded in written and oral discourse, promises to be a fruitful approach in discovering the reason for the credibility of any given urban legend or rumor. In 1968 Roger D. Abrahams, relying heavily on the theoretical framework advanced by Kenneth Burke, applied modern rhetorical method to expressive folklore, particularly to the structural and performative differences between riddles and proverbs. For Abrahams the rhetorical method reconciled the sometimes divergent methods of the anthropological and literary schools of folklore. We can see in Abrahams's defense of the rhetorical method just how uniquely suited it is for the study of urban legends and rumors:

> As the rhetorical approach considers the techniques of argument, it assumes that all expression is designed to influence, and that we must simply discover the design. Folklore, being traditional activity, argues traditionally; it uses arguments and persuasive techniques developed in the past to cope with recurrences of social problem situations. . . . Each item of traditional expression articulates conflict in some way; it also provides some manner of temporary resolution. Its very traditional nature promotes community. It can do this mediating because it is a "play" phenomenon, a projection of conflict in an impersonal and harmless milieu.[23]

Like the proverbs and riddles analyzed by Abrahams, rumors are short forms of artful expression. Understanding their power requires an understanding of the environment from which black performers interpret these texts.

What follows is a description of one telling of the rumor provided to me by an informant who recalled quite clearly his first hearing of it. In 1984, when this student was twenty-three years old he had a summer job in a Shawmut Bank, one of the largest banks in the New England area. In this branch there was one other black employee, a "young lady," in the same age group as my informant. The two became friendly. One day when they were discussing the pros and cons of various kinds of fast food, the "young lady" warned my informant about the potential hazards of eating at Church's chicken. She told him that Church's was owned by the Klan and that they were adding an ingredient to the recipe calculated "to make black men sterile and effectively wipe out the continuity of the black community." My informant first claimed that his friend had seen the *60 Minutes* exposé herself. When I pressed him on this, he conceded that perhaps a friend or relative of hers had actually seen the program. Between this day in the summer of 1984, when my informant first heard this item, and February 13, 1986, when I collected it from him, my informant had not eaten at Church's. Although he claims to believe that the rumor is false, he responded to my question as to whether or not he would eat there again by saying in a joking fashion that he didn't see why he should take any chances. He says that he believed it for three reasons: he trusted the young lady who told him the story; he trusted *60 Minutes*; he reasoned that this was why there was an abundance of Church's franchises in black neighborhoods.

Using Burke's terms, the above rhetorical situation can be described in terms of the young lady (agent) in the bank (scene) who recounts (act) the ostensibly true story (agency) in order to communicate with and warn my informant (purpose).[24] The reasons that the informant believed and re-told the story stem from this original situation. First of all, he and the young lady, as young black adults working in a bank, were members of the same folk group by virtue of their race, age, and occupation. The bank environment may well have provided the catalyst for the telling (act) of the story. Most of the other bank employees were white. Located in Boston, the bank reflected the community at large in that the integration that can be observed proves to be quite superficial. Although my informant claims that the black and white employees worked together fairly harmoniously, the two groups did not socialize outside of the bank. My informant felt that he underwent a proving period during which he was observed particularly closely by whites anxious to see if this young black male was smart and honest enough to work in the bank. Black employees commiserated about having to prove their mettle in a way not expected from the whites. Needless to say, blacks were poorly represented at the higher levels of the bank's management. Racial tension was still quite pervasive in this part of the country. My informant, the young lady, and all of the other bank employees and customers no doubt expected periodic racial unrest. My informant and the young lady also knew that there were many whites in Boston who did not want to see them working in a bank or attending the public schools.

Given the complexity of this scene, it is rather easy to understand the young lady's purpose in performing this text. By sharing this rumor about Church's with my informant, she was adding credence to what they both already knew and solidifying the bonds between them. In a sense, the purpose of the Burkean act was to identify themselves as potential victims of racist activity, as well as to identify the potential aggressors. The rumor flourished because it satisfied so many of the uncertainties of the informants' lives. As blacks outnumbered and outranked by whites, much of their life was reduced to an "us versus them" situation. They ventured out into the white world to work and to attend school, not ever really knowing if or when they would be confronted by racism. In contrast to the contexts of their lives, this rumor offered one certainty, one situation they could control. They might not know when a racist comment would come their way, but they did know that they could protect themselves by avoiding this restaurant and encouraging others to do likewise.[25]

The rumor also explained the peculiar presence of a white business in a black neighborhood. Other fast food franchises operated in black neighborhoods, but they were also evident in white ones as well. Here in their own neighborhoods and communities was this strange chain efficiently providing them with the kinds of delicacies that they are accustomed to enjoying in their own kitchens. Such behavior was suspect because it was so uncharacteristic. Most Boston-area informants expressed a great deal of surprise when I told them that in other regions Church's does operate in predominantly white areas as well as inner-city ones. More than one informant then speculated that the contamination was selective, that the chicken was tampered with only in the restaurants in black neighborhoods.

Like other folk groups, blacks maintain symbolic associations about food and its preparation. At first glance, a fast food chain that provides decent familiar foods at a reasonable price is in some sense doing its customers a favor. But by removing the preparation of an ethnic food from the kitchens of the group most strongly identified with it, the Church's corporation has unwittingly intruded itself into sacred territory. In a discussion of ethnic foodways, Abrahams notes that the "question of food choice is entailed in the larger symbolic ordering process by which humans endow the environment with meaning and feeling."[26] Abrahams goes on to discuss the normal process whereby ethnic foods are prepared and consumed by the people who have devised or perpetuated the recipes. So on special occasions or in special settings these food are shared with outsiders anxious to participate in "equal opportunity eating."

The Church's company has reversed this process by pushing the food on those people for whom the food has the strongest symbolic associations. Not all of these associations are necessarily positive. American popular culture has long perpetuated a stereotype in which blacks are portrayed as inordinately fond of foods that can be eaten without utensils—fried chicken and watermelon. Given these circumstances, it is not surprising that blacks want to approach these foods cautiously. Anthropologist Mary Douglas has lucidly pointed out that people with a minority status in their society are likely both to be suspicious of cooked food and to be protective of the body's orifices. "If we treat ritual protection of bodily orifices as a symbol of social preoccupations about exists and entrances," she writes, "the purity of cooked food becomes important. I suggest that food is not likely to be polluting at all unless the external boundaries of the social system are under pressure."[27] Clearly the black community perceives itself as vulnerable to the hostile desires of the majority population. The Church's rumor confirms for its believers the notion that the majority population is anxious to use cooked, polluted food to weaken individual sexual strength and thereby control the minority population as a whole. Once again we can see just how significant the name "Church" is in the perpetuation of this rumor. The threat to the teller's sexuality is coming from a familiar food prepared by an unfamiliar source that employs the name of the very religious structure presumed by the black community to offer the most safety.

This rumor fits Abrahams's discussion of rhetorical theory in every way save one. To be sure, the agents who share the rumor are using techniques "developed in the past to cope with recurrences of social problem situations." The Church's rumor clearly "articulates conflict in some way; it also provides some manner of temporary resolution." Unlike the proverbs and riddles being scrutinized by Abrahams, however, the Church's rumor does not genuinely allow for the "projection of conflict in an impersonal and harmless milieu." After all, a corporation that has endeavored to keep its doors open to minorities is suffering. The Church's corporation is being victimized by an unfortunate set of social circumstances that are for the most part beyond its control.

The Church's item's existence sheds light on several aspects of the rumor-telling process in the black community. The traditional nature of the motifs that comprise the rumor indicate that blacks and whites use a shared set of symbols to articulate their rumors and legends. Its structure reveals that blacks do in fact use rumors to verbalize and share their unresolved doubts and fears. When these doubts and fears reflect black perceptions of white racial animosity, blacks are unlikely to relate these rumors to whites. Travelling with the more mobile members of the black community such as college students, members of church groups, or those who visit the birthplaces from where they have migrated, the rumors proceed from one black enclave to another, across the country, with only a negligible number of whites privy to them. The rumors become a part of a larger corpus of information shared by blacks and used to shape their perception of their place in contemporary America.

The perpetuation of this rumor illustrates that we have a long way to go in race relations. Blacks have no trouble accepting the idea that a scandal of such devastating magnitude could be scrutinized on national television without any adverse effect on the culprits. This fact is not a demonstration of any particular gullibility, but rather an unfortunate reminder of how vulnerable blacks perceive themselves to be in American society.

Notes

1. Certainly it could be argued that racist jokes offer the clearest insights into the nature of bigotry, but the overt content of these jokes excludes certain kinds of conclusions. Such jokes don't tell us very much about the individuals who, though unwilling to tell an offensive joke, still may harbor ambivalent sentiments about members of another race. To understand these individuals we need access to those genres of folklore that at least superficially reflect the performer's notion of the "truth."

2. For a detailed discussion of the distinctions between legend and rumor, see Patrick B. Mullen, "Modern Legend and Rumor Theory," *Journal of the Folklore Institute* 9 (1982): 96.

3. Numerous contemporary urban legends are described in the Brunvand trilogy: Jan Harold Brunvand, *The Vanishing Hitchhiker* (New York, 1981); *The Choking Doberman* (New York, 1984); and *The Mexican Pet* (New York, 1986).

4. Frederick Koenig, *Rumor in the Marketplace: The Social Psychology of Commercial Hearsay* (Dover, DE, 1985), 84, 94.

5. Ibid., 84.

6. Gary Alan Fine, "The Kentucky Fried Rat: Legends and Modern Society," *Journal of the Folklore Institute* 17 (1980): 232–33.

7. Ibid., 233.

8. Koenig, 39.

9. Gladys-Marie Fry, *Night Riders in Black Folk History* (Knoxville, TN, 1975), 159.

10. Personal conversation with Gladys-Marie Fry, February 27, 1986.

11. Gary Alan Fine, "The Goliath Effect: Corporate Dominance and Mercantile Legends," *Journal of American Folklore* 98 (1985): 63–84.

12. "Is Frank Perdue Chicken?," *Forbes* 5, November 1984, 224.

13. "Church's: A fast-food recipe is light on marketing," *Business Week,* 20 February 1978, 110–112.

14. "Church's Fried Chicken: Cutting Loose From Its Penny-Pinching Past," *Business Week,* 27 February 1984, 72.

15. Personal communication with J. David Bamberger, August 8, 1986.

16. Ibid.

17. Ibid.

18. For an extended discussion of this motif see Florence H. Ridley, "A Tale Too Often Told," *Western Folklore* 26 (1967): 152–6 Robert Schwartz, "'Rappaccini's Daughter' and 'Sir Hugh, or, The Jew's Daughter,'" *Western Folklore* 45 (1986): 21–33; and Barre Toelken, *The Dynamics of Folklore* (Boston, 1979), 176–79.

19. Brunvand, *The Choking Doberman,* 12.

20. George W. Rich and David F. Jacobs, "Saltpeter: A Folkloric Adjustment to Acculturation Stress," *Western Folklore* 32 (1973): 164–79.

21. James H. Jones, *Bad Blood: The Tuskegee Syphilis Experiment—a Tragedy of Race and Medicine* (New York, 1981).

22. Brunvand, *The Choking Doberman,* 52.

23. Roger D. Abrahams, "Introductory Remarks to a Rhetorical Theory of Folklore," *Journal of American Folklore* 81 (1968): 146, 148.

24. Kenneth Burke, *A Grammar of Motives and A Rhetoric of Motives* (Cleveland, 1962), xvii.

25. The most recent comprehensive study of Boston racial conflict is Phillip L. Clay, ed., "The Emerging Black Community of Boston," A Report of the Institute for the Study of Black Culture, October 1985.

26. Roger D. Abrahams, "Equal Opportunity Eating: A Structural Excursus on Things of the Mouth," *Ethnic and Regional Foodways in the United States: The Performance of Group Identity,* ed. Linda Keller Brown and Kay Mussell (Knoxville, 1984), 24.

27. Mary Douglas, *Purity and Danger: An Analysis of the Concepts of Pollution and Taboo* (London, 1985), 126.

CHAPTER 30

MOTHER CORN AND THE DIXIE PIG: NATIVE FOOD IN THE NATIVE SOUTH

Rayna Green

Native food is in the news. Every day. All over the country, except in the South, foodies, farmers, chefs, environmentalists, and food writers are excited about Native food and foodways. That excitement usually comes from a "discovery" (or rediscovery) of the many virtues of old "slow" foods in the now hip vernacular—local, fresh, and seasonal foods that are good for you, good for the land, and good for the small food producer. Often, these rediscovered foods come from "Native" varieties that seed savers, naturalists, nutritionists, and Indians have propped up, from animals that regulators, commercial producers, and advocates have brought back from the brink of extinction, and from habitats redeemed from under middens of waste and neglect.[1]

Some Native communities, in revitalizing their own cultural histories and economies, have begun again to raise, catch, and market crops and critters long associated with them, but just as long ago replaced. Hopis and other Pueblos farm and market native varieties of corn, beans, and other vegetables to provide a better diet and income for their people, while Ojibwas do the same with wild rice in the Great Lakes. In the Plains, where once the death of bison was synonymous with the defeat and death of Indians themselves, buffalo herds now thrive on tribal and public lands. Northwest Coastal people fish for salmon, pack and ship it to an audience eager for it, and serve it at salmon feasts, some for the communities, some for the income generated by cultural tourism.

In spite of the good press, Native food and foodways are, as ever, subject to massive assaults on their maintenance and survival. What hunters, hat makers, the cavalry, miners, and trains didn't deplete or destroy in the eighteenth and nineteenth centuries, industrial and domestic polluters, ranchers, big farmers, dams, cities, and roads rolled over in the twentieth century. Modern tribal efforts at resource revitalization still meet resistance because they interfere—as Indians always have—with large non-Indian economic and cultural interests. Native people and park rangers in the Plains fight ranchers over the renewed presence of brucellosis-carrying buffalo in proximity to the huge cattle herds that graze, subsidized by federal money, on public lands. Northwest Coastal people struggle against international agency regulators, Japanese fish factories, and sport fishers for the right to catch the fish emblematic of their survival as a people. Always, Native Alaskans battle with the state and federal governments and with animal rights activists to continue their traditional subsistence diet, and thus maintain cultural skills and legal rights. They all know, out there in Indian Country, that the loss of traditional diet and the cultural skills needed to maintain it has killed more Indians than Andy Jackson. And they all know that the food fights, like the struggles to restore language and ceremony, are modern fights for survival. Where they are known to be central to

Rayna Green, 'Mother Corn and the Dixie Pig: Native Food in the Native South', *Southern Cultures* 14 (4) (2008), 114–126.

Copyright © 2008 by the Center for Study of the American South. Used by permission of the University of North Carolina Press. www.uncpress.unc.edu.

the economies and cultural histories of the entire region, Native food and the politics that govern Native resources are at the top of regional discussion.

Native food and foodways in the South, however, neither attract the rabid enthusiasms nor wild resistances of other parts of the country. Four hundred years ago, the settler-saving "gifts" of Indian food and food production technologies, along with the salvation of an English adventurer by the Indian chief's beautiful daughter, anchored colonial mythology; three hundred years ago Indian corn and tobacco centered the new growth economy; two hundred years ago Indian food resources still constituted, in essence, the base diet of the region. Yet this history seems nearly irrelevant today—as do Indians themselves—to popular conceptions of the South.

It was not always thus. Native food was once the only food story. Early travelers and colonists of the Americas spoke at length of the abundance and richness of the natural environment, the good that Indians made of it, and the absolute dependence of the would-be colonists upon Indian mastery of that environment. Archaeologists of Jamestown and other southern sites echo and reinforce these early accounts, confirming that Natives in pre-colonial Virginia and North Carolina, the Upland South, Coastal Mississippi, Florida, and Alabama ate well and often from a huge and diverse larder.[2] In most instances, they cultivated appropriately and well, renewing their resources by methods of complementary planting, crop rotation, nutritional enhancement, and resource-restorative rules for the gathering of plants and hunting of animals. Meat, fish, shellfish, vegetables, fruits, and nuts made for a better, richer, more abundant, and more nutritious diet than available to most of the Anglo-Europeans that journeyed to the South and a more dependable, consistent, diverse diet than most Indians elsewhere (except those in the Southwest and Pacific Northwest).[3]

From their indigenous relatives in Mexico, Southeastern (and Southwestern) Indians had centuries ago learned the knowledge and skills associated with cultivating corn, which they shared with receptive settlers.[4] Essential Native practices included combining corn and beans to create protein and amino acid-rich meals; consuming hominy, cornbreads, soups, drinks, and mushes (grits, tamales) made from limed corn (*nixtamalization*); using nitrogen-enriching leguminous ash in various corn dishes; interplanting corn with nitrogen-replacing or nitrogen-fixing varieties (e.g., legumes); and rotating nutritionally exhausted croplands with alternate crops.[5] It didn't take the Spanish very long at all, merely twenty years into their sixteenth-century invasions, to substitute many of their own imports for Native food resources. But well into the seventeenth century—in the remainder of the British-occupied Southeast—Native diet and Native knowledge formed the core of the new southern foodways even as the British process for amending and replacing that diet, Native knowledge and skills, and Indians themselves escalated. It took nearly a hundred years for the agricultural- and hunting-challenged British, in particular (at least the classes of Brits who first came to the Southeast), to begin amending the Native larder and food technologies for their own foods and technologies from home. It took two centuries more of dismantling Indian food technologies and land management skills to understand the errors of doing so, with once good agricultural lands farmed out and eroded by 1900, the population plagued by niacin deficiency, and pellagra reaching epidemic proportions.[6]

By the eighteenth century, when most colonists had succeeded in breaking the exclusive hold that the Native diet had on their survival, the "new" foods from Europe (Spain, France, the British Isles), Africa, and the Caribbean merged with native staples to create the complex mélange that is today's southern cuisine. These changes affected Indian and non-Indian alike. From Indians, the new southerners had developed the taste for and habit of eating more vegetables, particularly greens (fresh and cooked), than did other Americans. These native vegetables, both gathered and cultivated, joined Spanish-imported varieties like melons, peaches, and peppers. African food tastes and habits reinforced the Indian vegetable/greens complex and brought in new and healthful crops like sesame and okra, and legumes like black-eyed peas and peanuts thrived in the Lowland and southeastern climate.[7] From Africans as well, many acquired the taste for hot peppers and spices and for the technique of frying. Later, all would adopt dairy products—as they were able to raise the dairy cattle, wheat flour, and sugar when they could afford them—and more liquor when they could make it. Pigs, introduced in the sixteenth century, rooted their way into Indian communities in the late eighteenth century. Women, the primary farmers of the southern Indian world, first resisted the feral beasts that ravaged their fields and crops, but they eventually accepted the domesticated (and wild) food source that meant meat on the Indian table.[8] And Indians, like other southerners, learned to use pigs not only as their main meat source but as sources of cooking grease, side meat, and flavoring. They "nativized" the once alien animal, just as the newcomers once normalized and accepted the American animals and plants new to them, and incorporated pig into dishes featuring Mother Corn alone. These foods remain some of those most beloved by southern Indians.

Indian Removal in the 1830s was supposed to settle the resource fights begun in the seventeenth century. Cherokees, Choctaws, Creeks, and Chickasaws stood in the way of land grabbers, gold seekers, and farmer/landowners with cash crops based in a slave economy. The forced land cessions accompanying Indian Removal did indeed take most of the prime farm, hunting, and fishing lands held by Indians in the South, leaving behind many small communities with little but the weakened cultural skills essential to their survival. Those removed retained something of the skills and knowledge regarding the basic foods and foodways, which they tried, only partially successfully, to restore in Oklahoma. Indian losses would be the miner's canary, as they always were, for the environmental and economic disasters that were yet to unhinge large parts of the agrarian South.

The small group of Choctaws, once stellar farmers, who managed to stay in Mississippi were eventually reduced to the poorest of sharecroppers by the turn of the twentieth century. Their hunter-fisher-gatherer Houma relatives, in the Louisiana bayous since the late seventeenth century, would become French-speaking, forced to take protective cover in the ways and manners of their neighbors. They and the Seminoles and Miccosukees who had fled to Florida before Removal had become masters of their environments, persisting in food sourcing from small farms and watery habitats into the twenty-first century. But Houmas, unlike the Seminoles who resisted assimilation in any visible way, would remain unrecognized and relatively obscured as Indians to the world around them. Cherokees who avoided Removal in North Carolina remained in the hills, as poor and isolated as their Appalachian neighbors but able to continue a reasonably successful survival exploitation of the environment left to them. The menu from a 1949 feast given for anthropologists suggests not only how deeply Cherokee foodways had burrowed into the now all-but-Native diet of the Upland South, but how natural, how unexotic, how *southern* that diet was.

Other remaining Indians in the South—in South Carolina, Virginia, and North Carolina, in particular—faced a fate different from their removed relatives. Fragmented into small isolated communities, impoverished, collectively landless for the most part, with no federal treaties and a continuing lack of federal recognition, they most often "disappeared" as Indians. They kept what they could of the old ways and blended through intermarriage and interaction, as they always had done, with white and black folks, with Christians, with English-speakers. They ate more and more like the people with whom they lived, just as their neighbors had once learned to eat like them. But they remained at the edges of that society, further and further segregated into smaller units, with their identity as Indians virtually erased after the Civil War, the end of slavery, and Reconstruction by the South's primal obsession with black and white. Indian extinction had not succeeded; marginalization had.

Virginia's Indians, for example, so essential to the founding identity of the place, and so embedded in its historical memory, found themselves without any viable social niche. In 1924, via the Racial Integrity Act, they found themselves in a state that declared most Indians non-existent or illegal entities. This declaration of their legal non-existence drove Virginia Indians to rise up and insist on repeal of the invidious law that separated them from their historic identity. One of the ways in which they did that was to reenact the historic relationship, forged in Native food, between them and the colonists. In the Colonial era, "Powhatans" (a collective term for all Virginia Indians of the day) had delivered tribute deer to the governor of Virginia every year in lieu of taxes on lands held by Indians. Continuing this practice into the late twentieth century reinforced the survival and continuity of Virginia's Indians, several groups of which eventually obtained state recognition. Relatively recently, that recognition resulted in the restoration of their right to use the lands' more abundant larder so praised by early colonists for more than three hundred and fifty of the last four hundred years. By 2005, Pamunkeys and Mattaponi could again hunt deer and fish for shad off their state reservations and collect oysters from the Bay without a state license. Still, the Mattaponi in Virginia currently are trying to stop a proposed reservoir that would divert water from the Mattaponi River, endangering their shad fisheries and the shreds of a traditional life they have remaining. Still, much-loved Virginia spring shad feasts, like those offered the colonists four hundred years ago by Virginia's Indians, have come to be reserved for Virginia political events that exclude Indians (and women). In many ways, the complex relationship of Virginia's citizens to Indians, as expressed through the acceptance and rejection of Native food and foodways—as well as Virginia natives' persistence toward their food and food-ways—may act as a paradigm for the southern Indian story.

A few Native dishes never passed into the mainstream southern culinary repertoire and remain distinctly and exclusively Indian, very much a part of native identity, cherished and propped up in a public way, served to strangers and friends and certainly in revitalized Green Corn or stomp dance communal dinners. Bean bread and *so-chan* among the North Carolina Cherokees are dishes likely not found elsewhere in Appalachia. Choctaws and Chickasaws in Oklahoma eat *banaha,* a tamale-like corn mush with field peas and/or pea shell ash, and hominy in every form it comes in, including *tamfula* (often pronounced "tomfuller"), a hominy and hickory nut soup/cream unlikely to be on a restaurant menu even in Oklahoma. *Sofkee,* a soup or drink of soured cornmeal, links Seminoles and Miccosukees in Florida to Seminoles, Yuchis, and Creeks in Oklahoma and is never found outside Indian communities.[9] Many of these precious foods listed above may indeed have been the staples of the long-ago diet. Others, like the various corn-and-pig dishes or berry dumplings (often "cobblers" or "pies") that have characterized Indian cooking since the late eighteenth century, represent the beginnings of dietary change long ago, yet became enshrined within their communities as uniquely Cherokee, uniquely Choctaw, uniquely Indian. Today these foods and foodways belong to the communities that cook and serve them, in spite of the profound changes they represented when first introduced. Some foods maintain the ancient Indian relationships with and responsibilities to plants and animals, and most native communities worry about passing on their skills and tastes, just as they worry about the death of language. Even when they can get canned hominy, frozen corn, bottled grape juice, and four different kinds of greens at the grocery store, they still organize cultural camps and plant native gardens where younger Indians can learn traditions that now represent physical and cultural survival.

In the late 1970s, America began to look with favor on marginalized cuisines. Ethnic pride and cultural rights movements of the 1960s demanded acknowledgment for the cultural contributions of those once repressed. The long tradition of African American foodways became a distinctive and redemptive badge of cultural pride, and the new term "Soul Food" became synonymous with both traditional African American cuisine and the best of "southern cooking." Thus, Soul Food, Cajun food, so-called "White Trash" cooking, and good old country cooking started to have their day alongside Plantation (Antebellum) food, French/ Creole, and Low Country haute cuisine. The new southern food historians, a multivocal collection of people of good faith, mind, and heart, respectfully acknowledge the many peoples and ethnicities that have created and amended the delightful fusion that is southern cuisine. But discussions based solely on black and white relationships still dominate, and roiling underneath the civilities of new acknowledgments remains the intensely southern spat over which group really gave the most to this beloved food, planting old and ever volatile claims to the kingdom right in the middle of a plate of barbecue.

No Indian claims to a rightful place within southern foodways surfaced in these tangles, and no one has made any claims on Indians' behalf. Indians have not established restaurants that serve up ethnic pride along with the foods that underpin the southern diet; no PR campaign, protest, or demand for respect has accompanied the recent elevation of grits and greens to nearly sanctified status in New South cuisine. Some might say southern Indians have been too busy putting their cultural and physical survival, their very existence, on the agenda to pursue a more substantive acknowledgment of their historic contributions. But could the focus on Native food provide more than simply some suggestions for what historical curiosities might be served to interested patrons at the casino restaurant or for what might amount to just a little more political correctness regarding Native people by the next cookbook writer? Just what might a little attention to Native food history in the South be worth and to whom might that worth be manifest?

It's true that southern Indians and their foods do not have the competitive edge granted Indians in the West with their national attachments to the charismatic megafauna—buffalo, whales, seals—so emblematic of Native place and history in the West and Far North. But a different kind of repatriation might do us all good, and we could start by bringing back those native varieties that appear lost, to say nothing of showing interest in the reasons that certain foods were *not* lost to Native communities. The new small farms and farmer's markets, the new chefs that care so deeply about the restoration of southern food might want join forces with the oldest farmers to their mutual benefit. We could start in Mississippi where, just last year, a Choctaw woman sold Mason jars filled with a kind of shoepeg hominy she had raised and processed without a subsidy. Getting her grits on the menu somewhere would do more than simply lend chic credibility to this revitalized southern cult food. We might all find ways to support and extend the kinds of *so-chan* and ramp gardens that the Eastern Band of Cherokees have started in North Carolina. The story (and the action that needs to follow a good story) is missing in the South, where Native food might bring good news. And with that news could come a cultural construct that might be surprisingly useful—a region of the mind called "Native South"—a good name, perhaps, for the chain of restaurants that could appear in Indian casinos. The food served there would be shockingly familiar, albeit a tad underseasoned, to all good southerners, and once again Indians will welcome everyone to eat. Come on in where you see the neon cornstalk flashing over the smiling Dixie pig.

Notes

1. For the best account of the need for study and restoration of Native habitats, plants, and animals and Euro-American/African American heritage plants and animals, as well as the agricultural and animal management technologies necessary for restoration, see Gary Nabhan, ed., *Renewing America's Food Traditions: Saving and Savoring the Continent's Most Endangered Foods* (White River Junction, VT: Chelsea Green Publishing Company, 2008). This volume includes a redlist of endangered foods, as well as descriptions of foods thus far restored. See also Gary Paul Nabhan, *Enduring Seeds: Native American Agriculture and Wild Plant Conservation* (Berkeley, CA: North Point Press, 1989). For generalist accounts of Native food and foodways, see Rayna Green, "Native American Food," in *Smithsonian Folklife Cookbook,* ed. Katherine and Thomas Kirlin (Washington, D. C.: Smithsonian Institution Press, 1991) and Linda Murray Berzok, *American Indian Food* (Westport, CT: Greenwood Press, 2005). Quite a number of glossy Native cookbooks, good on highly modernized Indian recipes, but generally thin on cultural history, have appeared in the last ten years. These are mostly devoted to the popular modern Southwestern style, but may include a few "classics" from the Native Northwest and Northeast. Rare is the mention of Native food in the South. For a modern Indian cookbook that does contain a section on Southeastern foods, see Beverley Cox and Martin Jacobs, *Spirit of the Harvest: North American Indian Cooking* (New York: Stewart, Tabori and

Chang, 1991). Some small cookbooks—issued within and often by Indian communities and cooks—document Native cooking in the "old days" of the nineteenth century and include some mid–twentieth century variations on older foodways. These do not, in general, offer much about the historical contexts of and changes in these foods and food technologies, though the recipes themselves note changes in ingredients and cooking technologies. Most include only Cherokee and Choctaw recipes, with occasional mentions of Seminole and Creek foods; see Frances Gwaltney, compiler, *Corn Recipes From the Indians,* intro. Mary Frances Chiltoskey (Cherokee, N.C.: Cherokee Publications, 1988 and 1991); Frances Lambet Whisler, *Indian Cookin'* (Nowega Press, 1973); Mary Ulmer and Samuel E. Beck, *Cherokee Cooklore: Preparing Cherokee Foods,* published by Mary and Goingback Chiltoskey, in cooperation with Stephens Press, Inc. (Cherokee, N.C.: Museum of the Cherokee Indian, 1951), which contains an interview and demonstration of traditional foodways with Aggie Lossiah and others, a reprint of William Bartram's 1789 account of the foods of Cherokee and Creek Indians, and a newspaper account and menu of a 1949 feast given by North Carolina Cherokees for the N.C. Anthropological Society. Some Oklahoma Indian publications from the 1930s–1970s also contain recipes and information about southern Indian foodways; see Eula Doonkeen, ed., *Indian Cookbook* (Oklahoma City, OK: Alco Printing Co., 1975); Nettie Wheeler, *Indian Recipes From Cherokee Indians of Eastern Oklahoma* (Hoffman Printing Co., *n.d.*); and for a rare (not Cherokee, Choctaw, etc.) commentary on foodways in a contemporary southern Indian group, see Karen I. Blu, "Lumbee," in *Handbook of North American Indians* 14 (Washington, D.C.: Smithsonian Institution Press, 2004), 314.

2. William Bartram, *Travels Through North & South Carolina, Georgia, East & West Florida, the Cherokee Country, the Extensive Territories of the Muscogulges, or Creek Confederacy, and the Country of the Chactaws; Containing An Account of the Soil and Natural Productions of Those Regions, Together with Observations on the Manners of the Indians* (James & Johnson 1791; repr., Charlottesville: University of Virginia Press, 1980); Thomas Hariot, trans. Richard Hakluyt, illust. John White; *A Briefe and True Report of the New Found Land of Virginia, Part 1* (Theodore deBry, America 1588, 1590; J. Sabin & Sons, 1871); Samuel Cole Williams, ed., *Adair's History of the American Indians* (1775; repr., Promontory Press, 1930); David Stick, ed., *Indian Food and Cooking in Coastal North Carolina 400 Years ago,* expanded by Lebame Houston and Wynne Dough (Harpers Ferry, WV: National Park Service, *n.d.*); Jane Buikstra, "The Lower Illinois River Region: A Prehistoric Context for the Study of Ancient Diet and Health," in *Paleopathology at the Origins of Agriculture,* ed. Mark Nathan Cohen and George Armelagos (Burlington, MA: Academic Press, 1984).

3. Some, like the Chickasaws, who were frequently in conflict with the new settlers, whose lands and stability were rarely threatened, and who were not as committed to agriculture as their neighbors, were not always so successful at feeding themselves. Their Choctaw neighbors, who were prolific farmers, often shared or traded enough with them to fill the gaps.

4. For a readable general history of corn, including information about the Native science of growing and preparing corn and the demise of serious corn agriculture in the South, see Betty Fussell, *The Story of Corn: The Myths and History, the Culture and Agriculture, the Art and Science of America's Quintessential Crop* (New York: Knopf 1994). See also Muriel H. Wright, "American Indian Corn Dishes," *Chronicles of Oklahoma* 36, no. 2 (1958): 155–66.

5. Contemporary commentators, Indian and non-Indian, often use the term "The Three Sisters" in referring to the common Native method of interplanting corn, beans, and squash. While this popularized poetic reference comes from and is applicable to actual Iroquoian usage, no other Indian group ever referred to these foods or to interplanting in this manner.

6. Pellagra is a disease of malnutrition and poverty, long associated with folks who were dependent on a nutritionally inadequate diet of corn and little else. Research also suggests that pellagra was further exacerbated, or rather, the epidemic triggered, by turn-of-the-century changes in milling corn that left corn degerminated. See A. J. Bollet, "Politics and Pellagra: the epidemic of pellagra in the U.S. in the early twentieth century," *Yale Journal of Biological Medicine* (May/June 1992): 211–21. Scientists continue to offer even more support for the efficacy of Native agricultural and food preparation technologies and for the restoration of technologies that produce the same conditions in food products, e.g., whole grains in the instance of corn.

7. Peanuts came to the Americas via the slave trade. From the Incas (Peru), the Spanish brought peanuts to Africa, where they were grown to support the slave trade, eventually making their way to the Americas on slave ships. Corn had a similar role in the slave trade in Africa, where, like peanuts, it was introduced from outside and formed an easily and cheaply grown and stored commodity for the feeding of slaves on their journey to enslavement, where they would, in turn, grow corn and peanuts for their masters in the New World.

8. Theda Perdue, *Cherokee Women: Gender and Culture Change, 1700–1835* (Lincoln: University of Nebraska Press, 1998); Wilma A. Dunaway, "Rethinking Cherokee Acculturation: Women's Resistance to Agrarian Capitalism and Cultural Change, 1800–1838," *American Indian Culture and Research Journal* 21, no. 1 (1997): 128–149; Margaret C. Scarry, "Native American 'Garden Agriculture' in Southeastern North America," *World Archaeology* 27, no. 2 (June 2005): 259–274; Thomas M. Hatley, "Cherokee Women Farmers Hold Their Ground," in Robert Mitchell, ed., *Appalachian Frontier Settlement, Society, and Development in the Preindustrial Era* (Lexington: University Press of Kentucky, 1991), 37–51; Robert Newman, "The Acceptance of European Domestic Animals by the Eighteenth Century Cherokee," *Tennessee Anthropologist* 4, no. 1 (Spring 1979): 102–105. To further explore gender role changes and cultural and environmental shift and their connections to foodways and food technologies in Cherokee history, see Sarah H. Hill, *Weaving New Worlds: Southeastern Cherokee Women and Their Basketry* (Chapel Hill: University of North Carolina Press, 1996).

9. Regarding Choctaw/Chickasaw *tamfula,* some settlers ate these dishes early on in their settlements, but most certainly gave them up after the Indians who shared them were removed from their former co-residence with settlers. Joseph Dabney recounts in *Smokehouse Ham* (Nashville: Cumberland House Publishing, 1998) that the early southern Appalachian settlers liked the *sofkee* that the Creek Indians (and possibly Chickasaws) made, though they called it "Tom Fuller," and the author was never able to learn why.

PART V
FOOD IN PUBLIC AND APPLIED FOLKLORE

248
PUBLIC POLICE AND APPLIED FOLKLORE

INTRODUCTION TO PART FIVE

In the 1970s and 1980s, applied and public folklore developed within folklore studies in order to research and develop strategies and theories for using folklore materials and scholarship outside of academia. Although today applied folklore is usually included within public folklore, the two are not always in agreement over goals and practices. Also, each has been and can be applied to food studies differently.

Public folklore

The field of public folklore focuses on the documentation, uses, and presentations of the materials of folklore. In their 1992 edited volume, *Public Folklore*, folklorists Robert Baron and Nicholas Spitzer offer the following definition:

> Public folklore is the representation and application of folk traditions in new contours and contexts within and beyond the communities in which they originated, often through the collaborative efforts of tradition bearers and folklorists or other cultural specialists. (1992:1)

Throughout the history of the discipline, many folklorists, some university trained, others not, have worked in the "public sector," developing ways to preserve and present folk cultures and traditions. Documentation and artifacts were stored in archives, libraries, and museums where scholars could then study them. Historically, individuals influenced by the romantic nationalist movement also used these materials to forge or invent new works of art, music, dance, customs, and other products in order to construct a sense of cultural heritage and identity based on the past.

While such "invented traditions" have been effective in bringing people together and giving them a sense of identity and heritage, they have been used, in some cases, by political movements promoting cultural purity and superiority, with devastating results. Such uses of folklore materials made it suspect, interestingly by both governments and scholars, depending on the era and place.[1] Referred to as "folklorismo," such displays are common throughout the world and oftentimes serve as marketing tools for tourism, economic development, trade, and support for specific political parties. Also, stereotypic folkloric images and materials were, and are, frequently used in literature, music, dance, and visual arts to tap into people's sense of identity, community, and heritage and to evoke memories and emotions. Marketing, branding, politics, education, health, and public policy oftentimes do the same in order to manipulate people's spending, voting, and life practices, frequently commercializing if not trivializing and trinketizing those folk traditions. This "fakelore," as folklorist Richard Dorson (1950)[2] termed these products, undermined public recognition of the contemporary nature of folklore.

On the other hand, citizens and groups oftentimes used folk traditions to rally support for challenging those in power or the dominant paradigm of the times. Folk music in the United States played such a role first in the 1930s with Woody Guthrie who wrote "this machine kills fascists" on his guitar case and then in the 1950s McCarthy era, when the Weavers, Pete Seeger, and other "folk" singers were accused of communist sympathies. Even if not openly antiestablishment, folklore materials were oftentimes used to promote the "voice of the people" and to gain economic and political power for the disenfranchised individuals and groups.[3] Some proponents also see folklore materials as having a democratizing effect as well as offering the potential for intercultural and cross-cultural understanding and respect.[4]

In the meantime, folklore in the academy in the 1950s (as well as into the present) was fighting its own battles for recognition as a serious discipline, and some folklorists felt that associations with "fringe elements" did not help. Nor did the popular assumptions that folklore consisted of out-dated and backward superstitions and simplistic arts and crafts. The seeming triviality of folklore and folklife clouded the acceptance of it as a subject for study (and still does!). Furthermore, the shift to applying scientific methods to cultural and social phenomena that began occurring in the late 1800s created divisions between arts, sciences, and the humanities, as well as between "pure" and applied research. Folklore, as a discipline, did not easily fit into these categories, and had to fight for respect and recognition. Although it had long been recognized in Europe under the name ethnology, and the American Folklore Society was established in 1888 by highly respected scholars, it has always held a tenuous place within academia. This background of dismissal by other scholars meant that folklorists in the academy felt they needed to be vigilant against any lack of scholarship or misuse. (Baron and Spitzer 1992)

Public folklore arose out of this contentious atmosphere, but today it is recognized as an academic discipline as well as a career track, and many folklorists work in both. Programs training students in public folklore offer grounding in folklore theory and methods as well as in ways of addressing practical and ethical concerns surrounding the representation of folklore and applications of folklore scholarship. Public folklore has also contributed to contemporary debates specifically over the "false dichotomy" between pure and applied scholarship, the nature of tradition, authenticity, and intellectual property ownership and rights, along with issues and impacts of representing and displaying people's cultural forms and traditions.[5] Today, public folklore is distinguished from academic folklore in that the audiences being addressed and the products resulting from research differ, but the field is accepted as contributing to folklore scholarship, grounding, theory in the actual lives of people and traditions. Public folklore has also contributed by developing venues for the presentation and representation of folklore, including folklife festivals, museums (both permanent and traveling exhibits), media productions (documentary films, recordings, podcasts, and websites), educational programming in school and community settings, and arts administration and cultural organizations. Many regions in the United States (and other nations) now have folklore centers, archives, and programs supporting and promoting traditional cultural forms and groups.[6]

Foodways traditions are frequently included in public folklore work and are oftentimes used to present to public audiences a group's history and culture as well as an individual's perspectives and experiences. They do so through museums,[7] festivals,[8] educational settings,[9] documentaries (videos, podcasts),[10] popular publications, websites,[11] and even newer social media (personal websites, blogs).

Applied folklore

Although now frequently included within Public Folklore, applied folklore was defined in 1991 "as the utilization of the theoretical concepts, factual knowledge, and research methodologies of folklorists in activities or programs meant to ameliorate contemporary social, economic and technological problems" (Jones 1994: 11). Michael Owen Jones, a leader in the field, pointed out that the stated purpose was problematic since some folklorists felt that "social reform" was not their job. The ultimate use of folklore scholarship has continued to be debated into the present, with public folklorists emphasizing that there should be a strong sense of ethical responsibility for the materials of folklore and the people they belong to, along with concerns that folklore be used neither to manipulate others nor to enable those in power to unfairly or unjustly wield more power.[12]

Jones's edited volume, *Putting Folklore to Use*, suggests applications for folkloristics to a variety of professions and practical issues, and some of these, such as medicine, education, museums, environmental planning, tourism, art therapy, and economic development, have been developed further by folklorists (1994). As academic institutions in the United States lose funding and shift their emphasis from well-rounded education to job training, there seem to be fewer positions for folklorists, and many teach in other departments with folklore only a component of some of their courses. Many folklorists find themselves, however, ideally suited for work in other areas of academia (service-learning; multicultural and diversity initiatives; events programming; and others) as well as outside the university in a variety of occupations. Any field or career that involves human beings engaging with one another, with their cultures, histories, and places can use the perspectives and skills developed in folklore studies.

Folklore scholarship, unfortunately, has rarely been applied directly to contemporary food systems and eating habits, but it has much to offer, both by shedding light on the issues and in offering perspectives for developing solutions. Since folklore enables us to better understand the meanings foodways practices hold for individuals and groups and how those meanings emerge, it offers insights into how and why those practices are significant to them. Such understanding then contributes to recognizing the role of tradition and culture in issues surrounding health and nutrition, environmental sustainability and conservation, economic and gender equity, tourism, cultural heritage, intellectual property rights, and cross-cultural communication and conflict, as well as movements directly related to changing the contemporary industrial food system.[13] Activist groups, such as the international Slow Food organization, the current community garden and farmers market trend in the United States, and the global "eating local" movement are closely aligned with the folklore concepts of face-to-face communication, small reference groups which can develop into communities, individual agency, the artistry of food, the ritualistic power of food, and the meaningfulness of everyday foodways activities. By taking a holistic view of foodways as a system of connectedness, folklore perspectives can be used to understand why and how these groups are effective and what their larger impacts might be.

Creative expressions by folklorists

While many individuals have used folklore materials in fashioning their own artistic expressions, folklorists also draw from folklore theories and methodologies in creative explorations and productions. Folklorists apply these perspectives to art, music, and, particularly, literature, since many of them are also trained and teach in literature departments.[14] Such works raise questions about the ownership of folklore materials and the politics of representation, so folklorists take care in presenting themselves and their work accurately and honestly and with appropriate references to their sources. They also address the ethical and economic considerations of using materials that come from another individual or group, a consideration sometimes addressed by collaboration and sharing profits with "community scholars."

There are a small number of individuals who write about food for popular audiences, work in the food industry, or in the culinary arts, who draw upon folkloristic perspectives.[15] Since foodways traditions and practices tend to be considered "intangible heritage" whose ownership cannot be claimed, using the recipes, the cooking methods, or the ingredients learned through fieldwork is generally not an issue for individual creativity among folklorists.

Conclusion

Public folklore encourages us to think about how best to represent foodways in all of its complexity and totality. It also suggests ways in which folkloristic perspectives are useful and effective in viewing the world of food outside of academia. In doing so, it offers a framework for an activism based on an understanding of the complexity of individual choices within larger systems.[16]

Articles in *Reader*

The articles included in this section give examples of public and applied folklore, illustrating ways in which folklore concepts and methodologies can be used outside of academia. One of the key characteristics of public folklore products is the intended audience for whom they are addressed—usually the general public rather than a defined field of scholars. This usually means that they present content and ways of interpreting that content, but do not explicitly tackle theoretical issues raised by other scholars, as expected in academic publications. This does not mean that they lack scholarly rigor. Theory is oftentimes implied, rather than stated, and it serves as the foundation for what is presented.

The first article, "Laying a Place at the Table: Creating a Public Foodways Model from Scratch," by Millie Rahn, gives an overview of her extensive work with foodways in public folklore. She describes how such work frequently involves documentation of a community's foodways tradition, then developing public programs and educational materials around that documentation. Writing in first person, she explains here some of the steps and thought processes she goes through in developing a public program around food, along with the various issues that arise. The excerpt of her article includes descriptions of two projects she has conducted: a foodways exhibit and festival programs in the city of Lowell, Massachusetts; and a tourism plan around foodways in a coastal county in Maine. These examples demonstrate the potential uses and impacts of public folklore as well as effectiveness of developing programs around foodways. Rahn also points out that she uses her training as a folklorist to be an advocate for the people she has documented and to help them find a place in economic development and the tourism industry.

Rachelle H. (Riki) Saltzman has also worked extensively in public folklore. "Pork, Place, and Praxis: Foodways in Iowa" reflects her time as Folklife Coordinator of the Iowa Arts Council and her collaborations with the Aldo Leopold Center to research and present issues surrounding the role of food in tourism, economic development, and "branding" of a place. Using the concept of "place-based foods," (first coined by Rich Pirog, then of the Leopold Center, in 2004) she argues that there are food traditions in Iowa that distinctively represent the state, comparable to European designations of geographic origin. The place-association of those foods can be an effective component for marketing them. Using pork tenderloin as illustration, Saltzman cautions her audience to be mindful of issues surrounding authenticity, representation, and intangible heritage.

The article "[African] Food at the Smithsonian Folklife Festival," comes from the 1997 festival booklet. Co-written by Betty Belanus, a long-time folklorist and education specialist at the Smithsonian Institution, the article draws from fieldwork she conducted with a South African scholar on African immigrant foodways in the Washington, DC, area. It was written for the general public but demonstrates the use of folklore theory in the breadth of foodways processes covered and the attention to the meanings given to these foods by the individuals involved. Program books were published for each of the annual festivals, and most contain essays on foodways traditions. They are available through the Office of Folklife and Cultural Heritage at the Smithsonian Institution.

Museums pose a different set of issues from festivals for representing food, since they historically hold artifacts of material culture, not ephemeral and perishable items such as food. Sarah Conrad Gothie looks at these issues in her essay, "Food and Drink in the Museum: The Problem of Edible Heritage," asking how foodways can be accurately represented and interpreted in museum settings. Gothie explores the multisensory nature of food and discusses the complications that arise in museum settings. These complications reflect the larger issues with museums—the politics surrounding representation and inclusion as well as philosophical questions concerning knowledge and the experiencing of domains of life out of context. Gothie recognizes practical concerns around including food in museums, but raises questions about the purpose and function of museums as well as issues of interpretation of the objects in museums.

Attention to food in formal education has historically been primarily in home economics or culinary arts classes. Food, however, offers numerous opportunities for active, experiential learning in a variety of subjects. The essay "You Eat What You Are: Food in Education" was the introduction to a special issue of a newsletter on folklore in education, C.A.R.T.S, published by the nonprofit organization, Local Learning. It addresses the use of food in K-12 classrooms, giving examples of how food can be used to explore local culture, learn about specific cultures, and recognize connections between food and identity. Including this subject in education should enable children to make food choices that better contribute to their health and nutrition, as well as to sustainability in general.

Mary Hufford's article, "Ginseng and the Idea of the Commons," addresses the concept of sustainability, a key issue of our time referring to the wise use of resources in the present so that they will endure into the future. The concept was articulated initially around economic development and was posited to contain three "pillars," all of which were necessary—economic, environmental, and socio-cultural. The cultural part of sustainability tends to be the most vague, intangible, and difficult to achieve and assess. Folklorists are contributing to international dialogues about it by bringing their perspective on tradition, identity, and groups as dynamic and fluid constructions. They look particularly at the sense of community that develops from having shared traditions and that serves to sustain other aspects of the group.[17] Hufford's article addresses these issues through an ethnographic study of ginseng in the mountains of West Virginia and the historical traditions of sharing the public spaces—"the commons"—where it is hunted. Ginseng is a root used in traditional medicine in the Appalachian region, but it is also a commodity highly valued in the marketplace. Since it grows wild, its ownership comes into question, along with how to make sure access to such shared spaces is equitable. The issue also raises questions about the sustainability of ginseng as a resource since over-poaching is threatening it.

Zilia Estrada raises questions about the sustainability of communities themselves in "An Aesthetic of Community and an Activism of Embodiment in Two Collaborative Community Gardens in Bloomington, Indiana." She looks at how communities around a garden and an orchard in a university town in the American Midwest have been constructed through various strategies, but also have been contested by participants with different concepts of what constitutes community.

Folklore perspectives can also contribute to understanding issues of healthy eating. Michael Owen Jones argues for a "place at the table" for such discussions in "Food, Folklore and Nutrition." This excerpt from a longer article argues that understanding the meanings of food can shed light on why people eat the way they do—and what needs to be done to change harmful habits. He also examines the processes by which food acquires meaning and emphasizes that all the activities surrounding food and eating, not just food itself, can be symbolic. He encourages researchers to recognize the wide range of identities expressed through food choices and to acknowledge those identities in discussions on diet and health.

Tourism is frequently thought of as a superficial way of observing other cultures for our own entertainment. In "Culinary Tourism: Eating and Otherness," Lucy Long investigates the meanings and implications of "eating out of curiosity." Exploring tourism as a negotiation between the exotic and familiar, she expands the usual topics of tourism from just food to foodways and from gourmet food to any type of food. She also identifies five strategies frequently used in presenting food to make it either more or less exotic, edible, and palatable.

Margaret R. Yocom's "Poetry and Folklore: Partners in Practice" includes an introduction to two poems. She discusses similarities in poetry and folklore, how both were a part of her personal life, but also as disciplines, they encourage similar attention to details and everyday life. Both are ethnographic in that they preserve and share experiences. Also folklorists attend to the poetry in speech, in oral performance. She explains that writing poetry offers her a way to explore issues in her fieldwork as well as her own life. The poems included here are both food related. The "Last Piece" retells a memory told her by her grandfather of surreptitiously watching a funeral dinner as a boy. The title refers to raisin pie but is actually about the loss of heritage and identity. The poem "Eating Alone" describes the foods on the tables of her Pennsylvania German grandparents and how they simultaneously celebrate that heritage and set them apart, isolating them from others.

Discussion questions

1. Look for examples of food being used in the following mediums or contexts: Festivals, international dinners in schools, museums, films, television shows, literature, magazines, Internet blogs.
    What messages come across through food in these examples? How accurate are they, and what issues might there be? How can folklore concepts contribute to these uses?

2. Design a cooking demonstration or workshop that teaches audiences about the culture surrounding that food. What are some of the practical concerns (food safety, age appropriateness, audience interest, etc.)?

3. Design an exhibit, cookbook, or culinary tourism trail of a group's foodways. What foods and aspects of foodways do you include? Why?

4. Are you aware of food security issues within your own community or family? What stereotypes are assigned to those with such issues? What happens when others determine which foods those individuals should be consuming? Is there any way in which you can contribute to such needs?

5. What does a deeper understanding of food as folklore, and as a personal, social, and cultural construct contribute to understanding issues and developing solutions in the following areas: food in economic development, food systems activism, culinary tourism, community and individual health and wellness, access to healthy food, environmental sustainability, and community and cultural sustainability.

Notes

1. The phrase "invented tradition" comes from E. J. Hobsbawm and Terence Ranger in their edited volume, *The Invention of Tradition* (Cambridge: Cambridge University Press, 1984). An example of the politicized use of folklore is the dictator of Spain (1936–75), Francisco Franco, who encouraged displays of folklore (dance, music, and celebrations) in order to promote his socialist regime. Nazi Germany also made use of traditional folk narratives to instill a sense of national pride.

2. Folklorist Richard Dorson used the term fake lore to criticize popular publications about American folklore as "sugarcoating" traditions and presenting tales and customs that were not actually in oral tradition in any communities. In this article, he calls for more ethnographic research and for attention to the diversity of folk communities in the United States as well as the sometimes negative or unpleasant items of folklore. Richard

M. Dorson, "Folklore and Fake Lore," *The American Mercury*, March 1950, 335–42 (http://www.unz.org/Pub/AmMercury-1950mar-00335).

3. Archie Green was one of the most influential proponents of this view, and he spoke for numerous others.

4. Philosopher-musicologist Charles Seeger (father of Pete) promoted this last idea in his work with Latin American relations with the US, laying the groundwork for folksong and dance to be a key component of creating positive relations. The Smithsonian Folklife Festival includes an element of this approach, although its mission includes much more, including bringing to life artifacts in the museum collections and giving "a voice to people and cultures not otherwise likely to be heard in a national setting" ("Why We Do the Festival," ed. Richard Kurin, *American Folklife Festival Program Book 1989*, Washington, DC: Smithsonian Institution Office of Folklife and Cultural Heritage, 1989, 51–2). It has been vigorously critiqued, with scholars questioning its impact as well as cultural politics. See for example, Heather A. Diamond, "A Sense of Place: Mapping Hawai'i on the National Mall," *Journal of American Folklore* 121, no. 479 (2008): 35–59; Emily Satterwhite, "Imagining Home, Nation, World: Appalachia on the Mall," *Journal of American Folklore* 121, no. 479 (2008): 10–34; and Robert Cantwell, *Ethnomimesis: Folklife and the Representation of Culture* (Chapel Hill: University of North Carolina Press, 1993).

5. An overview and discussion of programs and issues in public folklore was published in *Folklore Forum* 1999, vol. 30. The following year, that journal published a special issue devoted to Public Folklore (vol. 31/2), edited by Betty Belanus and Gregory Hansen.

6. A list of such programs and organizations can be found on the website of the American Folklore Society.

7. The Smithsonian Institution hosted a travelling exhibit on American foodways, "Key Ingredients" (http://www.keyingredients.org.) Designed by folklorist, Charlie Camp, the exhibit has been displayed throughout the country, usually paired with additional exhibits and programming around local foodways. For a review of this exhibit and its impact, see Yvonne Lockwood and Lucy Long, "Key Ingredients Exhibit (Review)," *Journal of American Folklore* 122, no. 483 (2009): 92–5.

8. Folklife festivals, large public events meant to educate about as well as to entertain with folk culture, also frequently include food demonstrations, hands-on participation in foodways activities, and tastings of traditional foods. The Smithsonian Institution's Folklife Festival has included foodways demonstrations and presentations since the beginning, developing a model that emphasized the past and present contexts of those foodways. Food preparation was oftentimes the centerpiece of presentations, not as cooking instruction, but as a display, so that audiences see the complexity and nuances of techniques and ingredients. "Community scholars" demonstrated how to prepare traditional foods, and recipes were offered to audiences (unfortunately, samples were not, although food vendors sold selected dishes). Folklorists at the Smithsonian also developed the role of "presenters" who introduced the community scholars, adding contextual information, informally interviewing the demonstrator on stage, assisting in the demonstration if needed, and acting as a "mediator" between the demonstrator and audiences, encouraging them to ask questions and clarifying information. Ideally, the presenter and the community scholar collaborate, with each contributing their own knowledge and skills in order to create an effective educational event. For further discussion on the role of a presenter, see "Interpreting Food at the Smithsonian Folklife Festival," Legacy: Magazine of the National Association for Interpretation, ed. Lucy Long with Betty Belanus, March/April 2011, 22–5. A review of the 2006 Smithsonian Festival that featured food is in Anne Pryor, "Food Culture USA, 39th Annual Smithsonian Folklife Festival (review)," *Journal of American Folklore* 120, no. 476 (2007): 245–7. Also related to the festival were smaller events organized by the Smithsonian. For an analysis of the implications of some of these, see Jack Santino,"The Tendency to Ritualize: The Living Celebrations Series as a Model for Cultural Presentation and Validation," in *The Conservation of Culture: Folklorists and the Public Sector*, ed. Burt Feintuch (Lexington, KY: University of Kentucky, 1988), 118–31.

9. Educational settings for the presentation of foodways traditions include schools and universities as well as community venues, such as centers and libraries. Teachers have long used food as a medium for introducing other cultures to students, and "ethnic" foods are oftentimes offered at gatherings as a way of bringing people of diverse backgrounds together. Unfortunately, these are sometimes done with a simplistic view of multiculturalism and without an understanding of the complexity of food, culture, and taste, so that they sometimes actually affirm stereotypes and create prejudices. A number of folklorists have developed curriculum materials to be used in presenting traditional foods that address these issues. The sharing of traditional and ethnic foods can be an effective way of creating greater cultural understanding and respect, and it is frequently an underlying goal of a public

folklore work. For examples and more discussion, see Paddy Bowman and Lynne Hamer (2011) and organizations and websites such as Jan Rosenberg's Heritage Education Resources, Inc., Local Learning: The National Network for Folk Arts in Education (http://locallearningnetwork.org), and Louisiana Voices, an on-line guide to folklife resources in education in Lousiana (http://www.louisianavoices.org). Also Local Learning began publishing the *Journal of Folklore and Education* in 2014.

10. For examples of this work, see websites for the Southern Foodways Alliance, Traditional Arts Indiana, Louisiana Voices, and Center for Food and Culture.

11. See for example, http://www.iowaartscouncil.org/programs/folk-and-traditional-arts/place_based_foods/index.htm; and www.foodandculture.org.

12. Similar debates arise in any discussion on the role and uses of the humanities. The field of public humanities addresses these issues.

13. A number of recent publications on food systems issues are relevant to the concerns of folklorists, particularly Carole Counihan and Valeria Siniscalchi (eds), *Food Activism: Agency, Democracy and Economy* (London: Bloomsbury, 2014); Brian Gardner, *Global Food Futures: Feeding the World In 2050* (New York: Berg, 2012); Cristina Grasseni, *Beyond Alternative Food Networks: Italy's Solidarity Purchase Groups* (Bloomsbury Academic, 2013); Moya Kneafsey, Lewis Holloway, Elizabeth Dowler, Laura Venn, and Helena Tuomainen, *Reconnecting Consumers, Producers, and Food: Exploring Alternatives* (Oxford: Berg, 2008); Raj Patel, *Stuffed and Starved: Markets, Choice and the Battle for the World's Food System* (Toronto: HarperCollins, 2008). An example of how folklore perspectives can be used in better understanding the personal and emotional implications of food insecurity is Eileen Cherry-Chandler, "After the Reapers: Place Settings of Race, Class, and Food Insecurity," *Text and Performance Quarterly* 29, no. 1 (2009): 44–59.

14. See for example, *Seasonal: A Novel*, Round Barn Press, 2004, by folklorist Betty Belanus, who draws on her work as a fieldworker and public folklorist for her fiction writing. An example of creative writing being used to develop community identity and solidarity is Chicago's Neighborhood Writing Alliance, co-founded by folklorist Sue Eleuterio. Also see the poems included in this *Reader* by Dr. Peggy Yocum, a professor of folklore at George Mason University.

15. See for example, writings by Terese Allen (http://www.tereseallen.com/articles.html) and others. Not all folklorists are identified as such, and not all people who have taken folklore classes consider themselves folklorists.

16. See for example, the "Composting Connections Project" developed by the Center for Food and Culture (www.foodandculture.org).

17. Folklorist Jeff Todd Titon has explored cultural sustainability in relation to music and offers insights applicable to food. In his article, "Music and Sustainability: An Ecological Viewpoint" (*The World of Music* 51, no. 1 (2009): 119–37), he argues that conserving traditions through economic initiatives such as tourism oftentimes creates "staged authenticity" that crystalizes and destroys the vitality of the tradition. Instead, ecological sustainability suggests principles that allow resources to remain dynamic and responsive to the changing needs and conditions. Also see his blog: sustainablemusic.blogspot.com/.

References

Baron, Robert. "Sins of Objectification? Agency, Mediation, and Community Cultural Self-Determination in Public Folklore and Cultural Tourism Programming." *The Journal of American Folklore* 123, no. 487 (2010): 63–91.

Baron, Robert. "Theorizing Public Folklore Practice - Documentation, Genres of Representation, and Everyday Competencies." *Journal of Folklore Research*, (Special Double Issue: Cultural Brokerage: Forms of Intellectual Practice in Society) 36, no. 2 (1999): 185–201.

Baron, Robert and Nick Spitzer. *Public Folklore.* 2nd edn. Jackson, MS: University Press of Mississippi, 2007. (Washington: Smithsonian Institution, 1992.)

Bauman, Richard, Patricia Sawin, and Inta Carpenter. *Reflections on the Folklife Festival: An Ethnography of Participant Experience.* Bloomington: Indiana University Folklore Institute, Special Publications, 1992.

Belanus, Betty and Gregory Hansen, eds. *Folklore Forum*. 31, no. 2 (2000). Bloomington: Indiana University Folklore Institute.

Botkin, Benjamin A. "Applied Folklore: Creating Understanding through Folklore." *Southern Folklore Quarterly* 17, no. 3 (1953): 199-206.

Bowman, Paddy, and Lynne M. Hamer. *Through the Schoolhouse Door: Folklore, Community, Curriculum*. Logan, UT: Utah State University Press, 2011.

Brewer, Teri F. "Redefining 'The Resource': Interpretation and Public Folklore." *Journal of American Folklore* 119, no. 471 (2006): 80-9.

Chittenden, Varick A. "'Put Your Very Special Place on the North Country Map!': Community Participation in Cultural Landmarking." *Journal of American Folklore* 119, no. 471 (2006): 47-65.

Chittenden, Varick A. "The American Folk-Lore Society." *Milking It for All It's Worth: Foodways Projects and Local Identity* 16 (1996): 1-9.

Evans, Tim. "Toward Critical Theory for Public Folklore: An Annotated Bibliography." *Folklore Forum* 31, no. 2 (2000): 115-22.

Feintuch, Burt. *The Conservation of Culture: Folklorists and the Public Sector*. Lexington: University Press of Kentucky, 1988.

Hufford, Mary, ed. *Conserving Culture: A New Discourse on Heritage*. Urbana: University of Illinois Press, 1994.

Jones, Michael Owen. *Putting Folklore to Use*. Lexington: University Press of Kentucky, 1994.

Kirshenblatt-Gimblett, Barbara. *Destination Culture: Tourism, Museums, and Heritage*. Berkeley: University of California, 1998.

Kirshenblatt-Gimblett, Barbara. "Mistaken Dichotomies." In *Public Folklore*, edited by Robert Baron and Nicholas R. Spitzer, 29-48. Washington: Smithsonian Institution, 1992.

Klassen, Teri. "Representations of African American Quiltmaking: From Omission to High Art." *Journal of American Folklore* 122, no. 485 (2009): 297-334.

Kodish, Debora. "Cultivating Folk Arts and Social Change." *Journal of American Folklore* 126, no. 502 (2013): 434-54.

Kurin, Richard. *Reflections of a Culture Broker: A View from the Smithsonian*. Washington, DC: Smithsonian Institution Press, 1997.

Shuldiner, David, ed. *Folklore in Use: Applications in the Real World*. Middlesex, UK.

Staub, Shalom. "Folklore and Authenticity: A Myopic Marriage in Public Sector Folklore Programs." In *The Conservation of Culture: Folklorists and the Public Sector*, edited by Burt Feintuch, 166-79. Lexington, Kentucky: The University Press of Kentucky, 1988.

Wells, Patricia Atkinson. "Public Folklore in the Twenty-First Century: New Challenges for the Discipline." *Journal of American Folklore* 119, no. 471 (2006): 5-18.

CHAPTER 31

LAYING A PLACE AT THE TABLE: CREATING PUBLIC FOODWAYS MODELS FROM SCRATCH

Millie Rahn

Proverbial wisdom tells us that we are what we eat, but perhaps it is the other way around: we eat what we are. As a public folklorist who studies food and culture, I approach my work as another kind of archaeology, one that excavates the lives of people and their places of habitation over time and space through foodways. My contracted work crosses regions and sometimes national borders, ethnicities, ecologies, and historical periods. In every place, cultural inventories and ethnographies are the sources from which I develop model public programs for cultural and educational organizations, government economic development agencies, and the heritage and tourism industries. This kind of work falls outside prescribed foodways models of folk arts and folklife festivals, which I also curate, but many of the lessons learned from those models can be applied to community projects.

[…]

Feasting on community

Food—remembering and re-creating it, growing it, marketing it, cooking it, eating it—and sense of place are interconnected. Wherever we find ourselves—in the kitchen, garden, or field; at the corner shop, farmers market, or supermarket; or at festive events in sacred, seasonal, or ordinary time—foodways can show how family stories, community histories, and the significant events of humanity are regularly and traditionally expressed through food. By definition, folklorists are advocates for the people and the traditions with whom they work, both of which often are forgotten or invisible in official records and consensus histories. They often see people and things that mainstream culture and history do not see or do not wish to acknowledge, including refugees and recent immigrants, marginalized communities, once-prominent communities now swallowed up by sprawl, vestigial place names that have no apparent connection to present uses, and contested spaces.[1]

Long before actual fieldwork begins, as the client(s) and I are sitting around a conference table on their turf defining the project and refining timelines, budgets, and political agendas, I explain how it is second nature for folklorists to create partnerships and multidisciplinary approaches, which are often foreign concepts to others at the table. Frequently clients are vague about why they hired me in the first place. Usually, somewhere someone has heard that food is the way to attract audiences and tourists, so the charge to me becomes something like this: "Here's a pot of money, now go out and do it. Create a festival. Get restaurants and bed

Millie Rahn, 'Laying a Place at the Table: Creating Public Foodways Models from Scratch', *Journal of American Folklore* 119 (471) (2006), 30–46. (Excerpts printed here: 30, 32–33, 34–41, 43, 44, 45. Omitted text is indicated by ellipses.)

From *Journal of American Folklore*. © 2006 by the Board of Trustees of the University of Illinois. Used with permission of the University of Illinois Press.

and breakfasts to do special promotions. Just get those buses and credit-card-wielding city folks here and get them here soon. This place is dying. Young people are leaving. Farmers have to sell their land to developers. We need jobs. We need respect. Everybody eats, so what's the problem?"

Although this scenario is exaggerated, clients often are desperate, or at least eager, to become part of a trend. The problem is that there is no model, and usually no precedent, for different constituencies to speak to each other in a community, which can actually be an advantage for the folklorist. We know that people love to tell their stories or share their insights, yet here we are meeting in a conference room—the top-down model—instead of driving around the community, where I might see significant things that clients are so used to seeing that they fail to see potential. And often, from a car, they can point out things that I might otherwise overlook. But all that comes later.

So I begin by talking about how foodways can be a popular and multifaceted vehicle for looking at the community and its many components. Food, I tell them, is interwoven with a community's identity, its growth and development, its history of immigration and agricultural production and industrialization, and its balancing of tradition with change. The first step is to remind people that the food we grow to eat and drink, the people with whom we share this bounty, the languages we speak while gathered together, and where we feast all symbolize who we are, as individuals and as communities. Sometimes we want to keep these foods and traditions to ourselves, but increasingly we see potential benefits in sharing our culture with the larger world as tourism becomes a principal worldwide industry.

[...]

Program models based around food begin with basic questions: what do local people eat and why? In New England, these questions address political, economic, and ecological issues, for example, the fishery moratoriums and their impact on historic fishing communities such as Gloucester and New Bedford, Massachusetts; decades worth of mill closings; and families having to abandon their farms after many generations.[2] To make these ideas accessible, it helps to create a template that focuses on three areas where foodways are displayed and exchanged: the kitchen, the market, and the festival. These are the places where family stories, community history, and the significant events of humanity within a particular region are regularly expressed through food.

Conventional wisdom tells us that the kitchen is the heart of the home. I know from firsthand experiences in museums that if a kitchen vignette is installed, program success is nearly guaranteed. The kitchen, historically, is the place where families gather and where the everyday and the ceremonial meet and overlap. Here families interact and share private traditions, expressing identity through their food to each other and to the world. Creativity is alive in this space, from daily mealtimes to more elaborate feasts that mark rites of passage, religious and secular holidays, and other special events. This is where knowledge is passed on, from traditional ways of preparing and using various ingredients, implements, tools, and techniques to legends, stories, anecdotes, and cultural exchanges that have become part of familial and regional folklife.

Then there is food in the landscape, represented by growers and producers and markets and restaurants. Examples of local foodways can include signs for farm stands, local and farmers markets, and public suppers, as well as signs for social and agricultural organizations such as 4–H, the Grange, and university extension services. There might be visible evidence of historic or contemporary production, such as crop marks on fallow land or evidence of working orchards, fields, pastures, and farm buildings. Local foodways might also include family farms that advertise themselves as such on signs or outbuildings or display their designation as a Century Farm, meaning the land has been in production for more than a hundred years. The vitality of today's food market is evident in neighborhood stores, ethnic groceries, restaurants, and local businesses devoted to food. In many older places, literal signs of the commercial food past remain painted on the sides of old buildings and barns. Elsewhere it may be golden arches, diners, and billboards. The names and languages on the signs might be unfamiliar, but that is also significant.

Festivals are times to gather together at special events, set off from everyday time and space. Whether religious or secular, inclusive or exclusive, ancient or brand new, festivals are universally celebrated with an abundance of special food and drink. They are the venues where favorite foods, the most unusual utensils, and the fanciest presentations are likely to appear. In festivals, communities let what they eat symbolize who they are. The three case studies presented here illustrate how this model of food has been applied in my work in the public realm.

Feasting on lowell

Lowell, Massachusetts, is the quintessential American city, a microcosm of the evolving American experience from preindustrial to industrial and postindustrial life. Lowell is also the place where I have done the most extensive foodways studies, using the city as a laboratory in which to test theories about publicly presenting community identities. I have done contract work for the Lowell Historic Preservation Commission, the Lowell National Historical Park, and the Lowell Festival Foundation, and from time to time I have curated or co-curated foodways for the Lowell Folk Festival. For more than a decade, I have observed communities grow or decline, seen commercial signs fade on the sides of old factories and smokestacks, watched vacant mills be redeveloped into housing and office space, and generally seen the mix of cultures and sense of place celebrated at festival time each July.

In light of its layers of history, architecture, and cultures, Lowell is an ideal place to develop foodways projects. In the early nineteenth century, Yankee manufacturers from Boston built textile mills, boarding houses, and canals (essentially an entire company town and its works) alongside Native fishing grounds on the banks of the Merrimack River, launching an industrial revolution. Among those who originally came from all over the globe to work in the mills, and in the city's even more famous patent medicine industry, were "mill girls" from New England farms, as well as immigrants of Irish, French Canadian, Greek, Lithuanian, Polish, Portuguese, and other descent. Mill workers lived in neighborhoods like Petit Canada, the Irish and Greek Acre, or Little Lithuania, and made music in the ethnic hyphenated-American social clubs within walking distance of the factories. In the postindustrial late twentieth and early twenty-first centuries, Lowell continues to attract immigrants and has become home to large Central American, South American, and Southeast Asian communities, including the second-largest Cambodian population in the United States, as well as more recent arrivals from West African nations such as Cameroon and Sierra Leone. Like their predecessors, these newer arrivals bring their own traditions to the mix. Thus, Lowell epitomizes the old and the new, symbolizing contemporary America.

To many outsiders, Lowell is associated with Jack Kerouac, who captured much of the city and his Franco-American heritage in such books as *The Town and the City* (1950) and *Vanity of Dulouz* (1968), before he went *On the Road* (1957). Kerouac was born in Lowell on March 12, 1922, "at five o'clock in the afternoon of a red-all-over supper time," as he wrote in *Dr. Sax* (1959). Suppertime would have been at sunset at that time of year, and suppertime in Kerouac's Petit Canada neighborhood was legendary. Lowell's famous beans were baked on Saturdays and were the traditional Saturday night supper. Waiting in line for beans at local shops was a weekly social ritual, second only to Sunday mass at the (now-closed) St. Jean Baptiste Church.

Generations of Lowell's mill workers patronized local markets and diners. Where there were mills, there were also candy manufacturers, especially those that made hard candies for mill workers to suck on to avoid talking (once forbidden on the floor) and to reduce the danger from ingesting dust and fiber. Then there was "the cough," pervasive among mill workers, which supported a patent medicine industry. "Father John's" was perhaps the best-known remedy for "the cough." At one time, Father John's was marketed worldwide. Painted advertisements are still visible high on the wall of its former factory, now redeveloped into downtown condominiums and artists' lofts. The story goes that, in the mid-nineteenth century, Father John O'Brien took ill, went to a local pharmacy, and was given a "tonic" with cod liver oil and licorice flavor. Unlike other popular remedies, this one did not contain alcohol, so Father John started recommending it to his parishioners and it became known as "Father John's."[3]

Walking down Market Street today, few tourists know why there is a building with "Father John's" scrawled in nineteenth-century script on the top of the brick side wall, or why "Father John's" is picked out in gold-leaf letters on the front of a local apartment building. Nor do visitors from outside New England know why there are so many "spas," a regional urban institution that in Lowell are essentially corner shops in each neighborhood that have become contemporary purveyors of fast foods, hot coffee, and lottery tickets, or why the many diners—originally horse-drawn lunch wagons operated by immigrants— throughout the city proudly post metal signs proclaiming "home of Lowell's famous beans." Beans are still made in a second- and third-generation French-Canadian family grocery store and advertised on a sidewalk signboard on Saturdays reading: "Beans today. History that is here to be tasted." What was once an inexpensive, nutritious staple of mill workers' diets is marketed today as high-fiber protein, "with or without" [salt pork], as a taste of history.[4]

All of these ideas were featured in an ambitious exhibition called *Food, Glorious Food: Food Traditions of Lowell,* the culmination of nearly a year's fieldwork by folklorist Kathy Neustadt and me in the mid-1990s, work that presented historical and contemporary examples of the city's foodways, along with free programs for children and adults throughout the exhibition's run.[5] The venue was a downtown art gallery in a renovated mill with subsidized housing for seniors, across the complex from the Lowell National Historical Park's visitor center. Many visitors were nontraditional museum-goers who came because their own history, traditions, and objects were on display, an audience we had carefully cultivated. The gallery staff was surprised by and sometimes uncomfortable with these visitors; we were not, because we knew the opportunity to display culture publicly was a powerful draw, as was mere curiosity to see who was included and who was not.

Some of the park's artifacts on display had been used within living memory. Visitors recalled "rushing the growler" (an industrial lunch pail available in the Sears catalogue) to parents working at the mills. The pail was filled with a hot dinner (New Englanders' midday meal) and a locally brewed cup of beer on top, the rim greased with butter to keep the beer from spilling. Contemporary art by fourth graders adorned the refrigerator in the kitchen vignette, showing young, ethnically diverse, and mostly first-generation Americans' ideas about their native foods. The exhibition had many interactive components and a sophisticated message. Although the goal of bringing new audiences to the gallery to see *their* culture as part of the city's fabric was achieved, sustaining their level of visitation was not. But how do you measure success?

In the museum world where visitation numbers equal success, we were hugely successful. That year, the exhibition was part of opening festivities for local politicians and funders at the annual Lowell Folk Festival and attracted thousands, along with the exhibition-related programs such as kids' activities at the park and walking tours to diners and ethnic food shops. However well *Food, Glorious Food* showed off Lowell and its people to outsiders and other Lowellians, folklorists know that to sustain participation by those featured in the exhibition who usually have no tradition of patronizing what are perceived to be elite institutions, the folklorist has to continue to go into their neighborhoods and grocery stores and invite them to demonstrate and sell their community organizations' food at the festival. On the other hand, the Smithsonian Institution's

National Museum of American History solicited the gift of the 1940s stove out of a Lowell kitchen that we had on display. Again, how do you measure success? Lowell foodways have gone to Washington, D.C., or at least to a warehouse in the suburbs.

Nearly a decade later, the *Feasting on Lowell* series for the Lowell National Historical Park's Mogan Cultural Center built upon previous ethnographies to document the foodways of more recent immigrant communities.[6] The series featured culinary performances by members of Cambodian, Brazilian, Laotian, Cameroonian, and Sierra Leonean communities. Like festival foodways presentations, the concept of performances allowed flexibility and encouraged creativity, particularly in the makeshift kitchen of a national park meeting room. Programs emphasized traditional ways of preparing and using various ingredients, as well as tools and techniques and other cultural information mediated by folklorists. The idea was to introduce Lowell to itself publicly again, so folklorists were essential in using festival models for cultural content and interpretation. When the second series was launched several years ago, the pan-African community and Brazilians were still invisible to most Lowellians. That has changed, with the advent of an African festival each summer and because, with the huge influx of Brazilians into central and eastern Massachusetts in the past half decade, Portuguese is now the second-most-common language in the state, although it has long been heard in Lowell, where generations of Portuguese families handed down jobs at the now-derelict Prince spaghetti factory.

As foodways programs, these events were successful, toothsome, and packed with colorful performers and cultural content. Yet I wonder about their impact and ephemeral nature and whose interests are being served. As before, the goal of bringing the various communities and new audiences to the park was achieved, but at what cost and is the goal realistic? In truth, recent immigrants are often consumed by the mechanics of everyday survival, such as working multiple jobs, and are in need of locating a variety of social services. They scarcely have the luxury of engaging in their cultural traditions and rituals for themselves, much less performing them for the public or visiting cultural events. Many recent immigrants repeat the mantra of those who came before: earn lots of money in America and then go home, if you are fortunate enough to have a home place to which you can return. In reality, however, the children of immigrants often become the next hyphenated Americans as immigrant parents put down roots, buy property, and become American; and they stay. Many dream of opening restaurants so they can re-create the dishes they long for, as well as grow or import crucial ingredients for this purpose. Longer-established communities are more familiar with how to interpret their foodways in public settings, whereas at the other end of the spectrum are community elders who are desperate to pass on traditions they have maintained for several generations but have no one to whom they can pass them; younger people have moved away, intermarried, or become uninterested in cooking in the old ways or using unhealthy ingredients, no matter how central the foodstuffs once were to their parents' identity.

As models, these programs are important, but continuing the pattern of programming in a central place without context needs further thinking, work that is always subject to the whims of funding and other constraints. Foodways at festivals in a celebratory context is tried and true, but now the challenge is to develop ways to work on smaller, sustainable scales to build and strengthen communities.

Come see what's cooking in Hancock county

Another model is one that promotes foodways for economic sustainability as well as tourism. Maine already exudes a strong sense of place, with a long, venerable history promoting itself as a tourist destination. The concept of Maine as a rusticator's haven, as locals called the outsiders who first summered there, involves a sense of timelessness and New England self-sufficiency. For more than a century, visitors have come to Maine for its recreational pursuits and its foods.

Far from the simplistic tourist concept of lobsters and lighthouses, Maine has a working fishery, farms, smokehouses, sugarhouses, orchards, cultivated fields of grains and vegetables, livestock barns, canneries, and processing plants. It is a landscape of Grange halls, farm stands, urban markets, and community suppers. Mexican immigrants in the northern potato fields and various African refugees in urban centers are bringing a wealth of traditions to a previously rather homogenous population of rural Yankees, back-to-the-landers, Acadians, Québecois, and retirees. There are also former mill towns struggling to reinvent themselves and abandoned chicken barns everywhere, but those are usually off the tourist trails.

Summering in coastal Maine is a tradition in itself. Hancock County, the self-described "heart of 'Downeast,'" was among the earliest and largest places to lure nineteenth-century tourists from Boston, New York, and Philadelphia to its artists' colonies, ocean breezes, and natural beauty. The creation of Acadia National Park in 1916 on Mount Desert Island (MDI) institutionalized the tourism industry for the state and the region. Bar Harbor on the coast of MDI was a traditional Wabanaki hunting and fishing grounds; for more than two centuries, Maine Indians have been coming to the coast to sell their ash and sweetgrass fancy and work baskets to tourists.[7] The "summer people" are the ones who are, and long have been, perceived to be the key to economic development. More recently, the notion of summer people encompasses tourists in general—those who come to Maine from mid-April mud season through the end of "leaf-peeping" (fall foliage) and harvest in October, before winter closes in.

Hancock County has abundant resources upon which to develop a cultural tourism plan focused on food and local agriculture; there are islands, scenic vistas, blueberries, and rural and rustic architecture. There are also working fishing boats and seafood smokehouses, family farms, artists' colonies and painters, and back-to-the-landers who organize much of the organic growers and food cooperative initiatives, even though, after two or three generations, they are still not accepted as locals. Older Grange halls have become social centers for nonagricultural families. Signs for community suppers at Grange halls, churches, and community centers are part of the landscape, as are fields of vegetables, orchards, and stacked lobster pots. Historic farmhouses, bed-and-breakfast establishments, and restaurants of every size, budget, and culinary offering are also abundant. Agriculture and working in the fishery are the principal occupations in Downeast Maine, but the sustainability of both industries and ways of life is under threat for a number of reasons. The idea of marketing the area by capitalizing on the popularity of food and culture—connecting local people with their food and visitors with a regional rustic experience—was a progressive one in the mid-1990s, when cultural tourism was embraced by many institutions.

In early 1997, I was contracted by the regional planning commission to design a model program for this area, which I came to call *Come See What's Cooking in Hancock County*. Fieldwork and implementation over the course of eighteen months was funded by the state's arts, tourism, and agricultural agencies, along with some federal support. This was the planners' first cultural initiative, having grown out of a desire to build an economic sustainability plan for the local fishery and growers. They already had launched a program, *Hancock County Fresh, Locally Grown*, encouraging tourists and others to patronize restaurants, farms, bed and breakfasts, and food producers identified by the program's logo.

My charge was to develop and implement a model tourism plan to draw people away from the tourist magnets of Bar Harbor and Acadia on MDI. I was to concentrate my efforts on the forty-mile stretch of mainland coast from industrial Bucksport through Ellsworth, the municipal and mercantile center, to Gouldsboro at the top of the windswept Schoodic Peninsula, home of one of the few remaining sardine-processing plants in the state, and a local winery. Preliminary investigations showed that this kind of tour had strong potential in niche markets that had the demographic and economic profiles identified as "consumers of experiences." According to state economic planners and tour promoters, Hancock County was identified as an ideal mature tourism market, already drawing four million visitors seasonally, most of whom went to MDI and Acadia National Park. Creating destination awareness on the mainland was a challenge, but not insurmountable, because nearly all visitors to MDI must drive through most of the coastal towns featured on the tour just to get to Bar Harbor and Acadia.

Building on earlier cultural inventories of the area, my fieldwork concentrated intently on foodways and cultural and natural attractions that could be incorporated into self-guided weeklong spring or fall shoulder-season packages, a time when the area needed the infusion of tourist dollars before and after the summer. The *Come See What's Cooking* tour was initially offered in early autumn 1998, but the documentation and model were flexible enough that the planning commission or other entities could take it over and expand it after the initial development of the route. Research yielded about two dozen alternatives that could be offered at any time except darkest winter, including design of a formal annual tour week or simply letting people devise their own itineraries as they ate their way along the coast.

The 1998 *Come See What's Cooking* tour was built around six evenings, each scheduled at a different restaurant known for its traditional and/or local foods and offered programs drawn from local agricultural practices, traditional entertainment, and maritime history and culture. The tour culminated in a one-day, first-ever Downeast Folklife Festival, held on the green and along the waterfront of Blue Hill. The festival featured foodways demonstrations, entertainment, occupational folklife, and the opportunity for local residents, as well as tourists, to experience county-wide culture. The board of selectmen in Blue Hill, already experienced with decades of producing the Blue Hill Fair each September, contributed and organized the infrastructure, which served as an in-kind match to the cost of producing the festival, part of which was funded by a grant from the Fund for Folk Culture.

Tour brochures included a map of natural and cultural sites and attractions to visit during the day, descriptions of each nightly program and featured menu, and listings of bed and breakfasts that served local foods.[8] For those who chose not to participate in the formal programs, we provided a list of cooperating restaurants serving traditional Maine foods using locally produced products. Brochures were distributed at state tourism information centers and were available by mail by calling a toll-free number. The food press in regional newspapers and features in statewide and local media publicized the events. This was before websites were ubiquitous, and negotiating a budget from the state tourism office to fund the toll-free number was a major professional coup, another skill that one can learn only in the field.

Once the *Come See What's Cooking* tour was planned, however, my role became that of coach, grantwriter, publicist, go-between, and general factotum, coordinating all the various constituents, including the planners, selectmen (and -women), venue hosts, and program people, and reporting to key funding agencies. The idea of creating a model and implementing it, while simultaneously training planning staff and other community members to take over when my contract ended, was not only an ambitious task, but an unrealistic one. A project of this magnitude can be accomplished in little more than a year—we did it—but it really needs continuity and funding for several years to take root. The process of educating the client and the community had only just begun.

What happens when the folklorist moves on and the community redefines or discontinues the project? Funding that was contingent on hiring local tradition bearers worked in the first year, but some community members and organizations undervalued the quality of local talent and expertise, expecting to obtain future funding to bring in nationally recognized musical performers and dropping the idea of highlighting local folk culture, in essence doing a popular folk festival and little else. This negated the original idea of keeping money circulating in the local economy and favored seasonal elite institutions with bigger budgets and facilities. There were also conflicting notions between me, the folklorist "from away," and the community as to what constitutes "authenticity." For some, suggestions for participants often were based on family connections, political muscle, or who contributed most to the local chambers of commerce. This scenario is nothing new to folklorists who work in the field, but suffice it to say that foodways were almost completely lost along the way.

Situations like this give rise to two questions: (1) to whom do these models ultimately belong, and (2) how much weight can a foodways project be expected to bear as part of an economic development plan? Again, success was visible and in some ways measurable economically; however, it ultimately was not sustainable in Hancock County, although components of the model still exist there and lesser versions have been implemented elsewhere in Maine.

[…]

Conclusion

Why do we folklorists do these things? First, I believe we are incredibly fortunate to work in the field we do, almost always paid by public money, and to have the interdisciplinary grounding to take on opportunities to influence public perceptions of culture and policy, however slowly they change. Second, I firmly believe that in addition to doing the actual work of a public folklorist—cultural inventories, ethnographies, creating and presenting programs—the added educational value of often being the only advocate for vernacular culture on a project team is important to the client and the communities they serve, and to ourselves.

Public folklorists attempt to ensure that the living traditions that give identity to a place *as a place* are not forgotten or overlooked in the rush and change of modern life. We know that history and tradition keep us connected to each other and to our pasts, shape our present, and help determine our future. We all have multiple identities and many traditions to keep, and it is easy to lose our sense of ourselves and our communities in this age of chain eateries and grocery stores and agribusiness. With the globalization of economies and cultures, it may be more important now than ever to protect the traditional conditions that sustain us, as well as the unique places where we live and visit.

One way to maintain community through tradition is to keep it alive in the folklore and folklife of all the stakeholders; that is where we, as professional outsiders, can have a positive effect in a community. Outsiders like us notice the recent immigrants and ask questions about what we see and perhaps do not see, about place names, buildings, the history of the place, why it looks the way it does, who runs things, and why. We create programs that allow us to continue the conversation about how our foodways and our sense of place shape us in deep and lasting ways, for ourselves and for those who come after us.

[…]

Notes

1. Some of these ideas were identified in a pilot project, "Special Places," in which a team of historians and geographers looked at five communities across Massachusetts. As a folklorist, I helped adapt their research into a workbook format for teams of local organizations across the state to apply for funding to study their own community. The original studies and community grants were funded by the Massachusetts Foundation for the Humanities in the early to mid-1990s.

2. The Working Waterfront Festival, launched by folklorist Laura Orleans in New Bedford in 2004, is an excellent example of presenting the occupational folklife of the commercial fishery by and for fishermen and women. The Lowell Folk Festival, launched in 1987 as a National Folk Festival and, since 1990, presented by the Lowell National

Historical Park, the city of Lowell, the Lowell Festival Foundation, and the National Council for the Traditional Arts, shows how Lowell, one of the sites of the Industrial Revolution in the United States, has reinvented itself through culture in and around old mills. Similar festivals in Maine look at agriculture, such as the Acadian Festival in the St. John Valley, produced in part by the Maine Acadian Heritage Council/*Conseil d'Heritage Acadien du Maine*, and the Maine Organic Farmers and Gardeners Association's Common Ground Fair. The first two festivals have significant folklorist mediation; the latter two do not.

3. The story of Father John's cough remedy is from interpretive materials at the Lowell National Historical Park.

4. The proprietors of Coté's Market on Salem Street own what they say is the last authentic recipe for "Lowell's famous beans" and continue to bake them each Saturday.

5. The exhibition *Food, Glorious Food* appeared at the Brush Gallery in Lowell from July 22 to September 19, 1993. Fieldwork and the exhibition were funded by the Lowell Historic Preservation Commission, U.S. Department of the Interior. When we began, folklorist Martha Norkunas was director of cultural affairs in Lowell and an excellent resource; there was no functioning state folklorist at the time in Massachusetts, because of budget cuts.

6. Neustadt and I worked together again to document how Lowell had changed in a decade and paired many recent immigrants in programs.

7. For the past eleven years, the Maine Indian Basketmakers Alliance (MIBA) has been organizing the annual Native American Festival each Saturday after the Fourth of July on the grounds of the College of the Atlantic in Bar Harbor, after moving from its downtown site at the Abbe Museum. The festival is cosponsored by the Abbe Museum, the College of the Atlantic, and MIBA.

8. The events were billed as "a week-long self-guided food and heritage tour experiencing authentic history and culture from dawn to dark, including the Downeast Folklife Festival." The tour was a program of the Hancock County Planning Commission, with funding from the Maine Arts Commission, the Maine Office of Tourism, the Maine Humanities Council, the Maine Historic Preservation Commission, the Fund for Folk Culture/Lila Wallace Reader's Digest Community Folklife Program, and the U.S. Department of Agriculture. Folklorist Kathleen Mundell, then at the Maine Arts Commission, was an invaluable resource during this project.

References

Dooley, Norah. 1991. *Everybody Cooks Rice*. Minneapolis: Carolrhoda Books.

Fussell, Betty. 1986. *I Hear America Cooking: A Journey of Discovery from Alaska to Florida—the Cooks, the Recipes, and the Unique Flavors of Our National Cuisine*. New York: Viking.

International Institute of Lowell. 1989. *As the World Cooks: Recipes from Many Lands*. n.p.

Kerouac, Jack. *The Town and the City*. 1950. New York: Harcourt Brace Jovanovich.

—. 1957. *On the Road*. New York: New American Library.

—. [1959] 1987. *Dr. Sax: Faust Part Three*. New York: Grove Press.

—. 1968. *Vanity of Duluoz: An Adventurous Education, 1935–46*. New York: Coward-McCann.

Linck, Ernestine Sewell, and Joyce Gibson Roach. 1989. *Eats: A Folk History of Texas Foods*. Fort Worth: Texas Christian University Press.

Long, Lucy M., ed. 2004. *Culinary Tourism*. Lexington: University Press of Kentucky.

MacDowell, Marsha, ed. n.d. *Foodways: A 4–H Folkpatterns Project*. East Lansing, Mich.: State University Museum/ Cooperative Extension Service.

Martel, Jane, ed. 1974. *Smashed Potatoes: A Kid's-Eye View of the Kitchen*. Boston: Houghton-Mifflin.

Mundell, Kathleen, and Hillary Anne Frost-Kumpf. 1995. *Sensing Place: A Guide to Community Culture*. Augusta: Maine Arts Commission.

Neustadt, Kathy. 1992. *Clambake: A History and Celebration of an American Tradition*. Amherst: University of Massachusetts Press.

—. 1994. The Folkloristics of Licking. *Journal of American Folklore* 107(423):181–96.

Neustadt, Kathy, and Millie Rahn. 1993. *Food, Glorious Food: An Exhibit Celebrating the Amazing Things We Do with What We Eat*. Brush Gallery, Lowell, Massachusetts [exhibition brochure].

Rahn, Millie. 2000. Becoming a Public Folklorist: The "It Changed My Life" Syndrome. *Folklore Forum* 31(2):67–8.

—. 1998. *Come See What's Cooking in Hancock County: September 27–October 3, 1998* [exhibition brochure].

—. 1995. A Cornucopia of Traditional Foodways: The Lowell Folk Festival. *Radcliffe Culinary Times* 5(1): 3–4.

Rahn, Millie, and Dolores Root, eds. 1993. *Special Places: A Workbook about Community Cultural Programming.* South Hadley: Massachusetts Foundation for the Humanities.

Roberts, Kenneth. 1938. *Trending into Maine.* Boston: Little, Brown.

Weaver, William Woys. 1989. *America Eats: Forms of Edible Folk Art.* New York: Harper and Row.

Wood, Esther. 1976. *Country Fare: Reminiscences and Recipes from a Maine Childhood.* n.p.

Zeitlin, Steven J., Amy J. Kotkin, and Holly Cutting Baker. 1982. *A Celebration of American Family Folklore: Tales and Traditions from the Smithsonian Collection.* New York: Pantheon.

CHAPTER 32

PORK, PLACE, AND PRAXIS: FOODWAYS IN IOWA

Riki Saltzman

Iowa is a state with more pigs than people; they outnumber us over five to one (approximately 16 million pigs to just under 3 million people). The state leads the nation in hog production, with the ubiquitous pig almost overwhelming the corn and soybeans fields. According to Rich Horwitz, former Chair of the University of Iowa American Studies Department and author of *Hog Ties: Pigs, Manure, and Mortality in American Culture* (1998), "about 2/3 of all pigs in the US are raised on family farms within 200 miles of the state capital."

Pigs and Iowa have become almost synonymous, a sure marker of iconic status. Yet it wasn't always this way; Iowa's first in the nation status did not come about until after World War II, when pigs overtook beef cattle as the number one livestock commodity. According to the Leopold Center's then Associate Director, Rich Pirog, in his 2004 *A Geography of Taste*, prior to World War II and up until the 1950s, Iowa farms were highly diversified and relatively small.[1] The US Census of Agriculture notes that, in 1954, at least 1% of all Iowa farms produced these: cattle, hogs, chickens, horses, sheep, ducks, and turkeys as well as feed corn, oats, hay, soybeans, potatoes, orchard fruits, wheat, clover, timothy, popcorn, sweet potatoes, and sweet corn. While the major changes occurred between 1945 and 1964, by 1997 the differences from 50 years before are stark: commodities had shifted to just corn, soy, hay, cattle, hogs, oats, horses, sheep, chicken, and goats. Since 1920, Iowa commodities have plummeted from 34 items to 10. And although such products as Maytag Blue Cheese, rhubarb wine from the Amana Colonies, and Muscatine melons are known beyond Iowa's borders, few recognize such products and others as being particular to our state.

In fact, the flavors of Iowa derive from a variety of regional and ethnic traditions of those groups that have made Iowa their home over the years. Each has added its own distinct contribution to Iowa's cultural heritage—Meskwaki Indians, European Americans from other parts of the United States, Western Europeans, British, Irish, Southern Europeans, and African Americans. In the late twentieth century, Iowa become home to refugees from Southeast Asians, Middle Easterners (Iraqis, Palestinians), Africans, and Eastern Europeans. Agricultural and packing plant work has encouraged Latin American migration; many of those from Mexico are following the path of ancestors who started coming to Iowa over 100 years ago to work on the railroads. Also Iowa's universities as well as companies such as Pioneer Hi-Bred International, Inc. have attracted newcomers from India, Korea, China, and Thailand.

Iowa food specialties vary by region, with smoked, fried, or pickled fish available at river cafes along the Mississippi, Missouri, and inland waterways; flaekesteg (pork loin embedded with prunes) and rødkal (red cabbage) at the Danish Inn in Elk Horn; and *kolaches* in Cedar Rapids and Spillville. There are spring rolls and Southeast Asian curries and phở at Lao, Vietnamese, and Thai restaurants in central and western Iowa; marzipan-filled puff pastry "Dutch letters" found only in Pella; German sausage in western Iowa; and Italian sausages in Des Moines. Towns across the state with significant Latino populations produce tamales, tortillas, and pan dulces as well as feature butcher shops with fresh tripe, chorizo, and chicharones. In Tama, home of the

This article is based on a paper given by the author during the Food, Ethnic Identities, and Memory Symposium in 2008, sponsored by the University of Iowa's Center for Ethnic Studies and the Arts. Published with kind permission of the author, the former Folklife Coordinator for the Iowa Arts Council (1995–2012), now Executive Director, Oregon Folklife Network.

Meskwaki Settlement, Indian fry bread and tacos are available at annual powwows and in restaurants. Visitors to Decorah and Story City can savor Norwegian treats such as römmegrot (a sweetened cream pudding), lefse (a potato flatbread), and even lutefisk—also available in the frozen foods section of many Iowa food markets. And locker-smoked fish and meats can be found all over the state.

In Iowa, visitors and residents travel to the Amana colonies to experience the past, imagined as well as real, via the home-cooked German-style meals and fresh-baked breads and pies. While the sauerbraten served at every restaurant has more to do with tourists' expectations about German cuisine than with Amana foodways, there are other foods that do capture this still thriving settlement's cultural traditions: rhubarb wine, potato dumplings, homemade applesauce from local apples, and what I suspect may be the prototype for that all-American green bean casserole—but the cream is not from store-bought canned soup, and the string beans and onions are locally produced. Visitors to Cedar Rapids can experience Houby Days—in honor of the morel mushrooms that grow wild in Iowa in the early spring.

Pigs and Pork

Back to pigs. In Iowa, they are most famously found throughout the state as pork tenderloin—the dish most identified with Iowa according to members of RoadFood.com as well as an informal survey of state residents. Pork tenderloins have historically been available only in the upper Midwestern "I" states of Iowa, Indiana, and Illinois, not surprising given the region's predominant German and Czech immigrant heritage. Like (Philly) cheese steaks and (San Francisco) sourdough bread, their popularity has spread, though not necessarily reliably authentic preparation methods. Chowhound.com even has a list of restaurants that serve them in Minnesota's Twin Cities. While Iowa has its own pork tenderloin competition, sponsored by the Iowa Pork Producers, as of yet, there has been no formal competition among the states producing this regional specialty. Given the tenderloin's value and meaning to Iowans, notwithstanding those Indianans who also claim the tenderloin as theirs, I would certainly deem this dish an Iowa place-based food.

Before discussing definitions and the politics of those definitions, let's look at some examples of pork dishes that I would not consider place-based. At the 2008 Iowa trials for the National Pork Board's "Taste of Elegance" cook-off, one recipe "included more than 40 ingredients and required an entire weekend of preparation." Writes food dude Jim Duncan for Des Moines's *Cityview*, "Stroud's was the most time-consuming. He brined Niman Ranch pork shanks before smoking them in banana leaves, pulling the meat off the bones and mixing it with a puree of several different re-hydrated chilies he has toasted in pork lard, plus fresh chilies cooked in olive oil with tomatillos and tomatoes. He served that combo with a gremalata of pork belly, a pickled radish hay, scratch-made tortillas and momocho (crinkled fired pork skin)." Another dish included a pork shoulder, liver, and jowl sausage with pistachios and dried cherries stuffed in a Serrano ham and served with roasted fennel and a black-truffle risotto. Both dishes include ingredients and preparation methods that have no particular meaning in Iowa's culinary history.

On to the definitions—and why some foods are place-based and others are not.

Place-based foods

Place-based foods have a unique taste that often has to do with an ecological niche and/or the ethnic or regional heritage of their producers. These are the foods that we seek out to eat locally when we visit a particular place, purchase as souvenirs or gifts, or hunt down in specialty shops. Food is not just about sustenance, and we are increasingly interested in the stories behind our foods and their producers.

During 2005 and 2006, the Leopold Center funded the Iowa Foodways Project: Taste of Place, which surveyed the state to locate and document a variety of foods and the people who produce them.[2] The goal was to identify and document those foods that can be distinguished as uniquely Iowan in heritage (whether historical, ethnic, ecological, or geographic). Politics—local, regional, and global—make defining the term "place-based foods" not easy to put into words, even though identifying a food as "place-based" may be as deceptively simple and as inherently complex as "you know it when you see it."

In 1992 the European Union established specific definitions for "geographical indications" or GIs, which focus on place of origin and qualities that derive from that place, e.g. climate and soil. The EU did this to protect products from misuse or imitation and to give consumers reliable product information. Because geographic origin designations developed due to particular historic and economic conditions, heritage and artisanship are implied but not requirements of protected designation of origin (PDO) or geographical indication (PGI) criteria; they are part of the traditional specialty guaranteed (TSG) indication. These terms all have legal consequences and protections that differ from trademarks.

1. PDO—this label means that a food is produced, processed, and prepared using recognized methods.
2. PGI—this indication is less stringent and indicates that the geographical connection exists in at least one of the stages of production, processing or preparation.
3. TSG—this designation assures that a food's "main ingredients, composition or preparation, production method or processing are essentially traditional." TSG is not about geographical area of production.

Categorizing American foods in those terms is difficult, confusing, and possibly irrelevant, thanks to a lack of time depth for most American foods and because a different relationship with food has developed here than it has in Europe. Some foods, like California, Oregon, or Washington wines; Minnesota wild rice; New England lobsters; and Chesapeake blue crabs, are easy to declare place-based because they did originate in those places, have been grown and produced there for decades, or are tied to specific ethnic or occupational groups, processing/production methods, and eating traditions. But many foods are identified with either a specific origin or a particular heritage and not both. For example, a European PDO label means that a food comes from a specific, well-defined region, such as Champagne (the wine and the region) in France or Parmigiano-Reggiano cheese from Parma and Reggio-Emilia in Italy. A PDO designation also implies years, often centuries, of traditional heritage, both in terms of ethnicity or regionality and artisanship. Trademarked American foods such as Vidalia® onions from a 20-county region in Georgia or Idaho® potatoes are certified as grown in a particular locale or state. Both products claim that their taste is derived from their place of origin; heritage and artisanship are not relevant, e.g.

Idaho's growing season of warm days and cool nights, ample mountain-fed irrigation and rich volcanic soil, give Idaho Potatoes their unique texture, taste and dependable performance.[3]

The unique combination of low sulfur soil and the mild climate found in the 20 county production area of south Georgia produces the sweet flavor of the Vidalia Onion.[4]

Yet the where as well as the how and the why are substantive issues for growing and processing, especially given the ways in which definitions for *appellation* and *terroir*, both of which were once used to refer exclusively to wine are increasingly being tossed around.

Appellation refers to a designation, name, or title that refers to either an object, a place, or a product. With regard to wine labels, appellation refers to the ***place*** where the grapes are grown. Many appellations have official status, with either a government or trade bureau responsible for strictly delimiting and regulating usage in order to assure both quality and authenticity. An appellation may be as large as an entire region, encompassing hundreds of thousands of acres and many separate vineyards, or as small as a single vineyard of perhaps four acres or less. Most of the best-known wines from France are appellation wines. Appellations are also used to identify most of the wines of Italy, Germany, Spain and Portugal. Systems for officially identifying and regulating winegrowing regions are evolving in countries of the New World.[5]

"A *terroir* is a group of vineyards (or even vines) from the same region, belonging to a specific appellation, and sharing the same type of soil, weather conditions, grapes and wine making savoir-faire, which contribute to give its specific personality to the wine."[6] In *The Seattle Times* "Food and Wine," March 01, 2006, Paul Gregutt noted, "Terroir comes from an ongoing process of discovery, stewardship and passionate art." Terroir is about the "unique characteristics (e.g. soil composition, geography, climate) which exist in combinations found only in [an] area. These can be physical characteristics (such as soil acidity and mineral content), but may also be traditions (e.g. the tradition of producing a particular cheese in a particular way). . . . As each area has unique characteristics, the products traditionally produced in a given area are unique to that area."

Amy Trubek, food anthropologist, Executive Director for Vermont Fresh Network, Assistant Professor in Nutrition and Food Sciences at the University of Vermont, and author of *The Taste of Place: A Cultural Journey into Terroir* (2008), notes that place and quality as well as sustainable and artisanal production methods are critical; "food that tastes good . . . and that comes from known locales . . . [has a] taste of place." Trubek cites the French Ministry of Agriculture as an exemplar for officially recognizing "agricultural producers who can demonstrate a tradition of small-scale production in a region that is distinctive in terms of flavor and quality" (called the *goûte du terroir*).

Yet many heritage-based products in Iowa and elsewhere that are intimately associated with their *place* and *method* of production, are not made from locally or even American-grown ingredients. Like the TSG designation, these foods are about heritage preparation methods and taste—not *where* the ingredients are from. Nor does the advent and increasing popularity in this country of artisanal foods (hand-crafted or produced in a small shop versus a factory), from bread to cheese, jams to pastries, or smoked meats to wines, have anything to do with either place of origin or heritage; artisanal foods are merely those made in small batches or in small-scale production. In Europe, however, and in most traditional cultures, such a production method is intimately related to the producer's and consumer's *belief* in a food's traditionality—its authenticity.[7]

In fact, authenticity is the underlying issue for all these efforts to designate and describe place-based food—though authenticity means different things for different groups. Is it really from a particular region, and does it taste a certain way because of the soils, molds or bacteria, altitude, humidity, air or water quality of that region? Has a particular group prepared it in a certain way from time immemorial—or at least as long as anyone can remember? Did real people and not faceless machines create it? Is it uncontaminated by antibiotics, hormones, or GMOs? Various combinations of these criteria combine to determine just how "place-based" a particular food is.

Rich Pirog, in his conclusions to "A Geography of Taste: Iowa's Potential for Developing Traditional and Place-Based Foods" (2004) puts the issue succinctly: "Although American consumers value local foods, it is unclear which traits of place-based foods they value the most, and how they would perceive such foods among the confusing array of other differentiated foods already in the market." Within two years of Pirog's comments, the term "locavore" had become a ubiquitous term among foodies and food scholars, due partly to the overwhelming popularity of Michel Pollan's *The Omnivore's Dilemna* (2006) and Barbara Kingsolver's *Animal, Vegetable, Miracle* (2007).

Iowa place-based foods—examples

The survey provided nearly 50 suggestions for Iowa place-based foods. Most met at least two of the criteria for the designation, but we were looking for foods that carried all three. After conducting interviews with producers, eight food products met the test for out of four three benchmarks:[8]

- Maytag® Blue Cheese
- Maasdam's Sorghum
- Rhubarb wine from the Amana Colonies
- Muscatine Melons
- K&K Tiny but Mighty Popcorn
- Western Iowa mettwurst
- Southeastern Iowa black walnuts and pawpaws
- Iowa Pork Tenderloin

Most of the foods that Iowans and others identify with Iowa fall into four categories:

1. Those that are grown and processed here and have a heritage basis (pork tenderloins, Maasdam's sorghum syrup, Amana rhubarb wine, mettwurst, black walnuts, Muscatine melons, and pawpaws);

2. Those that are processed here and have a heritage basis (Dutch letters, lefse, kolaches, Swedish pancakes, Norwegian kringle, Danish aebleskivver, Mexican flour and corn tortillas, and other ethnic dishes);

3. Those that are grown and processed here, but have no substantive heritage basis (several kinds of tasty salsa made by non-Latinos; cows' milk and goats milk cheese from various makers; Java chickens and most other heritage poultry; emerging vineyards and wineries; a variety of delicious local organic and natural dairy products, some from re-emerging micro-dairies; and farmed fish from western Iowa); and

4. Those that are grown and processed here and that do have a heritage basis but are not necessarily produced organically or naturally, and as a result may prove problematic to market without having to contend with other political and economic issues (buffalo from northwest Iowa, Amana® meats, pork tenderloins, Maidrite® sandwiches, hybrid sweet corn, soy nuts).

The ecological basis of Iowa place-based foods stems from grasses the animals eat that affect the taste of the meat or the milk/cheese produced, the soils in which the crops grow (e.g., sorghum, Muscatine melons), the soil and climate for the grapes and fruits (e.g., Hawkeye apples, Amana rhubarb wine), and the effect of molds and humidity (Maytag® Blue Cheese). But if food comes from ingredients grown elsewhere, or is so common that it really doesn't matter where it comes from (e.g., potato chips, doughnuts, hamburgers, sweet corn), it is difficult to make the claim that the food has a uniquely specific Iowa origin and taste. Foods missing the heritage part that "tells the Iowa story" do not illustrate place-based foods. While more research needs to be done on precisely how these factors influence the taste of the food products, the ways that foods are identified with a particular ethnic group and place as well as the food itself seem to be the largest influence on whether or not it acquires iconic meaning for its culture group as well as for a particular place.

Pork, place, and praxis

So, this is where pork and its stories come in to play. Iowans produce a variety of pork dishes, old and new, traditional and innovative. Danes from Elk Horn and Kimballton are known for their röllepost, a brined pork meat roll, while the Amana Colonies have made famous the thick-cut pork chop that bears its name—though few Amana chops are actually produced in the Amana Colonies, much less in Iowa. Local varieties of locker-made pork sausages include the Doberstein of northwest Iowa (so-named for Father Doberstein, who built the Grotto of the Redemption in West Bend) to south and northwestern Iowa's mettwurst (a cold-smoked platt German delicacy). Des Moines's Grazziano and Scavo families both produce spicy Italian pork sausages, featured on pizzas and the regrettably named "guinea" grinders.

Responding to the market for additive-free pork products, fifth-generation farmer Tim Beeler produces ham, bacon, and sausage, including brats, under his company's Hogwild® label. Mexican restaurants from Des Moines to Columbus Junction feature tacos al pastor, a Mexico City street food with marinated chunks of slow-roasted pork piled on a soft corn tortilla. African Americans in Waterloo, whose parents and grandparents hailed from the Mississippi Delta, continue to prepare smoky chopped pork shoulder in their barbecue to use fatback to flavor slow-cooked greens. Iowa's Tai Dam community roasts several whole pigs for its New Year's festivities and other celebrations.

Mettwurst

Among the many sausages produced in the Midwest and in Iowa is *mettwurst*. This is a cold-smoked ring sausage, similar in texture to bratwurst but made in a bigger casing and produced by several small communities of *Plattdeutsch* from Schleswig-Holstein, Dutch, and Luxembourg heritage in southwest Iowa and northwest, Iowa. Typically made in midwinter (the traditional time to slaughter hogs, due to the cold weather and lack of other high intensity farm duties), the sausage is ground, mixed with spices, and then smoked at 70 degrees F for three hours. Although Germans in Europe eat the sausage without further cooking, Mineola community members of Platt German descent boil or grill the sausage after smoking to make sure that all bacteria are killed.

Gary Schoening, whose Plattdeutsch or low German community of Mineola in western Iowa celebrated its 125th anniversary in 2005, told me that his community commemorates its annual founders day with the local production of mettwurst—not bratwurst, which are not part of the community's heritage. Several families, including Schoening's, continue to make their own recipe for home or church consumption only, since the cold-smoked process is not a legal or commercially sanctioned method.[9]

Pigs and changing traditions

Beyond its role as a place-based food, pork has also changed ethnic food traditions in Iowa. For its annual food festival, the Des Moines Greek community uses pork for its souvlaki instead of the traditional lamb, which is more costly and not as readily available as pork. The latter also appeals more to the majority of Iowans, who are of northern and central European heritage—a consideration for this major church fundraising event. Jewish community members and self-confessed foodies, Herb and Kathy Eckhouse, opened La Quercia in 2005, and *Bon Appetit* named the couple among its 2007 Food Artisans of the Year for their salted, dry cured, and aged *salumi*, a group of meats that includes prosciutto.

When she read a short version of this presentation, Lauren Rabinovitz, American Studies professor at the University of Iowa, raised the question about Jews' being involved with the production of pork products. If ever there were an iconic forbidden food, pork is certainly it for Jews—something that "everyone" knows about Jewish foodways. According to former Iowan, Amy Scattergood, who interviewed the Eckhouses for "Prosciutto by way of Iowa," which appeared in the *LA Times*, 7/5/07, "The fact that he'd never made ham before, or that he wasn't Italian (Herb, who was born in Iowa and grew up in Chicago, describes himself as a 'Harvard-educated Jewish liberal,' while Kathy grew up in Berkeley) didn't faze him. The American tradition of reinvention, says Herb, smiling at the many implicit ironies, 'can be liberating.' So he [and Kathy] befriended a few of Parma's artisan *prosciutto* makers," lived and worked in Parma for over three years, and came back to Iowa determined to make their own way in the rarefied foodie world of artisanal speciality meats.[10]

Pork tenderloin

Back to Iowa and the pork tenderloin. Breaded tenderloin's historical ties to this specific region are indisputable, though, as with most folklore, it is next to impossible to pinpoint only one spot of origin. All immigrant groups have particular cultural traditions that they maintain in their new homes. And preparation methods, if not always a particular food, are especially likely to survive among later generations. Their ability to continue to raise food amenable to both Midwest and Central European growing conditions makes it relatively easy for the peoples who settled the "I" states to maintain their culinary traditions.

The breaded tenderloin likely has its roots in the Czech dish *veprovy rizek* rather than the German *schnitzel*, though both involve taking a thin-sliced piece of meat tenderized by pounding, dipping it in beaten egg or milk, then in wheat flour or bread crumbs and spices, and frying the meat in butter or lard, a preparation method common in the Slavic states as well. The Czech version uses pork, while German schnitzel uses veal.

Pork tenderloin preparation follows the same basics, though Iowa loins are sometimes run through a spiked tenderizer instead of pounded, and cooks occasionally use cracker crumbs in place of bread crumbs. The less common battered loins are dipped in an egg batter, and both battered and breaded loins are deep fried in vegetable oil or lard until crispy and golden and served on a bun with mustard and pickles—usually with a side of fries.

Size is of critical importance: the bigger, the better. There is some disagreement as to whether this meat lover's treat should be pounded thin (a quarter inch or less) before breading or left thicker and more succulent. The former method lends itself more to what Jane and Michael Stern describe as a "shatteringly crisp" texture—best exemplified by Smitty's on Army Post Road in Des Moines. The latter style is featured at many Iowa restaurants, in particular at Elk Horn's Larsen's Pub, which won the 2007 Iowa Pork Producers Best Breaded Tenderloin award; the Town House Supper Club in Wellsburg won the Iowa Pork Producers 2006 Best Breaded Tenderloin award with the Links at Lake Panorama placing second.[11]

Susie Lyon and Diane Cox make one of Iowa's best grilled tenderloins. The two sisters run the Suburban, a now 3rd-generation family restaurant in Gilbert, 5 miles north of Ames on Highway 69. Winners of the Iowa Pork Producers' 2004 Best Grilled Tenderloin Contest, the sisters also serve the more traditional breaded tenderloin, both made from the whole loin, from a local locker, which sources its meats from farmers in Story County.[12]

Conclusion

Food represents an interesting and complex way to explore issues endemic to twenty-first century issues of culture, environment, and heritage. Authenticity and purity seem to be at the center of current talk about food. The terms that describe food as unpolluted and somehow authentic—terroir, place-based, heritage, and heirloom—all refer to some connection with the past as well as to a particular place and, in some coded way, to the identity of the people who inhabit or who have inhabited the place. The phenomenon of iconization, a process whereby foods are marked as hyper-authentic, involves ethnicity, place, and preparation methods—the ingredients themselves become almost secondary to the symbolic value of a particular food item. The butter, flour, and certainly not the almond paste in Dutch Letters, does not have to come from Pella or even Iowa; the potatoes in lefse are not required to be grown in Decorah or Story City; and the pork in pork tenderloins is not necessarily Iowa grown. But in all three cases, the preparation methods and the place of production MUST be in Iowa for these foods to be considered authentic—for these foods to represent in some way what it is to be Iowan.

Ironically, the popularity of a food and success in marketing it can create disincentives for a place-based identification, which is what happened with Amana® meats. When demand outgrew supply, the label ceased to refer to pork actually raised in the Amana Colonies. Such a marketing strategy can "pollute" authenticity, leaving us with tasteless nostalgia, disconnected from any place.

Notes

1. See http://www.leopold.iastate.edu/sites/default/files/pubs-and-papers/2004-10-geography-taste-iowas-potential-developing-place-based-and-traditional-foods.pdf.

2. See http://www.leopold.iastate.edu/sites/default/files/grants/2005-M02.pdf.

3. See http://www.idahopotato.com/WhyIdaho.php.

4. See http://www.vidaliaonion.org/commercial/index.aspx.

5. Understanding Wine Labels (Part 2), APPELLATION LABELS, Professional Friends of Wine.

6. Terroir, French Wine Guide, http://www.terroir-france.com/theclub/meaning.htm.

7. See Regina Bendix, In Search of Authenticity (1997).

8. See Iowa Place-based Foods, Food Stories, http://www.iowaartscouncil.org/programs/folk-and-traditional-arts/place_based_foods/stories.htm.

9. To see and hear more on mettwurst, see http://www.iowaartscouncil.org/programs/folk-and-traditional-arts/place_based_foods/stories6.htm.

10. By way of a footnote to this American "fusion food," I should note that the Eckhouses are not the only American Jews to make their mark purveying pork specialities. Zingerman's Deli in Ann Arbor Michigan, which carries La Quercia's line, opened in 1982, starting "with a small selection of great-tasting specialty foods, a host of traditional Jewish dishes and a relatively short sandwich menu." Today, that menu, which has sections designated dairy, vegetarian, beef, fish, and chicken, also includes a pork section featuring Arkansas peppered ham and bacon as well as (Iowa's) Niman Ranch pork and Nueske's applewood-smoked bacon—that last Wisconsin specialty served with "leaf lettuce, tomato & mayo on Jewish rye bread."

11. For the best list of Iowa restaurants making and selling breaded tenderloins, check out Allen Bukoff's website http://www.allenbukoff.com/wildBPTiowa03/ as well as the Des Moines Register's 2004 list at http://www.dmregister.com/entertainment/stories/c2124444/23675061.html.

12. To read about and listen to Susie Lyon's and Diane Cox's pork tenderloin story, see http://www.iowaartscouncil.org/programs/folk-and-traditional-arts/place_based_foods/stories9.htm.

CHAPTER 33

A TASTE OF HOME: AFRICAN IMMIGRANT FOODWAYS

Nomvula Mashoai Cook and Betty J. Belanus

In almost all African cultures food is a traditional art. Simple or elaborate, frugal or opulent, food plays a vital role in affirming individual ethnic identities and in modeling cultural diversity. Recent African immigrants to the Washington metropolitan area come from different regions of the continent. And as they create a taste of home through their foodways, they discover the similarities and differences in their fellow immigrants' foods. They also come to know the common problems they share cooking -authentic' dishes and recreating the contexts of serving them. Immigrant groups sustain continuity by cooking everyday meals similar to those that nourish families in Africa, by using food in the context of traditional celebrations, and by establishing African restaurants.

Mealtimes in Africa bring families together: the generation gap between young and old can be bridged: in conversations, children may learn proverbs, their meanings, and other wisdom from their elders. Here in the United States, however, African immigrant families are often too busy to sit down to a traditional-style meal every day of the week, or sometimes even once a week. But great effort is made to introduce to children traditional foods and the etiquette of eating.

While most ingredients needed for traditional foods are now available in the Washington, D.C., area at specialized grocery stores serving African, Caribbean, Latin American, and Asian cooks, this was not always the case for earlier immigrants. Olaniyi Areke, a film maker originally from Nigeria, recalls trying to find something in an American grocery store resembling the staple *fufu,* made in West Africa from cassava flour. The closest thing he could find was Bisquick!

Some African immigrants with enough yard space and access to seeds from home grow their own vegetables and herbs. Different varieties of greens, many of them not to be found even in specialty stores, are popular garden items. Sally Tsuma, originally from the Kalenjian region of Kenya, grows five types of greens around her home. Sally cooks a large batch of greens on the weekend and serves them throughout the week, heating them in the microwave. The correct combination of greens is the secret to the taste, as Sally says, "When you cook [the greens] alone, it tastes like something's missing."

Comfort foods for African immigrants are staples like *fufu,* or the Southern African *papa* (made from corn flour), roughly equivalent to American mashed potatoes. Typical dishes accompanying the staples - depending on the region of Africa you hail from - are stews and soups made with palm oil, pureed peanuts, dried or fresh fish, okra, tomatoes, onions, hot peppers, black-eyed peas, lentils, many different kinds of meat, and an array of spices. But there are many foods considered more exotic by most Americans that also count among the comfort foods of some Africans: goat's head, for instance, or lamb's intestines. Foods served often reflect a combination of cultures, as Dorothy Osei-Kuffuor, originally from Ghana, says: "The main dishes in my house are African, though the children enjoy some American dishes, too."

Nomvula Mashoai Cook and Betty J. Belanus, 'A Taste of Home: African Immigrant Foodways', *Festival of American Folklife Program,* (1997), 51–53. Reproduced with permission from the Center for Folklife and Cultural Heritage, Smithsonian Institution.

Living in America, some African immigrant women break traditional food taboos. Nsedu Onyile wrote in a *Washington Post* article:

> Let me tell you about the goat head. Where I come from, the women fix and serve it in a big platter but only the men are entitled to eat it. As a child, I fantasized about the taste of the goat head and could not wait for an opportunity to eat one. Now in a total declaration of independence, I buy a goat from the slaughterhouse, fix the head first, and sit down to catch up on missed years. I eat every bit of this delicacy, appreciating what those men enjoyed during their roundtable goat conferences in our sunny yard back in Nigeria.

In the Washington, D.C., area, such splendid African foods are more often served at family or community celebrations. Every major rite of passage - birth, coming-of-age, marriage, and death - is celebrated with specific foods. At a traditional naming ceremony in the Yoruba community, for instance, a tray of symbolic ritual foods is prepared that includes salt (for joy and happiness), palm oil, cola nut, bitter cola and alligator pepper (for medicinal purposes), and honey (for sweetness). After the ceremony, a meal including fried plantains, two rice dishes, goat stew with fufu, boiled yam, and chicken is served to all the guests.

Other types of celebrations bring communities together seasonally. One example is the braai, a South African cookout celebrated in the summer. Typically, the women congregate in the kitchen, cooking and singing. The men bond with each other and with their sons while preparing imbuzi ne mvu (goat and lamb) for the barbecue grill with such savory condiments as South African curry or cumin.

The braai usually starts at noon and may last until midnight. Besides eating and reconnecting with old friends, people might listen to South African township music. Conversation might center around political, economic, or social issues and their effect on people back home. Children are encouraged to play games such as *lebekere* (hide-and-seek).

Community-bridging celebrations that are hybrids of American and African traditions also involve food. At the Cook household in suburban Maryland, this year's Kwanzaa celebration (an African-American holiday) brought together African immigrants from all parts of the continent, African Americans, and White Americans. The food was potluck and included roast turkey, Christmas cookies, Swedish-style meatballs, and a rice dish from an Egyptian guest. The centerpiece dishes, however, were cooked with great loving care (and no visible recipes) by Mimi Green, originally from Niger in West Africa. They included *yassa* chicken (a Senegalese dish), *egusi* spinach (spinach with ground melon seeds), and *mafi* (meatballs in a peanut butter sauce), all served with mounds of perfect white rice. As is the custom in many African cultures, a libation offering of drink for the ancestors was poured on the ground before the meal was eaten.

Other occasions bring generations together and reinforce language and customs. Amharic women in the Washington, D.C., area meet at one another's homes for a coffee ceremony. The coffee is roasted and prepared in a special pot and served with crunchy grain snacks. Kenyan women in the area try to meet once a month for *chai* (tea) and *mandazi* (doughnuts).

Restaurants offering many African cuisines have mushroomed around the metropolitan Washington area in the past ten years. Many find their homes in the ethnically diverse Adams Morgan area of the city including well-established Ethiopian restaurants like Meskerem, Addis Ababa, and The Red Sea, as well as newer ventures such as the Casa Africana, which serves West African food, and the South African Cafe. Cecelia Vilakazi, owner/proprietor of the South African Cafe, whose parents emigrated from South Africa to the United States when she was a teenager, explains her motivation to start her restaurant in 1995: "I looked and I saw Ethiopians have restaurants, people from Ghana, Nigeria, and Brazil, but no South Africa. So the timing was right to introduce the rich culinary spread that's there in South Africa. I saw an opportunity and said this was something I've always wanted to do."

These restaurants, of course, cater not only to African immigrant clients, but to culinarily adventurous Americans. Some attempt, therefore, is made to serve foods that appeal to a wide spectrum of people. Cecelia admits it takes some education for those unfamiliar with some of the dishes served at the South African Cafe, such as bobotie, a meat loaf with curry spices and raisins. "It's tasty, but you have to grow up eating it. When people do try it, we show them how to eat it, and they like it." She has toned down the heavily meat-oriented South African diet to accommodate American tastes.

There are also foods prepared exclusively for a busy African immigrant clientele. At lunchtime, taxicabs line the front of the Akosombo restaurant near Chinatown, where the African-born drivers can get cafeteria-style service like that in the restaurants back in Ghana. African immigrant caterers, some working out of their home kitchens, deliver traditional foods to wedding receptions, naming ceremonies, and birthday or graduation parties. Whether cooked as a simple dish at home, for an elaborate celebration, or for sale to the public, African immigrant foods embody cultural connections. They create a continuity with custom back home, and they reflect the circumstances of living in a new place. Like other aspects of African immigrant folklife in the Washington, D.C. area, foodways are continually recreated and offer a glimpse of a community in the process of defining itself.

References

Brown, Linda K., and Kay Mussell. 1984. *Ethnic and Regional Foodways in the United States.* Knoxville: University of Tennessee Press.

Grant, Rosamund. 1995. *Taste of Africa.* New York: Smithmark Publishers.

Hafner, Dorinda. 1993. *Taste of Africa.* Berkeley: Ten Speed Press.

Kirlin, Katherine, and Thomas Kirlin. 1991. *Smithsonian Folklife Cookbook.* Washington, D.C.: Smithsonian Institution Press.

Onyile, Nsedu. 1995. I'll Have the Goat's Head, Please. *Washington Post.* 5 March.

CHAPTER 34
NO FOOD OR DRINK IN THE MUSEUM?:
THE CHALLENGES OF EDIBLE ARTIFACTS
Sarah Conrad Gothie

Nora Ephron's 2009 film *Julie & Julia* juxtaposes the life of Julia Child writing her tour de force *Mastering the Art of French Cooking* in the 1950s with the contemporary life of Julie Powell, a civil servant attempting to cook each of the book's 524 recipes over the course of a year in post-9/11 New York City. After completing her project, Julie makes a pilgrimage to Washington D.C. to the "Julia Child's Kitchen" exhibit at the Smithsonian's National Museum of American History. Having spent a year rehearsing Child's recipes, Julie seeks to get closer—not to the 'meat' of Child's kitchen, which she has recreated in her own kitchen by proxy—but to a sacred domestic space and an aura of 'Julia' that Julie's mass-produced copy of the cook book, and her own attempts at its recipes, cannot approximate.

In the museum, Julia Child's custom countertops and a pan-adorned pegboard are recontextualized as a national shrine. When the kitchen was disassembled and packed to be shipped from Massachusetts, an inventory was taken of foodstuffs and their locations before the ingredients themselves were discarded.[1] Durable, non-perishable aspects of the kitchen are displayed (no food; no Julia). Julie's husband photographs her as she leans against a large portrait of Julia Child (as portrayed in the film by Meryl Streep), then Julie requests a private moment. At this shrine to an exceptional American, within the national space of the Smithsonian, Julie offers up a pound of butter. The butter is an ordinary, paper-wrapped brick. Julie places it on a ledge beneath Julia's photograph, and quickly departs, satisfied. The camera lingers a few seconds on Julia Child's beaming visage and the pound of butter. I viewed this scene with apprehension. *She's just going to leave that butter there?! It will melt under the lights! It will seep onto the guest book! Who will find it? A guard? A concerned museum visitor? How warm was it already from being in her bag?* Perishable, edible—these are not characteristics of typical museum artifacts. Julie crossed a line. She interacted with an exhibit in the *wrong way*. But in some sense, her instinct was right on. A perishable, absent essence of Child's legacy—her democratization of butter-rich French cooking—had been restored to the kitchen through Julie's offering. Museums have been accused of being dusty and dead—butter is alive and gathers no dust. *Or does it?*

The archaeology exhibits of the National Museum of Ireland display objects discovered in peat bogs, including partial, contorted human remains. These Iron Age bodies had been preserved (pickled, really) within anaerobic, humic acid-rich bogs, only to be dredged up centuries later by mechanized peat harvesting equipment. Bodies, it turns out, are not the only organic objects bogs preserve. In the same museum, a wooden vessel sits behind glass, packed to the brim with a porous, tan substance. This dirty, dry substance is *butter*—circa 11th to 13th century AD.[2] Urns of butter were likely placed in bogs for preservation or ritual purposes, and subsequently lost, forgotten, or abandoned—only to surface centuries later. The long-dead

Commissioned for this publication.

churners remain anonymous, but here is their butter, on display alongside brooches, boats, and bowls. Unlike the spontaneous, unsanctioned offering of butter by Julie, this bog butter, sacred by dint of its extremely unlikely survival, has been accessioned and responsibly housed within a climate-controlled case. Yet, both butters seem incongruous with their surroundings—after all, museums typically greet us with stern signs advising that food and drink are not permitted inside.

Food is essential to human life, but it is not durable like the buildings and tea pots classified as material culture.[3] The United Nations Educational, Scientific and Cultural Organization (UNESCO) categorizes foodways—the processes through which humans interact with food, including production, procurement, preparation, and performance[4]—as intangible heritage. While skills and techniques for preparation may reside intangibly in human minds and muscle memory, food itself—the product, not the process—is an undeniably tangible material. Food might be better understood as its own unique sub-category of material culture, residing in that hazy zone between the tangible and the intangible: the edible.[5] It is the *edibility* of food that sets it apart from the other material culture created by humans and displayed in museums. Edible artifacts are perishable, palatable, and most comprehensively understood through full sensory engagement. By focusing on the sensory features of edible material culture, we can better understand the complexities of representing and interpreting food in museums.

Food appeals to multiple senses and promises to excite and engage museum visitors, but can present challenges that durable, inedible collections do not. The challenges of integrating food-centered exhibits intersect, however, with larger challenges faced by museums in general: determining what constitutes 'knowledge,' logistics of conserving collections and balancing budgets, and crafting accurate and empathetic interpretion of multiple perspectives in ways that will be relevant to diverse audiences. This essay argues for a more robust effort to find a place for food in museums—a place that allows us to access its enormous potential to transmit heritage, represent identity,[6] and illuminate meaningful connections across diverse audiences.

'Please don't lick the art': Sensory biases

The first challenge to museological engagement with edible artifacts is epistemological: determining what constitutes *knowledge* of a food—and how one might best acquire that knowledge. Deane Curtin argues that food studies[7] has been marginalized in academia due, in part, to Plato's dictum that pleasures of the body must be eschewed by philosophers. Ideally, the philosopher "ignores the body and becomes as far as possible independent, avoiding all physical contacts and associations as much as it can in its search for reality" (qtd in Curtin 5). The notion that human perception of 'reality' ought to be separated from embodied physical sensations highlights the mind-body disconnect—the "reductionist dualism"—that underpins Western intellectual traditions and devalues ordinary, everyday interactions with food (6). Yet, to know a *food* would seem to require more information than a text panel in a museum can impart.

To know a food—not just facts *about* a food—requires visceral experience. Janet Flammang calls for "a worldview of mind-body *interdependence*" (author's emphasis, 134). She believes that knowing through smelling and tasting complement the work of the mind:

> The mind-body dualism, with its hierarchy of senses, devalues food preparation as mundane, routine, messy, smelly, something to get out of the way so that more important things can be attended to. Mind-body interdependence allows one to be sensual, to trust the sense of smell, to use taste to discriminate among flavors, to experiment with new aromas and tastes, and to create with approximate cooking instead of rigidly following recipes. (134)

Flammang connects expanded sensory consideration with the practical skills necessary for culinary agency and enhanced attention to food preparation. Rather than rushing obliviously through food procurement and preparation, she suggests that real benefits are gained by unifying mind and body in an intentional, meaning-making way. Michael Pollan, a food writer and critic familiar to many non-specialists interested in food, also advocates for home cooking and mindful eating to promote health and banish ignorance of the "web of social and ecological relationships" (18) in which American food consumption practices are embedded. Mind-body interdependence requires a balance of theoretical and practical knowledges—the former is not replaced by the latter, but is complemented by it.

Perceiving and analyzing food through a full complement of sensory interactions can enhance intellectual understanding of food's material and symbolic dimensions. Folklorists Simon Bronner and Kathy Neustadt question the Western sensory bias that privileges observation as the preferred means for attaining information. Bronner uses the example of hands-on exhibits in museums to make the point that "simply observing the object or activity is often inadequate for the full apprehension and cognition of the three-dimensional reality" (353). Though Bronner's ethnographic work focuses on Indiana wood chain cutters, his conclusion that sight may identify, but "touch verifies" (358), applies to edible things. For example, we can read the date on a carton of milk or observe the color of an avocado, but scent, taste, and touch are required to verify freshness. Neustadt goes a step further, proposing a phenomenological "methodology of licking" derived from the simultaneous engagement of scent, taste, and touch, the triad of 'lower' senses considered least legitimate for yielding intellectual evidence in a scholarly context (185):

> [...] by privileging—even if momentarily—the tongue over the eye, for instance, by making our historical and cultural sensory biases conscious, and by exploring new perceptual models of experience and interpretation, we might get a fuller mouthful of truth. (1994: 183)

The revelation that each of the senses can contribute meaningfully to 'knowing' is not immediately helpful in a museum setting. As it stands, tasting and eating museum objects is so obviously taboo that the transgression can be referenced for comedic effect. A 1983 television special found the cast of children's program *Sesame Street* visiting the Metropolitan Museum of Art and accidentally being locked in overnight. *Don't Eat the Pictures* features a subplot in which the omnivorous Cookie Monster must be reminded by his human friend Bob not to devour the artworks, no matter how delectable they appear. Cookie sings the show's titular song, instructing the audience in his newly learned museum etiquette: "Picture exciting, but not for biting! [...] Mummy look yummy, but not for tummy! [...] Statue for viewing, it not for chewing!" Cookie's ingestion of artifacts would be irreversibly destructive, and museums are premised on protecting cultural treasures. But what about just a 'taste'? Parody news publication *The Onion* advises: "If you don't experience a painting with all five senses, you aren't truly experiencing it" ("Museum-Appreciation Tips"). In 2009, a real-life museum visitor infamously sought to 'truly experience' a seventeenth-century portrait of French aristocrat Catherine Coustard, drawing the attention of a Minneapolis Institute of Arts guard. "Please don't lick the art," the guard reproved as the little girl "leaned in for another surreptitious slurp of the Marquise's delicious blueberry-colored gown" (Abbe). The Minneapolis Institute of Arts museum shop consequently sells a custom tee shirt featuring the guard's admonishment.

Common-sense sensory conduct typically prevails for mature museum visitors, though there are some exceptions; blogger Lawrence Edmonds has been photographed licking every Anglican cathedral in the United Kingdom (70+ churches) and has posted 'tasting notes' on his website. That the act of licking an inedible cultural resource strikes us as comical, or rather bizarre, testifies to the sensory biases that Curtin, Flammang, Bronner, and Neustadt challenge. In the study of inedible material culture, the case for knowledge through tasting may be difficult to argue. For edible material culture, however, the conspicuous absence of knowing-through-tasting (outside the realms of the culinary professions and connoisseurship) becomes more salient. Unfortunately, the introduction of edible objects among the inedible presents a host of practical concerns that hinder museum visitors from accessing Neustadt's 'fuller mouthful of truth.'

Can we eat our cake and display it too?

Museums customarily explain the importance of food to human civilizations by using a durable material record of tractors, tools and tureens to tell stories about cultivation, preparation, and consumption. To include actual *edible* food poses serious logistical challenges. Food attracts rodents, insects, and other pests that may nibble on fragile canvases, textiles, and taxidermy also housed in museums. Upkeep of edible exhibits intended for visitor consumption would be costly. Safety clearances would be required from regulatory agencies. The solution has been to represent food with non-perishable specimens, replicas, and images.[8]

Actual food, intended to be eaten once-upon-a-time but then abandoned, is sometimes displayed in museums. Bog butter at the National Museum of Ireland. Egg shells and bread retrieved from Pompeii at the Museo Archeologico Nazionale di Napoli. Peas and lentils from 1st - 4th century AD Egypt at the Kelsey Museum of Archaeology. Visitors are not permitted to taste these rare surviving foods, nor would they want to. These objects resonate with 'realness' and familiarity, but bread that has survived volcanic annihilation and butter that has been under water for centuries no longer comprise a tasty breakfast. There is something uncanny about a perishable object that resists decay.

Non-perishable replicas carefully crafted and arrayed on tables in period rooms offer a more immersive, contextualized museum experience. Culinary historian and educator Ivan Day has drawn upon his vast private collection of antique cookery books and kitchen utensils to recreate historically accurate period banquets at a number of historic houses and museums in Great Britain and the United States.[9] Early in his career as a museum consultant, Day realized that, because Renaissance dessert food primarily consisted of confectionary, he could bring to 'life' this particular course for a museum exhibition of Renaissance dining furniture and serving ware that he was guest-curating. More recently, at the Minneapolis Institute of Arts, Day enlivened a c.1600 Tudor period room for an exhibit titled "Supper with Shakespeare: The Evolution of English Banqueting," using edible sugar paste molded to create a castle centerpiece and pedestal dishes filled with sweets (Loos AR26). Sugar molds, once dry, are neutral objects—they won't decay, nor will they attract pests. Day reports that sugar paste structures he molded twenty-five years earlier remain perfectly sound.

Confectionary can be 'real' without decaying, but for other courses, Day isn't fond of "rubber ducks and plastic joints of meat." Video, he believes, can better represent a food's context and sensory texture. A compelling interactive video installation can be found at the Detroit Institute of Arts, where visitors are invited to revel in visual fantasies of a lavish 18th century feast. Quivering aspic and a shiny suckling pig are among the delicacies projected from above onto a white dining table. Classical music plays softly throughout this multi-course 'meal,' which features at its center the 1763 William Cripps silver epergne displayed in an adjacent case. The cinematic victuals provide context for finely wrought serving ware and inspire wonder in visitors, who embody (to an extent) guests at the feast.

The sensual qualities that make edible artifacts so precious and so compelling present the greatest representational challenges in a museum setting. Although visual and auditory forms of capture are imperfect, certain types of cultural performances—music and dance, for example—are easier to record for visitors to experience later, repeatedly, at the push of a button. Technologies to digitally record and 'replay' scent[10] and

Figure 34.1 Visitors at the Detroit Institute of Arts are treated to the visual splendor of a 18th-century feast. Photo by Sarah Conrad Gothie, 2012.

taste are not (yet) available to bridge the gap between food representations in museum exhibits and the multi-sensory experience of eating. The insistent, seductive scent of spit-roasted beef, the irrepressible squirt of a juicy lemon wedge, and the duality of cold and cool when mint ice cream melts on the tongue are left for the visitor to imagine.

Food representations in museums are often relegated to contextualizing *something else*—be it the serving ware or the furniture. It is easier to locate fresh, edible food in museum-like venues linked to commercial enterprises than in traditional museums. The Hershey's Chocolate World attraction in Hershey, Pennsylvania, features a dark ride-style journey through the cultivating, refining, and manufacturing processes that transform cacao beans into milk chocolate bars. As visitors disembark from the ride, they receive a miniature Hershey's chocolate treat. Corporate museums, of course, have a financial incentive to provide sensory experiences of the foods they manufacture.

In a restaurant, *real, edible* food is the focal point; the meals served are 'artifacts' that offer a complete sensory experience. Restaurants may cater to folk group insiders as well as culinary tourists, offering engagement with edible artifacts that are efficiently remade fresh daily. Historical ephemera and décor can provide ambiance while contextualizing a food geographically, historically, and culturally, rather than vice versa. In her study of Cuban restaurants in New York City, Lisa Knauer analyzes, in explicitly museological terms, how culture is constructed, packaged, and consumed. Her descriptions of the restaurants suggest a range of aesthetic and educational possibilities for diners. At the iconic Victor's Café, the decor consists of "artifactual displays and museological flourishes that invoke memories (or fantasies) of a [...] specifically Cuban setting" (433), including pre-Revolution cigar boxes, currency, and swizzle sticks in glass cases. Because Cuban food is often mistaken for Mexican cuisine by the uninitiated, Knauer notes that Victor's menus are written to educate any non-Cuban customers: "like a museum, [...] the restaurant has a pedagogic mission" (434). In contrast, La Esquina Habanera is a modest neighborhood restaurant with a mostly Latina/o clientele who are already knowledgeable about the food; the restaurant "does not try to translate Cubanness for non-Cubans" (437). Diners in a restaurant setting are less likely to be explicitly 'educated' as one might be on a museum visit, and probably more inclined to simply experience food than to learn about it.

It is rare to find a restaurant with an educational bent, or a museum that educates using fresh food. Most museum cafés predict contemporary visitor tastes (e.g. the ubiquitous chicken caesar wrap) instead of being mindfully curated to enhance the visitor's experience of the collections, be they historical, cultural, scientific or artistic. Few museums match the ambitions of the Smithsonian Institution's National Museum of the American Indian (NMAI) in Washington D.C., where food served in the museum restaurant is inspired by indigenous cuisines of the Americas. NMAI's large food hall showcases regional specialties from the Northern Woodlands, South America, the Northwest Coast, Meso America and the Great Plains. Zagat-rated, this commercially successful restaurant draws visitors to the museum with its unique cuisine, generating increased visitation and profit for the institution. According to Lucy Long, who has conducted interviews with staff at the Mitsitam Native Foods Café, menus are developed in consultation with tribal councils and educational materials are available to supplement the dining experience. Although the notion of creating cafe food that complements museum programming is admirable, as with any restaurant, traditional foods at Mitsitam Native Foods Café must be reworked to accommodate consumer tastes, pricing, seasonal ingredient availability, and food safety concerns (Long, personal correspondence).

Special events sponsored by museums are an alternative venue for the public to taste and learn about regional or traditional foods. The annual Smithsonian Folklife Festival unites scholars and practitioners from the United States and abroad to present foodways, music, dance, crafts, storytelling, and lectures about cultural issues. Organized by the Office of Folklife and Cultural Heritage, the folklife festival developed out of a desire to show cultural resources outside the confines of glass cases. Two weeks each summer since 1967, the festival has presented programs themed by state, region, country, or culture outdoors, on the National Mall.[11] Edible culture has always been a major component of the festival, with cooking demonstrations presenting every aspect of the foodways process. Belanus and Long highlight the importance of sociality to this event, which brings professional folklorists and performers into conversation with the public (2011). The Smithsonian Folklife Festival nurtures the social networks vital to the continued existence of intangible skills and knowledges: "The Festival is not an end in itself, but rather a means for the museum to engage in cultural research, public presentation and institutional legitimisation of cultural exemplars so as to encourage their continued practice and creativity" (Kurin 9). Multiple avenues for dialogue open as questions are asked and answered and local sources for ingredients are shared. Connections are forged among food specialists, who may not have otherwise met, and laypeople, who take home new practical knowledge and appreciation for a previously unfamiliar culture.

Both museums and restaurants are sites of ideological instruction, cultural encounter, and personal meaning-making, although this may seem less evident at the latter. The primary purpose of a restaurant is to serve food efficiently and profitably. Traditional methods, therefore, will be streamlined if they are deemed too time-consuming or labor-intensive. A commercial food service operation will prioritize gastronomic pleasure and profits over politics—that's why the Hershey's chocolate ride romanticizes industrial-scale milk production with animatronic singing dairy cows and neglects to mention histories of exploitative labor practices in developing countries that produce cacao beans. It is not typically in the interests of a for-profit restaurant to encourage *critical* thinking about their menu's relationship to identity or ethical consumption. While such conversations are educational and essential to understanding the complexities of our globalized contemporary moment, they may deter clientele merely seeking the celebratory ambiance of a Mexican cantina, or a warm bowl of pho on a frosty February afternoon. To sample and enjoy a new cuisine in a restaurant is a reasonable leisure activity, but for visitors to engage seriously with food in museums, a high pedagogic standard is imperative. Museum interpretation of edible artifacts ideally illuminates the symbolic *and* ideological content of the person-food relationship.

'A surfeit of meanings': Helping visitors make sense of edible culture

The third challenge posed by edible artifacts in museums is interpretive. Interpretation has been defined as "a mission-based communication process that forges emotional and intellectual connections between the interests of the audience and meanings inherent in the resource" (National Association for Interpretation). Museum curators and educators determine how the museum will interpet the objects in their collections, that is, they decide what stories will be useful, interesting, or important for visitors to hear. With well-conceived interpretation, even a mass-produced Hershey's chocolate bar rates museological attention. A chocolate bar might be framed as an exemplar of industrial food production, or, for its role in youth scouting culture as a s'mores ingredient. The Strawberry Banke Museum in Portsmouth, New Hampshire, displays vintage chocolate bars in the immersive setting of a full-scale WWII 'homefront' grocery store, teaching-by-showing how wartime rationing affected food procurement in a small town. In *Stealing Buddha's Dinner,* Bich Minh Nguyen's lively memoir of growing up as a Vietnamese refugee in the United States, Pringles and Kit Kat bars represent normativity and belonging for a young girl seeking to construct a new, hybrid sense of self. In the context of an exhibit about any of these historical periods and uses, a Hershey's chocolate bar might be tasted by visitors in a new way. How a museum frames edible culture for visitors determines in part what type of knowledge is transmitted—historical, scientific, or humanistic—but every story a museum tells about an artifact also transmits ideas about what is 'normal.'[12]

For a museum to interpret a food's meanings too strictly would foreclose different, possibly conflicting, interpretations in the elevation of a single narrative. This is why multiple perspectives are so important, especially when the foodways of a marginalized group or subculture are displayed. In folklorist José Limón's interpretive ethnograpy of expressive culture in South Texas, a "powerful yet contradictory sexual and scatological discourse" (129) surrounding the foodways of Mexican working-class men illustrates the effects of colonialism. Limón's investigation of an all-male barbecue event includes performance (speech and gestures), setting (a small camp they call a rancho), and finally the food itself—unadorned, low prestige steer parts ("the discards of capitalist cattle ranching") (137). His gastropolitical analysis of this food's procurement, preparation, presentation, and consumption reveals the non-hierarchical, minimalist, and almost affectionate relationship the men have with their food and with each other. Limón demonstrates how the men's discourse about *carne* is more nuanced than superficial explanations, such as anxiety about homosexuality, 'typical' working class aggression, or juvenile jesting, might suggest.

Limón produces an intricate interpretation of food meanings among marginalized laborers, but as he concludes the essay, he wisely acknowledges the possibility of alternative readings. Laura Cummings' feminist response to Limón emphasizes gender, exploring broader implications of his somewhat celebratory interpretations. Cummings' concern is that "a ritually enhanced sense of dominant masculinity [...] may be carried over into other spheres of lived experience with repressive consequences for women" (Limón 140). In the context of a museum exhibition, it would be tempting to unproblematically celebrate how the men's camaraderie helps them to cope with a disadvantaged class position, but to do so would irresponsibly neglect the implications of the dominating, hyper-masculine culture this food event upholds.

Museums surpass restaurants in their ability and, indeed, obligation, to explore the less palatable power dynamics that underpin human relationships with food. Inclusive exhibits that put diverse voices in conversation expose visitors to the range of possible (and, possibly conflicting) perspectives. Consider the foodways of the Mexican laborers Limón describes in contrast to other contexts in which diners consume offal or low-prestige meats. The trendiness of offal consumption among affluent hipsters and foodies has been well-documented by the media and bloggers. One chef describes the diners who order such dishes as: "All these people who are 20 being like, 'I eat everything!'; and people who are 60 saying, 'I haven't eaten sweetbreads since I was a little kid!'" ("We're Gaga for Guts"). Consumption of organ meats, including brains, livers, tongues, and testicles, may be motivated by nostalgia, curiosity, or necessity. To taste an offal meat is not, in itself, educational; it may be a memorable novelty, or furnish an ego-boosting story of 'surviving' an exotic food to recite to incredulous friends. A museum exhibit, however, might pose provocative, open-ended questions to visitors, such as: What does it mean to *choose* to eat a food that others eat out of necessity? Museum interpretations rich with contradictions and situational variety stimulate learning about the intersections of gender, race, and class that underlie the foods we eat.

Museums presenting multiple perspectives on food promote an educated and critical society, yet, regardless of a museum's 'official' narrative, subjective responses to objects still occur. A single object "may have a surfeit of meanings—simultaneously or sequentially" (Hein 15) and diverse human responses to sights, sounds, scents, and tastes make museums important dialogic spaces where visitor voices join the conversation and express their personal responses to displayed artifacts. Visitor studies scholar Lois Silverman bases her theory of visitor-object interactions on factors such as background, companions, and motivations for visiting. She concludes: "visitors find personal significance within museums in a range of patterned ways that reflect basic human needs" (161). "My mum had one of those whippers like that," a silver-haired woman announces as she leans over a Plexiglas barrier to gain better vantage of kitchen utensils in the dairy porch at Green Gables Heritage Place, a popular tourist attraction on Prince Edward Island, Canada. For this visitor, the intimate and singular memory of her mum's whipper may be more meaningful than the historic house's world-famous literary associations.

Traditional museums are in the business of representing broad periods, regions, and ideas through possession, display, and interpretation of *some* idiosyncratic things. The very acts of curating and culling exclude many objects, voices, and stories from exhibition. Museum staff must carefully consider how best to design a cohesive and evocative exhibit narrative from the objects and information available to them. Regardless of their interpretative guidance, however, objects will often resonate in unpredictable, subjective ways. Like an ingested food, the intimate meanings made in a museum reside within each individual visitor.

'It looks nice, but I can't eat it': Conclusion

On a recent visit to Oxford, I found myself lingering in the Ashmolean Museum gallery dedicated to Dutch, Flemish, and German still life paintings. As I marveled at translucent cherries, satiny petals, and gently flocked butterfly wings painted centuries ago, a pair of elderly women entered the gallery. After peering at a few paintings, one remarked, "I don't like still life, I can't see any point to it. It looks nice, but I can't eat it." Representations of food in museums help visitors understand the symbolic, political, artistic, and material significance of food to people of the past and their relation to the present. Mere visual representations, however, lack the intimacy of mouthfeel, scent, and flavor. Just looking at food always feels incomplete.

Despite epistemological, logistical, and interpretive challenges, edible culture does, indeed, belong in museums seeking to showcase human achievements and attract visitors. Food sustains the bodies *and* minds of human beings who create the precious cultural objects that populate museum collections. Food reflects the beliefs, values, and norms that structure our experience of culture, the environment, and interactions with animals, plants, and other people. For museums keen to draw, inspire, and educate increasingly diverse audiences, multisensory, multimodal interpretative schemes utilizing food are an obvious lure; people love eating, discussing, and reminiscing about food. The boom in lifestyle media and 'foodie' culture since the 1980s has generated a vast corpus of food-centered television programming, magazines, memoirs, documentary films, recipe books and blogs. For middle-class consumers, acquiring food knowledge and eating omnivorously can be perceived as a pleasurable hobby and as a means for attaining cultural capital (Johnston and Baumann, 2010; Finn 2011).

As pleasurable as eating food is, and as popular as learning about it has become, its *edibility* remains frustratingly difficult to represent. In restaurants, efficiency and profit pare away the traditional methods, ingredients, and care that make edible culture feel authentic. In museums, food decays—the only pheasant under glass we are likely to see is a taxidermic specimen in a natural history museum. From petrified specimens of actual foodstuffs and paintings of food to replica banquets and 'curated' cafe menus, museological approaches to food cover a spectrum from just-looking to full sensory engagement. We may not be treated to a fragrant scoop of Julia Child's *bœuf bourguignon* on a visit to the Smithsonian (or a pat of bog butter on warm toast at the National Museum of Ireland), but we can encourage museums to develop innovative approaches to food education and experiential programming. The potential exists to spark conversations about the pleasures of the palate, but also about the cultural differences and power dynamics embedded in production, procurement, preparation, and consumption of the food shared at tables past, present, and future.

Thanks to Evelyn Alsultany, Lucy Long, Ray Silverman and Aimee VonBokel for comments on various iterations of this essay.

Notes

1. Most of Child's ingredients were stored in a pantry not included in the Smithsonian installation; tea, spices, vinegars, and oils kept in the kitchen were recorded, but not collected, due to preservation concerns. For an account of the process of moving Child's kitchen from Cambridge, MA, to Washington, DC, see http://amhistory.si.edu/juliachild/jck/html/faqs.asp.

2. The National Museum of Ireland (NMI) displays three vessels containing bog butter in their Medieval exhibition, from County Galway and County Mayo. Bog butters continue to be discovered. NMI records over 240 bog butter finds in Ireland (Mulhall).

3. Material culture scholars study relationships between people and objects—be they tactual or imagined, comforting or unsettling, conscious or unnoticed. Scholars in anthropology, sociology, folkloristics, art history, and other disciplines may disagree about the definition of the term 'material culture.' The term can refer to a discipline, field, or method, depending on a particular scholar's project and the role of material objects in it (i.e. whether 'things' are the topic, evidence, or method). For a review of arguments for various definitions, see Schlereth's prologue to *Cultural History and Material Culture* (1990).

4. See Yoder (1972) and Long (2005) for folkloristic theorizations of foodways.

5. The phrase 'edible heritage' has appeared in a variety of non-academic contexts. For example, it is the trademarked name for a smartphone app for tourists visiting Aix-en-Provence and Banff (http://edibleheritage.com/) and was the title of a lab-style heritage potato exhibit at Trinity College Dublin's Science Gallery (https://dublin.sciencegallery.com/edible/time/heritage-lab/).

6. Identity includes gender, race, ethnicity, class, sexuality, ability, ethos, and other characteristics through which people understand themselves and others. Folklorists specializing in food studies have demonstrated food's aptness for the expression of individual and group identities throughout history and across cultures. One area that has

received focused attention from folklorists is the study of food in the expression of ethnic or regional identity. Brown and Mussell (1987), Laudan (1996), Lockwood and Lockwood (2000), Long (2004), Neustadt (1992), Wilson and Gillespie (1999), and many others take up this topic in a vast array of cultural contexts.

7. Scholars working in the interdisciplinary and humanistic academic field known as 'food studies' focus on the relationships people have with food (Miller and Deutsch 3), drawing upon the methods and conventions of their own academic disciplines (e.g. cultural studies, folkloristics, history, philosophy, literature, anthropology, etc.) See also, Belasco (2008).

8. The examples in this essay are drawn from 'traditional' museums dedicated to broad surveys of art and history, for the most part. While somewhat sparse, specialized museums dedicated entirely to food do exist, such as the Southern Food and Beverage Museum in New Orleans, the Ramen Museum in Yokohama, Japan, and the National Mustard Museum in Middleton, Wisconsin.

9. See Day's blog (http://foodhistorjottings.blogspot.com/) for accounts of his historical food reproduction projects and debunking of food history 'fairy stories'.

10. It is, however, possible to identify the chemical properties of a scent and create an olfactory likeness from the formula. The Jorvik Viking Center in York, England, engaged environmental scent company Dale Air to recreate odor profiles evocative of village life. Sensory historian Mark Smith notes that scents must be placed in context, and even then, it is not possible to know how they would have been subjectively experienced by people in the past (Humphries 3).

11. For more information about past and future festivals, see www.festival.si.edu.

12. A great deal has been written about the politics of representation in museums. For sound treatments of this topic, see Fusco, "The Other History of Intercultural Performance" (1995), Lidchi, "The Poetics and Politics of Exhibiting Other Cultures" (1997), and Barringer, *Colonialism and the Object: Empire, Material Culture, and the Museum* (1998).

References

Abbe, Mary. "Item-World: Lickin'-Good Art." *Minneapolis Star Tribune*. 4 Sep 2009. Web. 15 Oct 2013.

Barringer, T. J. *Colonialism And the Object: Empire, Material Culture, And the Museum*. London: Routledge, 1998.

Belanus, Betty, and Lucy Long. "Interpreting Food: at the Smithsonian Folklife Festival." *Legacy Magazine* 22.2 (2011): 22+. Academic OneFile. Web. 15 Oct. 2013.

Belasco, Warren. *Food: The Key Concepts*. New York: Berg, 2008.

Bronner, Simon J. "The Haptic Experience of Culture." *Anthropos*. Anthropos Institute. 77. 1982. 351–362.

Brown, Linda Keller & Kay Mussell. *Ethnic and Regional Foodways in the United States: The Performance of Group Identity*. U of Tennessee P, 1987.

Curtin, Deane W. "Food/Body/Person." *Cooking, Eating, Thinking: Transformative Philosophies of Food*. Deane Curtin and Lisa Heldke, eds. Bloomington: Indiana UP, 1992. 3–22.

Day, Ivan. Personal interview. 9 March 2013. Shap, UK.

Edmonds, Lawrence. "About." *Cathedral-Licking Diary*. <http://cathedrallicking.wordpress.com/about/>. Access 1 October 2013.

Ephron, Nora. *Julie & Julia*. Columbia Pictures, 2009.

Finn, Stephanie Mariko. *Aspirational Eating: Class Anxiety And The Rise of Food In Popular Culture*. Dissertation, University of Michigan, 2011.

Flammang, Janet A. *A Taste for Civilization: Food, Politics, and Civil Society*. Urbana: U of Illinois P, 2009.

Fusco, Coco. "The Other History of Intercultural Performance." *English Is Broken Here: Notes On Cultural Fusion In the Americas*. New York City: New Press, 1995.

Hein, Hilde S. *The Museum In Transition: a Philosophical Perspective*. Washington D.C.: Smithsonian Institution Press, 2000.

Humphries, Courtney. "A Whiff of History." *Boston Globe* 17 July 2011. Web. <http://www.boston.com/bostonglobe/ideas/articles/2011/07/17/a_whiff_of_history/?page=3>. Access 31 Jan 2014.

Johnston, Josée, and Shyon Baumann. *Foodies: Democracy and Distinction in the Gourmet Foodscape*. New York: Routledge, 2010.

Knauer. Lisa Maya. "Eating in Cuban." *Mambo Montage: The Latinization of New York*. Laó-Montes, Augustín and Arlene Dávila, eds. Columbia UP, 2001.

Kurin, Richard. "Museums & Intangible Heritage: Culture Dead or Alive?" *ICOM News* 57.4 2004. 7–9.

Laudan, Rachel. *The Food of Paradise: Exploring Hawaii's Culinary Heritage*. Honolulu: U of Hawaii P, 1996.

Lidchi, Henrietta. "The Poetics and Politics of Exhibiting Other Cultures." *Representation: Cultural Representations And Signifying Practices*. Stuart Hall, ed. London: Sage, 1997. 151–208

Limón, José. "Carnes, Carnales, and the Carnivalesque." *Dancing with the Devil: Society and Cultural Poetics in Mexican-American South Texas*. U of Wisconsin P, 1994.

Lockwood, Y. and W.G. "Continuity and Adaptation of Arab-American Foodways." *Arab Detroit: From Margin to Mainstream*, eds., Nabeel Abraham and Andrew Shryock. Detroit: Wayne State UP, 2000. 515–549

Long, Lucy M. "Foodways: Using Food to Teach Folklore Theories and Methods," *Digest* Vol.19/1999 (2005): 32–36.

Long, Lucy M. (ed.). "Introduction." *Culinary Tourism: Explorations in Eating and Otherness*. Lexington: U of Kentucky P, 2004.

Long, Lucy M. Personal correspondence. 30 Sept 2013.

Loos, Ted. "Setting a Place for History." *New York Times*. 24 Feb 2013. AR26.

Miller, Jeff, and Jonathan Deutsch. *Food Studies: An Introduction to Research Methods*. New York: Berg, 2009.

Mulhall, Isabella. Irish Antiquities Division, National Museum of Ireland. Personal correspondence. 18 July 2013.

"Museum-Appreciation Tips" *The Onion*. 39.9. 12 Mar 2003. Web. 1 October 2013.

National Association for Interpretation. "Definitions Project: Interpretation." 2007. <http://www.definitionsproject.com/definitions/def_full_term.cfm>.

Neustadt, Kathy. *Clambake*. U of Massachusetts P, 1992.

Neustadt, Kathy. "The Folkloristics of Licking." *Journal of American Folklore*. 107 (423): 181–196. 1994.

Nguyen, Bich Minh. *Stealing Buddha's Dinner*. New York: Penguin Books, 2008.

Pollan, Michael. *Cooked: A Natural History of Transformation*. New York: Penguin Press, 2013.

Schlereth, Thomas J. *Cultural History And Material Culture: Everyday Life, Landscapes, Museums*. Ann Arbor, Mich.: UMI Research Press, 1990.

Silverman, Lois H. "Visitor Meaning-Making in Museums for a New Age." *Curator* 38.3. 1995. 161–170

Stone, Jon, dir. *Don't Eat the Pictures: Sesame Street at the Metropolitan Museum of Art*. (1983). Children's Television Workshop. Random House Home Video, 1995.

"We're Gaga for Guts." *New York Observer*. 20 Jan 2010. < http://observer.com/2010/01/were-gaga-for-guts/>. Web. 4 Jan 2014.

Wilson, David Scofield and Angus K. Gillespie, eds. *Rooted In America: Foodlore of Popular Fruits And Vegetables*. Knoxville: University of Tennessee Press, 1999.

Yoder, Don. "Folk Cookery." *Folklore and Folklife: An Introduction*. Ed. Richard M. Dorson. Chicago: U of Chicago P, 1972.

CHAPTER 35

YOU EAT WHAT YOU ARE: FOODWAYS IN EDUCATION

Paddy Bowman, Amanda Dargan, and Steve Zeitlin

"Proverbial wisdom tells us that we are what we eat," writes folklorist Millie Rahn, "but perhaps it is the other way around: we eat what we are." The study of foodways in K-12 classrooms offers compelling ways to explore local and world customs and cultures through an accessible, universal, everyday practice. The foods we eat provide a firsthand, sensory experience that can build an appetite for learning in wide array of subjects.

Foodways study offers opportunities for active, experiential learning. Students can grow, prepare, cook, and taste food. They can conduct interviews about foodways, document food preparation and celebrations where food is a central focus, and draw on food memories as inspiration for creative writing and art making. Foodways can serve as an entry point for talking about culture, history, and identity. "Food – remembering and re-creating it, growing it, marketing it, cooking it, eating it – and sense of place are interconnected," Rahn continues in her essay, "Laying a Place at the Table." "Wherever we find ourselves – in the kitchen, garden, or field; at the corner shop, farmers market, or supermarket; or at festive events in sacred, seasonal, or ordinary time – foodways can show how family stories, community histories, and the significant events of humanity are regularly and traditionally expressed through food."

Food knowledge

Our ideas about food – what's fit to eat, when to eat, manners, taboos, well-being – are a dynamic part of our folk culture. We learn about food among our various subcultures and become cooks by informally apprenticing ourselves to family and friends. Almost by osmosis we acquire the skills required to set a table, buy ripe fruit, clean vegetables, bake a favorite cake. Mining such implicit everyday knowledge for the classroom, we gain explicit knowledge of individuals, families, communities, and regions as well as of history, health, science, math, narrative, economics, religion, agronomy, and artistry.

Foodways refers to the whole range of activities, beliefs, and expressive forms surrounding food and eating within a cultural group. As folklorist Lucy Long writes, "Foodways includes not only what people eat, but when, where, why, how, and with whom." Planning, acquiring, preparing, eating, and cleaning up after eating consume a part of each day. Some days we put extra endeavor into what we eat to mark rites of passage, celebrate holidays, and honor others. Food brings people together to create communities—think of potluck suppers, church dinners, crawfish boils, and food festivals.

Foodways provides a window into geography and cultural history. On a recent visit to a Filipino bakery in Queens, New York, for example, folklorist Bill Westerman ordered a traditional dessert, *halo halo*, from the Tagalog word *halò*, meaning "mix." "You can see the history of the Philippines in this dish," he said. The purple yam, plantains, garbanzos, mangos, and *macapuno* (sweetened coconut meat) are the indigenous and

Paddy Bowman, Amanda Dargan and Steve Zeitlin, 'You Eat What You Are: Foodways in Education', *C.A.R.T.S.: Cultural Arts Resources for Teachers and Students* 11 (2010), 1, 3. Reprinted with permission from the authors.

Asian ingredients; the ice cream and crème caramel come from the Europeans, beginning with Magellan who arrived in the Philippines in 1521.

Cross-cultural exchange

Two books by Mark Kurlansky, *Cod: The Biography of a Fish That Changed the World* and *Salt: A World History*, illustrate how the history of the world can be told through just a single dish. Foods provide tangible evidence of the journeys of people across continents and oceans. For example, students may be surprised to discover that the potato, so strongly associated with Ireland, originated in Peru, and Spanish explorers of the New World took home to Europe the tomato, central to the cuisine of Italy. Foodways introduces students to cultural blending, population shifts, and cross-cultural exchange.

Some dishes prepared by Romy Dorotan, owner and head chef of the New York City restaurant Cendrillon, illustrate the blending of different cuisines. Romy came to New York from the Philippines in the '70s and opened Cendrillon in 1995. Asked about the origin of an appetizer, curried goat in a pancake with mango salsa, he answered, "The origin of the goat curry is that we lived in Flatbush, Brooklyn, and it's a West Indian community. So that's my own take on the goat *roti* – I used a scallion pancake instead of the *roti* – the bread. It's what I call 'fusion confusion.'" Students can investigate dishes that blend different cuisines and reveal histories and contemporary examples of cultural contact, such as jalapeno knishes, a recent offering at Yonah Schimmel's a Jewish store on New York's Lower East Side, which clearly didn't serve those when they opened in 1910.

The exploration of local foods, groceries, and markets that cater to different immigrant and regional groups can take students beyond classroom walls to visit farms, stores, and factories. Students' own distinctive recipes and documentation of regional variations in local dishes tell a lot about community history and culture. Students in Southwest Louisiana, for example, researched the local spicy sausage called *boudin*. They interviewed local French-speaking butchers who make and sell *boudin* and created a map of the "*Boudin* Trail." They made tee shirts and wrote haiku poetry inspired by what they learned and tasted. They created a brochure featuring their map and profiles of *boudin* makers. Then they nominated their trail for a National Millennium Community Trail, and they won! (See the 2002 CARTS issue, A Sense of Place, for an article about this project www.locallearningnetwork.org/library.)

Food and identity

Foods not only sustain our bodies, but are also a powerful badge of identity – positive and negative. Folklorist Michael Owen Jones, in his essay "Food Choice, Symbolism, and Identity," writes that traditional dishes can evoke both warm memories of home or feelings of shame. He recounts a story told by film director Luis Valdez. "'Mother's tacos, I mean, they're wonderful things, especially if the tortillas are warm, they're hot off the stove, the beans are hot,' he said. 'And it is everything that symbolized the warmth of home, mother. It's a symbol of the solidarity of Mexican family life.'" But at school, as Valdez expresses in his 1982 film, *Zoot Suit*, the other children were eating real, squared-off sandwiches. "'And you look at it and suddenly that taco, which symbolized that warmth, is no longer the same thing.…For one thing, it's no longer warm, it's cold. So the tortilla has undergone, you know,… a wrinkling process that makes it look like this long, ugly, dried up thing with spots on it, and the beans are cold, and all of a sudden, it represents everything that you're ashamed of, and you don't want to pull that sucker out and eat it in public.'"

With food in the news and on the minds of millions of Americans today, marrying issues such as sustainability, eating local, food safety, and children's health with the cultural knowledge of foodways scholarship benefits all. We can't improve nutrition without awareness of the cultural and personal food preferences and associations, yet food scholars and food advocates do not always talk with one another. This issue of CARTS bridges these realms to share ways of teaching with foodways that engage young people and help prepare them to make healthy choices and to be advocates for food issues that matter to them.

Paddy Bowman, Local Learning Director, and Amanda Dargan, City Lore Education Director, co-edit CARTS. Steve Zeitlin directs City Lore.

CHAPTER 36
AMERICAN GINSENG AND THE IDEA OF THE COMMONS
Mary Hufford

The view from the Sundial Tavern

The Sundial Tavern, known up and down Coal River as "Kenny and Martha's," is a mom-and-pop-style beer joint on Route 3, in Sundial, West Virginia, just north of Naoma. Retired coal miner Kenny Pettry and his wife, Martha, now in their sixties, have been the proprietors for nearly thirty years. The bar's modest facade belies the often uproarious vitality of its evenings. On weekend nights the music of Hank Williams, Bill Monroe, and Dolly Parton flows from the jukebox to mingle with the haze of cigarettes, the clangor of pinball, the crack and clatter of pool, and the jocular talk and teasing of friends from neighboring hollows and coal camps.

Like many taverns, the Sundial Tavern is a dynamic museum of local history, its walls covered with photographs, artifacts, and trophies that register local perspectives on national events, the triumphs of patrons, and the passing of eras. Among the items displayed are photos of Dolly Parton (who is Martha's second cousin), an ingenious trigger-and-funnel mechanism for planting corn, and a souvenir cap that registers the present struggle of the United Mine Workers for survival on Coal River. On another wall hangs a photograph of John Flynn, a beloved science writer and forest advocate, deemed one of the three best pool players on Coal River. He spent many nights here talking, sympathizing, arguing, joking, and shooting pool. He died in March of 1996 and is buried not far from Sundial in his family cemetery on Rock Creek, the hollow he was born in fifty-seven years ago.

Tucked into the display on the wall behind the bar is a set of framed and laminated leaves. Most people would be hard put to identify this specimen, but for many of the tavern's regular patrons it represents an extraordinary trophy and object of desire: the stalk from a rare six-prong ginseng plant, *Panax quinquefolia*. Above the large specimen is a lesser but still remarkable five-prong. The display speaks to the high status accorded to ginseng in life and thought on Coal River.

Diggers call it "seng," and on Coal River the passion for seng runs deep. In 1994, the most recent year for which figures are available, the state of West Virginia exported 18,698 dry pounds of wild ginseng root from its fifty-five counties.[1]

Though ginseng grows wild throughout the Mountain State, more than half of the wild harvest came from eight contiguous counties in the state's southwestern corner (Kanawha, Boone, Fayette, Raleigh, McDowell, Wyoming, Mingo, and Logan). "It's always been like that," said Bob Whipkey, who monitors the export of ginseng for the state's Division of Forestry. "There are more diggers there because of the culture. People there grow up gathering herbs and digging roots."

Because of wild ginseng's limited range and extraordinary value (diggers are averaging $450 per pound for the dried wild root), the federal government has been monitoring the export of ginseng (both wild and cultivated) since 1978. Of nineteen states authorized to export wild ginseng, West Virginia came in second,

Mary Hufford 'American Ginseng and the Idea of the Commons', *Folklife Center News* 19 (1997), 3–18. Reprinted with permission of the author.

behind Kentucky, which certified 52,993 pounds. Tennessee came in third, with 17,997 pounds. In 1994 these three contiguous states certified more than half of the 178,111 pounds of wild ginseng reported among nineteen states.[2]

The commons

There is a story in these figures of a vernacular cultural domain that transcends state boundaries. Anchoring this domain is a geographical space, a *de facto* commons roughly congruent with two physiographic regions recognized in national discourse. One is the coal fields underlying the ginseng, most of which are controlled by absentee landholders. The other is the mixed mesophytic forest, known among ecologists as the world's biologically richest temperate-zone hardwood system.

This multi-layered region is increasingly the focus of debates pitting the short-term economic value of coal and timber against the long-term value of a diverse forest system and topography. Because the social and cultural significance of the geographical commons is unrecognized in national discourse, it is particularly at risk. As Beverly Brown points out in writing about the rural working class in the Pacific Northwest, the widespread loss of access to the geographical commons occurs in tandem with a shrinking civic "commons."[3]

This loss of access is one effect of the increasing privatization and enclosure of land that for generations has been used as commons. Rural populations with uncertain employment have typically relied on gardening, hunting, and gathering for getting through hard times. Over the past decade, processes of gentrification, preservation, and intensified extraction of timber and minerals have eliminated the commons in which communities have for generations exercised fructuary rights. However, this exercise is motivated by something that goes beyond the prospect of economic gain.

Ginseng provides a case in point. Dollar for pound, ginseng is probably the most valuable renewable resource on the central Appalachian plateaus.[4] A linchpin in the seasonal round of foraging, ginsenging is also essential to a way of life. "I'd rather ginseng than eat," said Dennis Dickens, eighty-five, of Peach Tree Creek. "Every spare minute I had was spent a-ginsenging."

"If you can't go ginsenging," said Carla Pettry, thirty, of Horse Creek, "it totally drives you crazy."

Ginseng's etymology and economic value both come from China and neighboring countries, where the root has long been prized for conferring longevity and vigor of all sorts on its users. The term ginseng is an Americanization of the Chinese *jin-chen*, meaning "manlike." The Latin term *Panax quinquefolia* alludes to the five whorled leaves on each branch and the plant's function as a panacea. The active ingredients in the fleshy, humanoid root are ginsenocides, chemical compounds celebrated for their capacity both to stimulate and soothe. Whether ginsenocides in fact warrant such claims is a matter of continuing controversy among scientists and physicians.[5]

According to Randy Halstead, a Boone County buyer, "stress rings," which give the wild root its market value, are linked with a higher concentration of ginsenocides. Nearly impossible to reproduce in cultivation, stress rings are produced as the root pushes through soil just compact enough to provide the right amount of resistance. The ancient, humus-laden soils in the mixed mesophytic forests of Tennessee, Kentucky, and southern West Virginia are ginseng's ideal medium. "The most prolific spreads of wild ginseng," writes Val Hardacre, in *Woodland Nuggets of Gold*, "were found in the region touched by the Allegheny Plateau and the secluded coves of the Cumberland Plateau."[6] Through centuries of interaction with this valuable and elusive plant, residents of the plateaus have created a rich and elaborate culture, a culture of the commons.

Historical background

The history of human interaction with ginseng lurks in the language of the land. Look at a detailed map of almost any portion of the region and ginseng is registered somewhere, often in association with the deeper, moister places: Seng Branch (Fayette County), Sang Camp Creek (Logan County), Ginseng (Wyoming County), Seng Creek (Boone County), Three-Prong Holler (Raleigh). The hollows, deep dendritic fissures created over eons by water cutting through the ancient table land to form tributaries of the Coal River, receive water from lesser depressions that ripple the slopes. These depressions are distinguished in local parlance as "coves" (shallower, amphitheater-shaped depressions), "swags" (steeper depressions, "swagged" on both sides), and "drains" (natural channels through which water flows out of the swag or cove). The prime locations for ginseng are found on the north-facing, "wet" sides of these depressions. "Once in a while you'll find some on the ridges," said Denny Christian, "but not like in the swags there."

"You just go in the darker coves," said Wesley Scarbrough, twenty-five, who grew up on Clear Fork, "where it just shadows the ground so it'll be rich for ginseng."

Occupying higher and drier ground are sandstone "camping rocks," formed on the bottoms of ancient seas. These natural ledges have sheltered people hunting and gathering in the mountains since prehistoric times, and during centuries of corn-woodland-pastureland agriculture such ledges sheltered stock as well. Named by early settlers who came to stay, sites like Jake Rock, John Rock, Turkey Rock, Crane Rock, and Charlie Rock served as bases for ginsenging expeditions.

"My granddad and all them used to go and lay out for weeks, ginsenging," said Kenny Pettry. "A rock they stayed at, they called it the Crane Rock, and they stayed back in under that. They'd be gone for weeks ginsenging."

"Did you ever hear tell of Charlie Rock?" asked Woody Boggs, of Pettry Bottom. "That's a famous place."

"I've camped out many a night under Charlie Rock," said Randy Sprouse, of Sundial. "People used to live under Charlie Rock two or three months at a time, camp out and dig ginseng."

The harvesting of ginseng (as well as other wild plants) flourished within a system of corn-woodland-pastureland farming. Crucial to this system was recourse to a vast, forested commons rising away from the settled hollows. Though nineteenth-century patriarchs like "Mountain Perry" Jarrell homesteaded portions of it, the mostly unsettled higher-elevation ridges and slopes supplied the community with essential materials and staples: wood for fires, barns, fences, homes, and tools; coal for fuel; rich soil for growing corn, beans, and orchards; nuts, herbs, mushrooms, berries, and game; an open range for hogs and cattle; and spaces for anonymous stills. Because of the abundant supply of tree fodder (wild nuts and fruit), the central Appalachian plateau in the nineteenth century furnished some of the best pastureland in the country. A seasonal round of plying the commons is registered in many of the names for swags and coves: Walnut Hollow, Paw-Paw Hollow, Beech Hollow, Red Root Hollow, Sugar Camp Hollow, and so forth. During the turbulent early decades of industry the suppressed civic commons survived in lofty thickets where miners met in secret to organize the United Mine Workers of America (UMWA).

As practice and concept, the commons is ancient, predating the idea of private property, which began exerting pressure on local commons in England at the time of the Norman Conquest.[7] Since then history has been marked by recurrent efforts to enclose the commons for use by wealthy non-local interests.[8] In England the social and environmental effects of such use included irreversible deforestation, degradation of soils and water, homelessness, and the emergence of the world's first industrial working class.[9]

What happened in the late nineteenth century on Coal River and throughout the plateaus may be viewed as an episode in the continuing history of transnational appropriation and enclosure of the commons. Throughout central Appalachia, newly formed land companies surreptitiously subverted the system of the commons, taking out deeds on its unclaimed portions, offering small amounts of money and the right to continue using the surface resources in exchange for mineral rights.[10] Hence, despite the flurry of "quit claim deeds" and "deeds in ejectment" on record for the early decades of the century, the condition of exile imposed on some people by those transactions has only gradually been realized. In the aggregate, whatever the terms of individual transactions, access to the land for fructuary uses like hunting, gathering, and farming has tempered the negative effects of corporate domination over the past century.[11]

Before the development of a wage-labor economy, ginseng was the most reliable source of cash income on Coal River. "The whole economy was built up around ginseng," said Quentin Barrett, of Beckley. "They had a few eggs and chickens, but most of it was the whole crew would go out and hunt ginseng in the fall."

"That's all my grandma used to do, years ago, she'd ginseng," recalled Shelby Estep, who now ginsengs with her daughter and granddaughter on Coal River Mountain. "That's the way she bought the kids clothes. She had twelve."

Around the export of ginseng a class of entrepreneurs emerged who would buy the ginseng from diggers and get it to the metropolitan centers to trade for goods that could not be produced locally. In 1871 Quentin Barrett's grandfather, R. E. Barrett, began trading merchandise for ginseng from his store on Dry Creek. "Just about his only source of cash was from ginseng sales," said Bob Daniel, R. E. Barrett's great-grandson. "The people would come out of the hollows in the fall and sell him their ginseng and they would buy their shoes and salt and staples and so forth and he in turn sold it to exporters in New York or a broker, and that sent some cash dollars back here."[12]

Fortunes and political careers were built on ginseng in the nineteenth century. Daniel Boone on a bad day lost two tons of the root when the barge carrying it sank in the Ohio River. Ginseng money helped build the fortune of John Jacob Astor as well as the political career of an early senator from California, according to a "ginseng tale" told by Quentin Barrett.

"There was an old man at Madison, over on Little Coal River," said Barrett, speaking of his great-grandfather. "His name was Griffin Stallings. And he was a wheeler and dealer. He was wealthy. So he puts up a store at Whitesville and he buys all the seng at Whitesville, and he buys all the seng at Madison and puts up another store somewhere toward Logan up in the head of Pond Fork.

"So he buys all the seng coming and going. So come fall, he's ready to ship it. How do you get your seng to market? Only place you could sell it, really a big bunch, was Philadelphia or Cincinnati or someplace like that. So he loads up his hired man, the wagons, and takes all the seng down to Huntington, puts him on a boat. The hired man was supposed to take all this seng, a year's supply of seng and sell it and bring the money back. He never saw the hired man again. He never got it back."

"Well, after the Civil War was over, he had a boy [Joel], and the boy was a high-ranking man in the Confederate army and so his son ran for office. Along about that time, he got elected, he goes to Washington. And the first man he run into was a senator from California, and that senator from California was the hired man who'd left with his daddy's ginseng!"[13]

During the first half of the twentieth century, ginseng continued to infuse cash into the scrip-driven economy of the coal camps. "My dad was a coal miner when the union was organizing," said Randy Halstead. "He was involved in that, so a lot of times he was out of work. So you send ten children to school, and working now and then, you had to make money whatever way you could. We would dig ginseng to buy our school clothes and buy our books so we could go back to school in the fall."

In the coal boom of the 1990s, when the coal industry no longer depends much on a resident population, many roads leading into the commons have been gated off. Ginseng nonetheless contributes a vital piece to an economic patchwork that includes recurrent outmigration to find temporary employment, odd jobs, fishing, flea-market work, and raising produce.

"Ginseng's getting rare because so many people's out of work and so many people's digging it," said Randy Sprouse, who was himself unemployed at the time.

Joe Williams, who ginsengs with Randy, disagreed. "I'd say most of the people that ginseng are people that works. They just love to ginseng. I miss work to go ginsenging."

"What do you like about it that you'd miss work for it?" I asked him.

"Well, it's really something to find a big old stalk of seng. That's what you're looking for. Five prongs. If you'd ever get into it, you'd like it."

Stalking the Wily Seng

Though in biological terms ginseng is properly flora, in the ginsengers' world it behaves like fauna. Ginseng is not merely "harvested," it is "hunted," and rare six-, seven-, and eight-prong specimens are coveted like twelve-point bucks. There is an agency assigned to ginseng unparalleled among the many plants valued on Coal River. "It hides away from man with seeming intelligence," wrote Arthur Harding in a 1908 manual for diggers and cultivators.[14]

"You never know where you're going to find ginseng," said Ernie Scarbrough, of Rock Creek.

Seng is a verb as well as a noun. "I senged in there, and senged in there, and senged in there," reported Cuba Wiley, of Peytona, "and I didn't find any." In stories about ginseng the plant appears unbidden, almost like a quarry sneaking up on its stalker. "I was standing there looking around," said David Bailey, of Stickney, "and there was a big four-prong brushing my britches legs before I looked down and saw it."

"Now a lot of times," said Joe Williams, "you'll walk up, be standing there, and look right down at your feet and it'll be there."

Ginseng's uniqueness is much vaunted. "It's the most beautiful plant in the woods," said Randy Halstead. "Especially when it changes its color and it's got the seed on it." In spring ginseng sends up a stem that branches into stalks, each terminating in a cluster of five toothed leaflets. The older the root, the more stalks, or "prongs," it sends up.[15] A cluster of yellow-green flowers, scented like lilies of the valley, appears in spring and matures through the summer into the bright red "pod of berries" that ginseng diggers look for in fall.

In late September ginseng begins to turn an opalescent yellow, utterly distinctive to diggers. "That is a different color to any other yellow," said Dennis Dickens. "You can spot that."

On a warm day in September photographer Lyntha Eiler and I are clambering around on the near-perpendicular slopes of Tom's Hollow near Whitesville. Joe Williams, of Leevale, selected this site because it contained poplar and sassafras growing on the "wet side" of the mountain. "You don't find it where oaks are at," he says. He peers out through the columns of maples, hickories, sourwood, black gum, walnut, poplar, and sassafras, searching for brilliant red berries and the distinctive yellow of ginseng.

Slung over Williams's shoulder is a bag for carrying ginseng, and in his hand he carries a "seng hoe." Seng hoes are essentially double-bladed mattocks modified to serve as walking sticks. You cannot purchase one. On Coal River seng hoes are produced by recycling implements made for other purposes.

Taken as a collection, seng hoes register in concentrated form a pool of experiential knowledge attached to the commons. "They used to take old mine picks when they'd wear out and cut them off at the blacksmith shop," said Mae Bongalis, eighty, of Naoma. "They make a good one."

Herman Williams, of Clear Fork, has adapted a fire poker for use as a seng hoe. Ben Burnside's is made, like his father's, from a modified automobile spring. A popular model generally has an axe blade for cutting and a mattock blade for digging. Its long handle serves as a walking stick and a weapon to be wielded in self-defense against copperheads and rattlesnakes.

"It's real light," said Shorty Bongalis. "Something you can carry through the woods."

"It's light," said Randy Sprouse, "to beat the weeds."

Brandishing his seng hoe, Williams calls out in jest, "Here Mr. Four-Prong!" Ginseng is notoriously unpredictable. It does not send up a stalk every year.[16] Added to this is the appetite for ginseng shared by deer, pheasants, groundhogs, squirrels, and other small birds and mammals which consume stalks and berries, unwittingly conserving the plant both by hiding the roots and serving as agents of dispersal. Thus theories of where to look for this seemingly peripatetic plant flourish.

"Everybody's got a different way of fishing," said Randy Halstead. "You know: 'My bait works.'"

Vernon Williams sengs in "the roughest, wildest, snakiest places" he can find. Denny Christian looks around "sugar trees" (*Acer saccharum*) and black walnut.

"If you look under the right tree," said Ernie Scarbrough, "you might find a stalk of seng. There's trees I go for yet, ginsenging…sugar maples and black gum, whenever you can find one. And the hickories. Squirrels is in the hickories, and they eat the ripe ginseng berries. So it makes a lot of ginseng around the hickories."

Ginseng orders the landscape around itself, providing a basis for identifying related flora. Look-alike plants like sarsaparilla and cohosh have been given nicknames like "fool's seng," "he-seng," and "seng pointer." "The reason why they call it 'seng pointer,'" said Randy Halstead, "it's got three branches, one goes this way, one this way, and one goes straight out this way, and the old people would say that one would be pointing towards the ginseng plant. Of course it probably is somewhere within a hundred miles out in front of it, but that's how that got started. They like the same kind of a place to grow."

Halstead said experienced dealers can tell which county a root came from because differences in soil conditions produce roots that are bulby like pearl onions, or elongated like carrots. "Now in this area we have dark, richer, loose soil, and the ginseng grows longer, like a carrot. But you get into some of the neighboring counties with clay soil, it's real bulby because the ginseng can't push down into the dirt."

Dealers can also tell at a glance whether a root is "wild" or "tame." "Wild" seng exhibits "stress rings" from pushing through wild soils. "Loosening the soil causes the roots to grow rapidly," explained Randy Halstead. "What makes the roots valuable is the ringiness, the rings that's on the ginseng."

Pausing for breath in Tom's Hollow, Joe Williams finds a four-prong, topped with a "pod of berries." Flailing away at its base he discovers to his chagrin that someone else has already taken the root, adhering to the local practice of replanting the stalk attached to the dog-legged rhizome pocked with stem scars. "That's called the 'curl,'" says Williams, carefully reinstating it. "I usually put maybe two joints of it back. It's a better way of keeping it going than the berries…I'll come back here some year and get another root off of that."

Other strategies for conserving ginseng include scattering seeds where ginseng is known to grow, snipping the tops off of "five-leaves" and "two-prongs" so that less scrupulous diggers won't find them until they are bigger in future years, and transplanting young plants to sites closer to home where they can be monitored.[17]

Many residents on Coal River propagate wild patches of ginseng in the woods surrounding their homes. "We didn't exactly cultivate it," said Dave Bailey. "See our back porch went up to here, and then up here was the woods. Me and my brother, we just got some of it and we set it, to see if it would come up next year, and when it did, it accumulated and accumulated, and whenever I got married and left, why the whole back of that hill was ginseng."

Left to its own devices, ginseng simply sheds the seeds for gravity to deliver downslope. Consequently, one mode of tracking ginseng is to look uphill from any "five-leaves" or immature plants for the big progenitor.

"I've done that many a time," said Dave Bailey. "You go up the hill, you come to a little flat area and if there's any seng growing there you always look above it for a big one."

Giles the Seng Man

One of the more famous buyers who infused cash into the economy during the boom-and-bust period of coal was "Giles the Seng Man." Diggers generally sell ginseng to centers that recycle scrap metal and broker other non-woody forest products like moss, mayapple, bloodroot, cohosh, and golden seal. During the thirties, forties, and fifties much of the ginseng on Marsh Fork was bought by "Giles the Seng Man," remembered for his woolly aspect and bibbed overalls and his annual trek along the roads tracing the tributaries of the Coal River's Marsh Fork.

"There used to be a gentleman," Denny Christian said. "Old Man Giles, they called him. The Seng Buyer. And he wore bibbed overhauls. Had no vehicle, no horse, nor nothing. He always come in a-walking. Every fall he would make his rounds. And I'd senged that summer with my grandpa, and old man Giles, he came through."

"He was a legend," said Jenny Bonds, quilting with the women who gather weekly on Drew's Creek.

"Nobody knows where that old man come from," said Mabel Brown. "And nobody knows where he went," Jenny finished. "He'd just walk by in his big old overhauls and strut, strut by."

"Old Man Giles many a time come to our house," Dave Bailey remembered. "He'd keep change in his pocket. Wore overalls, had a gray beard and an old hat and here's the way he'd walk, you know." Here Bailey demonstrates Giles' inimitable strut. "He'd say 'Hubert, you got any seng?' And Dad would get wood all the time, go out in the woods, cut a little timber, if he found seng he'd dig it. He'd have a handful dry, maybe fifty cents worth."

"Do you remember Giles the ginseng man?" I asked Dennis Dickens.

"Tommy Giles?" said Dennis Dickens. "I remember him well. I used to sell to him. He was originally from Germany, I think. Someone told me that they got him as an alien and kept him in prison through the war. I know he wasn't around here through the war. He was a great big man, black beard, and he always walked. Somebody'd stop and ask him, 'Want a ride Mr. Giles?'…'No, I'm in a hurry, I'll just walk!'"

Seng talk and ginseng tales

Conjuring the commons

For seng aficionados, the ongoing prospect of ginseng makes the mountains gleam with hidden treasure. "It's like catching a big fish," said Randy Halstead. "You're out here all day and you find this big fish, and you know it's everybody's desire to catch this big fish in the lake. You find this big enormous plant and you know everybody that's out there digging, this is the one that they'd like to find. So you get an adrenalin rush when you find them, and when you find a big one it's like showing off your daily catch. You bring it in and say, 'Look what I found today.'"

"You can't get out and dig it for the money," said Joe Williams. "It's like looking for Easter eggs. You're always looking for the big one. If I found one eight ounces, I believe I'd quit."

"The one that boy brought in up at Flats weighed a pound," said Randy Sprouse.

"I'd like to have seen that one," said Williams.

"It was a monster," Sprouse emphasized.

"That's what you get out for," Williams mused. "Always looking for the big one."

On Coal River, ginseng plays a vital role in imagining and sustaining a culture of the commons. Among the means of keeping the commons alive is talk about ginseng: where to hunt it, its mysterious habits, the biggest specimens ever found, and the difficulties of wresting the treasure from an impossibly steep terrain shared by bears, copperheads, rattlesnakes, and yellow-jackets. The ability and authority to engage in this discourse is indeed hard won.

Over generations of social construction in story and in practice, places on the commons accrue a dense, historical residue. Every wrinkle rippling the mountains has been named for people, flora, fauna, practices, and events both singular and recurrent: Beech Hollow, Ma Kelly Branch, Bear Wallow, Board Camp Hollow, and Old Field Hollow. "I guess there must have been a newground in there at one time," said Ben Burnside, of Rock Creek, alluding to the old-time practice of clearing woodland to grow corn and beans.

Overlooking the valley from its giant tightly crimped rim, places like the Head of Hazy, Bolt Mountain, Kayford Mountain, the Cutting Box, Chestnut Hollow, and Sugar Camp anchor realities spun out in a conversation that Woody Boggs videotaped in Andrew, West Virginia. In one exchange, Cuba Wiley and Dave Bailey conjure and co-inhabit a terrain so steep that seng berries would roll from the ridge to the hardtop.

"You know where the most seng is I ever found up in that country?" asked Cuba Wiley. "I'm going to tell you where it was at. You won't believe it."

"Chestnut Holler, I'll bet you," guessed Dave Bailey.

"I found one of the awfullest patches of it, left-hand side of Chestnut Holler," Cuba continued. "I never seen such roots of seng in my life, buddy. And where I found all my seng, the good seng, come right this side of Clyde Montgomery's, and come down that first holler, and go up that holler and turn back to the right. Buddy it is steep."

"Going toward the Cutting Box?" asked Dave Bailey, referring to a place named for a mining structure.

"I senged that through there," said Cuba, "from there to Stickney, and I have really found the seng in there. One time me and Gar Gobel was in there, and Clyde would start up the mountain, and we just kept finding little four-leaves, all the way up the mountain.

"Gar says, 'Cuba, there's a big one somewhere. It seeded downhill.' We senged plumb to the top of the mountain, Cutting Box, got on top, and that old big nettleweed was that high, Gar had him a big stick, was hunting for the big one. Right on tip top the mountain, directly beneath them, it was about up to my belt, buddy. It didn't have such a big root on it, and I still wasn't satisfied. Gar, he dropped over the Cutting Box, and I still searched around up on top, parting the weeds, and directly, I found them about that high [indicates a height of about three feet], two of them right on top of the mountain. It was so steep, [the berries] rolled plumb down next to the hard road, buddy. I got more seng in there than any place I ever senged in that part of the country. It's steep, buddy."

"It's rough too, ain't it?" said Dave Bailey.

"It's rough, buddy," Cuba agreed. "But I swear I dug some good seng in there, buddy. And I dug some good seng in Sugar Camp."

Cuba's amazing account reminds Woody Boggs of a tall tale he heard from his brother. "You remember that time Bud and French Turner was…up there sawing timber for Earl Hunter? Remember Bud telling you about that? He said he was sawing that big tree. Thought it was a buckeye. And stuff like tomatoes started hitting him in the head."

"It was seng berries," laughed Dave.

"It was seng berries," Woody deadpanned.

"Said it was big as tomatoes," said Dave, still chuckling.

"Boy, that was some stalk of seng," allowed Cuba, his eyes twinkling.

Such stories conjure the commons as a rich social imaginary. Through narrative the commons becomes a public space, its history played out before audiences who know intimately its spaces whether they have been there together or not. Inhabiting the commons through practice and narrative confers social identity and makes a community of its occupants. "I work in construction," wrote Dennis Price, forty, of Arnett, on a petition to document the cultural value of the mixed mesophytic forest. "But really I consider myself a ginsenger."

In the realm unfolded through ginseng stories and other tales of plying the woods, the commons becomes a proving ground on which attributes of courage, loyalty, belonging, stamina, wit, foolishness, stewardship, honesty, judgement, and luck are displayed and evaluated. Collective reflection on what it means to be a ginsenger gives rise to reflection on what in fact it means to be human. It is through such a process that the geographic commons nurtures a civic commons as a forum for consensus and dissent.

Ginseng and the future of the commons

"Understanding the commons and its role within the larger regional culture," writes Gary Snyder, "is one more step toward integrating ecology with economy."[18] Environmental policy, focused too narrowly on physical resources, loses sight of the web of social relationships and processes in which those resources are embedded and made significant. "They're taking our dignity by destroying our forest," as Vernon Williams, of Peach Tree Creek, put it.

Williams was referring to the landscapes taking shape on the plateaus during the present coal and timber boom. Since 1990 the state has permitted tens of thousands of acres in southern West Virginia for mountaintop removal and reclamation. Mountaintop removal is a method of mining that shears off the top of a mountain, allowing the efficient recovery of multiple seams of coal.[19] When the "topped" mountains are rigorously reclaimed under the terms of the Surface Mining Control and Reclamation Act of 1977, the rich soils essential to ginseng and hardwood cove forests are gone, and with them the multigenerational achievement of the commons.

What is missing in the environmental planning process is any recognition of the commons and its critical role in community life. Such recognition, not unusual in the countries of Europe, could reopen portions of the civic commons that is suppressed in environmental planning by an unwieldy and inaccessible process of technical assessment. For instance, a slurry pond that fills the evacuated hollow of Shumate's Branch was permitted on the grounds that there were no endangered species, no historic artifacts (with the exception of a cemetery, which was relocated), and no prime farmland (despite a history of subsistence farming at least three generations deep). With that testimony, the commons specified in Cuba Wiley's narratives was quietly erased.20

As vital cultural resources, ginseng, commons, and community life are inseparable, yet there are presently no means available for safeguarding that relationship. A standard recourse, declaring ginseng an endangered species, would clearly be culturally destructive, since it would make a vital cultural practice illegal. Wild ginseng in fact would seem to merit federal protection not because it is endangered but because within its limited range it is integral to the venerable social institution of the commons.

Ginseng may be a powerful resource for resolving some very thorny dilemmas. A touchstone for economic, cultural, and environmental interests, ginseng provides a tangible link between ecology and economy. Given ginseng's predilection for native hardwood forest and rich soils, national recognition of its cultural value would be a way to begin safeguarding both a globally significant hardwood forest and the cultural landscape to which it belongs.

Notes

1. Since 1978 the U.S. Department of the Interior's Fish and Wildlife Service has tracked the certification of ginseng for export under the Convention on International Trade in Endangered Species of Wild Fauna and Flora (CITES). Ginseng is listed in Appendix II.

2. Ginseng can be cultivated, and in fact cultivated ginseng comprises more than 90 percent of American ginseng exports (*ASPI Bulletin* 38). However "tame seng," as diggers call it, commands an average price of thirty dollars a pound. That sector of the industry is concentrated in Wisconsin, which in 1994 certified more than 1,000,000 of the 1,271,548 pounds reported nationally.

3. Beverly Brown, "Fencing the Northwest Forests: Decline of Public Access and Accustomed Rights," *Cultural Survival Quarterly* (Spring 1996), 50–52.

4. According to a study directed by scientist Albert Fritsch, who heads the Appalachian Center for Science in the Public Interest, the Chinese market alone will bear 12 billion dollars' worth of ginseng annually. "Ginseng in Appalachia," *ASPI Technical Series* 38 (Mt. Vernon, Kentucky: Appalachia-Science in the Public Interest, 1996). To provide a basis for comparison, according to the West Virginia Mining and Reclamation Association in Charleston, West Virginia, the coal industry meets a direct annual payroll of 1 billion dollars for the state of West Virginia.

5. Ibid. "Though ginseng is commonly prescribed by physicians in Asia and Russia for a number of ailments, Western medicine has been very skeptical of the herb. In the United States it is illegal to market ginseng for medical purposes because it has not been tested by the Food and Drug Administration. Instead, it is marketed as a health food or with vitamin supplements."

6. Val Hardacre, *Woodland Nuggets of Gold* (New York: Vantage Press, 1968), 56.

7. Beryl Crowe writes that "the commons is a fundamental social institution that has a history going back through our own colonial experience to a body of English common law which antedates the Roman conquest. That law recognized that in societies there are some environmental objects which have never been, and should never be, exclusively appropriated to any individual or group of individuals" ("The Tragedy of the Commons Revisited," in *Managing the Commons*, ed. Garret Hardin and John Baden[San Francisco: Freeman, 1977], 53–65).

8. Gary Snyder's brief history of the six-hundred-year struggle in England highlights the historical depth of contemporary issues. Wool corporations, an early form of agribusiness, played a role in fifteenth-century enclosures. Snyder writes, "The arguments for enclosure in England–efficiency, higher production–ignored social and ecological effects and served to cripple the sustainable agriculture of some districts." Gary Snyder, "Understanding the Commons," in *Environmental Ethics*, ed. Susan J. Armstrong and Richard G. Botzler (New York: McGraw-Hill, 1993), 227–31.

9. Snyder, 228–29.

10. Consequently, according to a study by the Appalachian Landownership Task Force, roughly 80 to 90 percent of the land is controlled by absentee owners. See *Who Owns Appalachia? Land Ownership and Its Impact* (Lexington: University Press of Kentucky, 1983). For more detailed documentation of the often illegal means of land acquisition, see David Alan Corbin, *Life, Work, and Rebellion in the West Virginia Coal Fields: The Southern West Virginia Miners 1880-1922* (Urbana: University of Illinois Press,1981), and Ronald Eller, *Miners, Millhands, and Mountaineers* (Knoxville: University of Tennessee Press, 1982). An abundance of stories persist in oral tradition on Coal River about how the company "took" the land.

11. Paul Salstrom argues that this use of the land for farming and hunting ultimately subsidized the coal industry. Compensating for depressed wages, it kept the union out of southern West Virginia longer than in other areas. *Appalachia's Path to Dependency* (Lexington: University Press of Kentucky, 1994). See also David Alan Corbin, *Life, Work, and Rebellion in the Coal Fields: The Southern West Virginia Miners 1880-1922* (Urbana: University of Illinois

Press,1981), 37–38. Two local land companies have publicly accounted for the recent enclosures by citing instances of lawsuits brought against them by persons injured while gathering wood on "the property."

12. Among the figures published by the U.S. Department of Agriculture from 1858 to 1896, the highest number of pounds exported from the United States was 630,714 in 1863; the lowest was 110,426 in 1859. The total for the thirty-six years was 13,738,415. No official records were kept by state or county in West Virginia. "American Ginseng: Its Commercial History, Protection, and Cultivation," *Bulletin Number 16* (Washington, D.C.: United States Department of Agriculture, 1896), 16–17.

13. According to records compiled by Janet Hager of Hewett in Boone County, Joel Stallings became an attorney following his service as a Confederate captain during the Civil War and was then elected to the state legislature. Tradition holds that, on a trip to Washington, Stallings encountered Senator James Thompson Farley of California (Democrat, 1879–85), and recognized him as the hired man who never returned. *The Biographical Directory of the United States Congress* states that Farley made his way from Albemarle County, Virginia, to California via Missouri.

14. Arthur Harding, *Ginseng and Other Medicinal Plants* (Boston: Emporium Press, 1972; reprint of 1908 original).

15. "Our data show that on an average a one-pronged plant will be 4.5 (plus or minus 1.6) years before it develops a second prong, that a two-pronged plant will be 7.6 (plus or minus 2.4) years before developing a third prong, and that a three-pronged individual will average 13.5 (plus or minus 3.3) years before adding a fourth prong." Walter H. Lewis and Vincent E. Zenger, "Ginseng Population Dynamics," *American Journal of Botany* 69 (1982): 1485.

16. Diggers and dealers observe that because ginseng does not send up a stalk every year, it is impossible to calculate precisely the age of a given specimen or to assess the extent of the population. "Some of this wild ginseng could be thirty or forty years old," said Randy Halstead. "If every plant would come up one year it would be plentiful. You have maybe 50 percent of it that'll germinate each year. If it gets in a stressful situation, it sheds its top." Research by Lewis and Zenger on cultivated ginseng found 10 percent of the population to be dormant in a given year.

17. Such seng is termed "woods grown," and if properly set may bring top dollar. "If it looks wild," said Halstead, "it sells for wild."

18. Snyder, 228–29.

19. The present boom is an effect of the Clean Air Act of 1990, which set acceptable levels for sulphate emissions from coal-fired facilities and increased the national demand for the low-sulphur bituminous coal found in the region.

Because the region's low-sulphur coal has to be washed to come into compliance with the Clean Air Act, valleys must be found for storing the "slurry"–fine, wet, black refuse from the coal-cleaning and separation process. To contain the slurry, towering impoundments are built at the mouths of hollows out of the coarse refuse. "There's a saying around here," said one storekeeper. "'We fear the river above more than the river below.'" A similar structure collapsed on October 30, 1996, near Pennington Cap, Virginia. See Spencer S. Hsu, "Rural Va. Coal Field Accident Turns Streams Black, Chokes Thousands of Fish," *The Washington Post*, November 1, 1996, p. B4.

CHAPTER 37

AN AESTHETIC OF COMMUNITY AND AN ACTIVISM OF EMBODIMENT IN TWO COLLABORATIVE COMMUNITY GARDENS IN BLOOMINGTON, INDIANA

Zilia C. Estrada

In Bloomington, Indiana, two collaborative community garden projects are being developed by community and gardening activists as sites for increasing food security and redefining the notions of community. These gardening projects reflect, and resonate with, a growing movement of grassroots efforts at the local, national, and international levels that have emerged in response to deepening economic and environmental crises at the end of the 20th century and the beginning of the 21st century. As the word "sustainability" has become the catch-all for a broad range of municipal initiatives and community self-help projects, environmental, gardening, and community activists have come together to create opportunities to enhance and redefine notions of aesthetics, community, society, leisure, work, activism, and tradition. A salient feature of these collaborative community garden projects centered on sustainability is the conscious invocation of self-created rituals and ceremonies to bring people together. These projects are not unproblematic. The hoped for and imagined sites of community food raising and self-creation have also become sites for contestation between community garden creators and others in the surrounding neighborhood and municipal environments. Notions of what defines a community have also been challenged as overlapping, and inter-nesting, groups come together to work, play, volunteer, and create in common spaces.

On November 23rd, 2011, on a drizzly gray morning, a group of approximately twelve people of a variety of ages, including a child, gathered on the garden lot at the corner of DeKist and Overhill in Bloomington, Indiana. They stood in a semi-circle facing the terra-cotta colored L-shaped wall that softly curved around a small section of the southwest corner of the garden and the cob oven[1] that rested on a shelf in front of the wall. They sang a song of unity and affirmation, converting the lyrics of "We Shall Overcome," a song popularized in the Civil Rights movement of the 1960s, to affirm the perseverance of community. They invoked a blessing, and then, one by one, starting with Ann Kreilkamp, the woman who had founded the garden, they each took a turn with the sledgehammer that was resting against the shelf on which the cob oven lay, and swung three times at the cob oven.

The sledgehammer passed from person to person. It took several rotations of the sledgehammer going from person to person, each person taking three swings at the cob oven, before the cob oven was reduced to chunks of clay, sand, soil, and the dusty debris of demolition. The cob oven was surprisingly sturdy, considering it was made of clay, sand, straw, water, earth, and the energy of hands that had shaped it, and feet that had blended the ingredients. The somber mood that prevailed at the beginning of the ceremony lifted slightly as the participants got physically engaged smashing the cob oven with the sledgehammer. Once the cob oven was thoroughly demolished, the people standing around it began picking up its pieces. Ann Kreilkamp invited the participants to take a piece of the cob oven for themselves, home to their own

Commissioned for this publication.

gardens as a memento and affirmation of community. One person here, one person there, chose a piece of clay and earth. Everyone present, except for the child who was now holding the leash of Ann Kreilkamp's small dog, Shadow, so that it would not be harmed in the proceedings, and me, busy taking photographs, began spreading the pieces and debris of the cob oven around the garden, this garden, the Green Acres Neighborhood Garden (GANG garden). At first, people picked up the clay-bound pieces one at a time and placed them on the ground around plants, or buried them in the soil. Then someone brought out a wheelbarrow. The rest of the pieces of the cob oven were placed and swept into the wheelbarrow. The pace of the dispersal of the pieces quickened.

Later that day, Ann Kreilkamp sent an e-mail message to the neighbors and friends of the GANG garden that included a link to her fresh posting on her blog. The subject line of Ann's e-mail message read: "The GANG garden: How we conducted the Ceremony of Impermanence." In her message, Ann wrote:

Dear neighbors and friends of the GANG,
Here's how we conducted Sunday's momentous event.
www.exopermaculture.com/2011/11/23/local-action-true-grit-how-we-and-the-gang-have-have-begun-to-transform-a-seemingly-destructive-situation/

The blog posting for that day, November 23, 2011, on Ann's Exopermaculture blog (one of four blogs and two websites she maintains and writes), is entitled, "Local Action "True Grit": How we and the GANG have begun to transform a seemingly destructive situation." The posting has numerous photographs of the southwest corner of the GANG Garden, the cob oven, and the ritualized destruction of the cob oven. The posting is divided into six sections: Introduction; 1. The cut in the wall; 2. The Ceremony; 3. The Blows; 4. Potluck; 5. Aftermath. The blog posting includes: a recounting of the events leading up to the ritualized destruction of the cob oven; the particulars of the morning's activities; a description of the potluck, the quiet sharing of food, talk, and conviviality that took place in Ann's home in the lot next to the GANG garden just after the demolition of the cob oven; and thoughts about what happens next. As carefully orchestrated as the morning's "Ceremony of Impermanence," Ann's blog posting is both reflection and ongoing performance, as well as embodiment, of the desire she and others are working to fulfill to bring about revitalized forms of community gathering, local and communal food production, and more sustainable lifeways in Bloomington, Indiana. As with one other gardening and community-creating project I will discuss in this essay, the people who are creating the GANG garden have consciously set themselves the task to create a communal site that will serve as touchstone and template for a new, or new-old, vision and embodiment of sustainable, creative, and vigorous community life.

Political and communal framework surrounding community gardens, sustainability initiatives, and environmental activism in Bloomington, Indiana, in the first decade of the 21st century

As a trained folklorist who has been conducting research in Bloomington, Indiana, studying community gardens, interviewing community activists and activist gardeners, I was, and continue to be, grateful for the self-conscious reflection of the people with whom I have been doing participant-observer fieldwork. My field research, conducted as part of the final phase of my graduate education in the Department of Folklore and Ethnomusicology at Indiana University, has taken place during a critical shift not only in this college town, but regionally, nationally, and internationally, in urban mores and aesthetics about gardens and gardening, and during a vibrant moment in grassroots activism spurred by concerns about environmental and economic crises.

In an earlier research project that I conducted in 2005, I had spoken with half a dozen gardening and community leaders in Bloomington, Indiana, whose home gardening practices stood out in independent celebration of their individual creativity and expressiveness in their gardening designs and practices, as well as in defiance of the aesthetics and mores of the gardening expectations in the neighborhoods in which they lived. These gardeners and leaders were concerned with promoting indigenous flowers and plants, welcoming wildlife into the gardens and spaces around their homes, eschewing the use of chemical pesticides, celebrating the lushness, variety, and abundance of "naturalized" micro environments created on their home grounds, and growing food close to home. The enthusiasm of that spectrum of gardeners and community leaders was infectious. These gardeners (that particular group of people was all women) were also committed to bringing about change in their communities. The fruits of their individual and communal efforts were evident when I began my later fieldwork.

Five years later, in 2010, when I began the research for my dissertation project, much had changed, quickened, and developed in Bloomington, Indiana, that favored projects centered on sustainable development and community gardening projects. The efforts of the gardeners and leaders whom I had first interviewed in 2005, particularly Lucille Bertuccio—long-time president of The Center for Sustainable Living in Bloomington, Indiana—and Maria (Ria) Collee, a long-time volunteer at The Center for Sustainable Living, had led to Bloomington being designated an official Habitat city by the National Wildlife Federation. The several-year long work of Bertuccio, Collee, and others to educate, encourage, and support people in turning their gardens and home grounds into Backyard Wildlife Habitats had resulted in a critical mass of Backyard Wildlife Habitats in Bloomington.

While this educational and practical work was going on, others in Bloomington, including Bertuccio and Collee, were working in their neighborhoods and at the level of city government to introduce more, and friendlier, policies and practices for sustainability and long-term resiliency within the City of Bloomington. Notions of local economic prosperity and environmental sustainability were invoked in City Council meetings, in the meetings and discussions of various groups under the aegis of the Center for Sustainable Living, by the local food cooperative Bloomingfoods, and by a Peak Oil Task Force that was created by Bloomington's City Council. The Peak Oil Task Force members worked together to research the key systems that would need to be addressed if Bloomington were to survive the expected Peak Oil crisis that many accepted was already underway. The work of the task force resulted in a report that was released in October 2009.[2] The recommendations of the Peak Oil Task Force were officially accepted by the City Council.

During this time frame of 2009 to 2010, two other events of significance took place in Bloomington that influenced, and continue to influence, the timbre of activities and discussions within the interlinked communities of people concerned with sustainability and resilience for themselves and their communities, and concerned with developing community gardens: Bloomington became an official Transition Town, part of an international movement of municipalities that have embraced, and are embracing, the commitment to work for a resilient present and future,[3] and Amy Countryman approached decision makers at Bloomington's Department of Parks and Recreation with a proposal for a public community orchard. The occasion of Bloomington's official inauguration to Transition Town status was celebrated with a large public meeting in the City Council chambers in City Hall. Amy Countryman's submission of her proposal for a community orchard was, initially, quietly done without any fanfare. Ten months later, that had all changed.

The Bloomington Community Orchard's first planting day: Marking the occasion

With ceremony and singing on a bright Saturday in October, 2010,[4] the first trees were planted in the Bloomington Community Orchard (Orchard). Enthusiasm was high. Over two hundred people came to take part—beckoned through announcements that went out on local radio, flyers posted around town, e-mail listservs, the new Orchard website, the Orchard Facebook site, and word of mouth. Months of preparation and hard work from a hardy core of volunteers preceded the day. Children of all ages were present among the adults of all ages.

Babies were held in their parents' arms; a toddler here and there hugged a parent's leg; young children danced on the crushed limestone paths in the elliptical curves that shaped the contours of the orchard-to-be, the orchard-becoming. A news crew stood by, recording interviews with tree-planting participants and organizers. A sound system had been set up for the opening remarks. At the center of the space, colorful flags, attached to wooden poles planted in the soil, waved in the strong breeze. At the center of the activity, key to the day's events, stood Amy Countryman, modest in her desire to give credit to the hundreds of people, and generous grants, that had led to this day, steadfast in her commitment to the vision of an orchard that she had initiated, and delighted with all that was taking place in that moment.

A scant ten months earlier, in January 2010, Amy Countryman had submitted her proposal to the City of Bloomington that laid the groundwork for establishing a community orchard. The proposal was the senior thesis she had submitted in December, 2009, to fulfill her graduation requirements as an undergraduate at Indiana University in the School of Public and Environmental Affairs (SPEA).[5] At the time, a single mother of a three-year old son, an organic farmer (then working on someone else's small-scale farm), a thirty-something student finishing her bachelor's degree after ten years of working her way through school, her proposal galvanized a number of discussions that had been going on in Bloomington, and elsewhere, concerning the usefulness and value of a metropolitan fruit orchard.

People with similar goals and hopes for the enhancement of local food security and strengthening community networks were drawn to Countryman's proposal. Shaun Ziegler, a member of the Orchard Board of Directors at the time of my fieldwork, told me that he, too, had been thinking about the idea of an urban orchard. Ziegler had served as an intern on the Bloomington Peak Oil Task Force, and had long had a passion for learning about gardening, and supporting the development of food security in Bloomington. When he heard about the Orchard proposal, it fit his own thinking and goals. It was the right idea at the right time. I heard similar thoughts from H. Michael Simmons, a master gardener and gardening teacher, who worked at the time for the Bloomington Department of Parks and Recreation, and who became an advisor for the Orchard. Amy Countryman's proposal crystallized, synthesized, and helped to focus the talks, discussions, and meetings that had been going on in Bloomington, and that were paralleled in many other locations around the world, about how to address concerns about diminishing oil resources that could lead to food scarcity.[6]

Even though there had been talks going on about an urban orchard in the gardening, city, and food security circles in Bloomington, Indiana, for some time, Amy Countryman's proposal was fresh and clear. For all the talk going on, in Bloomington and elsewhere, her vision, and the Orchard project that is growing out of it, were and are unique. The uniqueness of the project can be found in its idealism, in its vision of "free fruit for all," in its goal of a volunteer-run enterprise, and in the sense of good faith that permeates the project that people can be counted on to work together for the common good. The project is also unique in the ways it combines food growing, educational elements, and community engagement and community growing aspects. This multi-dimensional vision and proposal has attracted and inspired potential volunteers, participants, and funders. But visions are only viable when they are translated into action and reality. How they are translated and interpreted is the creative expression of individuals, and individuals creating together in community, the province of folklorists.

An aesthetic of community and an activism of embodiment

The creators and participants in both the GANG garden and the Orchard have developed creative forms and strategies of gardening and community making that are similar in intent and, often, similar in practice. While there is a respectable history of utopian projects in the United States,[7] community gardens, with the impetus of the growing sustainability movement, are only recently beginning to attract attention as sites of creative, political, and community production and expressiveness. In these two community garden projects in Bloomington, Indiana, it is not just the design of the gardens, the layout of the plants and trees, the placement of the benches and workspaces, the choices of apple trees, pear trees, kiwi, strawberries, blackberries, huckleberries, bee hives, and birdhouses that is of importance, and concern, to the creators of, and participants in, these gardens, it is the creation of community itself, a community imagined,[8] hoped for, idealized, depicted in words and images, projected in drawings and plans, invoked in grant applications, represented on tee-shirts and brochures, symbolized in logos, and performed and embodied in situ through planned activities, performed ceremonies, and shared celebrations involving music and food.

Through a multiplicity of activities and creative expressions, including workdays, workshops, potlucks, planting days, cider and wassail days (borrowing old English customs for performance on American soil), fall and spring planting days, and events centered on harvest and season, the people working and creating the GANG garden and the Orchard are bringing forth, and delineating, what I have termed an aesthetic of community. Whether under adversity, as in the instance of the removal of the cob oven, and eventually of the entire corner wall in the southwest corner of the GANG garden (because one neighbor complained to the city authorities), or in the celebratory tone of the first Planting Day at the Orchard, the people creating these gardens are basing their decisions largely on the concept of community, community invoked at many levels and in many permutations: the community of plants, the soil, water, insects, and the sun; the community of people of all ages working and celebrating together; creating spaces for people to gather together; and creating gardens that reach toward unknown others in a hoped for future—others who will eat the fruit of these gardens, both literally and figuratively.

The aesthetic of community in the Bloomington Community Orchard and the Green Acres Neighborhood Garden includes, and goes beyond, designing a space *with* people in mind, *for* people, and *by* people in re-iterative consensus building dialogues. It is an aesthetic in which not just people, but people working together in *friendly community*, in harmony with interacting communities of plants, bees, butterflies, and the soil, embody and enact the values, vision, ethics, and style of the co-creators of the Orchard space and GANG garden, idealized, realized, and coming into fruition. This aesthetic is part performance, part tableaux, part living sculpture, part narrative, and part artifact (both constructed and planted). This aesthetic is also part of an activist intent, an activism that plays out in embodiment as well as verbal, written, and visual argument.

The aesthetic of community is visible in the ways in which the GANG garden and Orchard, or any other gardens and space, are seen to be expressed as part of an overarching ideal of what the space is designed for. This aesthetic of community can also be seen in the various moments, steps, and expressions leading towards the unfolding, hoped for, final vision of the idealized communal space, so that the microcosms of a day's events, any workday, workshop, planting, or celebration, can be seen as evidences of the fulfillment of the idealized vision—a vision of people contentedly working together in harmony with nature, providing adequate sustenance for themselves and others, where the doing of work together is as much the goal as the fruit of the garden.

The invoking of the aesthetic of community necessitates that the garden space has people in it, both as actors in the landscape as well as components of that landscape. The aesthetic of community calls not just for people, but people related in community, in the examples about which I am writing, community formed by the very work and play space of the GANG garden and Orchard. People, not just one person (unless that single individual is emblematic, a touchstone, of the web of community), are as necessary to the GANG garden and Orchard as the plants and trees are. I have seen orchards and gardens that were not thus informed. When I witnessed them, they seemed complete in their identity and expressiveness. On the other hand, there have been times when I was in either the GANG garden or the Orchard when no other people were present. Those spaces seemed incomplete to me without the people at work. I have been well trained by the founders and thinkers behind both projects, as well as conditioned by my participation in these gardens, in recognizing the spaces as needing the people, and not just random people, but people in communal expression in order for the design and the gardens to be complete. In these ways, the co-creators of the GANG garden and the Orchard have invoked, knowingly or unknowingly, the work of Henri LeFebvre in his work on the production of space.[9] For these spaces, designated as particular community gardens, have become implicated in the larger project of societal transformation that valorizes local community living and enactment.

To further the discussion, though, from a simplistic celebration of community, there are other concerns at play. At the Bloomington Community Orchard, for example, the framing of community is more nuanced than one may suppose at first glance. Within the opportunity of the framing of workdays at the Orchard, when work tasks are posted on a board and a volunteer leader oversees work activities, university classes sometimes come as a group to participate in Orchard activities as part of a class assignment. In my role of participant-observer, I have witnessed and experienced the multi-layered groupings and communications that have taken place within groups that have arrived at the Orchard within their own delineations and framing of community, and with multiple agendas (such as being required to fulfill a class assignment or socialize with classmates), whose members are then invited, implicitly and explicitly, to engage with the broader community of volunteers at the Orchard. This visible and tangible inter-nesting of interests and goals has helped me to further problematize the notion of community, and to think about what the project of the Orchard, as well as the GANG garden, is aiming to achieve in the short term and in the long run. The name of the Orchard itself, as the Bloomington *Community* Orchard, signals the hope and intent of the visionaries behind the Orchard. The designation of community, and the design of the orchard with its inclusionary activities and layout, provides a framework of possibility, and an aesthetic that calls to the idea of community, but does not inevitably fashion that community.

The template and framing of the Orchard and the GANG garden by their creators encourages and allows for the possibility of communal interactions, but it is still within the individual's purview as to the extent of that identification. The opportunities provided by workdays, workshops, celebrations, and events such as the Planting Days and the Cider Fests at the Orchard, and the Planting Days and Workshops at the GANG garden, are exercises in the practice of community participation. Not everyone who visits the Orchard or GANG garden once will return again, but many do. The cohesive, and faithful, cohort of volunteers and regular workers who have been involved with the Orchard since the first planning meeting called by Amy Countryman in February, 2010, function as a thread of continuity in the development of the Orchard and the community of the Orchard. The same is true for the GANG garden, with the thread of continuity being embodied by Ann Kreilkamp and a faithful cohort of volunteers, and in the looping, and interlinking, steps of participation, new recruits, and volunteers, who have more recently arrived, taking on the mantle of commitment in the continuous authorship of what the these gardens are becoming and may yet become.

These are long-term projects. In the case of the Orchard, the first fruits of the trees planted in the fall of 2010, may not be viable until three or five years out. The same appears to be a possibility for how the community, or communities, of the Orchard, around the Orchard, and inter-nested with the Orchard is, or are, developing, and may continue to develop. The long-range goals are still emerging and emergent—as witnessed by the afternoon-long planning session held at Bloomington's City Hall in the Showers Building on Saturday, October 20th, 2012, that centered on what should be done with the fruit of the Orchard when it arrives in full.

For all of this discussion, and all of this planning, and delayed gratification, the immediate satisfaction of any workday can be experienced by any volunteer or casual visitor who drops by the Orchard for an event, to take a look, or to lend a hand. The fulfillment of the long-term promise can be experienced in microcosm in the present, through participation, playing, basking in the quiet space of the Orchard on a sunny day, and sharing in the food provided by volunteers. This experiencing within the design of a site and project artfully built and engineered for community manifestation, formation, cohesiveness, and enhancement is part of what I call the aesthetic of community, but there is more.

Both the Green Acres Neighborhood Community Garden and the Bloomington Community Orchard are volunteer run, with a wide gamut of volunteers from various walks of life, and a broad range of ages and vocations, who, nonetheless, often share a set of common worldviews: beliefs about the value of community gardening projects; concerns about the environment, as well as concerns about local and personal food security; an informed awareness about Peak Oil issues and the unfolding energy descent; and, in many cases, the belief that children are to be brought into the arena of stewardship of the earth at an early age so as to foster long-term stewardship and commitments. The shared worldviews of many participants in the Orchard and GANG garden, as well as the inclusion of children, has led to broad ripples into the places and ways in which participants in these garden spaces meet and interact, providing fresh opportunities for reinforcing shared goals and idealism.

The communities of the Orchard and the GANG garden extend well beyond the spaces of soil, fruit trees, strawberries, and squash. They have, also, extended into the spaces of social media through websites, blogs, Facebook, and community radio. They have reached into educational arenas through the inclusion of children playing alongside adults in the garden spaces, and children being introduced to the notions of gardening and stewardship through educational experiences at these sites, and in the classroom by representatives of these garden projects. The aesthetic of community and the activism of embodiment that have been displayed in these gardens continues to reach out to audiences at distances that have been breached by digital media, photography, and writing. In these spaces of articulation and representation, the notion of an aesthetic is more clearly expressed in the conventional ways of images and text, while it continues on in the spaces in which it has been planted and continues to be grown.

Notes

1. "Cob or cobb or clom (in Wales) is a building material consisting of clay, sand, straw, water, and earth, similar to adobe. Cob is fireproof, resistant to seismic activity, and inexpensive. It can be used to create artistic, sculptural forms and has been revived in recent years by the natural building and sustainability movements…" Wikipedia http://en.wikipedia.org/wiki/Cob_%28material%29 (accessed January 9, 2012)

2. Rollo, David (Chair), Peter Bane, Gary Charbonneau, Clay Fuqua, Christine Glaser, Stephanie Kimball, Jim Silberstein, and Gregory Travis. *Redefining Prosperity: Energy Descent and Community Resilience: Report of the Bloomington Peak Oil Task Force*. October, 2009.

3. The notion of resilience is different than the notion of sustainability. Sustainability as a concept holds the implication that if we change our activities, actions, and practices, we can gain an equilibrium in our lives and ways

that can be continued, that is sustained. The notion of resilience, as I have heard it discussed in the activist circles in Bloomington, Indiana, holds the implication that our communities and world are in for dramatic changes, changes that go well beyond "business as usual." According to this worldview, it is already too late for sustainability to make a difference; now is the time to prepare for society-wide changes that will alter the ways in which we live. Resilience as a notion is about more dramatic preparedness, with the acceptance that much is about to change. Sustainability as a notion still holds the hope that life can go on, more or less, as it has been going on.

4. October 9, 2010.

5. Countryman, Amy J. *An Edible Urban Forest: An Element of the Sustainability Equation.* December 2009. [unpublished]

6. See the Bloomington Peak Oil Task Force, *Redefining Prosperity: Energy Descent and Community Resilience,* as well as James Howard Kunstler's *The Long Emergency: Surviving the End of Oil, Climate Change, and Other Converging Catastrophes of the Twenty-First Century.* New York: Grove Press, 2006, c2005. There are numerous books, articles, and community initiatives world-wide addressing this urgent problem. The Peak Oil Task Force's report can be downloaded from the Bloomington City website accessible at this url http://bloomington.in.gov/peakoil (accessed January 18, 2012)

7. See Hayden, Dolores. *Seven American Utopias: The Architecture of Communitarian Socialism, 1790-1975.* Cambridge, Massachuesetts and London England: The MIT Press, 1976.

8. Playing on Benedict Anderson's notion of imagined communities. See Anderson, Benedict. *Imagined Communities: Reflections on the Origin and Spread of Nationalism.* London and New York: Verso, 1991.

9. Lefebvre, Henri. Translated by Donald Nicholson-Smith. *The Production of Space.* Cambridge, MA, and Oxford, England: Blackwell Publishers, 1974, 1992.

10. This is the British edition, the author's, Richard Reynold's, own copy, bought from the author after his presentation at the School of Public and Environmental Affairs at Indiana University, fall 2010.

Bibliography

Abram, David. *The Spell of the Sensuous: Perception and Language in a More-Than-Human World.* New York: Vintage Books, 1996.

Abrahams, Roger D. *Everyday Life: A Poetics of Vernacular Practices.* Philadelphia: University of Pennsylvania Press, 2005.

Andrews, Moya. Photography by Jeffrey Hammond. "Growing Your Own," *Bloom: Our 5th Annual Homes & Gardens Issue.* June/July 2011, Vol. 6 No. 3 (pp. 102–111).

Berry, Wendell. *Bringing It To The Table: On Farming and Food.* Introduction by Michael Pollan. Berkeley, CA: Counterpoint, 2009.

Bormann, F. Herbert, Diana Balmori, and Gordon T. Geballe. *Redesigning the American Lawn: A Search for Environmental Harmony* (Second Edition). New Haven and London: Yale University Press, 2001.

Brende, Eric. *Better Off: Flipping the Switch on Technology.* New York: Harper Perennial, 2004.

Bryan Park District <http://bloomington.in.gov/documents/viewDocument.php?document_id=2415> (accessed November 11, 2011)

Campbell, Lindsay and Anne Wiesen, eds. *Restorative Commons: Creating Health and Well-being through Urban Landscapes.* Newtown Square, PA: United States Department of Agriculture (USDA) Forest Service, January 2009.

Carlson, Allen and Sheila Lintott, eds. *Nature, Aesthetics, and Environmentalism: From Beauty to Duty.* New York: Columbia University Press, 2008.

Carter, Thomas and Elizabeth Collins Cromley. *Invitation to Vernacular Architecture: A Guide to the Study of Ordinary Buildings and Landscapes.* Knoxville, TN: The University of Tennessee Press, 2005.

City of Bloomington, Indiana website. *Backyard Wildlife Habitats: Local Habitats.* http://bloomington.in.gov/documents/viewDocument.php?document_id=3017. (Accessed February 2, 2010)

City of Bloomington, Indiana website. *Volunteer Spotlight: Lucille Bertuccio: Sharing a Passion for Organic and Sustainable Living:* http://bloomington.in.gov/documents/viewDocument.php?document_id=4316, September 23, 2009. (Accessed February 2, 2010)

Collier, Jr., John and Malcolm Collier. *Visual Anthropology: Photography as a Research Method* (Revised and expanded edition). Foreword by Edward T. Hall. Albuquerque: University of New Mexico Press, 1986.

Countryman, Amy J. *An Edible Urban Forest: An Element of the Sustainability Equation.* December 2009. [unpublished]

Esposito, Roberto. *Communitas: The Origin and Destiny of Community.* Stanford, CA: Stanford University Press, c2010.

Estrada, Zilia C. *In My Own Backyard.* 2005. [unpublished]

Findhorn Community, The. *The Findhorn Garden.* New York: Harper & Row, c1975.

Flores, Heather C. *Food Not Lawns: How to Turn Your Yard into a Garden and Your Neighborhood Into a Community.* White River Junction, VT: Chelsea Green Publishing, 2006.

Food Not Lawns International [website]. http://www.foodnotlawns.net/. (Accessed February 2, 2010)

Frazee, Gretchen. "Neighbor Garden Is A Vision For Larger Cooperative Movement," under heading of *Gang garden and Green Acres Ecovillage hit the news,* Ann Kreilkamp's Exopermaculture blog. <http://exopermaculture.com/2012/01/07/gang-garden-and-green-acres-ecovillage-hit-the-news/> (Accessed January 7, 2012) [also at: http://indianapublicmedia.org/news/green-acres-ecovillage-25329/]

Galloway, Scott and Brent Pierson, directors. *A Man Named Pearl.* 2006. (documentary film)

Glab, Michael G. "New to Bloomington? 5 More Things You Need to Know," *The Ryder.* Bloomington, Indiana: In the Dark Enterprises, September/October (September 7 thru October 12) 2012. pp. 27–28.

Gladwell, Malcolm. *The Tipping Point: How Little Things Can Make a Big Difference.* Boston: Back Bay Books, 2002.

Glassie, Henry. *Vernacular Architecture.* Bloomington: Indiana University Press, 2000.

Grampp, Christopher. *From Yard to Garden: The Domestication of America's Home Grounds.* Chicago, IL: The Center for American Places at Columbia College Chicago, 2008.

Guter, Eran. *Aesthetics A-Z.* Edinburgh: Edinburgh University Press Ltd., 2010.

Hayden, Dolores. *Seven American Utopias: The Architecture of Communitarian Socialism, 1790–1975.* Cambridge, MA: The MIT Press, 1976.

Heath, Jennifer. *The Echoing Green: The Garden in Myth and Memory.* New York: Plume, Penguin Group, March 2000.

Hiskes, Jonathan. "Knockin' the Suburbs: Cities vs. Suburbs: The next big green battle?" *Grist: Daily Grist: Top Environmental News from Around the Globe* January 29, 2010 2:13 pm. http://www.grist.org/article/2010-01-29-cities-vs-suburbs-the-next-big-green-battle (Accessed February 2, 2010)

Holmgren, David. *Permaculture: Principles & Pathways Beyond Sustainability.* Hepburn, Victoria, Australia: Holmgren Design Services, December 2002.

Hou, Jeffrey. *Greening Cities, Growing Communities: Learning from Seattle's Urban Community Gardens.* Washington, D.C.: Landscape Architecture Foundation with University of Washington Press, 2009.

Hufford, Mary. "American Ginseng and the Idea of the Commons." *Folklife Center News* 19, nos. 1 & 2, Winter-Spring 1997.

Humes, Edward. *Eco Barons: The Dreamers, Schemers, and Millionaires Who Are Saving Our Planet.* New York: Ecco, 2009.

Hunt, John Dixon, and Joachim Wolschke-Bulmahn, eds. *The Vernacular Garden.* Washington, D.C.: Dumbarton Oaks Research Library and Collection, 1993.

Indiana Living Green: A Hoosier's Guide to a Sustainable Lifestyle. Vol. 5, No. 1, March/April 2011 <IndianaLivingGreen.com>

Jackson, J. B. "The Past and Present of the Vernacular Garden." In *The Vernacular Garden,* edited by J. D. Hunt and J. Wolschke-Bulmahn, 11-17. Washington, D.C.: Dumbarton Oaks Research Library and Collection, 1993.

Jackson, Jason Baird. *On Mediated Aesthetics and Micro-Ethnography:* Comments prepared for the panel "Mediated Aesthetics and Micro-Ethnography" at the 2011 Indiana University/Ohio State University Folklore and Ethnomusicology Graduate Conference. March 26, 2011. Bloomington, Indiana. (unpublished manuscript)

Kolbert, Elizabeth. "Turf War: Americans Can't Live Without Their Lawns—But How Long Can They Live With Them?" *The New Yorker* July 21, 2008. (Available at: http://www.newyorker.com/arts/critics/books/2008/07/21/080721crbo_books_kolbert)

Kreilkamp, Ann. GANG garden and Green Acres Ecovillage hit the news. Exopermaculture blog. < http://exopermaculture.com/2012/01/07/gang-garden-and-green-acres-ecovillage-hit-the-news/> (January 7, 2012)

Kunstler, James Howard. *The Long Emergency: Surviving the Converging Catastrophes of the Twenty-First Century.* New York, N.Y.: Atlantic Monthly Press, 2005.

Lefebvre, Henri. Translated by Donald Nicholson-Smith. *The Production of Space.* Cambridge, MA, and Oxford, England: Blackwell Publishers, 1974, 1992.

Leopold, Aldo with an Introduction by Robert Finch. *A Sand County Almanac, And Sketches Here and There* (Special Commemorative Edition). Oxford: Oxford University Press, 1949, Introduction copyright 1987.

Lichtman, Richard. "Is this a revolution? We are far from living our understanding of this question, but I do know that its realization is the meaning of a free citizenry and a good society," posted by Ann Kreilkamp on her *Exopermaculture* blog <http://exopermaculture.com/2011/12/16/richard-lichtman-on-occupy-is-this-a-revolution-we-are-far-from-living-out-our-understanding-of-this-question-but-i-do-know-that-its-realization-is-the-meaning-of-a-free-citizenry-and-a-good-soci/> (accessed December 16, 2011)

Llewellyn, Steve, and Zilia C. Estrada, Megan Hutchison. *In Bloomington, An Orchard Grows.* (video) Produced for the Bloomington Community Orchard. August, 2011.

Mandelstam, Janet. "How to Become an Organic Gardener," *Bloom Magazine.* [on the Abundant Harvest Farm website: http://abundantharvestfarms.com/AHF_bloommagazine.php] (Accessed November 11, 2011)

Mechling, Jay. Reviewed Work(s): *The Good Society: A Personal Account of Its Struggle with the World of Social Planning and a Dialectical Inquiry into the Roots of Radical Practice* by John Friedman. *Winterthur Portfolio*, Vol. 16, No. 1. (Spring, 1981), pp. 130–133.

Nassauer, Joan Iverson, ed. *Placing Nature: Culture and Landscape Ecology.* Washington, D.C. and Covelo, CA: Island Press, 1997.

Nokes, Jill with Pat Jasper. *Yard Art and Handmade Places: Extraordinary Expressions of Home.* Austin: University of Texas Press, 2007.

Noyes, Dorothy. "Group," *The Journal of American Folklore*, Vol. 108, No. 430, Common Ground: Keywords for the Study of Expressive Culture (Autumn, 1995), pp. 449–478.

Noyes, Dorothy. "Humble Theory," *Journal of Folklore Research*, Jan-Apr 2008. Vol. 45 Issue 1, p 37–43.

Putnam, Robert D. *Bowling Alone: The Collapse and Revival of American Community.* New York: Simon & Schuster, 2000.

Reid, Herbert, and Betsy Taylor. *Recovering the Commons: Democracy, Place, and Global Justice.* Urbana and Chicago: University of Illinois Press, 2010.

Reynolds, Richard. *On Guerilla Gardening: A Handbook for Gardening Without Boundaries.* London: Bloomsbury Publishing, 2008.[10]

Rollo, David (Chair), Peter Bane, Gary Charbonneau, Clay Fuqua, Christine Glaser, Stephanie Kimball, Jim Silberstein, and Gregory Travis. *Redefining Prosperity: Energy Descent and Community Resilience: Report of the Bloomington Peak Oil Task Force.* October, 2009.

Royce, Anya Peterson. *Anthropology of the Performing Arts: Artistry, Virtuosity, and Interpretation in a Cross-Cultural Perspective.* Walnut Creek, CA: AltaMira Press, A division of Rowman & Littlefield Publishers, Inc., 2004.

Scarry, Elaine. *On Beauty and Being Just.* Princeton, N.J.: Princeton University Press, 1999.

Sharpe, Erin K. *Delivering Communitas: Outdoor Adventure and the Making of Community.* Indiana University: December, 2002. (unpublished dissertation)

Stoeljte, Beverly J. and Richard Bauman. "Community Festival and the Enactment of Modernity" in *The Old Traditional Way of Life: Essays in Honor of Warren E. Roberts.* Edited by Robert E. Walls and George H. Schoemaker. pp. 159–171. Bloomington, Indiana: Trickster Press (Indiana University Folklore Institute), 1989.

Thiselton-Dyer, T.F. *The Folk-Lore of Plants.* London: Chatto & Windus, Piccadily, 1889. (Reissued) Detroit, MI: Singing Tree Press, 1968.

Turner, Victor W., and Edward M. Bruner, eds. *The Anthropology of Experience.* Urbana and Chicago: University of Illinois Press, 1986.

Turner, Victor: edited by Edith Turner. *Blazing the Trail: Way Marks in the Exploration of Symbols.* Tucson & London: The University of Arizona Press, 1992.

2011 Summer Garden Walk, The Bloomington Garden Club. <http://bloomingtongardenclub.com/wordpress/?page_id=2> (Accessed November 9, 2011)

Upton, Dell and John Michael Vlach, eds. *Common Places: Readings in American Vernacular Architecture.* Athens and London: The University of Georgia Press, 1986.

Westmacott, Richard. *African-American Gardens and Yards in the Rural South.* Knoxville: The University of Tennessee Press, 1992.

Whitefield, Patrick. *Permaculture in a Nutshell.* East Meon, Hampshire, England: Permanent Publications, Hyden House Limited, The Sustainability Centre, 1993, 2002.

Wilson, David Scofield and Angus Kress Gillespie, eds. *Rooted in America: Foodlore of Popular Fruits and Vegetables.* Knoxville: The University of Tennesse Press, 1999.

Winne, Mark. *Food Rebels, Guerilla Gardeners, and Smart-Cookin' Mamas: Fighting Back in an Age of Industrial Agriculture*. Boston: Beacon Press, 2010.

Zeff, Robbin Lee. *Not in My Backyard/Not in Anyone's Backyard: A Folkloristic Examination of The American Grassroots Movement for Environmental Justice*. Ph.D. dissertation, Indiana University, Bloomington, Indiana. September 1989. (unpublished dissertation)

Blogs and websites

Abundant Harvest Farms. http://abundantharvestfarms.com/AHF_bloommagazine.php

Bloomington Peak Oil Task Force Report: *Redefining Prosperity: Energy Descent and Community Resilience*. It can be accessed and downloaded from the Bloomington City website at http://bloomington.in.gov/peakoil (accessed January 18, 2012)

"Banneker Community Center" page on the City of Bloomington, Indiana, website http://bloomington.in.gov/banneker (accessed April 1, 2012)

Bloomington Community Orchard website "About" page. http://www.bloomingtoncommunityorchard.org/site/about/ (accessed December 5, 2011)

The Bloomington Garden Club. <http://bloomingtongardenclub.com/wordpress/?page_id=18> (accessed January 9, 2012)

Bryan Park Neighborhood Association. "Davis Street Gardens update – April 2011" http://bryanpark.blogspot.com/search/label/Gardening (accessed January 18, 2012)

"Community Gardening" page on the City of Bloomington, Indiana, website http://bloomington.in.gov/documents/viewDocument.php?document_id=4695 (accessed April 1, 2012)

Guerilla Gardening: Richard Reynolds's blog and website: www.GuerillaGardening.org

National Wildlife Federation: "Community Wildlife Habitat designation is conferred by the National Wildlife Federation as part of its efforts to create landscapes and spaces welcoming of wildlife in urban areas. A list of community habitat cities can be found at http://www.nwf.org/Get-Outside/Outdoor-Activities/Garden-for-Wildlife/Community-Habitats/List-of-Community-Habitats.aspx#bloomington" (accessed January 7, 2012)

Trillium Horticultural Park project. http://www.trilliumhortpark.org/(accessed January 7, 2012)

"Willie Streeter Community Gardens" <http://bloomington.in.gov/documents/viewDocument.php?document_id=212> (accessed January 18, 2012)

CHAPTER 38

FOOD CHOICE, SYMBOLISM, AND IDENTITY: BREAD-AND-BUTTER ISSUES FOR FOLKLORISTICS AND NUTRITION STUDIES

Michael Owen Jones

One could not stand and watch [the slaughtering] very long without becoming philosophical, without beginning to deal in symbols and similes, and to hear the hog-squeal of the universe.

—Upton Sinclair, *The Jungle*

My points are simply stated. First, not only particular foodstuffs but also the procuring, preparing, and consuming of provisions figure largely in symbolic discourse regarding identity, values, and attitudes. Second, people have multiple identities—ethnic, regional, gendered, or classed, which have dominated inquiry, but also many others that rarely have been examined—and these identities are dynamic, subject to challenge and change through the life course. Third, eating practices reproduce as well as construct identity; in addition, both identity and alimentary symbolism, not just taste or availability or cost, significantly affect food choice. Finally, nutrition educators and counselors would benefit from drawing upon ethnographic investigations of the meanings of food in their efforts to design dietary programs, while folklorists should consider adding practical applications of foodways research to their plate.

[…]

"You are what you eat" may be true in a broad sense, but on closer examination the situation is more complex than this proposition suggests. We have seen that you become what you eat literally and figuratively, because consumption practices construct identity; you eat what you already are owing to the fact that alimentation reflects self-concept (as in the expression "If you are what you eat, then I'm fast, cheap, and easy"); you are how you eat in regard to comportment and class; you often eat what others think you are, which is conveyed by what they serve you; those who prepare food for you to eat may do so on the basis of who they think you think they are; and you sometimes eat what you wish you were or want others to think you are but might not be. Whoever we are, we express or symbolically construct an identity linked to eating practices related to the range and type of food consumed, personal characteristics of the eater (including values and lifestyle), and social categories and reference groups with which the individual is associated. If the proof of the pudding is in the eating, then it's time to submit some of the ideas in this essay to the test by considering their relevance to practical issues in nutrition studies.

[…]

The second application involves educating those in nutrition and health care fields about the significance of food customs and symbolism in everyday life, however seemingly commonplace. No one can compile

Michael Owen Jones, 'Food Choice, Symbolism and Identity: Bread-and-Butter Issues for Folkloristics and Nutrition Studies', *Journal of American Folklore* 120 (476) (2007), 129–177. (Excerpts printed here: 129–130, 159–177. Omitted text is indicated by ellipses.) Copyright 2007 by the Board of Trustees of the University of Illinois. Used with permission of the University of Illinois Press.

an encyclopedia of food symbols, owing to their vast numbers and context-derived meanings, nor would health care personnel be able to avail themselves of such a gigantic smorgasbord of items. They need to be informed, however, of basic principles regarding the iconic significance of meat in the American diet and in a "proper meal" as well as the gender symbolism of foodstuffs, investment of emotions in meals, emblematic uses of food and its preparation, service and consumption for signifying people and events, and ways in which alimentary activities relate to forming and signaling a sense of self. They should understand how class, ethnicity, family, peer relations, and other social groups and reference categories are indexed by gastronomy, and they should be aware of the fears of many people about having to give up cherished traditions in the name of health (whether a cuisine like soul food with some dishes that can be high in fat and calories, the "Provincial Cooking of New jersey" characterized by its abundance of processed and convenience fare, or the creative and expressive uses of Jell-O, Spam, and ramen noodles).

In the current climate of healthism, those with diabetes are often reproached for having failed to take responsibility for their health. However, "They might be more effectively supported by discourses and services that strive to restore agency without implicit or explicit judgement," write Dorothy Broom and Andrea Whittaker, "and that dispute the common cultural currency that blames people for their health problems" (2004:2381; see also Liburd 2003). The authors note that one diabetes sufferer commented on being "treated like a leper" (2373) while other patients employed metaphors such as naughty child, foolish adult, and child needing help in feeding by an authority. Earlier I quoted Mintz (1985:211) to the effect that people are increasingly *made* into what they eat, and eat what they do, owing to external forces such as food manufacturers, advertisers, and the entertainment industry. Perpetrators, not victims, should have their feet held to the fire.

As culprits in the problem of obesity-related diseases, video games and television have long been charged with turning youth into overweight couch potatoes. A few seem to be feeling the heat. In September of this year an Australian firm will release an interactive DVD called *Escape from Obeez City,* in which the heroine fights villains like cholesterol that are making people fat; when she is captured, kids must answer educational questions in order for her to be released (MacKeen 2005). Two other video games unveiled recently are designed for children with diabetes to teach them about self-management of their condition, provide coping skills in social situations, and address problems of self-image. In the world of television, the villainous Robbie Rotten in Nickelodeon's *LazyTown* keeps the children indoors, occupied with candy and video games; fitness-loving Sportacus and Stephanie back-flip to their rescue, bringing them fresh air and fitness. This is one of the new wave of shows attempting to "instill a desire for fruits, vegetables and cartwheels in young viewers" (Smith 2005). Clearly beginning to address health issues, network executives nevertheless stop short of admitting guilt for Americans' fat and lack of fitness. So does McDonald's, long the symbol of globalization (with its burgers and fries now available in 119 countries) and happy but unhealthful meals. The company dismisses as "frivolous" a class-action lawsuit filed in 2002 by two Bronx teenagers who blame it for making them fat, and it denies that it has been affected by Morgan Spurlock's 2004 documentary *Super Size Me,* which details the serious health problems he suffered on a thirty-day diet of McDonald's fare. However, the restaurant chain recently began offering a new line of "premium" salads, chicken sandwiches, bottled water as an option to soft drinks, apple slices instead of fries, and a bun-less burger wrapped in lettuce. Ronald McDonald appears in some TV commercials snowboarding, skateboarding, and serving as (in the words of marketing executives) "an ambassador for a balanced, active lifestyle" and "powerful force for good" (Piccalo 2005).

If clinicians are to maximize the good that they do, they should not only understand the impact of customs and symbolism on identity and food choice as well as help remove the stigma of having diabetes, but also begin taking the compliance model with a grain of salt (see Anderson and Funnell 2000, who discuss the dysfunctional consequences, for themselves and for patients, of health care educators relying on the concepts of adherence and compliance; they also describe how they have shifted to an approach that makes patients' lives the focus of education, which might serve as a model for other diabetes educators). A principal ingredient of the health and nutrition literature is reference to "improved adherence" as a goal and as a measure of the success of interventions. As David Hufford writes about folk medicine in the clinic (1994:125), the primary issue for many health care professionals is that of "How can we get patients to give up those health practices and beliefs that are not in accord with medicine or, failing that, how can we get them to follow medical advice regardless of those beliefs and practices?" From this perspective, food traditions and symbols are a complication or impediment in the treatment and control of diabetes. The ultimate goal should be to deliver the best medical care, however, which entails the creation of a cooperative relationship between caregiver and recipient (Hufford 1994:126; Kleinman 1980:114). Clinicians have to know patients' symbolic uses of food, what their impact on food choice and health is, and how to talk with individuals about these matters. Health care personnel "need to learn this material within a framework that will permit them to elicit the relevant information from their patients and then discuss it reasonably and ethically with them" (Hufford 1998:300).

Clinicians might draw upon a list of general questions to obtain information from patients. Several recent works include queries that could be modified or elaborated for this purpose. G. D. Coronado et al. (2004:578–9) list such topics (for focus group discussion) as the following: What is diabetes? What puts someone at risk for getting diabetes? What are some factors that help you prevent getting diabetes? What are some things that make it difficult for people to treat their diabetes? What are some things that help people treat their diabetes? Delores C. S. James (2004:354) provides a guide (again, for focus group interviews) asking: What comes to mind when you think of healthful eating? What factors in your life make it difficult for you to eat a healthful diet? Which foods are most difficult to limit or give up from your diet (and what special meanings are attributed to them)? Which foods would be the most difficult to add to your diet and why? What type of information do you need to help change your eating habits? And what would motivate you to improve your eating habits (and why)? Finally, Leandris C. Liburd (2003) proposes that clinicians ask patients the following: How. important is eating to your social interactions and why? How do certain foods represent an event? How would relationships with family and friends change if you radically altered your diet? How often do you use food as a gift or to celebrate special occasions? And what are foods that you are unwilling to eliminate from your diet (and why)?

Devising a list of questions is not a recipe for success, however. Clinicians' perspectives need to change from strict adherence to technological and compliance models to approaches that emphasize collaboration, negotiation, and the joint development of treatment plans that the patient can live with—plans that are appropriate to the symbolic significance of food in the patient's daily life, social relations, and self-making.

To gain this orientation, health care personnel should identify assumptions in their own system of beliefs—for example, patients who do not practice healthful behaviors do not care about their well-being, biomedicine is "right," traditional beliefs must be changed rather than built upon, people should and will follow instructions given by health practitioners, and adherence failure is the patient's fault and problem (Tripp-Reimer 2001). They can also reflect on their own symbolic uses of food socially and emotionally, which may generate greater understanding of and empathy toward patients. As Bisogni et al. write, "Learning about the identities that clients bring to and derive from eating can help practitioners to think about food through the eyes of their clients and forces practitioners to see beyond their own personal or professional meanings for food and eating" (2002:137). All of this requires another change analytically, one that anorexic-bulimic Kim Chernin (1981) finally realized after many years of struggling with food-related issues—namely, the "shift from literal to symbolic understanding" and research into the meanings of behavior.

Putting butter in the spinach

It requires a certain kind of mind to see beauty in a hamburger bun.

—Ray Kroc, franchiser of Mac and Dick McDonald's hamburger stand in San Bernardino, California

To bring this essay to a close, I will mention two matters, one regarding national and ethnic identity and the other concerning the application of folkloristic research to nutrition studies and health fields. In regard to discussions of ethnicity and culture, I am often reminded of the following traditional saying: "To a foreigner a Yankee is an American. To an American a Yankee is a Northerner. To a Northerner a Yankee is a New Englander. To a New Englander a Yankee is a Vermonter. To a Vermonter a Yankee is a person who eats apple pie for breakfast." This is not to suggest that breaking the fast by consuming pie (or cold pizza, as some people do) is necessarily a health risk but to emphasize that, like an onion, identity is a complex, many-layered thing. Food choice and meanings are influenced by numerous factors, including culture. In addition, while ethnic identity often has a bearing on symbols and consumption patterns, it exists in conjunction with other identities, some of which predominate in one or another context (Devine et al. 1999:89). A promising research direction in folkloristics and nutrition studies, then, is that of exploring a wider range of identities in relation to food choice and symbolism.

If issues concerning diet and health are the bread and butter of nutrition studies, then in folkloristics it is questions about how and why traditions are generated, why they are perpetuated, how and why they remain stable as well as change, and what their meanings are for people in their everyday lives (Georges and Jones 1995:317). Food customs and symbolism are among these traditions. Sociologists, psychologists, and those in fields related to nutrition have conducted most of the research on diet and health, but with too little attention to the traditional and symbolic aspects of food in people's day-to-day activities. My second point, therefore, is that there is room for folklorists at the table.

References

Anderson, Robert M., and Martha M. Funnell. 2000. Compliance and Adherence Are Dysfunctional Concepts in Diabetes Care. *The Diabetes Educator* 26(4):597–604.

Aykroyd, Wallace R. 1967. *The Story of Sugar.* Chicago: Quadrangle Books.

Babcock, Charlotte. 1948. Food and Its Emotional Significance. *American Dietetic Association Journal* 24(5):390–3.

Belcher, Jerry. 1980. Twinkies—An American Love Affair. *Los Angeles Times,* October 10, 1980.

Beoku-Betts, Josephine A. 1995. We Got Our Way of Cooking Things: Women, Food, and Preservation of Cultural Identity Among the Gullah. *Gender and Society* 9(5):535–55.

Bisogni, Carole A., Margaret Connors, Carol M. Devine, and Jeffery Sobal. 2002. Who We Are and How We Eat: A Qualitative Study of Identities in Food Choice. *Journal of Nutrition Education and Behavior* 34(3):128–40.

Brillat-Savarin, Jean Anthelme. [1825] 1926. *The Physiology of Taste: Or Meditations on Transcendental Gastronomy.* New York: Boni and Liveright.

Broom, Dorothy, and Andrea Whittaker, 2004. Controlling Diabetes, Controlling Diabetics: Moral Language in the Management of Diabetes Type 2. *Social Science & Medicine* 58:2371–82.

Camp, Charles. 1989. *American Foodways: What, When, Why and How We Eat in America.* Little Rock, Ark.: August House.

Carson, Gerald. 1957. *Cornflake Crusade.* New York: Rinehart.

—. 1969. Graham: The Man Who Made the Cracker Famous. *New-England Galaxy* 10(4): 3–8.

Chalmers, Irene. 1994. *The Great Food Almanac: A Feast of Facts from A to Z.* San Francisco: Collins.

Chernin, Kim. 1981. *The Obsession: Reflections on the Tyranny of Slenderness.* New York: Harper & Row.

Clendenen, Vanessa I., C. Peter Herman, and Janet Polivy. 1994. Social Facilitation of Eating among Friends and Strangers. *Appetite* 23(1):1–13.

Coleman, John P. 1986. Casting Bread on Troubled Waters: Grahamism and the West. *Journal of American Culture* 9(1):1–8.

Coronado, Gloria D., Beti Thompson, Silvia Tejeda, and Ruby Godina. 2004. Attitudes and Beliefs Among Mexican Americans about Type 2 Diabetes. *Journal of Health Care for the Poor and Underserved* 15:576–88.

Counihan, Carole M. 1985. What Does It Mean to Be Fat, Thin, and Female in the United States: A Review Essay. *Food & Foodways* 1(1):77–94.

—. 1999. *The Anthropology of Food and Body: Gender, Meaning and Power.* New York: Routledge.

Cummings, Richard Osborn. 1940. *The American and His Food: A History of Food Habits in the United States.* Chicago: University of Chicago Press.

Devine, Carol M., Jeffery Sobal, Carole A. Bisogni, and Margbaret Connors. 1999. Food Choices in Three Ethnic Groups: Interactions of Ideals, Identities, and Roles. *Journal of Nutrition Education* 31(2):86–93.

Dubisch, Jill. 1989. You Are What You Eat: Religious Aspects of the Health Food Movement. In *Folk Groups and Folklore Genres: A Reader,* ed. Elliott Oring, pp. 124–35. Logan: Utah State University.

Fleshman, Ruth P. 1973. Symposium on the Young Adult in Today's World: Eating Rituals and Realities. *The Nursing Clinics of North America* 8(1):91–104.

Flynn, Margaret Tailberi. 1944. Dining with Samuel Pepys in Seventeenth Century England. *American Dietetic Association Journal* 20(7):434–40.

Georges, Robert A. 1984. You Often Eat What Others Think You Are: Food as an Index of Others' Conceptions of Who One Is. *Western Folklore* 43(4):249–56.

Georges, Robert A., and Michael Owen Jones. 1995. *Folkloristics: An Introduction.* Bloomington: Indiana University Press.

Grivetti, Louis Evan, Sandra J. Lamprecht, Hans J. Rocke, and Allyn Waterman. 1987. Threads of Cultural Nutrition: Arts and Humanities. *Progress in Food and Nutrition Science* 11(3–4):249–306.

Guerrini, Anita. 1999. A Diet for a Sensitive Soul: Vegetarianism in Eighteenth-Century Britain. *Eighteenth-Century Life* 23(2):34–42.

Hilliard, Sam. 1969. Hog Meat and Cornpone: Food Habits in the Antebellum South. *Proceedings of the American Philosophical Society* 113(1):1–13.

Hufford, David. 1994. Folklore and Medicine. In *Putting Folklore to Use,* ed. Michael Owen Jones, pp. 117–35. Lexington: University Press of Kentucky.

—. 1998. Folklore Studies Applied to Health. *Journal of Folklore Research* 35:295–313.

James, Delores C. S. 2004. Factors Influencing Food Choices, Dietary Intake, and Nutrition-Related Attitudes Among African Americans: Application of a Culturally Sensitive Model. *Ethnicity & Health* 9(4):349–67.

Jones, Christine Kenyon. 1998. "Man Is a Carnivorous Production": Byron and the Anthropology of Food. *Prism(s)* 6:41–58.

Jones, Michael Owen. 1987. The Proof Is in the Pudding. In *Exploring Folk Art: Twenty Years of Thought on Craft, Work, and Aesthetics,* pp. 97–106. Ann Arbor, Mich.: UMI Research Press.

—. 1988. Afterword: Discovering the Symbolism of Food Customs and Events. In *"We Gather Together": Food and Festival in American Life,* ed. Theodore C. Humphrey and Lin C. Humphrey, pp. 235–46. Ann Arbor, Mich.: UMI Research Press.

—. 1995. Why Make (Folk) Art? *Western Folklore* 54(4):253–76.

—. 2000a. "Tradition" in Identity Discourses and an Individual's Symbolic Construction of Self. *Western Folklore* 59(2):115–41.

—. 2000b. What's Disgusting, Why, and What Does It Matter? *Journal of Folklore Research* 37(1):53–71.

Jones, Michael Owen, Bruce S. Giuliano, and Roberta J. Krell, eds. 1981. Foodways and Eating Habits: Directions for Research. Special issue, *Western Folklore* 40 (1).

Kalof, Linda, Thomas Dietz, Paul C. Stern, and Gregory A. Guagnano. 1999. Social Psychological and Structural Influences on Vegetarian Beliefs. *Rural Sociology* 64(3):500–11.

Klein, Dianne. 1991. Even an Apple a Day Can't Keep Twinkies Away. *Los Angeles Times,* March 17, 1991.

Kleinman, Arthur. 1980. *Patients and Healers in the Context of Culture.* Berkeley: University of California Press.

Kraft, Scott. 1995. France's Culture War Gets Cooking in Classroom. *Los Angeles Times,* July 11, 1995.

Laguerre, M. S. 1987. The Body, Blood, and Illness. In *Afro-Caribbean Folk Medicine,* pp. 64–72. South Hadley, Mass.: Bergin and Garvey.

Lee, Sing. 1996. Reconsidering the Status of Anorexia Nervosa as a Western Culture-bound Syndrome. *Social Science & Medicine* 42(1):21–34.

Liburd, Leandris C. 2003. Food, Identity, and African-American Women with Type 2 Diabetes: An Anthropological Perspective. *Diabetes Spectrum* 16(3):160–6.

MacKeen, Dawn. 2005. Fat Is the Villain Here in "Obeez City." *Los Angeles Times,* July 11, 2005.

Maxwell, Archibald Montgomery. 1841. *A Run Through the United States, During the Autumn of 1840.* Vol. 1. London: H. Colburn.

Mechling, Elisabeth Walker, and Jay Mechling. 1988. Sweet Talk: The Moral Rhetoric of Sugar. *Central States Speech Journal* 34(1): 19–32.

Mieder, Wolfgang. 1993. *Proverbs Are Never Out of Season: Popular Wisdom in the Modern Age.* New York: Oxford University Press.

Mintz, Sidney W. 1985. *Sweetness and Power: The Place of Sugar in Modern History.* New York: Elisabeth Sifton Books, Viking.

Nabhan, Gary Paul. 1998. Food, Health, and Native-American Farming and Gathering. In *Eating Culture,* ed. Ron Scapp and Brian Seitz, pp. 169–79. Albany: State University of New York Press.

Nye, Russel Blaine. 1974. *Society and Culture in America 1830–1860.* New York: Harper and Row.

Piccalo, Gina. 2005. Fries with That Fruit? McDonalds Marketing Campaign Touts Active Lifestyles and Good Nutrition. *Los Angeles Times,* July 18, 2005.

Pizzey, Erin. 1977. *Scream Quietly or the Neighbors Will Hear.* Short Hills, N.J.: R. Enslow.

Rikoon, J. Sanford. 1982. Ethnic Food Traditions: A Review and Preview of Folklore Scholarship. *Kentucky Folklore Record* 28(1–2):12–25.

Rudrum, Alan. 2003. Ethical Vegetarianism in Seventeenth-Century Britain: Its Roots in Sixteenth-Century European Theological Debate. *Seventeenth Century* 18(1):76–92.

Schlesinger, Arthur M. Sr. 1944–47. A Dietary Interpretation of American History. *Massachusetts Historical Society Proceedings* 68:199–227.

Shelley, Percy Bysshe. [1813] 2000. *A Vindication of Natural Diet. Being One in a Series of Notes to Queen Mab, a Philosophical Poem.* In Vol. 1 of *Radical Food: The Culture and Politics of Eating and Drinking 1790–1820,* ed. Timothy Morton, pp. 274–85. 3 vols. London: Routledge.

Smith, Lynn. 2005. Kids' TV: Off the Couch, Children. *Los Angeles Times,* August 14, 2005.

Spencer, Colin. 1993. *The Heretic's Feast: A History of Vegetarianism.* London: Fourth Estate.

Tripp-Reimer, Toni, Eunice Choi, Lisa Skemp Kelley, and Janet C. Enslein. 2001. Cultural Barriers to Care: Inverting the Problem. *Diabetes Spectrum* 14(1):13–22.

Trollope, Frances. [1832] 1949. *Domestic Manners of the Americans.* New York: Alfred A. Knopf.

Waldenberger, Suzanne. 1995. Our Daily Bread: A Look at Bible Breads. *The Digest: An Interdisciplinary Study of Food and Foodways* 15:17–9.

Yoder, Don. 1972. Folk Cookery. In *Folklore and Folklife: An Introduction,* ed. Richard M. Dorson, pp. 325–50. Chicago: University of Chicago Press.

CHAPTER 39
CULINARY TOURISM: A FOLKLORISTIC PERSPECTIVE ON EATING AND OTHERNESS
Lucy M. Long

Culinary tourism is about food as a subject and medium, destination and vehicle, for tourism. It is about individuals exploring foods new to them as well as using food to explore new cultures and ways of being. It is about groups using food to "sell" their histories and to construct marketable and publicly attractive identities, and it is about individuals satisfying curiosity. Finally, it is about the experiencing of food in a mode that is out of the ordinary, that steps outside the normal routine to notice difference and the power of food to represent and negotiate that difference.

Definitions

Folklorists, food scholars, and food aficionados have long been fascinated by occasions of exploratory eating—instances of eating the new, the unfamiliar, the alien—and by the institutions and artifacts that enable those occasions, such as "ethnic" restaurants, international cookbooks, and folklife festivals.[1] These occasions and institutions include a wide variety of food-related behaviors and reflect complex networks of cultural, social, economic, and aesthetic systems as well as individual preferences. The definition of what constitutes adventurous eating is a contextual one that depends on the perspective and motivations of the eater. In this essay I propose the concept of "culinary tourism" as a framework for tying together the notion of perspective and the variety of instances in which a foodways is considered representative of the other.[2] I define culinary tourism as the intentional, exploratory participation in the foodways of another—participation including the consumption, preparation, and presentation of a food item, cuisine, meal system, or eating style considered to belong to a culinary system not one's own.[3] This definition emphasizes the individual as active agent in constructing meanings within a tourist experience, and it allows for an aesthetic response to food as part of that experience.[4]

Exploration and intentionality define these instances as tourism. Participation occurs specifically because of the perceived otherness of the foodways, and that otherness elicits curiosity. Although scholarship concerning the anthropology of tourism primarily addresses exploration of new spaces, it has generated concepts applicable to the exploration of new culinary domains as well. Valene Smith defined a tourist as "a temporarily leisured person who voluntarily visits a place away from home for the purpose of experiencing a change" (1989:1). The culinary tourist anticipates a change in the foodways experience for the sake of experiencing that change, not merely to satisfy hunger. Nelson Graburn proposed that the tourist experience is a journey from the profane to the sacred as a way to embellish and add meaning to one's life (1989:22). The tourist experience offers not only new cultures and new sights, but also new ways of perceiving those sights, and these

Lucy M. Long, 'Culinary Tourism: A Folkloristic Perspective on Eating and Otherness' in Lucy Long (ed.), *Culinary Tourism*, (Lexington: University Press of Kentucky, 2004), pp. 20–50. (Excerpt printed here: 20–24, 32–35, 36–50. Omitted text is indicated by ellipses.) Used with permission.

new ways of perceiving ultimately enhance the individual. John Urry developed this notion of tourism as a qualitative category of experience, defining it as a kind of viewing he refers to as "the tourist gaze" (1990). This gaze is distinctive from "everyday looking" in that it attends to difference (1990, 1995). It notices contrast and distinctiveness; it shifts objects and actions out of the common and mundane world, enabling or encouraging viewers to recognize their power as symbols, entertainment, and art. In this sense, foodways may be one of the fullest ways of perceiving otherness. Sightseeing is only a partial engagement with otherness, whereas culinary tourism, utilizing the senses of taste, smell, touch, and vision, offers a deeper, more integrated level of experience. It engages one's physical being, not simply as an observer, but as a participant as well.[5]

A key concept in these definitions is the idea of tourism being voluntary; becoming a tourist is a choice, and with that choice there is an implied openness to the new. New experiences may be tried, however, for a variety of reasons, not all of which we would consider touristic. For example, individuals may participate in an exotic foodways out of consideration for one's host, in response to a challenge, as a statement of rebellion against the status quo, to conform to social obligations or norms, and so on. Tourism, on the other hand, involves new experiences for the sake of the experience itself. Through tourism, we satisfy our curiosity about otherness; we confront the impulse to explore the unknown, to climb the mountain because it is there. And we expect to find pleasure in seeking the unknown, perhaps not in the unknown itself, but in the conducting of that search; we may not like the food after all, but we can have fun trying it. Furthermore, the pleasure we find in food and eating can be of an aesthetic nature, satisfying our sensibilities of taste, proportion, and appearance, so that the pleasure stems from the food itself and not from what it represents.

Intentionality also assumes the perception, or categorization, of a food complex as other, and it is this perception that shapes our approach to the food. We must think of a food as being somehow different, new, or exotic in order to think of exploring it. This perception can shift with experience, and the shift can move us toward tourism or away from it. What may begin as touristic eating may change with familiarity. We may try a new food with trepidation, but once we discover the taste is pleasing, we may then eat that food for aesthetic enjoyment. An example of such a shift occurred personally during a meal at a Taiwanese restaurant in the United States in which I came across a chunk of unknown substance in a seafood stew. Because the other ingredients were sea creatures and the chunk resembled marbled fat, my dinner companions and I tried to identify what animal it may have belonged to. After a tentative taste, we realized it was plant—more specifically, taro—and we ate it with hunger rather than curiosity.

Similarly, we have probably all had the experience of unknowingly eating something that we otherwise would have considered inedible or unappealing and would have approached with curiosity, with the sense of trying something different. An example that plays upon ethnic stereotypes occurred while I was traveling in Burma and was served dog-fried rice at a small lunchroom. Not knowing the ingredients but recognizing the general category of the dish and being hungry, my Western traveling companions and I ate enthusiastically. During the meal, however, the cook responded to our questioning gestures about the meat in the dish with an "arf, arf." We immediately lost our appetites. Those of us who continued to eat did so out of curiosity rather than hunger, and with a definite sense of eating something outside our usual boundaries of what was edible. Our initial consumption of this food was not a voluntary participation in an other, but a misperception of the familiar. We moved from eating to satisfy physical hunger to eating as outsiders.

Foodways

"Participation in foodways" implies the full spectrum of activities surrounding food. [...] The concept of foodways opens up the range of activities available for tourism. Since food is more than the dishes we eat, we can be tourists by exploring these other aspects of the food systems. Similarly, foodways can help to ground tourism in the everyday. By turning normally routine activities, such as shopping, cleaning up, and storing foods, into tourist sites, we can more easily contrast and negotiate the sense of difference with the familiar.

Otherness

"Other" in this definition refers to the anthropological notion of humans defining the world according to their own socially constructed perceptions of reality, perceptions that divide the world into the known and familiar as opposed to the unknown or other.[6] Otherness is a construction by the individual as well as by the culture within which that individual moves. Foods are not inherently strange or exotic; the experiences of an individual are what determine the status of a food. In this sense, tourism depends on a perception of otherness rather than an objective reality of an item's relationship to that individual.

[...]

All of these others can be enacted in a variety of arenas, commercial and domestic, public and private, festive and ordinary. Restaurants, festivals, cookbooks, grocery stores, private festive food events, cooking classes, televised cooking shows, advertising, and tourism brochures are some specific sites for culinary tourism. These arenas serve as interfaces between individuals and cultures, reflecting the expectations and contexts bearing upon each exchange. Interactions with foodways are seen through the lenses of our own experiences and cultural history; our perceptions of another are uniquely our own. Simultaneously, our expectations will shape the interchange. Using the term "interface" highlights the self-reflexive potential of such sites and the possibility for dynamic, negotiated interactions within them. The term also reminds us that encounters with the other frequently teach us more about ourselves than about the other.

Each enactment of such tourism involves at least two actors, real or imagined, the host and the guest, the producer and the consumer—each having their own perspectives on what defines otherness. Consumers select those foodways contrasting with their own culinary system; while producers, individuals, or institutions attempting to present potentially other foodways must take into account the foodways systems of their audience. An individual shapes the presentation of his or her ethnicity according to the cognitive model held of the audience's culture (Coggeshall 1986). Producers of instances and artifacts of culinary tourism will likewise adapt their presentations to their understanding of their audience's culinary aesthetics and experiences. Studies of culinary tourism, then, need to address instances of such tourism as interactive, communicative events within a larger conceptual symbolic system.[7]

Realms of culinary experience

In the context of foodways, the crux of otherness involves three realms of experience—what I call the realms of the exotic, the edible, and the palatable. The *exotic* is a continuum from the familiar to the strange that defines the similarity of things to our known socially constructed universe. It is based on our individual histories and personal tastes as well as on the collective cultural experience and the generally accepted culinary aesthetic.

The realm of the *edible* consists of cultural categories of what can and cannot be eaten, in the sense that one's humanity is tied to observing such categories. While this realm has similarities with Claude Lèvi-Strauss's categories of raw and cooked (Lèvi-Strauss 1966; 1978), I do not treat it as expressive of universal cognitive structures. Edibility is culturally specific, and as Mary Douglas has demonstrated in her work on taboos and food patterns, it can be a reflection of a culture's social structure. The question of edibility automatically occurs at the extreme end of the exotic continuum since the unknown raises questions not only about whether a food can be eaten, but also whether it should be eaten (Douglas 1966).

The realm of the *palatable* is an aesthetic rather than cognitive one, dealing with what is considered pleasing within a culinary system. Foods may be considered edible, but their selection for consumption will depend on whether or not they are considered savory, appetizing, or appropriate for particular contexts. Palatability can be seen as a "shadow" realm of edibility, since the two tend to be collapsed by many eaters. Certain food items or aspects of a food system may be considered culturally edible but unpalatable to a particular eater or group of eaters, and therefore would appear inedible. Vegetarians, for example, may find meat not only unpalatable, but also inedible. The children's categories of "yuk" and "yum" also blur the distinction between these realms, translating them into a culinary philosophy shaping everyday consumption, much to the dismay of nutrition-minded parents.

The difference between the realms of edible and palatable is perhaps most clearly seen in how we use them to evaluate other eaters. The eater of the "not edible" is perceived as strange, perhaps dangerous, definitely not one of us, whereas the eater of the unpalatable is seen as having different tastes. Both realms refer to the potential consumption of a particular food or aspect of foodways, but edibility refers to the categorical possibility; palatability to the aesthetic. The first is what we can eat; the second is what we want to eat.

By treating these categories as dynamic cultural resources available for individual manipulation and responsive to change, I hope to leave the model open to the historical, the situated, the contingent, and the diversity within cultures. In keeping with this approach, it is perhaps more accurate to portray these realms as axes that cross each other, forming four quadrants. These quadrants allow for overlapping, so there can be foods that are exotic but edible and foods that are familiar but inedible.

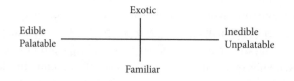

Since the boundaries of these realms depend on the past experiences, personal tastes, and personalities of the potential eaters and producers, as well as on the cultural categories and aesthetics of those actors, these realms are flexible and dynamic. Food items can shift in their location within these realms, because individuals' and society's perceptions of edibility and exoticness can shift. This shifting can occur in any direction along these axes: from the exotic to the familiar or the familiar to the exotic, and from the edible to the inedible or the inedible to the edible. It can occur on an individual basis or on a larger scale as a regional or national trend, either informal or institutionalized. It can also occur with any aspect of foodways—a specific ingredient, a particular dish, eating style, or preparation method—as well as entire cuisines.

Shifts in perspective and the multivocality of food

The shifting from the exotic to the familiar and the inedible to the edible occurs constantly in the marketing of new foods to the American public. A good example is kiwi fruit, ten years ago a rarity in grocery stores in my part of the Midwest, but now commonplace enough to be included in school lunches. Pizza provides another example, beginning as an ethnic food with some question as to its palatability. With acceptance it has become a common meal for many Americans and has lost much of its otherness, to the extent that it is now considered a genre of food with certain structural features: dessert pizzas consist of a sweet dough or cookie base covered with whipped cream or sweetened cream cheese and topped with fruit or candies; ice-cream pizzas are similar but with an ice cream base. Ironically, some producers are shifting pizza back to the exotic end of the continuum by the addition of trendy, expensive, or unusual items—whole-wheat crusts, sun-dried tomatoes, shiitake mushrooms, goat cheese, grilled shrimp, and lobster. A pizza carryout restaurant in Philadelphia owned by a Korean couple deftly mixed the familiar and the exotic by offering a dish called "Korean Pizza," a standard pizza crust with Korean grilled beef and vegetables. Similarly, tostados and tacos have moved from the realm of questionable edibility to such familiarity that they are being served in school cafeterias. Chopsticks, rice steamers, shish kebab, barbecue, hot pepper sauces, and salsa dips are other common examples of this type of shift.

While American foodways appear to be expanding, the opposite directional shift occurs also, particularly in the definitions based on ethos. Some foodways that were once mainstream, even normative, have been moved to the inedible by some segments of the population because of nutritional or health concerns. Cooking green beans (and other vegetables) for hours with lard or bacon, as is common in traditional Southern cooking, is no longer in favor in health-conscious restaurants in the South. Butters and creams are suspect, as are traditional sauces and gravies that call for these ingredients. Rich desserts full of fats and sugar are deemed taboo for those who are health-conscious, and women's magazines frequently give alternative recipes and cooking methods for popular but cholesterol-laden foods like fried chicken, grilled cheese sandwiches, and ice cream. Similarly, vegetarians have placed animal products in the realm of the inedible, sometimes replacing them with foods formerly treated as exotic (bean curd, mashed bean pastes, and bean and grain patties) or even inedible (soybeans, seaweed, fermented dairy products). In these cases, the foodways that have shifted to inedible remain familiar to the larger population.

These shifts occur on a personal level as well, reflecting an individual's history, personality, experiences, and circumstances. Food, like any cultural product, is multivocal and polysemic, and new meanings can be recognized in new contexts. This frequently occurs when one's perceptions of foods are challenged in some way. An example of such a shift in perspective is an incident in which a friend requested suggestions of an exotic food that his young daughter could make for a school project. When I suggested that he look to his own background, he stated that he remembered only "normal foods" like bubble and squeak, toad-in-the-hole, tudgies (mashed turnips), Yorkshire pudding, and odds and sods. Although he had grown up in the urban Midwest, he lived with his Irish immigrant grandparents and was raised with their foodways, assuming that that was standard to the area. When he realized that these foods represented his Irish heritage, he looked at them differently, recognizing that they could be exotic to the Midwest. He then helped his daughter select a recipe for potato pancakes from an Irish cookbook. (The project was very successful; her classmates found the pancakes both foreign and tasty.)

[…]

Tourism as negotiation

As this anecdote illustrates, exoticness, edibility, and palatability, like any cultural categories, are contextual, social and personal constructs that can undergo redefinition by specific cultures as well as by individuals. Likewise, they are a resource to be potentially manipulated for creative, expressive, economic, even political ends. The maneuvering between the realms of the exotic and the edible is a dynamic, creative process that is perhaps best thought of as a negotiation of the realms with the needs, interests, and aesthetics of all the actors involved. This negotiation should be examined, then, from the point of view of both the producer and the consumer, and in terms of individual choices as well as group inclinations. There will always be some individuals who are more conservative in their tastes than others, just as there are individuals who will "push the palate," so to speak. Likewise, some populations, for whatever reason, will be more open to new culinary experiences than others. One of my children's preschool teachers actively taught the children to be good taste testers, willing to take at least one bite of everything. Her concern was primarily a nutritional one, but she was teaching an exploratory approach to food that contrasted dramatically with the "better safe than sorry" approach pushed by some parents who cautioned children against trying new foods.

While exploratory eating can be a matter of personal preference and accessibility, it can also be promoted for commercial or ideological reasons. Individuals may want to introduce new foodways as a matter of ethnic or regional pride, as a statement of identity, as a demand for public recognition, or as social or cultural capital. They may also be a way to consolidate group belonging, define difference, and demonstrate distinctiveness. New foods may also be presented as a commodity, either as an innovation based on a tradition or as a tradition viable for new groups or uses. In such cases, producers explicitly manipulate the realms of the exotic, the edible, and the palatable to attract consumers.

Strategies of negotiation

In examining attempts to present and explore new foods, I found five basic strategies for negotiating these realms: *framing, naming* or *translation, explication, menu selection,* and *recipe adaptation.* In the following discussion of these strategies, I focus on the producers/presenters of food, and I draw data primarily from two kinds of arenas: ethnic restaurants, specifically Korean restaurants in Philadelphia in the mid-1980s, and community-based seasonal festivals in the Midwest.[8] Ethnic restaurants are a particularly valuable arena for observation, because the need to be commercially viable forces restaurant owners to be aware of their potential customers' tastes, pocketbooks, and prior exposure to different foodways systems. The anticipated clientele, then, is a major factor in the negotiation of edibility and exoticness, and ethnic restaurants must frequently emphasize the edibility of the exotic in order to attract non-native customers.

Community-based festivals, on the other hand, tend to exoticize the familiar; they present the mundane as celebratory and the ordinary as extraordinary. In the Midwest, many of these festivals highlight the region's agricultural roots by using as a theme a particular food item or crop associated with the locale— northwest Ohio, for example, boasts apple butter, cherry, radish, tomato, and pumpkin festivals as well as an "Eggstravaganza" featuring eggs.

Framing, the first strategy of negotiation, involves designing a context surrounding a food item that then defines that food's edibility and exoticness. I draw here on ideas from Richard Bauman (1977) and Erving Goffman (1963) to emphasize the need to situate performances in particular physical contexts. The languages used on menus and signs, the decor, the spatial arrangement of tables, and the location of public and private areas are means by which actors can emphasize the exotic or the familiar. The Korean restaurants in Philadelphia signaled their anticipated clientele through such framing. Those catering to primarily Korean customers frequently displayed signs and menus only in Korean, had Korean paintings or objects, but had none of the stereotypical Asian decor. Those anticipating both Korean and non-Korean customers had menus and signs in Korean and English and more of the Asian decor. They also had designated back rooms for in-group customers. These usually were rooms upstairs set aside for large group dinners and parties where the eaters would sit on cushions on the floor at low tables. One establishment even had a disco and bar that was not publicly advertised to non-Koreans. The restaurants expecting a non-Korean clientele tended to use the more stereotypical Asian decor, such as beaded curtains, dragon motifs, and red napkins, with a familiar large dining room seating arrangement.

Similarly, placing an otherwise familiar food in an unusual context can signal a potentially new interpretation of that food. The community-based festivals in Ohio juxtaposed local history with particular foods, assigning those foods associated (both imagined and actual) with cultural heritage and identity. Such framing essentially signifies the need to recognize familiar foods as potentially other, to see them as outsiders would.

The second strategy of negotiation, naming or translation, involves the identification of items. This may be a literal translation of the name of a dish or food item or the invention of a new name. For example, the Korean dish *bulgogi* is translated literally as "fire meat" but is frequently identified as "grilled beef strips." Such names frequently draw from the familiar end of the continuum in order to demonstrate their similarities to the larger foodways system. In doing so, the naming places the food analogously within a framework accessible to Americans. For example, the Korean dish *kimchi* is frequently identified as a pickle, although it is not made with vinegar. It could more accurately by identified as "cabbage and turnip fermented with salt, garlic, hot pepper, and rotted shrimp," but such a description would push it toward the inedible—or at least the unpalatable—for many American consumers.

Festivals also used this strategy to draw attention to the exotic quality of otherwise familiar foods. Prefixes such as "old-tyme" or "old-fashioned" emphasize the foods' representativeness of the past. Similarly, local regional or geographic ties may be made explicit by adding place names to the identification of a food item— Grand Rapids apple butter, Cincinnati chili, Ohio buckeyes (for a chocolate and peanut-butter confection made to resemble horse chestnuts). Religious identities associated with an area were also highlighted—Amish chickens and eggs, Mennonite whole-grain breads—as were characteristics felt to be representative of the region's ethos—homegrown, family-farmed, handpicked.

A third strategy is that of explication: description and explanation of the ingredients, manner of cooking, context for eating, or history and symbolism of the item. In this strategy, the consumer is drawn into the foodways system of the item and given a "native" perspective on it. In an intentionally humorous use of this strategy, a Thai restaurant in Milwaukee, The King and I, identified the spiciness of the dishes on their menu according to a scale that began with one star for "coward," two stars for "careful," three stars for "adventurous," and four stars for "Native Thai." Similarly, waiters and waitresses in most Korean restaurants were prepared to give a complete description of the ingredients and preparation methods of the dishes being offered. Likewise, they would demonstrate techniques for holding chopsticks, for cooking one's meal with the tableside grill—the *sinsullo*, and for serving oneself from the communal dishes. I played a similar role at the Festival of American Folklife at the Smithsonian Institution in Washington, D.C., in the early 1980s when I was a presenter for a Korean food-ways section. While two older Korean women, neither of whom spoke a great deal of English, demonstrated preparation techniques for a number of dishes, I fielded questions, most of which were about the edibility of those dishes, particularly *kimchi*. This dish is known among Americans for its extreme spiciness and powerful odor, features that have been played upon in American images of Koreans. In my explanations of the diversity of recipes for the dish and of its central role in Korean foodways, I attempted to make the audience familiar enough with *kimchi* to see it as at least edible. They may not personally like the item, but they gained an appreciation for why some people do.

Many cookbook authors attempt a similar negotiation of the exotic by including introductions to the food system being presented or by including narratives and anecdotes about the recipes. For example, a Korean cookbook written in English specifically for Americans provides descriptions of the basics of Korean cuisine and of Korean table settings and has photographs of ingredients potentially unfamiliar to that audience. Another cookbook compiled of recipes used at various Smithsonian folklife festivals includes descriptions of the significance of a recipe in a community or family tradition along with quotations from the original cooks. Such a strategy personalizes, and therefore humanizes, otherwise exotic, potentially inedible foods. A recipe for octopus, for example, is accompanied by the cook's memories of her family's procuring and eating of the creature (Kirlin and Kirlin 1991:95).

The local festivals in Ohio, on the other hand, frame the commonplace as worthy of attention through descriptions of the history and social uses of the item and through explanations of the otherness of familiar foods. Frequently, the food items are familiar, but the cooking methods are not, being "old-fashioned" ones used historically in that region. The Grand Rapids Apple Butter Festival, for example, offers apple butter prepared in large iron pots over outdoor fires, a method that used to be common in the region. While apple butter itself is still a familiar item in the region's foodways, that preparation method is not. During the festival, volunteers demonstrate the cooking method and discuss it with the audience. Similarly, some dishes are not recognized as being representative of the region until their distinctiveness—and their potential exoticness to an outsider—is pointed out. Items such as potpie (a thick chicken or turkey stew with large flat noodles) or Cincinnati chili, apple butter, and tomato ketchup are now being included as part of presentations of regional identity. Other food items may be presented as representative because of their commonness and therefore interrelatedness to other aspects of the regional culture. Recognizing a food item does not shift it toward the realm of the exotic so much as it clarifies the symbolic weight of that food.

Menu selection, the fourth and perhaps the most common strategy, is the selecting of particular dishes thought to best appeal to the consumer. This strategy involves the producer's cognitive model of the tastes of the potential eater as well as the producer's notions of which dishes best represent the cuisine. In Korean restaurants, waitresses frequently suggest the blander dishes to American customers, assuming that too much garlic and hot pepper is offensive to most Americans.

[...]

Menu selection clearly reflects the intentions of the producer and the anticipated consumer. Korean restaurants catering to a primarily Korean clientele featured specifically Korean dishes prepared in an "authentic" manner, that is, using more spices. Those anticipating a mixed clientele, frequently highlighted on the menu those dishes thought to appeal to non-Koreans. Restaurants targeting mostly non-Koreans selected those dishes using ingredients and quantities of spices known to be acceptable and liked by most American customers. A common strategy among these last establishments was to offer Korean food alongside other Asian cuisines, such as Japanese or Chinese, already established in the United States. By juxtaposing the relatively unfamiliar Korean cuisine with the others—still exotic but more familiar—Korean food was brought into the realm of the edible.

Similarly, a Cantonese restaurant owner in Memphis described to me how he "educated" American children to eat Chinese food by offering them Chinese dishes such as egg rolls and chop suey that he felt would not be too strange to them. Once they were familiar with these foods, he gradually offered them a larger selection until they had acquired a taste for Chinese cuisine. Ironically, his teaching was too effective, and the children, when they became adults, went on to acquire tastes for the Peking and Szechwan styles offered by other restaurants. He concluded that his Cantonese-style cooking was too bland for them, too familiar, and no longer offered the excitement of the exotic.[9]

Using the same strategy, the community-based festivals selected dishes thought to be familiar to the crowds but also fitting of a particular public identity, one that was usually based on an imagined past. Apple butter or popcorn was standard demonstration fare at these festivals; neither needed explanation to regional audiences. By grounding foodways in the familiar, these festivals emphasized the similarities, the unity of the area, thereby helping it qualify as a cultural region, one of the underlying themes of many of these festivals.

The final strategy, recipe adaptation, involves the manipulation of the ingredients and preparation methods of particular dishes in order to adapt to the foodways system of the anticipated consumers. Potentially offensive ingredients, or those not easily obtained, may be omitted or replaced with more familiar ones. Again, *kimchi* provides an excellent example. The dish comes in numerous variations of ingredients depending on the season, the locale, the occasion, and the social status of the eaters. The most typical kind, a winter *kimchi,* is made of, among other things, Chinese cabbage, turnips, green onions, garlic, red pepper, ginger, shrimp and oysters, water, and salt. The mixture is left in a cool place to marinate for at least four to five days, preferably several months. As mentioned above, the result is very hot and pungent. When preparing *kimchi* for American customers, most of the Korean restaurants in Philadelphia made a less spicy version. One cook described how she left out the shrimp and decreased the amount of pepper and garlic for her "American *kimchi.*" She also told of another restaurant that substituted paprika for the red pepper normally used, keeping the red color of the *kimchi* but reducing its spiciness.

In a reverse process, festivals frequently adapted recipes to produce foods that would seem familiar yet still out of the ordinary and with an aura of exoticness. These adaptations often emphasized the rural background and "hands on" attitude of the region. Instead of store-bought, canned, or frozen foods, festivals used homegrown, freshly picked ingredients prepared home style in a family setting, such as freshly picked cherries, homegrown pumpkins, farm fresh eggs, or apple butter prepared over outdoor fires instead of in crock pots.

This look at some of the strategies used in negotiating the realms of exoticness and edibility confirms the need to locate culinary tourism in the perspectives of the individuals involved; that is, tourism is in the eye of the beholder—or on the tongue of the taster. What to one individual is a culinary adventure may be mundane and familiar to another and vice versa. As with any cultural tradition, there can be a discrepancy between the meanings assigned to food by the producers and those assigned by the consumers. Furthermore, foodways serve a multitude of functions in our culture; culinary tourism is but one.

Concluding thoughts

Locating culinary tourism in the perspectives of individual consumers and producers addresses the question of why it occurs. Some scholars have interpreted the impulse to eat the other as a colonialist, hegemonic act, a taking over of another group by appropriating its cultural traditions, or as representing the capitalist inclinations to display superiority by mastery over ever-expanding arenas, including new cuisines (Goody 1982; Mintz 1985; Montano 1997; Heldke 2001). Culinary tourism can also be seen as a sign of prosperity, allowing producers and consumers to elevate food from being mere sustenance to the realms of art and recreation, and therefore tools for the expression and manipulation of social power (Appadurai 1981, 1986; Bourdieu 1984). A more optimistic interpretation sees culinary tourism as the willingness of humans to experience the cultural worlds of other people, as the result of curiosity about other experiences and other ways of life. This is not to deny the political implications of tourism or the ethical responsibilities attached to it. Nor does it ignore the fact that tourism turns culinary traditions into commodities to be bought and sold. Beginning at the level of individual involvement in tourism, however, illuminates the complexity of cultural productions and allows us to see the workings of personal meaning within larger institutional meanings.

In my research, I found the motivations for culinary tourism to be complex and to reflect what appears to be a basic and universal impulse. People intentionally consume an other because they are curious, and that curiosity stems from any number of reasons: because they are bored with .the familiar, they do not want to be rude to a host, they want to balance their nutritional intake, they want to belong to a specific community of eaters, they feel pride in the heritage represented by a foodways, or they want to authenticate an experience by relishing it, so to speak. As both social system and aesthetic system, food is a powerful medium through which to enter another culture. Through food we can communicate identity, relationships, ideologies, and emotions, as well as fulfill basic physical needs. Food offers us an aesthetic experience, and like other aesthetic realms—music, dance, art—it draws us into its own universe of meaning. The materiality of food allows an individual to experience an other on a sensory level, not just an intellectual one. By consuming the foods of a group distinct from us, we may be acting out larger cultural impulses, but the aesthetic and material nature of food, I think, explains the pervasiveness of food in tourist sites. The act of eating offers a way to share our basic humanity, while also acknowledging and negotiating our differential identities.

The model of culinary tourism suggested here provides a framework for seeing, the varieties of interfaces in which adventurous eating occurs as instances of negotiating individual and social perceptions of the exotic. As such, they represent a movement toward expanding the definitions of edibility and palatability and the horizons of the familiar. These instances are connected to a multitude of culinary experiences occurring throughout our culture, all characterized by the dynamic exploration and redefining of our culinary universes. As destination and vehicle for tourism, food expands our understanding of both food and tourism.

Notes

1. For contemporary folkloristic approaches to the study of food and foodways see Jones, Giuliano, and Krell 1983; Brown and Mussell 1984; Neustadt 1992; Gutierrez 1992; and Lockwood and Lockwood 1991. For examples of a folkloristic approach to recipe collections see Kirlin and Kirlin 1991, and Kaplan, Hoover, and Moore 1986.

2. I borrow here from folklorist Barbara Kirshenblatt-Gimblett's use of the phrase "gastronomic tourism" (personal communication, February 1996). Kirshenblatt-Gimblett is well known for "pushing" the boundaries of folklore and for her insightful critiques of the discipline (see, for example, Kirshenblatt-Gimblett 1988). She has also been a major influence in the folkloristic study of foodways.

3. I draw here from the extensive body of literature on the anthropology of tourism and on the critique of touristic productions. Three classics in the field are Smith 1989; MacCannell 1976; and Jules-Rosette 1984. For more experiential and ethnographic-based approaches, see Urry 1990, 1995; Smith and Eadington, 1992; Baranowski and Furlough 2001; and Desmond 2001. The journal *Annals of Tourism Research* specializes in tourism. Tourism has also been of particular interest to folklorists, partly because it raises questions over such issues as the nature of authenticity, the relationship between producer and consumer, and the aesthetic and political quality of cultural representations.

4. This conception of culinary tourism draws heavily from contemporary folklore theory, hence the title, "a folkloristic perspective." Some scholars use the term "folkloristic" to distinguish the field of folklore studies from its subject matter (Georges and Jones 1995). The definition of folklore offered by Dan Ben-Amos in 1972—"artistic communication in small groups"—is still useful today, succinctly characterizing folklore. Folklore is generally thought of as those products and patterns of behavior expressing a communal ethos and aesthetic and being transmitted over time and place in a way that allows for individuals and groups to create variations, enacting their particular histories, identities, and circumstances in each performance. I draw from a number of scholars in my own formulation of folklore as the processes and products by which individuals construct, negotiate, and maintain meaningful connections with past, place, and people (see Toelken 1996).

5. Jane Desmond's work on public displays of bodies as sites for tourism demonstrates the power of the materiality of things to ground experience. She states that Western thought reflects a philosophy "dependent on the body to anchor systems of knowledge that articulate social difference" (2001:xiv). Furthermore, she points out that "live performers not only authenticate these packages' differences: they also offer the possibility of contact with them" (2001:xv). Food similarly grounds the tourist experience in our own bodies and physicality.

6. The notion of other has informed the field of folklore studies since the 1970s and has drawn from both anthropological models and literary theory as well as from philosophical inquiries into the nature of knowledge. See, for example, Turner and Bruner 1984.

7. This approach draws from performance theory (see Bauman 1977) to attend to actual incidents of consuming an other with awareness of the varying levels of context present. It also reframes Dell Hymes's ethnography of speaking model as "ethnography of eating" (see Hymes 1962 and 1974).

8. In the fall of 1983, for a course in folklife taught by Don Yoder, I began an ethnography of Korean foodways in the Philadelphia area, looking specifically at the varieties, uses, and symbolic meanings of the dish *kimchi*. This work resulted in a term paper, a paper on *kimchi* read at the 1986 American Folklore Society meeting, and an unpublished paper on varieties of restaurant experiences. My work on festivals in the Midwest began in 1986 and has continued to the present. In 2002, I produced a documentary video on a local apple butter festival titled *Stirring Up the Past: The Grand Rapids Apple Butter Fest.*

9. This interview was a part of a larger survey on Asian communities in Memphis that I conducted for the Center for Southern Folklore in Memphis, Tennessee, from January through June of 1980.

References

Appadurai, Arjun. 1981. "Gastropolitics in Hindu South Asia." *American Ethnologist* 8: 494–511.

—. 1986. "Introduction: Commodities and the Politics of Value." In *The Social Life of Things: Commodities in Cultural Perspective.* Ed. Arjun Appadurai, 3–63. Cambridge, U.K.: Cambridge University Press.

Baranowski, Shelley, and Ellen Furlough, eds. 2001. *Being Elsewhere: Tourism, Consumer Culture, and Identity in Modern Europe and North America.* Ann Arbor: University of Michigan Press.

Bauman, Richard. 1977. *Verbal Art as Performance.* Rowley, Mass.: Newbury House.

Bourdieu, Pierre. 1984. *Distinction: A Social Critique of the Judgement of Taste.* Cambridge, Mass.: Harvard University Press.

Brown, Linda Keller, and Kay Mussell, eds. 1984. *Ethnic and Regional Foodways in the United States: The Performance of Group Identity.* Knoxville: University of Tennessee Press.

Coggeshall, John M. 1986. "One of Those Intangibles: The Manifestation of Ethnic Identity in Southwestern Illinois." *Journal of American Folklore* 99:273–90.

Desmond, Jane C. 2001. *Staging Tourism: Bodies on Display from Waikiki to Sea World.* Chicago: University of Chicago Press.

Douglas, Mary. 1966. *Purity and Danger: An Analysis of Concepts of Pollution and Taboo.* New York: Praeger.

Georges, Frank and Michael Owen Jones. 1995. *Folkloristics: An Introduction.* Bloomington: Indiana University Press.

Goffman, Erving. 1963. *Behavior in Public Places: Notes on the Social Organizations of Gatherings.* New York: Free Press of Glencoe.

Goody, Jack. 1982. *Cooking, Cuisine and Class: A Study in Comparative Sociology.* Cambridge, U.K.: Cambridge University Press.

Graburn, Nelson H.H. 1989. "Tourism: The Sacred Journey." In *Hosts and Guests: The Anthropology of Tourism, 2nd ed.* Ed. Valene L. Smith, 21–36. Philadelphia: University of Pennsylvania Press.

Gutierrez, C. Paige. 1992. *Cajun Foodways.* Jackson: University Press of Mississippi.

Heldke, Lisa. 2001. "Let's Cook Thai: Recipes for Colonialism." In *Pilaf, Pozole, and Pad Thai: American Women and Ethnic Food.* Ed. Sherrie A. Inness, 175–98. Amherst: University of Massachusetts Press.

Hymes, Dell. 1962. "The Ethnography of Speaking." In *Anthropology and Human Behavior.* Eds. T. Gladwin and William.C. Sturtevant. Washington, D.C.: Anthropological Society of Washington.

—. 1974. "Ways of Speaking." In *Explorations in the Ethnography of Speaking.* Eds. Richard Bauman and Joel Sherzer, 433–52. New York: Cambridge University Press.

Inness, Sherrie A., 2001. *Pilaf, Pozole, and Pad Thai: American Women and Ethnic Food.* Amherst: University of Massachusetts Press.

Jones, Michael Owen, Bruce Giuliano, and Roberta Krell, eds. 1983. *Foodways and Eating Habits: Directions for Research.* Los Angeles: California Folklore Society.

Jones, Suzi. 1976. "Regionalization: A Rhetorical Strategy." *Journal of the Folklore Institute* 13: 105–18.

Jules-Rosette, Benetta. 1984. *The Messages of Tourist Art: An African Semiotic System in Comparative Perspective.* New York: Plenum Press.

Kaplan, Anne R., Marjorie A. Hoover, and Willard B. Moore, eds. 1986. *The Minnesota Ethnic Food Book.* St. Paul: Minnesota Historical Society Press.

Kirlin, Katherine S., and Thomas M. Kirlin, eds. 1991. *Smithsonian Folklife Cookbook.* Washington, D.C.: Smithsonian Institution Press.

Kirshenblatt-Gimblett, Barbara. 1988. "Mistaken Dichotomies." *Journal of American Folklore* 101:140–55.

—. 1998. *Destination Culture: Tourism, Museums, and Heritage.* Berkeley: University of California Press.

Lèvi-Strauss, Claude. 1966. "The Culinary Triangle." *Partisan Review* 33: 586–95.

—. 1978. *The Origin of Table Manners.* Trans. John and Doreen Weightman. New-York: Harper and Row.

Lockwood, Yvonne R., and William G. Lockwood. 1991. "Pasties in Michigan's Upper Peninsula: Foodways, Interethnic Relations, and Regionalism." In *Creative Ethnicity: Symbols and Strategies of Contemporary Ethnic Life.* Eds. Stephen Stern and John Allan Cicala, 3–20. Logan: Utah State University Press.

Lowenthal, David. 1985. *The Past Is a Foreign Country.* Cambridge, U.K.: Cambridge University Press.

MacCannell, Dean. 1976. *The Tourist: A New Theory of the Leisure Class.* New York: Schocken Books.

Mintz, Sidney W. 1985. *Sweetness and Power: The Place of Sugar in Modern History.* New York: Penguin.

—. 1996. *Tasting Food, Tasting Freedom: Excursions into Eating, Culture, and the Past.* Boston: Beacon Press.

Montaño, Mario. 1997. "Appropriation and Counterhegemony in South Texas: Food Slurs, Offal Meats, and Blood." In *Usable Pasts: Traditions and Group Expressions in North America.* Ed. Tad Tuleja, 50–67. Logan: Utah State University Press.

Neustadt, Kathy. 1992. *Clambake A History and Celebration of an American Tradition.* Amherst: University of Massachusetts Press.

Stern, Stephen, and John Allan Cicala. 1991. *Creative Ethnicity: Symbols and Strategies of Contemporary Ethnic Life.* Logan: Utah State University Press.

Smith, Valene L., ed. 1989. "Introduction." In *Hosts and Guests: The Anthropology of Tourism, 2nd ed.* Ed. Valene L. Smith, 1–17. Philadelphia: University of Pennsylvania Press.

Smith, Valene L. and William R. Eadington, eds. 1992. *Tourism Alternatives: Potentials and Problems in the Development of Tourism.* Philadelphia: University of Pennsylvania Press.

Toelken, Barre. 1996. *The Dynamics of Folklore.* Logan: Utah State University Press.

Turner, Victor W., and Edward M. Bruner. 1984. *The Anthropology of Experience.* Urbana: University of Illinois Press.

Urry, John. 1990. *The Tourist Gaze: Leisure and Travel in Contemporary Societies.* London: Sage.

—. 1995. *Consuming Places.* London: Routledge.

Yoder, Don. 1972. "Folk Cookery." In *Folklore and Folklife: An Introduction.* Ed. Richard M. Dorson, 325. Chicago: University of Chicago Press.

CHAPTER 40
"THE LAST PIECE/S'LETSCHT SCHTICK"
AND "EATING ALONE"
Margaret R. Yocom

The Last Piece/S'Letscht Schtick

For Elmer Christman Keck, 1893–1982

Through the crescent hole, down
between stove pipe and floor, down
he and his cousins peer
into the hushed dining room, its closed windows.
His stove-pipe-peering would be too hot, except
it's summer, early, the full heat
not come onto his father's fields,
no need yet to thin the shoots of corn, walk
row after row, pinch
what is not wanted.

I have never wanted raisin pie,
but he does. Badly.
His nose follows the journey round
the funeral table,
one adult hand to another adult hand,
its hovering above the tatted white tablecloth.

One adult hand after another adult hand
lifts the silver server,
slices through buttery dough
into that dark center,
deep and dense,
scents of cinnamon, brown sugar,
hand over hand,
passing it on.

Margaret R. Yocom, 'Eating Alone' was originally published in Frank de Caro (ed.) *The Folklore Muse: Poetry, Fiction and Other Reflections by Folklorists* (Boulder: Utah State University Press, 2008), p. 212. Reproduced with permission of Utah State University Press in the format 'Republish in a book' via Copyright Clearance Center. 'The Last Piece/S'Letscht Schtick' and the accompanying commentary have not previously been published and have been commissioned for this publication.

If the mourners looked up,
they would have seen that ring of eyes,
that warm halo of desire.
Had he spoken to them, below,
no pie, ever, for days.
No dinner.

Had he spoken, I would
not have understood
his German sweetened, smoothed by
two hundred years of Pennsylvania Freindschaft,
of Karrich un Kich,
Kinner un Kieh.
His ears trail the words.
His eyes, the pie.
I have never wanted raisin pie.
I want those words.

He watches the slices disappear,
whispers the alarm:
Vier!
Drei!
Zwee!
Eens!
Fork in hand, his
uncle reaches once more for the pie.

From his faraway perch, he
calls to them, and me,
telling my tape-recorder his first memory,
that last piece,
his words blurted out in a language
lost to me,
ripped by war, and war again,
by "victory cabbage"
    Can you say it? zzzz- Sawwergraut
by "hot dog"
    Can you say it? frrrr- Frankfurter

He cries, my grandfather, as do I,
"Datt geht s'letscht Schtick!"

Notes:

—My thanks to Dr. Irmgard Wagner, George Mason University, emerita, for checking my German, and to Dr. Mark Louden, University of Wisconsin, for translating my German into Pennsylvania German.

—Translation.

Pennsylvania German (German, English):

Freindschaft (Freundschaft, relatives)
Karrich un Kich (Kirche und Küche, church and kitchen)
Kinner un Kieh (Kinder und Kühe, children and cows)
Vier! Drei! Zwee! Eens! (Vier, Drei, Zwei, Eins; four, three, two, one)
Sawwergraut (Sauerkraut, sauerkraut)
"Datt geht s'letscht Schtick!" ("Dort geht das letzte Stück!" "There goes the last piece!")

Eating Alone

I am from fields of manure and wheat,
from cow corn high enough to hide in, from
creek beds of violets, daffodils

I am from stone springhouses, from
bottles of milk and cream
shuttered, cool in August noons

I am from smokehouses, from
hooks and hatchets, from
blood and feathers

I am from farms with two houses,
one for grandfather, grandmother
when deep-veined hands turn from tractors, from

cauldrons of corn meal mush
I am from winding staircases, from attics, from
gauzy curtains in summer's night breezes

I am from jar after glass jar of tomatoes, green
beans, peaches, applesauce, but
I am also from chow-chow, dried corn, scrapple

shoo-fly pie, schmierkäse, sauerkraut, souse, and
all those other foods you
won't eat with me

Thanks to George Ella Lyon and her poem "Where I'm From."

Artist's statement to accompany poems "The Last Piece/S'Letscht Schtick" And "Eating Alone"

Poetry and Folklore: Partners in Practice

I had been writing poems for a few years when my parents put in my thirteen-year-old hands a wondrous gift: a scarlet red hardcover book protected by a gauzy white jacket that announced: *The Life Treasury of*

American Folklore. Page by page, I read stories of Joe Magarac, Pecos Bill, Paul Bunyan, and, my favorite, the ghostly tale of the "Girl in the Lavender Dress."[1] Since then, folklore and poetry have been companion practices for me.

Throughout my university years, I took courses in folklore and in poetry. I learned that the first American university folklorist, Francis James Child of Harvard, came to his devotion for traditional ballads through his scholarship in poetry. When I began my fieldwork projects in Pennsylvania and then in Maine in the 1970s, poems by Adrienne Rich and many others sang me to sleep. As I collected folklore, I met people who composed poems orally and recited them to hometown friends (Yocom and Wilcox, 2000).

This melding of poetry and folklore goes beyond my personal circumstances, though, because writing poems and writing ethnographic folklore studies converge in so many ways. One practice vital to both is the loving, scrupulous attention to detail. For poet Stephen Dunn, attention has a moral force: "All poems are moral to the extent that they are evidence . . . of an attentiveness to the details and circumstances of our lives. They get right the things they pay attention to, which always implies a correction of some sort. The issue is not right versus wrong. It's right versus off (the imprecise, the superficial, etc.)" (41).

Jane Hirshfield writes of a necessary concentration in poetry that pertains to folklore, too, a "particular state of awareness: penetrating, unified, and focused, yet also permeable and open. . . . It may come as the harvest of long looking." Great art, she notes, is "thought that has been . . . honed and shaped by a silky attention brought to bear on the recalcitrant matter of earth and of life" (5). The writer must, in the words of Henry James, become "a person on whom nothing is lost. What is put into the care of such a person will be well tended. Such a person can be trusted to tell the stories she is given to tell . . ." (223).

When folklorists enter the "field," we take tools with us, according to our talents, to help us attend: pen and ink to sketch, blank journals, computers, audio and visual recording equipment, and digital cameras. We record what we see, hear, smell, and taste; and we return to our recordings and photographs to see what we did not see at first, to hear what we did not hear. We want to "get it right" or come as close to "right" as mortals can. We want to be observers on whom "nothing is lost." Ethnographic practice is a moral practice: the great responsibility of preserving and sharing others' lives and talents is in our hands and hearts, and we take our charge and our code of ethics seriously. And, since so many of us work with our own family, community, ethnic, and work groups, our responsibilities often feel double- and triple-weighted.

A second practice common to both folklore and poetry attends to the translation of oral performance into the written word through ethnopoetics. This practice of breaking prose into short, poetry-like lines began in the United States among poets such as Jerome Rothenberg and Gary Snyder with training in anthropology, folklore, or linguistics, as well as anthropologists, folklorists, and linguists who wrote poetry: Nathaniel Tarn, Stanley Diamond, Dennis Tedlock (Tedlock, 1992). Working with orally-collected speech, we who use ethnopoetics break our story's lines where a speaker pauses; we signal tone, loudness, speed and more with typographic symbols such as dashes, spaces, bold typeface, and more.

To do this work, we listen deeply: we hear the voice rise at the end of a fragmented line, the telling pause, and the sudden, long silence. We mark the shifting climates of the story in hopes of keeping alive these words that live on the breath. One Master of Fine Arts: Poetry student in my graduate seminar "Living Words: Folklore and Creative Writing" described ethnopoetics as "life-changing" because it helped him attend to "how people actually speak." Another observed that ethnopoetics reinforced her "process of figuring placement, break, breath, punctuation, emphasis—exactly the kind of motion [she goes] through when [she works] on [her] own [poetry]" (Yocom, 2009).

Because poetry and folklore form such a creative partnership, I combine them regularly. I use my poetry writing to learn more—and in a different way—about those traditions that matter most to me. Writing poetry offers me a way of freedom and imagination, of permission and wide-open doors. "[O]ur house is open, there are no keys in the doors,/and invisible guests come in and out at will" writes Czeslaw Milosz in "Ars Poetica?" And from Emily Dickinson: "I dwell in Possibility – /A fairer House than Prose – /More numerous of Windows – /Superior – for Doors –"

I use poetry writing, for example, to explore issues I wonder about as I do fieldwork, questions that I will never be able to answer using the data-rich methods that a folklore researcher must. What is she thinking? Why does she do that? As a poet, though, I can create a world where a person answers a question that, in the real world of our fieldworker-informant relationship, she cannot. So, in flights of fancy, I can picture what is just out of sight, and beyond understanding.[2]

With my poetry, I can also approach a folklore text from a different direction. For example, as a scholar of folktales, I wrote a scholarly essay, based on textual proof, about the Grimm Brothers' "Allerleirauh" ("All Kinds of Fur"), a little-known version of "Cinderella" that includes an incestuous father from whom Allerleirauh escapes, in disguise as a dirty, rough-pelt-covered being. She works in a castle kitchen, and, helped by the cook, effects her transformation into a queen (Yocom, 2012).

I have also been interested, though, in what Allerleirauh would say, in her own words, if she told her own story. As a scholar, I cannot prove what Allerleirauh thinks; but, as a poet, I can write her words and worlds into being. Using the contemporary poetic practice of "erasure,"[3] I am writing a book-length poem, all KINdS of FUR. I "erase" some of the Grimms' words and letters; the words that remain are Allerleirauh's as she tells her own tale of incest, escape, survival, and re-creation.

I also use my poetry to find out more about my own traditions and my reactions to them, as I have with the poems published in this Reader. As I write, inviting the unknown and opening to what comes, I rarely know where a poem will take me. I did not expect these poems about my Pennsylvania German heritage—and foodways—to swerve as they did.

"Write a poem about your first memory" read one of the prompts my colleague and poetry workshop professor Eric Pankey handed out at the beginning of a class. Immediately, the story my grandfather Elmer Keck told me about his earliest memory came to mind, and I wrote down a few, quick notes. Later, as I wrote more, I found myself thinking about my grandfather's first languages: Pennsylvania German at home, German in church. Then a great wave of loss swept over me as I felt, once again, how incomplete I feel being Pennsylvania German but living without the language. My thoughts turned to World War I, how my grandfather would never speak of what it was like to grow up German American, then, in our hometown, even when I would ask why he and his father carefully named their slaughterhouse "The Abbatoir," not "Das Schlachthaus." How much ethnic culture and language, I considered, is lost during war times?[4]

In later drafts of the poem, my grandfather's desire for that disappearing piece of raisin pie linked itself with my desire for Pennsylvania German and for those last pieces of the language now gone, pinched off, from our family. The poem's turn also allowed me to show how an orally told personal story can shift in meaning for each person who hears it: in my life, my grandfather Elmer's tale of a lost, last piece of pie morphed into something quite different.

My poem "Eating Alone" took its unexpected turn as it neared its end. As I listed the things I loved about my grandparents' Yocom family farm, I found myself listing additional things that I loved but that others found quite strange, even suspect, those cultural objects—especially in the intimate circle of the meal-time table—that set me quite apart. What traditions influence me, and where am I from, I wondered as I wrote, living as I did in Virginia and do now in Maine, and feeling the pull of my Pennsylvania hometown.[5]

All told, with my poetry I call myself to another way of writing, one that approaches prose with the sensibility of a poet: listening for sound, feeling for rhythm, and sitting still so images and story-lines can rise. I want to write ethnography to the heartbeat of poetry. Poetry and folklore, folklore and poetry—my true guides. I step into the days ahead, hands reaching out to both.

Notes

1. Later, I would learn the complicated histories behind these so-called "folk heroes." As Edward Ives writes in his 1963 *Midwest Folklore* review of this book: "All told, there is absolutely nothing in this book of any importance to a folklorist. . . . If it gets people to say they 'just love folklore,' it will also give a lot of folklorists a busy time helping these same people sort out the real article from the bogus" (250).

2. For a discussion of this practice of mine and my poem "First Wash," see Yocom, 2012.

3. To see examples of erasure poetry, see http://erasures.wavepoetry.com

4. Cultural loss in the context of war through foodways. Myung Mi Kim, for example, in "Siege Document" writes of her family's experience in Korea during and after the war: "We are allowed to keep one bag of potatoes or carrots after working a ten-hour day / pulling these vegetables and loading them onto trucks / . . . Bitter, bitter roots" (91, 93). Brian Turner, veteran of the second Iraq War, documents the loss of local foods in "Jameel": "They say to produce one pound of honey / bees must travel from flower to hive / at least twelve thousand times" (57).

5. I am attracted to Lucy Lippard's discussions [1997] of our "multicentered" lives in contemporary society, and our several "homes."

Bibliography

Dickinson, Emily. "I dwell in Possibility" (466). http://www.poetryfoundation.org/poem/182904 Accessed 19 June 2013.

Dunn, Stephen. 2001. *Walking Light: Memoirs and Essays on Poetry*. Rochester, NY: BOA Editions.

Hirshfield, Jane. 1997. *Nine Gates: Entering the Mind of Poetry*. New York: HarperCollins.

The Editors of Life Magazine 1961. *The Life Treasury of American Folklore*. New York: Time, Inc. Illustrated by James Lewicki.

Kim, Myung Mi. 2002. Commons. Berkeley: University of California Press.

Ives, Edward D. Ives. 1963–64. Review of *The Life Treasury of American Folklore*. *Midwest Folklore* (13:4 Winter) 249–251). http://www.jstor.org/stable/4318052 Accessed 22 June 2013.

Lippard, Lucy. 1997. *The Lure of the Local: Senses of Place in a Multicentered Society*. New York: New Press.

Milosz, Czeslaw. 2003. *New and Collected Poems: 1931–2001*. New York: Ecco.

Tedlock, Dennis. 1992. "Ethnopoetics." In *Folklore, Cultural Performances, and Popular Entertainments: A Communications-centered Handbook*, edited by Richard Bauman. New York: Oxford University Press.

Turner, Brian. 2005. *Here, Bullet*. Farmington, ME: Alice James Press.

Yocom, Margaret R. 2009. "Writing Down the Breath." Forum Presentation. Association of Writers and Writing Programs Conference, Chicago, 11–14 February.

Yocom, Margaret R. 2012. "But who are you really?" Ambiguous Bodies and Ambiguous Pronouns in "Allerleirauh" (ATU 510B). In *Transgressive Tales: Queering the Grimms*, ed. Pauline Greenhill and Kay Turner, pp. 89–118. Detroit: Wayne State University Press.

Yocom, Margaret R. 2012. "Keeping Watch." *Voices: The Journal of New York Folklore* (38:1–2 Spring-Summer) 20–24.

Yocom, Margaret R. and Gaylon "Jeep" Wilcox. 2000. "'Just Call Me Sandy, Son': Poet Jeep Wilcox's Tribute to Sandy Ives." *Northeast Folklore: Essays in Honor of Edward D. Ives*. Ed. Pauleena MacDougall and David Taylor, pp. 405–409. Orono: University of Maine Press and the Maine Folklife Center.

APPENDIX OF SOURCES

Grateful acknowledgement is made to the following sources for permission to reproduce material for this volume.

Part One: Foundations: History, Definitions, and Methodologies

1. Don Yoder, 'Folk Cookery' in Richard M. Dorson (ed.), *Folklore and Folklife: An Introduction*, (Chicago: University of Chicago Press, 1972), pp. 325–350. © 1972 by The University of Chicago. Reprinted with permission from the University of Chicago Press.

2. Günter Wiegelmann, 'Innovations in Food and Meals', *Folk Life* 12 (1974), 20–30. Reproduced with permission of Maney Publishing in the format 'Book' via Copyright Clearance Center.

Part Two: Food in Groups, Community, and Identity

3. Anne R. Kaplan, '"It's All from One Big Pot": Booya as an Expression of Community' in Theodore C. Humphrey and Lin T. Humphrey (eds), *Food and Fesitval in American Life*, (Logan: Utah State University Press, 1991), pp. 169–189. Reproduced with permission of Utah State University Press in the format 'Republish in a book' via Copyright Clearance Center.

4. William G. Lockwood and Yvonne R. Lockwood, 'Continuity and Adaptation in Arab American Foodways' in Nabeel Abraham and Andrew Shyrock (eds), *Arab Detroit: From Margin to Mainstream*, (Detroit: Wayne State University Press, 2000) pp. 515–549. Copyright © 2000 Wayne State University Press, with the permission of Wayne State University Press.

5. Timothy Lloyd, 'Paterson's Hot Texas Wiener Tradition', *Folklife Center News* 17 (1995), 8–11. Reprinted with permission of the author.

6. Konrad Köstlin, 'A New Ascension of Regional Food' in Patricia Lysaght (ed.), Food and Meals at Cultural Crossroads: Proceedings of the 17th Conference of the International Commission for the Ethnological Food Research, Oslo, Nowray, September 15–19, 2008 (Oslo: Novus Press, 2010), pp. 36–45. Reprinted with permission from the author.

7. Holly Everett, 'Newfoundland and Labrador on a Plate: Bed, Breakfast, and Regional Identity', *Cuizine: The Journal of Canadian Food Cultures* 3 (2011), 12–22. Reprinted with permission of *Cuizine: The Journal of Canadian Food Cultures/Cuizine: revue des cultures culinaires au Canada* (www.cuizine.mcgill.ca).

8. Robert Smith in 'The Dog's Eye: The Pie in Australian Tradition' in Graham Seal and Jennifer Gall (eds), *Antipodean Traditions: Australian Folklore in the 21st Century*, (Perth, WA: Black Swan Press, 2011), pp. 157–69. Courtesy of Black Swan Press, Curtin University, Western Australia.

Part Three: Food as Art, Symbol, and Ritual

20. Jay Allan Anderson, 'Thanksgiving in the USA: The Meal as Medium and Message' in Nilo Valonen and Juhani Lehtonen (eds), Ethnologische Nahrungsforschung: Ethnological Food Research: Reports from the Second International Symposium for Ethnological Research, 1973. (Helsinki, 1975), pp. 9–14. Reprinted with permission from the author.

21. Yrsa Lindqvist, 'When Producers Became Consumers: Cultural Processes in Daily Life' in Patricia Lysgaht (ed.), Time for Food: Proceedings of the Eighteenth Conference of the International Commission for Ethnological Food Research, Abo Akademi University, Turku, Finland, 2010. (Abo, 2012), pp. 57–67. Reprinted with permission from the author.

22. Luisa Del Giudice, 'Sicilian St. Joseph's Tables in Los Angeles, California'. An earlier version of this article appeared as 'Rituals of Charity and Abundance: Sicilian St. Joseph's Tables and Feeding the Poor in Los Angeles', California Italian Studies 1 (2010), 1–30. Revised and excerpted by the author for this publication.

Part Four: Food as Communication, Performance, and Power

23. Janet S. Theophano, '"I Gave Him a Cake": An Interpretation of Two Italian-American Weddings' in Stephen Stern and John Allan Cicala (eds), Creative Ethnicity: Symbols and Strategies of Contemporary Ethnic Life, (Logan: Utah State University Press, 1991), pp. 44–54. Reproduced with permission of Utah State University Press in the format 'Republish in a book' via Copyright Clearance Center.

24. Amy Shuman, 'The Rhetoric of Portions', Western Folklore 40 (1981), 72–80. © Western States Folklore Society.

25. Eve Jochnowitz, 'Foodscapes: The Culinary Landscapes of Russian-Jewish New York' in Julia Brauch, Anna Lipphardt and Alexandra Nocke (eds), Jewish Topographies: Visions of Space, Traditions of Place, (Aldershot: Ashgate, 2008) pp. 294–308. © 'Foodscapes: The Culinary Landscapes of Russian-Jewish New York', Eve Jochnowitz, 2008, Ashgate.

26. Diane Tye, '"A Fruitcake Always Makes Me Think of Grandma": Food and Memory in L. M. Montgomery's Creation of Female Landscapes', CREArTA: Journal of the Centre for Research and Education in the Arts 5, Special issue: 'L. M. Montgomery's Interior and Exterior Landscapes', edited by Rosemary Ross Johnston (2005), 112–24. (Excerpts printed here. Omitted text is indicated by ellipses.) Reprinted with permission from CREArTA.

27. Mario Montaño, 'Appropriation and Counterhegemony in South Texas: Food Slurs, Offal Meats, and Blood' in Tad Tuleja (ed.), Useable Pasts: Traditions and Group Expressions in North America, (Logan: Utah State University Press, 1997) pp. 50–67. Reproduced with permission of Utah State University Press in the format 'Republish in a book' via Copyright Clearance Center.

28. Luanne Roth, 'Beyond Communitas: Cinematic Food Events and the Negotiation of Power, Belonging and Exclusion', Western Folklore 64 (3/4) (2005), 163–187. (Excerpts printed here. Omitted text is indicated by ellipses.) © Western States Folklore Society.

29. Patricia A. Turner, 'Church's Fried Chicken and the Klan: A Rhetorical Analysis of Rumor in the Black Community', Western Folklore 46 (4) (1987), 294–306. © Western States Folklore Society.

30. Rayna Green, 'Mother Corn and the Dixie Pig: Native Food in the Native South', Southern Cultures 14 (4) (2008), 114–126. Copyright © 2008 by the Center for Study of the American South. Used by permission of the University of North Carolina Press. www.uncpress.unc.edu.

Part Five: Food in Public and Applied Folklore

31. Millie Rahn, 'Laying a Place at the Table: Creating Public Foodways Models from Scratch', *Journal of American Folklore* 119 (471) (2006), 30–46. (Excerpts printed here: 30, 32–33, 34–41, 43, 44, 45. Omitted text is indicated by ellipses.) From *Journal of American Folklore*. © 2006 by the Board of Trustees of the University of Illinois. Used with permission of the University of Illinois Press.

32. Riki Saltzman, 'Pork, Place, and Praxis: Foodways in Iowa'. This article is based on a paper given by the author during the Food, Ethnic Identities, and Memory Symposium in 2008, sponsored by the University of Iowa's Center for Ethnic Studies and the Arts. Published with kind permission of the author, the Folklife Coordinator for the Iowa Arts Council.

33. Nomvula Mashoai Cook and Betty J. Belanus, 'A Taste of Home: African Immigrant Foodways', *Festival of American Folklife Program* (1997), 51–53. Reproduced with permission from the Center for Folklife and Cultural Heritage, Smithsonian Institution.

34. Sarah Conrad Gothie, 'No Food or Drink in the Museum?: The Challenges of Edible Artifacts'. Commissioned for this publication.

35. Paddy Bowman, Amanda Dargan and Steve Zeitlin, 'You Eat What You Are: Foodways in Education', *C.A.R.T.S.: Cultural Arts Resources for Teachers and Students* 11 (2010), 1, 3. Reprinted with permission from the authors.

36. Mary Hufford 'American Ginseng and the Idea of the Commons', *Folklife Center News* 19 (1997), 3–18. Reprinted with permission of the author.

37. Zilia C. Estrada, 'An Aesthetic of Community and an Activism of Embodiment in Two Collaborative Community Gardens in Bloomington, Indiana'. Commissioned for this publication.

38. Michael Owen Jones, 'Food Choice, Symbolism and Identity: Bread-and-Butter Issues for Folkloristics and Nutrition Studies', *Journal of American Folklore* 120 (476) (2007), 129–177. (Excerpts printed here: 129–130, 159–177. Omitted text is indicated by ellipses.) Copyright 2007 by the Board of Trustees of the University of Illinois. Used with permission of the University of Illinois Press.

39. Lucy M. Long, 'Culinary Tourism: A Folkloristic Perspective on Eating and Otherness' in Lucy Long (ed.), *Culinary Tourism*, (Lexington: University Press of Kentucky, 2004), pp. 20–50. (Excerpt printed here: 20–24, 32–35, 36–50. Omitted text is indicated by ellipses.) Used with permission.

40. Margaret R. Yocom, 'Eating Alone' was originally published in Frank de Caro (ed.) *The Folklore Muse: Poetry, Fiction and Other Reflections by Folklorists* (Boulder: Utah State University Press, 2008), p. 212. Reproduced with permission of Utah State University Press in the format 'Republish in a book' via Copyright Clearance Center. 'The Last Piece/S'Letscht Schtick' and the accompanying commentary have not previously been published and have been commissioned for this publication.

Every effort has been made to trace copyright holders and to obtain their permission for the use of copyrighted material. The publisher apologizes for any errors or omissions in the above list and would be grateful if notified of any corrections that should be incorporated in future reprints or editions of this book.

INDEX

Index

Index

Index